Stalingrad

Stalingrad

David M. Glantz

and

Jonathan M. House

University Press of Kansas

Published by the University Press of Kansas (Lawrence, Kansas 66045), which
was organized by the Kansas Board of Regents and is operated and funded by
Emporia State University, Fort Hays State University, Kansas State
University, Pittsburg State University, the University of Kansas, and
Wichita State University

Library of Congress Cataloging-in-Publication Data

Names: Glantz, David M., author. | House, Jonathan M. (Jonathan Mallory), 1950– author.
Title: Stalingrad / David M. Glantz and Jonathan M. House.
Description: Lawrence, Kansas : University Press of Kansas, 2017. | Series: Modern war
studies | Abridged version of the Stalingrad trilogy, which appeared in 5 volumes between
2009 and 2014. | Includes bibliographical references and index.
Identifiers: LCCN 2016047601
ISBN 9780700623822 (cloth : alk. paper)
Subjects: LCSH: Stalingrad, Battle of, Volgograd, Russia, 1942–1943. | Soviet Union.
Raboche-Krest'ianskaia Krasnaia Armiia—History—World War, 1939–1945. | Germany.
Heer—History—World War, 1939–1945.
Classification: LCC D764.3.S7 G589 2017 | DDC 940.54/21747—dc23
LC record available at https://lccn.loc.gov/2016047601.

British Library Cataloguing-in-Publication Data is available.

Printed in the United States of America

10 9 8 7 6 5 4 3 2 1

The paper used in this publication is recycled and contains 30 percent
postconsumer waste. It is acid free and meets the minimum requirements of
the American National Standard for Permanence of Paper for Printed Library
Materials Z39.48-1992.

For Professor John Shy,
who has contributed so much to the advancement of military history

Contents

Maps, Tables, and Photographs

TABLES

PHOTOGRAPHS
(*following page 240*)

Adolf Hitler meeting with Army Group South's staff

Field Marshal Fedor von Bock, commander of Army Group South and
Army Group B

Colonel General Ewald von Kleist, commander of First Panzer Army and
later commander of Army Group A

Colonel General Maximilian *Freiherr* von Weichs, commander of Army
Group B; General of Panzer Troops Friedrich Paulus, commander
of Sixth Army; General of Artillery Walter von Seydlitz-Kurzbach,
commander of LI Army Corps

General *der Flieger* Wolfgang von Richtofen, commander of Fourth Air Fleet

Josef Vissarionovich Stalin, People's Commissar of Defense and Supreme
    High Commander of the Armed Forces of the USSR
Army General Georgii Konstantinovich Zhukov, deputy Supreme High
    Commander of the Armed Forces of the USSR and commander of the
    Western Front
Colonel General Aleksandr Aleksandrovich Novikov, commander of the
    Red Army's Air Forces and deputy People's Commissar of Defense for
    Aviation
Colonel General Aleksandr Mikhailovich Vasilevsky, chief of the Red Army
    General Staff
Marshal of the Soviet Union Semen Konstantinovich Timoshenko,
    commander of the Southwest Main Direction and Southwestern Front
Lieutenant General Filipp Ivanovich Golikov, commander of the Briansk
    Front
Lieutenant General Rodion Iakolevich Malinovsky, commander of the
    Southern Front and later of 2nd Guards Army
Marshal of the Soviet Union Semen Mikhailovich Budenny, commander of
    the North Caucasus Main Direction and North Caucasus Front
Red troops fighting in the suburbs of Voronezh, July 1942
German tanks advancing into the Great Bend of the Don
German troops overlooking the Don River
Red Army riflemen counterattack in Stalingrad's suburbs
Colonel General Andrei Ivanovich Eremenko, commander Southeastern
    Front (later Stalingrad Front); chief of artillery, Major General of
    Artillery V. N. Matveev; commissar, Nikita Sergeevich Khrushchev
Major General N. I. Krylov, chief of staff of 62nd Army; Lieutenant
    General V. I. Chuikov, commander of 62nd Army; Lieutenant General
    K. A. Gurov, member of 62nd Army's Military Council (commissar);
    and Major General A. I. Rodimtsev, commander of 13th Guards Rifle
    Division
Red Army infantry defending the foothills of the Caucasus Mountains,
    August 1942
A German cemetery in the Caucasus Mountains
Central part of Stalingrad under assault
Central Stalingrad in flames
Street fighting in central Stalingrad
Ships of the Volga Military Flotilla transport naval infantry across the river,
    October 1942
Soviet tanks entering the penetration in Operation Uranus
Soviet troops and tanks assaulting Kalach-on-the-Don
Major General of Tank Forces Vasilii Mikhailovich Badanov, commander of
    24th (later 2nd Guards) Tank Corps

Preface and Acknowledgments

In 1998 we set out to replicate our study of the struggle at Kursk in 1943, attempting to write a one-volume history of the 1942–1943 campaign that culminated at Stalingrad. As in our previous collaborations, we hoped to bring balance to Western perceptions of this campaign, comparing German and Soviet accounts to approach a more objective understanding of what occurred and why.

Almost from the first, however, we discovered significant contradictions within and between sources. They often disagreed not only on interpretations but also on the very facts at issue, such as which units fought at what locations on what dates. Rather than a triumphal German Army falling into a trap laid by hordes of Soviet opponents, we found an ongoing struggle between two nearly equal adversaries, neither of which could mass sufficient combat power to achieve a decisive victory. Some units appeared to be in two places simultaneously, while other units went unreported. The reason for many of these discrepancies gradually emerged. The best-known memoirs of Stalingrad, such as Field Marshal Erich von Manstein's *Lost Victories* and Marshal of the Soviet Union Vasilii Ivanovich Chuikov's *The Battle for Stalingrad*, had been written from memory, without access to the primary records of the struggle. Official historians, most notably Earl Ziemke and Magna Bauer of the US Army Center of Military History, had incorporated many captured German records, but other such documents were believed lost in the war, and the Soviet archives and detailed after-action reports were largely unavailable until the 1990s. Even now, there are undoubtedly some records of the campaign that have yet to come to light.

The focus of the original project therefore changed. David Glantz undertook the arduous task of assembling and translating the available Soviet records as well as numerous studies by Russian historians. Recent Western histories, most notably the multivolume German official history (*Germany in the Second World War*), complemented these Soviet accounts, as did numerous analyses by gifted Western historians such as Jason Mark, Joel Hayward, Von Hardesty, and Ilya Grinberg. There is also a new generation of post-Soviet Russian historian-archivists, especially Aleksei Isaev and V. A. Zolotarev, as well as recently published, unexpurgated versions of participants' memoirs. We attempted to merge all these interpretations and documents into the ambitious *Stalingrad Trilogy* that, with supplemental documents, appeared in five volumes between 2009 and 2014.

This present volume returns to the original project, with Jon House using David's groundbreaking research to write a balanced history of Stalingrad in an accessible one-volume format. Of necessity, this version omits some of the detail of the original series of books. Except during the street fighting in Stalingrad, this account is told primarily at the operational, rather than the tactical, level. Nonetheless, we believe that the result gives readers a comprehensive account of how and why one of the pivotal campaigns of World War II played out as it did. The enormous sacrifice of participants on both sides deserves to be not only remembered but also understood, and we hope this study will find a different, larger audience than the multivolume trilogy.

As in our previous efforts, we are indebted to the professional efforts of the staffs of the Military History Institute in Carlisle, Pennsylvania, and the Combined Arms Research Library at Fort Leavenworth, Kansas. We also profited by the advice of numerous colleagues who read portions of the manuscript, especially Professor Christopher Gabel at the Command and General Staff College. That said, we are ultimately responsible for any errors in this study, which in no way reflects the official position of the US Army that we both served for so many years.

David M. Glantz
Colonel, Field Artillery (Retired)
Carlisle, Pennsylvania

Jonathan M. House
Colonel, Military Intelligence (Retired)
Leavenworth, Kansas

Stalingrad

Prologue

The German Army was poised to launch Operation *Blau* (Blue), its second summer offensive to conquer the Soviet Union. After great efforts, the Germans had replaced most but not all the equipment and personnel losses of 1941, at least in Army Group South, which would conduct the main attack southeastward to the Caucasus Mountains. Then, less than two weeks before the scheduled start of the main offensive, and with preliminary attacks already under way, a staff officer compromised a significant portion of the *Blau* plan.

The cause was one of the recurring weaknesses of German operational procedures: the lack of operations security. *Auftragstaktik*, loosely translated as mission-type orders, allowed subordinate commanders to exercise considerable initiative, depending on the situation. To do this, however, commanders and staff officers believed they needed to know the plans of higher and adjacent units, so that a local decision would support the commander's intent. Unfortunately, widespread sharing of such information caused a geometric increase in the probability that the enemy would also learn of German plans.

This problem had compromised a number of earlier German operations. On 10 January 1940, for example, a German aircraft inadvertently made a forced landing near Mechelen, in neutral Belgium.[1] On this plane was the logistics planner for the *Luftwaffe*'s 7th Parachute Division, carrying significant extracts from the German plan (Case Yellow) to invade the Low Countries. This event forced the Germans to completely rework their campaign plan. Next, during the invasion of Crete, the British found a regimental operations order on the body of a dead officer. Such compromises had prompted Adolf Hitler to demand stringent restrictions on information. For example, no operations order was to be taken forward of corps headquarters prior to an attack.

Unfortunately, many German officers continued to follow their usual habits, violating the spirit if not the letter of Hitler's instructions. One such well-intentioned meddler was General of Panzer Troops Georg Stumme, commander of XXXX Motorized Corps. At the urging of his subordinates, Stumme dictated a one-page summary of the first phase of the forthcoming offensive (*Blau* I) and distributed that summary, along with a map overlay, to his division commanders.[2] In turn, each division commander shared

1

this information with his own operations officer (known as "Ia" in the German system), grossly circumventing standing security orders. Major Joachim Reichel, the Ia of 23rd Panzer Division, compounded the problem by taking the overlay and summary on an aerial reconnaissance of his division's assigned axis of advance. On the afternoon of 19 June 1942, Reichel's Fieseler *Storch* (Stork), a small liaison aircraft identical to the one that had landed in Belgium in 1940, disappeared behind Soviet lines after suffering a fuel leak from ground fire. A German combat patrol found the downed aircraft and, nearby, the graves of Reichel and his pilot, but there was no sign of the missing order.

An investigation led to General Stumme's relief from command, effective 9 July, which in turn necessitated a reshuffling of panzer commanders in the midst of the *Blau* campaign. Meanwhile, at Hitler's insistence, a court-martial convicted Stumme, his chief of staff, and the division commander of gross negligence, for which the penalty was death. A number of senior officers appealed on behalf of these three men, so Hitler permitted Stumme to be reassigned to North Africa, where he died in October while serving as acting commander of the panzer army during Field Marshal Erwin Rommel's temporary absence.

Reichel's escapade occurred too late to change the plans for Operation *Blau*, so the Germans went ahead with them, despite the potential compromise. Fortunately for the attackers, Joseph Stalin suspected that the captured plan was a deliberate deception; it seemed incredible to him that the Germans would jeopardize their plans in such a foolish manner. The Soviet commanders were, in any event, fixated on defending Moscow rather than the road to the Caucasus. Stalin did, however, hedge his bets. In a series of orders issued in late June, he directed the transfer of various units to Marshal of the Soviet Union Semen Konstantinovich Timoshenko's Southwestern Front and Lieutenant General Filipp Ivanovich Golikov's Briansk Front, the apparent targets of the upcoming *Blau* attack.[3] By the time XXXX Motorized Corps attacked as part of German Sixth Army, the Southwestern Front alone had 640 tanks to oppose Sixth Army's 360, and the Briansk Front was even stronger, with 1,600 tanks compared with Fourth Panzer Army's 733. These new Soviet armored units were still inexperienced, but their persistent counterattacks hampered and weakened *Blau* almost from the first day. Reichel's death was an inauspicious start to Germany's last full-scale offensive and a further step in the steady decline of Hitler's relations with his generals.

PART ONE

The Limits of Maneuver
Warfare, 1942

CHAPTER ONE

Opposing Forces

BARBAROSSA

Major Reichel's ill-fated reconnaissance came almost exactly one year after Germany had invaded the Soviet Union. Operation Barbarossa not only surprised the Soviet leadership but also caught the Red Army and Air Force in the midst of multiple transitions. The Soviet armed forces were changing their leadership, equipment, organization, doctrine, mobilization status, and defensive plans, making them incredibly vulnerable to the Axis onslaught. One hundred fifty-two German divisions, including 19 panzer and 15 motorized divisions, thrust rapidly into Soviet territory and created a series of vast encirclements that, by December 1941, had killed, wounded, or captured 4.5 million Red soldiers.[1] The German Air Force, or *Luftwaffe*, achieved air superiority within the first two days, supporting the German advance with both air strikes and limited aerial resupply of spearhead units. By October, the Germans and their Axis allies, especially Finland and Romania, had captured many of the largest population and industrial centers in European Russia, blockaded Leningrad, and threatened Moscow and Rostov.

Yet, for all their advantages and successes at the tactical and operational levels, the Germans failed to achieve strategic victory for a number of reasons. The sheer scale of European Russia, complicated by the shortage of railroads and paved highways, meant that the invaders were unable to deliver a decisive blow to the Soviet state. The German Army's logistics planners, led by Major General Edouard Wagner, had predicted these problems with uncanny accuracy in a series of briefings they gave to Colonel General Franz Halder, the chief of the Army General Staff (*Oberkommando des Heeres*, or OKH), in November 1940. Wagner estimated that the army could carry sufficient fuel to advance to a maximum depth of 500 to 800 kilometers, with enough food and ammunition for a 20-day operation. After that, the army would have to pause several weeks for resupply, and it would be dependent on forced labor to convert the captured Soviet rail network to the narrower German gauge to support a deeper penetration.[2] As Wagner had predicted, for the rest of the year and indeed during the deep operations of 1942 as well, German offensives became intermittent and spasmodic. Each cycle began with the mechanized spearheads pausing to build up supplies and repair vehicles. They then lunged forward, usually succeeding in encircling their foes, but having to pause again to wait for the hard-marching infantry to catch up and seal off the resulting pocket, followed by another wait for resupply. Each time, the Germans not only lost their offensive momentum but also failed to prevent large portions of the Red Army from escaping the trap.

To offset this logistical challenge, Hitler, Halder, and other German leaders had planned to destroy the Red Army as far westward as possible, thus minimizing the size of the force needed to occupy the depths of the Soviet Union. However, this plan failed because of two German intelligence mistakes. First, they believed the Communist regime had only a fragile hold on its population and that the whole structure would collapse after a few defeats. Although there were certainly millions of Soviet citizens, especially ethnic minorities, who hated the Moscow government, the Germans' harsh occupation policies discouraged collaboration with the invaders, while Stalin's government proved remarkably resilient in controlling and inspiring its population. Second, the Germans had focused on destroying the active-duty Red Army, either ignorant or contemptuous of the huge mobilization capacity represented by a pool of 14 million trained reservists.[3] As quickly as the Germans destroyed enemy units, the Soviets used these reservists to generate new ones—often poorly trained and equipped, but still capable of inflicting casualties—to replace them. As early as July 1941, these Soviet units began to exact significant casualties and impose costly delays on the invaders. In a Darwinian process that took place throughout 1941 and 1942, the surviving Red commanders of these early defeats acquired a growing competence in battle, something that most German leaders ignored.

Delay was the one thing the Germans could not tolerate because their third problem, in addition to underestimating the resilience and strength of their opponents, was the very fragile nature of their own war machine.[4] German industry suffered severe shortages of raw materials even in 1939, and the growing demand for soldiers left German factories permanently undermanned. Hitler had not anticipated a general war when he invaded Poland in 1939, so his armed forces were only partially equipped for combat. Despite its reputation for mechanized modernity, the majority of the *Wehrmacht* was still dependent on draft animals to move artillery and supplies. Even the 34 panzer and motorized divisions included a hodgepodge of German tank designs and captured French and Czech tanks, trucks, and guns. This mixture of designs, for which there was a shortage of spare parts and appropriate repair tools, broke down with alarming frequency, especially on the unpaved "mud canals" that constituted most Russian roads. The German Panzer III and Panzer IV tanks, as well as the standard German antitank guns, were obsolescent. These weapons needed significant improvements to stand up to the better-armored and -armed T-34 and KV-1 tanks coming off Soviet

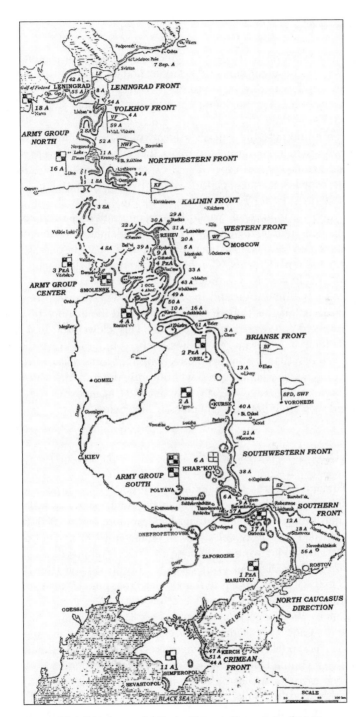

Map 1. The Situation on the Soviet-German Front, 1 April 1942

assembly lines. Even the *Luftwaffe*, which had priority for production and manpower, was primarily a tactical air force, and it had lost many of its most experienced pilots during the Battle of Britain. Germany never produced the armadas of four-engine, long-range strategic bombers employed by the British and Americans.

Moreover, because the Versailles Treaty of 1919 had limited the size of Germany's armed forces during the 1920s, they experienced severe shortages of trained manpower and especially of experienced midlevel leaders—the sergeants, captains, and majors who actually led combat battalions.[5] To form the final 20 divisions for Barbarossa in 1941, three classes of conscripts, including youths who normally would have been drafted in 1942, completed their individual training in May 1941, only a month before the invasion. Outside of those divisions, no more than 321,000 men on active duty were available as trained replacements.[6] Combat losses in the first three months of the war absorbed all these replacements.

Thus, by the time it ground to a halt outside of Moscow, the German Army was in tatters due to both enemy action and the extreme demands of its environment and overstretched logistics. This allowed the Red Army to achieve a temporary advantage, leading to the counteroffensive that began on 5 December 1941. Hitler instinctively refused to retreat and relieved a number of generals who disagreed with him. By the time the winter battles ended, both combatants were severely depleted in manpower and equipment, and their front lines were hopelessly intertwined.

REBUILDING THE *WEHRMACHT*

By 31 January 1942, the Germans had suffered 917,985 army and 18,098 *Luftwaffe* casualties; their allies, especially the Romanians, had suffered proportionately even more.[7] The Germans had lost more than 41,000 trucks and at least 207,000 horses, as well as 13,600 guns and mortars and 4,903 aircraft.[8] After the trying winter campaigns, German commanders considered only 8 of their 162 divisions in the East to be fully capable; the 16 panzer divisions in the East had only 140 functioning tanks among them, equivalent to one full-strength division.[9]

In January 1942 General of Infantry Georg Thomas, head of the Office of War Economy and Armaments, convinced Hitler that rebuilding the existing formations had to take precedence over creating new units. Manufacturers melted down church bells and textile manufacturing cylinders to obtain the copper necessary for wiring and ammunition casings. The Germans requisitioned thousands of trucks and almost 300,000 replacement draft animals from Western Europe, although neither vehicles nor horses could withstand the harsh Russian climate. Ruthless officials increased the use of slave labor and controlled the food supply more tightly. Perhaps most significantly, armaments minister Fritz Todt died in a plane crash in February and was succeeded by Hitler's architect, Albert Speer. Given the divided nature of German government and industry, it would be simplistic to argue that Speer single-handedly forced through the necessary arms production. However, he did cooperate with numerous officials and industrialists, establishing committees and controlling resource priorities in a manner that helped achieve the necessary production.[10]

The more difficult task was finding military manpower to fill at least half a million vacancies. Despite oppressive occupation policies, a significant number of young men from the Baltic states, Ukraine, and other non-Russian areas wanted to fight against Moscow, but at this stage in the war, the *Schutzstaffel* (SS) and *Wehrmacht* generally sought only ethnic Germans for their ranks. So the Nazi regime had to conscript more German industrial workers at precisely the time it sought to redouble production. In December 1941 alone, 282,300 German men, two-thirds of them working in the armaments industry, received orders for military service.[11] Another 200,000 followed during the first half of 1942, as Germany lowered the ages for conscripted and voluntary military service to 18 and 17, respectively. Forced laborers from Russia were supposed to replace German farmers, who in turn shifted to the factories, but due to the general transportation shortage and the abuse prisoners had suffered at German hands, slave laborers were largely unavailable until well into 1942.

Thus, despite its efforts, Germany could not make good all its losses, except in privileged formations such as the *Waffen* (Combat) SS divisions and the *Grossdeutschland* Division. Colonel General Friedrich Fromm, who as head of the Reserve Army was responsible for training new recruits, suggested to Hitler that the available reinforcements be funneled to Army Group South, in preparation for an offensive to reach the Caucasus oil fields.[12] This expedient brought the divisions of that army group up to 80 to 85 percent of their authorized strengths, even though some panzer divisions in First Panzer Army fielded only one tank battalion each, as opposed to the two or three battalions of 1941 divisions. To pay for this limited improvement in the southern divisions, however, 69 of the 75 infantry divisions in Army Groups North and Center shrank from nine to six infantry battalions each, with their artillery batteries cut from four guns to three and proportionate reductions in horses and motor transport.[13] Only the *Luftwaffe* began the 1942 campaign with substantially the same numbers it had possessed a year earlier—2,635 aircraft in the East, as opposed to 2,770 in 1941; even these figures concealed the loss of many experienced air crewmen.[14]

In March 1942 German factories began to produce the new model F2 of the workhorse Panzer IV, which included a long-barreled 75mm gun with increased armor penetration. Yet such tanks remained a rarity in the field, as did the new 50mm antitank gun intended to replace the inadequate 37mm in infantry units. Thus, the armor-piercing capacity of the average German weapon remained inferior to the standard Soviet medium tank, the T-34/76, armed with a 76.2mm gun.

Based on the Red Army's dismal initial performance in 1941, German commanders remained confident of their superior tactical ability at maneuver. Still, the Soviet counteroffensive before Moscow had been a great shock, and Hitler wished to ensure that his inexperienced recruits and shaken veterans experienced renewed success in several low-risk operations prior to the main *Blau* offensive.

SATELLITE ARMIES

If the German Army was only moderately prepared for the second summer offensive, the other Axis armies were even weaker. The sole exception was the Finnish Army, but once it reconquered the territory lost to Moscow in 1940, that army set up defensive positions and refused to move farther east. Despite a general contempt for the fighting qualities of the other satellites, German planners recognized the need for more troops in the upcoming campaign. Every step Germany took eastward would lengthen the front lines, especially the left flank of the long advance southeastward to the Caucasus. Given Germany's overall lack of manpower and reluctance to use local recruits, the only source of more troops was the Axis. Intense diplomatic pressure generated 52 non-German divisions for the 1942 campaign—27 Romanian, 13 Hungarian, 9 Italian, and 2 Slovak divisions, plus the volunteer Spanish "Blue" Division.

Benito Mussolini increased the Italian contingent in the East from 60,000 to 227,000, even though his commanders warned him that their forces were utterly unequipped for either the climate or the kind of mechanized warfare prevalent in Russia.[15] From a smaller population, Romanian dictator Ion Antonescu made an even greater contribution, peaking at 267,000 men, including a significant air force contingent, by November 1942. However, the Romanian 1st Armored Division had lost many of its obsolescent tanks in 1941 and received only a few German vehicles as replacements. The Hungarian armored division was even weaker, including 85 locally assembled Czech 38t tanks and 22 Panzer Is, the tiny light tanks the German Army had virtually retired from service.[16]

Thus, the satellite troops were lacking not courage but weaponry. To complicate matters further, the Hungarian and Romanian troops were more interested in fighting each other than the Soviets, so the Italian Eighth Army had to be inserted between the two national contingents at the front. Differences in language, doctrine, and equipment meant that the German liaison officers to these Axis units had to possess diplomatic skills of the highest order.

REBUILDING THE RED ARMY

While the *Wehrmacht* struggled to rebuild its existing combat units, the Red Army faced the even greater task of creating new headquarters and organizations from nothing, reinventing itself in the midst of war.[17]

Under the shock of the initial German invasion, the Soviet Headquarters of the Supreme High Command, usually referred to as the *Stavka*, had decided to simplify its force structure, creating smaller, less complex units at every level to match the limited experience and span of control of the average Red commander and staff. The majority of new units raised during 1941 were rifle (infantry) divisions (6,000 to 10,000 men) or brigades (4,000 to 6,000 men). In both instances, the new units were equipped with only rifles, machine guns, mortars, and a few guns or howitzers. Casualties sometimes reduced the effective strength of these divisions and brigades to as few as 1,000 bayonets (riflemen and sappers) each. The initial invasion had been even more disastrous to Soviet mechanized forces, although some remnants of the prewar mechanized corps and tank divisions survived. All new tank production went to tank brigades and separate tank battalions intended to support the infantry. When the first such brigades appeared in September 1941, each had an authorized strength of 93 tanks. By December, that authorization had fallen to 46, while the separate battalions increased in strength from 29 to 36 tanks each. Beyond the tanks, these units received only a minimum of support and maintenance troops. Many of these brigades and battalions died as quickly as they sprang to life, but their surviving commanders and troops provided cadres whose hard-won experience was essential to the formation of larger organizations in 1942.[18]

The Red Army had a distinguished history of using horse cavalry, which could move where swamps, snow, and fuel shortages blocked motorized and mechanized formations. During the first eight months of the war, the People's Commissariat of Defense (*Narodnyi Komissariat Oborony*, or NKO) fielded 15 cavalry corps consisting of 2 to 3 small divisions each. Such units had proved effective operating behind German lines under the confused conditions of the winter of 1941–1942. Cavalry could not actually fight on horseback, and such forces often had no weapons larger than a 50mm mortar, making them vulnerable in conventional battle. However, horses still facilitated movement in frozen and swampy terrain.

Stalin and his generals were convinced they needed larger, combined-arms mechanized units to fight the German panzers on equal terms. Fortunately, Soviet industry provided the tools to build these new units. Having packed up and moved beyond the Ural Mountains soon after the German invasion, many armaments factories somehow managed to resume production early in 1942. Three thousand aircraft, 4,500 tanks, 14,000 field pieces, 50,000 mortars, and thousands of additional weapons came off the assembly lines between January and May.[19] Some of these weapons were obsolescent, such as the T-60 light tanks, but the Soviets continued to produce them simply because they were easy to build on automobile assembly lines. Overall, however, the Red Army achieved a renaissance in armaments, significantly supplemented by Lend-Lease equipment provided by Britain and the United States. American all-wheel-drive trucks were especially important to supply mobile forces once they left their railroad lines behind.[20]

Organizing this wealth of equipment into a new generation of mechanized units was the task of Lieutenant General of Tank Forces Iakov Nikolaevich Fedorenko, chief of the Red Army's Main Auto-Armored Directorate. On 31 March 1942 Fedorenko formed the first four tank corps, which were actually small combined-arms divisions. By December, there were 28 such tank corps, many built by expanding a veteran tank brigade of 1941. Each of the first four tank corps consisted of two tank brigades, one truck-mounted rifle brigade, and very limited support, for a total strength of 5,603 men and 100 tanks (20 KV heavy, 40 T-34 medium, and 40 T-60 light). Almost immediately, however, Fedorenko added a third tank brigade plus various combat support elements necessary for sustained operations. By July, a typical tank corps included three tank brigades of 53 tanks each (32 medium and 21 light); one motorized rifle brigade; a motorcycle reconnaissance battalion; battalions of mortars, antiaircraft guns, and multiple-rocket launchers ("guards mortars," the famed *katiushas*); a combat engineer (sapper) company; and, somewhat later, a transportation company with two mobile repair teams. The total authorized strength of this organization grew to as much as 7,600 men and 180 tanks.[21]

Even these units proved to be too armor-heavy, lacking infantry and armored personnel carriers (APCs) for sustained operations. Beginning in September, therefore, Fedorenko began to organize another type of formation known as a mechanized corps. Again, there were a number of organizational variants, but all mechanized corps had a nucleus of three mechanized brigades, each with a regiment of 39 medium tanks as well as trucked infantry, plus one or two tank brigades or regiments and most of the supporting arms found in a tank corps. The mechanized corps, which still lacked APCs, were authorized 175 to 204 tanks each, depending on the exact table of organization.[22]

The tank and mechanized corps were roughly equivalent to panzer divisions, although the German units had more infantry, APCs, and artillery than the tank corps. Such units were increasingly effective at the tactical level, but the Red Army wanted a larger organization—equivalent to a German motorized corps or panzer army—for sustained, deeper attacks at the operational rather than tactical level of war. On 25 May 1942 the NKO combined some of the newly created tank corps into the 3rd and 5th Tank Armies. Two additional tank armies (1st and 4th) formed in July, but they were thrown into battle before their organization was complete and therefore suffered heavy damage at German hands. In any event, the structure of these tank armies was experimental and varied widely due to shortages of trucks and other equipment. As a result, these first tank armies included horse cavalry and rifle divisions whose mobility and armored protection were far inferior to those of the tank corps. A typical 1942 tank army included two or three tank corps, one cavalry corps, and two to six rifle divisions, plus supporting units. Their average strength was 35,000 men, 350 to 500 tanks, and 150 to 200 towed artillery pieces.[23]

Fedorenko and other senior leaders intended for these new organizations to permit a return to the prewar doctrine of "deep operations," a sophisticated set of concepts that had languished after Stalin purged many of its advocates in 1937. In theory, the experience of 1941 had prepared the surviving tank commanders to manage these new tank corps and tank armies. In practice, however, the commanders and especially their staff officers still had much to learn before they could concentrate, maneuver, and resupply their troops with the skill exhibited by the Germans. After a number of disasters beginning in May, the Red Army gradually learned from its experience, creating more effective organizations, tactics, and staff procedures by the end of 1942.

The same could be said for other Soviet efforts to improve field performance, such as concentrating artillery, tanks, and infantry on narrow frontages both to halt German penetrations and to create their own breakthroughs when they attempted to counterattack. Yet, time after time in 1942, Stalin and the *Stavka* badgered field commanders into attacking before their troops and supplies were completely assembled and coordinated. The resulting failures only confirmed German stereotypes about the incompetence of their opponents, making the November encirclement of Stalingrad all the more startling when it occurred.

Meanwhile, just as in the *Wehrmacht*, the Soviet decision to field these mechanized units meant that the average rifle division had a low priority for replacement soldiers and new equipment. The one exception was units with the "Guards" designation, which conferred not only supply priority but also better food and pay. The *Stavka* generally awarded this designation to successful divisions and higher units, rewarding its most skillful commanders. Just like the mechanized forces, the guards units became a means to return to prewar complexity in doctrine and organization. The 1st Guards Army was sacrificed in the defense of Stalingrad, but by late fall 1942, a new generation of such armies began to form, and they were authorized the full structure of corps, divisions, and fire support that the Red Army had jettisoned during the crisis of 1941.

In terms of weaponry, newly produced 45mm antitank guns were much more effective against German armor. Yet the Soviet tank designs, like their German counterparts, were almost identical to those of the previous year, which meant that the Red Army retained a technical superiority over its opponents. Thus, the T-34 medium tank had both thicker armor and better armament (a 76.2mm high-velocity main gun) than the German Panzer III and the short-barreled variant of the Panzer IV, although its engine and transmission were inferior. The T-34 still had significant design problems with regard to its turret layout, but its ability to operate in extreme weather with minimal maintenance made it a formidable weapon.[24] The KV-1 heavy tank, with the same main gun and even thicker armor, was virtually invulnerable to anything smaller than the famous German 88mm antiaircraft gun. However, because the KV-1 required a massive investment in material and production man-hours, Fedorenko focused on increasing the production of T-34s.[25]

The Red Air Force also began to recover its strength during the spring of 1942. Its new commander, Lieutenant General of Aviation Forces Aleksandr Aleksandrovich Novikov, established larger tactical headquarters, including 1st Air Army and a number of shock aviation groups, to mass aircraft under centralized control. However, the Red Air Force lagged behind its ground counterparts and did not present effective opposition to the *Luftwaffe* until the fall.[26]

CORRELATION OF FORCES

It is almost impossible to make a genuine one-to-one comparison between Axis and Soviet forces in 1942. Each side had other theaters to defend (France, North Africa, and the Far East), and each had some strategic reserves. The Soviet Supreme High Command (VGK) Reserve was almost exponentially larger than its German counterpart; even after committing many of these reserves during the winter campaigns, the VGK Reserve still numbered 218,276 men on 1 May.[27] It would soon grow much larger, a factor that repeatedly prevented strategic German victory. Moreover, many of the promised Axis satellite divisions had yet to reach the front lines in the East when the summer battles began. In any event, since the 1942 campaign focused on only the southern portion of the theater of operations, forces on both sides could shift from one region to another as the situation required.

Suffice it to say that in early April 1942 Germany had approximately 2.5 million troops in the East, reinforced by almost a million allied troops either on hand or en route—450,000 Finns and 440,000 Romanians, Hungarians, Italians, and Slovaks. By June, Army Group South (including Eleventh Army in the Crimea) would grow to 71 German divisions—46 infantry, 4 *Jäger* (light infantry), 2 mountain, 7 motorized (including 2 SS), 9 panzer, and 3 rear-area security—plus an SS motorized brigade. In addition, there were 22 Axis divisions, including the Romanian 1st Armored and Slovak Mobile Divisions, giving Field Marshal Fedor von Bock's Army Group South a potential of 1 million German and 300,000 Axis soldiers.[28] His weakened panzer divisions totaled 1,700 tanks, of which 300 were obsolete Panzer II light tanks. The Fourth Air Fleet supported Army Group South with almost half—1,002—of the aircraft in the East, although only 548 of this fleet were operational on 20 May 1942.[29]

The Soviet forces opposite Army Group South on 1 June included four and a half *fronts*—Briansk (one-half), Southwestern, and Southern, later backed up by the North Caucasus and Trans-Caucasus, numbering over 1.7 million troops. Among them, these commands mustered 102 rifle divisions, 19 separate rifle brigades, 5 cavalry corps, 19 cavalry divisions, 8 tank corps (with 24 tank and 8 motorized rifle brigades), 1 separate motorized rifle brigade, and 29 separate tank brigades. Behind them stood the VGK Reserve, which included 1 tank and 7 reserve armies (including 3 tank corps with 8 tank brigades and 4 separate tank brigades), roughly half of which were in place behind the fronts in the southern Soviet Union.[30] Many of these formations, especially the corps and army headquarters to control the mechanized brigades, were still in the process of activation and training. Across the entire front, the Red Army's field and reserve units reported 4,197 tanks on 1 May; another 5,128 newly produced tanks had not yet reached the combat units. Moreover, of the 4,197 tanks in the field, many were outside the region of the principal German offensive, and more than half of them were light tanks of limited capacity.[31] In practice, therefore, in the southern region the Red Army began the second year of the war with an overall tank ratio, in comparison to the Germans, of less than 2:1.

THE TWO DICTATORS

Popular histories of the Soviet-German conflict frequently focus on Adolf Hitler and Joseph Stalin, blaming them for every mistake and defeat.

Although both men made significant military errors, the reality of their leadership was both more nuanced and more successful than the legends suggest.

To begin with, one must recognize that the ultimate leader—the *Führer* or *Vozhd'*—had to *lead*, both to satisfy his propaganda image and to discourage any potential rivals. Men who took and held power by the threat of violence could not afford to appear passive or indecisive. Moreover, Hitler in particular had accumulated a number of diplomatic and military successes that encouraged even his closest associates to assume that the Führer really *did* know best in any crisis. Living up to this image sometimes compelled him to interfere in matters the General Staff officers had always considered their private area of expertise. Hitler was a gifted amateur, while his "professional" subordinates were by no means infallible, as evidenced by his decision, perhaps for the wrong reasons, to defend in place outside Moscow.

That said, until mid-1942, Hitler often deferred to his commanders and advisers, so long as these individuals were generally effective. Even when Hitler issued a military pronouncement, he did not necessarily enforce that edict if his generals provided a logical explanation for a different course of action. Halder and the field commanders continued to circumvent the dictator's desires, often without penalty or punishment. However, the Reichel incident represented both a genuine lack of security awareness and a deliberate intent to thwart the essence of Hitler's instructions. As the 1942 campaign progressed without a decisive victory, the dictator began to suspect that his subordinates were overly cautious at best and perhaps genuinely obstructionist. He became increasingly impatient at what he perceived to be a closing strategic window, perhaps the last chance to establish his empire on a stable basis before American and Soviet production overwhelmed the Germans. From this perspective, he became more and more convinced that his subordinates were letting tactical opportunities slip away. Small wonder, then, that he relieved a number of senior commanders during the campaign while inserting himself more aggressively into it.

Not surprisingly, Stalin's conduct was a mirror image of Hitler's. His initial response to the defeats of 1941 was to centralize his control further while increasing the power of political officers and secret police and imprisoning or executing failed commanders on suspicion of treason. By the end of 1941, the Soviet leader had identified a small number of men, such as Deputy Commander in Chief G. K. Zhukov, Chief of the General Staff A. M. Vasilevsky, and Front and Main Direction Commander S. K. Timoshenko, who possessed the necessary competence and ruthlessness to succeed in battle. Even then, however, Stalin retained control of key decisions, such as committing the strategic reserve outside Moscow. Over the course of 1942, the very German failures that bothered Hitler eventually prompted Stalin to give greater trust and authority to his generals.

GERMAN LEADERS

Hitler's senior leaders in 1942 were all experienced generals. The two army group commanders most involved in the upcoming offensive were typical products of the older German officer corps. Field Marshals Fedor von Bock and Sigmund Wilhelm List were both 62 years old (born in 1880); both were veterans of World War I, the General Staff system, and the interwar German Army. Being slightly senior in rank, Bock had been given the plum assignment of commander of Army Group Center during the Barbarossa campaign; Hitler expressed his continuing faith in Bock by posting him at the head of Army Group South for the *Blau* campaign. When, as planned, this campaign achieved its initial successes, Army Group South would split into two parts, with Bock heading Army Group B to advance into the bend of the Don River, and List, who had spent the previous year commanding in the Balkans, assuming leadership of the newly formed Army Group A. This new headquarters was to direct the drive to the Caucasus oil fields in the later phases of the *Blau* campaign.

Below the army group level, there were a number of younger leaders, one in the *Luftwaffe* and six in the army, who would figure prominently in the campaign. Most of them began the campaign with the rank of colonel general, just below field marshal.

Wolfram *Freiherr* (Baron) von Richthofen, a cousin of the famous World War I aviator, was born in 1895 and served as an army officer on both fronts during World War I before becoming a pilot. In early 1942 he commanded *Fliegerkorps* (Air Corps) VIII, the *Luftwaffe*'s premier close air support formation that reinforced the main army effort in various locations. Throughout the 1942 campaign, Richthofen was frustrated and impatient with ground commanders who relied on his aircraft to blast through any Soviet resistance; like most airpower advocates, he considered this a poor use of his airmen's potential power. Nonetheless, he went to unusual lengths to coordinate not only with German Army commanders but also with their Romanian allies.[32]

Colonel General Hermann Hoth, born in 1885, had been an infantry commander before leading XV Motorized Corps in the 1940 campaign. During the Barbarossa campaign, Hoth commanded Third Panzer Group and Seventeenth Army, surviving the December crisis in which many of his contemporaries lost their positions. For the 1942 campaign, Hoth commanded Fourth Panzer Army, which was key to both the initial advance under *Blau* and the later vain efforts to relieve the encirclement at Stalingrad.[33]

Colonel General Fritz-Erich von Manstein had the most meteoric rise of any officer on either side during 1942. When the fighting resumed in May, he commanded a virtual sideshow, the German-Romanian Eleventh Army in the Crimea; six months later, he was Germany's last hope, a field marshal leading the improvised Army Group Don that eventually pushed the Red Army back in early 1943. Born Erich von Lewinski in 1887, he assumed the name of his stepfather and rose as an imperial guardsman and General Staff officer. Manstein was an abrasive, demanding, anti-Semitic leader who was nonetheless a brilliant planner and tactician. Self-confident to the point of arrogance, he rose rapidly once the war began, commanding LVI Motorized Corps in 1941 before leading Eleventh Army to victory in the Crimea.[34]

If Manstein had an equal as an operational commander, it was probably the handsome Colonel General Ewald Paul Ludwig von Kleist. Born into a long line of Prussian soldier-aristocrats in 1881, Kleist was a committed royalist and Christian who did not hide his distaste for Nazism. This attitude led to his temporary retirement in 1938. Once the war began, however, the former cavalryman was recalled to active duty, where he proved to be a consummate operational commander. This was reflected most famously in Panzer Group Kleist, the four-corps formation that broke through the Ardennes and raced to Dunkirk in 1940. Kleist then commanded First Panzer Group, later redesignated First Panzer Army, in 1941–1942. By the time the Red Army counterattacked at Stalingrad, Kleist had succeeded List in command of Army Group A in the Caucasus. While Manstein fought to relieve Stalingrad, Kleist conducted a brilliant fighting retreat from that region, a performance that earned him a marshal's baton.[35]

Perhaps the most famous and controversial name associated with the Stalingrad tragedy was Friedrich Wilhelm Ernst Paulus (sometimes erroneously identified as "von Paulus"), who commanded the German Sixth Army in that city.[36] Born in 1890, Paulus was an intelligent workaholic from a middle-class background who aspired to a place in the aristocratic officer corps of imperial Germany. In 1912 he acquired quasi-aristocratic status by marrying a Romanian noblewoman. Tall, lean, and always immaculately dressed, the young soldier was the model of a German officer. By 1918, he was a captain who had served as a staff officer at battalion and regimental level. Between the world wars, Paulus left the General Staff only twice for brief, obligatory assignments with troops, commanding at company and battalion level. The latter assignment was particularly auspicious, since Lieutenant Colonel Paulus commanded the 3rd Motor Transport Battalion, the model for future armored reconnaissance units at a time (1934–1935) when the Versailles Treaty still forbade Germany to possess tanks. Thereafter, he reverted to his normal role, becoming in succession chief of staff of three key organizations: panzer forces in 1935, Heinz Guderian's XVI Motorized Corps in 1938, and Army Group 4 in 1939.

For the invasion of Poland, Colonel Paulus was a chief of staff yet again, this time for the German Tenth Army commanded by Colonel General Walter von Reichenau, an early convert to Nazism. The two men's personalities were perfectly complementary; Paulus provided the methodical staff work that kept the headquarters functioning, while the earthy and assertive Reichenau led his troops from the front. After the 1940 campaign, Paulus reached the penultimate position in his career as *Oberquartiermeister* I, or deputy chief of the General Staff. As such, he helped plan for Operation Barbarossa, although when he war-gamed that plan, he reluctantly concluded that the Germans might well fail to achieve a decisive victory over the Red Army.[37]

The introverted, refined Paulus was never comfortable arguing with coarser, more assertive men such as Hitler and Reichenau, but he recognized their considerable ability; they, in turn, valued his loyal service as a meticulous subordinate. It retrospect, therefore, it appears almost inevitable that Paulus would have a starring role in the forthcoming campaign. On 5 January 1942 the man who had never commanded anything more significant than a peacetime battalion received a promotion to colonel general and command of Sixth Army, one of the spearheads of Operation *Blau*. Despite his inexperience, he proved worthy of the task.

At the time, Reichenau was Paulus's immediate superior as commander of Army Group South. Reichenau undoubtedly expected that they would reprise their respective roles from earlier operations, with Reichenau leading from the front while his protégé applied his usual thoroughness to the details of the operation. Less than two weeks after Paulus received his new position, however, Reichenau died unexpectedly, probably as a result of exercising in the extreme cold of the Russian winter. Fedor von Bock succeeded him as army group commander, and Paulus was on his own.

Colonel General Maximilian *Freiherr* von Weichs an dem Glon commanded Second Army during the first year of the war and then led an ad hoc army group that bore his name during the initial phases of Operation *Blau*. Like Kleist, Weichs was somewhat old for field command, having been born in 1881; also like Kleist, he was a cavalryman and rather outspoken—in his case, insisting on the army's political neutrality. A corps commander in the Polish campaign, he rose to field army command in 1941 and helped encircle the Red Army's Southwestern Front at Kiev in September. Weichs was known as the "antiaircraft general" for his innovative use of the *Luftwaffe*'s 88mm antiaircraft guns in a ground combat role. Illness took him away from his command in November 1941, but he returned a month later in time to contain the first Red Army winter offensive.[38]

The most junior army commander in this group was Colonel General Richard Ruoff. Born in 1891, Ruoff commanded V Army Corps from 1939 through 1941. As such, he halted the counterattack of two Soviet mechanized corps near Minsk in June 1941 and assisted in the encirclement battle of Smolensk a month later. This performance led him to command Army Group

Center's Fourth Panzer Army in January 1942 and Army Group South's Seventeenth Army five months later. In the latter position, Ruoff conducted one of the Germans' deepest advances into the Caucasus Mountains.

One key difference between the two sides was the relative experience of German commanders in their current positions. Because of equipment and manpower shortages, Germany could form only a few "new" units—such as converting 1st Cavalry Division into 24th Panzer—in 1942. Thus, many German commanders led the same units, or at least units of similar size and complexity, in both 1941 and 1942. By contrast, many Soviet commanders and their staff officers took on greater responsibilities and had to "grow" into their new positions. This was especially true of the successful tank brigade headquarters that now supervised tank corps and even armies. Many of the Soviet failures in 1942 were due to this inexperience in critical tasks such as operations planning and logistical support.

RED ARMY LEADERS

In contrast to their foes, the senior leaders of the Red Army were a much more diverse mixture of groups and individuals. Almost all of them were younger than their German counterparts. This included even the most senior Red officers, such as Marshal S. K. Timoshenko (born in 1895), who had Stalin's confidence because of their performance in the Russian Civil War two decades earlier. However, these veterans generally failed to adjust to the demands of mechanized, high-intensity conflict. Stalin's most trusted lieutenants, Deputy Commander in Chief G. K. Zhukov (born in 1896) and Chief of the General Staff A. M. Vasilevsky (born in 1895), have already been mentioned and are considered in detail in connection with strategic planning in chapter 2. Political officer Nikita Sergeevich Khrushchev (born in 1894) had also earned the dictator's confidence before the war and managed to retain it in battle by a combination of courage, competence, and political agility.

Below the highest levels, a number of *front* (army group) and field army commanders came and went, often relieved before they could gain control of their wavering formations. For our purposes, however, three men commanded the key *fronts* seeking to halt the German offensive in 1942. Lieutenant General Filipp Ivanovich Golikov was only 42 years old when he took command of the Briansk Front in April of that year. Golikov had had a varied career, including political commissar, mechanized corps commander, head of the General Staff's Main Intelligence Directorate (*Glavnoe Razvedyvatel'noe Upravlenie*, or GRU, where he managed to keep his job while warning Stalin of the impending German invasion), and Stalin's personal representative to London and Washington in 1941. He returned home in time to command 4th Shock Army successfully in the spring of 1942; this performance plus Golikov's political survival skills led to his elevation to *front* command.[39]

The second such commander was 43-year-old Lieutenant General Rodion Iakovlevich Malinovsky, who had begun his career in 1914, served in the Russian imperial expeditionary corps to France, and returned home to fight in the Russian Civil War. A peacetime cavalry corps commander, Malinovsky also served in the Spanish Civil War. His performance as a rifle corps commander in 1941 was more successful than that of many of his contemporaries, leading to his rapid promotion, including command of 6th Army (August–December 1941) and of the Southern Front thereafter. As such, he had helped defeat Kleist's First Panzer Army at Rostov in November and then pushed the Germans west to the Khar'kov area during the counteroffensive.[40]

The oldest of the three *front* commanders, Lieutenant General Dmitri Timonfeevich Kozlov, was 44 years of age when he became commander of the Trans-Caucasus Front in August 1941. A noncommissioned officer during World War I and the Civil War, Kozlov had commanded battalions and regiments and fought against central Asian insurgents. He attended the Frunze General Staff Academy in the 1920s and returned to teach at that school during the 1930s. Kozlov commanded the Trans-Caucasus Military District during the first half of 1941 and then became *front* commander of the same area upon mobilization. In the latter capacity, he had startled the Germans with a successful amphibious operation to regain control of the Kerch' Peninsula in the eastern Crimea during December 1941.[41]

Beyond these three men, one must include the *front* commander who directed the final destruction of Sixth Army, Lieutenant General Konstantin Konstantinovich Rokossovsky. Born in Warsaw and a veteran of the Tsar's army in World War I, he had risen in the Red Army as a cavalryman until he was swept up in the Great Purge and spent three years in prison after being implicated by another prisoner. Released in March 1940, he commanded a mechanized corps and a field army during 1941. He began the 1942 campaign as commander of the Briansk Front, but in September Zhukov brought him to Stalingrad.[42] There, Rokossovsky assumed various positions, ultimately commanding the Don Front that surrounded and destroyed Sixth Army between November 1942 and February 1943.

In addition to these *front* commanders, at least 15 other officers led field armies during the 1942 campaign, and some of them went on to command at higher levels. Almost all of them had benefited from the 1937–1941 purge of senior Soviet officers. Although many of these men figured in the events that followed, three deserve special mention because of their performance in 1942 and after; in terms of their background and behavior, they were typical of their peers.

First was Kiril Semenovich Moskalenko, a 39-year-old major general who assumed command of the Southwestern Front's 38th Army in March 1942. An enlisted cavalryman during the Russian Civil War, Moskalenko held a variety of commands in every active theater, including the Winter War with Finland (1939–1940), the occupation of Romanian Bessarabia (1940), and the disastrous Kiev encirclement (1941). After surviving Kiev, his pre-war experience with mechanized forces led to his command of a cavalry-mechanized group, followed by leadership of 6th Army in the partially successful Barvenkovo-Lozovaia offensive early in 1942.[43]

The two generals most responsible for the defense of Stalingrad were not yet on stage when Operation *Blau* began. Both had suffered disgrace in previous defeats, and both were thrown into battle after more favored commanders had failed. Colonel General Andrei Ivanovich Eremenko, born in 1892, had been drafted into the Tsar's army in 1913 and volunteered for the Red Army in 1918. Like many successful Red officers, he had served in Semen Budenny's cavalry army during the Civil War and remained in that branch, commanding 6th Cavalry Corps when the USSR invaded eastern Poland in 1939. Eremenko was wounded three times between July 1941 and January 1942, twice while commanding *fronts* that vainly tried to halt the German advance to Moscow. In August 1942 he became commander of the Southeastern Front, later redesignated the Stalingrad Front. There, assisted by his commissar Khrushchev, Eremenko had the grim task of feeding units into the meat grinder of urban warfare. Their *front* headquarters was located on the east bank of the Volga throughout the fall of 1942, allowing them to remain aloof from the tactical battle itself.[44]

The actual defense of Stalingrad fell to Lieutenant General Vasilii Ivanovich Chuikov, the 41-year-old commander of 62nd Army.[45] The son of a peasant, Chuikov had risen to command a regiment during the Russian Civil War. Thereafter his career was divided almost equally among military schools, troop commands, and repeated assignments as an adviser in Mongolia and China. Disgraced as commander of 9th Army during the Finnish Winter War, Chuikov went into de facto exile as the Soviet military attaché to the Nationalist Chinese government. Even when he wrangled his way back to European Russia after the German invasion, an automobile accident sidelined him for more than a year. Thus, he did not meet the Germans in battle until the summer of 1942, when he managed to salvage something from the repeated defeats of that period. His hard-headed perseverance and competence led him to the perilous command of 62nd Army in September, just as the defense of Stalingrad began. Chuikov was an energetic rather than a brilliant soldier, but he had a knack for inspiring his subordinates. In the house-to-house struggle for the ruins of the city, the earthy, pragmatic Chuikov proved at least as effective as the cerebral, meticulous Paulus.

THE GERMAN SOLDIER

Germany's soldiers, like its commanders, were a mixed bag of veteran professionals and new enthusiasts. After three years of uninterrupted triumph, the winter campaign of 1941–1942 had cost the German Army in experience and confidence as well as in blood and equipment.

To meet the urgent need for replacements in the spring of 1942, infantry divisions received soldiers with as little as two months of training and scant time in their new units.[46] An army that prided itself on tactical skill and training now had to deal with half-trained recruits and inexperienced units. This began a deadly spiral that continued for the rest of the war: inexperienced, inadequately trained soldiers were more likely to become casualties than were experienced ones, which led to a renewed demand for replacements and forced the training base to send out men with steadily decreasing periods of training.

The high turnover in manpower, with its resulting influx of younger Germans, also contributed to a trend that existed even in 1941—what might be termed the Nazification of the German Army. With certain exceptions such as Reichenau, during the first part of the war, senior commanders were still the products of the conservative, professional army of World War I and the Weimar Republic, albeit this conservatism was often tinged with old-fashioned anti-Semitism. As time went on, however, many company-grade officers and rank-and-file soldiers had grown up under the Nazi regime and often reflected Nazi attitudes.[47] They tended to regard their opponents as uncivilized subhumans, an attitude that encouraged the Germans to fight with great bravery because they feared capture more than death. Yet this same belief structure had a darker side. Isolated from German society in a strange and frightening land, German soldiers were guilty of constant callousness and casual atrocities against Soviet civilians as well as prisoners of war. Despite later denials, in practice, their senior commanders did little or nothing to correct these excesses.

THE SOVIET SOLDIER

As the training level of the average German soldier declined, that of his Soviet counterpart rose. Wartime training in the Red Army varied greatly, depending on the date and location of entry into service. In general, units formed in the interior had achieved some level of competence and cohesion before they entered battle. The legends of draconian discipline were exaggerated; the main function of "blocking detachments" behind the front lines was not to punish deserters but to return stragglers to their units. Thousands of Soviet soldiers still died in the summer of 1942, but a year of painful experience gave both the surviving troops and their commanders a growing measure of competence.[48]

Soviet histories tend to glorify the socialist spirit of the Red Army, and indeed, millions of the bravest and most competent soldiers were rewarded with membership in the Communist Party. Reading between the lines, however, the average Soviet soldier was apparently actuated by the more traditional motives of loyalty to comrades and patriotic defense of the nation. Indeed, beginning in 1941, the Soviet state consciously identified itself with Mother Russia in the struggle against the invaders, gaining a loyalty that Marxism alone had never inspired. There were, of course, misunderstandings and friction between the officer corps (largely Great Russian) and various minority groups from all over the Soviet Union.[49] Some nationalities provided significant numbers of armed auxiliaries to support the Germans or, like the Ukrainians, fought as guerrillas against both sides.[50] However, the Germans' harsh occupation policies and their initial reluctance to arm Slavs tended to drive many potential supporters into the Soviet camp.

The desperate struggle to defend the Motherland meant that women as well as men bore the burdens of war. The NKO was initially reluctant to enlist large numbers of females, often restricting them to "traditional" but dangerous tasks such as medics, drivers, and communications operators. In the course of 1942, however, the government gradually widened the use of female soldiers, eventually training them as antiaircraft troops, pilots, snipers, and even tank drivers.[51] Like their male counterparts, these women exhibited the traditional Russian ability to endure unimaginable hardship while fighting with great intensity.

In 1942, therefore, the average German soldier might have been marginally more competent than his Soviet counterpart, but neither side needed lessons from the other about the ferocity of a struggle for survival.

CHAPTER TWO

Plans and Preparations

In retrospect, both the German and Soviet plans for 1942 appear unrealistic and overly ambitious. Perhaps subconsciously, each side expected the other to display the weaknesses of the previous year. Senior German commanders and staffs—at least at the level of the OKH (*Oberkommando des Heeres*, the Army General Staff) and OKW (*Oberkommando der Wehrmacht*, the joint staff responsible for all theaters except the one in the East)—assumed that the Red Army would make the same bumbling mistakes it had committed in 1941, when Soviet units had often allowed themselves to be surrounded and then fell apart. Stalin, the *Stavka*, and many senior Red commanders subconsciously expected the Germans to be in the same parlous state they had been in during the winter months—undermanned, undersupplied, and almost immobilized by equipment failures. Both sides would be disappointed.

THE STRATEGIC PICTURE

Prior to the 1941 invasion of Russia, Adolf Hitler had dominated Western Europe, with only Great Britain still openly opposing him. One year later, Germany was fighting the two largest industrial powers in the world—the United States and the Soviet Union—in two separate theaters. Thus, even as the OKH and OKW prepared for a 1942 offensive in the East, they had to consider the demands of other theaters of war. The United States, which had just begun its mobilization, had to balance any actions in Europe against the more pressing needs of the Pacific war. Still, Hitler could not rid himself of the fear that the British, aided by the Americans, might attempt to reduce the pressure on the Soviets by launching a limited invasion of Norway or France. The Soviet government repeatedly demanded such a "second front," dismissing the logistical and tactical problems involved.

Hitler's fears were not entirely unfounded. From his perspective, which his army commanders in the East rarely understood, any attack in the West would pose a much more immediate threat to the core of the German Reich than an equivalent enemy advance in Russia because of the relative distances involved. Therefore, at a 28 March conference on the upcoming *Blau* campaign, the dictator insisted that several high-priority units remain in the West

25

as a strategic reserve. These included the *Luftwaffe*'s improbably named Hermann Göring Parachute Panzer Division as well as three reconstituting panzer divisions. Hitler also focused on the difficulties of resupplying Field Marshal Erwin Rommel's small *Afrika Korps* in North Africa. In particular, he diverted significant air assets to help the Italians bombard the British island of Malta, which straddled the sea-lanes between Italy and North Africa.[1]

Germany's strategic position in the spring of 1942 was not completely negative. The United States' sudden entry into the war had given the German submarine service an unprecedented opportunity to attack the poorly protected merchant shipping in US waters. Hitler could reasonably expect these U-boat victories to damage the US and British economies and delay the deployment of American forces to Europe. Yet the very complexity of a wider war, with conflicting demands on resources for U-boats, for North Africa, and for Western Europe, complicated decision making and made Germany less likely to accept risk than it had been in 1941.

Even in the East, the Germans had to be more disciplined, focusing on one objective rather than attempting to capture everything at once, as they had done the previous year. In the north, the besieged city of Leningrad beckoned. Capture of this great city, birthplace of the Bolshevik Revolution, would not only yield psychological advantages but also permit the German troops to link up with their capable allies the Finns. With luck, a northern offensive might cut off the Soviet arctic seaports and thereby reduce the flow of Allied Lend-Lease supplies into the Soviet Union. As a result of the confused winter fighting, there were also large pockets of surrounded Germans to be rescued and, similarly, significant groupings of Soviet troops that might be choked off behind German lines. All this promised, at the very least, to shorten the German defensive lines and thereby free forces for further offensive operations.

South of Khar'kov, that great industrial city in the northern Ukraine, German intelligence analysts detected a combination of enemy troops near a westward bend of the front at the Northern Donets River. This protrusion, the remnant of the Soviet Barvenkovo-Losovaia offensive of January and February 1942, was variously known as the Izium or Barvenkovo salient. The Germans suspected correctly that their opponents intended to use this salient as a bridgehead for offensive operations; therefore, German planners wished to eliminate both the salient and any Soviet troop concentrations before launching a major offensive. The German plan for this preliminary attack was known as Operation Fridericus, but the Soviets preempted it with their own failed offensive in May 1942.

Finally, the Germans had to clear two Soviet positions on the Crimean Peninsula. The fortified city of Sevastopol', which had repulsed Axis attacks in 1941, posed multiple threats. Its port allowed the Red Navy to harass the

German-occupied coastlines, while its airfield was a natural base for the Red Air Force to attack the vital oil fields of Ploesti, Romania.[2] In addition to Sevastopol', the Soviets held the Kerch' Peninsula at the extreme eastern end of the Crimea. To eliminate this threat, Erich von Manstein's combined German-Romanian Eleventh Army planned Operation *Trappenjagt* (Bustard Hunt). Large German siege guns and significant *Luftwaffe* ground support aircraft gathered to assist in clearing both Kerch' and Sevastopol'.

FALL BLAU

All these possible objectives, from Leningrad to Sevastopol', were sideshows to the main objective for 1942: seizure of the Caucasus oil fields. The small oil field at Maikop and the much larger one centered around Baku (in what is now Azerbaijan) together produced approximately 80 percent of all Soviet petroleum products; seizing them would not only strike a major blow against the USSR but also solve the greatest limitation on the German economy and war machine. In October 1941 Germany had managed to refuel its spearheads only by coercing the Romanians into providing more of their limited fuel supply. By 1942, the German and Italian surface fleets were almost immobilized by a lack of fuel, and the U-boats were hampered by a 50 percent reduction in supplies. For Hitler and his military and economic planners, the Caucasus oil fields appeared to be the solution to most of their problems.[3]

The Caucasus offered other advantages to the German prosecution of the war. The region contained not only petroleum but also extensive reserves of coal, peat, manganese, and other materials; however, moving bulk materials from such a remote location would pose a formidable problem. In addition, the Caucasus was the natural gateway to the Middle East; its seizure would eliminate another major conduit of Lend-Lease aid coming through Iran. Some Germans even dreamed of a gigantic pincer movement, pushing south beyond the Caucasus to link up with Rommel's *Afrika Korps* east of the Suez Canal and seize control of the vast oil reserves of the Middle East.

For all these reasons, control of the Caucasus had been part of German thinking since July 1940, when Hitler initiated planning for the invasion of the Soviet Union. Long-range aerial reconnaissance took extensive photographs of the region as the Barbarossa plan progressed. Yet by October 1941, it was clear that Germany could not reach the oil fields that year, so the OKH pushed the date for such an operation forward into 1942. Throughout the difficult defensive battles during the winter of 1941–1942, Hitler frequently returned to this prospect, insisting that specialized mountain troops remain ready to push through the Caucasus as early as possible the following spring.[4]

Once the winter battles shuddered to a halt, the plan for the next campaign took final form.[5] On 28 March 1942 General Halder, as head of the OKH, presented Hitler with the draft for the summer offensive. Originally code-named *Fall* (Plan or Case) Siegfried, this plan had already received the more neutral name *Blau* (Blue), apparently because the failure of Barbarossa had made further references to German mythology seem embarrassingly grandiose. After the dictator commented extensively on the OKH proposal, General Alfred Jodl, the operations chief of the *Wehrmacht* High Command (OKW), revised the plan and again presented it to the dictator a week later.

Halder and Jodl had produced the kind of plan that the German General Staff system expected: it established an overall concept of operations and responsibilities of subordinate headquarters but left many decisions to the field commanders, especially Bock as head of Army Group South. However, as noted in the prologue, Hitler was developing some suspicions about his generals' willingness to fulfill his intent. He therefore insisted that Jodl add detailed instructions about the conduct of the campaign. The result was a curious mixture of operations order, strategic evaluation, and wishful thinking.

Führer Directive (*Weisung*) No. 41, issued on 5 April 1942, assumed that the Soviet Union had been so exhausted by the previous year of warfare that one additional push would rupture the Red Army and clear the way to the Caucasus oil fields. Still, the directive tacitly recognized that no single campaign was likely to crush the Soviet Union completely, which had been the goal of Operation Barbarossa. Instead, the most Hitler could hope for was to destroy Stalin's military forces and push the remnants of the Communist regime eastward toward the Ural Mountains. The stated objective of the 1942 campaign was to "wipe out the entire defense potential remaining to the Soviets and to cut them off, as far as possible, from their most important centers of war industry."[6] To this end, Hitler envisioned another series of encirclement battles but reemphasized his 1941 concern that these pockets be sealed off tightly so the Soviets could not escape to fight again.

The directive discussed all aspects of the 1942 effort in the East, beginning with a renewed assault on Leningrad, a series of limited offensives to straighten the German lines, and preparatory operations to eliminate Soviet capabilities in the Crimea and around Izium. Only after these operations reached completion would the Germans launch the main offensive for the summer. The distances involved were so great and the transportation lines so tenuous that the operation would be conducted in phases, later referred to as *Blau* I, *Blau* II, and so on. This portion of the directive was still expressed in fairly general terms; only later did the field commanders assign specific tasks to the various maneuver armies. What follows, therefore, is an attempt to flesh out the ambiguous outline of the original plan.[7]

What we now refer to as *Blau* I would begin with a German advance from

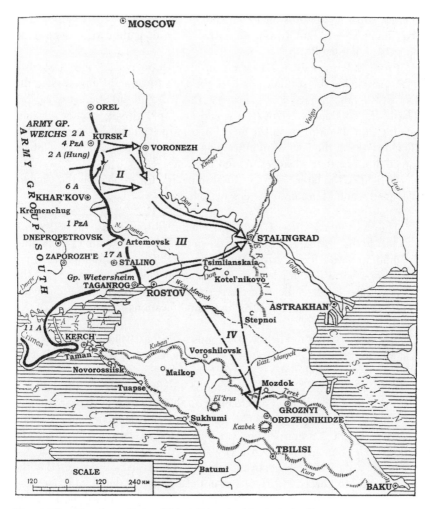

Map 2. Plan *Blau* According to Hitler's Directive No. 41, 5 April 1942

the region south of Orel eastward to the Don River where it approached Voronezh. Attacking from the areas of Kursk and Belgorod, two larger pincers of panzers and motorized forces, especially the northern group led by Fourth Panzer Army, would advance to establish a strong left or northern defensive flank from Orel to Voronezh and, in the process, destroy the Soviet forces of the Voronezh Front. During *Blau* II, the mechanized forces that had reached the Don would turn southward along the river's right bank to link up near Millerovo with Sixth Army, advancing eastward from Khar'kov, thereby creating another encirclement. As the panzers moved southward, Axis forces were to build strong defensive works along the Don to secure the operation's left flank.

From Millerovo, *Blau* III called for a much deeper advance eastward, again paralleling the southern bank of the Don River and then crossing the Don at the point where it was closest to the Volga, in the Stalingrad region. There, the southeasterly advance would link up with yet another advance coming from Taganrog near the Sea of Azov, which would also seize the Don River bridges at the key communications center of Rostov, the obvious starting point for further advances to the Caucasus.

In light of the later course of the campaign, it is ironic that the original plan paid scant attention to the city of Stalingrad:

> The third attack [*Blau* III] in this scheme of operations will be so conducted that formations thrusting down the Don can link up in the Stalingrad area with forces advancing from the Taganrog-Artemovsk area . . . every effort will be made to reach Stalingrad itself, or at least to bring the city under fire from heavy artillery so that it may no longer be of any use [to the Soviets] as an industrial or communications center.[8]

Clearly, the city that today is synonymous with the 1942 campaign was *not* part of the original German objective. Neutralizing it was considered desirable but not essential to the real objective in the Caucasus.

Führer Directive No. 41 went on to specify supporting tasks for the *Luftwaffe* and the German Navy and to insist on absolute secrecy in preparing for the offensive. To this end, the Germans had already launched an operation known as *Kreml* (Kremlin), a deception designed to play on Soviet fears of a renewed German advance on Moscow.[9]

Blau IV, the subsequent advance into the Caucasus, was projected in the introduction to Directive No. 41 but not elaborated in detail. Still, German staff officers were well aware of the dictator's intentions. Once the Don and Volga River lines were secure, panzer and motorized troops would spearhead the attack southward, except in the high Caucasus Mountains, where the German and Italian mountain troops would come into their own. A special 10,000-man organization, the Oil Brigade Caucasus, waited to move into the oil fields and restore production as quickly as possible. Meanwhile, the Axis satellite armies, reinforced by antitank batteries and backed by a few mobile German divisions, would protect the ever-lengthening left flank of the German advance.

Such an advance would pose an operational and logistical challenge greater than that of any previous German offensive. The straight-line distance from the starting point at Kursk to the Chechen city of Grozny, center

of the Soviet petroleum industry, was 760 kilometers; the various encirclements for the plan meant an overall distance of more than 1,000 kilometers.
Thus, the total advance would be greater than that achieved in 1941, and it
would be done over a combination of semi-desert and mountainous terrain.
To control this daring penetration, Hitler and his generals foresaw the need
to split Army Group South into two separate entities—Army Groups A and
B—at some point in the campaign because the German forces would be
pursuing two divergent objectives. On 14 April Hitler directed the OKH to
prepare for this eventuality by creating an additional army group headquarters under Field Marshal List.[10]

Lacking the resources for two full-blooded offensives, Hitler had turned
to the artificial expedient of splitting his force into two groups with diverging
strategic objectives. This field expedient failed to recognize that *Blau* actually involved three strategic axes: defending the Voronezh flank, securing
the Don-Volga River area near Stalingrad, and moving into the Caucasus. At
most, the Germans had sufficient combat and logistics capacity to support
one of these axes, but not all three. This divided objective proved particularly ominous because, once again, the Red Army was much more resilient
that German intelligence had expected. As previously noted, the shortage of
German troops meant that the poorly equipped Axis armies, acting as a full
army group, would have to protect the Voronezh flank.[11]

THE SOVIET STRATEGIC DEBATE

The Soviet leadership was well aware that the Germans were gathering
strength for another offensive; unfortunately, the Soviets failed to identify
either the true objective of that offensive or an appropriate response to it.
Mesmerized by the desperate battles of the previous winter, Stalin and his
subordinates were convinced that the next German offensive would again
make Moscow its primary objective, with a possible secondary offensive in
the south. Soviet commanders and intelligence analysts calculated that 70
German divisions could strike from the center of the enemy front eastward
toward Moscow; these same analysts and commanders tended to ignore the
possibility that many of the same divisions could pivot and strike southeastward.[12] The defense of Moscow therefore received first priority for weapons,
units, and the construction of field fortifications. It is ironic that a group of
dedicated Marxists, who supposedly believed that the basis of all power lay
in controlling the means of production, focused on defending their political
capital rather than the economic value of the southeastern region of the Soviet Union.

Even as the guns fell silent in March, the Soviet senior leadership began planning for the next campaign. Stalin was convinced he had been within inches of victory during the winter battles; like Hitler, he continued to hope for decisive success in the coming months. The Soviet dictator therefore wanted to launch a new general offensive as soon as his troops had regained some strength and the spring mud had dried out. His subordinates tried to dissuade him, and the resulting Soviet strategy was an almost incoherent compromise between offensive and defensive.

The chief of the Soviet General Staff at the time was Marshal of the Soviet Union Boris Mikhailovich Shaposhnikov, a scholarly, courtly 60-year-old who was one of the last tsarist officers still serving in the Red Army. In the spring of 1942 a combination of overwork and respiratory distress was slowly destroying Shaposhnikov's health; on 10 May he retired to the less demanding position of head of the Higher Military Academy. Meanwhile, he labored to convince Stalin of the dangers of a premature Soviet advance. Shaposhnikov was convinced that the Germans would launch a new offensive as soon as the spring thaw ended. Just as in the previous year, therefore, any Soviet attack must wait until this threat had expended itself on the Red Army's defenses.

Shaposhnikov's former operations chief and hand-picked successor, Aleksandr Mikhailovich Vasilevsky, supported his chief's arguments, even at the risk of the dictator's displeasure. Vasilevsky had earned Stalin's trust in part because, as a key staff officer, he had remained in Moscow with the *Vozhd'* (leader) during the city's 1941 defense, when most of the government evacuated. Vasilevsky had risen from colonel to colonel general in four years, becoming chief of the Operations Directorate and deputy chief of the General Staff in August 1941. He helped plan most of the major Red Army operations in 1941–1942 and, at the same time, served as a "Representative of the *Stavka*"—a trusted troubleshooter sent out from the capital to supervise critical field operations. Although Vasilevsky failed to dissuade Stalin from his plan for new attacks in the spring, he became chief of the General Staff in his own right in June 1942 and deputy commissar for defense in October.[13]

At age 45, Georgii Konstantinovich Zhukov was already Stalin's favorite general in the spring of 1942. Since his victory over the Japanese at Khalkhin-Gol, Mongolia, in August 1939, he had experienced rapid promotion, becoming chief of the General Staff in January 1941. By the fall, he was a member of the *Stavka* as well as the Red Army's most influential *front* commander, and Stalin dispatched him to each successive crisis along the front lines. Zhukov understood the wisdom behind Shaposhnikov's and Vasilevsky's cautious counsel in the second year of the war. However, Zhukov was a naturally pugnacious man who was not above currying favor with his master. In his own recollections, Zhukov claimed he had warned against the danger of dissipating Soviet strength in too many local offensives. Still, it was entirely in character for Zhukov to urge Stalin privately to undertake limited offensive actions within the context of an overall strategic defense. Even Zhukov admitted to advocating a limited offensive in the Rzhev-Viaz'ma region in the north, which he regarded as the starting point for a renewed advance on the capital.[14]

The outcome of this internal debate was disastrous for the Soviet military. In early March Stalin's initial guidance for the next campaign called for an "active strategic defense" but directed planning for seven local offensives, from the Kerch' Peninsula in the south to Leningrad in the north.[15]

Stalin's field commanders responded to the dictator's obvious preference for offensive action. Although they must have known the limitations of their own units, they gave Stalin overly optimistic assessments of the proposed offensives. Nowhere was this truer than in the Southwestern Main Direction, one of three regional super-headquarters established on 10 July 1941. Marshal of the Soviet Union Semen Konstantinovich Timoshenko commanded this grouping, which included both the Southwestern and Southern Fronts. Timoshenko's reputation had soared in 1940 when he defeated Finland in the Winter War after his predecessors had bungled the job. After this success, the marshal became commissar of defense and, once the war broke out, chief of the *Stavka* and commander of a number of crucial headquarters. As head of both the Southwestern Direction and its subordinate Southwestern Front during the winter of 1941–1942, Timoshenko pushed the Germans back with offensives near Rostov and the Izium region. The result was a large salient that both Stalin and Timoshenko wished to use for a spoiling attack against the Germans; as noted earlier, the German planners correctly identified this salient as a weakness they needed to eliminate prior to the main *Blau* offensive.[16]

In response to Stalin's planning guidance, Timoshenko called a meeting of his principal subordinates, the Military Councils of both the Southwestern Direction and the Southwestern Front. Most such Military Councils consisted of three men: the commander, his political officer or commissar, and the chief of staff. In this instance, the commissar was N. S. Khrushchev, who had headed the Communist Party in the Ukraine before the war. In this instance, however, the chief of staff position was split between two men because of the dual direction-*front* command. Lieutenant General I. Kh. Bagramian, a 45-year-old ethnic Armenian, was both chief of staff of the Southwestern Direction and operations chief in the Southwestern Front; the chief of staff of that *front* was Lieutenant General P. I. Bodin.

Whether because of professional belief or political expedience, these three men all agreed with Timoshenko's proposal for an offensive in the Khar'kov-Izium region. On 20 March Bagramian presented his plan for this operation to a larger group of Timoshenko's subordinates.[17] Khrushchev reportedly emphasized that Stalin himself had ordered the plan and stated that it was guaranteed to succeed.[18] Not surprisingly, the assembled commanders acquiesced to the plan. The most charitable explanation is that these officers believed the Khar'kov offensive to be part of a larger *Stavka* plan about which, in keeping with the Soviet mania for secrecy, they had not been informed.

The 20 March meeting resulted in a series of highly optimistic reports from the Southwestern Direction to the *Stavka*. On 22 March, for example, Timoshenko, Khrushchev, and Bagramian forwarded their overall assessment for the spring-summer period. This report assumed falsely that the desperate conditions of midwinter, when German units had become dispersed and fragmented, still existed. At this stage of the war, Soviet military intelligence assessments were often inaccurate about German order of battle and capabilities, let alone future intentions. While noting that 3,500 German tank crewmen were assembled at Poltava to receive new vehicles, Timoshenko insisted there was no sign of reinforcement at the front. The 22 March report therefore contended that, to forestall the anticipated German attack on Moscow, the Southwestern Direction should launch a series of minor attacks that, after the spring thaw ended, would lead to a major counteroffensive pushing some 240 kilometers westward to the middle Dnepr River. In retrospect, the poor state of readiness of the Soviet units, other than the fledgling armored units, makes this optimistic assessment even more astonishing—in the same report, Timoshenko indicated that his divisions averaged only 51.2 percent of authorized rifles and less than 24 percent of machine guns.[19]

Such recommendations only encouraged the Soviet dictator's aggressive tendencies. Summoned to Moscow, the three leaders of the Southwestern Direction presented their plan to Stalin and Shaposhnikov on 27 March. At this stage, however, the Soviet preoccupation with defending their capital intervened. Although Stalin wanted an offensive against Khar'kov, he was unwilling to weaken Moscow's defenses by providing the extensive reinforcements Timoshenko requested to implement his proposal. Instead, the Military Council of the Southwestern Direction went through several iterations of its plan, each more modest than the last, until the council members finally satisfied their chief by requiring only modest reinforcements.[20]

At the same time, the other sectors of the Soviet defense prepared for lesser offensives. On 9 April the *Stavka* directed the Leningrad and Volkhov Fronts, on either side of Lake Ladoga, to prepare an attack to rescue 2nd Shock Army, which had been encircled south of Leningrad since January.[21] On 20 April Moscow instructed the Briansk Front, just north of Timonshenko's proposed Khar'kov offensive, to plan a supporting attack along the Kursk-L'gov axis. The next day, another order required the Crimean Front to break out of the Kerch' Peninsula and relieve the besieged port of Sevastopol'. On 22 April the Northwestern Front received instructions to make another attempt to reduce II Corps of German Sixteenth Army, encircled near Demiansk; Vasilevsky traveled in person to supervise these preparations.[22] In the far north, the Karelian Front planned to push Finnish forces back to the 1940 border.[23]

The overall concept was that all these operations would occur in late April and early May 1942, preventing the Germans from shifting reserves from one sector to another. However, Khar'kov remained the crown jewel of this spoiling counteroffensive plan. As the professional soldiers of the *Stavka* had feared, these limited offensives merely dissipated resources that would have been better employed to stop the renewed German onslaught.

THE KHAR'KOV PLAN

On 10 April 1942 Timoshenko issued the scaled back but still ambitious plan for the Khar'kov offensive.[24] Even after it was amended on the twenty-eighth, it remained complex and daring; he intended to encircle and destroy the German Sixth Army in the Khar'kov region by enveloping it with two pincers. Northeast of Khar'kov, the Southwestern Front's 21st, 28th, and 38th Armies would advance out of the Staryi Saltov bridgehead on the western bank of the Northern Donets River. Then 3rd Guards Cavalry Corps, reinforced by a tank brigade, would exploit southwestward to link up with the other pincer. This second attack, 110 kilometers to the south, was composed of the South-western Front's 6th Army plus an ad hoc, army-sized formation called Group Bobkin, led by the deputy commander of the Southwestern Front's cavalry, Major General L. V. Bobkin. Supported by two of the new tank corps, this formation would advance out of the Barvenkovo bridgehead over the North-ern Donets, pushing first west and then north toward Khar'kov. This thrust was focused on the poorly equipped Hungarian 108th Division.

The Soviets deployed much of their new materiel to penetrate the Axis defenses, presaging later heavy concentrations in the breakthrough sectors. The main effort in the north, Lieutenant General D. I. Riabyshev's 28th Army, allocated 59.2 guns and mortars and 12 infantry support tanks per kilo-meter of front. Given Stalin's reluctance to reinforce Timoshenko, however, these concentrations could be achieved only by allocating almost all available forces to the field armies involved, with very little held in reserve. Timos-henko had only two rifle divisions, the three-division 2nd Cavalry Corps, and three separate tank battalions under his direct control, a force far too small to respond to unexpected situations.

In making these plans, Timoshenko and his subordinates seriously under-estimated their opponents. Soviet intelligence reported that General Pau-lus's Sixth Army consisted of only 12 understrength infantry divisions and the equally threadbare 23rd Panzer Division. While this may have been accurate in March, by May, Paulus had 15 much stronger infantry or security divisions, with another one en route from France, plus the 3rd and 23rd Panzer Divisions and two smaller ad hoc battle groups.

Moreover, the Soviet planners largely ignored First Panzer and Seventeenth Armies, which were yoked together under Kleist's command, located south of Barvenkovo. Given the mistaken belief that the Germans intended to concentrate on Moscow, they perhaps assumed that these units were low priority. In reality, Kleist commanded 26 divisions and 15 smaller combat groups. His strongest striking force was III Motorized Corps, including 13th, 14th, and 16th Panzer and 60th Motorized Divisions, as well as the well-equipped SS Motorized Divisions *Leibstandarte Adolf Hitler* and *Wiking*. These units fell outside the Soviet operations area, but they were perfectly capable of attacking northward into Timoshenko's flank. Every kilometer the Soviets advanced westward only increased this vulnerability. The Red Army was about to thrust its head, eyes closed, into the lion's mouth.[25]

Overall, the Southwestern Direction intended to employ an impressive force of 765,300 men and 923 tanks against the 392 German tanks available for this battle.[26]

In short, both the German and Soviet plans for 1942 were exercises in wishful thinking. The Germans lacked both the combat power and the logistical reach to achieve their ambitious goal along the Volga and in the Caucasus; the Soviets had sufficient resources to halt and counterattack the proposed German offensives but still had much to learn about maneuvering and supplying their field forces effectively. This residual German advantage in command, control, and planning declined as 1942 wore on, but it was conspicuously evident in May, June, and July, when the invaders achieved one last string of lopsided tactical victories.

CHAPTER THREE

Preliminary Battles, April–June 1942

Before the main effort in the summer of 1942, both the *Wehrmacht* and the Red Army conducted operations intended to create favorable conditions for the pursuit of their strategic aims. As noted in chapter 2, the Germans wanted to jockey into the most favorable position to launch Operation *Blau*, whereas Stalin had authorized a series of spoiling offensives intended to weaken the looming German offensive. Neither side was ready to attack on schedule, and both dictators had to approve delays of their projected start dates. The Germans got in the first punch in the Crimea.

OPERATION BUSTARD HUNT: THE BATTLE FOR KERCH'

General von Manstein, commander of Eleventh Army, knew he had to eliminate the Red Army's 44th, 47th, and 51st Armies from the Kerch' Peninsula before he turned to the main prize: the fortress of Sevastopol'.

General Kozlov (see chapter 1), commander of the Crimean Front, had crammed 259,622 men, 347 tanks, 3,577 guns and mortars, and 400 aircraft into an area that measured only 18 kilometers across by 75 kilometers deep (see map 3).[1] In theory, this elongated peninsula would force the attacking Germans to penetrate four successive defensive lines before reaching the port of Kerch' itself. Yet Kozlov's forces—including 23 rifle and 2 cavalry divisions, 6 separate rifle and 4 tank brigades, 17 artillery regiments, and numerous smaller units—were densely packed in preparation for their own attack; they had little room to maneuver to defend themselves.[2] Moreover, all Kozlov's supplies had to cross the Sea of Azov, interdicted by German air and light naval units.

Kerch's importance was self-evident, but the Soviets mishandled the situation. Under repeated urging from the *Stavka*, Kozlov began in mid-January to submit plans for an offensive to relieve the Separate Coastal Army inside Sevastopol'. The first of these offensives failed in late January after negligible gains, prompting an impatient Stalin to intervene directly.

At the end of the month, Moscow sent not one but two representatives of the *Stavka*, with their usual broad authority, to supervise Kozlov's operations. In this case, Stalin's lingering distrust of generals caused him to send

37

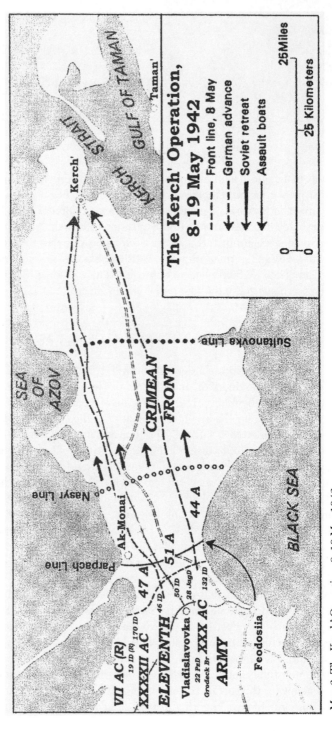

Map 3. The Kerch' Operation, 8–19 May 1942

a political hatchet man rather than an experienced soldier. By 1942, Lev Zakharovich Mekhlis, chief of the Red Army's Main Political Directorate and a deputy chief of the General Staff, already had a daunting reputation for purging the officer corps. During the 1941 German advance, he had condemned several defeated commanders to die in front of impromptu firing squads. In the Crimea, Mekhlis openly bullied the men on the scene, disrupting working relationships by reshuffling senior officers. In particular, he replaced Kozlov's experienced chief of staff, Major General (and future marshal) Fedor Ivanovich Tolbukhin, with the other visiting *Stavka* representative, Major General Pavel P. Vechnyi.[3]

The combination of a mediocre commander (Kozlov), a domineering commissar (Mekhlis), and an inexperienced staff proved disastrous. The resulting confusion, in conjunction with the crowded situation on the Kerch' Peninsula, had disastrous effects on troop readiness and morale. With Mekhlis and Vechnyi interfering in every aspect of planning, 47th and 51st Armies attacked again on 27 February, only to bog down and then totally collapse in less than a week. Another series of assaults in mid-April also ended in abject failure.[4] The Crimean Front suffered 226,370 casualties between February and April 1942, with nothing to show for them.[5]

To attack Kozlov's densely packed force, Manstein could spare only two army elements: General of Artillery Maximilian von Fretter-Pico's XXX Corps and Lieutenant General Franz Mattenklott's XXXXII Corps, with one panzer and five infantry divisions, aided by three poorly trained Romanian divisions. The remaining three German infantry and two Romanian divisions of Eleventh Army were barely sufficient to maintain the siege of Sevastopol'. The Soviet defenders at Kerch' outnumbered the attackers by more than two to one in infantry and artillery and even more in tanks, but in practice, the narrowness of the peninsula prevented Kozlov from bringing all his forces to bear at one location.[6]

Manstein had several other advantages over his more numerous foes. First, at this stage of the war, German staff officers were still better prepared to plan and coordinate an offensive than were their Soviet counterparts. Second, Hitler provided airpower to supplement Manstein's limited ground capability. Richthofen's VIII Air Corps, the premier tactical air support unit in the *Luftwaffe*, furnished more than 600 aircraft and flew up to 2,000 sorties per day. The vast distances of European Russia often diluted the effectiveness of the German Air Force, but in the confined space of the Crimea, Richthofen's pilots achieved almost total air superiority while providing massive fire support to Manstein's advance.[7]

Third, Manstein misled his opponents. During the winter battles, the Crimean Front's 51st Army on the northern (right) portion of Kozlov's front lines had pushed forward 5 to 6 kilometers on its right flank. This left a vul-

nerable bulge that seemed to invite a limited German attack. Using Mattenklott's weak XXXXII Corps, composed largely of Romanians, Manstein
convinced his opponents that this northern bulge was his principal objective in a forthcoming attack. Instead, Manstein planned a much more daring
main effort on the opposite end of the front. Here, Fretter-Pico's XXX Corps,
with one panzer and four infantry divisions plus an improvised force known
as the Grodeck Motorized Brigade, was supposed to breach the southern
Soviet defenses. Then, while ignoring its open northern flank, the German
force was to thrust rapidly along the length of the peninsula, seizing the port
of Kerch' before the Soviets could organize an effective defense.

Operation Bustard Hunt (*Trappenjagt*) began with the roar of German
artillery at 0315 hours (Berlin time) on 8 May 1942.[8] In addition to conventional field artillery and close air support, Manstein had the services of *Ne-
belwerfer* multiple-rocket launchers, the *Luftwaffe*'s 88mm antiaircraft guns,
and even some of the heavy siege artillery assembled to bombard Sevastopol'.
The fires shifted eastward after ten minutes of shelling, allowing German engineers and infantry to begin the hazardous task of clearing land mines and
barbed wire in front of the Soviet positions. Soviet counterfire artillery and
machine guns joined the barrage.

The overwhelming din of this firing covered another clever if risky German maneuver. During the previous night, four companies of the 436th Infantry Regiment, in engineer assault boats, had paddled out into the darkness
of the Crimean Sea opposite the southern end of the front line. Under cover
of the artillery preparation, these troops from the Bavarian 132nd Infantry
Division started their outboard engines and sailed straight up the artificial
waterway created by a broad Soviet antitank ditch. The assault boats appeared unexpectedly in the midst of the Soviet defenders, disrupting their
defensive plans and attacking bunkers from an unexpected direction. By
noon on 8 May, the German-Romanian Grodeck Brigade began crossing the
ditch over a hastily erected bridge and soon left the first Soviet defensive line
behind in a mad dash to the east.

Late that same morning, 22nd Panzer Division also penetrated the main
defensive line at a point farther north. As the Germans pressed eastward,
they surprised a Red tank brigade in its assembly area, and the assault guns
and panzers shattered their opponents in a brief but vicious firefight.

Heavy rains on the night of 9–10 May turned the peninsula into a swamp,
briefly slowing Manstein's advance. This respite did not save the poorly led
defenders, however. Mekhlis appeared more concerned with escaping responsibility than stopping the rout. As soon as the German offensive began,
the commissar telegraphed Stalin personally, demanding that Kozlov be replaced and claiming that the Crimean Front had ignored his warnings. The
Soviet dictator proved as implacable with his henchmen as he was with his

generals, replying, "You are not a mere onlooker but the representative of the [*Stavka*], who answers for all the successes and failures of the *front*."[9] Mekhlis was demoted and never again served as a *Stavka* representative, although he continued to meddle in military affairs. Lieutenant General S. P. Cherniak and Major General K. S. Kolganov of 44th and 47th Armies were relieved of command and reduced to the rank of colonel, while Lieutenant General V. N. L'vov of 51st Army perished in the fighting.

From the Soviet viewpoint, Mekhlis's disgrace was perhaps the only positive result of the Kerch' debacle. In a single day (15 May), the German 170th Infantry Division's 213th Regiment covered more than 80 kilometers to reach the port itself, which fell the next day. Throughout 16 and 17 May, Manstein's howitzers and Richthofen's dive-bombers reduced the surrounded Soviet troops to a demoralized, formless mob. Only a few escaped the trap by swimming across the chilly waters of the Kerch' Strait. The Germans claimed to have captured 170,000 prisoners while suffering only 7,588 casualties themselves.[10] This lopsided victory confirmed the Germans' confidence in their own abilities and contempt for their foes.

DISASTER ON THE NORTHERN DONETS, 12–29 MAY

The only Soviet action that had any effect on Manstein's success was Timoshenko's offensive in the Khar'kov area, which began four days after Bustard Hunt and prompted the diversion of part of Richthofen's aircraft northward from the Crimea.

As described in chapter 2, Timoshenko's staff had planned an attack from bridgeheads across the Northern Donets River to encircle German Sixth Army with two pincers. The 21st, 28th, and 38th Armies would emerge from the Staryi Saltov bridgehead northeast of Khar'kov, while 6th Army and the ad hoc Group Bobkin formed the southern pincer, attacking westward and then northward out of the Barvenkovo bridgehead.

Unfortunately, the relevant headquarters staffs were not yet capable of such a complex operation. Instead of detailed written schedules for redeployments, staff officers issued verbal instructions that often caused confusion. The need to move under cover of darkness made these deployments more difficult, while German air strikes repeatedly demolished key bridges and delayed the construction of a road network. Moreover, many of the units involved had to move laterally behind the lines, a crablike motion that interfered with the normal east-west flow of supplies and replacements for other formations. Divisions found themselves reporting to new higher headquarters with unknown personalities and procedures.[11]

The original plan called for all headquarters to be in place by the start of

April, leaving two weeks to prepare for the offensive. In reality, many units arrived at the last minute, forcing Stalin to reluctantly approve a delay from 4 to 12 May. Even then, the troops were far from ready. Of 32 nondivisional artillery regiments assigned to reinforce the Southwestern Front, only 17 were in their firing positions by 11 May. On average, these units had less than a 2-day supply of ammunition on hand, even though they were scheduled to expend 5.5 days' worth of shells.[12]

Still, the Soviet attack caught the Germans unprepared and achieved considerable initial success (see map 4).[13] Beginning at 0630 on 12 May, a one-hour artillery preparation preceded 15 minutes of air attacks against the German XVII Army Corps, located opposite the northern shock group of 28th Army, with 38th Army on its left flank and 21st on the right. Although Riabyshev's 28th Army had the most resources, its lack of experience meant that the flanking armies actually advanced more quickly, unintentionally forcing the Germans to commit reserve forces earlier than they wished.

In the south, Lieutenant General A. M. Gorodniansky's veteran 6th Army, with Group Bobkin on its left, had even greater initial success, smashing the lightly equipped Hungarian 108th Infantry and German 464th Security Divisions. Sixth Cavalry Corps and the infantry-support tank brigades of Gorodniansky's army advanced as much as 15 kilometers on the first day. Stalin was so pleased that he used this success to poke fun at the naysayers in the Red Army General Staff.[14]

In his first operation as Sixth Army commander, General Paulus was cautious and even nervous about the unexpected strength of the Soviet attacks. He intended to conduct a purely defensive battle, but Bock, the army group commander, urged him to counterattack and authorized Paulus to use several divisions, including 23rd Panzer, that had been earmarked for the *Blau* offensive. Supported by aircraft redeployed from the Crimea, 3rd and 23rd Panzer Divisions launched a counterattack against Major General Moskalenko's 38th Army at noon on 13 May. Moskalenko contained this attack the next day, but his army had to abandon its offensive role. This, in turn, left 28th Army's flank exposed as it continued to advance. Meanwhile, poor staff coordination delayed the commitment of the 3rd Guards Cavalry Corps, which was supposed to be the main exploitation force in the north.[15]

The southern penetration continued to have more success, having advanced up to 40 kilometers by the evening of 14 May. Again, however, inefficient staff work delayed the forward movement of the two tank corps designated to exploit the breakthrough. These units received no instructions to move out of their assembly areas.

In the crisis, Bock again asked permission to use troops earmarked for *Blau*. Although Hitler would not approve the transfer of units between field armies, he did allow Kleist to conduct a wider counteroffensive by turning

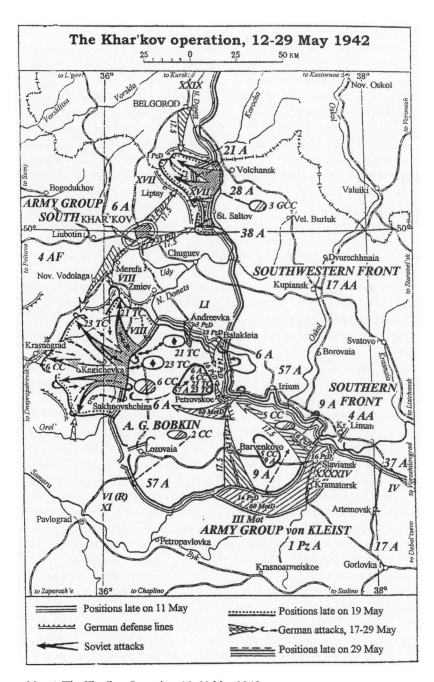

The Khar'kov operation, 12-29 May 1942

25   0   25   50 км

to L'gov   36°   to Kursk   38°   to Kastornoe   38°   Nov. Oskol
XXIX
Vorskla
Vorsklitsa   BELGOROD   N. Donets   Korocha   Oskol   to Voronezh
to Sumy   21 A
3 PzD   Volchansk
XVII   Bogodukhov   Liptsy   XVII   28 A   Valuiki
ARMY GROUP   6 A   3 GCC
SOUTH   KHAR'KOV   St. Saltov   Vel. Burluk
50°   Liubotin   38 A   50°
4 AF   Chuguev   Dvurechhnaia
Nov. Vodolaga   Merefa   Udy   SOUTHWESTERN FRONT
VIII   Zmiev   Kupiansk   17 AA
N. Donets   to Starobel'sk
21 TC   LI
23 TC   VIII   Andreevka   3 PzD   Oskol   Svatovo
Krasnograd   23 PzD   Balakleia   Borovaia
6 CC   21 TC   6 A   57 A   Krasnaia
Kegichevka   23 TC   6 CC   6 CC   Izium   SOUTHERN   to Lisichansk
6 CC   23 TC   9 A   FRONT
6 A   Petrovskoe   69 MotD   9 A   4 AA
Sakhnovshchina   6 A   5 CC   Kr. Liman
Orel'   A. G. BOBKIN   2 CC   37 A
Lozovaia   Barvenkovo   5 CC   16 PzD
9 A   9 A   Slaviansk   to Voroshilograd
Samara   57 A   XXXXIV   Kramatorsk   IV
VI (R)   14 PzD   17 A
XI   60 MotD   Artemovsk
Pavlograd   III Mot   to Debal'tsevo
Petropavlovka   ARMY GROUP von KLEIST
Byk   1 Pz A   17 A
Krasnoarmeiskoe   Gorlovka   to Stalino
to Zaporozh'e   36°   to Chaplino   to Stalino   38°

Positions late on 11 May   Positions late on 19 May
German defense lines   German attacks, 17-29 May
Soviet attacks   Positions late on 29 May

Map 4. The Khar'kov Operation, 12–29 May 1942

part of First Panzer Army northward, into the rear of the southern Soviet pincer. In effect, Kleist launched the southern half of Operation Fridericus, an existing plan intended to pinch off the Barvenkovo bulge west of the Northern Donets River.[16]

This counteroffensive kicked off on 17 May 1942, just as Timoshenko belatedly committed 21st and 23rd Tank Corps to exploit northwestward from 6th Red Army toward Khar'kov. Thus, the entire Southern Front was off balance, focusing its attention and forces to the northwest while the Germans attacked into its southern flank. Kleist's leading edge was General of Panzer Troops *Freiherr* (Baron) Geyr von Schweppenburg's III Motorized (Panzer) Corps, which by this time included 14th and 16th Panzer Divisions, 60th Motorized Division, 1st Mountain Division, 20th Romanian Infantry Division, and a separate battle group, for a total of 170 tanks. In two days, this corps and flanking German divisions broke through the defenses of the Southern Front's 6th and 57th Armies, advancing northward deep into Soviet rear areas.[17] At the same time, Paulus shifted 23rd Panzer Division laterally along the northern bulge to launch another attack against 28th Army. This forced Riabyshev to commit 3rd Guards Cavalry Corps to contain the counterattack rather than to continue the exploitation of the northern pincer.

Soviet responses to the new threat were remarkably slow. Vasilevsky, acting as chief of the Red Army General Staff for the first time, failed to convince an optimistic Stalin to recall the tank spearheads and redirect them against Kleist's counteroffensive. By the time Timoshenko acknowledged the danger on the evening of 19 May, only immediate flight would save any of the forces in the Khar'kov offensive. Yet Southwestern Front had no contingency plans for withdrawal and proved unable to refuel and rearm the forward units. Soviet armies, corps, and divisions lost communication with and control over their subordinate units. Once again, as in the Crimea, a huge, disorganized force of Soviet troops was hemmed in and destroyed by German firepower. Officially, the Soviets acknowledged the loss of 266,927 casualties, of which 46,314 were evacuated to hospitals, as well as 652 tanks, 1,646 guns, and 3,278 mortars. German claims were even higher. Among the Soviet casualties were three army commanders and virtually all the division commanders in 6th and 9th Red Armies.[18] Poor staff work, lack of intelligence and reconnaissance, logistical problems, and delays in committing the new tank corps had sacrificed whatever chance the offensive originally had. The Germans lost only 20,000 casualties, and Paulus received the Knight's Cross for his effective defense. The Axis did, however, lose valuable equipment and training time for the panzer divisions. Moreover, thoughtful observers were dismayed by the seemingly bottomless resources of the Red Army.

In the wake of the Crimean and Khar'kov failures, Stalin canceled several other ambitious offensives and issued the first of many directives creating seven new armies within the *Stavka* VGK Reserve. This array was imposing on paper, but the new units needed time to organize and train. Moreover, the Soviet dictator remained focused on the defense of Moscow, sending four of the new armies there. By the first week of June, however, he had reinforced Timoshenko's *front* with seven rifle divisions, four separate tank brigades, and three tank corps, a force that he wrongly believed would be sufficient to contain the Germans in the south.[19]

Meanwhile, the invaders undertook various minor offensives to shorten and simplify their defensive lines in front of Leningrad and Moscow. On 28 May 1942 Halder won Hitler's approval for several similar operations in the south. These included a continued counteroffensive in the Khar'kov area, pushing northeastward to take Volchansk.[20]

On 1 June Hitler flew from his headquarters in Rastenburg, East Prussia, to Poltava in the Ukraine. There he conferred with Army Group South commander Bock and three of his field army commanders—Kleist of First Panzer, Hoth of Fourth Panzer, and Paulus of Sixth. Hitler focused on two goals: destroying Soviet troop units and seizing the Caucasus oil fields. Based on input from Halder and Bock, the dictator established a revised timetable. On 7 June the Germans would simultaneously attack in the Volchansk area (Operation Wilhelm) and at Sevastopol' (Operation *Störfang* [Sturgeon Trap]). Five days later, Kleist would attack to reduce the Izium salient (Operation Fridericus II). Once these preliminaries were completed, the *Wehrmacht* could launch Operation *Blau* on 20 June.[21]

SEVASTOPOL', 7–30 JUNE

Although rain delayed Wilhelm until 10 June, Manstein began his final attack in the Crimea on schedule. He had already failed to reduce the fortress once, in late 1941. The attackers faced a combination of obsolescent tsarist-era fortifications, modern concrete casements, and 350 kilometers of trenches with minefields and barbed wire. These defenses formed two belts: an outer ring near Balaklava, 15 to 20 kilometers from the port, and an inner ring approximately 5 kilometers from the center. The overall commander was Vice Admiral Filipp Sergeevich Oktiabr'sky, commander of the Black Sea Fleet, but most of the defenders belonged to Major General I. E. Petrov's Coastal Army. Petrov controlled seven rifle divisions, three naval brigades, and two naval regiments fighting as infantry, as well as two separate tank battalions and seven artillery regiments.[22] Two additional rifle brigades arrived by sea during the second siege, for a total of 130,100 troops, supported by 38 tanks, 1,667 guns and mortars, and an armored train.

To overcome these formidable defenses, Manstein had approximately

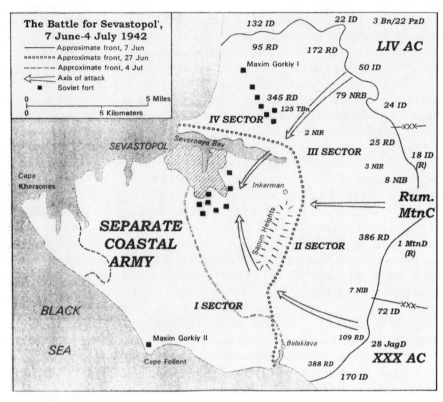

The Battle for Sevastopol',
7 June-4 July 1942
———— Approximate front, 7 Jun
ooooooo Approximate front, 27 Jun
– – – – – Approximate front, 4 Jul
⟵——— Axis of attack
■ Soviet fort
0   5 Miles
0   5 Kilometers

132 ID   22 ID   3 Bn/22 PzD

95 RD   172 RD   LIV AC

Maxim Gorkiy I   50 ID

345 RD   79 NRB   24 ID
125 TBn
IV SECTOR ■
                        —XXX—
2 NIR
                   25 RD
III SECTOR   18 ID
        3 NIR   (R)
SEVASTOPOL   Severnaya Bay   8 NIB

Cape
Khersones   Inkerman   Rum.
                                        MtnC
SEPARATE
COASTAL   386 RD   1 MtnD
ARMY   (R)
                II SECTOR

                7 NIB

BLACK   I SECTOR   —XXX—
                            72 ID

Maxim Gorkiy II   109 RD   28 JagD
SEA   Balaklava
Cape Folient   388 RD   XXX AC
                    170 ID

Map 5. The Battle for Sevastopol', 7 June–4 July 1942

167,000 soldiers, 80 tanks and assault guns, and 1,300 guns and mortars, supported by up to 600 of Richthofen's aircraft. The failed Soviet offensive at Khar'kov had diverted all but one tank battalion of 22nd Panzer Division from Manstein, but he also had three assault gun battalions. The attacking forces were organized into General of Cavalry Erik Hansen's LIV Corps in the north, with four German infantry divisions, and General Fretter-Pico's XXX Corps, consisting of two Romanian and three German infantry divisions, although the latter units were slow to arrive as they mopped up in the Kerch' Peninsula. The 46th German Infantry Division and a Romanian corps (two divisions plus a cavalry brigade) provided rear-area security for the entire Crimea, leaving the Romanian 4th Mountain Division as Manstein's only reserve.[23]

Higher Artillery Command (*Harko*) 306 orchestrated the German guns, including Dora, an 800mm railroad cannon whose seven-ton shell could penetrate more than seven meters of concrete. The Germans also had three

533mm and six 430mm siege mortars, but their rate of fire and accuracy were relatively low. Richthofen had diverted most of his famous 88mm antiaircraft guns to ground support but insisted that they remain under *Luftwaffe* rather than army command, creating some miscommunications during the battle.[24]

After five days of air and artillery bombardment, the infantry and engineers of Eleventh Army began their assault at 0350 on 7 June.[25] LIV Army Corps made the main attack against the northern sector, as described by one of the German assault troops:[26]

> Companies, platoons, and groups one after the other move forward in the blue-gray powder smoke and thick dust. . . . The going is slow through the thick bushes. There is no chance for the groups and platoons to maintain contact [with one another] here. The Bolsheviks hide in their numberless holes, and they let us pass and then fall on us from the rear. . . .
>
> An enemy machine gun nest suddenly appears in a small depression. Due to our fire, three men come out of it with their hands up. As we approach slowly, two others, who are still in the shelter, fire on us with the machine gun. Another takes his life. As we pass, another jumps up and fires at us from the rear. This is the Bolshevik method of combat. On the ground there is mine after mine. Next to me a company commander is flung into the air; he falls back, and almost lands, uninjured, on his feet. However, not everyone has such luck.[26]

Three days of such attacks led to nothing but failure, and both Hitler and Bock considered suspending the Sevastopol' operation to focus on Operation *Blau*. In particular, the continued commitment of VIII Air Corps meant that these aircraft would be late to redeploy to support the main offensive.[27]

Manstein persisted in the attack, however, and XXX Corps joined the assault on 10 June. The defenders used everything, including the corpses of their comrades, to shore up positions. German flamethrowers, hand grenades, and satchel charges increased the carnage, yet the Red Army and Navy fought to the last breath. In 12 hours of fighting on 13 June, every officer in two battalions of German 16th Regiment, 22nd Infantry Division, was killed or wounded, leaving a replacement lieutenant to continue the attack with the remnants of the regiment. By the time the attack was over, other regiments were also led by lieutenants in place of colonels.[28]

To make up for such losses, Army Group South gave Eleventh Army an additional infantry regiment and allowed it to swap two depleted regiments for stronger units left with the division still occupying Kerch'. On 13 June LIV Army Corps captured Maxim Gorki I, a massive fortification that anchored the northern end of the outer defensive belt. Four days later, the Germans finally swept six other forts nearby and pressed forward to Severnaia (Northern) Bay, a thin finger of water that divided Sevastopol' proper from its northern defenses. There, however, XIV Corps had to halt, waiting for the other corps to come on line to the east and south.[29] The depleted German units slowly eliminated bypassed centers of resistance, while the Soviet defenders, resupplied only by submarine, ran low on ammunition, food, and water.[30]

Manstein again took a calculated risk in the final assault. At 0100 on 29 June troops from 22nd and 24th Infantry Divisions used engineer assault boats to cross Severnaia Bay, seizing the city's power plant by surprise. An hour later XXX Corps began the artillery preparation for its assault on the Sapun Heights, overlooking the town to the southeast. The new offensive was so successful that the next day Admiral Oktiabr'sky persuaded the *Stavka* to authorize an evacuation. During the next four nights, key commanders and staff officers escaped by boat, leaving their subordinates to defend the fortresses. Some political officers committed suicide by blowing up their positions, seeking to take their attackers with them.[31]

Soviet records claim that the Sevastopol' Defensive Region lost 200,000 soldiers from 31 October 1941 to 4 July 1942, including 156,880 killed, wounded, and missing, as well as 95,000 prisoners, 1,380 guns and mortars, and 26 tanks.[32] Yet the only advantage the Soviets gained from this heroic defense was the temporary diversion of German dive-bombers and other resources away from the main *Blau* offensive. Recognizing the ferocity of the battle, the Soviet government awarded the Order of Lenin to the entire city collectively, while the Germans authorized all participants to wear the special Crimea Shield on their left sleeves. A jubilant Hitler promoted Manstein to field marshal on 1 July.

OPERATIONS WILHELM AND FRIDERICUS II

The conquest of the Crimea removed the threat of Soviet air attack from that peninsula toward the Romanian oil fields. Before the main summer offensive could begin, Army Group South still needed to seize favorable jumping-off positions. It did so in two related operations, Wilhelm (10–15 June 1942) and Fridericus II (22–25 June).

For Wilhelm, General Paulus received temporary control of III Motorized Corps to form the southern part of an encirclement operation against the Southwestern Front, reaching some 75 kilometers due east of Khar'kov. The Soviet defenders were still recovering from their defeat in Timoshenko's abortive offensive and could offer little resistance to the German attack. However, a steady rain returned on 11 June, slowing the German advance; this allowed Riabyshev to evacuate much of his 28th Army while using several

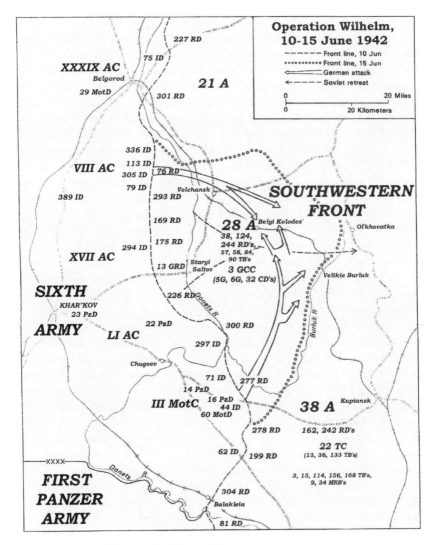

Map 6. Operation Wilhelm, 10–15 June 1942

new tank units to block and delay the German spearheads. As a result, the Germans captured only 24,800 prisoners in this encirclement. Still, Wilhelm not only seized the desired terrain east of the Donets River but also further weakened the center of the Southwestern Front.[33]

Stalin reacted forcefully to this further German advance. On 13 June, in the midst of the battle, he conducted an extended conference with the

Southwestern Direction's Military Council by means of a secure Baudot radio-teletype (known as BODO). The dictator denied Timoshenko's request for additional rifle divisions, saying he had no ready units available. Stalin scolded his marshal for poor command and control, noting that the defenders had more tanks than the attackers. He urged Timoshenko to concentrate his three available tank corps (13th, 22nd, and 23rd) in one place; two days later he ordered Briansk Front to dispatch two additional tank corps, the 4th and 16th, and released Major General A. I. Lizuikov's newly formed 5th Tank Army to further bolster the Southwestern Front.[34] This represented almost 980 additional tanks, but the units' commanders and staffs, like so many other Red Army headquarters at that time, were too green to function effectively.

On 21 June Stalin disestablished the Southwestern Direction's headquarters, leaving the Southwestern Front (commanded by Timoshenko) and the Southern Front (commanded by General Malinovsky) as coequal units under direct *Stavka* supervision.[35] In practice, the three regional super-headquarters established in June 1941 had never functioned well, but this abrupt decision was a clear vote of no confidence in Timoshenko on the eve of the second German summer offensive.

The next day, 22 June, Kleist's First Panzer Army, on the southern flank of Paulus's Sixth Army, launched Fridericus II, the final preliminary to Operation *Blau*. The ubiquitous III Motorized Corps, transferred yet again from Paulus to Kleist, launched the main attack in a southeasterly direction, threatening to encircle Moskalenko's 38th Army west of the Oskol River. Simultaneously, General of Artillery Maximilian de Angelis's XXXXIV Army Corps advanced northward from Kleist's right flank, brushing past Izium to the east to link up with III Corps' panzers near Gorokhovatka. Once again, however, most of the defenders in the 38th and 9th Red Armies managed to escape the intended encirclement. At Kupiansk on the Oskol River, III Motorized Corps' spearhead, 16th Panzer Division led by the one-armed legend Major General Hans Hube, encountered stiff resistance from 9th Guards Rifle Division, reinforced by 6th Guards Tank Brigade and 1st Destroyer Division. The commander of 9th Guards, Major General A. P. Beloborodov, represented the new crop of Soviet commanders who had won their spurs in the defense of Moscow the previous year. Fridericus II came to a halt, having achieved most of its objectives.[36]

These two preliminary operations went far to restore German confidence while setting the pattern for subsequent encounters throughout the summer campaign. The Germans could still attack and penetrate at will, but they now encountered significant resistance from the new Soviet tank forces and were rarely able to achieve the huge encirclements of the previous year. Consequently, the invaders had to resist the temptation to advance too far with too

Table 3.1. Axis and Red Army Force Dispositions in Operation *Blau*, 28 June 1942 (First and Seventeenth Armies as of 7 July) (from north to south, with army groups, separate armies, and tank forces in bold)

AXIS	SOVIET
The Army of Lapland (later Twentieth Mountain Army) (Colonel General Eduard Dietl)	**Karelian Front** (Lieutenant General V. A. Frolov) 14th, 19th, 26th, and 32nd Armies 7th Separate Army
Finnish Army **Army Group North** (Colonel General Georg von Küchler) Eighteenth Army Sixteenth Army Eleventh Army (in July)	**Leningrad Front** (Colonel General L. A. Govorov) 23rd, 42nd, 55th, and 8th Armies and Coastal Operational Group **Volkhov Front** (Colonel General K. A. Meretskov) 54th, 4th, 59th Armies, 2nd Shock Army, and 52nd Army **Northwestern Front** (Colonel General P. A. Kurochkin) 11th, 34th, and 53rd Armies and 1st Shock Army
Army Group Center (Field Marshal Günther von Kluge) Ninth Army Third Panzer Army Fourth Army Second Panzer Army	**Kalinin Front** (Colonel General I. S. Konev) 3rd and 4th Shock Armies and 22nd, 30th, 39th, 29th, and 31st Armies **Western Front** (Colonel General G. K. Zhukov) 20th, 5th, 33rd, 43rd, 49th, 50th, 10th, 16th, and 61st Armies

Army Group South—Field Marshal Fedor von Bock

***Armeegruppe* von Weichs** SECOND ARMY (Colonel General Maximilian *Freiherr* von Weichs an dem Glon) LV Army Corps (General of Infantry Erwin Vierow) 45th, 95th, 299th IDs and 1st SS IB FOURTH PANZER ARMY (Colonel General Hermann Hoth) XIII Army Corps (General of Infantry Erich Straube) 82nd and 385th IDs and **11th PzD** **XXIV Panzer Corps** (General of Panzer Troops Willibald *Freiherr* von Langermann und Erlenkamp) 377th ID, **9th PzD**, and **3rd MotD** (11th PzD on 4 July) **XXXXVIII Panzer Corps** (General of Panzer Troops Werner Kempf) **24th PzD** and "**GD**" **MotD** (**16th MotD** on 4 July) HUNGARIAN SECOND ARMY (Colonel General Gusztav Jany)	**Briansk Front** (Lieutenant General F. I. Golikov) 3rd Army (Lieutenant General P. P. Korzun) 60th, 137th, 240th, 269th, 283rd, and 287th RDs, 104th and 134th RBs, and **79th** and **150th TBs** 48th Army (Major General G. A. Khaliuzin) 6th Gds., 8th, 211th, and 280th RDs, 118th and 122nd RBs, 55th CD, and **80th** and **202nd TBs** 13th Army (Major General N. P. Pukhov) 15th, 132nd, 143rd, 148th, and 307th RDs, 109th RB, and **129th TB** 40th Army (Lieutenant General M. A. Parsegov) 6th, 45th, 62nd, 121st, 160th, and 212th RDs, 111th, 119th, and 141st RBs, and **14th** and **170th TBs**

(continued on next page)

Table 3.1. (*continued*)

AXIS	SOVIET
VII Army Corps (German) (General of Artillery Ernst-Eberhard Hell) 387th ID and Hungarian 6th LtD Hungarian III Army Corps Hungarian 7th and 9th LtDs and **16th MotD** RESERVES 88th, 323rd, 34th, and 383rd IDs VIII Air [*Flieger*] Corps (Fourth Air Fleet)(General *der Flieger* Hans Seidemann) Rear Area Command Hungarian 105th Infantry Brigade 213th SecD	5th Tank Army (Major General A. I. Liziukov) 340th RD and **19th TB** **2nd Tank Corps** (Major General I. G. Lazarev) (**26th**, **27th**, and **148th TBs** and 2nd MRB) **11th Tank Corps** (Major General N. N. Parkevich)(**53rd, 59th**, and **160th TBs** and 12th MRB) 2nd Air Army (Major General of Aviation K. N. Smirnov) 205th, 207th, and 266th FADs, 208th FBAD, 223rd BAD, and 225th, 227th, and 267th AADs 6th Sapper Army (Lieutenant General A. S. Gundorov) 17th, 18th, and 19th SBs *Front* units 1st Gds. and 284th RDs, 2nd DD, and **118th**, **157th**, and **201st TBs** **1st Tank Corps** (Major General M. E. Katukov) (**1st Gds.**, **49th**, and **89th TBs** and 1st MRB) **4th Tank Corps** (Major General V. A. Mishulin) (**45th**, **47th**, and **102nd TBs** and 4th MRB) **16th Tank Corps** (Major General M. I. Pavelkin) (**107th**, **109th**, and **164th TBs** and 15th MRB) **17th Tank Corps** (Major General N. V. Feklenko) (**66th**, **67th**, and **174th TBs** and 31st MRB) **24th Tank Corps** (Major General V. M. Badanov) (**4th Gds.**, **54th**, and **130th TBs** and 24th MRB) 7th Cavalry Corps (Major General I. M. Managarov) (11th, 17th, and 83rd CDs) 8th Cavalry Corps (Colonel I. F. Lunev) (21st and 112th CDs)
SIXTH ARMY (General of Panzer Troops Friedrich Paulus) XXIX Army Corps (General of Infantry Hans von Obstfelder) 57th, 168th, and 75th IDs VIII Army Corps (Lieutenant General Walter Heitz) 389th, 305th, and 376th IDs **XXXX Panzer Corps** (General of Panzer Troops Georg Stumme) 100th JD, 336th ID, 3rd and **23rd PzDs**, and **29th MotD**	**Southwestern Front** (Marshal of the Soviet Union S. K. Timoshenko) 21st Army (Major General A. I. Danilov) 76th, 124th, 226th, 227th, 293rd, 297th, 301st, and 343rd RDs, 8th NKVD RD, **10th TB**, and 1st MRB, 478th TBn **13th Tank Corps** (Major General P. E. Shurov) (**85th** and **167th TBs** and 20th MRB)

XVII Army Corps (General of
  Infantry Karl Hollidt)
  113th, 79th, and 294th IDs
LI Army Corps (General of Artillery
  Walter von Seydlitz-Kurzbach)
  297th, 71st, 44th, 62nd, and 384th
  IDs
IV Air Corps (Fourth Air Fleet)
  (General *der Flieger* Kurt Pfflugal)

First Panzer Army (Colonel General
  Ewald von Kleist)

28th Army (Lieutenant General
  D. I. Riabyshev)
  13th and 15th Gds., 38th, 169th,
    and 175th RDs and **65th, 90th,**
    and **91st TBs**
23rd Tank Corps (Colonel A. M.
  Khasin) (**6th Gds.** and **114th TBs**
  and 9th MRB)
38th Army (Major General K. S.
  Moskalenko)
  162nd, 199th, 242nd, 277th, 278th,
    and 304th RDs, **133rd**, **156th**,
    159th, and **168th TBs**, 22nd
    MRB, and **92nd TBn**
22nd Tank Corps (Major General
  A. A. Shamshin) (**3rd, 13th,** and
  36th TBs)
9th Army (Lieutenant General A. I.
  Lopatin)
  51st, 81st, 106th, 140th, 355th,
    296th, 318th, and 333rd RDs,
    18th and 19th DBs, **12th TB,**
    and **71st** and **132nd TBns**
5th Cavalry Corps (Major General
  F. A. Parkhomenko) (30th, 34th,
  and 60th CDs)
57th Army (Major General D. N.
  Nikishov)
  no subordinate units
8th Air Army (Major General of
  Aviation T. T. Khriukhin)
  206th, 220th, 235th, 268th, and
    269th FADs, 226th and 228th
    AADs, 221st and 270th BADs,
    and 271st and 272nd FBADs
7th Sapper Army (Major General
  V. S. Kosenko)
  12th, 14th, 15th, 20th, and 21st SBs
Front units
  9th Gds., 103rd, 244th, and 300th
    RDs, 1st DD, and 11th, 13th, 15th,
    and 17th DBs,
  57th, 58th, 84th, 88th, 158th, and
    176th TBs, 21st MRB, and
    composite **TBn**
  14th Tank Corps (Major General
    N. N. Radkevich) (**138th** and
    139th TBs)
  3rd Gds. Cavalry Corps (Major
    General V. D. Kriuchenkin) (5th
    and 6th Gds. and 32nd CDs)
  52nd, 53rd, 74th, 117th, and 118th FRs
Southern Front (Lieutenant General
  R. Ia. Malinovsky)

(continued on next page)

Table 3.1. (*continued*)

AXIS	SOVIET
XI Army Corps (Group Strecker) (General of Infantry Karl Strecker) (with Romanian VI Army Corps) 1st MtnD and Romanian 1st, 4th, 20th, and 2nd IDs	37th Army (Major General P. M. Kozlov) 102nd, 218th, 230th, 275th, and 295th RDs and **121st TB**
III Panzer Corps (General of Panzer Troops Leo *Freiherr* Geyr von Schweppenburg) **16th** (temporarily in XIV PzC) and **22nd PzDs** and **SS "LAH" MotD** (temporarily in OKH reserve south)	12th Army (Major General A. A. Grechko) 4th, 74th, 176th, 261st, and 349th RDs
XIV Panzer Corps (General of Infantry Gustav von Wietersheim) **14th PzD** and **60th MotD**	18th Army (Major General F. N. Kamkov) 216th, 353rd, 383rd, and 395th RDs and **64th TB**
XXXXIV Army Corps (General of Artillery Maximilian de Angelis) 257th and 68th IDs and 97th and 101st JDs	56th Army (Major General. V. V. Tsyganov) 3rd GRC (2nd GRD and 68th, 76th, and 81st NRBs) 30th, 31st, and 339th RDs, 16th RB, 70th and 158th FRs, and **63rd TB**
IV Army Corps (General of Infantry Viktor von Schwedler) 295th, 76th, 94th, and 9th IDs (to Eleventh Army by 7 July) 444th SecD 454th SecD	24th Army (Lieutenant General I. K. Smirnov) 73rd, 228th, 335th, and 341st RDs
	4th Air Army (Major General of Aviation K. A. Vershinin) 216th and 217th FADs, 218th FBAD, 219th BAD, and 230th AAD
	8th Sapper Army (Colonel D. I. Suslin) 10th, 11th, 23rd, 24th, 25th, 26th, 28th, 29th, and 30th SBs
	Front units 347th RD, 89th and 73rd FRs, **5th Gds.**, **15th**, and **140th TBs**, and **62nd** and **75th TBns**
Seventeenth Army (Colonel General Richard Ruoff) LII Army Corps (General of Infantry Eugen Ott) 111th and 370th IDs	
Italian Expeditionary (Mobile) Corps 3rd Celere Mobile, 9th Pasubio, and 52nd Torino Mobile IDs	
XXXXIX Mountain Corps (General of Mountain Troops Rudolf Konrad) 198th ID and 4th MtnD	
LVII Panzer Corps (Group Wietersheim) (General of Panzer Troops Friedrich Kirchner) **13th PzD, SS "Viking" MotD, Slovak Mobile Div.**, and 125th, 73rd, and 298th IDs	

Reserves
371st ID and **SS "LAH" MotD**
(temporarily from III Panzer Corps)

Note: As of 24 June, First Panzer and
Seventeenth Armies' panzer and
motorized forces were organized as
follows:
III Panzer Corps (Group
Mackensen), with 14th and 16th PzDs,
part of **22nd PzD** and **60th MotD**
  XIV Panzer Corps, with **13th PzD**, ·
"LAH" and **"Viking" MotDs**, Slovak
Mobile Division, and parts of 73rd and
125th IDs.
  Army Group A reorganized its
panzer and motorized forces and
activated **LVII Panzer Corps** (Group
Wietersheim) prior to the beginning of
Blau II.

Third Army (Romanian)
Army Group Reserve:
  V Army Corps (General of Infantry
    Wilhelm Wetzel) (HQ only)
  HQ, Italian Eighth Army
    Italian II Army Corps
      Italian 2nd Sforcesca, 3rd
      Ravenna, and 5th Cosseria IDs
  Hungarian IV Army Corps
    Hungarian 10th, 12th, and 13th
    LtDs
  HQ, Hungarian V Army Corps
  Hungarian VII Army Corps
    Hungarian 20th and 23rd LtDs
  Eleventh Army (Colonel General Fritz-
    Erich von Manstein)
    XXXXII Army Corps (General of
      Infantry Franz Mattenklott)
      132nd ID
    XXX Army Corps (General of
      Artillery Maximilian von Fretter-
      Pico)
      72nd and 170th IDs and 28th JD
    LIV Army Corps (General of Cavalry
      Erik Hansen)
      22nd, 24th, and 50th IDs, two
      regiments of 132nd ID, and 4th
      Romanian MtnD
    Romanian Mtn. Corps (General
      Gheorghe Avramescu)
      Romanian 1st MtnD and 18th ID

North-Caucasus Front (Marshal of
  the Soviet Union S. M. Budenny)
  47th Army (Major General G. P.
    Kotov)
    32nd Gds. and 77th RDs, 86th
      NRB, 103rd RB, and **126th TBn**
  51st Army (Colonel General A. M.
    Kuznetsov)
    91st, 138th, 156th, and 157th RDs,
      110th and 115th CDs, 255th CR,
      and **40th TB**
  Coastal Army (Major General I. E.
    Petrov)
    25th, 95th, 109th, 172nd, 345th,
      386th, and 388th RDs, 79th and
      138th NRBs, 7th and 8th NIBs,
      and **81st** and **125th TBns**
  5th Air Army (Lieutenant General of
    Aviation S. K. Goriunov)
    132nd BAD, 236th, 237th, and
      265th FADs, and 238th AAD
  Front units
    1st RC (236th and 302nd RDs and
      113th and 139th RBs)
    83rd, 142nd, and 154th NRB, **136th**
      and **137th TBs**, and **79th TBn**
    17th Cavalry Corps (Major General
      N. Ia. Kirichenko) (12th, 13th,
      15th, and 116th CDs)
Trans-Caucasus Front (Army General
  I. V. Tiulenev)
  44th Army (Major General
    A. A. Khriashchev)
    223rd, 414th, and 416th RDs and
      9th and 10th RBs

(continued on next page)

Table 3.1. (*continued*)

AXIS	SOVIET
	46th Army (Major General V. F. Sergatskov)
	3rd RC (9th and 20th MtnRDs)
	389th, 392nd, 394th, and 406th RDs, 155th RB, 63rd CD, and 51st FR
	Front units
	417th RD and **52nd TB**
	Stavka Reserve
	1st Reserve Army
	18th, 29th, 112th, 131st, 164th, 214th, and 229th RDs
	2nd Reserve Army
	25th Gds., 52nd, 100th, 111th, 237th, and 303rd RDs
	3rd Reserve Army
	107th, 159th, 161st, 167th, 193rd, and 195th RDs
	4th Reserve Army
	78th, 88th, 118th, 139th, 274th, and 312th RDs
	5th Reserve Army
	14th Gds., 1st, 127th, 153rd, 197th, and 203rd RDs
	6th Reserve Army
	99th, 141st, 174th, 206th, 219th, 232nd, and 309th RDs
	7th Reserve Army
	33rd Gds., 147th, 181st, 184th, 192nd, and 196th RDs
	8th Reserve Army
	64th, 126th, 221st, 231st, 308th, and 315th RDs
	9th Reserve Army
	32nd, 93rd, 238th, 279th, and 316th RDs
	10th Reserve Army
	133rd, 180th, 207th, 292nd, 299th, and 306th RDs
	3rd Tank Army
	154th RD and **2nd**, **89th**, **166th**, and **179th TBs**
	12th Tank Corps (Colonel S. I. Bogdanov) (**30th**, **86th**, and **97th TBs** and 13th MRB)
	15th Tank Corps (Major General V. A. Koptsov) (**96th**, **105th**, and **113th TBs** and 17th MRB)
	7th Tank Corps (Colonel P. A. Rotmistrov) (**3rd Gds.**, **62nd**, and **87th TBs** and 7th MRB)

18th Tank Corps (Major General
I. D. Cherniakhovsky) (**110th**,
180th, and **181st TBs** and 18th
MRB)
25th Tank Corps (Major General
P. P. Pavlov) (**111th**, **162nd**, and
175th TBs and 16th MRB)
2nd Gds. Cavalry Corps (Major
General V. V. Kriukov) (3rd and 4th
Gds. and 20th CDs)
6th, 7th, 8th, and 10th DBs

Sources: Axis Forces: Horst Boog, Werner Rahn, Reinhard Stumpf, and Bernd Wegner, *Germany and the Second World War*, Vol. VI, *The Global War*, trans. Ewald Osers, John Brownjohn, Patricia Crampton, and Louise Willmot (Oxford: Clarendon Press, 2001), 965, for Army Group South's order of battle on 24 June 1942, as amended to the dates shown by "Lagenkarten, Anlage zum KTB Russland, 12 June–31 Dec 1942," *AOK II, Ia 29585/207*, in NAM T-312, Roll 1206; "Ia, Lagenkarten zum KTB 12, May–Jul 1942," *AOK 6, 22855/Ia*, in NAM T-312, Roll 1446; "Lagenkarten Pz. AOK 1, Ia (Armee-Gruppe v. Kleist), 1–29 Jun 1942," *PzAOK 1, 24906/12*, in NAM T-313, Roll 35; and "Lagenkarten, Anlage 9 zum Kreigstagebuch Nr. 3, AOK 17, Ia., 29 May–30 July 1942," *AOK 17, 24411/18*, in NAM T-312, Roll 696.

Red Army Forces: *Boevoi sostav Sovetskoi armii, Chast' 2 (ianvar'–dekabr' 1942 goda)* [Combat composition of the Red Army, Part 2 (January–December 1942)](Moscow: Voenizdat, 1966), 124–128, 134–135. Prepared by the Military-Scientific Directorate of the General Staff.

Notes:

1. Soviet order of battle as of 1 July, *Armeegruppe* Weichs and Sixth Army as of 28 June, and First Panzer and Seventeenth Armies as of 7 July.

2. The OKW redesignated German motorized corps as panzer corps in late June.

Abbreviations

German
ID—infantry division
PzD—panzer division
MotD—motorized division
JD—jäger division
LtD—light division
MtnD—mountain division
SecD—security division
IB—infantry brigade

Soviet
A—army
RC—rifle corps
TC—tank corps
RD—rifle division
CD—cavalry division
DD—destroyer division
FAD—fighter aviation division
FBAD—fighter-bomber aviation division
BAD—bomber aviation division
AAD—assault aviation division
RB—rifle brigade
TB—tank brigade
MRB—motorized rifle brigade
NRB—naval rifle brigade
NIB—naval infantry brigade
DB—destroyer brigade
FR—fortified region
TBn—tank battalion

small a force, exposing themselves to counterattacks; German commanders for the first time had to watch their flanks and avoid excessive risks. Under pressure, some Red units dissolved, while others conducted a more disciplined withdrawal, but both types escaped to fight another day. In either event, the Soviet defenses were weakened, yet decisive victory continued to elude the German commanders. Meanwhile, the unfortunate Reichel affair described in the Prologue further frayed the nerves of Hitler and his generals.

CHAPTER FOUR

Punch and Counterpunch:
Blau I and II, June–July 1942

Two factors delayed the onset of Operation _Blau_ until 28 June: III Motorized Corps had to refit after its advances during Fridericus II, and frequent rains further interfered with the German plans.

AREA OF OPERATIONS

The battles of _Blau_ I occurred between the Oskol and Don Rivers, focusing around the great city of Voronezh on the river of the same name just east of the Don. Numerous rivers traversed this area, with most streams flowing diagonally to the southwest or southeast, thereby complicating east-west maneuvers by both sides. Although all these rivers except the Don were easily crossed at existing fords and bridges, the steep banks—usually higher on the western side than on the eastern—and plentiful ravines, or _balkas_, severely limited movement. For example, the Oskol River could be easily crossed only at major towns such as Staryi Oskol, Chernianka, Novyi Oskol, and Volokovka. If the attackers failed to seize such bridge sites quickly, they would have to pause and conduct a more conventional river crossing at each major stream.

In addition, the overall scarcity of paved roads made the rail lines especially important for maneuver and resupply, a generalization that was true throughout European Russia. Although there were three north-south rail lines in this area, only one significant line ran east-west, connecting Kursk and Voronezh. This railroad and its associated vehicular roads figured prominently in German planning and go far to explain why General von Weichs's Second Army, with Fourth Panzer Army and Hungarian Second Army under its operational control, advanced toward Voronezh even though that city was originally outside the designated area for _Blau_ I. Paulus's Sixth Army moved generally parallel to and south of Weichs's forces, planning to turn southward and advance parallel to the Don once it approached that river.

FIRST ENCIRCLEMENT, 28 JUNE–3 JULY

At dawn on 28 June, Weichs's ad hoc army group began its attack with a half-hour artillery bombardment and reconnaissance probes of Soviet defensive positions. More than half of Bock's 68 German divisions were involved in this attack, in which XXIV and XXXXVIII Motorized (soon redesignated Panzer) Corps led the northern thrust of a plan to encircle two Soviet armies, Lieutenant General M. A. Parsegov's 40th on the southern wing of the Briansk Front and Major General A. I. Danilov's 21st on the right (northern) wing of the Southwestern Front. In terms of equipment, these two panzer corps massed more than 700 tanks, primarily Panzer IIIs, against some 250 tanks (a mixture of KV-1 heavy, T-34 medium, and T-60 light) under Parsegov's command. Worse still for the defenders, under the pressure of the German penetration, Parsegov's headquarters quickly lost control of its subordinate units.[1] On the very first day, the German spearheads brushed by the defenders and seized crossings over the Tim River, 10 to 16 kilometers from the start line. In its first attack as an armored unit, 24th Panzer Division, converted from horse cavalry that spring, led XXXXVIII Panzer Corps' advance and seized an intact railroad bridge over the Tim, quickly tearing lit fuses and explosive charges from the structure. Twenty-five kilometers farther north, General of Panzer Troops Hermann Balck's 11th Panzer Division and Lieutenant General Johann Bassler's 9th Panzer Division, spearheading General of Panzer Troops Willibald *Freiherr* von Langermann's XXIV Panzer Corps, were equally successful.[2]

Frequent thunderstorms and heavy rain hampered the German attackers and forced Bock to postpone the advance of Paulus's Sixth Army, which was scheduled to form the southern pincer of the encirclement. Despite these difficulties, Weichs's northern panzer attack continued to spread chaos in the rear of the Briansk Front on 29 June. The 9th and 11th Panzer Divisions reached the Kshen' River, 30 kilometers beyond their start point, before being checked by 160th Rifle Division and 16th Tank Corps, respectively, in 40th Army's second echelon. While *Grossdeutschland* Division protected his left flank, General of Panzer Troops Bruno von Hauenschild and his 24th Panzer Division also crossed the Kshen' River. The converted cavalrymen not only dispersed 40th Army's 6th Rifle Division but also overran Parsegov's army headquarters in the village of Bykovo. The Soviet staff escaped, leaving behind its maps and radios as well as any hope of coordinating the battle.[3] Indeed, the attackers were moving so quickly that a *Luftwaffe* pilot bombed a spearhead of *Grossdeutschland*, ignoring aircraft recognition panels in the belief that no Germans could have moved that far east.[4]

General Golikov, the Briansk Front's commander, and the *Stavka* worked frantically to repair the situation. Golikov attempted to assemble 4th, 24th,

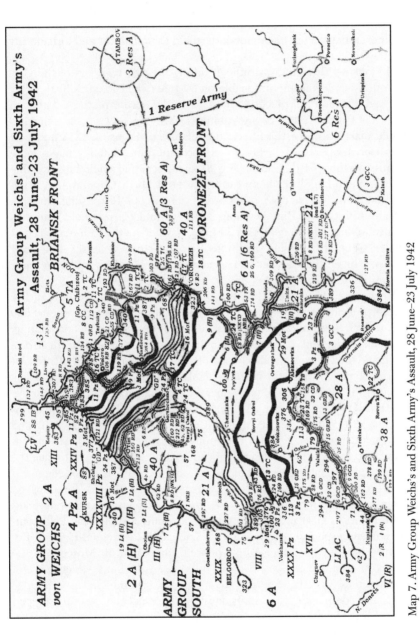

Map 7. Army Group Weichs's and Sixth Army's Assault, 28 June–23 July 1942

and 17th Tank Corps near Staryi Oskol to launch a counterstroke, but all these units were too inexperienced to move quickly; 17th Tank Corps even ran out of fuel. Stalin, thinking purely in terms of Golikov's overall numerical superiority in tanks, could not understand these failures and forbade any withdrawal.[5]

If Golikov's situation was difficult during the first two days of the German offensive, it became untenable on 30 June when Paulus's Sixth Army launched the southern pincer 48 hours after the northern attack. Although General of Panzer Troops Georg Stumme's XXXX Panzer Corps was the designated main effort for this attack, the infantry divisions of XXIX and VIII Army Corps, operating on Stumme's northern flank, actually made more progress on the first day, advancing 20 kilometers and encircling two rifle divisions and a tank brigade on the left wing of Major General A. I. Danilov's 21st Army. By contrast, other Soviet defenders—169th Rifle Division, 13th and 15th Guards Rifle Divisions, and 13th Tank Corps—held Stumme's advance to only 10 kilometers on 30 June. Farther south, 28th Army's commander, General Riabyshev, attempted to erect a new defensive line along the Oskol River, but the German success against Danilov's left wing made this position tenuous at best.

Between 29 June and 5 July the Briansk Front launched a total of five tank corps against the Germans, but despite outnumbering the enemy 600 tanks to 350, these efforts accomplished very little. Instead of cooperating, the green Soviet tank units, like their British counterparts in North Africa, fought and died separately. Balck's 11th Panzer Division severely attrited 1st and 16th Tank Corps on the northern flank, with the latter tank corps losing 137 of its 181 tanks. Even Major General M. E. Katukov, who would survive to outmaneuver his opponents six months later, was unable to coordinate his first attack as commander of 1st Tank Corps. Farther south, 4th, 24th, and 17th Tank Corps engaged 24th Panzer and *Grossdeutschland* Divisions but again failed to coordinate even the brigades within each corps, let alone the larger units. Vasilevsky relieved Major General N. V. Feklenko of command of the 17th, which lost 141 tanks and had to withdraw to the rear for refitting.[6]

Unfortunately for the Soviets, the *Stavka*'s response to these mistakes was to revert to 1941 attitudes, attempting to micromanage the field commanders and especially the tank units. Stalin sent Lieutenant General Fedorenko, head of the Main Auto-Armored Directorate in Moscow, to the Briansk Front command post in a vain effort to ensure more effective use of its armored assets. Still, experience continued to give the Germans an edge over Soviet commanders and staffs, most of which had only recently stepped up from brigade- to corps-level operations.[7]

Even before these tank battles concluded, the German threat to both flanks of 28th Army prompted Riabyshev to inform the *Stavka* on the evening of 2 July that he was withdrawing behind the Oskol River. Moscow had already recognized this danger, authorizing Golikov and Timoshenko to withdraw their respective *fronts*, including the tank corps still engaged, to establish a new defensive line along the Olym and Oskol.[8] However, communications were so unreliable that some units did not receive the withdrawal orders.

By nightfall on 3 July, General Sigfrid Heinrici's 16th Motorized Division of XXXXVIII Panzer Corps completed the encirclement of much of 40th Army, linking up with the infantry of VIII and XXIX Army Corps south of Staryi Oskol. As so often before, however, the pocket was not tightly sealed, allowing half of Parsegov's men to exfiltrate to the Don River and avoid capture. Much the same fate awaited Danilov's 21st Army and Major General P. E. Shurov's 13th Tank Corps, south of 40th Army; many small groups broke through Paulus's thin cordon of infantry, although Shurov and two of his brigade commanders perished in the process.[9] The Germans had wrecked their opponents as formed units but took only limited numbers of prisoners. Riabyshev's 28th Army remained an organized structure, even though it was severely depleted.

The first German attack had torn a large hole in the Soviet defenses. Stalin was increasingly alarmed by the prospect of losing Voronezh, thereby severing the railroad links to the south and making strategic troop movements far more difficult. On 2 July he responded to this threat by ordering four of his newly organized reserve armies to form a new, backup defensive line in front of Bock's forces. The 5th and 7th Reserve Armies, soon redesignated 63rd and 62nd Armies, respectively, went to plug the gap between the Briansk and Southwestern Fronts and thwart any subsequent German drive toward Stalingrad, while 3rd and 6th Reserve Armies, renamed 60th and 6th Armies, went to restore Golikov's defenses north and south of Voronezh. In addition, the dictator directed the transfer of 7th Tank Corps, commanded by the rising armored commander Colonel Pavel Alekseevich Rotmistrov, from the Kalinin Front southward to the Elets region. There, it would join 5th Tank Army as part of another large counterattack force under Golikov's control.[10] With this sole exception, however, the *Stavka* still refused to weaken the defenses of Moscow to meet the unexpected German offensive in the south. The dispatch of 60th, 62nd, and 63rd Armies would eventually give Golikov 22 fresh rifle divisions plus a rifle brigade, almost all of them newly formed. In the interim, however, Golikov also rearranged his own forces, transferring two rifle divisions, two tank brigades, and 8th Cavalry Corps from quiet sectors in an effort to bolster defenses in front of Voronezh.[11]

Despite such timely Soviet decisions, the German advance was so rapid that it was almost unstoppable. At 1930 on the evening of 4 July, a single company of the *Grossdeutschland* Division found an unguarded bridge over

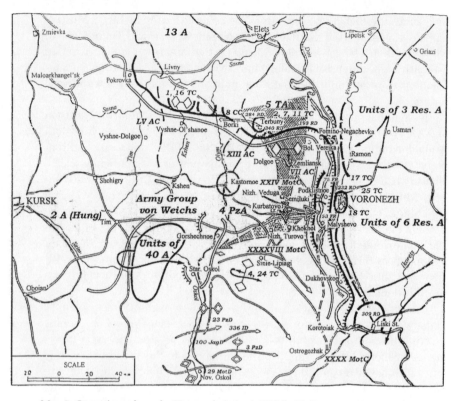

Map 8. Operations along the Voronezh Axis, 4–15 July 1942

the Don River at Semiluki. A German corporal waded underneath the bridge
to remove the demolition charges, with their fuses still burning, after which
a lieutenant rushed the bridge and took possession of the far bank.[12] Meanwhile, on 4 July, Langermann had turned 11th and 9th Panzer Divisions of
XXIV Panzer Corps northeastward, attempting to form a cordon protecting
Grossdeutschland and 24th Panzer Divisions. The next day, XXXXVIII Panzer Corps crossed the Don in force, and its 24th Panzer Division entered the
outskirts of Voronezh almost unopposed.[13]

5TH TANK ARMY'S COUNTERSTROKE, 6–12 JULY

This crisis prompted Stalin, shortly after midnight on 3 July, to order Golikov to prepare another counterstroke against the northern flank of the German thrust toward Voronezh. His chosen instrument was the fresh 5th Tank

Army—including 2nd and 11th Tank Corps, 340th Rifle Division, and 19th Separate Tank Brigade—now joined by the newly arrived 7th and the remnants of 1st and 16th Tank Corps, as well as 1st Guards Cavalry Corps.[14] This placed an excessive span of control on a green headquarters, but the dictator had considerable faith in 5th Tank's commander, A. I. Liziukov. Liziukov had displayed great audacity and skill while commanding 1st Motorized Rifle Division during the battle for Smolensk in August 1941, followed by equally impressive performances as deputy commander of 20th Army and then commander of 2nd Guards Rifle Corps during the battle for Moscow. The assigned mission of Liziukov's formidable (on paper) force, which included 641 tanks, was to attack southward, severing the communications of the German armored forces near Voronezh while assisting the escape of the surrounded elements of 40th Army.[15]

To ensure the success of this new counterstroke, Stalin directed Golikov to supervise 5th Tank Army personally while allowing his deputy commander, Lieutenant General N. E. Chibisov, to control the rest of the Briansk Front. Golikov, however, was often out of radio contact, and his *front* headquarters had to scramble for a new location after the fall of Voronezh on 5 July. By that time, the dictator had already dispatched his own chief of staff, Vasilevsky, to coordinate operations in the area.

German airpower continued to dominate the region, hindering all road and rail movements, especially during daylight hours. Although Rotmistrov's 7th Tank Corps reached its assembly area late on 5 July, 11th and 2nd Tank Corps did not begin to concentrate until the morning of the seventh. Under immense pressure from higher commanders, Liziukov directed Rotmistrov to attack at 0600 on 6 July, less than five hours after the order was issued. The 7th Tank Corps dutifully advanced on schedule, catching a *kampfgruppe* (battle group) of 11th Panzer Division near the village of Krasnaia Pliana, 55 kilometers northwest of Voronezh, and pushing it back 4 kilometers. Rotmistrov ordered his troops to "cling" to the retreating Germans to minimize the effects of German air strikes. Even on 7 July, however, only about half of Major General A. F. Popov's 11th Tank Corps, totaling no more than 50 tanks plus one battalion of 12th Motorized Rifle Brigade, was available to support him.[16]

The neighboring German division, Bässler's 9th Panzer, helped Balck halt the Soviet advance briefly at the Kobyl'ia Snova River, but the arrival of the rest of Popov's corps on 8 July pushed the defenders southward another 6 kilometers to the Sukhaia Vereika River. There, this almost unprecedented Red advance against German panzers came to a halt, hampered by German air strikes and artillery as well as the continuing problems of poorly directed vehicles stuck in river mud.

To further complicate Soviet command and control, on the evening of

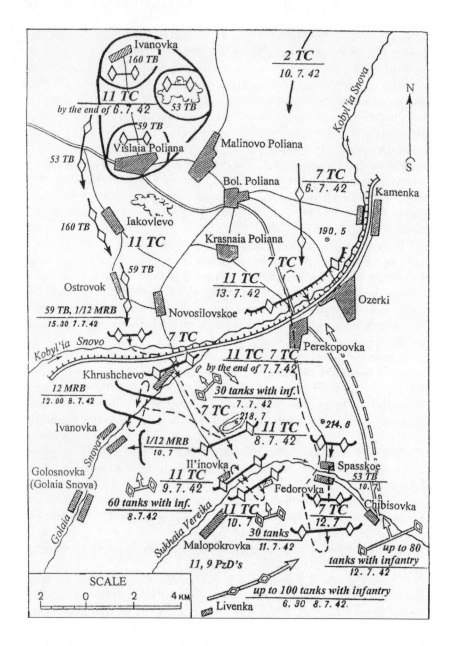

Map 9. 5th Tank Army Counterstroke, 7–14 July 1942

7 July Stalin decided to split the huge Briansk Front into two smaller organizations in an effort to reduce the span of control involved. Golikov retained control of the newly created Voronezh Front, using the arriving reserve armies to defend that region, while his former deputy, Chibisov, commanded a truncated Briansk Front to the north.[17] This reorganization was undoubtedly wise in the long run, but its immediate effect was to transfer control of 5th Tank's ongoing counterstroke to Chibisov, yet another senior officer who was unfamiliar with Liziukov's tactical situation. Meanwhile, Stalin continued to demand aggressive action, still believing that Liziukov faced only a single panzer division rather than the two panzer divisions with supporting infantry that were actually present.

On 9 July Liziukov mounted his first coordinated attack along the Sukhaia Vereika River, using all of Rotmistrov's 7th and Popov's 11th Tank Corps. After an initial success, however, the Soviet tankers were stymied by Stuka bombing and a local counterattack from 11th Panzer Division. At dawn on 12 July Langermann conducted a larger counterattack in which 11th Panzer advanced 5 kilometers along the boundary between the two committed tank corps, then swung eastward to outflank both Rotmistrov's corps and the second-echelon 2nd Tank Corps. The hard-pressed Soviet units had to withdraw northward to the next river line, where Liziukov managed to stabilize the situation on the thirteenth. Still, by 15 July, 5th Tank Army was short half its 641 tanks (including 261 permanently lost) and had suffered 7,929 casualties. Claims that it inflicted far more losses on its opponents were undoubtedly wishful thinking, but Langermann's corps certainly suffered significant attrition.[18] Liziukov had also attracted German air and ground reserves, leaving other elements of Weichs's *Armeegruppe* unsupported. On 8 July a mixed group, including Katukov's 1st and Major General M. I. Pavelkin's 16th Tank Corps, joined by 8th Cavalry Corps and several other formations, tried vainly to penetrate German XIII Army Corps on Weichs's left flank, northwest of the site where 5th Tank Army struggled with XXIV Panzer Corps.[19]

That same day, pressure from the *Stavka* prompted Golikov to attempt to retake Voronezh. To do this, he put new commanders in charge of the battle-weary 17th and 18th Tank Corps, the former reinforced to a total of 109 tanks. To these, Golikov added the fresh 25th Tank Corps. Major General Ivan Danilovich Cherniakhovsky, another rising young commander, displayed considerable aggressiveness in employing 18th Tank Corps but ultimately lost much of his force after an initial advance of 8 kilometers. Once again, the experienced Germans employed air, artillery, and antitank fires to stop a Soviet advance. The Soviet staffs were slow to react to changing tactical circumstances, in part because an obsessive concern for secrecy prompted them to avoid using the radio. That same day, in a final effort, Lieutenant General M. A. Antoniuk, commander of 60th Army, committed 25th Tank

Corps, together with two rifle divisions, against three German infantry divisions in the swampy lowlands north and west of Voronezh. Ultimately, however, the Soviets failed again, and Antoniuk was relieved of command.[20]

Outraged by the failure of such a large armored force, on 15 July Stalin ordered the dissolution of 5th Tank Army, with Liziukov himself demoted to command of 2nd Tank Corps. Golikov, in turn, found himself reduced to deputy commander of the Voronezh Front, being replaced by the brilliant young deputy chief of the General Staff, Lieutenant General Nikolai Fedorovich Vatutin. Konstantin Konstantinovich Rokossovsky, another general who had Stalin's trust, temporarily assumed command of the Briansk Front.[21]

HITLER, BOCK, AND ARMY GROUP A

If Stalin underestimated the problems facing his commanders in the Voronezh counterstroke, Hitler appeared unaware of the very existence of the Soviet effort. Instead, the German dictator became increasingly impatient with his generals, especially Field Marshal von Bock, for allowing their forces to become tied down around Voronezh.

On 3 July Hitler, his OKH chief Halder, and his OKW head Keitel boarded the Führer's four-engine Condor transport and flew to Army Group South headquarters at Poltava in an effort to get the offensive back on schedule. Despite the heat of the Ukrainian summer, Hitler was "in a receptive, friendly mood," but he remained convinced that the Red Army must be immediately encircled to avoid a further retreat to the Don River.[22] Bock readily agreed on the need to press the advance but noted that infantry forces alone would be insufficient to encircle the enemy, "who had gradually learned from past experience."[23]

Like other German field commanders, Bock believed he had the latitude to use his forces as he thought necessary to accomplish his mission—in this case, securing Voronezh, a key transportation hub that was under persistent Soviet counterattack, before resuming the offensive. He therefore retained all of Hoth's Fourth Panzer Army in that area for the next two weeks, fending off Soviet attacks and consolidating his gains. Unbeknownst to Bock, however, this disobedience irritated the German dictator considerably.[24] Neither Hitler nor Halder considered the Soviet counterattacks to be significant, whereas Bock was under no illusions about the danger posed by 5th Tank Army.[25] At about the same time, General Leo Geyr von Schweppenburg assumed command of XXXX Panzer Corps, replacing Stumme, who had been relieved for his part in the Reichel incident, an event that undoubtedly contributed to Hitler's irritation with his subordinates.

XXXX Panzer Corps, leading Sixth Army in its thrust to the northeast,

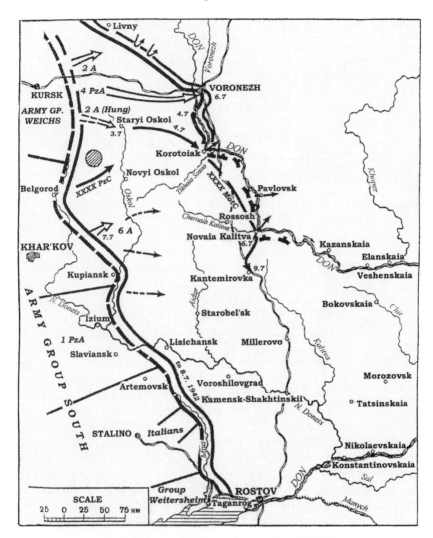

Map 10. Penetration of *Armeegruppe* Weichs to Voronezh and XXXX Panzer Corps' Turn to the South

reached Ostrogozhsk, 75 kilometers south of Voronezh, and Korotoiak on the Don River by 6 July, then wheeled south toward Rossosh'. In the process, Stumme's (and later Geyr's) panzers turned the right flank of Riabyshev's 28th Army, cutting off its line of retreat. Farther south, Sixth Army's VIII and XVII Army Corps pushed Riabyshev's troops out of their shaky defenses and forced them to withdraw southward toward Ol'khovatka and Rossosh' in

Table 4.1. Organization of Army Groups B and A, 7 July 1942

Army Group B—Field Marshal Fedor von Bock
   Armeegruppe von Weichs—Colonel General Maximilian von Weichs
      Headquarters, German Second Army
      Fourth Panzer Army—Colonel General Hermann Hoth
         XIII, VII, and XXIX Army Corps
         XXIV and XXXXVIII Panzer Corps
      Hungarian Second Army—Colonel General Gusztav Jany
         Hungarian III Corps
      German Sixth Army—General of Panzer Troops Friedrich Paulus
         VII, XVII, and LI Army Corps
         XXXX Panzer Corps
         Reserve—Hungarian IV Corps
         VIII Air Corps
Army Group A—Field Marshal Friedrich List
      First Panzer Army—Colonel General Ewald von Kleist
         XI and XXXXIV Army Corps
         III and XIV Panzer Corps
         Romanian VI Corps
      German Seventeenth Army (*Armeegruppe* Ruoff)—Colonel General
        Richard Ruoff
         IV and LII Army Corps and XXXXIX Mountain Corps
         LVII Panzer Corps
         Italian Expeditionary Corps
         Reserve—V Army Corps
         Headquarters, Italian Eighth Army—General Italo Gariboldi
           Italian II Corps
          Hungarian IV and VI Corps

Note: The OKH originally intended German-Romanian Eleventh Army to redeploy as part of Army Group A, but this was overtaken by events.

increasing disorder. Meanwhile, other units of German Sixth and Hungarian Second Armies continued to reduce the encirclement around Soviet 40th and 21st Armies.

The original plan for *Blau* II, developed in April, had foreseen the need to split Army Group South at this point. Bock would command a reduced Army Group B—essentially *Armeegruppe* Weichs plus Sixth Army—to continue the advance eastward toward the Volga River, while Wilhelm List's Army Group A headquarters assumed control of Seventeenth and First Panzer Armies for the advance to the Caucasus. Now that the split was at hand, Bock objected strenuously to dividing his command. Nonetheless, the split into two army groups took effect on 7 July. Bock bitterly confided to his diary that "the Army High Command is thus hanging on to *Blau* II and would like to encircle a foe who is no longer there."[26]

BLAU II: THE BATTLE FOR THE DONBAS, 9–17 JULY

Wasting little time, on 9 July List launched First Panzer and Seventeenth Armies on an offensive to the east and southeast toward Voroshilovgrad, moving parallel to the Northern Donets River. This was a modified version of *Blau* II, code-named Operation Clausewitz. Once again, the objective was to destroy remaining Red Army units in the region. However, because Bock was still dealing with the counterattacks around Voronezh, Fourth Panzer Army did not immediately join this attack. Instead, the northern pincer of this new offensive began with only Sixth Army's XXXX Panzer Corps, consisting of 3rd and 23rd Panzer Divisions and 29th Motorized Division. Yet even this limited effort soon ran short of fuel; the German offensive had already exceeded its logistical capacity, and for two weeks in mid-July, Army Group A had priority on gasoline. In the interim, XXXX Panzer Corps' advance was limited to a two-company *kampfgruppe* of 3rd Panzer Division. At dawn on 7 July this handful of Germans exploited surprise to seize the Kalitva River bridges at the transportation junction of Rossosh' and even captured one portion of Southwestern Front's headquarters.[27]

The German advance in *Blau* II was restricted not only by fuel but also by the rivers in the area, especially by the upper Don River, which formed the left boundary of Army Group B's advance. It also canalized the advancing German forces, especially Sixth Army, southeastward into the river's Great Bend. Similarly, the lower Don River formed the right boundary of List's Army Group A. This part of the river formed the limit of advance of *Blau* II; Army Group A raced eastward through open country, seeking to outflank the Southern Front's defenses along the Northern Donets and Mius Rivers. The ultimate objective was the city of Rostov-on-the-Don, a key collection of bridges and transportation links that formed the gateway to the Caucasus. In the process, however, the available mechanized units became scattered in a wide arc, and the limited river crossings made it difficult to encircle their opponents.

Thus, Army Group B's Sixth Army (and eventually Fourth Panzer Army) attacked southeastward, south of the Don, while Army Group A's First Panzer Army advanced eastward north of the Northern Donets River. The latter would cross the Northern Donets River at Voroshilovgrad, lunge eastward across the steppes south of Starobel'sk, and then turn southeastward along good roads to return to the Northern Donets at Kamensk-Shakhtinskii and ultimately reach Rostov.

Except for the Mius River line, held by the Southern Front's 56th, 18th, and 37th Armies, the remainder of the region was almost indefensible. The *Stavka* directed that the Southwestern Front erect barriers along a number of lesser rivers, but this only left the armies of both *fronts* open to penetration and encirclement.

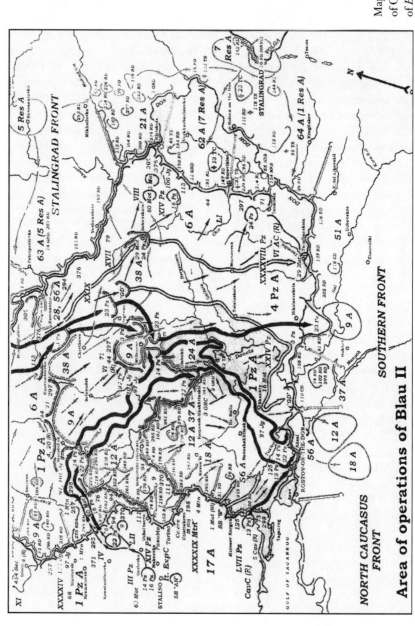

Map 11. Area of Operations of *Blau* II

Area of operations of Blau II

By 6 July, the shoestring advance of XXXX Panzer Corps, assisted by VIII Army Corps thrusting across the Tikhaia Sosna River, had unhinged the defenses of 28th Army. The *Stavka* had relieved Riabyshev of command of this army on 5 July, and his successor, Major General V. D. Kriuchenkin, had no choice but to retreat eastward. In an attempt to preserve a continuous front, on 6 July the *Stavka* reluctantly approved the withdrawal of all four armies of the Southwestern Front—21st, 28th, 38th, and 9th—eastward to the next river line. However, XXXX Panzer Corps, now refueled and led by 28th Motorized and 3rd Panzer Divisions, had already reached Ol'khovatka and Rossach' ón 7 July, deep behind the right wing of 28th Army, compromising the new defensive line before it was even established. A number of Soviet construction and logistical units were caught up in the chaotic withdrawal that ensued.[28]

Recognizing the opportunity, at dawn on 8 July Bock authorized the infantry of XI and XXXXIV Corps, on First Panzer Army's right wing, to begin a general exploitation; within a day they had reached the Krasnaia River and threatened both 9th Army and the right wing of 37th Army. Lieutenant General A. I. Lopatin's 9th Army had already suffered a severe drubbing during Operation Fridericus II and gave way quickly. By 9 July, Kleist has shifted III and XIV Panzer Corps to attack toward the Northern Donets River, completing the compromise of 37th Army in the Southwestern Front and neighboring 12th Army.

In this confusing situation, Timoshenko had to withdraw his auxiliary command post from the area near Rossoch', while the remainder of his staff was at Kalach, 50 kilometers northeast of the Don River. Neither headquarters had reliable communications with its field units. Moskalenko, commander of 38th Army, repeatedly warned of threats to both his flanks. After attempting to contact both Timoshenko and the *Stavka* representative, Vasilevsky, at 2000 hours on 9 July Moskalenko ordered a withdrawal on his own authority.[29] But it was too late.

By the evening of 9 July, XXXX Panzer Corps had cut a broad corridor through Timoshenko's defenses; together with XVII Army Corps on its right flank, this attack encircled 22nd Tank Corps and seven rifle divisions of 38th Army, as well as 13th Cavalry Corps and two rifle divisions from Timoshenko's *front* reserve. To the northwest and west, the remnants of Kriuchenkin's 28th Army were scattered across the countryside as the infantry corps of Sixth Army captured some units and pursued the others eastward.[30]

Like 21st Army, the 28th survived in name to withdraw across the Don, but its component divisions each mustered no more than 400 effective troops with a handful of guns and mortars. Moskalenko's 38th Army suffered a similar fate; its retreat was largely cut off by XXXX Panzer Corps, which repeatedly reached crossing sites over the Kalitva River before Moskalenko's troops

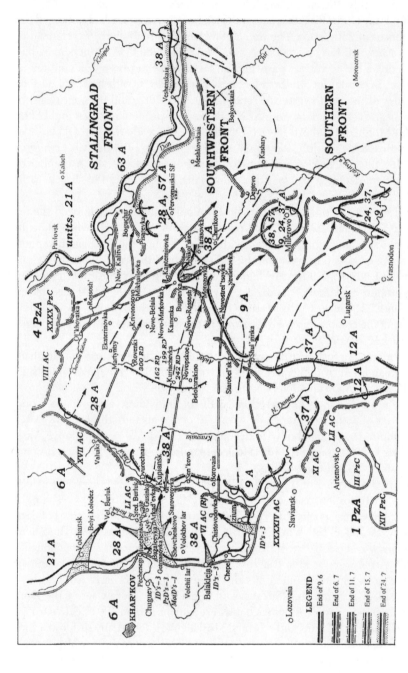

Map 12. Combat Operations of 28th, 38th, and 9th Armies between the Donets and Don Rivers, June–July 1942

could cross. Vasilevsky, as the *Stavka* representative, authorized further withdrawals while directing the construction of new defensive lines along the lower Don River, but again, German spearheads preempted such plans.[31] This rapid German advance endangered the Soviet airfields in the area, forcing Timoshenko on 10 July to order 8th Air Army to relocate eastward; this, in turn, deprived the Southwestern Front of the last vestige of friendly air cover.

Delayed by fuel shortages, XXXXVIII Panzer Corps, commanded by Lieutenant General Werner Kempf, nonetheless closed on the Tikhaia Sosna River at Nikolaevka and Ostrogozhsk by the end of 12 July. Meanwhile, the southern pincer of Bock's grand drive, composed of two panzer corps of First Panzer Army, was almost as successful. The 14th and 22nd Panzer Divisions of General of Cavalry Eberhard von Mackensen's III Panzer Corps, flanked on the left by Romanian VI Corps, advanced to the Aider River south of Starobel'sk. General of Infantry Wietersheim's XIV Panzer Corps, led by 16th Panzer and 16th Motorized Divisions, crossed the same river at Novyi Aidar. In the process, Kleist's panzers had outflanked the Southern Front's defensive lines and were herding the rear guards of 38th and 9th Armies eastward.

By 15 July, the spearheads had linked up, but as usual, the pocket was too porous to prevent large numbers of Red soldiers from escaping, albeit without any heavy equipment or organization. Once again, the Germans had outmaneuvered their foes, but in the process they suffered significant wear and tear and repeatedly had to stop due to fuel shortages. There were simply insufficient mechanized formations to achieve the ill-defined goals of the operation and too few infantry divisions to prevent Red Army soldiers from escaping the encirclement. XXXX Panzer Corps, which had begun with 230 tanks, had no more than 100 functioning by the end of *Blau* II.[32]

FORMATION OF THE STALINGRAD FRONT

The rapid advance of Bock's spearheads also exposed the severe limitations of the Soviets' command and control network, as suggested above. In addition to having inadequate communications, the senior leadership of the Southwestern Front was divided against itself. Reflecting Stalin's selective trust in his senior officers, the Soviet leader had dispatched General Bodin, formerly chief of the Operations Directorate in the General Staff, to become the *front* chief of staff. Marshal Timoshenko apparently regarded Bodin as a spy from the *Stavka*. On 6 July, without warning, Timoshenko and his political officer, Khrushchev, left the *front*'s main headquarters at Kalach to establish a new tactical or auxiliary command post at Gorokhovka, four and a half hours away, but they failed to take communications troops with them. For several days, the *front* commander was incommunicado with higher and lower units, while Bodin loyally attempted to answer for failures that were beyond his control. Ultimately, Vasilevsky had to order Timoshenko to return to his main headquarters to coordinate the retreat.[33]

Given such problems, it is not surprising that many retreating Soviet units lost their organization. By 11 July, Stalin recognized that previous attempts to restore the situation had been completely inadequate. He therefore ordered Major General I. Ia. Kolpakchi's 62nd Army (the former 7th Reserve Army) to move its six rifle divisions by rail from Stalingrad forward to a new defensive line still in preparation across the western base of the Great Bend of the Don. This new line, which Stalin demanded be completed by 14 July, was a gentle arc roughly halfway between the Chir River to the west and the Great Bend to the east, which in turn was only 50 kilometers from Stalingrad itself. To help Kolpakchi's 81,000 men in this task, the *Stavka* reinforced 62nd Army with 18 artillery–machine gun battalions of 52nd and 115th Fortified Regions, specialty units intended to add firepower to an otherwise weakly held sector of the front. Three additional rifle divisions would meanwhile assume Kolpakchi's previous positions in Stalingrad itself.[34]

This was only the first stage in a much larger reorganization. Early on the morning of 12 July Stalin and Vasilevsky discussed the crisis by Baudot teletype with the Southern Front commander, General Malinovsky. They followed this conversation with an order that put Malinovsky's headquarters in charge of the remnants of Southwestern Front, including 28th, 38th, 57th, and 9th Armies. Only the skeletal 21st Army would remain under Timoshenko's headquarters, which now became the Stalingrad Front. This *front*, controlling three former reserve armies, tried to form a new echelon of defense. Kolpakchi's 62nd Army, as already described, was deployed across the Great Bend of the Don; in addition to the fortified region battalions, it now included six divisions: 33rd Guards and 192nd, 147th, 184th, 196th, and 181st Rifle Divisions. Similar deployment orders were sent to 63rd Army, which was to extend the line on Kolpakchi's northern flank and block any further German advance north of the Great Bend toward Stalingrad.[35] The new commander of 63rd Army, Lieutenant General V. I. Kuznetsov, controlled five additional formations: 14th Guards and 1st, 153rd, 197th, and 203rd Rifle Divisions. Finally, General Chuikov's 64th Army (formerly 1st Reserve Army) was initially slated to form a second echelon behind the other two, between the Chir and Don Rivers. Chuikov had six subordinate organizations: 131st, 229th, 29th, 18th, 214th, and 112th Rifle Divisions.

The bulk of these formations consisted of officers and staffs that were almost as raw as their troops. The three army commanders, however, were all experienced officers, two of whom had survived the crucible of the battles of 1941. At age 42, Kolpakchi had been a Red soldier since the storming of the tsar's winter palace during the November Revolution of 1917. He had advised the Republicans during the Spanish Civil War and in 1941 assumed command of 18th Army to lead that unit's escape from encirclement; later he became chief of staff of the Briansk Front and then commander of a special shock group that recaptured the city of Belyi in April 1942.[36] The 48-year-old Kuznetsov—one of three generals with that last name who led field armies during the Soviet-German conflict—had commanded an imperial regiment before joining the Red Army in 1918. He had also led a field army's escape from German encirclement in 1941, after which he had headed 1st Shock Army during the Northwestern Front's offensive that encircled but failed to crush German II Corps at Demiansk in the spring of 1942.[37] As described in chapter 1, Chuikov, the 41-year-old son of peasants, had commanded 9th Army during the Winter War with Finland, but bad luck kept him away from the front during the first year of the German conflict.

Later on 12 July the *Stavka* took additional measures in an effort to block the German advance. It instructed Marshal Budenny, now commander of the North Caucasus Front, to concentrate three rifle divisions, each supported by a guards-mortar (multiple-rocket launcher) regiment, to act as a covering force along the southern bank of the Don River east of Rostov. The Southern Front was to dispatch a reserve tank brigade to Stalingrad, while concentrating its tactical air units against the German panzer columns.[38]

Still, even this extensive program went aground when, on 15–17 July, the survivors of 28th, 38th, and 57th Armies escaped not to Malinovsky's Southern Front in the south but eastward to the Stalingrad Front's forward positions along the Don River. Stalin's repeated rebukes of Timoshenko could not remedy the complete breakdown of command and control. To fill the resulting gap to the south, the *Stavka* instructed Budenny's North Caucasus Front to deploy Major General T. K. Kolomiets's 51st Army along the lower Don River near Rostov.[39] This makeshift defense could succeed only if the Soviets were able to predict the focus of the next blitzkrieg attack, something Germany's enemies had been remarkably unsuccessful in doing.

HITLER ALTERS COURSE

By 12 July, Hitler and the OKH believed the Soviets intended to defend the Millerovo, Kametsk-Shakhtinskii, and Rostov line. Millerovo was the critical rail junction on which any further resupply or withdrawal of the Southwestern Front depended. This assessment was accurate, but the dictator and his military advisers continued to underestimate the Soviet ability to rebuild shattered units and resist their advances, believing that the Red Army was on its last legs. For Fourth Panzer Army's tardy involvement in the previous attack, Hitler blamed Bock's willful commitment of *Grossdeutschland* and

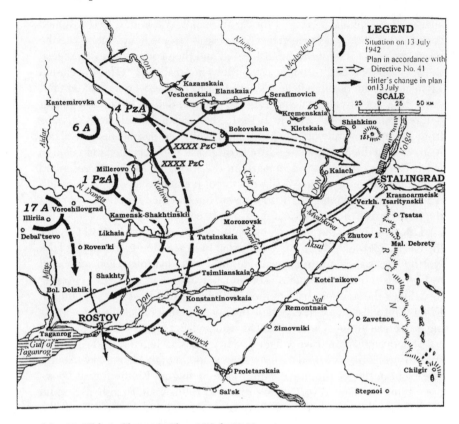

Map 13. Hitler's Change in Plan, 13 July 1942

24th Panzer Divisions to fighting in Voronezh, refusing to recognize that Soviet counterattacks in that area had necessitated a German response.[40] Bock
continued to object to the ensuing deployment of his panzer corps, arguing
correctly that, given the restrictive rivers in the Donets region, they would
be pursuing rather than encircling enemy forces there. Halder and Bock
disagreed when the OKH wanted to hold back the infantry corps of Sixth
Army in a vain attempt to allow the panzer corps to achieve an encirclement.
On 13 July Hitler decided that Bock's behavior was too obstructionist to allow him to continue in command. The Führer ordered Weichs to succeed
Bock as commander of the truncated Army Group B. Bock never again held
a significant command. General Halder persuaded Hitler to retain Major
General Georg von Sodenstern as army group chief of staff only by arguing
that Sodenstern had opposed Bock's plans.[41] Lieutenant General Hans von
Salmuth succeeded Weichs as commander of Second Army.

On that same eventful day, the OKH sent new orders by teletype to both army groups.[42] Discarding much of the preliminary planning for *Blau* III, the next operation, now code-named *Braunschweig* (literally, "liverwurst," but probably referring to the German city of Brunswick), shifted the main effort to List's Army Group A, which assumed control of XXIV, XXXXVIII, and XXXX Motorized Corps (now redesignated panzer corps) of Fourth Panzer Army, as well as VIII and LI Army Corps, which had previously belonged to Sixth Army. Although still short of fuel, Hoth's panzer army had a new mission to thrust southward, cross the Don River at Konstantinovskaia (120 kilometers east of Rostov), and then hook westward back to Rostov itself. Simultaneously, III and XIV Panzer Corps of Kleist's First Panzer Army would parallel Fourth Panzer Army, advancing eastward north of the Donets to encircle 9th Red Army at Millerovo, then cross the river and swing back westward toward the northern side of Rostov. In the meantime, Ruoff's Seventeenth Army would press the Southern Front's 12th, 18th, and 56th Armies eastward and southward, pushing the defenders into the path of First Panzer Army's flanking maneuver. Meanwhile, the truncated Army Group B, consisting of (west to east) German Second, Hungarian Second, and German Sixth Armies, was relegated to securing the Don River flank from Voronezh southeastward. Only the first of these three armies retained any mechanized forces, 9th and 11th Panzer Divisions.

Three days later, on 16 July, Hitler permanently moved Führer headquarters from East Prussia to Vinnitsa in the central Ukraine. This newly constructed headquarters, code-named *Wehrwolf*, included Halder but only the operations sections of the OKW and OKH, leaving many staff officers behind. From there, the German leader attempted—like his counterpart in the Kremlin the previous year—to supervise the conduct of battle in immense detail. The move was a clear indication of Hitler's growing impatience with and distrust for the German officer corps.

THE MILLEROVO ENCIRCLEMENT AND THE BATTLE FOR ROSTOV, 17–24 JULY

Hitler also redirected scarce reserves in a manner that further stretched German resources. By early July, he was worried that Churchill might launch a desperate attack to take pressure off the Soviets and respond to political criticism about Rommel's capture of Tobruk in North Africa. As a result, on 6 July the dictator placed restrictions on any use of 1st SS Motorized Division *Leibstandarte Adolf Hitler*, a major portion of First Panzer Army's striking power. Three days later, the German leader ordered that this division, the newly formed 2nd SS Motorized Division *Das Reich*, and other new units

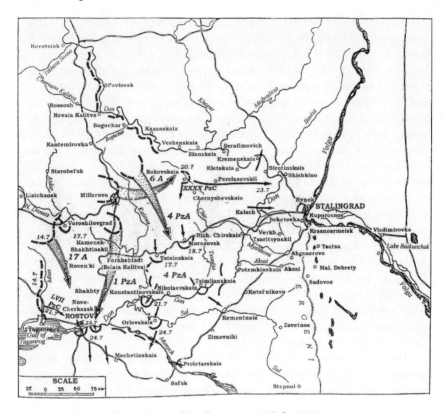

Map 14. German Operations to Seize Rostov, 14–24 July 1942

be sent to France rather than be committed to the East.[43] Historians and German generals have criticized such decisions, but it is worth recalling that the British-Canadian raid on Dieppe, France, happened in August 1942, indicating a kernel of validity in Hitler's strategic concerns.

On 11 July Führer Directive No. 43 specified that Manstein's Eleventh Army, fresh from its victory at Sevastopol', would now use part of its forces to advance across the Kerch' Strait. The objective was to secure the vital Soviet naval bases at Anapa and Novorossisk and facilitate a further advance into the Caucasus. Given the shortage of cargo vessels, such an amphibious movement was risky, but two days later, Manstein received new instructions to prepare for movement northward to the Leningrad region in early August.[44]

These ambitious plans reflected the continuing German belief, however mistaken, that the Red Army was near the end of its strength. The 62nd and 64th Armies were still trying to organize an effective defense and were ripe for preemption. At the same time, Paulus's army had torn a gap at the junction of the Southern and Southwestern Fronts. Again, however, exploiting these opportunities required quick movement by the German mechanized forces, forces that were already undersupplied and overstretched.

At first, despite persistent fuel shortages, both Hoth's and Kleist's panzer divisions performed brilliantly (see map 14). On 14 July 3rd Panzer Division of XXXX Panzer Corps struck southward to further block the withdrawal of 38th, 57th, and 9th Armies, while 23rd Panzer was already occupying Millerovo and fending off Moskalenko's attempts to break through it. That same day, west of this growing encirclement, 29th Motorized Division, now assigned to Kempf's XXXXVIII Panzer Corps, advanced halfway (25 kilometers) toward the key road junction at Morozovsk. At dawn on 15 July 3rd Panzer Division from Fourth Panzer Army linked up with 14th Panzer Division, which was leading First Panzer Army in its supporting attack eastward. On a map, this marked the sealing of the Millerovo encirclement. In reality, Hoth's and Kleist's infantry were still west of the town, unable to keep up with the armor. The other two units of XXXXVIII Panzer Corps, *Grossdeutschland* and 24th Panzer Divisions, could not begin their southward movement until 15 July because of fuel shortages. Meanwhile, the Millerovo pocket, which appeared so definitive on maps, hemorrhaged refugee Soviet troops, while to the south, most of the infantry of 37th Army retreated west of the Glubokaia River.[45]

This encirclement also brought the two panzer armies together as neighbors. As Bock had predicted, this meant they were competing for the same supply routes to support their advance, and they were too close together to launch another encirclement.

Field Marshal List was fully aware of this. He was also concerned that First Panzer Army, having begun the campaign at 40 percent strength, was now down to 30 percent. In addition, he recognized that Italian Eighth Army, which was supposed to guard his flank, was extremely inexperienced and ill equipped. List nonetheless had to continue the advance. On 16 July he brought together his army commanders and chiefs of staff at Gorlovka to discuss these plans. Using 14th and 22nd Panzer Divisions of Mackensen's III Panzer Corps, First Panzer Army would pass to the east of Kamensk-Shakhtinskii to outflank the Soviet defenses there and then capture Rostov from the east, thereby encircling the Southern Front's 12th, 18th, and 56th Armies before they could withdraw. Meanwhile, Fourth Panzer Army's XXXXVIII and XXXX Panzer Corps would advance southward from the Millerovo area to the Don. There, XXXX Panzer Corps would move into reserve with its 23rd Panzer Division, while 3rd Panzer Division, joined by 16th and *Grossdeutschland* Motorized Divisions from XXXXVIII Panzer Corps, would transfer to the control of General Langermann's XXIV Panzer Corps for mopping up around Rostov. Seventeenth Army, as already planned, would act as the anvil on which these panzer formations would pound the So-viet defenders.[46] Once again, the armored spearheads appeared headed for gridlock in the area of Rostov, although on 18 July Halder persuaded Hitler to approve a modification that permitted Army Group A to seize a broader stretch of the lower Don.[47]

Between 15 and 18 July the widely dispersed divisions of XXXXVIII and XXXX Panzer Corps each covered almost 200 kilometers to reach the lower Don. Dust and heat were greater obstacles than any defense offered by the Red Army. Everywhere they went that month, the Germans encountered long columns of Soviet troops hurrying eastward, seeking to escape encircle-ment. Captured Red soldiers appeared confused and sometimes surrendered en masse, but most of the defenders, however disheartened or disorganized, continued the struggle.

As a result, most of the German maneuvers came up empty-handed in the quest for prisoners. Malinovsky skillfully used his rear guard to enable more than half the troops of his 12th, 18th, and 56th Armies to withdraw southward toward Rostov. In fact, during the first two weeks of its existence, Army Group A captured only 54,000 Soviet soldiers, a far cry from the huge encirclements of the previous year.[48]

Meanwhile, on 17 July Hitler had returned control of VIII and LI Army Corps from Hoth to Paulus and reinforced them with 16th Panzer and 60th Motorized Divisions of Wietersheim's XIV Panzer Corps. Heavy rains again virtually halted Sixth Army's operations from 18 to 20 July. On the twenty-first, however, the newly transferred units spearheaded another advance, with 16th Panzer moving a third of the way between the Chir and Don Riv-ers on the first day. This brought Sixth Army into contact with the forward detachments of Kolpakchi's 62nd Army, beginning a monthlong struggle that eventually carried the Germans to the outskirts of Stalingrad.

With *Stavka* approval, on 16 July Malinovsky ordered all the armies of Southern Front to begin a phased withdrawal to the Don River south of Ros-tov. Two days later, the rapid advance of Kleist's panzers began to threaten Malinovsky's right wing, and he ordered all units to accelerate their retreat in an effort to break contact. On 21 July General of Panzer Troops Ferdi-nand Heim's 14th Panzer Division captured Novocherkassk, 25 kilometers northeast of Rostov, and the next day LVII Panzer Corps encircled Rostov's outer defenses; 13th, 22nd, and 14th Panzer Divisions converged from the west, north, and east, respectively. Although Malinovsky had repeatedly or-dered 56th and 18th Armies to defend the vital city, too many Soviet units, especially those in 18th Army, had fled across the river. Major General V. V. Tsyganov endeavored to organize the Rostov defenses using several divisions of his 56th Army, while the 70th and 158th Fortified Regions and NKVD security forces erected hasty positions within the city's streets and bridges.[49]

On 23 July 13th Panzer Division thrust rapidly through the city streets, bypassing opposition and reaching the main bridge across the Don. There, however, Tsyganov's troops destroyed the bridge in the nick of time. The panzer units were ill equipped for city fighting, so 125th Infantry Division drew the onerous task of clearing Rostov block by block. This struggle, from 24 to 27 July, proved to be a forerunner of the desperate fighting in Stalingrad. Meanwhile, on the night of 26–27 July, teams of Brandenburgers—the German Army's elite special operations troops—surprised the guards and seized several bridges south of Rostov. They had to defend these bridges for 24 hours before help arrived, but First Panzer Army now held the gateway for its projected advance toward the Caucasus.[50]

Official Soviet sources, based on partial German records, claim that 88,689 Red Army soldiers were captured during June and July 1942, covering the first three phases of the *Blau* offensive. Based on increases in forced laborers working in German industry, the actual prisoner count was probably closer to 150,000. Given that Soviet accounts often underestimate losses by up to 30 percent, the total irreplaceable losses (killed, captured, deserted, or missing) probably approached 500,000 soldiers out of 1.3 million engaged.[51] Overall, the Stalingrad Front retained only about 340,000 survivors of the 610,000 troops fielded by the Southwestern Front on 22 June.[52]

HITLER'S DIRECTIVE NO. 45

Once again, German tactical encirclements gave the illusion of an operational or strategic success, while many Red commanders and units escaped to fight another day. Although General Halder argued that the Soviets had conducted a phased withdrawal, Hitler became convinced that the enemy was at the end of his strength. Führer Directive No. 45, issued on 23 July, included the confident assessment that "only weak forces from Timoshenko's Army Group have succeeded in avoiding encirclement and reaching the southern bank of the Don. However, we must expect the retreating forces will be reinforced at the expense of forces in the Caucasus. In addition, a concentration of enemy force groups has been detected in the Stalingrad region, which he apparently intends to defend stubbornly."[53] Based on this assessment, and still feeling the pressure of time, Hitler decided to seek the two objectives of *Blau* III and *Blau* IV—securing the Stalingrad area and reaching the Caucasus oil fields—in a simultaneous operation. This new advance, code-named Edelweiss, had three phases. In the first phase, List's Army Group A would mount a pincer operation with Fourth and First Panzer Armies on the left and Seventeenth and Romanian Third Armies on the right, all aiming to achieve another encirclement at Tikhoretsk, 160 kilometers south of Rostov

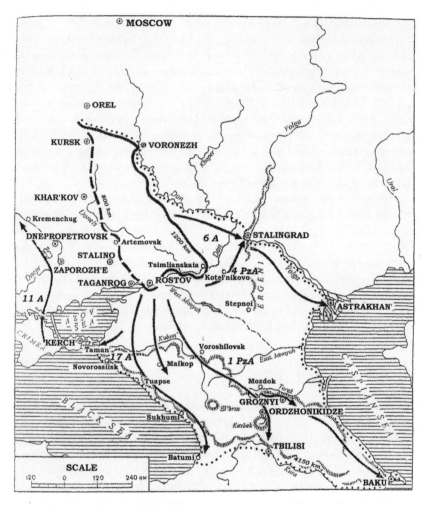

Map 15. Hitler's New Plans of 23 and 30 July 1942

and halfway from that key city to the Black Sea port of Novossisk. Simultaneous with this encirclement, Paulus's Sixth Army, reinforced by two army
and one panzer corps from Fourth Panzer Army, would advance eastward
toward Stalingrad. At the end of this first phase, List was to transfer 24th
Panzer and another panzer division to Army Group B for the final advance
on Stalingrad, while *Grossdeutschland* Division would prepare for transfer
to Western Europe.[54]

During the second phase of Edelweiss, List's army group, using First
Panzer Army and a truncated Fourth Army, was to capture the Black Sea

coast east of the Crimea to neutralize the Red fleet based there, while severing communications between the Caucasus and Stalingrad regions. In addition, to support the light and mountain troops of German Seventeenth Army, the Romanian Mountain Corps would cross the Kerch' Strait, after which Ruoff's reinforced army would seize the high ground in the Maikop area, the northernmost petroleum field. In the third phase, the mechanized forces of First Panzer Army, together with the rump of Fourth Panzer Army (XXXXVIII and XXXX Panzer Corps), would seize the oil center at Groznyi, interdict major highways at the Caucasus Mountain passes, and, if possible, continue on to the Azerbaijan oil fields near Baku.[55] In practice, however, the transfer of Fourth Panzer Army to Army Group B on 30 July spelled doom for Operation Edelweiss (see chapter 5).

In light of later events, perhaps the most significant aspect of Directive No. 45 concerned Weichs's Army Group B. In effect, this order split Fourth Panzer Army by transferring XXIV Panzer Corps headquarters, along with 24th Panzer Division, to Paulus. For the first time, this directive also explicitly charged Army Group B with capturing rather than neutralizing the city of Stalingrad. Thereafter, Weichs would prepare to advance southeast along the Volga to Astrakhan on the Caspian Sea, further disrupting Soviet rail and road communications. Meanwhile, Army Group A was weakened by the loss of this panzer corps as well as the *Leibstandarte Adolf Hitler* and *Grossdeutschland* Divisions. Moreover, the bulk of German Eleventh Army, originally intended to reinforce List, would now redeploy to reinforce the siege of Leningrad. In terms of *Luftwaffe* and logistical support, priority went to List, although the 23 July order forbade any air strikes on the oil facilities themselves.[56]

As a result of this organization, Paulus's Sixth Army now had two panzer corps headquarters—XIV (with 16th Panzer and 3rd and 60th Motorized Divisions) and XXIV (with only 24th Panzer Division)—to advance on Stalingrad. The big loser was General Hoth's Fourth Panzer Army, truncated to XXXXVIII Panzer Corps (controlling only 29th Motorized Division and a Romanian infantry division) and XXXX Panzer Corps (with 3rd and 23rd Panzer Divisions). By contrast, Kleist's First Panzer Army grew to two infantry and two panzer corps, the latter consisting of III Panzer Corps (14th Panzer, 16th Motorized, and, at least temporarily, *Grossdeutschland* Divisions) and LVII Panzer Corps (13th Panzer and 5th SS Motorized Division *Wiking*).

This reshuffling left almost every element of the two army groups shorthanded. In Army Group B, Paulus, though reinforced by another panzer division, had barely sufficient combat power to advance on Stalingrad, while Weichs's other field armies, including only one panzer division, stretched to protect the ever-growing left flank from Voronezh southeastward along the Don. By early fall, the *Stavka* had begun to exploit both these weaknesses.

In numerical terms, Weichs's army group had 37 divisions (including three panzer and two motorized) and 386 tanks along a front that would eventually reach 500 kilometers; they faced a Soviet force equivalent to 90 divisions (including 18 tank corps) and 1,939 tanks. Army Group A was initially better off, controlling 32 divisions (including six panzer and five motorized) and 435 tanks. They faced an initial Soviet force of 34 division equivalents (including 253 tanks), many of which were understrength.[57] One should note, however, that most of List's divisions had begun the campaign at lower strengths than their counterparts under Weichs, and the logistical demands of their extended advance soon wore down their capabilities. By 25 July, the six German and one Slovak mobile divisions assigned to Kleist and Ruoff fielded only 235 serviceable tanks.[58]

The most serious deficiency in this German plan was the relative weakness of the Voronezh axis and the adjacent Don River flank. Here, German Second and Hungarian Second Armies had only about 100 tanks, as opposed to a Soviet force of some 700 tanks. If the Soviets could ever coordinate their tanks effectively in this area, this could have devastating consequences for the *Wehrmacht*.

Stalin recognized this vulnerability and began to organize counterattacks against both the Voronezh sector and the nose of Sixth Army's advance. On 17 July he directed the Briansk Front to join the Voronezh Front in such attacks, beginning on or about 21 July. The next day he reinforced this region with 2nd and 4th Reserve Armies, which would later form a resurrected 38th Army to join the Briansk Front's main effort.[59] Later that day, Stalin directed the formation of two new organizations, 1st and 4th Tank Armies, by 28 July and 1 August, respectively, with each one consisting of two tank corps and three rifle divisions transferred from the Far East; their unstated purpose was to coordinate another major counterstroke. To ensure more experienced leadership, Stalin chose to form these new organizations around two experienced headquarters from the recent struggle: Moskalenko and his 38th Army staff would head 1st Tank, while Kriuchenkin and the headquarters of 28th Army would organize 4th Tank.[60]

CONCLUSIONS

During the first month of Operation *Blau*, German forces were still able to achieve their territorial objectives, although they had to move more cautiously because of Soviet resistance, especially the counterstrokes launched near Voronezh. For the Germans, the problem was how to interpret their success: was the enemy fleeing in panic, resisting in his usual clumsy manner, or withdrawing in good order? In fact, all three interpretations were correct, depending on the specific unit and situation. Overall, Stalin had attempted to conduct a resolute defense. Superior German experience had once again defeated this defense, resulting in the destruction or decimation of ten field armies—5th Tank, 28th, 38th, 9th, 12th, 37th, 18th, 56th, 24th, and 57th. Stalin was forced to bring forward six raw armies from his strategic reserves and create two additional tank armies, erecting two completely new echelons of defense. Still, the growing experience of Soviet commanders and staffs had both attrited the attackers and denied them the huge prisoner hauls of the previous year. This improvement in enemy performance was often invisible at the level of Hitler, the OKW, and the OKH, resulting in conflicts with more cautious field commanders and excessive optimism about the future. Meanwhile, some of the Soviet escapees joined local partisan forces, while many others eventually rejoined the Red Army to fight another day.

Hitler, at least, chose to believe that the Red Army was as incompetent and weak as it had been in 1941. The 7 July split of Army Group South and the subsequent change of direction embodied in Führer Directive No. 45 have often been characterized as disastrous examples of the dictator's excessive optimism. Germany had, at most, sufficient air and ground resources to achieve one major objective in 1942; splitting Army Group South into two forces that operated in three divergent directions—the Voronezh flank, Stalingrad, and the Caucasus—raised the possibility that none of these missions would succeed. However, as the authors of the German official history have argued, the dictator felt the pressure of time. He apparently believed that his window of opportunity would close soon as the United States and Britain prepared to challenge him in the West.[61] Based on his perceptions, he took what he regarded as a calculated risk, trying to achieve all his objectives on a shoestring in a very brief period. He came perilously close to succeeding.

CHAPTER FIVE

The German Advance to
the Don and the Volga

On 17 July 1942 the bulk of German Sixth Army was poised to advance into the Great Bend of the Don River, with the ultimate goal of reaching Stalingrad on the Volga. With German resources divided between the twin targets of Stalingrad and the Caucasus, General Paulus would be hard-pressed to reach that goal.

Joseph Stalin was equally determined to defend this region. He instructed the Stalingrad Front to hold on to its defenses in and just west of the Great Bend, while the Briansk and Voronezh Fronts unleashed another concentrated assault against Army Group B's lengthening left flank.

By a quirk of geography, the Don and Volga Rivers ran generally parallel to each other until they converged in the Stalingrad region—where the Don bent sharply eastward while the Volga curved more gently toward the west, bringing the two rivers within 70 kilometers of each other between Kalach and Stalingrad. After the war the Soviet Union built dams to flood this area and support a canal between the two rivers, but at the time of the German invasion, the Don was a formidable obstacle. The few bridges in the area, such as those at Trekhostrovskaia and Kalach, were key terrain for both attacker and defender.

West of the Don, the Chir River and numerous smaller streams, together with the *balkas* (ravines) and marshes created by them, presented additional obstacles. Just as elsewhere in European Russia, western banks tended to be higher than eastern ones, inhibiting Soviet defense of these streams. Similar streams and *balkas* also inhibited movement across the land bridge, where the land sloped gradually upward from the Don to the Volga. To compound these challenges, the Soviet defenders destroyed water wells and evacuated villages as they retreated.

The transportation network both within the Great Bend and on the land bridge had a few major roads that generally paralleled the rivers. The main east-west railroad ran from the Donbas area to Stalingrad, passing north of the Chir River. In addition to its industrial and propaganda significance, Stalingrad was the junction between this railroad and the north-south line from Moscow to Astrakhan' on the Caspian Sea.

Stalingrad was a man-made island in the midst of a vast, almost treeless steppe. The configuration of the land bridge, together with the concentration of bridges at the city, made Stalingrad an almost unavoidable target for the Germans. First, however, Paulus had to overcome the geographic and human obstacles west of the town.

SIXTH ARMY'S INITIAL ADVANCE TO THE DON, 17–25 JULY

On 23 July General Paulus completed his plan to capture Stalingrad, even as his troops made their initial advances eastward. His concept relied on speed to negate any remaining Soviet defenses in the area. Briefly, he wanted to seize crossings over the Don River both north and south of Kalach and then thrust due eastward with his available armor, flanked by infantry. General Langermann's XXIV Panzer Corps, with only one panzer division—the 24th—would advance toward the southern end of the city. North of and parallel to this advance was the main spearhead, built around General Wietersheim's XIV Panzer Corps, whose ultimate goal was the northern industrial suburbs of the city. Wietersheim's corps included 16th Panzer, 3rd Motorized, and 60th Motorized Divisions and received support from General of Artillery Walter von Seidlitz's LI Army Corps, including 297th, 71st, and 44th Infantry Divisions. North of Seidlitz's corps and protecting the left wing of the advance was Lieutenant General Walther Heitz's VIII Army Corps, consisting of 79th and 113th Infantry and 100th *Jäger* (light infantry) Divisions. This German concentration totaled about 120,000 men and 150 tanks and assault guns.[1]

Heavy rains delayed the concentration of this force along the Chir River, opposite Kolpakchi's 62nd Army, until late on 21 July. Kolpakchi had deployed five of his six rifle divisions uniformly across the Great Bend from Surovikino on the Chir northward to Kletskaia on the Don. Including nondivisional units, Kolpakchi had 383 guns, 1,138 mortars, and 277 tanks.[2] South of the Chir, Chuikov's 64th Army was just arriving to extend the defensive line with six rifle divisions, two naval rifle brigades, two weak tank brigades, and a mixture of various student units from nearby schools, giving him 226 guns, 622 mortars, and 55 tanks.[3]

On 22–23 July the three mobile divisions of XIV Panzer Corps, organized into combined-arms *kampfgruppen* (combat groups), advanced up to 40 kilometers into Kolpakchi's outpost zone, while the infantry of LI Corps also engaged Chuikov's outposts. Once Langermann's XXIV Panzer Corps with its single panzer division (the 24th) arrived, Paulus committed it to assist Seydlitz's LI Corps against Chuikov's green troops. Under a clear blue sky dominated by the *Luftwaffe*, remnants of shattered Soviet units once again roamed the steppe, confused and disheartened.[4]

In addition to being relatively weak in armor, Sixth Army had persistent supply shortages. Army Group A had logistical priority for the advance to the

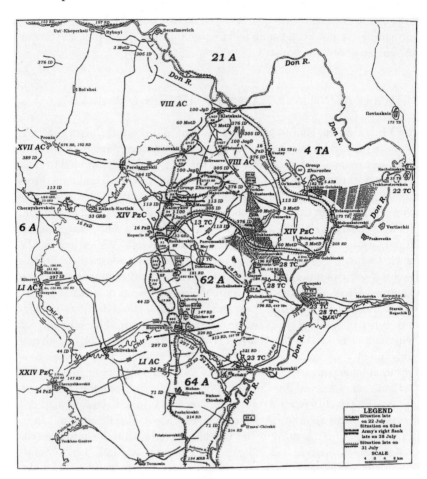

Map 16. Operations in the Great Bend of the Don River, 22–31 July 1942

Caucasus, while OKH planners failed to allow for the additional demands of
the two panzer corps transferred to Weichs's army group. At the end of July
Hitler redirected 750 tons of transport capacity from First Panzer Army to
Sixth Army. However, by that time, Paulus's forces had been shortchanged
for more than two weeks, creating a backlog of shortages that took some time
to correct. As the Germans advanced beyond their supply bases, they became
increasingly dependent on stopgap measures such as the aerial delivery of
fuel and ammunition to the spearheads. This not only diverted scarce Ju-52
transports from other missions but also involved the risky transport of highly
flammable materials by air.[5]

Fortunately for Paulus's advance, Chuikov's 64th Army had only begun to occupy its defensive positions when the German attack began. Because the bridges in its sector would support only light tanks, much of the Soviet armored support was left behind. Moreover, according to Chuikov (but unsubstantiated by other sources), on 19 July the *Stavka* reduced him to deputy commander and superimposed Major General Vasilii Nikolaevich Gordov (former commander of 21st Army) as commander of the 64th, only to restore Chuikov to command three days later. This latter change apparently occurred because Stalin decided to use Gordov to replace Timoshenko as commander of the Stalingrad Front, effective 23 July. By this time, Gordov's new command included eight ground armies (63rd, 62nd, 64th, 51st, 57th, 21st, 28th, and 38th), as well as 8th Air Army and the Volga River Flotilla.[6]

Stalin continued to micromanage the battle, refusing Gordov's request for permission to withdraw on 23 July. Instead, he directed a firm defense with nine-tenths of all air support to be concentrated against XIV Panzer Corps. Accompanied by increasingly strident orders from the Soviet dictator, Vasilevsky commuted between Moscow and Gordov's headquarters to ensure the defense of the Don's Great Bend.

Paulus's twin attacks penetrated 62nd Army's defenses with relative ease. By dusk on 24 July, Wietersheim's XIV Panzer Corps and the supporting 113th Infantry Division had loosely encircled a third of Kolpakchi's army on the high ground north of Manoilin. Inside the pocket were 33rd Guards Rifle Division and portions of 192nd and 184th Rifle Divisions, with a few supporting tanks. At this point, however, fuel shortages and stiffening enemy resistance forced the Germans to pause and consolidate. Stalin reacted with characteristic forcefulness, instructing Gordov to commit Moskalenko's embryonic 1st Tank Army. Only Colonel T. I. Tanaschishin's 13th Tank Corps was immediately available, but Kolpatchi cooperated with this corps in a counterattack on 25–26 July to rescue the surrounded wing of 62nd Army. Elements of Major General G. S. Rodin's 28th Tank Corps managed to join the fighting on the twenty-sixth. These Soviet efforts were poorly coordinated, but they did help halt Wietersheim's advance; some 60 tanks of 13th Tank Corps penetrated the panzer corps' rear area on 26 July, and behind Wietersheim, VIII Army Corps was fully engaged trying to keep the encirclement closed.[7] At about the same time, Chuikov's 64th Army began to gel, preventing XXIV Panzer Corps and LI Army Corps from linking up with Wietersheim. A 35 kilometer gap remained between Paulus's two spearheads, and the first attempt to advance on Stalingrad stalled only five days after it began.[8]

STALINGRAD FRONT'S COUNTERSTROKE, 26–31 JULY

While various German commanders reconsidered their options, Stalin pushed Gordov into renewed action. At 2000 hours on 26 July, Gordov ordered 1st and 4th Tank Armies, supported by 8th Air Army and by 21st, 62nd, and 64th Armies, to mount a concerted counterstroke against Paulus's northern pincer. However massive this force might appear on paper, its staffs and communications were inadequate, and Gordov had allowed fewer than seven hours, all at night, to prepare for the attack. As a result, only Moskalenko's 1st Tank Army was prepared to engage at the designated time of 0300 on 27 July. Most of Moskalenko's armored strength was already in contact, and two tank corps had suffered significantly in the previous fighting.[9] Still, XIV Panzer Corps was down to 100 functioning tanks, and the renewed assault by twice that many Red tanks had an immediate effect. Despite losing 40 tanks to German air attack, Tanaschishin's 13th Tank Corps briefly encircled two *kampfgruppen* of 16th Panzer Division, forcing the Germans to withdraw temporarily on the twenty-seventh.[10] The 16th Panzer Division's unit history recorded: "The division was split into three parts, all of which were involved in heavy fighting and were cut off from any supply. A truly testing time!"[11]

By nightfall on 28 July, 13th Tank Corps, now personally supervised by Major General E. G. Pushkin, the Stalingrad Front chief of armored forces, succeeded in linking up with the encircled elements of 62nd Army. This success had come at a terrible price, however. Without air cover or artillery support, Tanaschishin's corps had lost all but 40 tanks on the twenty-seventh; despite reinforcements, it suffered additional losses the next day. Meanwhile, Rodin's 28th Tank Corps pushed 3rd and 60th Motorized Divisions several kilometers northward, away from Kalach.

In response, Paulus ordered most of VIII Army Corps, on the northern flank, to wheel southward, reinforce 16th Panzer, and block any breakout attempt by Tanaschishin and the encircled infantry. Unfortunately for the Germans, this meant leaving only a screen—including one *kampfgruppe* of 16th Panzer—to defend against the Soviet bridgehead at Kremenskaia and Sirotinskaia. It was precisely at this point that 4th Tank Army's 22nd Tank Corps belatedly entered the fray. Gordov attempted to move another tank corps, the 23rd, forward through Chuikov's 64th Army, but there were the usual problems of staff and logistics coordination. Indeed, Major General A. A. Shamshin repeatedly committed the elements of his 4th Tank Army without reconnaissance preparation or infantry support.

In a battle without fronts, the two adversaries struggled and swirled between 29 July and 1 August. Continued German shortages of fuel and ammunition hampered their response to the attack. On 31 July one Red tank battalion overran the command post of XIV Panzer Corps, but *Luftwaffe* air support often made the difference on the battlefield. Eventually, the Soviet counterstroke lost momentum, and only remnants of the surrounded divisions of 62nd Army were able to rejoin the main defensive lines.[12] The Germans retained the battlefield but were still unable to advance to Kalach, and XIV Panzer Corps was reduced, at least temporarily, to 75 functioning tanks.[13] The wounded Stalingrad Front still retained some 500 tanks, if it could only coordinate their operations. Clearly, Sixth Army could not reach its objective with the available troops and supplies.

THE OREL AND VORONEZH AXIS, 20–26 JULY

While Bock's and List's Army Groups B and A were pummeling the Southwestern and Southern Fronts during the heat of July, the *Stavka* orchestrated a series of counterstrokes farther north in an effort to take the pressure off its troops in the south. These attacks had some success, but again, the combination of inexperienced staff planners and urgent pressure emanating from Moscow meant that such moves were hasty and ill prepared.

The first of these efforts occurred in Zhukov's Western Front, where General Rokossovsky's and Lieutenant General Pavel A. Belov's 61st Army attacked along the Zhizdra River north of Orel and Bolkhov. Both men were successful later in the war, but their efforts in this instance had no visible effect on the Germans. Attacking on 6 and 5 July, respectively, the two Soviet armies almost penetrated the German infantry defenses but could not coordinate their tanks, infantry, artillery, and engineers and suffered heavy losses. Rokossovsky's designated exploitation force, 10th Tank Corps, lost nearly all its 152 tanks, and 3rd Tank Corps under Belov's direction fared little better.[14]

Undeterred by this failure, Moscow continued to direct counterattacks against the German flanks, especially around Voronezh. On 17 July the *Stavka* ordered the Briansk and Voronezh Fronts to attack from three salients—Kazinka-Vereika, Podgornoe, and Semilutskoe—to cut off German VII Corps and free the city of Voronezh.[15] The main recipient of this order was once against Rokossovsky, recently transferred to command the Briansk Front. As was customary in Soviet staff procedures, he directed his deputy (and predecessor), General Chibisov, to command the main effort, attacking southward from Kazinka-Vereika. This effort bore Chibisov's name and included five rifle divisions, 8th Cavalry Corps, Katukov's 1st Tank Corps, and the three other tank corps that had previously constituted 5th Tank Army—Liziukov's 2nd, Rotmistrov's 7th, and A. F. Popov's 11th. The Soviet supply system had provided these four armored units with replacement vehicles to bring their total strength to 500 tanks, but the troops involved, especially the rifle divisions, were very green.

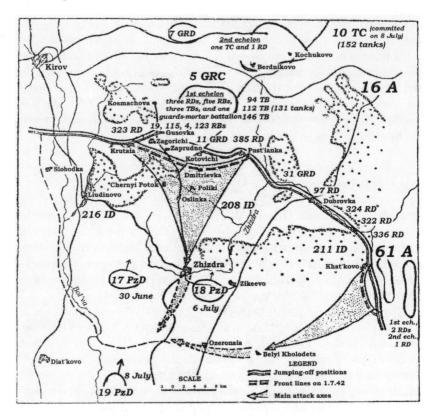

Map 17. 16th Army's Operations along the Zhizdra River, 6–14 July 1942

While Chibisov was launching the Briansk Front's main attack from the north, General Vatutin's neighboring Voronezh Front would conduct two supporting attacks from the east. General Antoniuk's 60th Army, with seven rifle divisions supported by 17th, 18th, and 25th Tank Corps, was to break out of the Podgornoe salient to cut the main supply road west of Voronezh. Farther south, Popov's 40th Army, with four rifle divisions and two tank brigades, was to penetrate the German defenses and then turn northward in an effort to link up with the other two attacks.[16] All told, Vatutin was committing some 300 tanks, 166 of them concentrated in Major General P. P. Pavlov's 25th Tank Corps. The defending German infantry relied primarily on antitank weapons of limited effectiveness, although 9th Panzer Division, with perhaps 120 tanks, was in reserve.

On 21 July 1942 Rokossovsky launched his offensive with considerable air support. While some of Chibisov's subordinates made little progress, in two days of fighting, Rotmistrov's 7th and Liziukov's 2nd Tank Corps tore a gap 20 kilometers wide and 10 kilometers deep in the defense of German VI Corps.[17] Reacting quickly, Lieutenant General Hans von Salmuth, commander of German Second Army, shifted two infantry regiments to slow the Soviet advance, then ordered General Bässler's 9th Panzer Division, supported by 385th Infantry Division, to prepare for a counterattack against Chibisov's penetration from the west, while two other infantry divisions advanced from the east.

By 23 July, the two leading brigades of 2nd Tank Corps were out of radio contact and almost encircled. Chibisov castigated Liziukov for his piecemeal commitment of troops and ordered the disgraced commander to find the missing brigades and accomplish the mission at all costs. Liziukov, who had repeatedly been trapped by inexperienced staffs and conflicting orders from higher commanders, apparently sought death on the battlefield. That same day, the hapless general and his political officer climbed into a KV-1 tank and led a vain attempt to free his subordinates. After this tank was immobilized by a German antitank gun, the crew bailed out, and Liziukov died instantly under German artillery fire.[18]

Salmuth sprang his counterattack at dawn the next day. By 26 July, 9th Panzer and 385th Infantry Divisions had penetrated the Soviet advance and encircled half of 7th Tank Corps, all of 2nd Tank Corps, and their supporting infantry west of Bol'shaia Vereika. Chibisov committed Katukov's 1st Tank Corps in a vain effort to rescue the encircled forces.[19]

Attacking a day late, on 22 July Antoniuk's 60th Army was unable to cut the German supply route but did penetrate the suburbs of Voronezh, where confused fighting occurred over the next several days. Heavy German air strikes and counterattacks virtually eliminated the Soviet gains.

Once again, the German defenders had contained a major Soviet counterstrike without having to call on outside reserves. Perhaps the best that could be said about the late July attacks around Voronezh was that they forced the Germans to maintain a panzer division in the area indefinitely. Moreover, this and subsequent Soviet efforts probably contributed to the fateful German decision to commit satellite armies to defend the overextended flanks of Paulus's Sixth Army between Voronezh and Stalingrad.

NOT A STEP BACK!

In this crisis, Stalin became even more insistent on the need to stand and fight. Frustrated by the repeated failures of his southern forces, the Soviet dictator decided to reemphasize the draconian defensive measures employed in 1941. The result was a 28 July 1942 order from the Commissariat of Defense, drafted by Vasilevsky and extensively rewritten by Stalin. Although its official designation was Order No. 227, this decree became famous for its title, *Ni Shagu Nazad!* or "Not a Step Back!"

Citing the Soviet Union's economic and manpower losses of the previous year against the backdrop of an apparent breakdown in military discipline, Stalin explained why further retreat had become impossible. He scorned the argument that the Soviets could continue to retreat indefinitely when such retreats meant the loss of resources and industry. Instead, the dictator declared, "We must stubbornly defend every position and every meter of Soviet territory to the last drop of our blood and cling to every shred of Soviet land and fight for it to the utmost."[20]

Order No. 227 asserted that "company, battalion, regimental, and division commanders, and associated commissars and political workers, who retreat from their combat positions without orders from higher commands must be treated as 'enemies of the Homeland.'" Stalin demanded that all commanders and commissars implement a series of stringent measures designed to restore "iron discipline" in the ranks.[21] The Red Army had habitually used blocking detachments, control points that returned stragglers to their parent units. Now, however, each *front* was to create penal battalions composed of those who had proved cowardly or unsteady, assigning such battalions to the most dangerous missions. Aleksandr Sergeevich Shcherbakov, a senior official of the Communist Party, had replaced Lev Mekhlis as head of the army's Main Political Directorate, but informers and NKVD security troops continued to enforce loyalty and punish failure on the battlefield. Even inside the *Stavka*, any appearance of defeatism was dealt with harshly.[22]

No amount of intimidation and effort could offset the inexperience and tactical disadvantages under which the Red Army labored that summer. On 25 July, for example, 24th Panzer and 71st Infantry Divisions, with strong *Luftwaffe* support, attacked the right wing of Chuikov's 64th Army south of the Chir River. The defending 229th Rifle Division had brought five of its nine infantry battalions into position, but its supporting 137th Tank Brigade could muster only 35 tanks, the majority of them light T-60s, with limited fuel supplies. By the afternoon of 26 July, the Germans had penetrated these defenses, but Chuikov managed to patch together a new defensive line using elements of 112th Rifle Division and 66th Naval Rifle Brigade.[23]

That evening, the psychological effects of blitzkrieg—the constant fear of being cut off by German armor—produced an unreasoning panic among Soviet rear-area units. While Chuikov was absent from his command post, his chief of staff ordered several units to withdraw east of the Don, even though a German air attack had destroyed the floating bridge at Nizhne-Chirskaia. Chuikov countermanded the order but lost several of his best staff officers to air attacks while these men rallied the mass of troops at river crossings. Finally, 64th Army reestablished its lines, but it was out of touch with neighboring 62nd Army, and Gordov continued to hector both armies with unrealistic orders to counterattack. On 31 July Stalin ordered the creation of blocking detachments in the rear of these two armies. Under these circumstances, it was astonishing that the Soviets in the Great Bend of the Don were able to put up a defense that 24th Panzer Division's history described as "tough" and "grimly obstinate."[24]

From the Soviet viewpoint, the most serious problem was the failure of division and higher commanders to concentrate their antitank weapons and artillery in coherent strongpoints to engage German panzer forces effectively. The same problem with the dispersal of antiaircraft guns and machine guns made it impossible to counter the effects of *Luftwaffe* air strikes, which were particularly deadly against Red armor, artillery, and supply lines. Failure to coordinate the actions of the new Soviet tank corps and armies meant that commanders squandered hundreds of tanks and their crews in piecemeal engagements or penny packets to support the infantry.

Despite all these errors, the defenders put up such a determined defense that Paulus's advance had ground to a halt by 28 July. The commitment of four rifle and two tank armies, in combination with Order No. 227, definitively disproves the notion that the Red Army fled or deliberately retreated in front of the invaders. Moreover, the attrition inflicted on the German units before they even approached Stalingrad would haunt Sixth Army when it finally reached its ultimate target in that city.

SHIFT IN PRIORITIES AND RENEWED OFFENSIVES

Adolf Hitler was just as frustrated as Joseph Stalin by the course of events on the battlefield, and he took out his frustrations on his staff officers. General Halder's diary entry on 23 July might have been written by a Soviet officer: "This chronic tendency to underrate enemy capabilities is gradually assuming grotesque proportions and develops into a positive danger. The situation is getting more and more intolerable. There is no room for any serious work. This so-called leadership is characterized by pathological reaction to the impressions of the moment and a total lack of any understanding of the command machinery and its possibilities."[25]

In an effort to revitalize Sixth Army's advance, Hitler decided on 30 July to return the headquarters of Hoth's Fourth Panzer Army, together with its XXXXVIII Panzer and IV Army Corps, to Army Group B. In addition to these two corps, Hoth controlled Romanian VI Corps, consisting of four divisions, and on 14 August 24th Panzer and 297th Infantry Divisions also reverted to his army. For the first time, on 30 July Hitler explicitly made the capture of

Stalingrad a high priority, even though he continued to insist that First Panzer and Seventeenth Armies must move quickly to trap a largely imaginary enemy force north of the Caucasus.[26] Meanwhile, the OKH began to deploy Italian Eighth Army to the Don River front, freeing four German infantry divisions to support Paulus's advance into the Great Bend.[27]

While Hitler shuffled his limited resources, Stalin also took a number of steps to replenish the supply of available units. On 29 July, for example, the Stalingrad Front was ordered to withdraw six rifle divisions from the shattered 21st, 28th, and 38th Armies for refitting under NKO control. Two days later, the NKO began redesignating its elite airborne divisions as guards rifle divisions; the first two began moving to Stalingrad on 5 August. Control of 51st Army was transferred from the North Caucasus to the southern wing of the Stalingrad Front.[28] Despite such actions, front-line Soviet rifle and tank units in the Great Bend had suffered considerable losses; the Stalingrad Front lost at least 600 tanks during the last ten days of July and more in early August. Thus, Paulus's 250 and Hoth's 150 tanks would have rough parity with their foes in the coming battles.

Kempf's XXXXVIII Panzer Corps (14th Panzer and 29th Motorized Divisions) and General of Infantry Viktor von Schwedler's IV Army Corps (94th and 371st Infantry Divisions) concentrated in the Tsimlianskaia bridgehead across the Don River, opposite the Red 51st Army, on the evening of 31 July. Because Paulus's troops were still waiting for more fuel, these two corps attacked alone at dawn on 1 August 1942, advancing up to 40 kilometers the first day. Reacting quickly, the *Stavka* tapped its reserves and dispatched the Far Eastern 208th Rifle Division, 6th Guards Tank Brigade, and a regiment of tank destroyers by rail to Kotel'nikovo and the Aksai River line. Gordov also directed 57th Army to move two understrength divisions, 15th Guards and 38th Rifle, from Stalingrad proper to new defensive positions backing up 64th Army. Unfortunately for the defenders, the Germans moved even faster. Major General Max Fremerey's 29th Motorized Division reached Kotel'nikovo by 1100 on 2 August, routing 208th Rifle Division as the latter detrained. As the advance guard of Heim's 14th Panzer Division, 64th Motorcycle Battalion bypassed Kotel'nikovo and drove northeastward another 25 kilometers virtually unopposed.[29]

Late on 2 August Lieutenant General M. S. Shumilov, who had replaced Chuikov as commander of 64th Army, put the latter (who was now his deputy) in charge of a "Southern Operational Force" composed of two new units— 29th Rifle Division and 154th Naval Rifle Brigade—with orders to defend the Aksai; additional units arrived piecemeal over the next week. Meanwhile, Gordov, the Stalingrad Front commander, transferred the three divisions of 64th Army's right wing to 62nd Army's control to simplify the defensive task.[30]

It was almost too late, however. On 3 August 14th Panzer Division advanced another 30 kilometers and sent patrols to the outskirts of the town of Aksai, where Chuikov had only four rifle battalions, five batteries, and almost no ammunition on hand to stop the attackers. The next day, XXXXVIII Panzer Corps, with its left flank protected by Romanian VI Corps and its spearheads supported by the *Luftwaffe*, pushed the forward elements of Chuikov's force out of their defenses. By sheer force of personal leadership, however, Chuikov managed to stabilize his defenses until 13 August, despite constant attacks by Romanian VI and German IV Army Corps. During this stalemate, Chuikov began to devise innovative responses to German tactics. Thus, he would disrupt an anticipated Axis attack by a sudden artillery raid or a short tactical withdrawal, thereby avoiding the artillery and air strikes aimed at his previous positions and forcing the attackers to recoordinate their plans.[31]

Stalin recognized that the Stalingrad Front could not coordinate operations across almost 800 kilometers of front, but his solution only added to the confusion. On the night of 1–2 August he summoned Colonel General Andrei Ivanovich Eremenko off convalescent leave to assume command of the new Southeastern Front, which would control the beleaguered 64th and 51st Armies as well as the weak 57th Army and 13th Tank Corps. The shattered 1st Tank Army was disbanded, and General Golikov, former head of the Voronezh Front, was ordered to assemble 1st Guards Army (five formerly airborne divisions) in Stalingrad but under *Stavka* control. General Gordov remained in command of a truncated Stalingrad Front, consisting of 63rd, 62nd, 21st, and 4th Tank Armies, all significantly weakened, as well as 18th Tank Corps.[32] Rejecting Eremenko's advice, the dictator drew the boundary of these two *fronts* through Stalingrad itself, where both *fronts* would have their headquarters. Four days later, Stalin recognized his error and further complicated matters by subordinating the Stalingrad Front to Eremenko's new Southeastern Front. The same order made Golikov Eremenko's deputy, while entrusting the garrison of the city itself to Colonel A. A. Saraev, commander of 10th NKVD Division. The order closed with a strong exhortation to the two *front* commanders concerning the decisive importance of defending Stalingrad.[33]

Meanwhile, German IV Corps consolidated control of the Aksai region. By 6 August, Kempf's XXXXVIII Panzer Corps, though rapidly declining in combat power, pushed 10 kilometers east of Abganerovo to the small town and rail station of Tinguta. The *Stavka*, not understanding the situation on the ground, demanded an immediate counterattack against this spearhead. However, Gordov and Shumilov took three days to prepare for this action. By the ninth, Shumilov had assembled Colonel Tanaschishin's 13th Tank Corps, with 68 functioning KV and T-34 tanks, as well as 38th, 157th, and 204th Rifle Divisions and a hodgepodge of artillery and other support elements. At dawn on 9 August the Soviets struck 29th Motorized and 14th Panzer Divisions

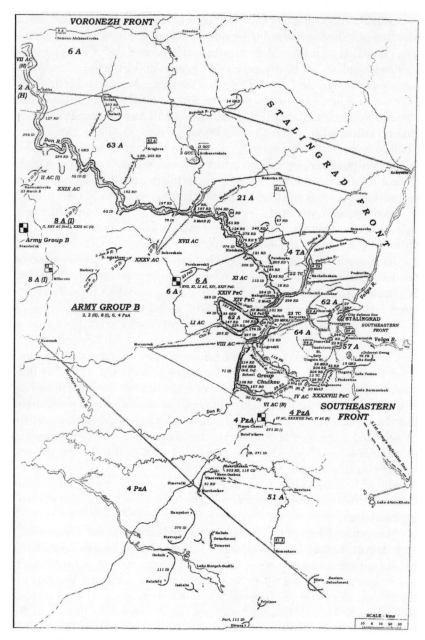

Map 18. Situation along the Stalingrad Axis, 8–10 August 1942

from three sides; in four days, Shumilov pushed the German mobile forces back to Abganerovo, while Chuikov continued to defend the Myshkova River until Shumilov withdrew him to create a more stable front. Kempf's two divisions were left with only 50 functional panzers between them, and the supporting Romanian infantry suffered heavily.[34]

Fourth Panzer Army, like Sixth Army before it, had proved unequal to the task of reaching Stalingrad. Hoth's further progress depended on the arrival of more armor, while attention shifted again to Sixth Army.

During the first week of August, Paulus's armor force worked to repair its tanks while preparing for another attempted encirclement operation aimed at Kalach. XIV Panzer Corps (16th Panzer and 3rd and 60th Motorized Divisions) would again form the northern pincer, using XI Army Corps to protect its right flank. The southern pincer still depended on XXIV Panzer Corps' 24th Panzer Division, with 71st, 76th, and 297th Infantry Divisions attached to that corps. This time, however, the deployment of Italian troops farther north had freed up two relatively fresh infantry divisions, the 44th and 295th, to give LI Army Corps additional combat power against the southern wing of 62nd Army along the Chir River. Moreover, Paulus's attack would initially get support from VIII Air Corps, now commanded by Lieutenant General Martin Fiebig, at a time when the Red Air Force was still struggling to reinforce the Stalingrad area.[35]

Lieutenant General A. I. Lopatin had replaced Kolpakchi as commander of 62nd Army on 3 August. The new commander incorporated remnants of the now-defunct 1st Tank Army and one wing of 64th Army, giving the 62nd a total of eight rifle divisions, 23rd and 28th Tank Corps, four tank brigades, and various other units, such as student regiments from two officer schools.[36] In all, Lopatin had 100,000 men supported by fewer than 150 tanks, whereas the enforced pause had allowed Sixth Army's four mobile divisions to reach a total of approximately 330 operating tanks.

Hitler remained convinced that the enemy was fleeing, so he rushed Paulus into attacking on 7 August. Despite ferocious counterattacks and Red Air Force bombing, the two pincers reached the Don near Kalach and then turned back, trapping a large portion of 62nd Army by 9 August. It took three more days to reduce the resulting pocket. For the first time since May, the Germans felt they had achieved a genuine encirclement based on the 1941 pattern, and they claimed to have taken almost 50,000 prisoners. The 62nd Red Army had indeed been heavily damaged, but in reality, about half of Lopatin's soldiers had escaped to the east without their heavy equipment.[37] Moreover, Paulus's tank strength declined by approximately 20 percent during this brief operation,[38] and he still had to clear 4th Tank Army from his left flank before he could leave the Don behind for an advance to the Volga.

ORGANIZING THE DEFENSE OF STALINGRAD

The fall of Kalach convinced the Soviet leadership that a climactic battle was imminent in the Stalingrad region. As previously noted, on 9 August Stalin subordinated Gordov's Stalingrad Front to Eremenko's new Southeastern Front; on the thirteenth he formally designated Gordov as Eremenko's deputy, while leaving each man in command of his own *front*. Not satisfied with this, Stalin added another level of supervision by dispatching three senior officials to guide Eremenko. This troika consisted of Vasilevsky, the chief of the General Staff; Georgii Maksimilianovich Malenkov, a close Stalin henchman from the Communist Party's Central Committee; and Lieutenant General Aleksandr Aleksandrovich Novikov, the new head of the Red Air Force.[39] Meanwhile, the *Stavka* gave rail priority to 1st Guards Army, now headed by Moskalenko, to establish a new defensive belt behind 4th Tank Army by 14 August; three more rifle divisions and a fortified region went to create a similar defense behind 64th and 57th Armies south of Stalingrad. The new 16th Air Army, with 447 aircraft, was to support the Southeastern Front; the *Stavka* also dispatched a rifle division and a separate railroad brigade to screen the immense gap around Astrakhan' between the Southeastern and North Caucasus Fronts.[40]

Vasilevsky and Eremenko went to work, devising multiple defensive belts in front of the probable German advance. They were too sanguine in their planning assumptions, unfortunately. The 1st Guards Army arrived piecemeal and without artillery or ammunition at its new destination, so that only 40th Guards Rifle Division was in place by the time the Germans resumed their advance.[41] The 62nd Army lost most of its combat power in the Kalach pocket, so it was unable to mount a planned effort to relieve that encirclement. More seriously, the German advances had captured two key railroad lines west of Stalingrad and exposed the remaining lines to aerial interdiction, constantly disrupting the flow of ammunition, food, and weaponry to defending units.[42] Thus, like their German counterparts, the Soviet defenders of Stalingrad had to operate on a logistical shoestring, improvising at every stage.

SIXTH ARMY'S ADVANCE INTO THE NORTHEAST CORNER OF THE GREAT BEND, 25–29 AUGUST

On 10 August Paulus paused for the third time to prepare for his next advance. He did not want to move directly from Kalach to Stalingrad because such a path would bring Fourth Panzer and Sixth Armies so close together that they would be competing for the same supply routes, while losing any

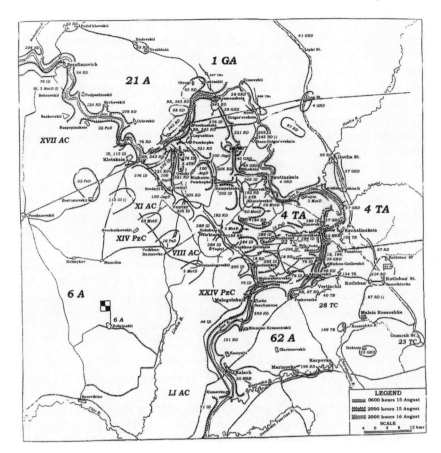

Map 19. 4th Tank and 1st Guards Armies' Defense, 15–16 August 1942

chance for another major encirclement. Moreover, such an advance would leave Paulus's left flank exposed to Major General V. D. Kriuchenkin's 4th Tank Army, which held a bridgehead south of Kremenskaia and Sirotinskaia on the Don. Although Kriuchenkin had only one effective tank corps—the 22nd—at his disposal (in addition to four rifle divisions and various other units), Paulus had learned that his opponents were still capable of reinforcing their forward armies rapidly.

Therefore, as his subordinate corps completed their part in the encirclement west of Kalach, Paulus transferred them northward. By 12 August, he had concentrated one panzer, two motorized, and eight infantry divisions in the 55 kilometer sector of the Don River stretching from Kletskaia to Bol'shenabatovskii. The main attack, as usual, fell to Wietersheim's XIV Panzer Corps in the German center, strongly supported on its right by VIII Army Corps and XXIV Panzer Corps, with five infantry divisions between them (24th Panzer Division was recovering in preparation to reinforce Hoth in the south). To distract the defenders, however, XI Corps, with 376th Infantry and 100th *Jäger* Divisions, was to attack the Soviet right (western) flank on 13 August, two days before the main assault.

Paulus's troops executed this plan almost flawlessly, but they encountered strenuous resistance. For example, 16th Panzer Division, task-organized into *kampfgruppen*, took the brunt of this resistance on 15 August:

> KG [*Kampfgruppe*] Sieckenius [2nd Panzer Regiment] rolled through the [advancing German] infantry and cut through the Russians' fortified positions south of Blizhniaia-Perekopka. The Russians defended fiercely and bitterly, and some elements held out in the steep *balkas*. After the tanks broke through [the defenders] renewed their attacks, destroyed the *Werfer* [six-tube mortar] batteries, and fired at vehicles transporting the wounded. Mues' battalion had to turn back to mop up the area. An intense battle began. Numerous antitank rifles were captured. Panzer Detachment von Strachwitz managed to move forward to the Don at Trekhostrovskaia. The bridges there had already been destroyed.[43]

Later that same morning, *Kampfgruppe* Strachwitz overran Kriuchenkin's headquarters, preventing a coordinated defense of the bridgehead. Gordov responded by ordering the uncommitted divisions of Moskalenko's 1st Guards Army to counterattack on the seventeenth, but the German advance was so rapid that it preempted this plan. In heavy fighting on 16 August, 3rd and 60th Motorized Divisions inflicted heavy losses on 37th and 39th Guards Rifle Divisions and secured the banks of the Don. Only the timely arrival of 38th and 40th Guards Rifle Divisions blocked XI Army Corps from completely eliminating the Soviet bridgehead west of the river.[44]

The 4th Tank Army was virtually destroyed. On the evening of 17 August, Gordov directed 1st Guards Army to take control of the remnants and hold the remaining bridgehead over the Don. Even with the addition of 23rd Rifle Division from the *front* reserve, the defenses of the northeastern Don bend were very weak, especially near the junction of 1st Guards and 62nd Armies along the eastern bank from the mouth of the Ilovlia River south to Lake Peschanoe. Between 16 and 18 August Paulus withdrew the three mobile divisions of XIV Panzer Corps to refit for renewed operations; only a *kampfgruppe* from 22nd Panzer Division, whose main body was supporting XVII Army Corps to the northwest, assisted the German infantry in holding the line of the Don.[45]

ASSESSMENT—THE DON RIVER BEND

Friedrich Paulus had finally reached the Don River, but it had taken him a month—from 17 July to 18 August—and four deliberate assaults—on 17 July, 23 July, 8 August, and 15 August—to advance about 100 kilometers. He had another 70 kilometers to go to reach his objective at Stalingrad. Hoth's Fourth Panzer Army had also lost momentum and come to a halt at Abganerovo. The Germans had destroyed or severely damaged six Red field armies during this month—the 21st, 28th, 38th, 62nd, 1st Tank, and 4th Tank. However, a seemingly limitless supply of new organizations rose up to replace Soviet losses.

German losses, though much smaller than those of their foes, were still worrisome. For example, 14th Panzer Division had fielded 102 tanks when Operation *Blau* began on 28 June, but only 24 were still operational on 12 August.[46] During the same period, some German divisions had suffered 1,500 casualties, or about 10 percent of their authorized strength, the majority of them infantrymen.

Early accounts of the 1942 campaign on both sides either obscured or ignored the long struggle for the Great Bend of the Don. Taken together, these battles represented a determined effort by Stalin and the *Stavka* to halt the German advance before it reached Stalingrad. Although that effort failed, it left Sixth Army seriously weakened before it ever entered the streets of the city.

OPPOSING PLANS

On the evening of 19 August 1942, Paulus issued yet another order for the attack on Stalingrad. The previous month's battles had left him in considerable doubt about the enemy's reaction: would the Soviets collapse, defend tenaciously, or launch renewed counterattacks? His concept of the operation was therefore very conservative in tone, directing Sixth Army to "occupy the isthmus between the Don and Volga north of the railway line Kalach-Stalingrad" and "protect its own northern and eastern flank."[47]

To accomplish this, Paulus assigned LI Army Corps, with two divisions, to seize a bridgehead across the Don River near Vertiachii. The three mobile divisions of Wietersheim's XIV Panzer Corps would then pass through the Vertiachii bridgehead and advance along the high ground to the northern end of Stalingrad while LI Corps protected its southern flank and linked up with General Hoth's Fourth Panzer Army, which was to conduct a mirror-image advance to the southern outskirts of the city. Kempf's XXXXVIII Panzer Corps, with 14th Panzer and 29th Motorized Divisions reinforced by 24th

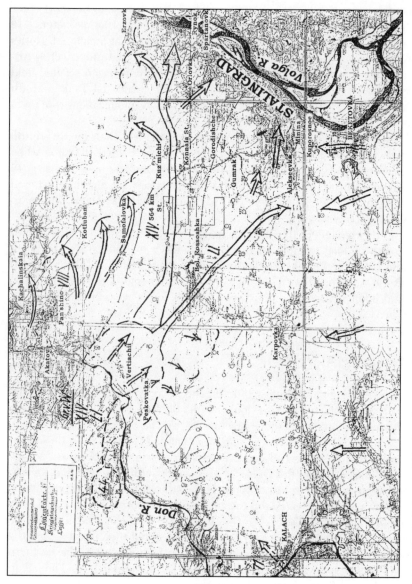

Map 20. Sixth Army's Offensive Plan, 19 August 1942

Panzer, was the spearhead of the southern pincer. Paulus also assigned XI Army Corps, with three divisions and temporarily reinforced by 22nd Panzer Division (arriving from the Voronezh sector), plus XVII Army Corps, with two infantry divisions and the Italian *Celere* Mobile Division, to screen the northern flank of this narrow advance. Aerial reconnaissance indicated little opposition east of the Don, encouraging the Germans to hope for a resumption of rapid and deep penetrations.[48] Still, the success of this plan depended on rapid movement and the seizure of Stalingrad before the Soviets could react and attack the lengthening flanks of the two armored pincers.

Sixth Army's rapid defeat of 4th Tank Army in mid-August had indeed placed Stalingrad in danger. During the first three weeks of August the *Stavka* had reinforced the Stalingrad Front with 15 rifle divisions and 3 tank corps, and 5 of these rifle divisions had already been committed at Kalach. Now Eremenko concluded that the next German advance would come north of Akatov, well away from Paulus's planned new bridgehead at Vertiachii. In preparation for this assumed advance, Eremenko ordered General Lopatin to form two shock groups, each consisting of a rifle division with one or more tank brigades, prepared to counterattack toward Akatov. Responding to urgings from Moscow, Eremenko directed his wavering armies to prepare for coordinated counterattacks that were beyond their capabilities. He also directed five additional rifle divisions, just released to him from the VGK Reserve, to establish a new defensive line, 20 to 30 kilometers east of the Don, by 22 August. Yet all these troop movements required time. At nightfall on 19 August, Sixth Army's main shock group of three mobile and six infantry divisions faced only five weak rifle divisions, plus the 20 remaining tanks of 28th Tank Corps, now redesignated 182nd Tank Brigade.[49] The Germans struck before Eremenko's preparations had even begun.

SIXTH ARMY'S ADVANCE TO THE VOLGA, 21–31 AUGUST

Under a clear, starry sky in the predawn hours of 21 August, the designated assault forces of LI Corps crossed the Don without any preliminary bombardment. The 516th Regiment of 295th Infantry Division crossed in less than two hours against minimal resistance, but other units, especially 76th Infantry Division, encountered strong Soviet reactions. German engineers erected two floating bridges on 21 and 22 August, and determined Red air attacks failed to damage them. The crossing cost Sixth Army 425 killed and wounded, as well as 19 assault craft and 26 rafts destroyed.[50] On the twenty-second the Soviets concentrated heavy howitzer and *katiusha* fires on the crowded bridgehead, inflicting an additional 427 killed and wounded.[51]

Leading the breakout of XIV Panzer Corps, 16th Panzer Division, followed by 3rd and 60th Motorized Divisions, burst out of the Vertiachii bridge-head at dawn on 23 August and advanced eastward in two columns. Stukas and Henschel-129 fighter-bombers of VIII Air Corps helped Hube's division brush aside the defenders of 62nd Army and lunge eastward across the arid grasslands in a cloud of dust. In the early afternoon of the same day, the Germans saw the chimneys, factories, and apartment houses of Stalingrad on the horizon. The *kampfgruppen* of 2nd Panzer and 64th Panzer-Grenadier Regiments moved so rapidly that they outstripped Soviet efforts to intercept them. Female factory workers manned the city's antiaircraft and antitank guns, but most of their shots missed; the German response was much dead-lier. By evening, 16th Panzer Division and XIV Panzer Corps headquarters had joined these leading elements on the high ground overlooking the Volga River from Akatovka to Rynok, in the northern suburbs of the city.[52]

That night the three mobile divisions formed a series of temporary hedgehog defenses to wait for the German fighter-bombers that would re-turn at dawn to resume the attack. On the operations maps in German higher headquarters, the panzer spearhead appeared poised to complete its mission of interdicting the Volga River barge traffic and occupying the northern in-dustrial suburbs of Stalingrad. Far to the south, 29th Motorized and 14th Panzer Divisions of Hoth's Fourth Panzer Army were engaged in a parallel, complementary advance to the southern edge of the city. Together, Paulus's and Hoth's troops hoped to catch the Stalingrad metropolitan area in a pincer and secure it rapidly.

Yet it soon became evident that the Germans, rather than their Soviet opponents, were the ones under siege. Lieutenant General Lopatin, com-manding the threadbare 62nd Red Army, made great efforts to shore up his defenses on the southern side of the German corridor, while other ele-ments of Eremenko's Stalingrad Front besieged the Vertiachii bridgehead from which Wietersheim had advanced. None of these Soviet counterattacks made any headway against the Germans, with their Stuka dive-bomber sup-port, but they did prevent Sixth Army from reinforcing XIV Panzer Corps. Meanwhile, Eremenko used every available force, from a regiment of NKVD internal security troops to gunfire from the Red Navy's Volga Flotilla, to build an internal defensive arc along the northern flank of the city. The city's De-fense Committee contributed 60 tanks manned by workers, 45 tractors, 150 machine guns, and 40 guns repaired in its factories. The improvised defense was under the command of N. I. Feklenko, who had earlier failed as com-mander of 17th Tank Corps. Other Soviet forces, including 2nd Tank Corps and 315th Rifle Division, gathered to attack from the north, seeking to inter-dict the long German salient in the Kotluban' area.[53]

To further bolster Stalingrad's defenses, Eremenko ordered the Stal-ingrad Training Center to form three antitank artillery regiments and one

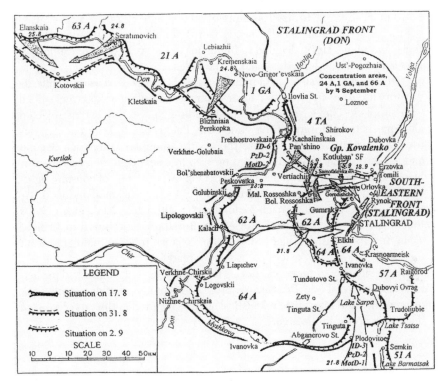

Map 21. Soviet Counterattacks and Counterstrokes, August–September 1942

gun artillery battalion and deploy them to the northern outskirts by 24 August. He concentrated all 560 available antiaircraft guns inside the city and designated three rifle brigades, scheduled to arrive by the twenty-seventh, as the city's reserves.[54] The *Stavka* also reacted, dispatching 4th and 16th Tank Corps and five additional rifle divisions to the Stalingrad region by rail. Moscow directed the deployment of 8th Reserve Army, redesignated 66th Army, to a town 150 kilometers north of Stalingrad. Lieutenant General S. A. Kalinin became commander of this new force, which included eight rifle divisions, three tank brigades, two *katiusha* regiments, and a mixed aviation corps.[55] The implied mission of the 66th was to block German movement northward if Stalingrad fell.

On 24 August 16th Panzer Division was unable to make progress against the suburbs of Rynok and Spartanovka. At one point, using T-34 tanks that had come directly off the assembly lines in the area, Feklenko's men overran the headquarters of 64th Panzer-Grenadier Regiment and forced Hube's troops to withdraw to defensive positions south of Rynok. The *Luftwaffe* failed in its attempts to air-drop supplies on the night of 24–25 August, leaving the three divisions of XIV Panzer Corps almost out of ammunition and fuel. That night, Hube decided to break out to the west, despite explicit orders from Hitler to hold the banks of the Volga.

On 25 August a supply column from 3rd Motorized Division fought its way forward to resupply 16th Panzer, bringing 10 tanks and 250 trucks filled with supplies. This gave Hube some breathing space, but Paulus rejected all requests to withdraw. At the same time, Paulus had to keep one nervous eye over his left shoulder, where the poorly equipped Hungarian Second and Italian Eighth Armies had been pressed into service to defend the ever-lengthening German left flank along the Don. After a week of constant fighting with up to 500 casualties per day, 16th Panzer Division abandoned Rynok on 31 August, pulling back 2 kilometers.[56] Ultimately, XIV Panzer Corps fought off the uncoordinated Soviet counterattacks and survived to fight again, but the Germans had lost their best chance to seize Stalingrad from the march before the Soviet defenses were ready.

Eremenko's counterattacks during the last ten days of August had pushed back but not crushed XIV Panzer Corps. Poor command and control, weak fire support, and intermittent logistical aid had resulted in the loss of most of the Soviet armor in the area.

IN THE AIR

While Paulus and Hoth advanced to the suburbs of Stalingrad, Richthofen's aircraft launched a murderous bombardment of the city, beginning with one of the most concentrated aerial bombardments of the German-Soviet conflict. On Sunday, 23 August, VIII Air Corps flew the first of a series of raids apparently intended to demoralize the defenders. After numerous false alarms, the inhabitants at first ignored the air-raid sirens; in any event, the city had far too few bomb shelters for its population. Although some of the bombers attacked prominent factories, rail yards, and the telephone exchange, most of the destruction fell on residential areas. The wooden houses at the southern end of the city were incinerated by firebombs. The petroleum storage tanks near the Volga River caught fire, and the flames and smoke persisted for several days. Streets began to fill with rubble, complicating the task of both defenders and attackers. On 25 August and on numerous subsequent days, the *Luftwaffe* returned in a round-the-clock series of air raids.[57]

The Red Air Force was still ill prepared to counter this threat. Like its German counterpart, it was overextended and could not support both the Stalingrad and the Caucasus defenses. Moreover, Soviet air operations were curtailed in the late summer by the need to train and build new formations for future operations. This, plus the technical and tactical inferiority of many Red air units, produced a sometimes one-sided air battle that allowed Richthofen to attack almost at will. Still, the Soviets could replace their air losses much more easily than the Germans could; later in the campaign the Red Air Force would pose a serious threat to the *Luftwaffe*.[58]

THE ADVANCE OF FOURTH PANZER ARMY, 20 AUGUST–2 SEPTEMBER

Supporting the effort to destroy XIV Panzer Corps, Lopatin's 62nd Army and part of 4th Tank Army had attacked Paulus's left wing but quickly ran into trouble near Vertiachii (see map 22). The 384th Infantry Division of VIII Corps and the neighboring 76th and 295th Infantry Divisions of LI Corps slowed and significantly weakened this attack. Overnight on 24–25 August the German infantry crossed the Don River and counterattacked, pushing Lopatin's troops steadily back. Lopatin repeatedly asked the Stalingrad Front and the *Stavka* first for assistance and later for permission to withdraw before his principal rail line for evacuation could be cut. Fortunately for 62nd Army, on the night of 27–28 August LI Corps suddenly ceased its attacks, shifting forces to help bolster XIV Panzer Corps' beleaguered corridor. In effect, Paulus was leaving any encirclement of 62nd Army to the advance of Hoth's Fourth Panzer Army.[59]

Despite the threat to 62nd Army's left, Eremenko's Southeastern Front repeatedly refused the *Stavka*'s suggestions that it withdraw both 62nd and 64th Armies eastward to create a more coherent front. In this respect, Eremenko was reflecting Stalin's own reluctance to cede any territory, but in this case, it left Shumilov's 64th Army exposed to Fourth Panzer Army's advance northeastward toward Stalingrad. To mount such an advance, Hoth had fewer than 200 tanks among 14th and 24th Panzer and 29th Motorized Divisions.[60] Moreover, while these mobile divisions advanced toward the city, the security of their lengthening left flank depended on the four lightly equipped infantry divisions of Romanian VI Corps.

Opposite them, the Southeastern Front probably outnumbered its attackers, but its defenses were still in flux. The 64th Army was deployed in two echelons, with 38th, 204th, and 126th Rifle Divisions facing southward between Vasil'evka and Tinguta, backed by 29th and 138th Rifle Divisions as well as 66th Naval Rifle Brigade in second echelon. Most of Shumilov's 100 tanks belonged to 13th Mechanized Corps, concentrated southeast of Tinguta Station.[61] To Shumilov's left, Tolbukhin's 57th Army extended this front with 15th and 36th Guards Rifle Divisions in first echelon, plus three other rifle divisions, an infantry school, and a fortified region in second echelon.[62] On

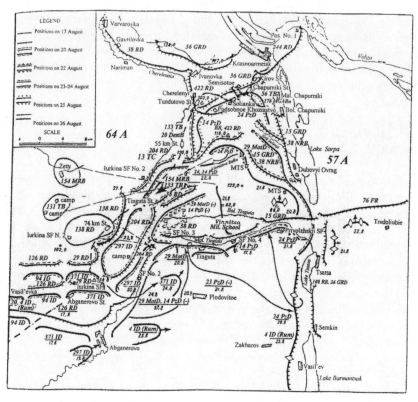

Map 22. 64th and 57th Armies' Defense, 17–26 August 1942

the left flank of the *front*, however, the three weakened divisions and three tankless tank brigades of T. K. Kolomiets's 51st Army were still withdrawing to their new assigned positions and were incapable of providing significant resistance to the German advance.

Delayed by fuel and lubricant shortages, Hoth did not begin his attack until 20 August, one day before Paulus. The 94th and 371st Infantry Divisions, aided by *kampfgruppen* from 29th Motorized and 14th Panzer Divisions, initially pushed 64th Army's troops back at Abganerovo Station, but Shumilov shifted forces and obtained Red air support that slowed the German advance late on the twentieth.[63] Hoth tried again the next day, farther to his left, sending 14th Panzer Division to split 64th Army from 57th Army and 24th Panzer to attack 15th Guards Rifle Division, but Tolbukhin shifted reserves and again halted the German advance. By now, though, Hoth had carved a wedge into the Soviet defenses.[64]

The Southeastern Front provided five antitank regiments to reinforce

57th Army; these guns inflicted significant losses on XXXXVIII Panzer Corps as it advanced slowly over the next several days. Extremely bitter resistance brought the Germans to a halt on 25 August, and Hoth pulled his mobile divisions back to refit.[65]

Careful German reconnaissance finally identified a Soviet weak point: the 20 kilometer sector between Vasil'evka and Abganerovo Station. Here, 126th Rifle Division had only 20 percent of its authorized artillery, and other units had been shifted away to stop German advances elsewhere. Hoth concentrated most of his remaining armor as well as supporting infantry there, attacking by surprise at dawn on 29 August. This thrust finally unhinged Eremenko's defenses and forced him to withdraw 64th Army well to the rear. The speed of Hoth's advance and heavy German air support preempted Soviet efforts to restore the defense; only 20th Destroyer Brigade brought 24th Panzer's exploitation to a halt just outside Stalingrad on 1 September.[66] Hoth had duplicated Paulus's northern advance, but in the process, his panzer forces had been severely reduced, boding ill for the coming urban battle.

Hoth's advance also permitted Sixth Army's LI Army Corps to almost encircle forward elements of 62nd and 64th Armies in late August. Fortunately for the defenders, their recent counterattacks against XIV Panzer Corps in the north of the city had made Paulus cautious. He therefore chose to shore up the flanks of his advance there rather than boldly trying to complete the encirclement with LI Corps. This caution allowed 62nd and 64th Armies to escape when, at 2000 on 1 September, Eremenko belatedly ordered their withdrawal.[67]

This withdrawal meant that when 24th Panzer Division resumed its advance on 2 September, it encountered no resistance. Still, the Southeastern Front retained significant forces, including (as of 31 August) 101 functioning tanks and 114 in various stages of repair.[68] As the Germans closed in on Stalingrad proper, the defenders were far from beaten.

OMINOUS SIDESHOWS: SERAFIMOVICH AND KLETSKAIA, AUGUST 1942

Amidst the German attacks of late August, General Kuznetsov's 63rd Army and General Danilov's 21st Army tried again to threaten the left flank of Army Group B's advance. Eremenko directed these two armies to cross the Don at Serafimovich, 160 kilometers northwest of Stalingrad (see map 23). Once across the river, the two armies were to expand their bridgeheads and exploit southward with 3rd Guards Cavalry Corps, a three-division force commanded by Major General I. A. Pliev.[69]

The attack at dawn on 20 August achieved considerable success against

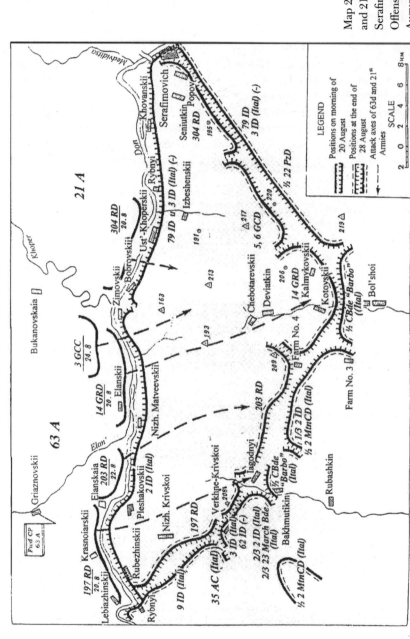

Map 23. 63rd and 21st Armies' Serafimovich Offensive, 20–28 August 1942

21 A

63 A

LEGEND

Positions on morning of 20 August

Positions at the end of 28 August

Attack axes of 63d and 21st Armies

SCALE

0 2 4 6 8 км

Griaznovskii

Bukanovskaia

Fwd CP 63 A

Khoper

Elan

Lebiazhinskii

Rybnyi

Krasnoiarskii

197 RD 20.8

Rubezhinskii

Elanskaia 203 RD 22.8

Nizh. Krivskoi

Pleshakovskii

2 ID (Ital)

Elanskii

14 GRD 20.8

3 GCC 24.8

Nizh. Matveevskii

Zimovskii

Bobrovskii

304 RD 20.8

Ust'-Khoperskii

Rybnyi

Khovanskii

Don

Serafimovich

Seniutkin

304 RD

Popov

79 ID 3 ID (Ital) (-)

79 ID u 3 ID (Ital) (-)

Izbeshenskii

△ 163

△ 193

△ 213

191 ◦

195 ◦

△ 217

220

5, 6 GCD

½ 22 PzD

219 △

Chebotarevskii

Deviatkin

206 ◦

14 GRD

Kalmykovskii

Kotovskii

½ CBde "Barbo" (Ital)

Bol'shoi

203 RD

Farm No. 4

209 ◦

Farm No. 3

½ 1/3 2 TD

½ 2 MtnCD (Ital)

Rubashkin

197 RD

Verkhne-Krivskoi

Iagodnyi

◦ 205

½ CBde "Barbo" (Ital)

Bakhmutkin

2/3 2 ID (Ital) 2/3 23 March Bde. (Ital)

3 ID (Ital) 62 ID (-)

9 ID (Ital)

35 AC (Ital)

½ 2 MtnCD (Ital)

Medveditsa

Italian Eighth Army, stiffened in this sector by the German 79th Infantry Division. Eighth Army eventually contained Pliev's corps and the other attackers by redeploying its Cavalry Brigade Barbo and 3rd *Celere* Division, the latter an unusual mixture of Bersiglieri light infantry, motorized artillery, and two companies each of light tanks and tank destroyers. By this time, the attackers had created a bridgehead 50 kilometers wide and up to 25 kilometers deep, which they then consolidated in a deeply echeloned defense.[70] Although higher headquarters criticized the Serafimovich offensive for its failure to achieve greater results, it did in fact create one of the starting points for the successful November counteroffensive, while demonstrating the weakness of the Italian defense. At the time, however, the Germans were focused on Stalingrad and the Caucasus and dismissed this weakness once the front stabilized.

The Germans also underplayed the success of another attack during the same period, this time working from an existing Soviet bridgehead in the northeast corner of the Don bend, east of Kletskaia. Here, about 50 kilometers southeast of Serafimovich and 110 kilometers northwest of Stalingrad, sat Moskalenko's 1st Guards Army. Although this organization was much weaker in August than in subsequent operations, it still included six rifle divisions, four of which were the favored guards organizations, plus a handful of tanks from the remnants of 4th Tank Army.

Opposite this, the German defenders of Sixth Army's XI Army Corps included 376th Infantry and 100th *Jäger* Divisions, as well as two regiments of 44th Infantry Division. Temporarily, XI Corps also controlled elements of Lieutenant General Wilhelm von Apell's 22nd Panzer Division, with about 60 tanks. Attacking on 22 August, Moskalenko pushed the Germans back some 8 to 10 kilometers. This modest advance established a recurring pattern of tying down German reserves and inflicting casualties on defending infantry units outside of the struggle for Stalingrad.[71] Like Serafimovich, the Kletskaia bridgehead provided a key starting point for the November counteroffensive.

CONCLUSION

The fighting during the last ten days of August had brought the Germans to the gates of Stalingrad, while stranding 62nd and 64th Armies on a narrow strip of the west bank of the Volga River. This fighting completed the destruction of 1st Tank Army and severely damaged 4th Tank, 62nd, and 64th Armies; the defeat brought the total Red Army losses since mid-July to well over 300,000 soldiers and 1,000 tanks. Undoubtedly, many German commanders believed or at least hoped that they were on the verge of occupying Stalingrad.

The triumphal dash of Wietersheim's XIV Panzer Corps from the Don to the Volga in just three days erased many memories of the repeated German failures that preceded that success. Still, this advance cost up to 500 men per day, a rate that threatened to eliminate the corps as a combat organization.[72] Even after reaching the Volga, Paulus was unable to begin his assault on Stalingrad until Fourth Panzer Army, a misnamed formation with even fewer tanks than Sixth Army, was able to close up on the southern end of the city.

At the same time, the Soviet counterstrokes at Serafimovich and Kletskaia illustrated the overall weakness of Army Group B in comparison to its opponents. Although these attacks were contained, they illustrated the continued resilience of the Red Army and the weaknesses of the Axis satellite armies. While the Germans focused on capturing Stalingrad and the Caucasus oil fields, their long left flank would continue to both drain effectives and pose a threat to the entire German advance.

PART TWO

To the Caucasus and the Volga

CHAPTER SIX

Struggles on the Flanks, 25 July–11 September 1942

Before considering the street battles for control of Stalingrad, we need to examine the simultaneous challenges of the German advance into the Caucasus—the original mission of Operation *Blau*—and the repeated Soviet counteroffensives of July–September 1942.

OPERATION EDELWEISS: ADVANCE INTO THE CAUCASUS

Field Marshal Wilhelm List, commander of Army Group A, faced a daunting task as he prepared to leave Rostov in late July. He was already operating at the end of a tenuous supply chain and soon would have to compete with Army Group B for available fuel and shipping space. Now, however, the Germans were pushing even farther forward. From Rostov to the Maikop oil fields was 290 kilometers, and to the refineries at Groznyi was almost 650 kilometers. If the Germans ever intended to reach the oil center of Baku on the Caspian Sea, they would have to advance 1,100 kilometers, greater than the distance the invaders had already covered to reach Rostov from the start of their invasion 13 months earlier.

Moreover, the terrain was extremely challenging. Immediately south of Rostov lay the fertile collective farms of the Kuban' River area, but that ground soon tapered off into a high plateau that was almost a salt desert. This region, in turn, led to the Caucasus Mountains, a chain 1,100 kilometers from west to east and up to 200 kilometers from north to south, with peaks as high as 5,600 meters, the highest in continental Europe, and few improved roads. Further complicating their task, the Germans had to advance on a front of almost 300 kilometers to reach their widely dispersed objectives.

Führer Directive No. 45, dated 23 July, outlined the first step in the projected advance: as he had from the beginning of Operation *Blau*, Hitler sought to encircle and destroy the Soviet forces that had withdrawn across the Don by launching two pincers toward Tikhoretsk.[1] List's left or eastern pincer consisted of Kleist's First Panzer Army and (until diverted to Stalingrad) Hoth's Fourth Panzer Army. On paper, Kleist had a formidable total of three panzer divisions (3rd, 13th, and 23rd), plus the 16th, 5th SS *Wiking*, and *Grossdeutschland* Motorized Divisions and the Slovak Mobile Division (see table 6.1). However,

Map 24. The Caucasus Region (West)

as noted earlier, these units had begun the campaign without their full complement of tanks, and *Grossdeutschland* had a number of restrictions on its employment, indicating that it might be redeployed. Still, at the end of July, this pincer fielded approximately 435 tanks. *Armeegruppe* Ruoff, composed of German Seventeenth and Romanian Third Armies, formed the army group's right or western pincer; when Manstein's Eleventh Army headquarters transferred to the Leningrad region, it left one German infantry division as well as the Romanian mountain troops behind to reinforce Ruoff. For the initial advance, Ruoff had the temporary support of First Panzer Army's LVII Panzer Corps to capture a bridgehead south of the Don at Bataisk; 13th Panzer and SS *Wiking* Divisions then had to catch up with the rest of Kleist's force, which had already crossed the Sal River and reached the Manych River.[2]

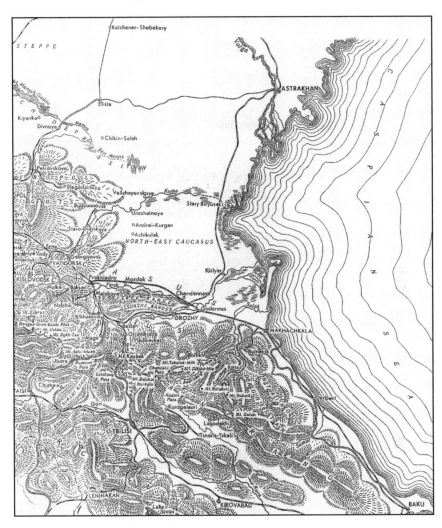

Map 25. The Caucasus Region (East)

The defending Soviet commanders confronted challenges almost equal to those facing the Germans. Any retreat would bring the Red Army closer to the petroleum supplies at Groznyi and the Lend-Lease aid coming through Iran. However, such a withdrawal would carry the defenders farther away from the centers of Soviet forces, the sources of troops and ammunition. The railroad line from Rostov southeast to Baku was jammed with trains carrying refugees and evacuated factory components, making that line as useless to the Soviets as it was to the Germans. As commander of the Southern Front, Lieutenant

Table 6.1. Organization of Army Group A, 1–13 August 1942

Army Group A—Field Marshal Wilhelm List
   First Panzer Army—Colonel General Ewald von Kleist
      XXXX Panzer Corps—General of Panzer Troops Leo *Freiherr* Geyr von
         Schweppenburg
         3rd and 23rd Panzer Divisions
      III Panzer Corps—Lieutenant General Eberhard von Mackensen
         16th Motorized and 13th Panzer Divisions
      XXXXIV Army Corps—General of Artillery Maximilian de Angelis
         97th and 101st Jäger Divisions, 373rd Walloon Battalion
      LVII Panzer Corps—General of Panzer Troops Friedrich Kirchner
         5th SS Wiking (Viking) and Slovak Mobile Divisions
      LII Army Corps—General of Infantry Eugen Ott
         11th and 370th Infantry Divisions; (to 13 August) *Grossdeutschland*
         Division
      XXXXIX Mountain Corps (from Armeegruppe Ruoff on 12 August)—General
         of Mountain Troops Rudolf Konrad
         1st and 4th Mountain Divisions, Romanian 2nd Infantry Division
   Armeegruppe Ruoff (Seventeenth Army)—Colonel General Richard Ruoff
      V Army Corps—General of Infantry William Wetzel
         125th and 198th Infantry Divisions; (by 12 August, from XXXXIX
         Mountain Corps) 9th and 73rd Infantry Divisions
      XXXXIX Mountain Corps (to First Panzer Army on 12 August)
      Romanian Third Army—General Petre Dumitrescu
         Romanian I Corps—General Mihail Racovita
             Romanian 2nd Infantry Division (to XXXXIX Mountain Corps by
               12 August), German 298th Infantry Division
         Romanian Cavalry Corps
             Romanian 5th, 6th, and (by 12 August) 9th Cavalry Divisions
         Romanian II Corps
   Eleventh Army—Field Marshal Fritz-Erich von Manstein (headquarters and
     most troop elements diverted to Leningrad region)
   Army Group Reserve
      Italian Alpine Corps (diverted to Army Group B in late August)
         3rd Alpine Division Julia, 4th Alpine Division Cuneense (by 13 August)
         2nd Alpine Division Tridentina
      Grossdeutschland Motorized Division (withdrawing after 13 August)
   Army Group Rear Area Command: 445th and 454th Security Divisions,
     4th Security Regiment

Source: Horst Boog Werner Rahm, Reinhard Stumpf, and Bernd Wegner, *Germany and the Second World War*, vol. vi, *The Global War: Widening of the Conflict into a World War and the Shift of the Initiative, 1941–1943*, trans. Ewald Osers et al. (Oxford: Clarendon Press, 2001), 1030.

General Malinovsky had four armies (see table 6.2) totaling only 112,000 combat troops, 169 guns, and 17 operable tanks, supported by 130 combat aircraft.[3] In early August Marshal Budenny's North Caucasus Front dispatched a small reinforcement to the Southern Front in the form of Major General N. Ia. Kirichenko's 17th Cavalry Corps. Meanwhile, Malinovsky assembled his threadbare armies into a defensive line on the southern bank of the Don,

Table 6.2. Southern and North Caucasus Fronts on 25 July 1942, and North Caucasus and Trans-Caucasus Fronts on 28 July 1942

25 July
Southern Front—Colonel General R. Ia. Malinovsky
  18th Army—Major General F. V. Kamkov: from the mouth of the Don River
    50 km eastward to Kizikerinka, opposite Seventeenth Army
      383rd, 395th, and 216th Rifle Divisions; 68th Naval Rifle Brigade, with
        remnants of 236th Rifle Division and 16th Rifle Brigade
  12th Army—Major General A. A. Grechko: from Kizikerinka 40 km eastward
    to Belianin, opposite First Panzer Army's III Panzer Corps
      4th, 261st, and 353rd Rifle Divisions, with remnants of three other
        divisions
  37th Army—Major General P. M. Kozlov: from Bogaevskaia 65 km eastward to
    Konstantinovskaia, opposite Fourth Panzer Army's XXXX Panzer Corps
      102nd, 218th, and 275th Rifle Divisions
  51st Army—Major General T. K. Kolomiets: from Konstantinovskaia 171 km
    eastward to Verkhne-Kurmoiarskaia, opposite Fourth Panzer Army's
    XXXXVIII Panzer Corps
      156th, 302nd, 91st, 157th, and 138th Rifle Divisions
      110th and 115th Cavalry Divisions
      135th and 155th Tank Brigades
  56th Army—Major General A. I. Ryzhov: front second echelon south of the
    Eia River
      Five rifle divisions and three rifle brigades
  24th Army—Major General V. N. Martsenkevich—and 9th Army—Major
    General F. A. Parkhomenko: reorganizing south of the Egorlik River and
    Sal'sk
North Caucasus Front—Marshal of the Soviet Union S. M. Budenny
  17th Cavalry Corps—Major General N. Ia. Kirichenko, supplementing the
    Southern Front's 18th Army
      12th, 13th, 15th, and 116th Cavalry Divisions, reinforced by 56th Army's
        30th and 385th Rifle Divisions
  47th Army—Major General G. P. Kotov, defending the eastern coast of the Sea
    of Azov
      32nd Guards and 77th Rifle Divisions, 103rd Rifle Brigade, and 126th
        Separate Tank Battalion
  1st Separate Rifle Corps—Colonel M. M. Shapovalov, reinforcing the Southern
    Front
      83rd Naval and 139th Rifle Brigades

28 July
(After the North Caucasus Front absorbed most of the Southern Front)
North Caucasus Front—Marshal of the Soviet Union S. M. Budenny
  Coastal (Maritime) Operational Group—Colonel General Ia. T. Cherevichenko
    47th, 56th, and 18th Armies
    1st Separate Rifle Corps
    17th Cavalry Corps (redesignated 4th Guards on 17 August)
    69th Fortified Region
  Don Operational Group—Colonel General R. Ia. Malinovsky
    12th, 37th, and 51st Armies (the last transferring to the Stalingrad Front)
    136th, 138th, 139th, 5th Guards, 2nd, 15th, 63rd, and 140th Tank
      Brigades
    21st and Special Motorized Rifle Brigades
  Front subordinate
    9th Army—Major General F. A. Parkhomenko

Table 6.2. (*continued*)

      51st, 81st, 106th, 140th, 24th, 255th, 296th, and 318th Rifle Divisions
      30th Cavalry Division
      18th and 19th Destroyer Brigades, 132nd Separate Tank Battalion
  24th Army (headquarters only)—redesignated 58th Army in mid-August
  4th Air Army—Major General of Aviation K. A. Vershinin
  5th Air Army—Lieutenant General of Aviation S. K. Goriunov
  8th Sapper Army—Colonel I. E. Salashchenko (19 construction
      battalions)
  Front strength—74 tanks and 230 combat aircraft
Trans-Caucasus Front—Army General I. V. Tiulenev, defending the Terek River
  and the Caucasus
  44th Army—Major General I. E. Petrov
      223rd, 414th, and 416th Rifle Divisions
      9th and 10th Rifle Brigades
  46th Army—Major General V. F. Sergatskov (K. N. Leselidze on 23 August)
      3rd Mountain Rifle Corps—Major General of Artillery K. N. Leselidze
        9th and 20th Mountain Rifle Divisions
      389th, 392nd, 394th, and 406th Rifle Divisions; 156th Rifle Brigade
      63rd Cavalry Division, 51st Fortified Region, 12th Separate Tank Battalion
  45th Army—Lieutenant General F. N. Remezov
      61st, 89th, 151st, 402nd, 408th, and 409th Rifle Divisions
      55th Fortified Region, 151st Tank Brigade
  Front subordinate
      417th Rifle Division, 3rd Rifle Brigade, Separate Parachute Assault
        Battalion
      52nd and 191st Tank Brigades

Sources: Boevoi sostav Sovetskoi armii, Chast 2 (ianvar'-dekabr' 1942 goda) [Combat composition of the Soviet Army, part 2 (January–December 1942)] (Moscow: Voenizdat, 1966), 150–151. For 1st Separate Rifle Corps, A. A. Grechko, *Bitva za Kavkav* [The battle for the Caucasus] (Moscow: Voenizdat, 1973), 55; V. A. Zolotarev, ed. "Stavka VGK: Dokumenty i materialy 1942" [The *Stavka* VGK: Documents and materials, 1942], in *Russkii arkhiv: Velikaia Otechestvennaia [voina]*, 16 (5-2) [The Russian archives: The Great Patriotic (War), vol. 16 (5-2)] (Moscow: Terra, 1996), 530.

while trying to withdraw the intact 56th Army into reserve positions south of the Eia River. Even farther to the rear, near Sal'sk, Malinovsky attempted to rebuild the remnants of previously decimated 9th and 24th Armies.

THE INITIAL ADVANCE, 25–31 JULY

While List's army group prepared for its main thrust into the Caucasus, on 25 July Geyr's XXXX Panzer Corps advanced southward from the Don at Nikolaevskaia. The 3rd Panzer Division and a *kampfgruppe* from 23rd Panzer pushed aside two divisions of 51st Army, seizing a bridgehead over the Sal River near Orlovka by nightfall. To the west of this advance, Heinrici's 16th Motorized Division of III Panzer Corps forced a crossing over the Don just

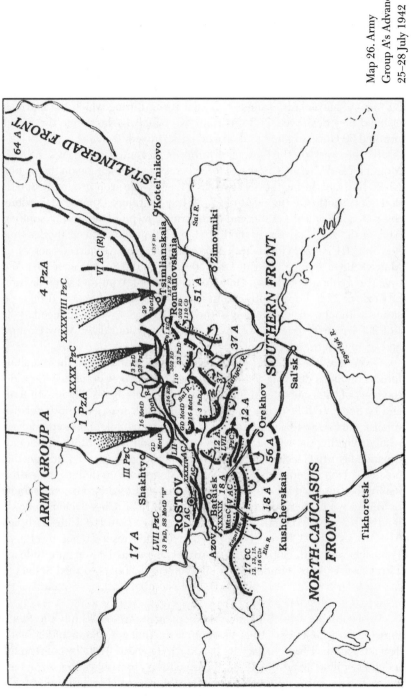

Map 26. Army
Group A's Advance,
25–28 July 1942

south of the junction with the Sal River, pushing back the demoralized 37th Army; lead elements of *Grossdeutschland* Division entered that bridgehead by nightfall.

At Malinovsky's direction, 51st Army conducted a number of local counterattacks against Major General Erwin Mack's 23rd Panzer Division on 28–29 July. A sharp clash ensued at the Sal River, during which the Germans claimed they destroyed 77 T-34s from two tank brigades, while the Soviets counted 60 German tanks as damaged or destroyed.[4]

To the west of this struggle, however, Seventeenth Army's XXXXIX Mountain and V Army Corps had forced crossings of the Don on the night of 25–26 July, and during the next two days, List's entire army group pressed the defenders south. On the night of 27–28 July, therefore, Malinovsky ordered the remnants of 18th, 12th, and 37th Armies to pull back to the southern bank of the Kagal'nik River and the Manych Canal and River. By this time, however, III Panzer Corps' 16th Motorized Division was already across the Manych River in the center of List's advance, so the Soviets were unable to organize a coherent defense. Only Kolomiets's 51st Army and some divisions of Kozlov's 37th Army continued to resist; other units abandoned their positions without a struggle. Many of the Soviet divisions were reduced to 300 to 1,200 bayonets (combat soldiers) each.[5] In only four days, Army Group A had again penetrated a Soviet defensive line.

Given this disaster, on 27 July Budenny recommended that the remaining forces conduct a delaying action while organizing a new defensive line along the crest of the Caucasus Mountains and the Terek River. Then 47th Army and 1st Separate Rifle Corps would shield the Black Sea Fleet's ports at Novorossiisk, Anapa, and Tuapse. Early on 28 July Stalin implemented this advice, resubordinating the remnants of Malinovsky's Southern Front to Budenny's expanded North Caucasus Front. To reestablish some control, Budenny then created a Don Operational Group under Malinovsky to defend the eastern half of the front and a Coastal or Maritime Operational Group, commanded by Budenny's former deputy, Colonel General Ia. T. Cherevichenko, to defend in the west. Malinovsky would control the shattered 12th, 37th, and 51st Armies, while Cherevichenko tried to defend Krasnodar and the Taman' Peninsula with 18th, 56th, and 47th Armies, as well as 1st Separate Rifle and 17th Cavalry Corps.[6] Budenny required all commanders to read Stalin's famous Order No. 227 (see chapter 5) to their subordinates, emphasizing the need to defend the oil region.[7]

In accordance with Budenny's recommendations, on 30 July the *Stavka* directed Army General Ivan Vladimirovich Tiulenev, commander of the Trans-Caucasus Front, to back up the North Caucasus Front by constructing a defensive line along the Terek River and the approaches to Groznyi and Baku; Tiulenev was supposed to complete this construction by 7 August. The

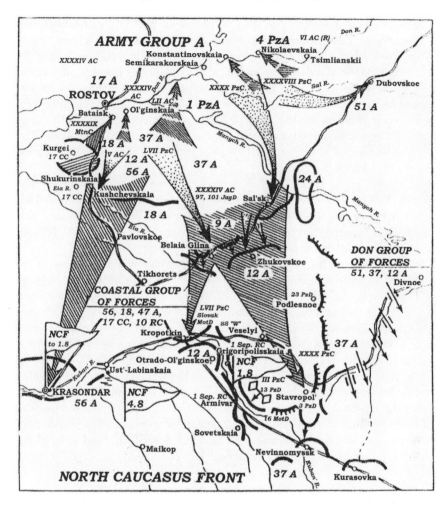

Map 27. Army Group A's Advance, 29 July–5 August 1942

task fell to Major General I. E. Petrov's 44th Army, with three rifle divisions and two rifle brigades. The following day, Tiulenev received orders to create two new guards rifle corps, the 10th and 11th, each with three brigades, from his local reservists and use them to erect yet another defensive line north of the mountain crest and centered on Groznyi.[8]

On 29 July, before these new defenses were even begun, List's armor was on the move again. Despite a shortage of fuel, the panzer-grenadiers of General of Panzer Troops Hermann Breith's 3rd Panzer Division crossed the Manych River at its widest point, immediately behind a cofferdam. The defending elements of 37th Army, including an NKVD division, contested the crossing bitterly until the morning of the thirtieth, when a few German armored vehicles boldly drove along the top of the dam and outflanked the Soviets.[9] While the defenders managed to contain this bridgehead, to their west, Seventeenth Army broke out of its bridgehead at Bataisk on 30 July. Led by the 109 tanks of 13th Panzer Division, this attack advanced 80 kilometers in two days, capturing Sal'sk and another bridgehead across the Srednyi River and then linking up with 3rd Panzer along the Manych River. The other division of Mackensen's III Panzer Corps, 16th Motorized, soon closed up with 13th Panzer.[10]

At this point, Hitler's 30 July decision to reinforce the Stalingrad effort with XXXXVIII Panzer Corps and IV Army Corps of Hoth's Fourth Panzer Army (see chapter 5) forced List to reorganize his eastern pincer. This left First Panzer Army with three weak panzer corps—the XXXX, III, and LVII—to continue the advance (see table 6.1).

Nonetheless, the restructuring occurred almost without a pause in the attack. Despite temperatures as high as 40 degrees Celsius (104 degrees Fahrenheit), SS *Wiking* Division of LVII Panzer Corps pushed deep into the Soviet defenses on 30 July, parallel to and west of the previous advance by XXXX Panzer Corps. Exploiting this success, the three infantry divisions of Seventeenth Army's V Army Corps smashed through Kamkov's 18th Army and reached bridgeheads across the Eia River by the end of 1 August. To the west, XXXIX Mountain Corps' divisions duplicated this feat, overrunning Kirichenko's 17th Cavalry Corps along the lower Kagal'nik River and reaching the Eia River west of Kushchevskaia, 80 kilometers south of the German starting point in Rostov. On 30 July Ruoff transferred one of the divisions of this mountain corps to reinforce Romanian I Army Corps and ordered the rest of his army to continue advancing.[11]

RESTRUCTURING THE ADVANCE

First Panzer and Seventeenth Armies had preempted the Soviet defenses and were poised for exploitation; the question was how long these forces could sustain the advance. Given the departure of most of Fourth Panzer Army to Stalingrad, List had to give up his plans for an encirclement at Tikhoretsk and instead send his two remaining armies southward toward Maikop and Krasnodar, respectively. With the departure of *Grossdeutschland* Division in mid-August, First Panzer Army was reduced to three panzer and two motorized divisions—about 350 tanks—to conquer an area almost the size of France.[12]

Mackensen's III Panzer Corps, with 13th Panzer and 16th Motorized Divisions, received the primary mission of capturing the oil fields and refineries of Maikop. Mackensen's eastern flank would be protected by Geyr's XXXX Panzer Corps (23rd and 3rd Panzer Divisions), which in turn would be secured by LII Corps, advancing to seize the headwaters of the Terek River. Kirchner's LVII Panzer Corps, with SS *Wiking* and Slovak Motorized Divisions, was on Mackensen's other flank, seeking to split Budenny's two operations groups in their defense of Krasnodar and Maikop. Meanwhile, Ruoff's German-Romanian *Armeegruppe* would advance in the west to Krasnodar and the Black Sea. V Army Corps, ultimately composed of 9th, 73rd, 125th, and 198th Infantry Divisions, led this advance. Castling to the left (east) flank of this advance and transferring two divisions to V Corps, XXXIX Mountain Corps, now consisting of 1st and 4th Mountain and Romanian 2nd Mountain Divisions, would assault the Caucasus Mountains. The corps' goal was to capture Sukhumi on the eastern coast of the Black Sea before snow closed the high mountain passes in late September. Unfortunately for Ruoff, he lost most of Eleventh Army to the Leningrad Front in August. This was followed by the loss of the Italian Alpine Corps in late August and Romanian Third Army in early September, both of which were redeployed to secure the long left flank of Army Group B.

Opposite the weakened Army Group A were the North Caucasus Front, already damaged by the battles of July, and the embryonic Trans-Caucasus Front. By this stage in the war, the defending Soviet tactical commanders were generally very experienced; for example, Petrov, commander of 44th Army, had already performed well in the Crimean battles earlier that year. By contrast, the North Caucasus Front commander, Budenny, had demonstrated that he was thoroughly ineffectual. Stalin retained a soft spot for his old cavalry warhorse, but he was not blind to the dangers in the region. The dictator, himself a native of Ossetia, suspected with some justification that the various minority groups of the Trans-Caucasus might welcome the German invaders over the Soviet oppressors. Lavrenti Beriia, the People's Commissar for Internal Affairs, unleashed the NKVD behind the lines, where they murdered or deported thousands of Chechens, Tartars, Volga Germans, and other minorities. Such repression made Stalin's fears self-fulfilling, and the Germans received passive and even some active armed support from the peoples they encountered.[13]

THE GERMAN EXPLOITATION TO STAVROPOL', MAIKOP, AND KRASNODAR

On 1 August Army Group A resumed its exploitation southward (see map 27). In First Panzer Army, XXXX Panzer Corps advanced on Stavropol', protecting the left flank of III and LVI Panzer Corps' thrust toward Armavir.

Simultaneously, Seventeenth Army departed its bridgeheads over the Eia River near Kushchevskaia and headed for Krasnodar.

As Soviet resistance melted away, Kleist's armored divisions accelerated, covering almost 100 kilometers in the first two days of August. In the process, this advance liquidated bypassed elements of 12th and 37th Armies. After a two-day struggle, 37th Army yielded the city of Stavropol' to XXXX Panzer Corps' 3rd Panzer Division on 5 August, while Mack's 23rd Panzer Division operated in small *kampfgruppen* to screen the lengthening eastern flank of the advance. That same day, SS *Wiking* fanned out along the northern bank of the Kuban' River while the Slovak Mobile Division occupied Kropotkin, pushing 1st Separate Rifle Corps south of the river.[14]

Seventeenth Army, with Romanian Third Army shielding its right (western) flank along the Sea of Azov, almost kept pace with the advance. Only Kirichenko's 17th Cavalry Corps and other depleted Soviet units briefly held up the right wing of XXXXIX Mountain Corps, and by 5 August, forward German elements were within 80 kilometers of Krasnodar.[15]

Alarmed by the continued German advance, on 5 August the *Stavka* sent a dire warning to Budenny while taking additional steps to shore up the front. Tiulenev's Trans-Caucasus Front received instructions to move 89th Rifle Division and 52nd Tank Brigade from Armenia to reinforce its northern defenses, and Moscow instructed the North Caucasus Military District, the administrative headquarters in the region, to form eight new rifle divisions under a new 66th Army headquarters to defend the Terek Valley. To prevent Malinovsky's Don Operational Group from being isolated, the *Stavka* ordered Budenny to expel German forces south of the Kuban' River and to hold the key railroad line from Armavir eastward to Prokhladnyi.[16] In a teletype conference late on 6 August, Vasilevsky directed Tiulenev to use his existing assets to organize a Northern Group of Forces commanded by Lieutenant General Ivan Ivanovich Maslennikov, one of the few senior NKVD officers to display any tactical skill. Maslennikov would control Petrov's 44th Army and the reorganized 9th Army, now commanded by Major General A. A. Khadeev. Vasilevsky also told Tiulenev that he would receive priority for newly produced aircraft, as well as Lend-Lease tanks sent through Iran.[17]

By the time these Soviet decisions occurred, however, XXXX Panzer Corps had already reached the railroad line 60 kilometers southeast of Armavir, effectively severing communications between the Don and Coastal Operational Groups. Only 11th NKVD Division and various detachments of school troops were available to plug this gap. In the first week of August, Kleist's spearheads had forced Soviet 51st Army to withdraw eastward and 37th Army to retreat to the southeast, leaving remnants of 18th and 12th Armies to fight a delaying action southeastward toward Maikop. To consolidate these gains, Kleist attempted to bring forward the infantry of XXXXIV

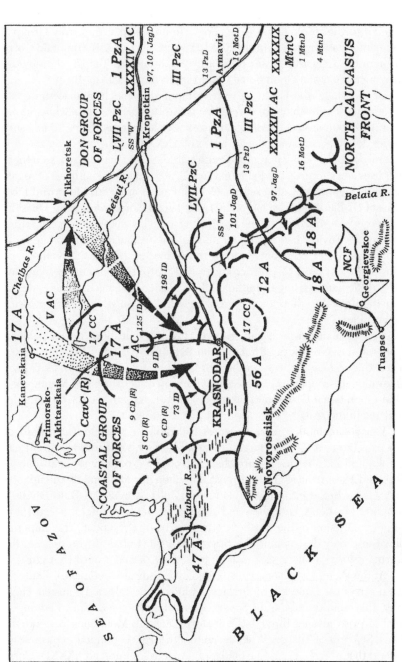

Map 28. The Krasnodar-Kuban' Operation, 12–15 August 1942

and LII Army Corps, but in the meantime, under pressure from Hitler, List urged a further exploitation to Maikop. Simultaneously, the Army Group A commander attempted to insert XXXXIV Army and XXXIX Mountain Corps through the Caucasus passes to capture Sukhumi and Tuapse, thereby destroying the Coastal Operational Group south of the Kuban' River.

At this stage, the Germans were hampered as much by inaccurate tsarist-era maps as by the local defenders; they often had to pause while *Storch* aircraft reconnoitered crossing sites over the numerous rivers.[18] Makeshift Soviet defenses contained the advances of XXXX Panzer Corps over the next several days, but on 9–10 August Breith's 3rd Panzer Division bypassed these defenses and captured the Piatigorsk area, 200 kilometers southeast of Armavir. More significantly, that same day, 13th Panzer and 16th Motorized Divisions of III Panzer Corps, joined by LVII Panzer Corps' SS *Wiking* Division, converged on Maikop from the north and east. This victory proved an empty one, as the Soviets had destroyed most of the wellheads and storage tanks and removed key components from the refineries; during the final several days of the advance, Mackensen's men had plotted their route by marching toward the flames rising from the oil field.[19] The Germans had succeeded in denying this oil to their enemies, but they did not solve their own pressing fuel problems.

The German advance had severed all communications between Major General A. A. Grechko's 12th Army and Kozlov's 37th Army. Budenny recognized this change and resubordinated Grechko to Cherevichenko's Coastal Operational Group; on 11 August the *Stavka* in effect abolished Malinovsky's Don Operational Group and directed Tiulenev to withdraw 37th Army for refitting in the rear.[20]

Krasnodar, another refinery center 150 kilometers inland from the Black Sea, was the next German target. After adjusting his dispositions, Ruoff had accelerated his advance toward that city, opposed only by skeletal units of 56th and 18th Armies. On 10 August, the same day Maikop fell, the infantry of V Corps broke into the city. However, 56th Army's 30th Rifle Division, supported by tanks, *katiushas*, and aircraft, suddenly counterattacked 198th Infantry Division in the northeastern suburbs of Krasnodar. This impetus, plus the timely destruction of a bridge over the Kuban' River, delayed the Germans for several days; they did not secure Krasnodar until 15 August.[21]

At this stage, List planned to consolidate his advance and secure all the areas north of the Caucasus Mountains, including the Taman' Peninsula. However, the rapid crumbling of Soviet defenses encouraged him to attempt a final surprise advance through the western Caucasus Mountains to secure the Black Sea port of Tuapse. While Seventeenth Army continued to push south toward that port, General Maximilian de Angelis's reinforced XXXXIV Corps of First Panzer Army would thrust southwestward from Maikop to form a

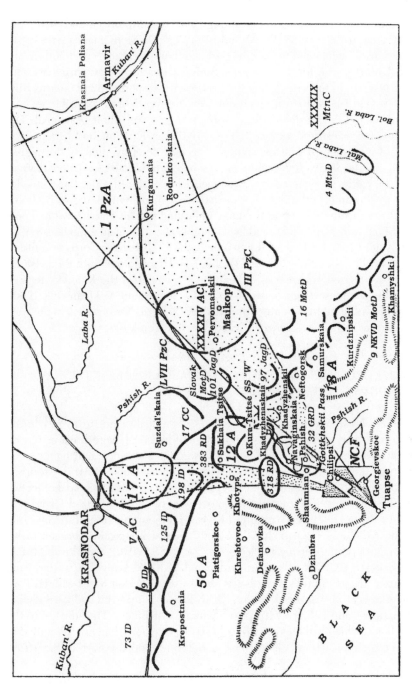

Map 29. The Tuapse Operation, 12–28 August 1942

second pincer consisting of two prongs. The 16th Motorized and 97th *Jäger* Divisions, paralleling SS *Wiking* and 101st *Jäger* Divisions, made up these two columns, which aimed to take the port and thereby cut off Soviet 56th Army.

Unfortunately for the Germans, Budenny was also restructuring his slender reserves in this area, while the Red Navy transported 32nd Guards Rifle Division to Tuapse to form a new defensive line north of the port. These measures halted the German advance on 18 August, well short of its goal. The 32nd Guards exacted a heavy toll on 101st *Jäger* Division, and Kirichenko's 17th Cavalry Corps, shifting south to this new defensive line, performed so well that the *Stavka* redesignated it as 4th Guards Cavalry Corps ten days after the battle. German attempts to reach Tuapse later in August also failed.[22]

By this time, both sides were worn down to a nub. On 13 August Budenny sent a dour situation report to Stalin, indicating that his entire *front* had only 24,500 bayonets, no tanks, and five operable aircraft.[23] Equally exhausted, on 16 August Kleist withdrew the two divisions of III Panzer Corps to refit before further operations. A week later, OKH detached one of these divisions, 16th Motorized, to act as a thin eastern screen across the Kalmyk Steppes, a wide, semidesert gap between Army Groups B and A. Meanwhile, List's attention shifted to Seventeenth Army's advance on Novorossiisk in the west and especially Kleist's panzer advance into the Terek River region.

ARMY GROUP A'S ADVANCE TO THE CAUCASUS MOUNTAINS, 16 AUGUST–11 SEPTEMBER

The remarkable series of German successes gradually came to an end during the latter half of August as a combination of logistical overextension, mountainous terrain, and Soviet resistance slowed List's advance. During the same period, the continued demands to screen the long flanks of Army Groups A and B siphoned off additional forces from the designated principal objective in the Caucasus. For example, the movement of 16th Motorized Division to cover the open left flank required Kleist to temporarily drain the tanks of a panzer division. Recognizing this, on 17 August List again reorganized his army group, transferring LVII Panzer Corps (SS *Wiking* and Slovak Mobile Divisions), XXXXIX Mountain Corps, and XXXXIV Army Corps from First Panzer Army to Ruoff's dwindling *Armeegruppe*. This left Kleist with III Panzer Corps (13th Panzer Division), XXXX Panzer Corps (3rd and 23rd Panzer Divisions), and LII Army Corps (two infantry divisions). The advance to the oil fields, which had begun with eight mobile divisions, had now dwindled to three such formations, all of which were losing combat power as they struggled southward.

The objective remained unchanged, however. Depleted Army Group A

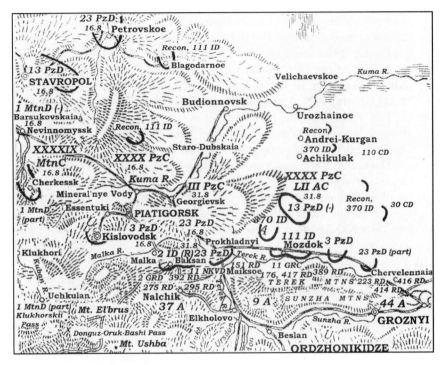

Map 30. The Mozdok Operation, 16–31 August 1942

found itself trying to advance in three directions simultaneously—into the Terek Valley, against the Taman' Peninsula and Novorossiisk, and through the high passes of the Caucasus Mountains. Kleist's First Panzer Army was to advance southeastward, parallel to the mountains, to seize in succession the Terek River Valley, the key cities of Ordzhonikidze and Groznyi, the eastern mountain passes, and ultimately Baku. Meanwhile, Seventeenth Army's V Corps aimed to capture Novorossiisk while the Romanian Cavalry Corps, reinforced by German 298th and 46th Infantry Divisions, cleared the Taman' Peninsula on the army's right. Together, XXXXIV Army, XXXXIX Mountain, and LVII Panzer Corps would seize the western Caucasus passes en route to the ports of Tuapse and Sukhumi. First, however, some of the German mountaineers paused on 21 August for a purely propaganda victory, planting the swastika flag on top of the volcanic Mount Elbrus, the highest peak in the Caucasus.[24]

Kleist initiated the renewed offensive by sending Geyr's XXXX Panzer Corps, reinforced by Romanian 2nd Mountain Division, southeastward on 16 August. Within a week, reconnaissance elements of Mack's 23rd Panzer Division reached the Terek River at a point 30 kilometers east of Mozdok. There,

Mack turned his gains over to the Romanian mountain troops and continued to press to the southeast. After shifting eastward behind 23rd Panzer, Breith's 3rd Panzer Division reached the outskirts of Mozdok late on 23 August. Despite support from 111th Infantry Division, Breith did not clear the city itself until two days later. By that time, the new commander of the Red 9th Army, Major General V. N. Martsenkevich, had reinforced the southern bank of the Terek River with the three brigades of 11th Guards Rifle Corps, blocking an immediate German crossing. Farther west, however, part of 13th Panzer Division seized a bridgehead across the Terek at Ishcherskaia on 26 August.[25]

Thereafter, Kleist again revised his command structure to reflect deployments on the ground. Mackensen's III Panzer Corps controlled only Romanian 2nd Mountain Division and one *kampfgruppe* of 23rd Panzer Division around Baksan, while 13th Panzer joined 3rd Panzer and most of 23rd Panzer under XXXX Panzer Corps, making the main effort farther east. To further complicate matters, General Mack and other members of 23rd Panzer's divisional staff were killed while visiting the front on 23 August; Lieutenant General Wilhelm Hans, *Reichsfreiherr* (Baron) von Boineburg-Lengsfeld, who had lost command the previous month in connection with the Reichel affair, returned to head the division.[26]

The Soviet leadership struggled to erect fresh barriers in the face of the weakening German spearheads. During the final days of August, three rifle divisions, one NKVD division, and one rifle brigade moved to the Makhachkala region under the headquarters of 24th Army, soon redesignated 58th Army. Thousands of civilians worked to build antitank obstacles in that area.[27] On 1 September the *Stavka* merged the two *fronts* into a single Trans-Caucasus Front, with Tiulenev as *front* commander and Cherevichenko, previously head of the Coastal Group of Forces, as commander of a reinforced Black Sea Group. The hapless Budenny received orders to return to Moscow. Two days later, secret police chief Beriia convinced Moscow to relieve Martsenkevich for alleged dereliction of duty as commander of 9th Army, the luckless focus of First Panzer Army's advance. Major General K. A. Koroteev, commander of 11th Guards Rifle Corps, succeeded Martsenkevich.[28]

These actions left the Trans-Caucasus Front's Northern Group of Forces controlling, from west to east, 37th, 9th, and 44th Armies, with 58th Army forming in second echelon. Lieutenant General K. A. Vershinin's 4th Air Army had 176 combat aircraft to support these armies. Opposite the weakened III Panzer Corps, Kozlov's 37th Army defended the Baksan River with one NKVD and four rifle divisions. In the center, opposite LII Corps, which now controlled two infantry divisions plus 13th Panzer, Koroteev's 9th Army occupied the southern bank of the Terek River, covering the route to Groznyi, with four rifle divisions, a naval rifle brigade, and the three brigades of 11th Guards Rifle Corps. On Maslennikov's right, Petrov's 44th Army extended the defensive line eastward with three rifle divisions, four rifle brigades, and 110th Cavalry Division. In depth behind this front, Maslennikov stationed 10th Guards Rifle Corps (with three brigades), two rifle divisions, 52nd Tank Brigade, and two separate tank battalions. This meant that, except in tanks, the defenders now substantially outnumbered the attackers. However, Maslennikov apparently misread the constantly shifting enemy order of battle, deploying only one rifle division, two rifle brigades, and 45 tanks along the Mozdok-Malgobek axis, where the Germans still had one infantry and two panzer divisions.[29]

While List advanced into the eastern Caucasus in the second half of August, Ruoff generally kept pace along the Black Sea coast. The Romanian Cavalry Corps, supported by one German and one Romanian division attacking across the Kerch' Strait from the Crimea, tried to clear Soviet forces from the Taman' Peninsula. Still, the main effort was against Novorossiisk, led along two axes by General of Infantry Wilhelm Wetzel's V Army Corps. The corps' 125th and 198th Infantry Divisions pushed southward from Krasnodar toward the crest of the western Caucasus, while 9th and 73rd Infantry Divisions, with 64 tanks and assault guns attached, swung westward along a railroad line to assault Novorossiisk from the northwest. The 125th Infantry later switched to the west to reinforce this second thrust.[30]

Leaving several naval infantry battalions to contest the Taman' region, 47th Army fell back on Novorossiisk. Meanwhile, 18th, 12th, and 56th Armies conducted a fighting withdrawal into new positions along the crest of the High Caucasus Mountains, seeking to defend the approaches to Tuapse. In the process, however, a 40 kilometer gap appeared between 47th and 56th Armies, leaving the defenders of Novorossiisk isolated. On 18 August, therefore, the *Stavka* designated Major General G. P. Kotov, head of 47th Army, as commander of the Novorossiisk Defensive Region, with Vice Admiral Sergei Georgievich Gorshkov, future chief of the postwar Soviet Navy, as his deputy. As a covering force, Kotov deployed 103rd Rifle Brigade in company- and battalion-sized outposts to delay the German advance, while various Red Army and Navy units defended seven sectors south of that covering force.[31]

Ruoff's new offensive commenced on 19 August. The Romanian Cavalry Corps forced the defending naval infantry of the Azov Military Flotilla to fall back and eventually to evacuate the Taman' Peninsula, withdrawing to Novorossiisk. On 1 September the Romanian cavalry captured the port of Anapa, just as German 46th Infantry and Romanian 3rd Mountain Divisions crossed the Kerch' Strait; these two divisions secured Taman' itself several days later.[32]

The main offensive by V Corps was initially equally successful, pushing aside Soviet naval and infantry covering forces to penetrate the mountain passes and advance within artillery range of the port of Novorossiisk by 23

August. On the twenty-fifth, however, Kotov launched 77th Rifle Division in a counterattack against one regiment of 125th Infantry Division, which had transferred westward to support V Corps' attack. This counterattack recaptured the railroad station near Neberdzhaevskaia, but 77th Rifle Division soon found itself forced back with heavy losses. On 29 August 73rd, 9th, and 125th Infantry Divisions resumed their attack from the northwest and northeast.[33]

Before his relief on 1 September, Budenny had reinforced the Novorossiisk defenses with every unit he could scrape up, including 16th Rifle Brigade; after the change took effect, the new *front* commander, Tiulenev, added 318th Rifle Division, deployed northwest of the city. Although the advancing Germans encircled a number of defending units, it took a solid week of bitter fighting before they even reached the city. Grechko, who replaced Kotov as 47th Army commander during this struggle, ordered the evacuation of the Black Sea Fleet on 9 September, and the next day V Corps announced that it had control of Novorossiisk. However, the defenders continued to hold the industrial districts in the city's southern suburbs. The front line came to a halt there on 11 September and remained frozen until the German withdrawal in late December. The invaders were thus never able to complete their conquest of the area.[34]

The defenders of Novorossiisk forced Ruoff to reinforce V Corps with most of the Romanian units at his disposal, thereby preventing the Germans from shifting additional forces eastward to reinforce their advances on other seaports, let alone to aid in the underresourced advance on the oil fields. The Soviets claimed they cost Ruoff's forces 14,000 casualties, 47 tanks, and 95 guns and mortars during this defense.[35] Such figures were probably optimistic, but the fighting at Novorossiisk further attrited and delayed Army Group A.

As the Romanians and the infantry of V Corps struggled for Novorossiisk and Kleist's panzers maneuvered into Mozdok, General Konrad's XXXXIX Mountain Corps stunned the North Caucasus Front with a sudden thrust into the mountains on 16 August. To attain speed in the attack, the German divisions were preceded by small detachments that moved first by truck and then with pack animals for equipment transport.[36] By 22 August, 1st and 4th Mountain Divisions had captured numerous passes, including the one near Mount Elbrus, almost without a fight.

The defending 46th Army, commanded by Major General V. F. Sergatskov until 27 August and by Lieutenant General K. N. Leselidze thereafter, had neglected to fortify several mountain passes that it considered unusable for military forces. Most of these passes had only company- and battalion-sized defensive units with inadequate reconnaissance. Complicating matters further, Stalin's henchman Lavrenti Beriia, clothed in the authority of a repre-

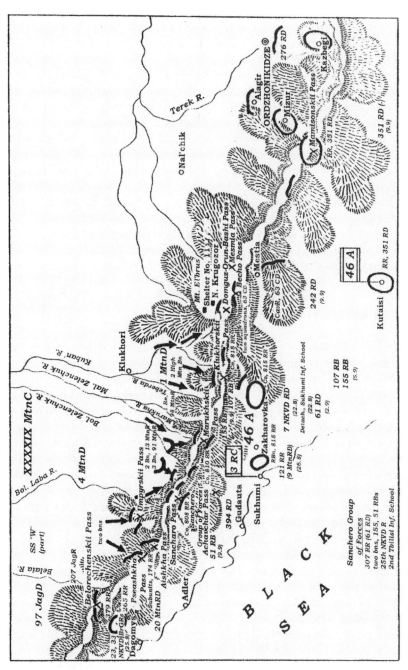

Map 31. Battle for the Caucasus Mountain Passes, 16 August–11 September 1942

sentative of the *Stavka*, had questioned and often reversed the decisions of local commanders. For these and other reasons, 46th Army's headquarters was completely unaware of the German advance until 17 August.[37]

The initial reactions by 46th Army began to slow the German advance in late August, but the confined frontages of the passes meant that all counterattacks had to be frontal. The *front* commander, Tiulenev, traveled to Sukhumi on 19 August and remained there until the twenty-eighth to organize defenses, especially against German 1st Mountain Division in the Klukhori Pass. By the end of the month, 46th Army finally had a coherent defense consisting of infantry with mobile engineer detachments to build obstacles on the southern slopes, but in most cases, it had lost the vital passes. During the first half of September, the defenders matched the German tactics of small mountain detachments and slowly drove the invaders back. The approaching winter snows boded ill for the Germans' continued advance; by mid-September, it was obvious that the invaders would not reach the seacoast here.[38] Once again, belated but effective Soviet responses had thwarted the Germans just short of their goals.

THE NORTHERN FLANK: VORONEZH DÉJÀ VU

While Army Group B struggled to conquer Stalingrad and Army Group A fell a few kilometers short of success in the Caucasus, Army Groups Center and North had their own challenges. As discussed in chapters 3 and 4, during July both sides had planned limited offensives in these areas to straighten their front lines. Tactically, neither side achieved its goals, and the Red Army suffered additional defeats. In the broader operational and strategic context, however, a series of Soviet attacks from late July through August helped strain German troop strength and logistics to the breaking point. These offensives tied down precious German divisions at a time when they were desperately needed at and south of Stalingrad. As such, these operations were important precursors or shaping operations for the ultimate Soviet victory at Stalingrad. Moreover, the existence of these persistent attacks—however unsuccessful—calls into question the traditional view that the Red Army deliberately avoided decisive engagement during the summer of 1942.

If perseverance alone ensured success, the Briansk and Voronezh Fronts would have been the Olympic gold medalists of the German-Soviet conflict. From early July until late September, a series of Red Army counterattacks near Voronezh continued almost without pause. General N. E. Chibisov, deputy commander of the Briansk Front, had already failed in July to break through the northern shoulder of the German *Blau* advance around Voronezh. Undeterred, the *Stavka* merged 4th Reserve Army with remnants of this first effort, forming a resurrected 38th Army under Chibisov. The resulting organization included six rifle divisions, seven rifle brigades, and 1st, 2nd, 7th, and 11th Tank and 8th Cavalry Corps, for a total of more than 400 tanks.[39]

Once again, however, the Soviet leadership was too impatient to permit adequate preparation for a renewed attack, allowing only five days (3–7 August) for Chibisov to form three shock groups, each consisting of a tank corps and a rifle division. As *front* commander, General Rokossovsky persuaded Moscow to delay the attack until 12 August, but even then, logistical shortages and inexperienced commanders produced another failure. German VII Army Corps moved its seven infantry divisions to halt the initial penetrations, *Luftwaffe* support pounded the attackers, and one tank brigade commander blundered into battle without reconnaissance, suffering heavy losses. The best one could say about this effort was that it taught the *Stavka* not to continue attacks that had clearly failed. In late August the staff withdrew Katukov's veteran 1st Tank Corps into central reserve, where it became part of the new 5th Tank Army that finally attacked with deadly effect in November.[40]

The Red Army continued its convulsive efforts to capture Voronezh, if only to prevent the reassignment of German units from that area. In late August the brilliant and audacious young commander of the Voronezh Front, Lieutenant General Nikolai Fedorovich Vatutin, persuaded Stalin to approve a reorganization that concentrated the shock groups under his command around the city. This transferred Chibisov's entire 38th Army to Vatutin's command, giving him control of three armies (38th, 60th, and 40th), as well as 11th, 18th, and 25th Tank Corps. The *front* also controlled six rifle, four destroyer (antitank), and seven tank brigades, in contrast to the six infantry divisions of German XIII and VII Army Corps. However, on 7 September the *Stavka* transferred four rifle divisions from the Voronezh Front to the Stalingrad region, and the remaining divisions averaged only 5,000 to 5,500 men each. Despite a ten-to-one superiority in armor, Vatutin's forces made little progress against prepared German defenses when they renewed their attacks on 15 September. Ignoring the *Stavka*'s advice to cut his losses, Vatutin persisted in attacking for the next two weeks, accomplishing almost nothing.[41]

THE RZHEV SALIENT, 30 JULY–23 AUGUST

Although the focus of the 1942 campaign was in southern Russia, the remainder of the front was by no means static. One particular bone of contention was the vital road and rail network of Rzhev, 200 kilometers north-northwest of Moscow. The Rzhev salient was the anchor between Army Groups North and Center. In July 1942 Army Group Center's Ninth Army defended this

sector with the low-priority VI and XXVII Army Corps; in the absence of the
ailing General of Panzer Troops Walter Model, General of Panzer Troops
Heinrich-Gottfried von Vietinghoff commanded Ninth Army. The city also
marked the boundary between the Kalinin and Western Fronts, commanded
by Colonel General Ivan Stepanvich Konev and Army General Zhukov, respectively. The presence of Zhukov on this sector of the front reflected Stalin's continuing concern for the defense of Moscow.

On 16 July the *Stavka* ordered an attack on the Rzhev salient as yet another means of distracting German resources from the south. The Kalinin
Front's 30th Army, commanded by Lieutenant General D. D. Leliushenko
and supported by Major General V. I. Shevtsov's 29th Army on its left, was to
attack Ninth Army north and northeast of Rzhev on 29 July. Three days later,
Zhukov's 31st Army (Major General V. S. Polenev) and 20th Army (Lieutenant General M. A. Reiter) would join the fight farther east, exploiting
westward with the goal of seizing bridgeheads over the Vazuza River around
Sychevka. To accomplish this, Zhukov's two armies would have the support
of 6th Tank, 8th Tank, and 2nd Guards Cavalry Corps.

Konev's initial attack on 29 July caught the Germans off guard, but it
began to bog down as the defenders recovered from their surprise and Vietinghoff dispatched reserves to the area. Zhukov was unable to launch his
own offensive until 4 August, but again he made progress, advancing up to
25 kilometers in the first two days. Late on the fifth, the *Stavka* gave Zhukov
control over both *fronts* to ensure coordination. On 6 August the mobile
group commanded by deputy *front* commander Major General I. V. Galanin
passed through the attackers to exploit. These 600 tanks, half of which were
KV-1s and T-34s, advanced more than 50 kilometers by day's end through the
remnants of German 161st Infantry Division. Only 5th Panzer Division stood
between the Soviets and the Vazuza River.[42]

Hitler had reacted promptly, sending 1st, 2nd, and 5th Panzer Divisions,
78th and 102nd Infantry Divisions, and XXXIX Panzer Corps headquarters
to Field Marshal Günther von Kluge, commander of Army Group Center.
Kluge intended to launch a powerful counterstroke using Second Panzer and
Fourth Armies to relieve the pressure on Ninth Army. Unfortunately, these
armies were committed piecemeal as they arrived, rather than massing for a
deliberate attack. When Kluge sought to execute the existing offensive plan,
code-named *Wirbelwind*, Colonel General Gotthard Heinrici replied that
his Fourth Army lacked the units to carry it out.[43]

Kluge insisted on launching *Wirbelwind* anyway, although rain delayed it
until 11 August. The southern pincer of the proposed counterstroke, led by
11th and 9th Panzer Divisions of Colonel General Rudolf Schmidt's Second
Panzer Army, soon ran into trouble. Lieutenant General I. Kh. Bagramian,
whose 16th Army protected the southern flank of Zhukov's advance, had es-

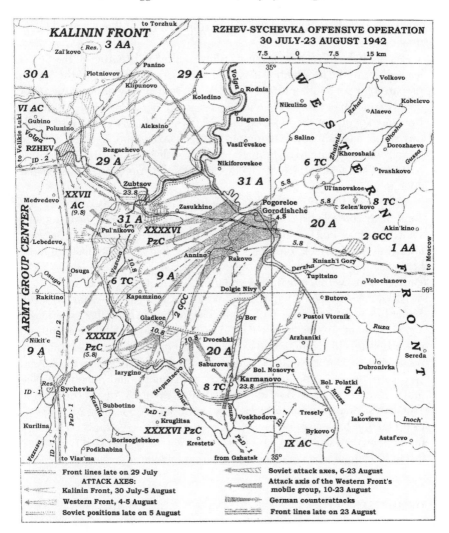

Map 32. Kalinin and Western Fronts' Rzhev-Sychevka Offensive,
30 July–23 August 1942

tablished elaborate fortifications that prevented the Germans from capturing more than a few leading rifle regiments. Hitler reluctantly redirected *Grossdeutschland* Motorized and 72nd Infantry Divisions, the latter en route to Leningrad, to this sector. However, the German defenders had to contain renewed Soviet attacks on the southern flank of the salient. Konev, who had succeeded Zhukov in command of the Western Front, reluctantly brought the battle to a close, although fighting continued around Rzhev until 24 September.[44]

As the Rzhev-Sychevka offensive slowly halted in late August, the Soviet leadership shifted its attention slightly to the south. On 15 August the *Stavka* prepared for yet another attack by the Western Front by designating a new deputy commander for that *front*. Lieutenant General Prokofii Logvinovich Romanenko, one of the most experienced armor officers in the Red Army, was simultaneously commander of 3rd Tank Army and Zhukov's deputy, thereby allowing him to coordinate his army with 16th and 61st Armies in a counterstroke against the eastern flank of Second Panzer Army's *Wirbelwind* operation.

On paper, this counterstroke was a formidable assembly of forces: 3rd Tank Army controlled 12th, 15th, and the attached 3rd Tank Corps, totaling some 610 tanks, and was reinforced by 9th and 10th Tank Corps in Bagramian's 16th Army, which, despite recent battles, had an additional 100 tanks between them. Second Panzer Army controlled XXXV Army and XXXXI Panzer Corps, with a total of four infantry, one motorized, and four panzer divisions that included roughly 200 tanks and assault guns.[45] Again, however, Soviet forces entered battle with inadequate planning, cohesion, experience, and air support. In four frantic days (15–19 August), 3rd Tank Army moved to Kozel'sk by rail and prepared to conduct its first attack since its formation. Advancing on 22 August, the Soviet tankers soon bogged down in the careful German defenses, supplemented by forests, swamps, and minefields. The initial advance achieved only about 5 kilometers. On 23 August the veteran 1st Guards Motorized Rifle Division had more success, pushing 25th Motorized Division back an additional 4 kilometers. Renewed attacks on 23 September accomplished little, however; up to 500 of the 700 Red tanks were lost in Romanenko's counteroffensive, with no significant results.[46]

DEMIANSK

In his spring guidance, Joseph Stalin had directed a number of limited offensives all along the front from the Crimea north to Leningrad. Although these operations failed spectacularly, they set the pattern for the summer's operations. While German Army Groups A and B conducted Operation *Blau* and Army Group Center found itself hard pressed at Rzhev, Army Group North also faced a persistent if vain series of Soviet attacks. Their objective was always the same—to pinch off the salient of German II Corps at Demiansk, south of Lake Il'men', and, in the process, to weaken the German siege of Leningrad.

Lieutenant General Pavel Alekseevich Kurochkin, commander of the

Northwestern Front, attempted this feat twice in attacks beginning on 5 May and 17 August. Each time the attackers had insufficient artillery support to penetrate the careful German defenses and therefore accomplished little beyond inflicting some casualties on the enemy.[47] A German counterattack during the first Soviet attack carved out a narrow corridor connecting the main German forces near Staraia Russa with II Army Corps defending the Demiansk salient. The second Soviet offensive by 11th and 27th Armies failed to capture either the corridor or the salient.

To maintain pressure on Demiansk, the *Stavka* directed Kurochkin to plan a third offensive, using Lieutenant General V. I. Morozov's 11th Army to attack the northern side of the Ramushevo corridor. After an internal review, Moscow added Lieutenant General V. Z. Romanovsky's 1st Shock Army to the operation, directing Romanovsky to attack the corridor from the south. By the time this attack began on 10 August, the Germans had built additional defenses to protect the corridor. In ten days of fighting, 1st Shock Army advanced only a few hundred meters against the German defenses.[48]

Dissatisfied with this failure, the *Stavka* insisted that Kurochkin attack Demiansk yet again, beginning on 15 September. The exhausted units of 1st Shock Army made no progress, although they provoked a series of minor German attacks to widen the corridor. The last of these, Operation *Winkelried*, loosened the Soviet hold significantly, although most of the Soviet defenders escaped encirclement.[49]

FLANK BATTLES: ASSESSMENT

In retrospect, it seems clear that Germany lacked the troop units and logistical support to simultaneously seize both Stalingrad and the Caucasus oil fields. Frequent shifting of air and ground assets to other assignments, including the Crimea, Leningrad, and Western Europe, only exacerbated this disparity. Hitler must bear a large measure of responsibility for this overextension. Yet at the time, many if not most of his subordinates were as optimistic as their Führer. Even Franz Halder, who expressed many doubts in his diary, remarked on 30 July, "The enemy is running for dear life and will be in the northern foothills of the Caucasus a good piece ahead of our armor."[50]

Thus, the German leaders continued to seek not only the economic target of the oil fields but also the operational goal of a decisive battle to destroy the Red Army, something they had tried and failed to achieve since the start of Barbarossa. Under the circumstances, Stalingrad appeared to be an opportunity to force the Soviets to stand and fight, as well as a chance to achieve a propaganda and psychological victory. Even if Germany had been capable of accomplishing victory under these circumstances, however, the battle for

Stalingrad was an improvisation that distracted troops and supplies from the original objective of Operation *Blau*—the Caucasus oil fields. Whether or not the oil fields were ever obtainable in 1942, they certainly could not be taken with 16 to 18 divisions while the rest of the available ground and air forces were concentrated farther north.

One might therefore evaluate the Soviet offensives outside the Stalingrad area by measuring the degree to which they diverted additional German forces from Operation *Blau*. By this standard, the repeated Soviet offensives on the Voronezh shoulder and the Demiansk salient were abject failures, squandering Soviet resources without retaking ground or attracting sufficient Germans to weaken the main effort of Operation *Blau*. Only the Rzhev-Sychevka offensive against Army Group Center succeeded in further extending the invaders. For example, 9th and 11th Panzer Divisions departed Voronezh in late July not to reinforce Sixth Army at Stalingrad but to help Second Panzer Army in the failed Operation *Wirblewind*. Indeed, Zhukov later argued in his memoirs that if he had been allocated one or two additional field armies, the Rzhev-Sychevka offensive might have decisively defeated Army Group Center.[51] He eventually received and employed those armies in November. Moreover, it is worth noting that Rzhev-Sychevka, like the second battle of Khar'kov in May and the various Soviet counteroffensives in July and August, represented additional painful steps in the Soviet process of learning how to employ large armored formations.

Regardless of the degree to which these Soviet flank operations actually tied down German resources, they compounded the psychological strain on Hitler and his commanders. Such pressure, in turn, made it more difficult for staff officers to voice doubts to the Führer, and it encouraged Hitler to be impatient with and distrustful of his most experienced subordinates. He was clearly driven by a sense that time and opportunity were running out, by the feeling that he must achieve his economic and military goals in the East before the Americans and British posed a greater threat in the West. Whether these incremental effects on the Germans were worth the enormous cost in Soviet blood and materiel remains an entirely subjective judgment.

CHAPTER SEVEN

The Initial Battles for Stalingrad, September 1942

THE TARGET

In 1942 Stalingrad was a long, thin strand of factories and apartment houses that snaked for more than 40 kilometers along the western bank of the Volga. Throughout the coming battle, the defenders had to bring every replacement soldier, every round of ammunition, and every loaf of bread across this broad river while exposed to German air and artillery interdiction. The same topography made it impossible for the Germans to encircle the defenders of the city; the attackers eventually had to conduct costly frontal attacks in an effort to break up the urban ribbon into less defensible segments. Much of the Soviet artillery remained on the eastern shore throughout the struggle, firing from that location. Moreover, the high western bank of the river provided the Soviets with a last protective barrier that was eventually honeycombed with caves. The lee of this bank was sheltered from German observation and direct fire, forming a narrow strip of land where the commanders could unload supplies and construct command posts.

By Soviet standards, Stalingrad was a model city, with many modern white apartment buildings and extensive gardens and parks. A series of landmarks, both man-made and natural, dominated the skyline. Inevitably, these landmarks became military objectives, the goals of both attackers and defenders. In the northern half of the city, four huge factories—the Dzerzhinsky tractor works, Barrikady gun factory (called Red Barricade by the Germans), Red October (Krasnyi Ok'tiabr) ironworks, and Lazur chemical factory—were the focus of events. During the early days of the battle, the Dzerzhinsky tractor works continued to produce T-34 tanks that went directly into the battle, but production soon halted. Between these major factories were smaller ones, such as the brick factory just south of the tractor works and the bread factory one block south of Barrikady. Northwest and west of these factories were workers' villages named for their corresponding factories, flanked on the west by the Mechetka River and its associated Vishnevaia *Balka*, a deep ravine suitable for defending the factory district from the west. On higher ground farther to the west were two outlying towns, Orlovka and Gorodishche, as well as the city's airport at Gumrak, some 10 kilometers northwest of the city.

147

Map 33. Stalingrad and Its Environs

South of the factories, closer to the center of the city, stood the Mamaev Kurgan, an ancient Tartar burial mound. Both sides coveted this 102 meter hill as an observation post. On the northern and southern flanks of Mamaev Kurgan were three deep *balkas*—the Bannyi to the north and the Krutoi and Dolgii to the south—forming formidable barriers to north-south movement while protecting their defenders from observation and artillery fire. West of these three ravines were a smaller airfield, its associated flying school, and a hospital on the heights south of Razgulaevka Station, part of the main railroad line into the city. Farther south stood the main railroad station (Station No. 1), a frequent bone of contention because it lay just west of the city's 9 January Square and near the principal ferry landing to cross the river.

The southern end of the city was separated from the center by the Tsaritsa River. This deep gorge divided the city and provided a natural axis for east-west movement, terminating at the Volga. This part of the city contained Railroad Station No. 2 and a huge grain elevator or silo. Between the elevator and the railroad line was a large collection of factory buildings and warehouses belonging to the city's food combine.

As 62nd and 64th Armies struggled to defend the approaches to the city, Eremenko and Stalingrad's civilian Defense Committee worked to shore up defenses. On 23 August, for example, the Defense Committee ordered all major factories to form workers' battalions to protect their enterprises and maintain order. The able-bodied population was mobilized to construct barricades and other obstacles. At this stage, however, Stalingrad was packed with refugees from the Great Bend of the Don River, in addition to the normal population of factory workers, children, and other noncombatants. By the time local authorities finally organized an evacuation, it was too late, and much of the population was trapped in the city during the ensuing battle.[1]

The internal defense of the inner city fell to the paramilitary 10th NKVD Division, commanded by Colonel A. A. Saraev. Although Saraev was under Eremenko's orders, the traditional rivalry between the NKVD and the Red Army created friction in organizing the city.

The terrain favored three approaches to conquer Stalingrad (see map 25). The first ran southward along the western bank of the Volga River from Rynok, where 16th Panzer Division had arrived on 23 August; through Spartanovka; across the Mokraia Mechetka River; and into the northern factory district. The second approach extended southeastward along the road and railroad line from Konnaia Station through Gorodishche and Gumrak Station and then west of Mamaev Kurgan in the center of the city, terminating at Station No. 1 and 9 January Square. The third approach began in the southwest, extended along the railroad and roads north of the El'shanka River, and terminated at Station No. 2. The first two approaches were the areas of operations of Sixth Army's XIV Panzer and LI Army Corps, while Fourth Panzer Army's XXXXVIII Panzer Corps entered the city along the third axis.

OPPOSING FORCES

The composition and strength of the two antagonists changed almost daily during the five months they struggled for control of Stalingrad. When the battle began on 3 September, the strength of Army Group B was roughly 980,000 troops, including 580,000 Germans and 400,000 Axis allies. During

August, as described previously, Army Group A had steadily lost forces to Army Group B, leaving approximately 300,000 German and Axis forces to advance into the Caucasus.

Along the extended left flank of Army Group B, stretching from Voronezh south to the Stalingrad area, were (in order) German Second Army (180,000 men), Hungarian Second Army (120,000 men, including two German infantry divisions), and Italian Eighth Army (another120,000 men, including two German infantry divisions). South of the Italians, along the Stalingrad axis itself, Army Group B had Sixth Army (roughly 200,000 men) and Fourth Panzer Army (150,000 men). Of these forces, about 30,000 combat troops of LI Army Corps (389th, 295th, and 71st Infantry Divisions) and perhaps 50,000 men in Fourth Panzer Army's XXXXVIII Panzer and IV Army Corps (24th and 14th Panzer, 29th Motorized, 94th Infantry, and Romanian 20th Infantry Divisions) conducted the initial assault on the city. The 100th *Jäger* and 305th Infantry Divisions later reinforced or replaced some of these assault units, joined in November by two regiments of 79th Infantry Division (see table 7.1).

The remainder of Sixth Army, including up to two-thirds of its strength, occupied defenses north of the city or farther west along the Don River. XVII and XI Army Corps, with approximately 35,000 and 45,000 men, respectively, faced the Soviet 21st Army and 4th Tank Army along the Don River from the Serafimovich bridgehead eastward to Kachalinskaia. Farther south, VIII Army and XIV Panzer Corps, each with approximately 32,000 men, faced the Soviet 24th, 1st Guards, and 66th Armies between the Don and Volga Rivers. During and after the Soviet Kotluban' counterstroke in September (see below), XIV Panzer Corps used the majority of its forces to defend outside the city, leaving only one-third of its troops facing south toward the city proper. Thus, although popular accounts link German Sixth Army with the name of Stalingrad, more than half its forces were involved in equally important but almost forgotten fighting north and northwest of the city.

Opposite the two German field armies, the Stalingrad and Southeastern Fronts defended the contested area with a force of 550,000 men, of which roughly 470,000 were assigned to the eight combat armies (see table 7.2). The two key formations within the city were 62nd and 64th Armies. The actual strengths of these two armies ebbed and flowed repeatedly during the prolonged struggle; during the course of the battle, the Germans actually drove the bulk of 64th Army's 50,000 men from the city, confining them to the Beketovka bridgehead south of Stalingrad.

Despite the critical psychological importance of the fight for the city, Stalin and his generals apparently gave 62nd and 64th Armies just enough men and materiel to continue the struggle. They funneled most of their resources to new formations outside the city, where they prepared a series of counteroffensives.

Table 7.1. Forces of Army Group B in the Stalingrad Area,
3 September 1942 (North to South)

Army Group B—Colonel General Maximilian von Weichs an dem Glon
Sixth Army—General of Panzer Troops Friedrich Paulus
    XVII Army Corps—General of Infantry Karl Hollidt
        79th Infantry Division—Lieutenant General Richard von Schwerin
        113th Infantry Division—Lieutenant General Hans-Heinrich Sixt von Arnim
        22nd Panzer Division—Lieutenant General Wilhelm von Apell
    XI Army Corps—General of Infantry Karl Strecker
        376th Infantry Division—Lieutenant General Alexander Edler von Daniels
        100th *Jäger* Division—Lieutenant General Werner Sanne
        44th Infantry Division—Lieutenant General Heinrich Deboi
        384th Infantry Division (transferred from VIII Army Corps in early
          September)
    VIII Army Corps—Lieutenant General Walter Heitz
        384th Infantry Division (transferred to XI Corps in early September)—
          Lieutenant General Eccard *Freiherr* von Gablenz
        305th Infantry Division—Lieutenant General Kurt Oppenländer
        76th Infantry Division (transferred from LI Corps in early September)—
          Lieutenant General Carl Rodenburg
    XIV Panzer Corps—General of Infantry Gustav von Wietersheim
        60th Motorized Division—Major General Otto Kohlermann
        3rd Motorized Division—Lieutenant General Helmuth Schlömer
        16th Panzer Division—Lieutenant General Hans-Valentin Hube
    LI Army Corps—General of Artillery Walter von Seydlitz-Kurzbach
        76th Infantry Division (transferred to VIII Corps in early September)
        389th Infantry Division—Lieutenant General Erwin Jänecke
        295th Infantry Division—General of Artillery Rolf Wuthmann
        71st Infantry Division—General of Infantry Alexander von Hartmann
Fourth Panzer Army—Colonel General Hermann Hoth
    XXXXVIII Panzer Corps—General of Panzer Troops Werner Kempf
        24th Panzer Division—Major General Bruno *Ritter* von Hauenschild
        Romanian 20th Infantry Division—General of Division Nicolae Tătăranu
        14th Panzer Division—Lieutenant General Ferdinand Heim
        29th Motorized Division—Lieutenant General Max Fremerey
    IV Army Corps—General of Infantry Viktor von Schwedler
        94th Infantry Division—General of Artillery Georg Pfeiffer
        297th Infantry Division—General of Artillery Max Pfeffer
        371st Infantry Division—Lieutenant General Richard Stempel
    Romanian VI Army Corps (later subordinated to Romanian Fourth Army)—
        Lieutenant General Corneliu Draglina
        Romanian 2nd, 1st, and 4th Infantry Divisions
Army Group B control
    Italian Eighth Army—Colonel General Italo Gariboldi
        Italian II, XXXV, and XXIX Corps headquarters
        Two German infantry divisions plus ten Italian formations: six infantry
          divisions,
    2nd Alpine Division *Tridentina*, 3rd Mobile Division *Celere*, two cavalry brigades
    Romanian divisions: one armored, two cavalry, two infantry
    16th German Motorized Division (screening the southern flank)—General of
        Panzer Troops Sigfrid Henrici
    298th German Infantry Division (Army Group Reserve)—Lieutenant General
        Arnold Szelinski

Table 7.2. Soviet Forces in the Stalingrad Area, 3 September 1942 (North to South)

Stalingrad Front—Colonel General A. I. Eremenko
  63rd Army—Lieutenant General V. I. Kuznetsov
    14th Guards, 1st, 127th, 153rd, 187th, and 203rd Rifle Divisions
  21st Army—Major General A. I. Danilov
    4th and 40th Guards, 23rd, 63rd, 76th, 96th, 124th, 278th, 304th, 321st, and
      343rd Rifle Divisions
    5th Separate Destroyer Brigade, three separate tank battalions
  4th Tank Army—Major General V. D. Kriuchenkin
    27th and 37th Guards, 18th, 214th, and 298th Rifle Divisions
    193rd Tank Brigade, 22nd Motorized Rifle Brigade, one armored train
      battalion
  24th Army—Major General D. T. Kozlov
    173rd, 207th, 221st, 292nd, and 308th Rifle Divisions
    217th Tank Brigade
  1st Guards Army—Major General of Artillery K. S. Moskalenko
    38th, 39th, and 41st Guards, 24th, 64th, 84th, 116th, and 315th Rifle
      Divisions
    4th, 7th, and 16th Tank Corps
  66th Army—Lieutenant General R. Ia. Malinovsky
    49th, 99th, 120th, 231st, 299th, and 316th Rifle Divisions
    10th, 69th, 148th, and 246th Tank Brigades
  8th Air Army— Major General of Aviation T. T. Kriukin
    206th, 226th, and 228th Assault Aviation Divisions
    220th, 268th, 269th, 287th, and 288th Fighter Aviation Divisions
    270th, 271st, and 272nd Fighter-Bomber Aviation Divisions
    23rd, 282nd, 633rd, and 655th Mixed Aviation Regiments
    8th Reconnaissance, 714th Light Bomber, and 678th Transport Aviation
      Regiments
  Front-controlled forces
    3rd Guards Cavalry Corps (three divisions)
    147th and 184th Rifle Divisions
    13th and 22nd Separate Destroyer Brigades
    54th Fortified Region
    22nd and 28th Tank Corps
    176th Tank Brigade, one separate tank battalion, two armored train battalions
Southeastern Front—Colonel General A. I. Eremenko
  62nd Army—Lieutenant General A. I. Lopatin (Lieutenant General V. I.
    Chuikov on 12 September)
    33rd and 35th Guards, 87th, 98th, 196th, 229th, 309th, and 10th NKVD Rifle
      Divisions; 115th Fortified Region
    115th, 124th, and 149th Rifle and 20th Destroyer Brigades
    2nd and 23rd Tank Corps
    20th and 38th Separate Motorized Rifle Brigades
    169th Tank Brigade
  64th Army—Lieutenant General M. S. Shumilov
    36th Guards, 29th, 38th, 126th, 138th, 157th, 204th, and 208th Rifle
      Divisions
    66th and 154th Naval Infantry Brigades, 10th Reserve (160th Separate) Rifle
      Brigade, six student rifle regiments from military schools, 118th Fortified
      Region
    13th Tank Corps
    One armored train battalion
  57th Army—Major General F. I. Tolbukhin
    15th Guards, 244th, and 422nd Rifle Divisions; 76th Fortified Region

Table 7.2. (*continued*)

6th Tank Brigade
51st Army—Major General T. K. Kolomiets
    91st and 302nd Rifle Divisions
    115th Cavalry Division and 255th Separate Cavalry Regiment
    One separate tank battalion, one armored train battalion
Front-controlled forces
    77th, 78th, and 116th Fortified Regions and 132nd Destroyer Detachment
    40th, 134th, 135th, 137th, and 255th Tank Brigades
    One separate tank battalion, one armored train battalion

In terms of armor, on 3 September Fourth Panzer and Sixth Armies contained between 250 and 300 tanks, supplemented by a total of 30 to 40 assault guns in 177th, 244th, and 245th Assault Gun Battalions.[2] By contrast, the two Soviet *fronts* began the battle with perhaps 550 to 650 functioning tanks, of which 146 supported 62nd and 64th Armies in Stalingrad proper.[3]

On paper, the Stalingrad and Southeastern Fronts together outnumbered Sixth and Fourth Panzer Armies in terms of personnel and armor, although actual strengths on any given day varied because of the logistical challenges faced by each side. From the beginning, the Germans operated with inadequate resupply over an extended rail network, while the Soviets had to bring their supplies and men across the Volga River. For example, *Luftflotte* 4 began September with 950 aircraft, but perhaps only 550 were operational on any given day. Even this reduced availability gave the Germans the edge over the Soviets' 226 assigned aircraft.[4]

ZHUKOV'S KOTLUBAN' OFFENSIVE, 3–12 SEPTEMBER

The struggle for Stalingrad took two forms during the first half of September. First, Sixth and Fourth Panzer Armies assaulted 62nd and 64th Armies in the suburbs of the city on 3 September, seeking to penetrate to the center. On the following day, the Stalingrad Front launched yet another offensive at Kotluban', attempting to pierce the narrow corridor connecting the Don River to the forward elements of Sixth Army in order to reestablish land contact with 62nd Army.

On 26 August Stalin had given Zhukov the unprecedented position of deputy supreme commander and dispatched him to supervise the defense of Stalingrad. He also ordered the creation of two new armies under the control of the Stalingrad Front—24th and 66th—to attack Sixth Army's northern flank.[5] The dictator then directed the relocation of Moskalenko's 1st Guards Army headquarters from the Kletskaia bridgehead northeastward to the village of Sadki, where it would participate in the renewed effort against the

Germans at Kotluban'. Moskalenko had only three days (30 August–1 September) to make the shift, which involved four divisions going into the attack after marches of up to 50 kilometers. More significantly, although his army had a total of 309 tanks, its motorized rifle brigades were short of infantrymen, while its artillery was understrength and equipped with ineffective weapons, such as 45mm antitank guns.[6] Despite the efforts of all concerned, the attackers and their supplies were not in position in time for the planned attack on 2 September, so Stalin reluctantly acceded to Zhukov's request for a one-day delay.[7]

While the Soviets prepared, Paulus directed that the relatively strong 305th Infantry Division swap defensive positions with the weakened 384th opposite the expected attack. This left VIII Corps' 305th and 79th Infantry Divisions and XIV Panzer Corps' three mobile divisions to defend the northern face of the corridor against attacks by the Stalingrad Front's 4th Tank, 24th, 1st Guards, and 60th Armies. The divisions of XIV Panzer Corps were all in hedgehog positions, with some of their subordinate *kampfgruppen* facing south in preparation for the attack on Stalingrad.[8]

On 2 September the left wing of Kriuchenkin's 4th Tank Army attacked 384th and 79th Infantry Divisions in an attempt to divert the Germans from Moskalenko's main effort. Instead, German counterattacks neutralized the preliminary attack, defeating its intent. Nevertheless, 1st Guards Army began its offensive at 0530 on 3 September with a weak 30-minute artillery preparation (see map 34). Moskalenko focused the main effort on his western flank, with 24th and 116th Rifle Divisions supported by the tanks of 16th and 7th Tank Corps, respectively. This blow fell on 3rd Motorized Division's 8th Grenadier Regiment and 9th Machine Gun Battalion, reinforced by *Luftwaffe* 88mm guns firing over open sights. Attacking over flat, treeless terrain crisscrossed with numerous *balkas* and smaller gullies, Moskalenko's soldiers suffered significant casualties but managed to advance half the distance across the 8 kilometer wide corridor separating them from 62nd Army.[9]

This advance attracted considerable German air support, as well as much of XIV Panzer Corps' infantry, away from the advance on Stalingrad. Nonetheless, late on 3 September Eremenko convinced Stalin that the city's fall was imminent, and the dictator telegrammed Zhukov that he must "demand the commanders of the forces standing north and northwest of Stalingrad attack the enemy immediately and go to the assistance of the Stalingraders. . . . No sort of delay is permissible."[10]

Despite a devastating 90-minute German counterpreparation, Moskalenko's troops resumed their attack at 0830 on 4 September but achieved little in the face of the enemy's air and artillery superiority. Danilov's 21st Army also launched a diversionary attack against the German 79th Infantry Division, seeking to tie down forces farther to the west. Malinovsky's inexperienced

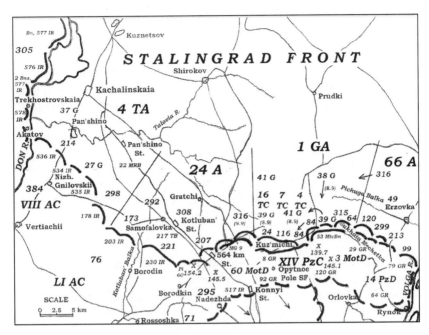

Map 34. Stalingrad Front's Kotluban' Offensive, 3–12 September 1942

66th Army was not prepared to attack until 0900 on 5 September, leaving Moskalenko, who had already lost half his tanks, to make a third unsupported effort earlier that morning. At 1500 hours, 4th Tank and 24th Armies assaulted 305th and 76th Infantry Divisions, with predictably dismal results, recoiling under withering German fire.

Zhukov's entire offensive had stalled, but driven by Stalin's entreaties, the four weakened armies continued to make convulsive efforts almost daily through 13 September. These costly frontal assaults did weaken the Germans' efforts to attack the city; by the afternoon of the sixth, General Wietersheim reported to Paulus that XIV Panzer Corps was "strained to the limit" and required more infantry and air support, "even if it meant putting off the attack into Stalingrad indefinitely."[11]

Summoned to Moscow on 12 September, Zhukov, supported by Chief of Staff Vasilevsky, finally convinced Stalin that the Kotluban' forces could advance no farther and needed a month to rebuild. Although the Russians have yet to release figures for this operation, at least one-third of the 250,000 soldiers involved were casualties, as well as up to 300 of the 400 tanks in these four armies. Throughout the battle, a steady stream of replacement troops and tanks had maintained the paper strength of the units involved, but this did not make up for the haste of the initial operation. As Rokossovsky wrote later:

> The grouping on the left wing of the Stalingrad Front was not suited to the existing conditions and did not have a clearly expressed main attack axis. . . . The armies attacked in sectors 12 kilometers wide, in dispersed combat formations. . . . The formations of the armies did not have time to orient themselves on the open terrain to the required degree and to organize cooperation and command and control. They were not able to determine the enemy's grouping and his defensive system before the start of the offensive . . . the enemy's air forces, operating in groups of 20–40 aircraft, bombed the combat formations of our infantry and tanks continuously.[12]

The Kotluban' offensive is a case study in the Soviets' recurring difficulties in 1942. Despite courage, superiority in numbers and equipment, and a growing tactical skill, the Red Army's counterattacks repeatedly failed because of hasty preparation by harried commanders and staffs. Yet, even with such weaknesses, the reality on the ground belied the legend of the invaders advancing almost unopposed into Stalingrad.

THE GERMAN ASSAULT ON STALINGRAD'S SUBURBS, 3–9 SEPTEMBER

On 1 September Eremenko, the commander of both *fronts* in the Stalingrad area, gave 62nd and 64th Armies detailed instructions to withdraw to a curved defensive line running from Rynok in the north via Gumrak Airfield, Alekseevka, and Elkhi to the Chervlennaia River near Ivanovka and thence back to the Volga River south of Krasnoarmeisk (see map 35).[13] This movement was complicated because portions of General Lopatin's 62nd Army had to move south of the Tsaritsa River, which had previously been the boundary between the two armies.

The northern face of 62nd Army's new positions, opposite XIV Panzer Corps, was relatively well anchored. By contrast, farther south, Lopatin's other units, beginning with 196th Rifle Division, were seriously depleted before the battle even began (see table 7.3). Although Lopatin had directed 87th Rifle and 35th Guards Rifle Divisions to counterattack westward, there was no guarantee that they would arrive in time to shore up his defenses. Recognizing this weakness, on the evening of 3 September Eremenko decided to reinforce Lopatin with Colonel M. S. Batrakov's 42nd Rifle Brigade, which was about to cross the Volga that night, as well as Major General

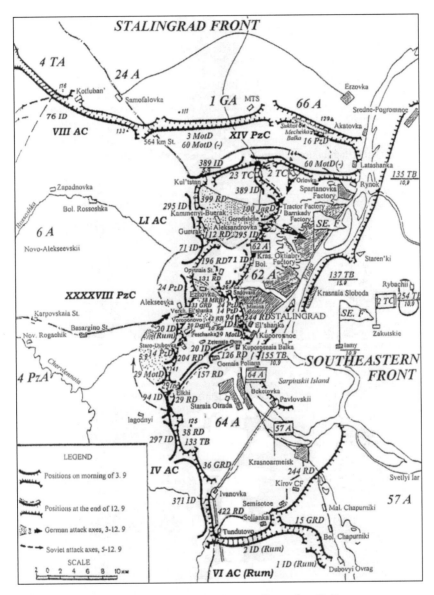

Map 35. Operations along the Stalingrad Axis, 3–12 September 1942

Table 7.3. Composition and Disposition of 62nd Army,
3 September 1942 (North to South)

Lieutenant General A. I. Lopatin, commanding
- Operational Group Gorokhov (Colonel S. F. Gorokov): 124th and 149th Rifle Brigades, 282nd NKVD Rifle Regiment, motorized infantry detachment, and 227th Separate Machine Gun–Artillery Battalion of 115th Fortified Region— Defense of Rynok, Spartakovka, and tractor factory village against German northern axis
- 2nd Tank Corps (Major General A. G. Kravchenko): 26th, 99th [31 tanks], and 27th [31 tanks] Tank Brigades; 2nd Motorized Rifle Brigade; 98th Rifle Division; 724th Rifle Regiment; and 115th Rifle Brigade— Defense of prepared positions near Gumrak airfield and Orlovka
- 23rd Tank Corps (Major General A. F. Popov): 189th, 169th, and 39th Tank Brigades; 20th Motorized Rifle Brigade; and 399th Rifle Division—Initial defense on the northwestern shoulder of 62nd Army, opposite 389th Infantry Division
- 112th Rifle Division (Colonel I. E. Ermolkin): with 157th and 158th Separate Machine Gun–Artillery Battalions of 115th Fortified Region—Defense west of Aleksandrovka
- 196th Rifle Division (Colonel V. P. Ivanov): with 50th Separate Machine Gun– Artillery Battalion of 115th Fortified Region, four guns of 398th Tank Destroyer Regiment, and 236th Rifle Regiment—Defense of Opytnaia Station and Erzhovka line
- 33rd Guards Rifle Division (Colonel A. I. Utvenko): with 52nd Separate Machine Gun–Artillery Battalion of 115th Fortified Region and 651st Tank Destroyer Regiment—Defense of Erzhovka and the Kruten'kii suburb
- 20th Motorized Rifle Brigade (commander unknown): with 160th, 174th, and 175th Separate Machine Gun–Artillery Battalions of 115th Fortified Region— Defense of Alekseevka, Kuporosnoe, and Talovoi
- Shock groups
  - 87th Rifle Division (Colonel A. I. Kazartsev): with 139th Separate Machine Gun–Artillery Battalion of 115th Fortified Region—Occupy the area from Aleksandrovka to Opytnaia Station and be prepared to counterattack toward Gorodishche or Talovoi
  - 35th Guards Rifle Division (Major General V. A. Glazkov, Colonel V. P. Dubiansky on 8 September): with two batteries of 651st Tank Destroyer Regiment—Occupy the area from Opytnaia Station southward and be prepared to counterattack toward Krasnyi Oktiabr', Gorodishche, and Verkhniaia El'shanka
  - 131st Rifle Division (Colonel M. A. Pesochin)—Occupy three positions in the Verkhniaia El'shanka defensive area and be prepared to counterattack toward Peschanka and Zelenaia Poliana
  - 169th Tank Brigade (Colonel A. P. Kodonets)—Concentrate in the Minima suburb and be prepared to counterattack in various directions
- Artillery Group (General of Artillery N. M. Pozharsky): Five subordinate units initially containing only 9 guns and 18 M-8 *katiusha* rocket launchers

Source: "Boevoi prikaz no. 114. Shtarm 62 2.9.42. 10.30" [Combat order no. 114, headquarters, 62nd Army, 1030 hours, 2 September 1942], in *62nd Army Combat Journal.*
Note: Known tank strengths are listed in brackets.

G. A. Afanas'ev's 244th Rifle Division and supporting 20th Destroyer Brigade, which the *front* had transferred from 64th Army. Lopatin, in turn, directed 42nd Brigade, composed primarily of soldiers from the White Sea Military Flotilla, to reinforce the defenses at the army's northwestern shoulder. When 244th Rifle Division reached Stalingrad before dawn on 3 September, Lopatin directed it to the same vulnerable area. Within hours, however, German LI Corps had thoroughly disrupted all of Lopatin's plans.

As the commander of Army Group B, General von Weichs planned to take the city in a pincer, with Wietersheim's XIV Panzer Corps of Sixth Army, supported by LI Army Corps, pushing in from the north, while Kempf's XXXXVIII Panzer Corps of Fourth Panzer Army attacked from the south. Simultaneously, VIII Air Corps, reinforced by most of IV Air Corps' aircraft transferred from the Caucasus, would begin round-the-clock air raids on the city itself.

In the south, 24th Panzer Division attacked at dawn on 3 September and pushed 62nd Army's left-wing units—35th Guards Rifle Division and 20th Motorized Rifle Brigade—back to Voroponovo, but the reinforcing 131st Rifle Division held on there. Farther south, 64th Army repelled initial attacks by the two other mobile divisions of XXXXVIII Panzer Corps, 14th Panzer and 29th Motorized.[14]

On the northern shoulder, General von Seydlitz's LI Corps made much more significant progress. Rolf Wuthmann's 295th Infantry Division smashed the defenses of 399th Rifle Division and one brigade of 23rd Tank Corps west of Konnaia (Konnyi to the Germans) Station, while Alexander Hartmann's 71st Infantry Division inflicted heavy casualties on 196th Rifle Division and captured Talovoi, Opytnaia Station, and Ezhovka. Counterattacks halted the 71st's advance in the afternoon, but by that time, it had driven a deep wedge south of Gumrak Station. The 87th and 196th Rifle Divisions, already understrength, literally disappeared from the Soviet order of battle within days.

In contrast to LI Corps' success, XIV Panzer Corps initially could not advance against Group Gorokhov at the northern end of Stalingrad. The ongoing Kotluban' offensive distracted the majority of Wietersheim's combat power, and the remaining small *kampfgruppen* had little effect. The result, in combination with Seydlitz's nearby success, was to fashion a Soviet salient west of the northern suburbs of the city. This salient soon separated the forces of XIV Panzer and LI Army Corps and stymied Weichs's operational plan for a double pincer advance into the city. On 4 September Kravchenko's 2nd Tank Corps surprised the Germans by counterattacking 60th Motorized Division, although this effort failed to break through the German corridor.[15]

That same day, however, Seydlitz's infantry continued to make progress south of the salient. General Erwin Jänecke's 389th Infantry Division completed its movement from VIII Corps to the left flank of LI Corps, permitting Wuthmann's 295th Division to shift slightly southward and clear the remnants of 112th Rifle Division from the vicinity of Gumrak Airfield and Station. Hartmann's 71st Infantry Division pushed the weakened rifle units completely away from Gumrak; 112th and 87th Rifle Divisions withdrew northeastward toward Gorodishche, while the remnants of 196th Rifle and 33rd Guards Rifle Divisions retreated southeastward toward Opytnaia Station and the wooded northern slopes of the Tsaritsa River. Lopatin began to organize a counterattack by 244th Rifle Division to contain 71st Infantry's advance.[16]

On the southern flank, 24th Panzer Division again led the advance on 4 September, capturing Voroponovo from 35th Guards Rifle Division even though the Stukas mistakenly inflicted casualties among their own troops. Strong resistance by 64th Army's 126th and 204th Rifle Divisions stalled an advance by 14th Panzer Division short of Peschanka. Farther south, the remaining divisions of XXXXVIII Panzer Corps—29th Motorized, 94th Infantry, and Romanian 20th—forced 157th and 29th Rifle Divisions and 154th Naval Rifle Brigade to abandon Elkhi.[17] During the night of 4–5 September, however, Soviet bombers, mortars, and rocket launchers almost smothered Kempf's panzer corps; its renewed attack on the morning of the fifth gained minimal territory while incurring significant casualties. By nightfall, 24th Panzer Division reported only 34 functioning tanks.[18]

Anticipating a possible loss of the city to the German breakthrough, Lopatin deployed five tank brigades (135th, 137th, 155th, 254th, and 169th), all of them tankless after previous battles, to defensive positions on the eastern bank of the Volga, where they awaited new equipment. Shumilov's 64th Army made similar preparations while shoring up his defenses from Peschanka south to Elkhi and assembling 160th Separate Rifle Brigade as a counterattack force behind its northern wing.[19]

The heavy fighting at Kotluban' limited German efforts against the city on 6 September, but the next day, once the situation had stabilized, Paulus again launched Seydlitz's LI Corps on what he hoped would be the final assault of the city. Advancing abreast with both assault gun and Stuka support, 389th and 295th Infantry Divisions ground their way eastward across the steppe toward the bluffs overlooking the city, while 71st Infantry drove eastward along the high ground north of the Tsaritsa River Valley. By this time, the defenders were too depleted to offer significant resistance and yielded Gorodishche and Aleksandrovka to the attackers. The 399th, 112th, and 87th Rifle Divisions had only 675 infantrymen among them, and Kravchenko's 2nd Tank Corps was so weak that by 11 September Eremenko had reassigned its headquarters to the eastern bank, where it took control of the reconstituting tank brigades there.[20]

Still preoccupied by the Kotluban' offensive, XIV Panzer Corps could do little to support the advance into the city. Concerned by the Soviet threat on his left center, Paulus temporized, ordering LI Corps to turn northeastward on 9 September and eliminate the Orlovka salient. Meanwhile, the battle raged along most of the front throughout the eighth. On Fourth Panzer Army's front, General Afanas'ev's 244th Rifle Division contained a furious attack by 24th Panzer Division, temporarily commanded by Colonel Fritz Brioch after General Bruno Hauenschild was wounded. However, this defense led to the complete destruction of two rifle battalions and prompted a distraught Lopatin to send 10th Rifle Brigade, transferred to him from 64th Army, to shore up the 244th's defenses at Sadovaia Station and Minina.[21] Still farther south, 29th Motorized Division, reinforced by a *kampfgruppe* from 14th Panzer, pressed 64th Army's left wing back to new defenses southeast of Peschanka; 126th Rifle Division was so weakened that Shumilov withdrew it to a second-echelon position.[22] Overall, the heavy fighting between 5 and 9 September halved the distance between the German front line and the Volga River while threatening to split 62nd and 64th Armies.

CHUIKOV TAKES COMMAND

The Germans were undoubtedly worried by the high cost of advancing through the suburbs,[23] but for the defenders, the situation was catastrophic. Lopatin had become so despondent that on 7 September his *front* commander, Eremenko, recommended his relief. Stalin agreed almost immediately but then took another 35 hours to designate his replacement: Vasilii Chuikov, then deputy commander of 64th Army.[24] Stalin accepted Eremenko's recommendation only after the *front* commander personally vouched for Chuikov. The reasons for this choice may never be known, but certainly Chuikov's behavior in rallying the troops in the Don bend suggested that he was the type of dogged defender the situation demanded.

The fighting in 64th Army was so desperate that Chuikov did not report to Eremenko and his commissar, Nikita Khrushchev, until 1000 hours on 12 September. When Khrushchev asked the new commander how he interpreted his new mission, the response (at least in Chuikov's recollection) was melodramatic and almost fatalistic: "'We cannot surrender the city to the enemy,' I replied, 'because it is extremely valuable to the whole Soviet people . . . I don't ask for anything now, but I would ask the [Southwestern Front's] Military Council not to refuse me help when I ask for it, and I swear I shall stand firm. We will defend the city or die in the attempt.'"[25]

That evening, after darkness had halted the German air attacks, Chuikov and his aides crossed the Volga River by ferry. In a truck with covered headlights, he drove through a dead city, a maze of burned-out ruins where civilians dug through the rubble searching for lost possessions. His way was lit by the fires started by German bombers. Eventually, Chuikov arrived at his new headquarters on the slope of Mamaev Kurgan, a primitive earthen dugout rocked by near misses from enemy artillery. He later described the scene:

> I find myself in the dugout of the Army Chief of Staff, General N. I. Krylov, who has been Acting Commander. He is a thick-set, stocky man with a determined face. . . .
>
> There were two people in the dugout—General Krylov, with a telephone in his hand, and the telephonist [switchboard operator] on duty, Elena Bakarevich, a blue-eyed girl of about eighteen. Krylov is having strong words with someone or other. His voice is hard, loud, angry. The telephonist is sitting near the entrance with headphones on, answering someone, "He is speaking on the other telephone. . . ."
>
> I take out my papers and put them in front of Krylov. Continuing to tell somebody off, he glances at the papers, then finishes the conversation, and we introduce ourselves. In the poor light of a paraffin lamp, I see a vigorous, stern, and at the same time friendly face. . . . The telephone rings continually. Elena Bakarevich hands the telephone to Krylov. He is giving instructions for the following day . . . I realize that he has no time to give me a report on the situation.[26]

As a veteran of Odessa and Sevastopol', Krylov had extensive experience in organizing a desperate defense. Chuikov and Krylov formed two-thirds of the Military Council, the troika that alternately cajoled and threatened 62nd Army's commanders to hang on to Stalingrad despite enormous German efforts and unimaginable human hardships. Krylov was intellectual and precise; Chuikov, though equally analytical, gave the appearance of being more down-to-earth, alternating between joviality and ruthlessness. The third member of the command team was Kuz'ma Akimovich Gurov, by rank a divisional commissar and later a lieutenant general.[27] At this stage of the war, commissars were still more hatchet men than cheerleaders, motivating by fear more than by patriotic fervor. Even Gurov's bald head and contrasting dark, thick eyebrows conveyed a sense of menace. Together, Chuikov and Gurov used encouragement, embarrassment, fear, and ruthless punishment to motivate any whose faith wavered. NKVD guards at the ferry landings closely questioned anyone who sought to leave the city.[28]

The army that Chuikov inherited had, on paper, 12 divisions and 7 separate brigades. In reality, however, only 10th NKVD Division (8,615 soldiers) and a few recently arrived formations such as 42nd Rifle Brigade (5,032 soldiers) were anywhere near their authorized strength. On 11 September the entire 62nd Army consisted of roughly 54,000 soldiers; of these, the combat units contained 48,360 men and 115 tanks.[29] Even these figures exaggerate the rifle strength of the army, because a significant number of these soldiers were assigned to essential support and maintenance positions.

THE FALL OF STALINGRAD'S SUBURBS, 10–12 SEPTEMBER

On 10 September XXXXVIII Panzer Corps' 29th Motorized Division pierced the junction of 62nd and 64th Armies along the railway line; despite bitter house-to-house resistance by 35th Guards Rifle Division and 20th Tank Destroyer Brigade, one battalion of 29th Motorized broke through to the Volga River on a narrow front near Kuporosnoe.[30] Overnight on 10–11 September, however, furious attacks by 131st Rifle and 35th Guards Rifle Divisions eliminated this foothold on the river. Still, the OKW triumphantly announced the penetration, suggesting that the city's fall was imminent.[31]

Of equal importance to the defenders, at dawn on the tenth Weichs's two pincer movements resumed their general advance against the city. In the north, 295th and 389th Infantry Divisions of LI Corps applied unrelenting pressure, threatening to create multiple breakthroughs in the area from Gorodishche south to the Tsaritsa River. Ermolkin's and Afanas'ev's 112th and 244th Rifle Divisions were only shadows of their former selves, and even Batrakov's newer 42nd Naval Rifle Brigade hemorrhaged strength in a matter of days. To provide some depth to his defenses, Chuikov had already ordered the remnants of 399th and 112th Rifle Divisions to withdraw to new positions along the heights west of the city, less than 6 kilometers from the northern factory district and no more than 2 kilometers west of the city center. Meanwhile, despite the temporary setback experienced by 29th Motorized Division, its parent XXXXVIII Panzer Corps continued to grind forward in the southern portion of the city. On 11 September Heim's 14th Panzer Division encircled and destroyed 204th Rifle Division's 704th Regiment as the defenders attempted to pull back. By this time, most of the divisions of Shumilov's 64th Army were as worn down as those of the 62nd. Communications were so fragile that it took Shumilov more than 24 hours to learn that his troops had retaken Kuporosnoe.[32]

Encouraged, Weichs ordered Fourth Panzer Army to reorient its attack directly into the southern portion of the city. In the north, however, the defenders exacted a growing price for the advance of 389th Infantry Division, which was operating without armored support. Fortunately for the Germans, by this point they had contained the Kotluban' offensive. Early on 12 September, therefore, Paulus ordered Seydlitz to turn responsibility for the Orlovka battle over to Wietersheim's XIV Panzer Corps and prepare for a renewed attack toward the Volga on the next day.[33] To free 389th Division for this new mission, Paulus also reinforced LI Corps with Group Stahel, a *Luftwaffe* formation built around Colonel Rainer Stahel's 99th *Flak* (Antiaircraft) Regiment. This was a precursor to a more widespread use of *Luftwaffe* forces in a ground combat role beginning in December 1942; it also reflected the German airmen's reluctance to transfer their ground personnel to the increasingly understrength German Army.

The southern advance had also been costly for the Germans. By 11 September, for example, 24th Panzer Division reported a strength of 8,714 men, as compared with an authorized 15,401 soldiers. The division had only 14 operable tanks, prompting the corps commander, Kempf, to shuttle the available tanks back and forth between his two panzer divisions, depending on circumstances. Late that day, Hoth substituted 94th Infantry Division for 24th Panzer to continue the attack.[34]

As Weichs's ground forces advanced on downtown Stalingrad in the south and the factory district in the north, the air battle intensified above them. Between 5 and 12 September, *Luftflotte* 4 flew an average of 934 sorties per day, the majority of them over the Stalingrad area. In response, Major General Khriukin's 8th Air Army could generate only about 354 sorties per day.[35] It had 137 operable aircraft on 3 September. On the sixth the *Stavka* committed Major General P. S. Stepanov's 16th Air Army, previously in reserve, to support 62nd and 64th Armies. This new air army was inexperienced and underequipped, and Stepanov, better known for his political reliability than his combat ability, was not the right person to lead it. By October, he was replaced by Major General R. S. Rudenko, who directed his inexperienced pilots to avoid German fighters and instead ambush the bombers and reconnaissance aircraft.[36]

CONCLUSION

By nightfall on 12 September, the attackers held all the high ground west and southwest of the city, save for the shrunken salient around Orlovka in the north. The battle for the suburbs shaped the desperate fighting to come, which would focus around three regions: in Stalingrad city and its northern factory district, in the land bridge between the Don and Volga Rivers on the northern flank of the city, and on the banks of the Don and Volga far to the northwest and in the Beketovka bridgehead south of Stalingrad.

Although the Soviets continued to hammer away in areas such as the Voronezh shoulder and the Kotluban' flank, such attacks had only limited effect on the struggle in Stalingrad, as we have seen. Gradually, however, Zhukov came to believe that the Germans had committed so many forces at Stalingrad that they might be vulnerable to a concerted series of strategic counteroffensives along the entire front, especially near Moscow. Meanwhile, Stalin continued to feed just enough troops and munitions into 62nd and 64th Armies to keep those formations alive, tying up German strength. Most of the available forces were held back for grander offensive efforts. To this end, the dictator directed that local forces expand existing bridgeheads over the Don and Volga on either flank of the city that bore his name.

A thoughtful observer could derive three lessons from the first 12 days of September. First, while the Kotluban' offensive had been indecisive, it had pinned down forces that Weichs needed to assault the city proper. Second, the struggles in the suburbs reinforced the conclusion of the preceding month, which was that Paulus and Hoth had insufficient combat power to take the city promptly. An army dedicated to rapid, operational-level maneuver was now committed to a slow, grinding, attritional assault. Finally, although the Red Army had far more troops and supplies to commit to battle than did its opponent, those resources would be wasted until the Red Army command and staff cadre learned how to perform at a much higher level than they had displayed to date.

CHAPTER EIGHT

The Battle for Central and Southern
_____ Stalingrad, 13–26 September 1942

STALINGRAD AS A SYMBOL

Stalingrad, a city that had barely figured in the original German plan for Operation _Blau_, quickly became the psychological and emotional center of both sides' military efforts. Admittedly, the city had significant military value due to its weapons factories as well as its location on the remaining water and rail communications that connected Moscow with the Caucasus. Yet to the German leadership, the very name Stalingrad, identifying the city with the Soviet dictator and the beleaguered Communist regime, seemed to give it a psychological and political significance out of all proportion to its actual military worth. German propaganda centered more and more on the titanic struggle for Stalin's namesake city. As Army Group A's advance into the Caucasus ground to an inconclusive halt during the autumn, Stalingrad and the Volga River bend increasingly seemed to be the logical place to conclude Operation _Blau_ with at least some appearance of success. Even before Hitler's speeches staked German prestige on the outcome of the battle, German commanders, soldiers, and citizens began to acquire a kind of tunnel vision about Stalingrad. As one German commander ruefully reflected, "Politics, prestige, and emotions won the upper hand over sober military judgment."[1]

The defenders fought to the last for many of the same reasons. Stalingrad became a powerful political and psychological symbol of Soviet resistance. More practically, however, the Soviet commanders from Stalin down to Chuikov apparently realized that a prolonged defense of the city would immobilize the _Wehrmacht_, neutralizing its advantages in maneuver warfare while bleeding it white.[2] The daily rate of German advance was measured in city blocks rather than tens of kilometers. The time gained in this manner permitted the Soviets to launch a series of counteroffensives on the flanks of Army Group B; many of these counteractions were poorly prepared and generally ineffective, but in the long run, such efforts helped develop the command and staff skills necessary to succeed in November.

As the two sides exhausted themselves, they behaved more and more like two boxers stung hard in the ring: wobbly on their feet, no longer able to land a coordinated series of blows, yet refusing to concede defeat.

166

OPPOSING FORCES

In mid-September the main body of General Weichs's Army Group B appeared poised to capture Stalingrad, while simultaneously, Field Marshal List's Army Group A was battling for the seaports and mountain passes that were key to a further advance into the Caucasus. In reality, of course, the Germans were already overextended, and nowhere was this more true than along the Don River, where the majority of Sixth Army, including most of the armor in XIV Panzer Corps, had to defend the long German left flank. Therefore, the main German attack force in the northern factory district of Stalingrad came from Seydlitz's LI Army Corps, consisting of *Luftwaffe* Group Stahel and 389th, 295th, and 71st Infantry Divisions.

Similarly, only half of Hoth's Fourth Panzer Army was available to assault the city itself. In the south, IV Army Corps, consisting of Romanian 20th Infantry and German 297th and 371st Infantry Divisions, was containing the Southeastern Front's 64th Army in the bridgehead west of Beketovka. Farther south, the three divisions of Romanian VI Corps were defending Hoth's long right wing in the lake region south of Stalingrad. This lightly equipped force had to confront the Southeastern Front's 57th and 51st Armies.[3] Moreover, even 14th Panzer Division was deployed against the Beketovka bridgehead, leaving only three divisions—24th Panzer, 94th Infantry, and 29th Motorized—of Kempf's XXXXVIII Panzer Corps to assist in the city assault. Based on previous fighting, it was clear that Paulus and Hoth had insufficient forces to seize the city rapidly, so in mid-September the German commanders were already acting to reinforce Sixth Army.

On 12 September 1942 Adolf Hitler held a planning conference at *Wehrwolf*, his headquarters in the Ukraine. Accounts of this conference are somewhat suspect because the participants tended to blame Hitler for their subsequent defeats. Apparently, however, Generals Paulus and Weichs arrived at Vinnitsa to find that the dictator considered the Battle of Stalingrad to be virtually over.[4] Based on repeated victories over the Red Army and on optimistic German intelligence estimates, Hitler believed his opponents were incapable of launching another major counteroffensive. Paulus and Weichs later claimed that they raised issues such as the difficulties of city fighting and the vulnerability of their northern flank, but their Führer dismissed such warnings—an action that was entirely in accord with his recent dismissal of generals he considered overly cautious. Instead, he transferred XXXXVIII Panzer Corps (with 24th Panzer, 94th Infantry, and 29th Motorized Divisions) to Sixth Army's control, effective 15 September, to facilitate the final defeat of Stalingrad. He also directed Army Group B to conduct other minor operations to straighten out its left wing and further defend Voronezh. The resulting order, dated 13 September, included various efforts to shorten and reinforce the defenses on the left flank. However, it authorized the temporary diversion of 22nd Panzer and 113th Infantry Divisions from the left flank of Army Group B to Stalingrad, deferring a plan for those units to improve the junction between German Sixth and Italian Eighth Armies.[5]

In retrospect, of course, this delay in eliminating Soviet bridgeheads over the Don, especially at Serafimovich, proved fatal in November. Moreover, the OKH authorized the movement of Romanian V Corps, including Romanian 1st Cavalry, 13th, and 6th Infantry Divisions, into the sector of Sixth Army's XVII and XI Army Corps. This allowed Paulus to redeploy German 113th Infantry and 100th *Jäger* Divisions closer to Stalingrad. Thus began the process that, by November, put General Petre Dumitrescu's Romanian Third Army on Paulus's left flank. In addition to freeing German troops to fight in Stalingrad, this redeployment was apparently part of Hitler's plan to give his loyal ally, Marshal Ion Antonescu, command of a proposed Romanian army group (Third and Fourth Armies) on a relatively quiet portion of the front. However, as Dumitrescu complained to the OKH on 24 September, his Third Army of 69 battalions, none of which had effective antitank guns, had to defend a sector of 168 kilometers, or more than 2.4 kilometers per battalion.[6]

These redeployments set the stage for the assault on Stalingrad proper (see tables 8.1 and 8.2). Most Soviet and German accounts describe 62nd and 64th Armies as fielding 54,000 and 36,000 troops, respectively, against Sixth and Fourth Panzer Armies' total of 170,000. In actuality, however, this latter figure includes XIV Panzer Corps and other German troops not actually engaged in the city fight; the true German strength available for street fighting was closer to 80,000. In terms of armor, the two Soviet armies had roughly 144 tanks on 13 September, compared with about 100 German tanks and assault guns.[7] As an illustration of the low density of German armor, consider 24th Panzer Division, which was a spearhead during most of the battle. That division had only 19 operational tanks on 13 September; it peaked at 34 operational tanks on 17 October, but during the ensuing four weeks, it averaged only 14 armored vehicles each day. Each of the three separate assault gun battalions—177th, 244th, and 245th—averaged 5 to 17 serviceable guns on any given day.[8]

Thus, to a considerable extent, the Battle of Stalingrad was a race between the two armies to see which could reinforce its attenuated forward units more quickly. The Southeastern Front began this race on the evening of 14 September by bringing the fresh 13th Guards Rifle Division across the Volga; Paulus responded on 19–20 September by shifting 100th *Jäger* Division eastward, committing it to the city fight beginning on 25 September.

At the outset of Weichs's assault on Stalingrad, the shallow depth of the Soviet positions limited 62nd Army to a two-echelon defense, with the second

Table 8.1. Opposing Forces on the Stalingrad Axis, 12 September 1942

GERMAN
Sixth Army
VIII Army Corps
305th Infantry Division (Vertiachii–
Samofalovka)

76th Infantry Division
(Samofalovka–564 km Station)

XIV Panzer Corps
60th Motorized Division (564 km
Station–7 km east of Kuz'michi)

3rd Motorized Division (7 km east of
Kuz'michi–Sukhaia Mechetka balka)
16th Panzer Division (Sukhaia
Mechetka balka–Akatovka on Volga
River)

16th Panzer Division (elements; Rynok–
east of Orlovka)
3rd Motorized Division (elements;
north of Orlovka)
60th Motorized Division (elements;
northwest of Orlovka)
LI Army Corps
Group Stahel (west of Orlovka)

389th Infantry Division (west of
Orlovka–east of Gorodishche)

295th Infantry Division (Motor Tractor
Station northeast of Razgulaevka
Station–west of Krasnyi Oktiabr'
village)

71st Infantry Division (west of Krasnyi
Oktiabr'village–Tsaritsa River)
Fourth Panzer Army
XXXXVIII Panzer Corps
24th Panzer Division (Tsaritsa River–
west of Sadovaia Station)

94th Infantry Division (west of Sadovaia
Station–Minina)

SOVIET
Stalingrad Front

4th Tank Army
27th, 37th Guards, 18th, 214th, 292nd,
298th Rifle Divisions; 193rd Tank,
22nd Motorized Rifle Brigades
24th Army
173rd, 207th, 221st, 308th, 315th Rifle
Divisions; 217th Tank Brigade

1st Guards Army
38th, 39th, 41st Guards, 24th, 64th,
84th, 87th, 116th Rifle Divisions;
4th, 7th, 16th Tank Corps

66th Army

49th, 99th, 120th, 231st, 299th, 316th
Rifle Divisions; 10th, 69th, 148th,
246th Tank Brigades
Southeastern Front
62nd Army (33rd Guards, 229th Rifle
Divisions; 129th Rifle Brigade
refitting)
124th (–), 149th (–) Rifle Brigades;
282nd NKVD Rifle Regiment
115th Rifle Brigade (–)

724th Rifle Regiment of 196th Rifle
Division

2nd Motorized Rifle Brigade (one
battalion), with 399th Rifle Division
in reserve
2nd Motorized Rifle Brigade (–), plus
one battalion each of 115th, 149th,
and 124th Rifle Brigades
6th Guards Tank Brigade, with 87th
Rifle Division, 189th Tank Brigade,
38th Motorized Rifle Brigade;
112th Rifle Division, with 27th Tank
Brigade in reserve
6th Tank and 42nd Rifle Brigades, one
regiment of 244th Rifle Division

244th Rifle Division (–), 10th Rifle
Brigade, 6th Tank Brigade (–), with
131st Rifle Division in reserve
133rd Tank Brigade, 271st NKVD Rifle
Regiment
(continued on next page)

Table 8.1. (*continued*)

GERMAN	SOVIET
29th Motorized Division (Minina–Kuporosnoe)	35th Guards Rifle Division

The Beketovka Bridgehead

IV Army Corps	*64th Army* 66th and 154th Naval Rifle Brigades (refitting), 118th Fortified Region (in Beketovka)
14th Panzer Division (Kuporosnoe–Gornaia Poliana)	126th, 204th, 138th Rifle Divisions; 13th Tank Corps (–); Krasnodar Infantry School
Romanian 20th Infantry Division (west of Gornaia Poliana)	157th Rifle Division
297th Infantry Division (north and south of Elkhi)	29th, 38th Rifle Divisions; 133rd Tank Brigade of 13th Tank Corps
371st Infantry Division (northwest and southwest of Ivanovka)	36th Guards Rifle Division
Romanian VI Army Corps	*57th Army*
Romanian 2nd Infantry Division (Tundutovo–Dubovoi Ovrag)	422nd, 15th Guards, 244th Rifle Divisions; 6th Tank Brigade; 76th Fortified Region

Note: Sectors are indicated in parentheses.

echelon only 1.5 to 3 kilometers behind the first. The 64th Army was even more restricted, operating generally in a single echelon except on its right (northern) wing opposite 14th Panzer Division. This shallowness precluded most Soviet efforts to maneuver forces laterally. Moreover, the German position on the heights west of the city provided superb observation and fields of fire into the city. However, once German artillery and bombs reduced the city and especially its factory district to rubble, the mountains of debris offered excellent concealment and considerable cover for the defenders.

To counter the German terrain advantages, 62nd and 64th Armies organized special artillery and mortar groups, each with two to four regiments, to provide fire support. As noted earlier, Eremenko took precautions against catastrophic defeat, positioning 2nd Tank Corps to defend the eastern bank of the Volga.

The ensuing German attack on Stalingrad may be divided into three phases. First, from 13 to 26 September, Paulus and Hoth attacked the central and southern portion of the city, while the Soviets launched a third counteroffensive at Kotluban'. Second, from 27 September through 13 October, Paulus's forces captured the outlying workers' villages north of the city and liquidated the remainder of Chuikov's Orlovka salient in that area. In the third and final stage, from 14 October through 18 November, Sixth Army struggled to capture the main factories at the northern end of the city, as well as 62nd Army's Rynok and Spartanovka enclaves even farther north. Throughout all

Table 8.2. Unit Commanders in Stalingrad, 12 September–18 November 1942
(North to South)

Sixth Army—General of Panzer Troops Friedrich Paulus
 XIV Panzer Corps—General of Infantry Gustav Wietersheim; (15 September)
  Lieutenant General Hans-Valentine Hube
  16th Panzer Division—Lieutenant General Hans-Valentine Hube;
   (15 September) Lieutenant General Günther Angern
  3rd Motorized Division—Lieutenant General Helmuth Schlömer
  60th Motorized Division—Major General Otto Kohlermann; (November)
   Major General Hans-Adolf von Arensdorff
 LI Army Corps—General of Artillery Walter von Seydlitz-Kurbach
  Group Stahel—Colonel Reiner Stahel
  389th Infantry Division—Lieutenant General Erwin Jänecke; (1 November)
   Major General Erich Magnus
  295th Infantry Division—General of Artillery Rolf Wuthmann;
   (16 November) Major General Otto Korfes
  71st Infantry Division—General of Infantry Alexander von Hartmann
 XXXXVIII Panzer Corps—General of Panzer Troops Werner Kempf;
  (1 November) Lieutenant General Ferdinand Heim
  24th Panzer Division—(12 September) Major General Arno von Lenski
  94th Infantry Division—General of Artillery Georg Pfeiffer
  29th Motorized Division—Lieutenant General Max Fremerey;
   (28 September) Major General Hans-Georg Leyser
62nd Army—Lieutenant General V. I. Chuikov
 Group Gorokhov—Colonel S. F. Gorokhov
  124th and 129th Rifle Brigades, 282nd NKVD Rifle Regiment
 Orlovka Grouping
  115th Rifle Brigade (Colonel K. M. Andriusenko), 724th Rifle Regiment,
   2nd Motorized Rifle Brigade; (in reserve) 399th Rifle Division (Colonel
   N. G. Travnikov)
 23rd Tank Corps—Major General A. F. Popov; (16 October) Colonel V. V.
  Koshelev
  6th Guards Tank Brigade (Colonel M. K. Skuva), 189th Tank Brigade
   (Lieutenant Colonel F. I. Bystrik), 27th Tank Brigade (Major P. F.
   Luchnikov), 9th Motorized Rifle Brigade (commander unknown)
  38th Motorized Rifle Brigade (Colonel I. D. Burmakov)
 112th Rifle Division—Colonel I. E. Ermolkin; (16 November) Major Ia. D.
  Filonenko
 6th Tank Brigade (reorganized as 19th Guards Tank and 73rd Tank
  Regiments, 12 October)—Lieutenant Colonel S. A. Khopko
 42nd Rifle Brigade—Colonel M. S. Batrakov
 244th Rifle Division—Colonel G. A. Afanas'ev
 10th Rifle Brigade—Colonel I. D. Driakhlov
 133rd Tank Brigade (Heavy)—Colonel N. B. Bubnov
 10th NKVD Rifle Division—Colonel A. A. Saraev
 35th Guards Rifle Division—Major General V. A. Glazkov; (8 September)
  Colonel V. P. Dubiansky; (21 November) Colonel F. A. Otashenko

these stages, Hoth continued lesser operations to eliminate 64th Army's Beketovka bridgehead, while the defenders prepared for a fresh counteroffensive.

THE INITIAL GERMAN ASSAULT, 13–18 SEPTEMBER

At 0630 on 13 September, Weichs began his first assault on the central and southern portions of the city. Chuikov had just assumed command of 62nd Army the previous night and was hard-pressed to counter this attack.

Seydlitz's LI Corps attacked the center of Chuikov's line, with Group Stahel containing the Soviet forces in the western portion of the Orlovka salient, while Jänecke's 389th Infantry Division pushed eastward from Gorodishche, seeking to compress the base of that salient. Meanwhile, 295th and 71st Infantry Divisions, in cooperation with 24th Panzer and 94th Infantry on Kempf's left wing, aimed to advance through the Krasnyi Oktiabr' village toward Mamaev Kurgan and the heights above the city center.

Simultaneously, Kempf's XXXXVIII Panzer Corps concentrated on the sector south of the Tsaritsa River but thrust northeastward and then east along the railroad line to seize the southern half of Stalingrad, thereby splitting 62nd Army in half. Meanwhile, 24th Panzer and 94th Infantry on Kempf's left sought to seize the Minina suburb, the southern heights of the city, and eventually Railroad Station No. 2.[9] On Kempf's right, 29th Motorized Division, supported by part of 14th Panzer Division, sought to clear the suburbs of El'shanka and Kuporosnoe.

At first, neither side had detailed knowledge of the other's exact dispositions. Thus, the initial German artillery preparation, supported by *Luftwaffe* bombers with incendiary weapons, was an area effort that reportedly killed more than 300 civilians and disrupted Chuikov's field telephone lines to his subordinate and higher headquarters.[10] These attacks were not concentrated, however, and caused only limited damage to defending units. *Katiusha* rocket volleys, launched from the far bank, also failed to hit many of their German targets. Still, the Germans made minor progress on 13 September, with Colonel Andriusenko's 115th Rifle Brigade halting 389th Infantry Division east of Gorodishche. Farther south, Wuthmann's 295th Infantry Division had more success, capturing Hill 153.7 and the hospital area from 23rd Tank Corps and 112th Rifle Division, respectively. Having lost at least 32 tanks and 250 men, 23rd Tank Corps' brigades had to withdraw to the outskirts of the Barrikady and Krasnyi Oktiabr' villages.[11] The progress of Kempf's panzer corps was slower, measured in hundreds of meters. German artillery forced Chuikov to move his headquarters to the banks of the Tsaritsa River, occupying the dugouts of the "Tsaritsyn bunker" that had once housed the *front* headquarters before it moved across the river.[12]

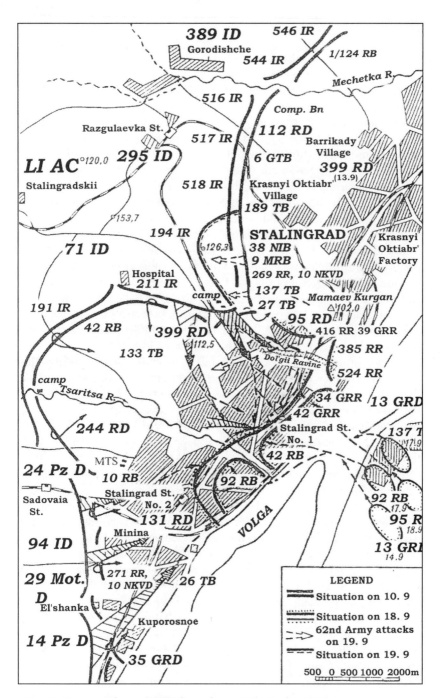

Map 36. German Advance into Stalingrad, 10–18 September 1942

That night, Eremenko directed both of his army commanders to launch counterattacks early the next morning. Chuikov focused available reserves against LI Corps' 295th and 71st Infantry Divisions, which threatened Mamaev Kurgan and the center of the city. Unfortunately for the Soviets, these attacks, attempted at 0330 on 14 September, accomplished little because they ran straight into the teeth of Weichs's advancing spearheads. Once the sun came up, German artillery and multiple groups of up to 60 Stuka aircraft abruptly halted the Soviet advance. German fire again disrupted Chuikov's wire communications, hampering his control of the battle.[13] The 191st Regiment of 71st Division penetrated Batrakov's reinforced 42nd Rifle Brigade north of the Tsaritsa, then infiltrated small groups along ridgelines and *balkas* until they were within 800 meters of Chuikov's command post. Small groups from the neighboring 194th Infantry Regiment also got behind the Soviet positions, cutting telephone lines and briefly reaching the Volga. A desperate defense, patched together from 6th Tank Brigade, NKVD units, local militia, and even Chuikov's headquarters troops, struggled to halt these advances. Railroad Station No. 1, governmental and party buildings, and the adjoining Red Square changed hands at least five times on 14 September and continued to be the focus of fighting in subsequent days.[14]

That afternoon, Chuikov's chief of staff, General Krylov, scraped together headquarters troops plus nine KV tanks from two different brigades and used them to slow 194th Regiment's advance. Despite this, the Germans reached the river late in the day, using antitank guns to sink two of the precious ferries. Fortunately for the defenders, 35th Guards Rifle Division slowed 29th Motorized Division's advance farther south, preventing an even wider breakthrough.[15]

The Red soldiers held on until nightfall, which brought the first significant reinforcements: 13th Guards Rifle Division. The division commander, Major General Aleksandr Il'ich Rodimtsev, became a mainstay of 62nd Army's defense, but initially his division was so short of transportation and even weapons that it took all night for the troops to arrive and take up positions.[16]

This arrival by no means solved the problems of 62nd Army, however, as the German counterattack continued on 15 September. The day began with what Chuikov described as "a colossal air raid."[17] The 295th Infantry Division again pressed toward the heights above the Krasnyi Oktiabr' village, pushing back 6th Guards Tank and 38th Motorized Rifle Brigades; at the same time, the division's 518th Regiment attacked 269th NKVD Regiment and 27th Tank Brigade northwest of Mamaev Kurgan. XXXXVIII Panzer Corps' advance farther south was even more threatening. Most of 24th Panzer Division's striking power was concentrated in a *kampfgruppe* led by Colonel Maximilian von Edelsheim, whose 26th Panzer-Grenadier Regiment, strongly reinforced by all the other arms of the division, attacked

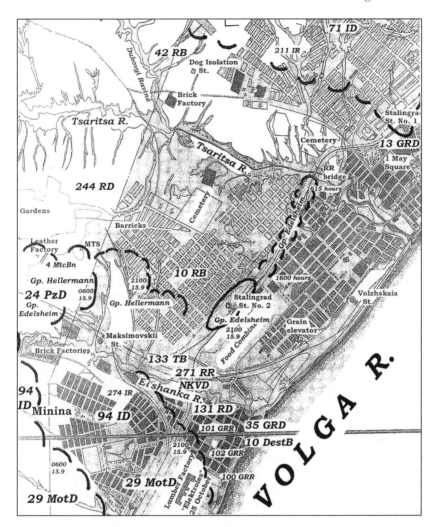

Map 37. XXXXVIII Panzer Corps' Advance, 15 September 1942

at 0330 on the fifteenth. Edelsheim advanced rapidly on a narrow frontage along the railway embankment; by midmorning, he had reached a railroad junction only 2 kilometers west of the Volga River. There, strong Soviet defenses briefly checked his advance. Once Edelsheim made contact with 94th Infantry Division, advancing on his right, and coordinated artillery support, he wheeled 90 degrees to the left and pressed northward through the city's cavernous blocks along Komitetskaia Street and the main north-south railroad line. The attackers had to dislodge each small group of Soviet infantry as they fought hand to hand, but by midafternoon the panzer-grenadiers had reached the area just west of Railroad Station No. 2. Following a pause to allow for air and artillery "softening up," *Kampfgruppe* Edelsheim captured this station at 1600 after only a brief fight. At that point, some of the Stuka bombs fell short among the German attackers. Undeterred, Edelsheim then turned west to help clear enemy forces from the high terrain to his left rear. This triumphant advance had cost 24th Panzer Division 5 of its 25 functioning tanks, at least 3 of which were mistakenly hit by *Flak* (antiaircraft) gunners when the panzer-grenadiers linked up with 94th Infantry Division.[18]

Despite the linkup between the two German divisions, elements of the Soviet 10th Rifle Brigade and the NKVD division still held a narrow strip of land between the north-south railroad line and the Volga River. Meanwhile, on XXXXVIII Panzer Corps' right wing, 29th Motorized Division, supported by a few tanks from 14th Panzer Division, had assaulted the left flank of 62nd Army south of the El'shanka River. The bulk of 35th Guards Rifle and 131st Rifle Divisions, aided by elements of 281st NKVD Regiment and 133rd Tank Brigade, suffered heavily and conducted a disorganized fighting withdrawal into the southern section of Stalingrad.[19]

To facilitate coordination of the continuing attack, that evening the OKH announced that XXXXVIII Panzer Corps would temporarily pass to the tactical control of Sixth Army, effective at midnight on 15–16 September.[20] Still, Kempf's mobile units were so short of dismounted infantry that, as had been the case so often in this war, they could not effectively encircle and capture the shattered Soviet forces. The Germans took up hedgehog positions while several groups of defeated Red infantrymen took the initiative to convert key buildings into fortified strongpoints. When the Germans resumed the advance the next day, they met unexpected resistance in areas that had supposedly been cleared of defenders.

In Stalingrad's center, the arrival of two regiments of 13th Guards Rifle Division on 14–15 September cleared some of the infiltrating German infantrymen. Two battalions of this division, plus the remnants of 269th NKVD Regiment and of Group Krylov, took up defensive positions on Mamaev Kurgan.[21] The rest of the division recaptured Railroad Station No. 1 from 71st Infantry Division's 194th Regiment. The Soviet defense was extremely chaotic, with newly arrived troops running short of ammunition and other supplies; there was often no means to evacuate the wounded, and the NKVD actively apprehended—and occasionally executed—stragglers.[22]

The arrival of 13th Guards Rifle Division marked the first step in a constant struggle for manpower effectives, a struggle waged by both sides over the next two months. Not counting replacements that arrived as reinforcements in ad hoc march units, 62nd Army received nine rifle divisions and

Table 8.3. Major Reinforcements to 62nd Army, September–October 1942

Date Crossed the Volga River	Organization	Commander
14–15 September	13th Guards Rifle Division	Major General A. I. Rodimtsev
16 September	92nd Naval Rifle Brigade	Lieutenant Colonel Tarasov
16 September	137th Tank Brigade	Lieutenant Colonel K. S. Udovichenko
19–20 September	95th Rifle Division	Colonel V. A. Gorishnyi
21–23 September	284th Rifle Division	Colonel N. F. Batiuk
25–27 September	39th Guards Rifle Division	Major General S. S. Gur'ev
30 September	42nd Rifle Brigade (reconstituted)	Colonel M. S. Batrakov
30 September	308th Rifle Division	Colonel L. N. Gurt'ev
3 October	37th Guards Rifle Division	Major General V. G. Zholudev
4 October	84th Tank Brigade	Colonel D. N. Belyi
12 October	524th Rifle Regiment of 112th Rifle Division (reconstituted)	Unknown
15 October	138th Rifle Division	Colonel I. I. Liudnikov
26 October	45th Rifle Division	Colonel V. P. Sokolov

Note: Beginning in mid-October, at Chuikov's request, replacements were sent primarily in march battalions and companies rather than formed divisions.

numerous separate brigades over the next seven weeks. Several of these formations actually deployed twice as their skeletons withdrew to the east bank, filled with replacements, and returned to the fight. These reinforcements totaled more than 100,000 soldiers, yet the attrition was so ferocious that Chuikov rarely commanded more than 50,000 at any one time.

If 62nd Army was constantly hemorrhaging effectives, German Sixth Army was even worse off because it had no ready source of replacements, other than soldiers recovering from wounds. After fighting its way to Stalingrad, Sixth Army was already emaciated when the city battle began. Instead of 132 full-strength combat battalions, the army had consolidated units so that only 109 infantry, panzer-grenadier, and *Jäger* battalions remained. For example, on 14 September LI Corps' 295th Infantry Division had only seven of nine infantry battalions, of which two were rated weak and three average. Overall, 19 of the army's infantry battalions were "weak," including 12 of the 21 battalions of LI Corps, which had already borne the brunt of the city fighting.[23] The most that Weichs and Paulus could do was to rotate units between Stalingrad and the defensive positions outside the city.

Heavy fighting continued on 16 September, with two regiments of Wuthmann's 295th Infantry Division inching their way east toward the western edge of Krasnyi Oktiabr' village, where that division's 518th Regiment began a prolonged seesaw battle for Mamaev Kurgan, opposed by two battalions each of 13th Guards Rifle and 112th Rifle Divisions. Farther south, Hart-

Table 8.4. Major Reinforcements to and Departures from Sixth Army's Assault Forces in Stalingrad, September–October 1942

Date	Organization (Commander)
11–12 September	Group Stahel (Colonel Rainer Stahel)
19–20 September	24th Panzer Division (Major General Arno Lenski) withdrawn
20–21 September	16th Panzer Division (part)
25–26 September	100th Jäger Division (Lieutenant General Werner Sanne)
26 September	24th Panzer Division recommitted
29 September	29th Motorized Division (Major General Hans-Georg Leyser) withdrawn
29 September	14th Panzer Division (Lieutenant General Ferdinand Heim) part withdrawn
13 October	14th Panzer Division recommitted
13 October	305th Infantry Division (Lieutenant General Kurt Oppenländer)
20 October	79th Infantry Division, two regiments (Lieutenant General Richard von Schwerin)

mann's 71st Infantry Division struggled through the rubbled area around 9 January Square and Railroad Station No. 1. The 1st Battalion, 42nd Guards Rifle Regiment, clung resolutely to the station and adjacent ruined buildings. Meanwhile, *Kampfgruppe* Edelsheim of 24th Panzer Division attacked shortly after dawn, pushing northward along the railroad and seizing a foothold across the Tsaritsa River against resistance from 42nd Rifle Brigade. On the panzer division's right, however, 94th Infantry Division ground to a halt in the late afternoon against determined resistance around the storage buildings of the Stalingrad Food Combine. The 71st Infantry Division also bogged down in the center of the city, leaving 24th Panzer Division's flanks exposed; by the end of the day, the division had only 19 operational tanks. Nonetheless, the threat to Soviet positions in the central city was so great that, on the evening of 16 September, 62nd Army's headquarters displaced to the Krasnyi Oktiabr' sector.[24]

The threat reached a climax the next day. Despite ferocious resistance by small groups of defenders, during the afternoon 71st Infantry Division linked up with 24th Panzer Division at the railroad bridge southwest of 1 May Square and Railroad Station No. 1. This created an oval encirclement along the Tsaritsa River, although some remnants of 42nd Rifle Brigade and 244th Rifle Division escaped from this loose trap. General von Lenski, commander of 24th Panzer, proposed a concerted attack on 18 September to clear this encirclement and finalize the German occupation of southern Stalingrad. Instead, General Paulus decided to transfer 24th Panzer to LI Corps, a tacit admission that Sixth Army was not progressing well against the northern factory district.[25] Nor did 29th Motorized Division make much progress farther

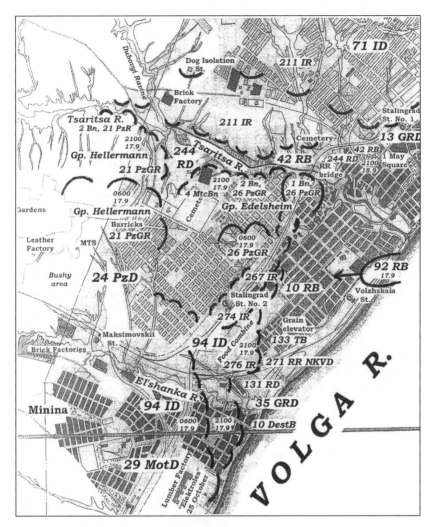

Map 38. XXXXVIII Panzer Corps' Advance, 17–18 September 1942

south, where survivors of 35th Guards Rifle Division, reinforced by what remained of 131st Rifle Division and 270th NKVD Regiment, continued to hold out in strongpoints near the banks of the Volga.

Chuikov had already asked the Stalingrad Front for major reinforcements to stave off disaster. Eremenko transferred 92nd Naval Rifle Brigade and 137th Tank Brigade to 62nd Army control on the evening of 16 September, although it took time to move these units across the river and into position. The 137th was one of the depleted elements of 2nd Tank Corps and had only 15 T-60 light tanks with 45mm guns. By the morning of 20 September, however, three battalions of the naval brigade reinforced 35th Guards Division and other units holding the buildings and streets from the Tsaritsa River south to the El'shanka.[26]

Meanwhile, by the close of 17 September, Chuikov's defenses were compressed into a shallow area less than 4 kilometers deep and 18 kilometers wide. Only north of Mamaev Kurgan did the Soviets retain some room to maneuver, and even there, the troops of XIV Panzer Corps and 389th Infantry Division of LI Corps were slowly hemming the Red soldiers in from the south and east. German determination was reflected by the announcement that, effective 14 September, General von Wietersheim was no longer in command of this panzer corps, apparently because he had protested too vigorously about the exposed position of his troops north of the city. Hans Hube, the phlegmatic commander of 16th Panzer Division, succeeded Wietersheim, despite his willingness to defy Hitler's orders when his division had been surrounded in August.[27]

Recognizing the threat to Stalingrad, on 17 September the *Stavka* also released Major General F. N. Smekhotvorov's 193rd Rifle Division to the Southeastern Front, which in turn assigned it to an assembly area on the east bank. Late on the seventeenth the *front* commander also instructed Chuikov to conduct another counterattack, aimed at ejecting the invaders from Stalingrad city. To prepare for this, Chuikov could only recognize reality, consolidating most of his remaining units under four headquarters: Batrakov's 42nd Rifle Brigade was to protect the right wing of Rodimtsev's 13th Guards Division in the city center, while Tarasov's 92nd Rifle Brigade and Dubiansky's 35th Guards Rifle Division confronted the immediate threat south of the Tsaritsa River.[28] However, these units were already hopelessly intermingled, and the planned assault by XXXXVIII Panzer Corps threatened to split these defenses apart.

Thus, 62nd Army had few formed units to oppose the renewed German advance on the eighteenth. Nonetheless, dozens of small groups, ranging from one or two men to a decimated company, stubbornly held on to strongpoints such as the concrete grain elevator, the buildings around Railroad Station No. 2, and various factories at and south of the Food Combine. German infantry received support from 50mm antitank guns and 105mm howitzers firing over open sights, while the defenders had a few 76.2mm field pieces, 37mm antitank guns, and 50mm infantry mortars. Even the famous 88mm antiaircraft guns had little effect on the Soviet positions. A naval infantryman of 92nd Brigade described the defense around the grain elevator:

> In all, ten attacks were beaten off on September 18. . . .
> In the elevator, the grain was on fire, the water [coolant] in the ma-

chine guns evaporated, the wounded were thirsty, but there was no water nearby. That was how we defended ourselves twenty-four hours a day for three days. Heat, smoke, thirst—all our lips were cracked. During the day many of us climbed up to the highest points in the elevator and from there fired on the Germans; at night we came down and made a defensive ring around the building . . . during a short lull, we counted our ammunition. There did not seem to be much left. . . . We decided to break out to the south, to the area of Beketovka, as there were many enemy tanks to the north and east of the elevator.

During the night of the 20th . . . we set off. . . . We passed through the gully and crossed the railway line, then stumbled on an enemy mortar battery that had only just taken up position under cover of darkness. We overturned the three mortars and a truckload of bombs. The Germans scattered, leaving behind seven dead, abandoning not only their weapons, but their bread and water. And we were fainting with thirst. "Something to drink! Something to drink!" was all we could think about. We drank our fill in the darkness. We then ate the bread we had captured from the Germans and went on.[29]

While this struggle continued, Paulus resubordinated 24th Panzer and 94th Infantry Divisions to LI Corps, effective 19 September.[30] The Sixth Army commander believed that southern Stalingrad was all but secure and sought to reinforce his attack in the northern factory district. Unfortunately for the Germans, continued Soviet counterattacks in that area not only stalled the intended offensive but also drew the depleted 24th Panzer Division back into combat before it could rest and refit.

THE TACTICS OF CITY FIGHTING

During the fight for Stalingrad, units on both sides appeared on operational maps and in written accounts as coherent divisions, brigades, and regiments. Yet this was true only for the set-piece fighting along the heights west of the factory district and on the slopes of Mamaev Kurgan. From 16 September onward, much of the fighting for the city was actually conducted by small groups of no more than 50 men each. When the Germans succeeded in capturing a building, survivors escaped and joined the nearest group of soldiers still capable of fighting. For both sides, the battle assumed a nightmarish quality of constant tension. Evening darkness brought a reduction in air and artillery attacks but left German and Soviet infantrymen marooned within a vast expanse of ruins, surrounded on all sides by strange noises and unseen dangers. Snipers and skirmishing became facts of daily life.

For the Germans, the failure to capture the city in the first daring rush and their subsequent heavy casualties prompted them to adopt a more cautious, methodical approach to operations. For the Soviets, every day they survived, every day they thwarted and attrited the Germans, only increased their fatalistic determination to die in place. With the Volga River and NKVD blocking detachments at their backs, the Soviet soldiers really had no choice but to fight on. Yet, given the heavy attrition among Red forces, even blocking detachments sometimes had to fight as ground units on the front lines.

During the chaotic first days of his new command, General Chuikov continued to study German tactics with a finely honed, analytical mind.[31] He observed, for example, that the terrain of urban warfare exacerbated the usual problems associated with coordinating close air support with the infantry and supporting arms. Although Stuka dive-bombers were more accurate than high-altitude medium bombers, their pilots still had only limited control over the exact impact point of their bombs. Thus, except where a large and visible no-man's-land existed, German pilots were understandably reluctant to drop bombs close to their own troops. The friendly fire incident in 24th Panzer's sector on 15 September only reinforced this cautiousness. Moreover, German air operations were confined almost exclusively to daylight attacks in fair weather.

Chuikov quickly reached the obvious conclusions: to stay alive, the defenders needed to "hug" the attackers, staying within 100 or even 50 meters of the German infantrymen so that neither Stuka pilots nor artillery forward observers would dare engage them, for fear of causing casualties among their own forces. Moreover, early Soviet counterattacks, which were usually conducted during daylight hours, simply provided more targets for the Germans. Therefore, with the exception of a few nighttime raids, Chuikov ceased launching organized counterattacks unless the threat was so great that he had no choice. Instead, the general encouraged his troops to operate in small combat groups, attacking and defending more like urban gangs than like organized battalions and regiments. These gangs would ambush individual German tanks and small infantry units, then retreat and move through the sewers to take up defensive positions elsewhere. If the Germans captured a fortified house at a corner, they were likely to discover that the Soviets were taking up new positions *behind* the German spearheads rather than falling back closer to the Volga. Attackers and defenders—often separated only by a single wall in a building—snatched a few moments of fitful sleep each night.

From these unorthodox beginnings, Chuikov gradually evolved a set of tactics for urban warfare. Although such tactics might not guarantee Soviet success, they would at least make German victory extremely time-consuming and expensive, particularly when combat shifted to the elemental struggle in the ruins of Stalingrad's factory district. They also immobilized the invaders for further counterattacks on the flanks.

THE THIRD KOTLUBAN' OFFENSIVE,
18 SEPTEMBER–2 OCTOBER

The Stalingrad Front's third offensive north and northwest of the city was yet another exercise in poor coordination and missed opportunities. Just as Hitler underestimated the extent of resistance in Stalingrad, his Soviet counterparts believed that Sixth Army was far weaker than it actually was. Before he departed for Moscow on 12 September, General Zhukov directed Eremenko to conduct yet another major counterattack in the Kotluban' area beginning on 18 September. Eremenko was convinced that his previous offensive had failed because its main shock groups had attacked the panzer and motorized divisions of XIV Panzer Corps. To avoid a repetition of this disaster, he shifted the axis of his main attack westward to the areas of Samofalovka and 564-km Station. There, due south of Kotluban' itself, the defenders were primarily the infantry of VIII Army Corps and the left flank of XIV Panzer Corps. Eremenko believed there was a weak point on the boundary between VIII Corps' 76th Infantry Division and the reconnaissance battalion of 60th Motorized Division. Of course, this area was the kind of open steppe that had left previous attackers exposed, but this time, Eremenko directed 62nd and 64th Armies in Stalingrad to launch simultaneous counterattacks, thereby attracting German attention and reserve forces. Eremenko also transferred 422nd Rifle Division from 57th to 64th Army and gave the counterattacks priority for artillery and air support.[32]

The *front* commander next directed that Moskalenko's 1st Guards Army exchange sectors with the weak 24th Army so that the former could provide concentrated combat power on a narrow frontage against 564-km Station. To minimize troop movements, however, this meant that Moskalenko would assume command of the rifle divisions previously controlled by 24th Army, as well as 4th, 7th, and 16th Tank Corps previously subordinated to 4th Tank Army. This was the third time in 30 days that the headquarters of 1st Guards Army had completely swapped out its subordinate units. In only three days, Moskalenko's staff had to shift positions, establish control of new subordinates, and concentrate supplies and armor for the new offensive.[33] Moreover, the three tank corps were still rebuilding after the previous campaign and were short of both trained crews and medium and heavy tanks. For example, 45 of Rotmistrov's 93 tanks in 7th Tank Corps were light T-60s, while a significant number of other tanks were Lend-Lease imports.[34] Overall, Moskalenko's nine rifle divisions and three tank corps began the new operation with a total of 123,882 men, 340 armored vehicles, 611 guns, and 1,956 mortars.[35] Of these, roughly 44,000 men and 170 tanks were targeted in two echelons against the junction between the two German corps. Smaller shock groups from 24th and 66th Armies, each with only a handful of tanks, would attack on Moskalenko's left and right, respectively.

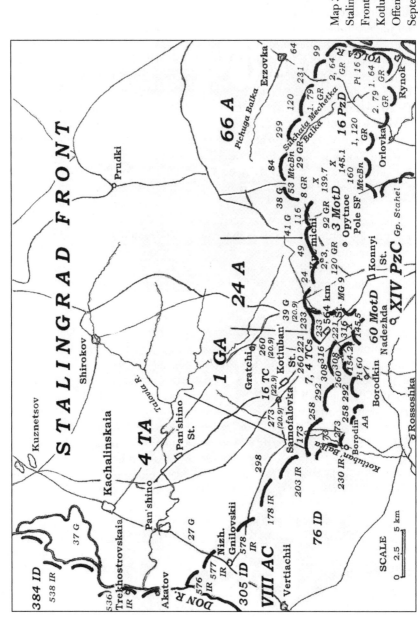

Map 39. Stalingrad Front's Kotluban' Offensive, 18–22 September 1942

By this time, however, the German defenders manned an extensive strongpoint defense in depth based on the best German practices of World War I.[36] This, plus Eremenko's hasty preparation and the decision to attack in broad daylight, doomed the attack in Kotluban' even before it began, while the two armies inside Stalingrad were in no condition to launch a coordinated attack.

After a 90-minute artillery preparation, Eremenko's third Kotluban' offensive began at 0830 on 18 September. As was typical of German defense systems, the forward positions were lightly held by a small number of troops, so the preparation largely fell on empty space. By sheer determination, the riflemen of 1st Guards Army advanced 3 kilometers, with 316th Rifle Division capturing 564-km Station. In the afternoon, *kampfgruppen* from 60th and 3rd Motorized Divisions halted this advance and drove the inexperienced Soviet troops back to their starting points. Elsewhere, the supporting attacks by the other two armies had no success.[37] The intense fighting on 18–19 September cost the three Red armies involved some 88,715 casualties, as well as half of Moskalenko's tanks.[38]

At Stalin's instigation, Zhukov and Eremenko recast the offensive, shifting the main axis of attack westward 5 kilometers while maintaining pressure on 564-km Station. Moskalenko repositioned his forces in accordance with this plan, but a renewed attack on 23 September initially had no more success than the previous efforts. On the next day, however, Moskalenko's two shock groups finally penetrated the forward defenses of 76th Infantry Division and 9th (Separate) Machine Gun Battalion, respectively.[39] Malinovsky's 66th Army rejoined the attack on 24 September but advanced only a kilometer in the face of German counterattacks that cost Rotmistrov 75 tanks, including 29 completely destroyed.[40]

Despite appalling losses, Eremenko continued to insist that Moskalenko continue his attack until 4 October, seeking to take some of the pressure off the two armies inside Stalingrad. In addition to capturing some 20 square kilometers, these persistent efforts forced the divisions of XIV Panzer Corps to divert armor that otherwise could have helped in the attacks on the northern factory district. Moreover, on 29–30 September Paulus relieved 76th Infantry Division with the much stronger 113th Infantry; according to German estimates at the time, the nine infantry battalions of the 76th had declined from five medium-strong and four average on 14 September to three weak and six exhausted by 5 October. The infantry units of 60th and 3rd Motorized Divisions also experienced a decline in effectiveness, though far less drastic.[41]

THE STRUGGLE FOR MAMAEV KURGAN AND THE CITY
CENTER, 19–26 SEPTEMBER

The third Kotulban' offensive gave the defenders of Stalingrad a breathing spell; even *Luftwaffe* air attacks halted for a day and a half, and a cautious Paulus slowed the rate of advance of Seydlitz's LI Corps.[42] Pressured by Eremenko, however, Chuikov attempted another offensive beginning at noon on 19 September, seeking to destroy the leading regiments of German infantry divisions west of the factory district and in the city center.[43] This effort promptly brought down renewed German air strikes that severely impeded or even halted the forward progress of 62nd Army. The first two battalions of the next Soviet reinforcement, Colonel V. A. Gorishnyi's 95th Rifle Division, arrived in time to join 112th Rifle Division's attack against Mamaev Kurgan and up the Dolgii ravine, an effort that retook the railroad embankment connecting these two terrain features. Farther south, Rodimtsev's 13th Guards Rifle Division suffered heavy losses when it attacked in the center of the city but had no impact on 71st Infantry Division.[44] By the end of 19 September, all the Soviet units in southern Stalingrad had no choice but to withdraw, block by block, delaying the German advance toward the Volga River.

Beginning on 20 September, an intense fight for control of Mamaev Kurgan dominated the struggle for southern Stalingrad. Chuikov committed the third regiment of Gorishnyi's 95th Rifle Division there, where it tried to dislodge 295th Infantry Division. Ermolkin's 112th Rifle Division fended off repeated attacks south of Mamaev Kurgan, blocking a continued German advance toward the river. However, Seydlitz, as LI Corps commander, had already directed 24th Panzer Division to shift its 26th Grenadier Regiment to reinforce the attack on the mound.[45] By 22 September, *Kampfgruppe* Sälzer, with a company of antitank weapons and a company of engineers, had joined the grenadiers, while 4th Motorcycle Battalion from the panzer division was in contact with 295th Infantry Division's 516th Regiment on the crest of Mamaev Kurgan.

On the twentieth Chuikov ordered Colonel Dubiansky, commander of the depleted 35th Guards Rifle Division, to transfer his defenses north of the El'shanka River to Tarasov's composite 92nd Rifle Brigade and then withdraw 35th Guards, together with the attached remnants of 131st Rifle Division and 271st NKVD Regiment, for evacuation to the eastern bank. However, as Dubiansky fought his way back to the landing site, 94th Infantry Division encircled one of his surviving groups near the grain elevator, where the guardsmen were obliterated. The next day the commander and commissar of 35th Guards' 101st Regiment sustained severe wounds in a desperate bayonet charge to break through to the rest of 94th Infantry Division as the Germans threatened to cut off the Soviet retreat near the mouth of the Tsaritsa River.

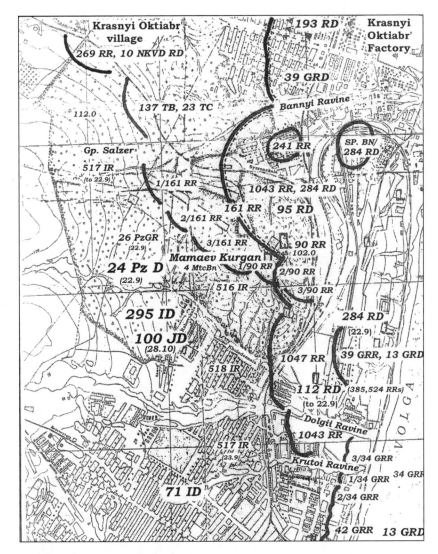

Map 40. The Struggle for Mamaev Kurgan, 20 September–5 October 1942

Only Dubiansky's division headquarters and support elements survived to cross the river on the night of 22–23 September, leaving behind 9,000 dead in Stalingrad. A rebuilt 35th Guards Division emerged in December.[46]

Meanwhile, on 21 September Chuikov tried in vain to continue the counterattacks ordered by Eremenko but found himself under continuous German pressure. The most intense fighting in the city center occurred between

13th Guards Rifle Division and 71st Infantry Division. The German infantry pushed back and partially encircled one Red battalion east of Railroad Station No. 1, while another Soviet battalion barely halted German infantry and assault guns northwest of 9 January Square. In the southern part of the city, Batrakov's 42nd Rifle Brigade and the remnants of 244th Rifle Division, cut off from communications with army headquarters, tried to hold their shrinking bridgehead south of the Tsaritsa River. By evening, 94th Infantry Division's 276th Regiment had almost cut off Tarasov's 92nd Rifle Brigade in the Tsaritsa gully, while the division's 267th Regiment finally snuffed out resistance at the grain elevator.[47]

That night, the 1043rd Regiment of Colonel N. F. Batiuk's 284th Rifle Division reached the western shore of the Volga, but the division was so underequipped that it had only enough rifles for one regiment.[48] Despite this deficiency, Chuikov felt compelled to throw the regiments into combat as soon as they arrived on 21–23 September, defending the sector south of Mamaev Kurgan. Meanwhile, the exhausted 112th Rifle Division, relieved by Batiuk, had to shift northward to reinforce Krasnyi Oktiabr' village.

The new Soviet regiments arrived just in time to deprive 295th Infantry Division of tenuous footholds on the Volga River bank, which the Germans had reached after a final assault on Mamaev Kurgan on the morning of 22 September. That same day, small elements of 71st Infantry Division moved through the sewers to reach the Volga at two points east of Railroad Station No. 1, but they had to withdraw that night.

By the evening of 23 September, the remnants of Rodimtsev's 13th Guards Division found themselves compressed into a narrow strip of land along the riverbank and were virtually combat ineffective. Meanwhile, Chuikov discovered that Colonel Tarasov, who commanded the survivors of 92nd and 42nd Rifle Brigades, had abandoned his troops, moving onto Golodnyi Island in the Volga and submitting false reports from there.[49] Chuikov promptly relieved Tarasov, but in reality, Rodimtsev represented the only remaining element of 62nd Army's left flank. In reaching this limited victory, the German 71st Infantry Division was also depleted, to the point where one of its eight battalions was dissolved and three more were rated "exhausted."[50]

To maintain communications with his left flank, on 23 September Chuikov ordered Batiuk's 284th Division to attack southward across the Dolgii and Krutoi ravines toward the city center, seeking to link up with Rodimtsev. The 62nd Army also dispatched 2,000 replacements to 13th Guards Rifle Division.[51] In fierce struggles between 23 and 26 September, the Germans continued to attrit and even penetrate 13th Guards' remaining positions. Chuikov's counterattacks stalled by 25 September without achieving any of their objectives, while the invaders captured the central landing stage on the twenty-second.[52] By 26 September, the Germans effectively controlled the

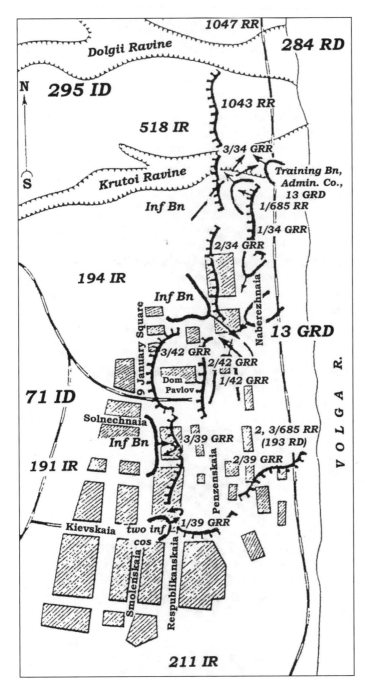

Map 41. The Battle for Central Stalingrad, 20 September–
1 October 1942

southern two-thirds of Stalingrad, with only Mamaev Kurgan and the Dolgii and Krutoi ravines remaining in Soviet hands.

With the loss of the main landing stage, larger vessels could no longer evacuate the Soviet wounded, a task that fell to Lieutenant Colonel A. N. Vertiulin's 3rd Division of cutters. These small, fast gunboats, operating under withering German fire, evacuated 350 wounded from the mouth of the Tsaritsa River on the night of 25–26 September. Meanwhile, virtually every civilian and military vessel on the river suffered damage from German air attacks while they continued to supply men and ammunition to 62nd Army. Soviet antiaircraft guns did their best to protect the landings from both air and ground attack; four batteries were destroyed in a single day of intense fighting, often firing at German vehicles over open sights. East of the river, a special group of antiaircraft trains and 38 fighter aircraft took on the assignment to defend supplies arriving by rail.[53]

Despite the loss of terrain, Chuikov professed himself well satisfied with his men's performance, as they continued to charge the attackers a blood toll for every meter they gave up.[54] Moreover, the closer the Germans came to the river, the more they suffered from Soviet artillery firing from the far bank. Between 23 and 25 September, 24th Panzer Division alone sustained 71 killed and 256 wounded.

Farther north, between Gorodishche and Mamaev Kurgan, the understrength tank and motorized brigades of 23rd Tank Corps were equally weak, barely holding on against 389th Infantry Division's 544th Regiment in the north and 24th Panzer Division's 26th Grenadiers, the latter scheduled for relief by that division's 21st Grenadier Regiment.

ASSESSMENT

Under enormous pressure from Hitler, Paulus planned to renew the attack on 27 September, aiming to take the factory district. Yet his combat power to accomplish this task continued to shrink on a daily basis. In the two weeks between 13 and 26 September, Paulus's assault forces dwindled from six divisions (389th, 295th, 71st, and 94th Infantry, 24th Panzer, and 29th Motorized) with roughly 80,000 men and 100 tanks and assault guns to only five and a half divisions (389th, 295th, 71st, and 94th Infantry plus half of 24th Panzer) with perhaps 65,000 men and fewer than 25 tanks.[55] Attrition in the actual combat battalions was proportionally higher. The 94th Infantry Division's seven infantry battalions all declined from "medium strong" on 14 September to "exhausted" by 5 October.[56]

The Soviet losses were even higher, including at least 69 of Chuikov's 100 tanks. To offset this, the *Stavka* reinforced the Stalingrad and Southwestern Fronts with ten rifle divisions, two tank corps, and eight tank brigades during the same two-week period. Chuikov alone received five divisions or brigades, totaling 40,000 reinforcements; this enabled 62nd Army to maintain a strength of approximately 51,000 as of 25 September.[57]

Stalin's decision to defend the city had deprived the Germans of their traditional advantages of mobility, maneuver, and precisely focused firepower. This forced the attackers to gnaw their way through Chuikov's defenses in fighting that resembled that of 1916–1917 rather than 1941–1942.

In turn, this loss of momentum gave the Soviets a much greater opportunity to achieve the counteroffensive they had sought in vain since late July. From the perspective of Stalin and the *Stavka*, the cold-blooded sacrifice of Chuikov's men in the ruins of Stalingrad, including whatever replacements were necessary to sustain that defense, was a small price to pay for victory by the million-plus men who would conduct the Red Army's planned counteroffensive. Even the brutal, repetitive failures at Kotluban' forced Paulus to divert combat power to defend his flanks, while adding 76th Infantry Division to the list of German units that were effectively hors de combat. In turn, this steady pressure eventually led to a growing German reliance on lightly equipped satellite forces.

The next act, a continued struggle between the exhausted units of 62nd and Sixth Armies, would be fought over the ruined factories and villages of northern Stalingrad.

CHAPTER NINE

The German Assault on
the Workers' Villages

PAULUS'S OFFENSIVE PLAN

By nightfall on 26 September, General Paulus had every reason to believe that southern and central Stalingrad was within his grasp. In the north, however, Seydlitz's LI Corps had faltered well short of its objectives. The 389th Infantry Division was marking time in front of the Soviet defenses west and southwest of Orlovka and east of Gorodische, while on Seydlitz's right, 295th Infantry Division, reinforced with half of 24th Panzer Division, had made little headway against 23rd Tank Corps and the remnants of other Soviet units west of Krasnyi Oktiabr' village and south to Mamaev Kurgan and the Dolgii and Krutoi ravines.

Paulus therefore reconfigured his units, bringing in a few fresh elements to form two shock groups for the continuing attack in the north. On LI Corps' left wing, he concentrated nine regiments: the 545th, 546th, and 544th Infantry Regiments of Jänecke's tired 389th Division; the 24th Panzer Regiment and 26th and 21st Panzer-Grenadier Regiments of Lenski's equally worn 24th Panzer Division; and the 54th and 227th *Jäger* Regiments of General Werner Sanne's 100th *Jäger* Division, with the attached Croat 369th Infantry Regiment. Their initial positions extended from west of Hill 112 and the Krasnyi Oktiabr' village to Mamaev Kurgan. With the support of 100 tanks and assault guns, these three divisions had to penetrate deep into the workers' villages and, if possible, into the factory district of northern Stalingrad.[1] To the south, a second shock group consisted of the 516th, 518th, and 517th Regiments of Wuthmann's 295th Infantry Division, together with the 194th Regiment of Hartmann's depleted 71st Infantry Division. This group was to attack eastward across the middle portions of the Dolgii and Krutoi ravines to reach the bank of the Volga River, then pivot northward and clear Soviet forces from the "Tennis Racket," a railroad marshaling yard east of Mamaev Kurgan, while 71st Division's 194th Regiment turned south to outflank the remaining defenders in the city center.

These 13 regiments were insufficient in themselves to achieve the desired results. In the north, Hube's XIV Panzer Corps would provide company- and battalion-sized *kampfgruppen* from 60th Motorized and 16th Panzer Divisions to assist in the attack on the Orlovka salient, but Hube had to focus most of his combat power on protecting Sixth Army's northern flank rather than clearing the city. General Paulus therefore directed that, once 94th Infantry Division finished clearing operations in the south, its 267th and 274th Regiments would transfer to reinforce Hube's thrust. Moreover, the main advance by 389th Infantry Division was to angle northeastward and eastward to help cut off the salient. In practice, continued Soviet attacks in the Kotluban' area and resistance in the southern city prevented Hube from mounting any serious effort against Orlovka.

Paulus allocated most of his air and artillery support to Seydlitz's main advance; 17 batteries supported 24th Panzer Division, with orders to fire a 12-minute preparatory concentration and then shift their fires as the mechanized troops advanced.[2] The limited duration of this concentration is a reminder that the entire German attack on Stalingrad was conducted on a shoestring with often inadequate logistical support, both because of the great distances involved and because of the competing demands of Army Group A. Limited transportation not only hampered the German attack on the city but also meant that Sixth Army had few supplies on hand when it was encircled in November.

The final step in Paulus's plan was that, once southern Stalingrad was secure, General Hoth would rest and refit 29th Motorized and 14th Panzer Divisions for a week, then launch them eastward toward Astrakhan' on the lower Volga.

CHUIKOV'S COUNTERATTACK PLAN

Correctly identifying the outline of future German plans, Chuikov issued an amendment to previous orders at 2300 hours on 25 September.[3] In the revised order he directed 284th Rifle Division to relieve 112th Division and establish an antitank defensive line along the northern bank of the Dolgii ravine. Colonel Ermolkhin's 112th Division, with the attached 186th Antitank Regiment, was to form a second defensive line just west of Krasnyi Oktiabr' village by 0400 on 26 September. This left Gorishnyi's 95th Rifle Division to hold Hill 102 (Mamaev Kurgan) and Rodimtsev's 13th Guards Division to defend the central landing stage and continue the contest with the enemy for control of the city center. Chuikov's order reflected the almost microscopic scale of the battle, specifying exact defensive positions in great detail.

The 26 September advance of 295th Infantry Division on Mamaev Kurgan prompted the 62nd Army commander to react yet again that evening, when he issued a revised counterattack order at 1940 hours. The 95th Rifle Division received priority of fire support for a planned counterattack at 0500 on 27 September toward Mamaev Kurgan and the southern spur of the Dolgii ravine. Simultaneously, the remaining tanks of Popov's 23rd Tank Corps, as well as the infantry of 184th Rifle Division, would conduct local counter-attacks. Chuikov's coordinating instructions in this order illustrate the nature of his urban tactics: "I again warn the commanders of all units and formations not to carry out operations or battles with whole units such as companies and battalions. Organize the offensive primarily on the basis of small groups, with sub-machine guns, hand-grenades, bottles of incendiary mixture [Molotov cocktails], and anti-tank rifles. Use regimental and battalion artillery to support the attacking groups by firing point-blank into windows, embrasures, and garrets."[4]

THE INITIAL GERMAN ASSAULT ON THE WORKERS' VILLAGES, 27 SEPTEMBER–1 OCTOBER

In the event, the Soviet forces ran straight into the teeth of Paulus's new thrust, faltering within minutes after they began the attack. At 0800 on 27 September, massed Stuka attacks not only broke up the Soviet advance but also destroyed 95th Rifle Division's strongpoint on the crest of Mamaev Kurgan. They also set fire to oil storage tanks near Chuikov's command post, rendering that post untenable. Chuikov, his chief of staff, and his commissar each took signal officers and went forward to a different threatened division headquarters but could see little in the smoke. At 1030 the 389th Infantry, 24th Panzer, and 100th *Jäger* Divisions began a coordinated attack toward the base of the Orlovka salient, the Krasnyi Oktiabr' village, and Mamaev Kurgan.

One participant described the bold thrust of 24th Panzer Division to the northeast, alongside the Vishnevaia *balka*:

> Encounters came at close range. A burst of fire from the bushes, a man would be hit and then crumple to the ground, his comrades also diving to the ground and opening fire on the suspected area. Grenades were thrown and the bushes stormed, usually ending in the death of the Russians. Then they moved on until fired on again. In this nightmarish terrain, which provided excellent cover and camouflage for the Russians, [3rd Squadron] under *Oberleutnant* Jurgen Pachnio suffered 11 casualties, including *Oberleutnant* Pachnio himself, who was severely wounded by a shot to the lungs.[5]

In the course of the day, the two main *kampfgruppen* of 24th Panzer Division, Edelsheim and Winterfeld, shattered the 137th and 27th Tank Brigades of 23rd Tank Corps, as well as an attached NKVD regiment, advancing up

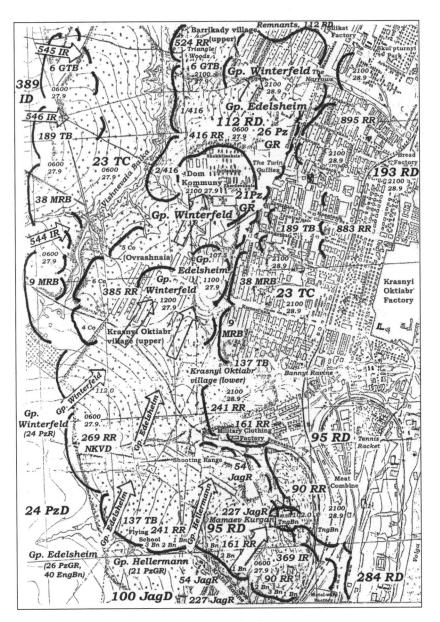

Map 42. LI Army Corps' Assault, 27–28 September 1942

to 3 kilometers to the upper section of the Krasnyi Oktiabr' village and the military clothing factory. This bold thrust threatened to cut off large portions of 23rd Tank Corps and 112th Rifle Division west of the Vishnevaia *balka*. Meanwhile, against desperate resistance by the 90th Regiment of Gorishnyi's 95th Rifle Division, the relatively fresh 100th *Jäger* Division finally secured the crest of Mamaev Kurgan, although the defenders still held on to the eastern slope and the railroad line to the southeast. These Soviet positions meant that as 24th Panzer Division continued to advance northward, its right flank would be increasingly exposed. Only fanatical resistance by Batiuk's 284th Rifle Division prevented 295th Infantry Division from reaching the Volga and splitting Chuikov's army in half. The depleted 71st Infantry Division swept away the remains of two equally exhausted Soviet brigades to secure the lower reaches of the Tsaritsa River. Although individual Red strongpoints held out in the center of the city, General Pfeiffer began transferring regiments of the 71st out of the southern city and sending them northward, as planned.

On the evening of 27 September Chuikov committed his latest reinforcement, two regiments of General Smekhotvorov's 193rd Rifle Division, to shore up defenses in front of the workers' villages, while the remnants of 23rd Tank Corps shifted into second-echelon positions near the factories. Gorishnyi's 95th Rifle Division got the mission to counterattack Mamaev Kurgan the next morning, and Chuikov directed his artillery to shell the hill constantly so as to disrupt German consolidation efforts.[6]

The Germans preempted many of these redeployments, however. On 28–29 September the *kampfgruppen* of 24th Panzer Division advanced more than 6 kilometers in and between the Krasnyi Oktiabr' and Barrikady suburbs. The 389th Infantry Division also made steady if slower progress. The armored unit suffered additional casualties—28 killed and 94 wounded—while the supporting 95th Infantry and 100th *Jäger* Divisions had great difficulty keeping pace with the panzers in the face of determined resistance by 124th and 149th Rifle Brigades and the depleted 23rd Tank Corps.[7]

Chuikov sensed that the German attacks were less confident and not as well coordinated, and he used available artillery and air support to delay the enemy advances. Nonetheless, 62nd Army was also approaching its breaking point. The concluding paragraphs of the army order issued on the evening of 28 September reflected the sense of crisis and repeated Stalin's famous Order No. 229:

Complete the initial work (mainly the antitank obstacles) by the morning on 29 September 1942, making the defenses of the city and its industrial centers impregnable. Every obstacle should be reliably covered by all types of fire.

Explain to all personnel that the Army is fighting on its last line of defense; there can be no further retreat. It is the duty of every soldier and commander to defend his trench, his position—NOT A STEP BACK! The enemy MUST BE DESTROYED AT WHATEVER COST!

Shoot soldiers and commanders who willfully abandon their foxholes and positions on the spot as enemies of THE FATHERLAND.

[signed] Chuikov, Gurov, Krylov[8]

At 0430 on 29 September two regiments of 193rd Rifle Division conducted a reconnaissance in force against 26th Panzer-Grenadier Regiment of *Kampfgruppe* Edelsheim in the "twin gullies" area between the two workers' suburbs. Although the Germans were initially surprised, they quickly stopped this attack and resumed their own advance northward toward the tractor factory village, although as previously noted, their long right (eastern) flank was increasingly exposed. To the left of 24th Panzer Division, 389th Infantry Division crossed the Mechetka River and also wheeled northward, in this case toward Orlovka. Meanwhile, *Luftwaffe* attacks created a fiery backdrop by setting the tractor factory ablaze.[9] Only the bravery of Smekhotvorov's 193rd Rifle Division prevented the Germans from consolidating their hold on Krasnyi Oktiabr' village.

Beginning about noon on 29 September, the regiments of 100th *Jäger* Division fought a bitter and ultimately successful battle for Hill 107.5, freeing up 212th Panzer-Grenadier Regiment to rejoin the rest of its division farther north. On the *Jäger* division's right, the attached Croatian troops took part of the Meat Combine from the weakened 95th and 284th Rifle Divisions, but still they could not quite reach the Volga.[10]

On 30 September and 1 October the fighting in the northern suburbs degenerated into a vicious slugfest of small-unit actions. Seydlitz was finally able to consolidate all his divisions for a push northward toward Orlovka but made only limited progress. On the opposing side, Chuikov concentrated the remaining armor of 23rd Tank Corps under 6th Guards Tank Brigade, which on the thirtieth had 21 operable tanks (14 T-34s and the remainder light vehicles) but only four 76.2mm field guns and 16 mortars.[11] By the end of 1 October, 24th Panzer Division faced the depleted companies of 112th Rifle Division but was still unable to penetrate the Silikat Factory. The 100th *Jäger* and 295th Infantry Divisions clung to the crest of Mamaev Kurgan, but the defending 95th Rifle Division and portions of 284th Rifle Division refused to concede the northern and eastern slopes to them. Similarly, south of the burial mound, Rodimtsev had created a virtually impregnable defense based on numerous building strongpoints only three to four blocks west of the Volga. On 28 September–1 October multiple attacks by 295th Infantry Division's 517th Regiment and 71st Division's 194th Regiment failed to dis-

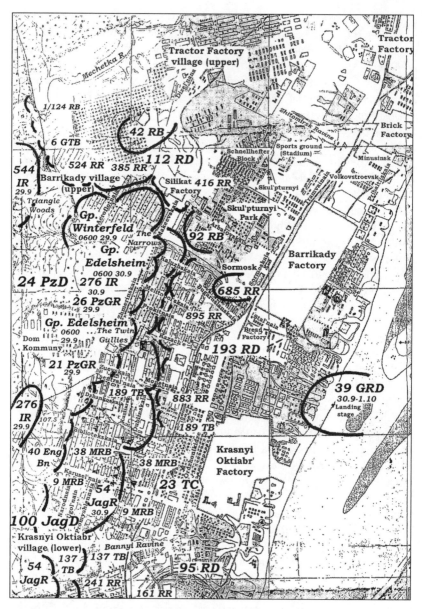

Map 43. LI Army Corps' Assault, 29–30 September 1942

lodge the defenders. Although the invaders could still advance incrementally, the battle for the central city appeared to be approaching a standstill as German combat power waned and new Soviet forces arrived.[12]

SOVIET REORGANIZATION

While the Sixth and 62nd Armies struggled inside the city, the Soviet High Command took its own precautions against further defeat. Between 25 and 28 September 1942, the *Stavka* ordered the redeployment of five rifle divisions, three rifle brigades, and two tank brigades to create reserves in the rear area of the Stalingrad and Southeastern Fronts.[13]

More significantly, on 28 September Stalin acted to reorganize the command structure in the region, dividing it into two separate *fronts* to direct the two portions of the struggle. The order transferred K. K. Rokossovsky from the Briansk Front to command the new Don Front, which controlled 63rd, 21st, 4th Tank, 1st Guards, and 66th Armies conducting the flank battle northwest of Stalingrad. With him, Rokossovsky took his chief of staff, Major General M. S. Malinin, to be the deputy *front* commander, while A. S. Zheltov became the *front* member of the Military Council (commissar). Eremenko remained commander of the Stalingrad Front to control the close-in battle with 62nd, 64th, 57th, 51st, and 28th Armies.

Beginning on the night of 29–30 September and over the course of several succeeding nights, Chuikov received almost 20,000 reinforcements, including the reconstituted 42nd and 92nd Rifle Brigades, as well as 37th Guards, 39th Guards, and 308th Rifle Divisions. These fresh troops replaced the 16,174 casualties the Stalingrad Front reported between 26 and 30 September; their arrival helped stabilize the front lines in the factory district.[14] In fact, a local counterattack by Batiuk's division recaptured part of the Meat Combine at the eastern base of Mamaev Kurgan. Meanwhile, 39th Guards Division now manned a secondary defensive line behind 193rd Rifle Division, building various strongpoints inside the workshops of the Krasnyi Oktiabr' Factory. By late on 1 October, 62nd Army once again had more than 44,000 men in Stalingrad, and the 6,695 men of 37th Guards were still waiting to cross the Volga.[15]

THE REDUCTION OF THE ORLOVKA SALIENT, 29 SEPTEMBER–3 OCTOBER

Paulus could not match this influx of new Soviet troops, yet he had no choice but to continue the fight. Beginning on 29 September he shifted part of his resources to reduce the 10 kilometer long salient along the Orlovka River, north of the workers' villages (see map 44). This salient separated XIV Panzer Corps from LI Army Corps and tied down German forces that could be better employed clearing the industrial areas. Still, the Soviet units to the north continued to occupy the attention of XIV Panzer Corps.[16] Thus, to attack the northern face of the salient, 16th Panzer Division could spare only a battalion of 79th Grenadier Regiment, working with 501st Artillery Battalion and two pioneer (combat engineer) battalions, the 194th and 651st, that Sixth Army had attached to the panzer corps. On 16th Panzer's right (western) flank, 60th Motorized Division committed 160th Motorcycle Battalion plus various detached companies from other units within the division. On the southern face of the Orlovka salient, the 94th (from XIV Panzer Corps) and 389th (from LI Corps) Divisions each deployed two infantry regiments, but all eight of the battalions involved were rated "weak."

Thus, despite several hours of German air and artillery strikes on the morning of 29 September, 2nd Motorized Rifle and 115th Rifle Brigades initially put up a strong defense, giving ground grudgingly even when faced with the relatively fresh pioneer battalions. The *kampfgruppen* of General George Pfeiffer's 94th Infantry Division had more success near Orlovka itself, splitting Andriusenko's 2nd Motorized Brigade and forcing his battalions to withdraw eastward.[17] In succeeding days, two battalions of this brigade, as well as elements of 115th Brigade, found themselves cut off and surrounded east of Orlovka; the Soviets abandoned that village on 2 October. The defenders received a brief respite on 3 October, when Paulus reshuffled his weary forces to generate a renewed attack. Moreover, Zhukov's exhausted forces came to a halt in the Kotluban' region on 4 October, freeing more elements of XIV Panzer Corps to concentrate on their southern front.

When the German attack resumed on the fourth, small *kampfgruppen* from 60th Motorized and 16th Panzer Divisions began to systematically reduce the remnants of seven Soviet battalions around Orlovka. Unable to reinforce the surrounded units, Chuikov organized *katiusha* barrages against German troop concentrations north of the Mokraia Mechetka River.[18] This supporting fire enabled small groups of Andriusenko's surrounded soldiers to exfiltrate successfully, rejoining 62nd Army's lines on the western edge of the tractor factory workers' village. The Germans overran the last defenders of these encirclements during the afternoon of 7 October. Of the 6,500 men originally encircled in the area, no more than 220 soldiers of 2nd Motorized Rifle Brigade, plus a few others from NKVD and other rifle units, escaped.[19]

Chuikov's forces had unquestionably suffered serious defeats at the end of September and during the first three days of October. The attackers had not only brushed off repeated counterattacks but also captured Orlovka, most of Mamaev Kurgan, and large portions of the Krasnyi Oktiabr' and

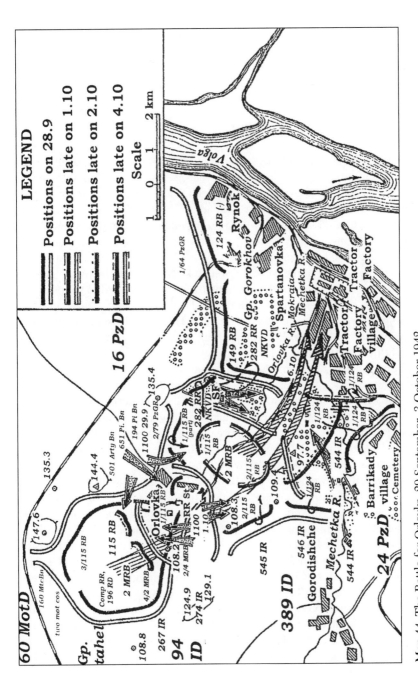

Map 44. The Battle for Orlovka, 29 September–3 October 1942

Barrikady workers' villages. Seydlitz's LI Corps appeared poised for a subsequent advance on the tractor factory. Yet Chuikov was receiving a steady flow of replacements, while Paulus had no new source of manpower. By 5 October, of 54 infantry and 9 pioneer battalions, only 3 were considered "medium-strong," while 16 were rated "average," 20 "weak," and 24 "exhausted."[20]

THE GERMAN PAUSE, 1–3 OCTOBER

Paulus had hoped to continue the advance without a pause, but by midnight on 30 September, it was already clear that he needed new combat power. As of 1 October, for example, 24th Panzer Division's three regiments—24th Panzer and 21st and 26th Panzer-Grenadier—reported combat strengths of 1,089, 896, and 923 men, respectively, as compared to ration strengths of 2,064, 1,213, and 1,293.[21] Seydlitz's infantry divisions were no stronger. Paulus therefore had to pause for several days while Jänecke's 389th Infantry Division shifted south of the Mokraia Mechetka River; then the two regiments of Pfeiffer's 94th Infantry Division in turn moved southward to the northern bank of this river. Meanwhile, 24th Panzer Division had reorganized into two *kampfgruppen,* each supported by artillery. The main division striking force remained *Kampfgruppe* Edelsheim, built around the 21st and portions of the 26th Panzer-Grenadier Regiments, with attached companies of pioneers and tank killers. *Kampfgruppe* Winterfeld included most of the division's remaining tanks, plus the half-track mounted 1st Battalion, 26th Panzer-Grenadiers, and one squadron (company) of 4th Motorcycle Battalion.[22]

During this German pause, Chuikov deployed the hastily refurbished 42nd Rifle Brigade to the wooded area south of Dizel'naia, behind the left wing of 112th Rifle Division. The 351st Rifle Regiment, the first element of Gurt'ev's 308th Division to arrive on the west bank, took up positions at the boundary between 112th and 193rd Rifle Divisions, southeast of the Silikat Factory, to protect the approaches to the Barrikady Factory. If Gurt'ev's remaining two regiments arrived in time, they would block *Kampfgruppe* Edelsheim on the right flank of 24th Panzer. Meanwhile, on 30 September–1 October the refurbished 92nd Rifle Brigade and 39th Guards Rifle Division arrived to thicken the defenses of 193rd Rifle Division at the Krasnyi Oktiabr' Factory. Given the dwindling manpower and equipment of the attackers, Paulus's advance would now be reduced to a snail's pace.

Chuikov attempted to exploit the German lull by mounting a limited counterattack on 1 October to feel out and, if possible, push back the enemy front line, but 24th Panzer easily thwarted this effort.[23] Chuikov tried again the next day, ordering 92nd and 42nd Rifle Brigades, as well as 351st Regiment of Gurt'ev's 308th Rifle Division, to clear the Germans from the

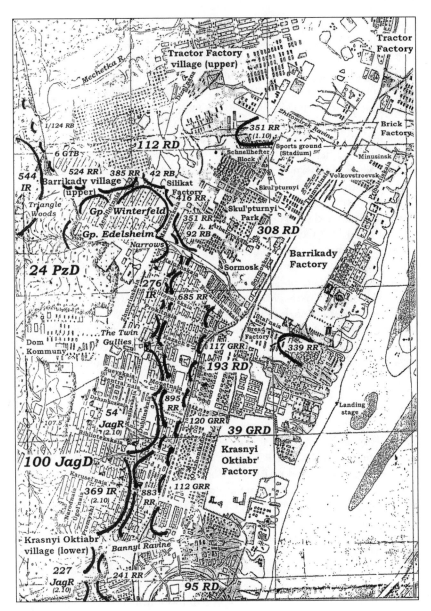

Map 45. LI Army Corps' Situation, 1–2 October 1942

narrows and the upper Barrikady village to the cemetery on the Vishnevaia *balka*. As had happened so often before, however, battlefield coordination eluded the Soviets; only 351st Regiment attacked on time, failing to dent 24th Panzer Division's *Kampfgruppe* Winterfeld and making only minor progress against the neighboring *Kampfgruppe* Edelsheim. Indeed, the panzer division believed the Soviets had made only light "reconnaissance probes."[24] In the midst of this unsuccessful attack, *Luftwaffe* bombers first ignited a small petroleum reservoir near 62nd Army's headquarters and then hit the headquarters bunker itself, briefly knocking out all wire communications. Krylov, the army chief of staff, managed to restore some control using radios, but the reservoir continued to burn. When Eremenko's *front* headquarters inquired as to the location of Chuikov and his staff, the response was, "We're where the most flames and smoke are."[25]

That night, 2–3 October, Chuikov reconfigured his defenses. The newly arrived regiments of 39th Guards Rifle Division allowed 193rd Division to place one of its three regiments in second echelon, while 112th Rifle Division moved to the left flank of Gorokhov's northern group in the Spartanovka region, north of the Mokraia Mechetka River. The result was a more coherent defense, with 39th Guards in front of the Krasnyi Oktiabr' Factory and 93rd Rifle Brigade to its right (north), followed (from south to north) by 92nd Rifle Brigade and 308th Division (in front of the Barrikady Factory) and 42nd Brigade and 37th Guards Division near the Silikat Factory (see map 46).

THE FIGHT FOR THE WORKERS' VILLAGES, 3–7 OCTOBER

On 3 October the German attack resumed, focused on the upper tractor factory village and the Silikat Factory. On the left, 389th Infantry Division encountered unexpected resistance from the redeployed 112th Rifle Division, reinforced by the remaining armor of 6th Guards Tank Brigade. The slow German advance here forced General von Lenski to postpone the main attack by 24th Panzer Division, which began at 1400 with Stuka attacks and a brief artillery barrage against the Silikat Factory. The armor-heavy *Kampfgruppe* Winterfeld, on the division's left, skirted the Barrikady Factory, reached its assigned objective, and dug into the shattered remains of various workers' buildings, still defended by elements of 42nd Rifle Brigade. On the right, *Kampfgruppe* Edelsheim had more difficulty and was unable to secure the massive building the Germans called the *Schnellhefter* block.[26] By the end of 3 October, 112th Rifle Division had to abandon Hill 97.7, west of the Dizel'naia section, as the division's regiments fell to 200 men each. To the south, the neighboring 193rd Division had more success containing 100th *Jäger* Division in the rubble-filled streets west of the railroad line and

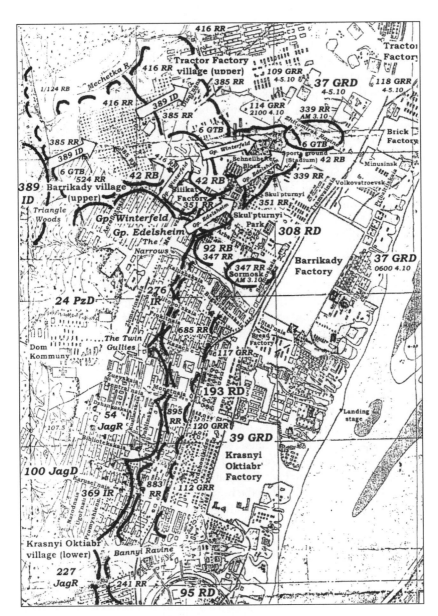

Map 46. LI Army Corps' Assault, 3–4 October 1942

the Krasnyi Oktiabr' Factory, but here the Soviet rifle regiments suffered even more, reduced to no more than 150 men each.[27]

Not content with this progress, General Seydlitz urged 389th Infantry and 24th Panzer Divisions to press forward and capture the dominating heights on the western edge of the northern part of Stalingrad. Accordingly, Lenski issued a divisional order to attack on 4 October at 0900. After the two *kampfgruppen* seized the *Schnellhefter* block and the nearby sports stadium, Edelsheim was to wheel southeastward to repulse expected counterattacks. Beyond this, however, the absence of German replacement troops meant that Paulus and Seydlitz had to settle for limited assaults.[28]

With the defending units in this area decimated, Chuikov persuaded the Stalingrad Front to release Major General V. G. Zholudev's 37th Guards Rifle Division to his control. Although one of the three rifle regiments of this fresh unit crossed the Volga on the night of 3–4 October, a shortage of cutter transports meant that the division headquarters and antitank artillery remained behind. The next morning, staff officers from 62nd Army led the new infantry into position just in time to engage the renewed LI Corps attack.[29]

At 0910 hours on 4 October 24th Panzer Division, led by the 36 operational tanks of *Kampfgruppe* Winterfeld, jumped off after a brief artillery and aerial fire preparation. Catching the defenders by surprise, the two *kampfgruppen* seized their respective objectives, the *Schnellhelfer* block and the sports stadium, and destroyed nine Soviet tanks in the process, including seven T-34s, from the remnants of 6th Guards Tank Brigade. Lenski's grenadiers cleared Soviet troops from the *Schnellhelfer* block, but the newly arrived troops of 37th Guards Division's 114th Regiment halted a German attempt to exploit between the tractor and Barrikady factories. Simultaneously, 389th Infantry Division penetrated several blocks into the upper tractor factory village along Shchelkovskaia Street, encircling and destroying 351st Rifle Regiment of Colonel Gur'tev's 308th Division.[30]

On the night of 4–5 October the remaining rifle elements of 37th Guards Division crossed the river. The 109th Regiment reinforced the depleted 112th Rifle Division protecting the tractor factory village, while the 118th Regiment took up positions to protect the tractor factory from the southwest.[31]

The Germans were clearly conscious of their manpower problem. In an entry late on 4 October, Sixth Army's chief of staff observed, "Without reinforcements, the army is not going to take Stalingrad very soon. The danger exists, were the Russians to make fairly strong counterattacks, our front might not hold because there are no reserves behind it."[32]

After suffering another 23 killed and 89 wounded on 4 October, Lenski informed Seydlitz that his panzer division had insufficient strength for further offensive operations. Moreover, on 24th Panzer Division's right, 100th *Jäger* Division had been unable to keep pace with the armored advance, forcing the panzer troops to protect an ever-lengthening right flank. On Lenski's left flank, 389th Infantry Division had thrust northward along the Mechetka River and established contact with Hube's XIV Panzer Corps, but this effort had left the 389th equally depleted.[33]

The defenders had their own issues with replacement units. In addition to 37th Guards Rifle Division, Eremenko attempted to dispatch Colonel Daniil Nikitovich Belyi's 84th Tank Brigade across the river to reinforce the defenses around the factories. Unfortunately, lack of appropriate shipping vessels meant that only 20 T-70 light tanks could cross, leaving behind 5 KV-1 heavy and 24 T-34 tanks. The light tanks were broken up into small groups for infantry support.[34] Even this limited effort strained the Volga River Flotilla, which was also moving 45th Rifle Division to defend the Golodnyi and Sarpinskii Islands opposite the southern suburbs of the city.

Effective 5 October, Paulus authorized his exhausted troops to go over to the defense in order to recover for future operations. However, both sides engaged in limited but bloody fighting over the next three days (see map 46).

On the fifth, a tank squadron from 24th Panzer and hundreds of aircraft sorties aided 389th Infantry Division in advancing 400 meters into the lower tractor factory village, bringing the infantry on line with the neighboring panzer division. Only antitank guns and the newly arrived T-70 tanks helped 37th Guards Rifle Division contain this attack.[35]

The next day, 6 October, the Germans confined themselves to continued air strikes, prompting Eremenko to encourage Chuikov to launch yet another round of counterattacks. Chuikov reluctantly signed an order for 37th Guards and 308th Rifle Divisions to attempt to regain ground, but renewed German activity preempted this on the seventh. Once again, Jänecke's 389th Infantry Division made a limited advance with borrowed tank and air support. Given the emaciated units on both sides, this successful attack appeared on situation maps to be much greater than it was.[36] Eventually, 114th and 118th Regiments of 37th Guards Rifle Division halted the Germans, and Seydlitz and Paulus concluded that they needed significant reinforcements to conquer the tractor factory. An eerie lull set in along Sixth Army's front lines.

THE STRUGGLE ON THE FLANKS, 29 SEPTEMBER–11 OCTOBER

As fighting raged along the Orlovka salient and the factory district, the *Stavka* once again sought to distract German forces by mounting attacks north and south of the city. In addition to directing the Don Front to make yet another effort against XIV Panzer Corps north of the city, Moscow demanded that the Southeastern Front mount diversionary offensives to the south. The 57th and 51st Armies were to conduct regimental-sized probes on the night of

28–29 September, while 8th Air Army attacked seven sites within the city in the hope that this would disorganize the next German offensive.[37] The *Stavka* sent General Vasilevsky to the Southeastern Front (soon redesignated the Stalingrad Front), where he urged local commanders to attack south of the city and seize the entrances to the gaps between Lakes Sarpa, Tsatsa, and Barmantsak; at the time, this area was defended by Romanian 1st and 4th Infantry Divisions of Romanian VI Army Corps.[38]

To penetrate Romanian 1st Division between Lakes Sarpa and Tsatsa, General Tolbukhin, commander of 57th Army, formed a composite detachment consisting of 1334th and 115th Rifle Regiments and 155th Tank Brigade, supported by an antitank regiment and two guards-mortar (*katiusha*) regiments. General Kolomiets, who headed 51st Army, formed a smaller task force under the control of Colonel E. F. Makarchuk, commander of 302nd Rifle Division. Makarchuk's force, consisting of 254th Tank Brigade, one rifle battalion, and a guards-mortar regiment, focused on Romanian 4th Division between Tsatsa and Barmantsak. The 15th Guards Rifle Division provided artillery and other support to both attacks.

This dual thrust, launched on the night of 28–29 September, caught the lightly armed Romanians off guard. In two days of fighting, Makarchuk penetrated up to 18 kilometers, while 57th Army's detachment to his north advanced about 5 kilometers to the Dubovoi ravine. Romanian 4th Division, which had been screening a front of 60 kilometers, was particularly hard hit as the attackers even penetrated the divisional command post.[39]

Paulus recognized the danger to his southern flank and immediately ordered 14th Panzer Division, then in reserve preparing for a planned thrust to Astrakhan', southward to rescue the Romanians. Heim's division went into action at midday on 1 October; it managed to contain but not eliminate the Soviet thrust. Thus, Vasilevsky's southern diversion denied Paulus the use of 14th Panzer and 29th Motorized Divisions in the factory district until at least 9 October.[40]

On the night of 1–2 October Shumilov's 64th Army followed suit, launching six rifle divisions and a naval infantry brigade against the German 371st Infantry Division near Peschanka, at the extreme southern end of Stalingrad. This attempt to link up with 62nd Army failed, but it tied down additional German forces.[41]

No sooner did the assaults south of the city falter than the *Stavka* directed Rokossovsky's Don Front to launch yet another offensive—its third—in the Kotluban' and Erzovka regions northwest of the city. Although Rokossovsky's forces had not yet recovered from their previous actions in late September and early October, they attacked again on 9 October. Within two days, the feeble attempts by 1st Guards and 24th Armies came to a halt without any measurable results, except for more Soviet casualties.

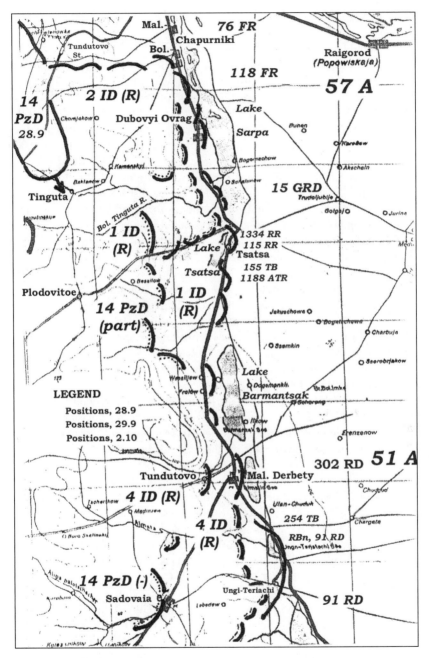

Map 47. 57th and 51st Armies' Counterstroke, 28–30 September 1942

THE LULL, 8–13 OCTOBER

Paulus could see no easy way to make good on Hitler's demand for the immediate conquest of Stalingrad. Victory had become even more important psychologically during September, however, when Erwin Rommel's Panzer Army Africa came to a halt in western Egypt, unable to advance farther after the Battle of Alam el Halfa. On 6 October the OKH informed Hitler that the German Army was a million men below strength, primarily due to casualties in the East. The dictator therefore authorized the reassignment of 400,000 *Luftwaffe* air-defense troops to the army, but this process would take too long to solve the immediate shortages in Army Groups A and B.[42]

Meanwhile, after failing to take the factory district on 7 October, the Germans virtually ceased offensive operations for several days while preparing for a renewed attempt. Sniping and small firefights went on as each side jockeyed for position with company- and battalion-sized attacks. Chuikov even planned for 37th Guards Division, reinforced with tanks and artillery, to conduct a limited attack late on 9 October to push the German 389th Infantry Division back beyond the ravines north of Zhitomirsk, near the brick factory and midway between the Barrikady and tractor factories. This attack did not take place, however, because the Soviets used the quiet time to reorganize their defending units. Chuikov moved the relatively strong 95th Rifle Division into the Zhitomirsk sector, narrowing the defensive frontage of 37th Guards, and directed units of 284th Rifle Division to assume the 95th's former sector south of the Bannyi ravine.[43]

The reduced strength of Sixth Army forced Hitler, reluctantly, to cancel the projected advance to Astrakhan', freeing 14th Panzer Division for eventual redeployment to the factory district. At Army Group B, General Weichs decided to shift two divisions from the long northern flank to reinforce the shock groups in Stalingrad. XVII Army Corps, opposite the Soviet Serafimovich bridgehead on the Don River, gave up 79th Infantry Division, while VIII Corps, which faced northward along the Don and Volga Rivers on the extreme left of Sixth Army's sector, released 305th Infantry Division.[44] However, 79th Infantry Division took days to redeploy and arrived with only two of its regiments. Meanwhile, Paulus also withdrew the battered 76th Infantry Division, reduced from nine to six battalions, into reserve and replaced it with 113th Infantry Division, also from XVII Corps.

These German movements away from the flanks climaxed during the first ten days of October, when the entire Romanian Third Army (171,256 men) occupied defenses along the southern bank of the Don, opposite the Serafimovich bridgehead and the western end of the Kletskaia bridgehead. By assigning this vital sector to the Romanians, both Hitler and Weichs took the fatal gamble that the Red Army would not, or could not, attack there in any strength. Deployed in thinly spread positions on the open steppe, the Romanians lacked the firepower, ammunition, and provisions necessary to defend their sector. The best that could be said for them was that Third Army had higher morale than the Romanians south of the city, who were scheduled to be redesignated as Fourth Army.[45]

To further complicate the situation, the Romanians were not even defending along the Don River itself, except on their extreme flanks. Rather, their defensive line dipped southward as much as 30 kilometers from the river in a straight line to save manpower, allowing the Soviets ample bridgeheads to prepare for future attacks. General Petre Dumitrescu, the commander of Third Army, was no fool. From the moment he assumed the defense of this new sector, he repeatedly asked for permission and reinforcements to conduct local counterattacks up to the river line. However, Army Group B was stretched so thin that it regularly deferred such actions until after the prospective victory at Stalingrad.[46] Instead, the Soviet forces conducted repeated probes of the Romanian front lines.

Meanwhile, Paulus reshuffled his scant resources inside the city. The two regiments of Pfeiffer's 94th Infantry Division transferred from LI Army Corps to XIV Panzer Corps, where they were to support 16th Panzer Division in attacking Soviet defenses north of the Mokraia Mechetka River. Seydlitz's LI Army Corps retained 24th Panzer, 389th Infantry, 100th *Jäger*, and 295th Infantry Divisions but now gained three more subordinates. Heim's 14th Panzer and Kurt Oppenländer's newly arrived 305th Infantry would join the assault on the factory district. One regiment of Hartman's 71st Infantry Division would continue clearing the central city, while two others defended the west bank of the Volga southward to Kuporosnoe. Fourth Panzer Army, on the defensive, retained only German IV and Romanian VI Corps, plus the headquarters (only) of XXXXVIII Panzer Corps and 29th Motorized Division in reserve.

After the fact, Soviet accounts claimed that Paulus had concentrated 90,000 men, 2,300 guns and mortars, 300 tanks and assault guns, and 1,000 aircraft in the city at this point.[47] However, these figures ignored the reality that most of XIV Panzer Corps was still facing northward rather than toward the city, and they assumed a maintenance availability that rarely occurred. On an average day, the actual attackers in Stalingrad had the services of roughly 50 tanks from 16th Panzer Division and 30 from 24th Panzer, supplemented by perhaps 30 vehicles from 244th and 245th Assault Gun Battalions. All the repair efforts of German maintenance units could not halt a steady decline in these numbers.[48] Despite a ration strength of 334,000 men on 17 October, Sixth Army reported only 66,549 combat troops, many of them north and south of the city itself.[49]

The combat ratings of the Sixth Army battalions about to resume the

Table 9.1. Combat Ratings of German Infantry and Pioneer Battalions Fighting in Stalingrad, 26 September–12 October 1942

26 September	5 October	12 October
54 infantry battalions	54 infantry battalions	61 infantry battalions
16 medium strong	3 medium strong	2 medium strong
20 average	12 average	21 average
14 weak	18 weak	19 weak
4 exhausted	21 exhausted	19 exhausted
9 pioneer battalions	9 pioneer battalions	10 pioneer battalions
2 strong	0 strong	1 strong
5 average	4 average	1 average
2 weak	2 weak	4 weak
0 exhausted	3 exhausted	4 exhausted

Source: Florian Freiherr von und zu Aufsess, "Betr.: Zustand der Divisionen, Armee-Oberkommando 6. Abt. 1a, A.H. Qu., den 26 September 1942," "Betr.: Zustand der Divisionen, erstmalig nach neu festlegter Bestimmung des Begriffes 'Gefechsstärke,' Armee-Oberkommando 6. Abt. 1a, A.H. Qu., den 5 Oktober 1942," and "Betr.: Zustand der Divisionen, Armee-Oberkommando 6. Abt. 1a, A.H. Qu., 12 Oktober 1942, 10:00 Uhr," in *Die Anlagenbänder zu den Kriegstagebüchern der 6. Armee vom 14.09.42 bis 24.11.42*, book 1 (Schwabach, Germany: self-published, 2006), 59–62, 128–132, 156–160.

attack against the factory district underscored Paulus's plight (see table 9.1). Despite an increase in the total number of battalions, their average rating was still "weak." By 12 October 1942, 295th, 389th, and 71st Infantry Divisions were virtually hors de combat, while 24th Panzer Division was nearing complete combat exhaustion. Of necessity, the new advance would rely on the nine added "average" infantry battalions of 305th Division.

While the German commanders faced the coming fighting with a bleak sense of resignation, Joseph Stalin was angered by his field commanders' continued failure to halt the German advance in the city that bore his name. On 5 October he sent a stinging rebuke to Eremenko, the Stalingrad Front commander, with a copy to Rokossovsky at the Don Front:

You must press the enemy back from the Volga and once again seize those streets and buildings in Stalingrad which the enemy has taken from you. To do so, it is necessary to convert every building and every street in Stalingrad into a fortress. Unfortunately, you have not succeeded in doing this and are still continuing to give block after block to the enemy. This testifies to your poor performance. You have more forces in the Stalingrad region than the enemy, and, in spite of this, the enemy is continuing to press you. I am dissatisfied with your performance in the Stalingrad Front, and I demand you undertake every measure for the defense of Stalingrad. Stalingrad must not be abandoned to the enemy, and those parts of Stalingrad which the enemy has occupied must be liberated.[50]

To underscore his dissatisfaction, the Soviet dictator shunted Eremenko's chief of staff, Major General G. F. Zakharov, aside, making him deputy commander and replacing him with Major General Ivan Semenovich Varennikov. The 45-year-old Zakharov had extensive experience as a *front* chief of staff, whereas his younger successor (aged 41) had previously served only at field army level. The previous deputy *front* commander, Lieutenant General F. I. Golikov, found himself relieved without a specific future assignment.[51]

Anticipating future reverses, on 7 October the *Stavka* assigned additional antiaircraft artillery regiments to Eremenko, with instructions to strengthen the defenses of Golodnyi and Sarpinskii Islands. In anticipation of a possible defeat in Stalingrad, on 10 October the *Stavka* assigned 4th Cavalry Corps and 300th Rifle Division to reinforce the eastern bank of the Volga.[52]

Speaking for Stalin, the *Stavka* also called for yet another offensive on the Kotluban' front, beginning about 20 October; this was to be accompanied by a similar strike south of the city, in the lakes region, seeking to link up with the Kotluban' attack. The Don Front commander, Rokossovsky, objected strenuously to such an offensive because of the strength of German defensive positions and the weakness of rifle units in his *front*. Instead, he proposed a much shallower plan whereby 24th Army would advance southeastward from Kuz'michi to link up with 62nd Army in the Orlovka area. But even this plan was unrealistic and required at least seven new rifle divisions to reinforce 24th Army.[53] Stalin rejected this proposal but confined Rokossovsky's mission to conducting active, limited attacks on the eastern part of his frontage to attract German units away from the Stalingrad fight. At the Stalingrad Front, Eremenko also responded to Stalin's order for a new offensive at Kotluban', offering a counterproposal that would ultimately become the plan for the successful November counteroffensive (see chapter 12). Yet, as early as 15 October, the continued pressure on 62nd Army prompted the dictator to revisit the possibility of renewed offensives on the flanks, only this time with far greater consequences.

During the lull, General Chuikov also reshuffled his forces, forming a relatively dense and deep defensive alignment around the factory district. North of the Mokraia Mechetka River, Group Gorokhov continued to defend the approaches to the tractor factory and its associated village with 124th and 149th Rifle Brigades, the latter minus its 1st Battalion, manning positions from Hill 93.2 to the north side of Spartanovka and to the Volga River just north of Rynok. On the left flank of Group Gorokhov, the remnants of 115th Rifle and 2nd Motorized Rifle Brigades occupied the ravine from Hill 93.2 down to the Mokraia Mechtka River.

South of the river, 416th and 385th Regiments of Ermolkhin's 112th Rifle Division, now rebuilt to a total of 2,300 men, defended the western and southwestern approaches to the tractor factory. This included positions along the river as well as the upper tractor factory village.[54] The third regiment of the 112th was located behind 39th Guards Rifle Division's 117th Regiment. On the left flank of Zholudev's guards division, Gorishnyi's 95th Rifle Division, which had absorbed 42nd Rifle Brigade, defended the sector from the western end of the Zhitomirsk ravine south to the northwestern corner of Skul'pturnyi Park, covering the area between the tractor and Barrikady factories.

Farther south, the defensive line was extended by the two surviving regiments of Gurt'ev's 308th Division, all three regiments of Smekhotvorov's 193rd Division, and 112th and 120th Regiments of Gur'ev's 39th Guards Rifle Division. These units covered the western approaches to the Barrikady and Krasnyi Oktiabr' Factories. At the southern end of the factory district, Colonel Batiuk's 284th Rifle Division clung to positions on the northern half of Mamaev Kurgan and the Meat Combine, while also providing a narrow link to Rodimtsev's 13th Guards Rifle Division. Rodimtsev still defended shallow positions in central Stalingrad as far south as 9 January Square.

All told, 62nd Army's combat units included 44,017 men as of 10 October (see table 9.2); another 11,000 men, mostly in artillery battalions, supported the army from the eastern bank. Despite frequent influxes of replacements, the Soviet units were as weak as their German counterparts, with an average of 4,304 men per division and 1,598 per brigade. They were supported, however, by 1,400 guns and mortars and 80 tanks, of which 33 were light.[55]

Table 9.2. Personnel Strengths of 62nd Army Units, 10 October 1942

Unit	Number of Men
13th Guards Rifle Division	6,053
37th Guards Rifle Division	4,670
39th Guards Rifle Division	5,052
95th Rifle Division	3,075
112th Rifle Division	2,277
193rd Rifle Division	4,168
284th Rifle Division	5,907
308th Rifle Division	3,225
42nd Rifle Brigade	760
92nd Rifle Brigade	1,050
115th Rifle Brigade	1,135
124th Rifle Brigade	3,520 (as of 5 October)
149th Rifle Brigade	2,556
2nd Motorized Rifle Brigade	569
Total	44,017

Source: Aleksei V. Isaev, Stalingrad: Za Volgoi dlia nas zemli net [Stalingrad: There is no land for us beyond the Volga] (Moscow: Iauza, Eksmo, 2008), citing TsAMO RF, f. 48, op. 451, d. 41, l. 136.

In addition to these units of 62nd Army, the Stalingrad Front had erected a network of defensive strongpoints on the islands in the Volga River, as well as on the river's eastern bank. That bank belonged to the artillery–machine gun battalions of 77th Fortified Region and the largely dismounted men of 2nd Tank Corps.

By late September, General Novikov, chief of the Red Army Air Force, and Major General P. S. Stepanov, his deputy for Stalingrad, had made some progress in air support for the city's defense. Soviet air logistics and command and control became more efficient during this period. Between 27 September and 8 October, for example, 8th Air Army flew 4,000 sorties in the Stalingrad region, at a time when the number of *Luftwaffe* sorties were plummeting. Red air operations were particularly effective in night raids over the city, but the Red Air Force still needed considerable improvement.[56]

Thanks largely to Stepanov's efforts, Chuikov's air defenses also improved during the lull. Large numbers of light 37mm and medium 85mm antiaircraft guns, many with female crews, fired from both banks of the Volga and the midstream islands to make German interdiction of the river more difficult. The hard-pressed Volga River Flotilla needed all the defenses it could get. In addition to the large troop units added to 62nd Army, the flotilla hauled immense quantities of ammunition westward, returning home with wounded soldiers and evacuated civilians.

CONCLUSIONS

Between 27 September and 13 October 1942, Sixth Army took control of the workers' villages at the northern end of Stalingrad and cleared the Orlovka salient in preparation for an attack on the major factories themselves. At the same time, Sixth Army fended off repeated assaults on the Kotluban' region with relative ease, while Fourth Panzer Army contained smaller Soviet attacks in the lakes region south of the city.

Before resuming the attack in the factory district, however, General Paulus had to accept repeated delays and risky redeployments of troops from the flanks. In effect, during October, his army replicated the events of late July, August, and September. Four times during the summer, and several times in September–October, Sixth Army found that it had insufficient combat power to defeat the opposing Soviet forces. On earlier occasions, Hitler and Weichs had furnished additional units to continue the attack, but by October, the German cupboard was almost bare. Moreover, even though Sixth Army had overcome its obstacles in previous operations, each time it did so exacted a toll on dwindling personnel and equipment. As reflected in table 9.1, by early October, roughly one-third of the infantry and pioneer battalions that had to clear Soviet strongpoints were rated as "exhausted." Once again, Weichs provided additional units, this time in the form of 305th Infantry and 14th Panzer Divisions. However, this redistribution further increased the risks along Army Group B's flanks without guaranteeing victory in the city. The time delay also enabled the defenders to reorganize and prepare for the next act.

In some ways, therefore, the fate of Stalingrad depended not on the actual fighting in the streets but on the ability of the rival commanders, Paulus and Chuikov, to find reinforcements in time to counteract the constant scourge of attrition. The ensuing monthlong struggle for Stalingrad's factory district would provide the answers for both commanders.

CHAPTER TEN

The Struggle for the Factories

COMPETING PLANS

General Paulus did everything possible to muster the necessary combat power to push the remaining elements of 62nd Army the final 400 to 1,400 meters to the chilly waters of the Volga. To capture the tractor factory, Sixth Army and LI Corps formed a special Group Jänecke, named for the commanding general of the tired 389th Infantry Division. For this operation, Jänecke had operational control of not only his own division but also the newly arrived 305th Infantry Division. The group also included 83 functional tanks from 14th and 24th Panzer Divisions, as well as 31 *Sturmgeschützen* drawn from 244th and 245th Assault Gun Battalions.[1]

All the commanders involved carefully task-organized their other forces, assigning them specific grid squares and objectives within the factory district. In the north, General Hube's XIV Panzer Corps assigned 16th Panzer Division to attack eastward, north of Spartanovka and Rynok—the same area the division had briefly seized in August. To free 16th Panzer for this mission, Hube reestablished *Luftwaffe* Group Stahel, which had been dissolved when the Germans destroyed the Orlovka salient. Now, Colonel Stahel assumed the defense of an 8 kilometer stretch from the Volga westward, taking over the left wing of the panzer division's previous sector facing northward. This left 16th Panzer's *Kampfgruppe* Krumpen, composed of two panzer-grenadier battalions, one panzer battalion, the divisional antitank battalion, and 651st Pioneer Battalion, to push eastward north of Rynok.

Farther south, General Heim's 14th Panzer Division would spearhead Group Jänecke's assault against the lower tractor factory village and into that factory, in close cooperation with 576th and 578th Regiments of 305th Infantry Division. On Heim's left, two regiments of Jänecke's 389th Division were to collapse the other Soviet defenses in the upper tractor factory village. Meanwhile, on Heim's right, 577th Regiment of 305th Infantry Division, supported by ten tanks from 24th Panzer, was to advance across the railroad line and penetrate into the southern sector of the tractor factory. This left the bulk of 24th Panzer Division to both seize the remainder of the sports stadium and protect the southern flank of LI Corps' advance.[2] Farther south, the remaining divisions of LI Corps—100th *Jäger*, 295th, and 71st Infantry—would remain largely on the defensive.

As the Germans openly prepared to renew the assault, Stalin and his generals sought once again to prepare distractions on the flanks. The outline was familiar: the Don Front's 24th and 66th Armies were to attack southward toward 62nd Army, while 64th Army prepared to threaten Paulus's right from the Beketovka bridgehead.

INITIAL ASSAULTS ON THE TRACTOR AND BARRIKADY FACTORIES, 14–18 OCTOBER

Neither of these Soviet attacks was ready when the Germans struck on 14 October. For two and a half hours, Sixth Army's artillery and 1,250 *Luftwaffe* aircraft concentrated on the northern half of the factory district. Then, as General Paulus observed from the outskirts of Gorodische, Group Jänecke began its assault at 0730 (see map 48). Led by two battalions from 36th Panzer Regiment, each cooperating with a single panzer-grenadier battalion, Heim's 14th Panzer Division advanced northeastward toward the lower tractor factory village and the factory beyond. The assault, supported by 305th Infantry Division, struck the Soviet defenses at a vulnerable angle between the village and the factory. This well-coordinated attack split Zholudev's 37th Guards Rifle Division, destroying two battalions of 109th Guards Regiment as well as the second-echelon defenses that included 112th Rifle Division. German dive-bombers struck Zholudev's command post, disrupting all communications. In the ensuing retreat, the attackers encircled and virtually destroyed 416th Regiment of 112th Division. The furious German advance carried across the railroad line, through the lower tractor factory village, and into the northern and central parts of the factory itself; the Germans later withdrew to allow further artillery preparation of the remaining defenses.[3]

On the left wing of the main German attack, battalion *kampfgruppen* from Jänecke's own 389th Division smashed the other defenses of 112th and 37th Guards Divisions. On Heim's right (southern) flank, 305th Division's 577th Regiment, supported by a tank squadron from 24th Panzer Division, crushed 90th Regiment of Gorishnyi's 95th Rifle Division. Farther south, *Kampfgruppe* Edelsheim of 24th Panzer forced 161st Regiment of 95th Rifle Division to abandon its defenses east of the sports stadium and draw back its flank to the north, along the Zhitomirsk ravine.[4] Elsewhere, the Germans conducted numerous probes and raids to prevent Chuikov from shifting forces northward to the critical sector.

Even 62nd Army had to acknowledge that "the enemy captured the Tractor Factory and Minusinsk by the end of the day and reached the Volga

Map 48. LI Army Corps' Assault, 14–15 October 1942

River."[5] The army's journal contained numerous terse descriptions of the fierce struggle:

> 112th Rifle Division . . . 385th R[ifle] R[egiment] was defending the Mechetka River line in the sector of the railroad bridge and the separate building (450 meters south of the railroad bridge). After leaving 10 men in its defensive region, 80 fighters counter-attacked towards the Stadium at 1700 hours but, while advancing, were subjected to a fierce enemy air strike and strong artillery fire. Suffering heavy losses, the regiment had no success and, together with 524th RR, dug in. . . .
> 37th Guards Rifle Division . . . 118th G[uards] RR fought with 12 enemy tanks and more than two companies of infantry and, as a result,

suffered heavy losses. Its remnants of up to 20 men were fighting in the vicinity of the school south of the Tractor Factory at 2100 hours.

As a result of its withdrawal from the positions it occupied, 524th RR and 109th G[uards] R[ifle] R[egiment]'s C[ommand] P[ost]s were encircled and were fighting with the enemy under their chiefs of staff. . . .

95th Rifle Division . . . 90th RR, because of its heavy losses, could not hold onto its positions and its remnants (11 men) joined the right flank of 161st RR by the end of the day.[6]

Seydlitz's assault ultimately carried the German forces to within 300 meters of Chuikov's command post on the bank of the Volga. German bombers also struck headquarters, killing 30 staff members and again disrupting wire communications with subordinate units, many of which also lost their command posts. This forced Chuikov to use unreliable radios for command. In one of the few positive events, troops from Chuikov's headquarters rescued General Zholudev from his buried command post.[7]

This remarkable German advance was purchased at a relatively modest cost, including 534 soldiers killed, wounded, and missing on 14 October. The two panzer divisions lost 9 of their 83 available tanks, and the two assault gun battalions lost 13 of their 31 operational vehicles. As always, the German mechanics repaired many of these armored vehicles quickly, restoring much of the lost combat power. By contrast, Chuikov estimated that the Volga Flotilla ferried 3,500 wounded across the river that night, a new record.[8] Overall Soviet losses on 14 and 15 October probably exceeded 10,000 men.

In a telephone conversation with *front* commissar Nikita Khrushchev on the first evening, Chuikov argued that sending more troops into the tractor factory would only speed the attrition process, so the Soviets should base their defenses on the remaining factories. Khrushchev promised to satisfy the most urgent need, which was for ammunition, and Eremenko later agreed to release the fresh 138th Rifle Division to 62nd Army on the fifteenth.[9] At 0100 on the morning of 15 October, Chuikov ordered 92nd Rifle Brigade to turn over its sector of the Barrikady Factory to 308th Division and move north to reinforce the shattered 37th Guards; there was little else he could do before the German attack resumed.[10]

This resumption included a predawn attack by XIV Panzer Corps against Group Golikov north of the Mokraia Mechetka River. After some initial progress, however, 16th Panzer Division stalled against the elaborate defenses of what the Germans nicknamed *Grossen Pilz* (large mushroom), a knobby hill northwest of Spartanovka (see map 49). The attacking elements of 64th and 79th Panzer-Grenadiers took some of the outer works but generally failed to clear the Soviet defenses.[11] A frustrated Hube, as XIV Corps commander, tried to hasten the shift of two regiments of 94th Infantry Division north-

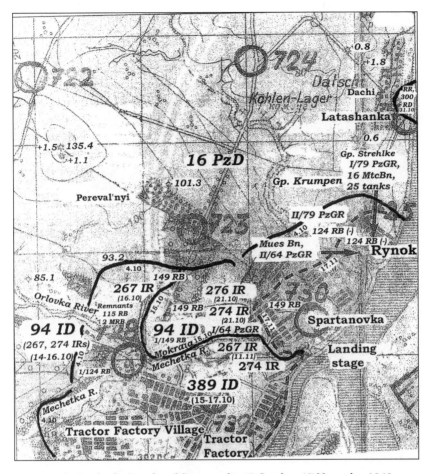

Map 49. The Battles for Rynok and Spartanovka, 15 October–17 November 1942

ward to accelerate the attack on Spartanovka. For his part, Gorokhov found his ammunition cut off and began to send urgent messages to Chuikov and Eremenko. This shortage of ammunition enabled the Germans to take additional positions on 16 October, surrounding most of Group Golikov near Spartanovka. However, by this time, all the battalions in 94th and 389th Infantry Divisions were exhausted, so the Germans could not complete their victory. This gave Eremenko several days to mount a relief effort from across the Volga.[12]

Meanwhile, by midday on 15 October, 14th Panzer and 305th Infantry Divisions had secured virtually all of the tractor factory, a success the OKW announced to the world.[13] By the end of the day, remnants of 112th Rifle

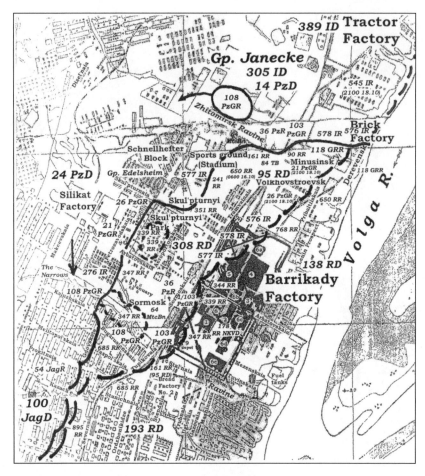

Map 50. LI Army Corps' Assault, 16–18 October 1942

Division and battalions sent from Group Golikov had set up forlorn strong-points in the tractor factory village, while Seydlitz's forces controlled almost the entire area. Farther south, however, 95th Rifle and 37th Guards Rifle Divisions, reinforced by security troops from Chuikov's headquarters and dug-in tanks of 84th Tank Brigade, had contained the German advance short of the Barrikady Factory.

Shortages of basic weapons and river transportation delayed the commitment of 138th Rifle Division, commanded by Colonel Ivan Il'ich Liudnikov, until 17 October. Having already been attrited as part of 64th Army in the approach battles of August, Liudnikov's division had only 2,646 men in October.

It did, however, have 11 122mm guns, 31 76mm guns, and 21 antitank guns, which proved critical in the vicious fighting around the factories.[14]

During the night of 15–16 October, Group Jänecke reconfigured its forces into an east-west line facing southward, in preparation to clear the factories from north to south (see map 50). Two regiments of 305th Infantry Division held the left wing between the Volga and the railroad line south of the brick factory, while the third regiment of that division reinforced 14th Panzer Division from the railroad line west to the sports stadium, where it linked up with 24th Panzer Division. The resulting force numbered some 10,000 combat troops, 70 tanks, and 18 assault guns facing perhaps 6,000 Red soldiers of the depleted 95th Rifle and 37th Guards Rifle Divisions, with roughly 20 surviving tanks of 84th Tank Brigade. The 650th Regiment, the first of Liudnikov's 138th Rifle Division to arrive, backed up 95th Division east of the stadium. Most of the Soviet forces were in well-prepared defensive positions.

All morning on the sixteenth, Soviet and German tanks traded rounds at close range, resulting in almost equal losses on both sides. Once the dug-in Soviet tanks were eliminated, however, the Germans renewed the assault with 103rd Panzer-Grenadier and 576th Infantry Regiments, taking the northern half of the Barrikady Factory by nightfall.[15] The shattered 95th Rifle Division took up defensive positions at the bread factory, just south of the Barrikady. Fortunately for the defenders, much of 138th Rifle Division arrived that night, occupying positions in and east of the Barrikady Factory.

Stalin and the *Stavka* were understandably angered by the rapid fall of the tractor factory and demanded explanations. On the evening of 16–17 October, Eremenko and his deputy *front* commander, Lieutenant General M. M. Popov, visited the ash- and dust-covered command post of 62nd Army. General Zholudev, commander of the decimated 37th Guards Division, broke down repeatedly while briefing Eremenko on the enormous casualties in the battle. Chuikov asked his superior to send individual replacements rather than formed units; above all, he requested more ammunition. Eremenko promised to give him what he asked for, although in retrospect, it appears that the Red Army was already husbanding resources at Chuikov's expense, in preparation for another counteroffensive.[16]

For 17 October, Paulus ordered Seydlitz to reorganize his forces, using 14th Panzer and 305th Infantry Divisions to make the main attack southward to capture the remainder of the Barrikady Factory. Meanwhile, 24th Panzer Division, reinforced with 276th Infantry Regiment and later with part of 14th Panzer's 108th Panzer-Grenadier Regiment, made a supporting attack to destroy Soviet forces in the Skul'pturnyi Park area and then penetrate the southern section of the Barrikady from the west. This plan promised to surround 308th Rifle Division and one regiment of 193rd Division, while expelling other Red forces from the factory area.[17] However, the plan belied the rapid decline of combat power among German units. Although 24th Panzer still reported 33 tanks as operational, many of them were in disrepair; the panzer squadron supporting 108th Panzer-Grenadiers was reduced to five tanks.[18]

Still, the 17 October attack progressed almost as planned. By the end of that day, the eastern pincer had forced all three of Liudnikov's weak regiments to fall back to the south, exposing 308th Rifle Division's left wing in Skul'pturnyi Park. By midday, the leading elements of 36th Panzer and 103rd Panzer-Grenadier Regiments had reached the southwestern corner of the Barrikady Factory, where they linked up with the forward elements of 18th Panzer-Grenadier, advancing from the west. It took another three days of bitter fighting inside the park and the dense network of defensive positions before the Germans completely cleared Gurt'ev's 308th Division from the area. The surviving riflemen of this division suffered more casualties when they withdrew eastward through a porous German encirclement. Similarly, the survivors of Liudnikov's 138th Division conducted a slow fighting withdrawal into new defensive positions in the western half of the Barrikady Factory.[19]

Meanwhile, on 17 October XIV Panzer Corps made yet another effort to destroy Group Gorokhov in the Rynok-Spartanovka region. However, this attack was weakened because Paulus directed Pfeiffer to shift one of 94th Infantry Division's regiments south of the Mokraia Mechetka River in order to release two regiments of 389th Infantry Division to reinforce the assault on the Barrikady. Nonetheless, the understrength 1st Battalion of 64th Panzer-Grenadiers reinforced the main attack of 16th Panzer Division on the Soviet positions northwest of Spartanovka; the Germans actually broke into the Red positions briefly, but the supporting attack by 94th Infantry Division, now reduced to one regiment, failed to link up with 16th Panzer's attack. When Colonel Gorokhov asked permission to withdraw his remaining troops to Spornyi Island east of Rynok, General Chuikov refused and sent his operations officer, Colonel S. M. Kamynin, to bolster Gorokhov's resolve.[20]

The attacks of 17 October cost the Germans 576 casualties, including 91 killed, 469 wounded, and 16 missing. The Soviets suffered much more heavily, losing 860 prisoners of war, including 103 deserters, as well as hundreds of additional casualties. Still, 24th and 14th Panzer Divisions, which had begun the day with 33 operational tanks each, found themselves reduced at least temporarily to 4 and 19, respectively.[21] Despite this weakness, Paulus ordered LI Corps to continue the advance on 18 October, pushing south toward Krasnyi Oktiabr' with the main shock group of 14th Panzer and 305th Infantry Divisions, while the weaker 24th Panzer Division, with 276th Infantry Regiment and elements of 14th Panzer in support, continued to clear the bypassed Soviet forces around Skul'pturnyi Park. It was at this point that the Sixth Army commander also began to shift regiments of 389th and 79th

Infantry Divisions into the factory district. Once 545th Regiment of 389th Division had relocated, it was supposed to capture the brick factory, with support from 24th Panzer, by the end of 18 October.[22]

Although the Germans failed to capture the factory in a single bound, their partial success forced Chuikov to shift his army command post repeatedly, eventually coming to rest in a new site located 800 meters south of Bannyi ravine and west of the Tennis Racket, 800 meters behind 284th Rifle Division's trenches on Mamaev Kurgan. Here the headquarters remained for the rest of the city fighting.[23]

When 305th Infantry and 14th Panzer Divisions renewed their attack on 18 October, they were able to advance through the Barrikady Factory, but only at an excruciatingly slow pace. The 138th Rifle Division, together with fugitives from the shattered 308th, defended every foot of the complex. Moreover, the closer the Germans got to the banks of the Volga, the more exposed they were to Soviet artillery fires from the far bank. Ostensibly, the Germans controlled the Barrikady Factory even before this attack, but in reality, the battle for the Barrikady and brick factories was fought out in a pitiless room-by-room struggle.

Late on the afternoon of 18 October, 24th Panzer Division's two panzer-grenadier regiments, cooperating with 545th Infantry Regiment, secured the brick factory and, overcoming one regiment of 138th Rifle Division, reached the gully-scarred western bank of the Volga River. They immediately came under fire from Soviet bunker positions, as well as from a nearby island. West of the Barrikady Factory, the Germans struggled to overcome the remnants of Gurt'ev's 308th Division, reporting that "enemy resistance has come back to life in the districts captured on 16. and 17.10."[24] Sixth Army, for its part, noted that an NKVD company and supporting workers' detachment were reduced to only five survivors by the time the Germans broke through the Barrikady Factory and reached the railroad station to the west.[25]

Despite their advances, the Germans had still failed to clear their objectives. The 14th Panzer Division's 103rd Panzer-Grenadiers and 64th Motorcycle Battalion, together with 577th Regiment of 305th Infantry Division, were still fighting against survivors of 138th and 308th Rifle Divisions in the crumbled halls and shops deep within the Barrikady Factory. Farther east, the other two regiments of 305th Infantry Division, with some support from the panzer-grenadier regiments of 24th Panzer, were still fighting with 138th Rifle and remnants of 37th Guards Divisions in the northern part of the factory and in the streets and gullies to the east. The three battalions of Liudnikov's 344th Regiment, together with the few survivors of Gurt'ev's 308th, still held out in the Barrikady Factory, while the bread factory and the ravine southeast of the Barrikady remained in the hands of 161st Regiment of Gorishnyi's 95th Division. By holding the strip of land between the Barrikady

Factory and the riverbank, Liudnikov's division was still able to feed in reinforcements and supplies. Despite this, during the night of 18–19 October, for
the first time in the battle, a hard-pressed Chuikov ordered a deliberate withdrawal by 308th Rifle Division, away from Skul'pturnyi Park, to straighten
the army's lines.[26]

In the north, XIV Panzer Corps was equally frustrated in the battle for
Rynok and Spartanovka; in fact, Colonel Kamynin informed Chuikov that the
defenders had eliminated the German incursion inside their positions. By
19 October, the heavy casualties in Gorokhov's group were largely replaced,
leaving him 3,953 men, 22 45mm antitank guns, and 20 76mm field guns.
Chuikov heaved a sigh of relief that his right flank had been resupplied.[27]

Daily German casualties had been modest, but they were beginning to
add up over time. Between 13 and 18 October Sixth Army suffered 13,343
casualties, bringing its total losses since crossing the Don River on 21 August to 40,068 officers and men. Although the army had captured 57,800
prisoners during those same two months, this total was much lower than
previous German prisoner hauls for equivalent periods. Though expressing
confidence that the battle could be completed in another two to three days,
Paulus brought 79th Infantry Division forward as a precaution.[28]

OPERATIONAL LULL, 19–22 OCTOBER

Heavy rains on 19–21 October hindered the movement of German supplies,
delaying Paulus's next major attack. Meanwhile, the first two regiments of
General Richard von Schwerin's 79th Infantry Division arrived and prepared
for a concerted assault in the Krasnyi Oktiabr' Factory and in the remainder
of the Barrikady Factory. At the same time, Paulus instructed LI Corps to
keep up the pressure with local attacks, denying both sides any opportunity
for rest.

On the morning of 19 October, two battalion-sized *kampfgruppen* of
305th Infantry Division stormed the northern sector of the Barrikady Factory. As they compressed the defending 768th Regiment of 138th Rifle Division, the Germans splashed through water-filled shell craters and clawed
their way over heaps of debris. Soviet small-arms, machine gun, mortar, and
light artillery fire promptly stalled this attack; the close-quarters fight did
not permit *Luftwaffe* support. The German division commander, Oppenländer, called off the assault to avoid a protracted struggle, and Seydlitz soon
ordered all his forces to cease such attacks. Liudnikov responded with a surprise counterattack that recaptured the northern part of the factory, prompting Seydlitz and his divisional commanders to dig in against further attacks.[29]
According to Sixth Army reports, the day cost Seydlitz's corps 186 casualties,

including 34 killed, 137 wounded, and 15 missing, plus 29 tanks that were put out of operation at least temporarily.[30]

Because of the continued lack of progress against Group Gorokhov, on 20 October Seydlitz directed Lenski's 24th Panzer Division to release 276th Infantry Regiment; the next day the regiment moved to rejoin its parent 94th Infantry Division north of the Mokraia Mechetka River. On 21 October the corps commander directed the newly arrived 79th Infantry Division to take control of 100th *Jäger* Division's 54th Regiment and make a limited attack against the cooking factory, 600 meters northwest of the Krasnyi Oktiabr' Factory. The purpose of this attack was to establish a firm link with the neighboring 24th Panzer. To this end, one squadron of the panzer division would support three companies of 54th Regiment in attacking the cooking factory, which was defended by the 1st Battalion of 685th Regiment, 193rd Rifle Division.[31] After a daylong fight on 21 October, the German attack built around 54th *Jägers*—by a force named *Kampfgruppe* Weber, after its regimental commander—secured its objectives. In the process, however, the *Jägers* suffered 154 casualties, while the accompanying squadron of 24th Panzer lost two killed (including its commander) and seven of ten tanks destroyed breaching a Soviet minefield. Chuikov responded by reinforcing the defenders, drawn from 193rd Rifle Division, with a battalion of 284th Division, an example of how the Red commander continually moved small elements around to maintain his defenses.[32] Yet Chuikov realized that he was scraping the bottom of the barrel. In addition to requesting additional personnel and antitank regiments, he committed his flamethrower company to defend the main landing stage along with the army's blocking detachment, which had previously prevented unauthorized troop withdrawals.[33]

Throughout 22 October, similar struggles continued in and around the Barrikady Factory. Intense German aerial bombardment inflicted additional casualties, including the entire command and staff element of 141st Mortar Regiment.[34]

Recognizing that Paulus was preparing for a renewed assault on the Barrikady Factory, on 20–21 October General Chuikov used the lull to withdraw all surviving elements of Ermolkin's 112th Rifle Division, as well as the headquarters of 115th Rifle and 2nd Motorized Rifle Brigades and 95th Rifle and 37th Guards Rifle Divisions. The combat troops of these brigades and divisions reorganized into 161st Regiment, which held the bread factory and adjacent blocks, and 650th Regiment, which was subordinated to Liudnikov's 138th Division to defend the Volga bank northeast of the Barrikady Factory. Eremenko had assigned 87th and 315th Rifle Divisions, which had completed refitting, to Chuikov as replacements, but those divisions were still on the eastern bank of the river.[35]

The *Stavka* also made various administrative reorganizations during the lull. On 18 October, for example, it reassigned General Moskalenko from 1st Guards to command 40th Army, withdrew the headquarters of 1st Guards Army, and reassigned its subordinate units to other headquarters in the area. On 21 October it belatedly redesignated 4th Tank Army as 65th Army. The 4th Tank had become known, sarcastically, as the "four tank army" because of its lack of mechanized units; under its new commander, Lieutenant General Pavel Ivanovich Batov, the redesignated 65th Army became much more effective.[36]

On 22 October the *Stavka* went even farther, creating a new Southwestern Front using the staff of 1st Guards Army and giving it control of the Don Front's 63rd and 21st Armies, as well as the Briansk Front's 5th Tank Army. The new *front*'s sector stretched along the Don River from Verkhnyi Mamon eastward to Kletskaia, opposite Third Romanian Army. Vatutin assumed command of the Southwestern Front, and Golikov replaced him as head of the Voronezh Front.[37]

FOURTH KOTLUBAN' COUNTERSTROKE, 20–26 OCTOBER

In response to the German success in the factory district, on 15 October Stalin had Zhukov and Vasilevsky direct Rokossovsky (Don Front) and Eremenko (Stalingrad Front) to launch renewed flank attacks by the end of 19 October.[38]

Rokossovsky responded promptly with a proposal that focused on four relatively strong divisions of Malinovsky's 66th Army, supported by a secondary attack on the left wing of 24th Army, which was now commanded by Lieutenant General I. V. Galanin. Although 664 guns, mortars, and rocket launchers would support this attack, Rokossovsky had almost no tanks, and most of his divisions were severely undermanned. He therefore had few hopes that the assault would accomplish anything.[39] Moreover, at Stalin's behest, Zhukov and Vasilevsky directed that the attack be moved forward to the morning of 19 October and that the secondary attack be eliminated to strengthen the primary thrust. Once again, a Soviet *front* launched its attack prematurely, without having accumulated sufficient force or conducted thorough staff coordination. Small wonder, then, that the well-developed defensive positions of XIV Panzer Corps easily contained Rokossovsky's attack, launched in the same rainy weather that postponed the German assault in Stalingrad.[40] Under pressure from Moscow, the attacks continued from 19 through 26 October without success. Considering that XIV Panzer Corps was already stretched thin, this weak attack wasted Soviet lives without deflecting any German forces from the factory district. Still, 3rd Motorized Division suffered considerable casualties and saw its tank park reduced to 30 vehicles, many of them in need of repair.[41]

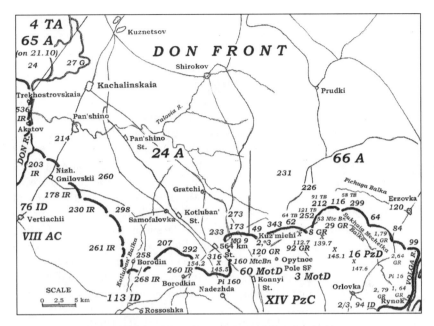

Map 51. Don Front's Kotluban' Counterstroke, 20–26 October 1942

As Paulus prepared to resume his offensive on 23 October, both sides were worn to a nub. The German commander had been able to conduct one last surprise maneuver on 15–17 October, bringing 14th Panzer and 305th Infantry Divisions forward in relative secrecy. Thereafter, however, the Germans had few remaining large forces to commit and no real opportunities for maneuver. Seydlitz's infantry, panzer-grenadiers, and pioneers would have to pry the Soviet defenders from their holes one by one. Yet it was precisely these dismounted German troops that melted away, day by day, in the merciless struggle.

Similarly, Eremenko had saved 62nd Army by providing Liudnikov's 138th Rifle Division to restore some balance in the Barrikady Factory. Whereas the Germans still had the morale advantage of advancing, the defenders were faced with inevitable death or captivity. Desertions began to rise, and the NKVD counterintelligence cells, censoring military mail, found increasing complaints of near starvation, lice, and disease. One soldier wrote to his aunt, "I want you to come to me and bring me whatever food you can. True, it is embarrassing for me to beg, but hunger compels me." Another wrote his wife, "I am sick with dysentery. The food is scarce and crude, and we have no sugar or tobacco at all. We already have lice—the initial breeding ground for disaster."[42] Yet, in their misery, the soldiers of both sides had no choice but to continue fighting.

PLANNING THE RENEWED ATTACK

The one new element available for the next German offensive was the truncated 79th Infantry Division, which passed to the control of LI Army Corps on the evening of 18 October. Having left his 226th Regiment to defend another sector, Lieutenant General Richard von Schwerin, commander of the 79th, assumed control of 54th *Jäger* Regiment when the "new" division moved in between 14th Panzer and 100th *Jäger* Divisions on the night of 19–20 October (see map 52). The main attack would be by 14th Panzer Division, aiming to seize the bread factory and the southern portion of the Barrikady Factory en route to the Volga, and by 79th Infantry Division, which was to assault the "metal" factory, the Germans' term for Krasnyi Oktiabr'.[43] The 14th Panzer organized into three *kampfgruppen* built around its 64th Motorcycle Battalion and its 103rd and 108th Panzer-Grenadier Regiments, respectively. The first two task forces, supported by 12 tanks, were to assault the bread factory and the adjacent ravine, while the 108th, with another dozen tanks, aimed for a large building slightly to the north, midway between the bread and Barrikady factories.

In addition to 54th *Jäger* Regiment, Schwerin's division had the support of seven tanks from 24th Panzer Division, as well as 244th and 245th Assault Gun Battalions. The tanks, attached to a battalion-sized *kampfgruppe* from 54th *Jägers*, were to attack in bounds eastward across the railroad line and then wheel south to capture Halls 1 and 2 of the Krasnyi Oktiabr' Factory (see map 53). The center *kampfgruppe* of 79th Division included its 208th Infantry Regiment, a company of assault guns, a company from 179th Pioneer Battalion, and a heavy *Werfer* battalion; its objectives were the fortified administrative buildings known by their shapes as "H," "Ladder," and "Hook." Finally, 212th Infantry Regiment, reinforced by most of the divisional reconnaissance battalion, a company each of assault and antitank guns, and a light *Werfer* battalion, aimed to seize the southernmost buildings of the factory (Halls 8–10 and 8a). Between them, 14th Panzer and 79th Infantry Divisions had a combat strength of just under 15,500 men, plus at least 523 Russian auxiliaries known as *Hiwis* (**Hilfswilliger**, or volunteer helpers).[44]

As a secondary effort, 305th Infantry Division was to advance its 578th Regiment through the Barrikady Factory and then swing north to meet a mirror-image thrust by *Kampfgruppe* Below, built around 26th Panzer-Grenadier Regiment of 24th Panzer Division. Between them, these two forces aimed to encircle most of 138th Rifle Division and clear the bank

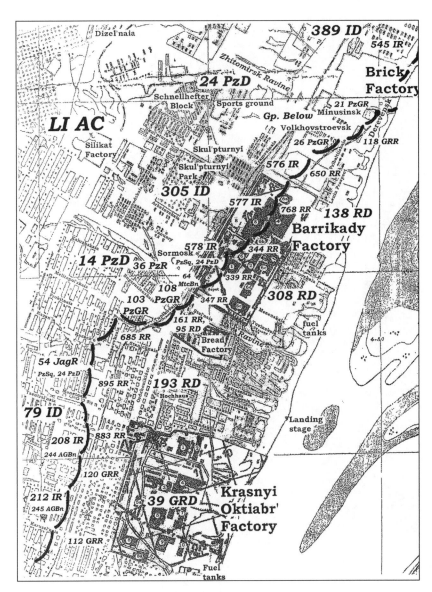

Map 52. LI Army Corps' Dispositions, 23 October 1942

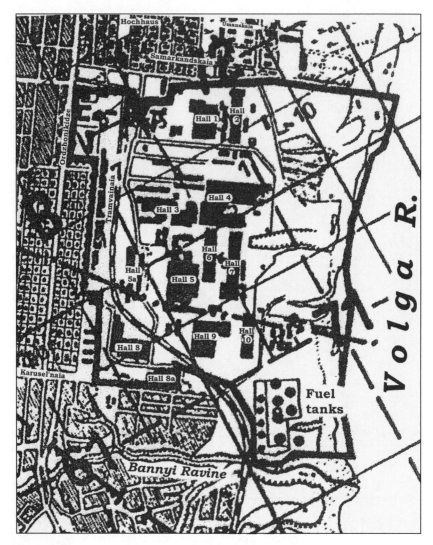

Map 53. The Krasnyi Oktiabr' Factory

of the Volga. The combat strength of these two German divisions totaled 8,700 men, plus as many as 3,322 *Hiwis*.[45] Thus, although Paulus and Seydlitz had high hopes for success, both men were concerned about the waning manpower of their assault forces. When the commander of 79th Infantry Division's 208th Regiment, Lieutenant Colonel Richard Wolf, met his counterpart in 54th *Jägers*, the latter warned him, "You can't expect anything more from my troops. In the long days, we've been completely exhausted and bled dry. The fighting spirit is gone. Just wait until your troops have fought here for fourteen days, you'll be no different."[46]

THE BATTLE FOR THE BARRIKADY AND KRASNYI OKTIABR' FACTORIES, 23–31 OCTOBER

At 0100 on 23 October battalion- and company-sized elements of 305th Infantry Division began a series of nighttime attacks to clear Soviet forces from the gullies and ravines along the western bank of the Volga, northeast of the Barrikady Factory (see map 54). The Soviet defenders had some success in repelling these attacks, but they were only the prelude to the main event.

For ten minutes beginning at 0700, Stuka attacks struck the Soviet outposts, followed by an hour of artillery, *Werfer*, and mortar fire. Next, 14th Panzer Division's initial assault into the bread factory and nearby buildings stalled after penetrating only about 100 meters, but it inflicted so many casualties on 308th Rifle Division that Gurt'ev, operating from a command bunker in the ravine south of the Barrikady, withdrew his 339th Regiment deeper into the factory and his 347th Regiment farther east into the adjacent ravine. Similarly, attacks by 103rd Panzer-Grenadier and 54th *Jäger* Regiments, south of 305th Division, generally failed to advance but tore holes in 193rd Rifle Division that could no longer be plugged.[47]

The relatively fresh regiments of 79th Infantry Division had more success, with 2nd Battalion, 208th Infantry Regiment, seizing Halls 3 and 6 of the Krasnyi Oktiabr' Factory and actually reaching the Volga by 1530 hours on the twenty-third. However, even German officers acknowledged that the stubborn Soviet defenders threatened the open flanks of 208th and 212th Infantry Regiments. By day's end, Gur'ev's 120th Guards Rifle Regiment had regained some positions inside the southern portion of Hall 8, leaving the German advance in this area split in two.[48] The failure of 54th *Jäger* Regiment's attack also left the northern halls (1, 2, and 3) in Soviet hands. To achieve these partial results, 79th Infantry Division lost 83 officers and men killed, 364 wounded, and 1 missing—almost 10 percent of its starting force.[49]

On the northern face of the Barrikady, where 305th Infantry Division attacked on 23 October with tank and artillery support from 24th Panzer, the German effort was even less successful. In most areas the Germans advanced only 100 meters before bogging down. Worse still, from General Seydlitz's viewpoint, 138th Rifle Division counterattacked, recaptured Hall 4 (see map 53), and held it in the face of Stuka attacks that resumed when the weather cleared that afternoon. When General Paulus visited the area, Op-

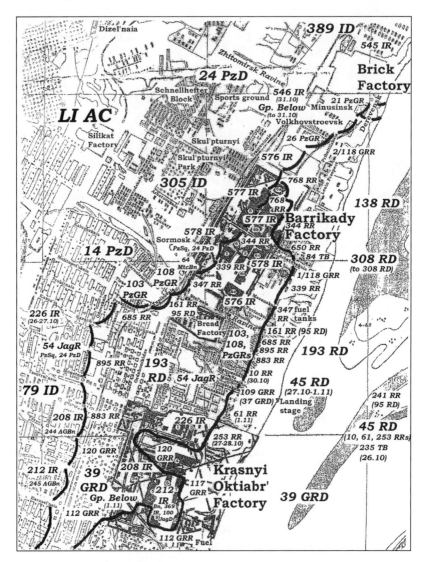

Map 54. LI Army Corps' Assault, 23–31 October 1942

penländer told his army commander that 305th Infantry Division was no longer capable of large-scale assault.[50]

Stubborn Soviet defenses had once again denied the invaders victory, giving Chuikov more time. Having lost more than 60 percent of his effective strength in recent days, the army commander faced the possibility that the

Germans would encircle 138th and 308th Rifle Divisions. He again appealed to Eremenko for aid, including all possible artillery and rocket launcher support in the area.[51]

Seydlitz ordered almost identical attacks for the next day, 24 October. The 79th Infantry Division's regiments spent the day locked in a bitter struggle for the Krasnyi Oktiabr' Factory, beginning with the administrative building (Hall 5a) at 0300. The Germans took portions of several buildings in the factory, but in the afternoon Gur'ev, commander of 39th Guards Division, counterattacked, eliminating the German penetration by nightfall. On the western (right) wing of 79th Division, 212th Infantry Regiment received so much Soviet fire from the ravine south of the factory that it could not advance. To the south, the decimated *kampfgruppen* of 14th Panzer Division dutifully engaged 95th Rifle Division in the bread factory and 308th Rifle Division but made only limited gains, most of which were eliminated when 161st Regiment of 95th Rifle Division counterattacked in the afternoon. Likewise, 54th *Jäger* Regiment advanced only 100 meters before its attack fell apart. Soviet artillery fire from the height of Mamaev Kurgan blanketed the Germans. Despite the lack of actual success on the battlefield, the daily OKW news report claimed that all but one building was in German hands, and most of the factory area had been cleared of enemy forces.[52] Later in the day, 305th Infantry Division partially justified this claim by a renewed offensive that captured the main mechanical shops and part of Hall 4 in the north. That building, built to house huge blast furnaces, was a natural fortress with very thick walls.[53] The 39th Guards Rifle Division now held only the southern half of Halls 4, 8, and 8a, as well as all of Halls 9, 1, and 2. Thanks to a continuous stream of replacements, 39th Guards and 138th Rifle Divisions probably still had about 2,500 effectives each, although Chuikov believed they had lost their combat effectiveness.[54]

The second day's assault had again cost the Germans heavily (see table 10.1). This time it was Heim, commander of 14th Panzer Division, who reported that his unit had been reduced to 750 dismounted infantrymen and could make no significant advances without reinforcements.[55] That division was down to 11 functioning tanks, while 24th Panzer fielded 11 tanks, and the 2 assault gun battalions had only 7 operational armored vehicles between them. In essence, LI Corps had lost its armored teeth for the moment.[56] In hindsight, Chuikov concluded that, although the Germans had split his army and taken the tractor factory, "Paulus could not repeat an attack on the scale of the one on 14 October unless he had 10–15 days to bring up fresh supplies of ammunition, bombs, and tanks as well as reinforcements."[57]

Over the next six days, 25–30 October, 398th Infantry and 24th Panzer Divisions could do little more than routine patrolling and fire support from the Mokraia Mechetka River south to the Barrikady Factory. The remainder

Table 10.1. Combat Ratings of German Infantry and Pioneer Battalions
Fighting in Stalingrad, 19 October–9 November 1942

19 October	26 October	9 November
63 infantry battalions	69 infantry battalions	62 infantry battalions
1 strong	1 strong	2 strong
13 medium strong	8 medium strong	8 medium strong
11 average	11 average	15 average
20 weak	37 weak	26 weak
18 exhausted	12 exhausted	11 exhausted
11 pioneer battalions	12 pioneer battalions	12 pioneer battalions
1 medium strong	0 strong	0 strong
1 average	4 average	5 average
7 weak	5 weak	5 weak
2 exhausted	3 exhausted	2 exhausted

Source: Florian *Freiherr* von und zu Aufsess, "Betr.: Zustand der Divisionen, Armee-
Oberkommando 6. Abt. 1a, A.H. Qu., 19 Oktober 1942, 12:35 Uhr," "Betr.: Zustand der Divisionen,
Armee-Oberkommando 6. Abt. 1a, A.H. Qu., 26 Oktober 1942, 10.15 Uhr," and "Betr.: Zustand
der Divisionen, Armee-Oberkommando 6. Abt. 1a, A.H. Qu., 09 November 1942, 16.20 Uhr," in
Die Anlagenbänder zu den Kriegstagebüchern der 6. Armee vom 14.09.42 bis 24.11.42, book 1
(Schwabach, Germany: self-published, 2006), 185–189, 212–216, 248–253.
Note: The reduction in infantry battalions in November represents the consolidation of
weakened units.

of LI Corps, however, continued a difficult and generally futile struggle to
clear 62nd Army's divisions from the Barrikady and Krasnyi Oktiabr' Factories. The 305th Infantry, 14th Panzer, and 79th Infantry Divisions fought
vicious small-unit actions against Red Army soldiers in the ravine south of
the Barrikady, in the bread factory, and in the rubble of destroyed buildings
between the two factories. Sixth Army continued to make spasmodic assaults
against the shrinking Soviet bridgehead. All this fighting occurred in an area
measuring no more than 2,000 meters wide and 100 to 1,000 meters deep—
less than 1.5 square kilometers. No more than 6,000 German and 3,000 Soviet troops were directly involved, and the average readiness rating of Sixth
Army's infantry divisions declined to "weak" (see table 10.1). Moreover, on 26
October LI Corps could muster only 28 tanks and 9 assault guns.

To combat the convulsive attacks of the declining German force, Chuikov
juggled his slender forces and launched frequent counterattacks to keep the
invaders at bay. He also asked Eremenko to provide two full-strength divisions to relieve 39th Guards, 308th, 193rd, and 138th Rifle Divisions, but in
the interim he demanded that these decimated units continue to hold their
positions.[58]

On 25 October LIV Panzer Corps seized Spartanovka itself, but as one
German historian acknowledged, "there were still hundreds of Russians
holding out in the lower sections of the *balkas* running west to east between

Spartanovka and Rynok. In fact, Group Gorokhov's two brigades defended Rynok with fanatic efforts."[59] The Volga River Flotilla landed reinforcements and provided fire support to these beleaguered brigades.

On 27 October another crisis loomed for the defenders as German submachine gunners infiltrated through the depleted Red units and attacked the headquarters bunker of 39th Guards Division. Chuikov dispatched a company of his own headquarters guard that pushed the Germans back and pursued them into the Krasnyi Oktiabr' Factory, where the rescue force remained with the guards defenders.

That same day, elements of 14th Panzer Division almost reached the northern ferry landing on which Chuikov's entire defense depended, but again, the Soviets beat them back.[60] This threat prompted Eremenko to release the relatively green 45th Rifle Division, rebuilt from scratch after the Donbas fighting in early July, to 62nd Army. A 40-year-old veteran, Major General Vasilii Pavlovich Sokolov, commanded the 45th. Although Sokolov had roughly 6,400 soldiers, the continuing shortage of rifles meant that the division could cross the river only a few battalions at a time, as each became properly armed. Moreover, the landing stages had suffered heavy damage, further delaying the process.[61]

General Chuikov later recalled the extremes to which he resorted to hold his bridgehead while waiting for the new division to arrive:

> We collected about a dozen men [from support roles] and put them together with thirty soldiers discharged from the medical centers by the banks of the Volga. And—oh joy!—we had found, or rather had dragged from the battlefield, three broken-down tanks—two light tanks and one with a flame-thrower. We had them rapidly repaired, and I decided to give the enemy a "shock"—to send the three tanks and fifty infantrymen into an attack . . . [at] the junction point between Smekhotvorov's [193rd] and Gur'iev's [39th Guards] divisions along Samarkandskaya Street, where the enemy had almost reached the Volga. . . .
>
> The counterattack began in the early morning [27 October], before dawn. It was supported by artillery from the left bank and by Yerokhin's "Katyushi" regiment. We did not manage to advance very far, but the results were impressive. The tank with the flame-thrower sent three German tanks up in flames. . . . In this way, we gained a whole day on this sector.[62]

The first two battalions of 45th Rifle Division crossed the Volga that evening, followed by a company of tanks from Colonel D. M. Burdov's 235th Tank Brigade. A cadre of experienced junior officers stiffened the green troops of this brigade.

Even these reinforcements did not ease the sense of crisis among the defenders on 28–29 October. The 305th, 14th Panzer, and 79th Divisions continued to press their counterparts hard in the ravine east of the Barrikady Factory and in the buildings within it.[63] After 20 separate German assaults during these two days, 138th and 39th Guards Divisions finally found themselves pushed out of the Barrikady Factory, leaving them in the 500 to 700 meter strip of gullies and ravines that separated the factory from the Volga (see map 54). Much of this German success was due to the late arrival of 79th Infantry's remaining subordinate unit, 226th Infantry Regiment, which was immediately thrown into battle on the twenty-eighth. But the German losses, coming on top of previous attrition, were heavy. In the three days of fighting on 27–29 October, Oppenländer's 305th Infantry Division lost 78 killed, 250 wounded, and 19 missing. Heim's 14th Panzer, already very weak, suffered an additional 50 killed, 174 wounded, and 19 missing. The 79th Infantry Division lost 54 killed, 216 wounded, and 7 missing during the same period. Late on 29 October 14th Panzer Division had only nine tanks still in action, while the two assault gun battalions had only ten vehicles between them.[64]

The German advance was almost spent. On 31 October, as it gathered to support 79th Infantry Division in yet another assault, 24th Panzer Division's remaining dismounted rifle strength, including two panzer-grenadier regiments, a motorcycle battalion, and a pioneer battalion, totaled only 41 officers and 960 men.[65]

That day, 39th Guards Rifle Division and one newly arrived regiment of 45th Rifle Division surprised the Germans with a strong counterattack that recaptured Halls 4, 7, 8a, and 10 in the Krasnyi Oktiabr' Factory. Although Schwerin's 79th Infantry Division managed to push the attackers out of Hall 10 by nightfall, Chuikov could rightly boast that he had got in the last punch. Farther north, on Halloween night Eremenko launched a reinforced battalion of 300th Rifle Division in an amphibious assault aimed at distracting the Germans and aiding the beleaguered Group Gorokhov in the north. The attack failed, with at least 900 casualties for the Red Army and the Volga River Flotilla, but the fighting was so serious that one German lieutenant earned the Knight's Cross. The Soviets attempted to repeat the process on subsequent nights, but the alerted Germans used artillery to scatter the landing vessels.[66]

Paulus generally halted offensive action after 30 October, causing his casualties to decline from an average of 100 per day to 35. Paulus and his army group commander, Weichs, still had to find some means of completing their task in Stalingrad.

64TH ARMY'S COUNTERSTROKE, 25 OCTOBER–2 NOVEMBER

On 15 October Stalin had directed Eremenko to launch another assault by 64th Army in the area south of Stalingrad. Ostensibly intended to clear German forces from the southern end of the city, in reality, the *front* commander had a more limited goal of attracting German divisions away from the struggle with 62nd Army.

Shumilov's 64th Army thought it was facing the German 71st Infantry and 29th Motorized Divisions, backed by part of 371st Infantry. In reality, however, the main attack would fall on only two regiments of 371st Division. Against this slender force, Shumilov focused the three fresh brigades (93rd, 96th, and 97th) of 7th Rifle Corps, as well as 126th and 422nd Rifle Divisions. Two tank brigades provided 55 tanks in first echelon and 25 in second echelon, while 169th Rifle Division was in general reserve. Overall, Shumilov had 30,000 troops to attack 5,500.[67] The usual staff and logistical problems made the preparation more difficult, but the attack finally began at 0900 on 25 October.

The result was very poor from the Soviet point of view. The 371st Infantry Division lost several hundred meters of ground to the initial assault, but thereafter it shifted local reserves and restabilized the front. A single German division had halted the best that 64th Army could offer, without attracting any forces away from Paulus's attack in the city. Given the crisis in the factory district, Shumilov had little option but to continue his attacks, with the same result.[68]

In the minds of senior German commanders, the relative ease with which Fourth Panzer Army repelled 64th Army's limited attacks south of Stalingrad confirmed the twin ideas that the *Wehrmacht* was invincible and that the Soviets were at last scraping the bottom of their manpower barrel. As a result, many German officers were unconcerned about reports of yet another Soviet counteroffensive, and they failed to anticipate the effect of such an offensive if it were aimed at satellite rather than German units.

CONCLUSIONS

By the end of October, Paulus and Seydlitz had again failed to clear Soviet forces from the factory district. Worse still, their infantry and armor units were depleted to the point of being combat ineffective, causing Paulus and his army group commander, Weichs, to accept greater and greater risks by redeploying troops from their vulnerable flanks. Inside Stalingrad, the Germans had no further opportunities for any form of maneuver. Under pressure from Hitler, however, Sixth Army continued to make convulsive efforts

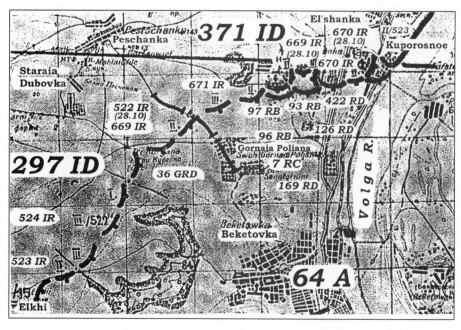

Map 55. 64th Army's Counterstroke, 25 October–2 November 1942

to achieve complete victory; these were often reduced to company-sized attacks that accomplished little, other than increasing the casualties on both
sides.

Chuikov's position was scarcely better. Despite frequent reinforcements,
62nd Army might have had fewer than 15,000 combatants on the western
bank at the end of October. German forces had divided his bridgehead into
three separate enclaves, leaving only narrow strips of land in Soviet hands
around the various landing stages. As winter arrived, ice floes on the partially
frozen Volga River would soon increase the already daunting problems of
resupply and reinforcement. Still, as long as Eremenko provided a minimum
number of troops and supplies, Chuikov could deny Paulus victory simply by
condemning his troops to die in place.

Casting about for some means of breaking the stalemate, Paulus understandably coveted the troops of neighboring Army Group A. By this time,
however, List's army group was as overextended as Weichs's and faced multiple crises of its own.

Hitler meeting with Army Group South's staff

Field Marshal Fedor von Bock, commander of Army Group South and Army Group B

Colonel General Ewald von Kleist, commander of First Panzer Army and later commander of Army Group A

Left to right: Colonel General Maximilian *Freiherr* von Weichs, commander of Army Group B; General of Panzer Troops Friedrich Paulus, commander of Sixth Army; and General of Artillery Walter von Seydlitz-Kurzbach, commander of LI Army Corps

General *der Flieger* Wolfgang von Richtofen (second from right), commander of Fourth Air Fleet

Josef Vissarionovich Stalin, People's Commissar of Defense of the USSR and Supreme High Commander of the Armed Forces of the USSR

Army General Georgii Konstantinovich Zhukov, deputy Supreme High Commander of the Armed Forces of the USSR and commander of the Western Front

Colonel General Aleksandr Aleksandrovich Novikov, commander of the Red Army's Air Forces and deputy People's Commissar of Defense for Aviation

Colonel General Aleksandr Mikhailovich Vasilevsky, chief of the Red Army General Staff

Marshal of the Soviet Union Semen
Konstantinovich Timoshenko,
commander of the Southwest Main
Direction and Southwestern Front

Lieutenant General Filipp Ivanovich
Golikov, commander of the Briansk
Front

Lieutenant General Rodion
Iakolevich Malinovsky, commander
of the Southern Front and later of
2nd Guards Army

Marshal of the Soviet Union Semen
Mikhailovich Budenny, commander of
the North Caucasus Main Direction
and North Caucasus Front

Red troops fighting
in the suburbs of
Voronezh, July 1942

German tanks advancing into the Great Bend of the Don

German troops overlooking the Don River

Red Army riflemen counterattack in Stalingrad's suburbs

Left to right: Colonel General Andrei Ivanovich Eremenko, commander Southeastern Front (later Stalingrad Front); his chief of artillery, Major General of Artillery V. N. Matveev; and his commissar, Nikita Sergeevich Khrushchev

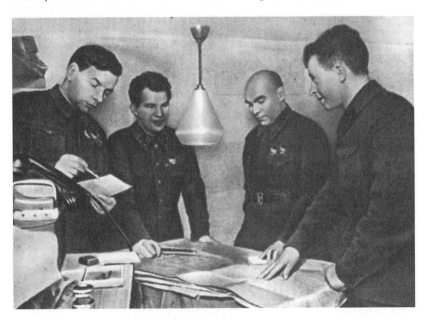

Left to right: Major General N. I. Krylov, chief of staff of 62nd Army; Lieutenant General V. I. Chuikov, commander of 62nd Army; Lieutenant General K. A. Gurov, member of 62nd Army's Military Council (commissar); and Major General A. I. Rodimtsev, commander of 13th Guards Rifle Division

Red Army infantry defending the foothills of the Caucasus Mountains, August 1942

A German cemetery in the Caucasus Mountains

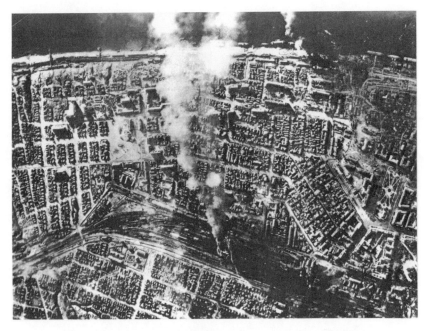

The central part of Stalingrad under assault with 9 January Square and Pavlov's House in the upper center, Railroad Station No. 1 at the left center, and "Red Square" at the lower center

Central Stalingrad in flames

Street fighting in the central part of Stalingrad

Ships of the Volga Military Flotilla transport naval infantry across the river in
October 1942

Soviet tanks entering the penetration in Operation Uranus

Soviet troops and tanks assaulting Kalach-on-the-Don

Major General of Tank Forces
Vasilii Mikhailovich Badanov,
commander of 24th (later 2nd
Guards) Tank Corps

Lieutenant General Markian
Mikhailovich Popov, deputy
commander of the Stalingrad
Front, commander of 5th Shock
Army and later of 5th Tank Army

Field Marshal Erich von Manstein,
commander of Army Group Don

Colonel General Hermann Hoth,
commander of Fourth Panzer Army

General of Panzer Troops Otto von Knobelsdorff, commander of XXXXVIII
Panzer Corps

6th Panzer Division on the attack in the Bystraia River Valley, December 1942

A German Ju-52 transport aircraft landing at Pitomnik airfield in January 1943

Soviet artillery preparation during Operation Ring, January 1943

Troops of 21st and 62nd Armies linking up in Stalingrad on 26 January 1943

Field Marshal Paulus at 64th Army's headquarters on
31 January 1943

German prisoners on the streets of Stalingrad, 4 February 1943

Red flag over Stalingrad's center city

CHAPTER ELEVEN

The Final German Advances

HITLER TAKES COMMAND

As Operation *Blau* dragged onward, Adolf Hitler became increasingly frustrated with his field commanders. German memoirs often seek to place all the blame on his shoulders, portraying him as micromanaging and unreasonable, without considering the strategic situation in which he found himself. From Hitler's viewpoint, the field commanders were being excessively cautious, frittering away the narrow window of strategic opportunity that Germany possessed before the United States mobilized and intervened in the war. His generals had repeatedly disputed or ignored his wishes, thereby (in his mind) permitting the Red Army to escape a series of encirclements. The creative gambler in this strange genius felt that his only hope was to achieve his goals rapidly, regardless of risks. Nor was he the only senior German leader who failed to sense the growing competence and lethality of his opponents.

During the course of 1942, while Joseph Stalin was beginning to trust his key subordinates, his German counterpart was losing his last ounce of patience with the General Staff professionals. As described in the Prologue to this study, those staff officers regularly flouted security regulations as well as their leader's stated intentions. The Germans' attempt to seize divergent objectives at Stalingrad and in the Caucasus suffered from insufficient troops and supplies for either goal. Even the German Army's successes of 1942 accomplished little; the capture of Maikop yielded no immediate supplies of petroleum to ease German shortages. Finally, Field Marshal List had come to a halt in the Caucasus, stopped by a Red Army that Hitler believed was already destroyed.[1]

On 13 July Field Marshal Bock, the commander of Army Group South since January, had lost his command because of this impatience. For the next six weeks of Operation *Blau*, Hitler still permitted his subordinates quite a bit of independence, while his principal staff officers absorbed the brunt of their leader's impatience. On 24 August, however, List indicated that fuel shortages, German casualties, and continued Soviet resistance had seriously retarded the progress of Army Group A. Two days later he reported that snowstorms were already impeding operations at higher elevations and suggested that, without reinforcement, he would have to go into winter quarters in mid-September.[2] In response, Hitler summoned first Army Group A's chief of staff, General Gylenfeldt, and then List himself to *Wehrwolf* headquarters near Vinnitsa in the Ukraine. After the second meeting, on 31 August, Hitler diverted air support from Stalingrad to permit Eleventh Army to attack from the Crimea into the Taman' Peninsula on 2 September, but otherwise, matters were left unsettled. Hitler and List each believed that the other understood his concerns, beliefs that proved to be incorrect.

On 7 September General Alfred Jodl visited Army Group A's headquarters at Stalino, where List convinced him that XXXXIX Mountain Corps could not continue its advance over the narrow mountain passes. Instead, List intended to redeploy this corps to support XXXXIV Army Corps in operations against Tuapse. When Jodl attempted to explain this to Hitler the next day, arguing that List was following orders, the dictator's patience snapped. He immediately implemented a requirement for verbatim stenographic records of all conferences. On 9 September Hitler relieved List outright but did not appoint a new army group commander for several months. Instead, the Führer nominally performed this task himself, conferring by telephone with the two army commanders, Ruoff (Seventeenth Army) and Kleist (First Panzer Army). In reality, he had little attention to spare for this new task, so Major General Hans von Greiffenberg actually ran the army group as chief of staff.[3]

Next to go was the chief of the OKH, General Halder, who acquiesced to Hitler's obvious desire for fresh advisers and turned his position over to Colonel General Kurt Zeitzler effective 24 September. Keitel and Jodl, the two principal staff officers of the OKW, remained in their positions, although at one point Paulus was slated to replace the latter.[4]

These command changes had little effect at the front, where the undermanned German units continued to struggle with terrain and logistics as much as with their Soviet opponents. Just moving sufficient ammunition, fuel, and food to the units was a significant problem. The standard infantry equipment, including high boots, greatcoat, and Gewehr 98 rifle, was ill suited to mountainous, forested terrain. Casualty evacuation was very difficult, so the few villages in the region were entirely occupied with medical aid stations.[5]

OPPOSING FORCES

For both sides, the order of battle in the Caucasus changed so frequently, especially on the Soviet side, that any listing can provide only a snapshot (see tables 11.1 and 11.2).

Table 11.1. Organization of Army Group A, Late September 1942

Army Group A—Vacant
First Panzer Army—Colonel General Ewald von Kleist
    XXXX Panzer Corps—General of Panzer Troops Leo *Freiherr* Geyr von
      Schweppenburg
      3rd Panzer Division
    III Panzer Corps—Lieutenant General Eberhard von Mackensen
      13th and 23rd Panzer Divisions, 370th Infantry Division
    LII Army Corps—General of Infantry Eugen Ott
      5th SS *Wiking* Division, 111th Infantry Division
    Group Steinbauer (disbanded in late October)
      Romanian 2nd Mountain Division (to III Panzer Corps in late October)
      Army Artillery Command (ARKO) 311
Seventeenth Army—Colonel General Richard Ruoff
    V Army Corps—General of Infantry William Wetzel; designated "Group Wetzel"
      9th and 73rd Infantry Divisions; Romanian 5th and 9th Cavalry Divisions
    XXXXIV Army Corps—General of Artillery Maximilian de Angelis
      97th and 101st *Jäger* Divisions, 46th Infantry Division (to XXXIX Mountain
        Corps in early October)
    XXXIX Mountain Corps—General of Mountain Troops Rudolf Konrad
      1st and 4th Mountain Divisions (each temporarily minus one regiment)
    LVII Panzer Corps—General of Panzer Troops Friedrich Kirchner
      1 25th and 198th Infantry Divisions; Slovak Mobile Division
Military Commander Crimea
    Romanian Mountain Corps
      Romanian 1st and 4th Mountain Divisions
    Reserve: 50th Infantry Division, Romanian 8th Cavalry Division
Army Group Rear Area Command: 444th and 454th Security Divisions

---

Source: William McCrodden, *German Ground Forces Orders of Battle, World War II*, rev. ed. (self-published, 2002).

THE MOZDOK-MALGOBEK OPERATION, 2–28 SEPTEMBER

As described in chapter 6, Ruoff's Seventeenth Army came to a halt in mid-September, just short of securing Novorossiisk. Farther east, First Panzer Army, which in early September controlled III Panzer, XXXX Panzer, and LII Army Corps, made equally slow progress against the bitter opposition of the Soviet Northern Group of Forces.

When General Ott's LII Corps first thrust across the Terek River in the Mozdok sector on 2 September, 9th Brigade of 11th Guards Rifle Corps conducted a counterassault, seizing a foothold on the northern bank that had to be eliminated by a *kampfgruppe* from 13th Panzer Division.[6] On 3–4 September XXXX Panzer Corps' 111th Infantry Division, reinforced by 25 tanks from 23rd Panzer Division, captured Terskaia, but only against strong resistance by 9th Red Army. Using this as a base of operations, on 6 September Colonel Otto Herfurth led a *kampfgruppe* consisting of two

Table 11.2. Organization of Trans-Caucasus Front, 1 October 1942

Trans-Caucasus Front—Army General I. V. Tiulenev
Northern Group of Forces—Lieutenant General I. I. Maslennikov
   9th Army—Major General K. A. Koroteev
      11th Guards Rifle Corps—Major General I. P. Roslyi (four rifle brigades)
      89th, 176th, and 417th Rifle Divisions
      19th, 59th, 60th, 131st, 256th Rifle, and 62nd Naval Rifle Brigades
      5th Guards Tank and 52nd Tank Brigades
      Two separate tank battalions, two armored train battalions
   37th Army—Major General P. M. Kozlov
      2nd Guards, 151st, 275th, 295th, and 392nd Rifle Divisions
      11th NKVD Rifle Division and 113th Separate NKVD Rifle Regiment
      127th Cavalry Regiment (of 30th Cavalry Division)
   44th Army—Major General M. E. Petrov (K. S. Mel'nik, 11 October)
      223rd, 317th, 337th, and 389th Rifle Divisions
      9th and 157th Rifle Brigades
      Separate cavalry regiment and three armored train battalions
   58th Army—Major General V. A. Khomenko
      271st, 319th, and 416th Rifle Divisions
      Makhachkala NKVD Rifle Division
      43rd Rifle Brigade
   4th Air Army—Major General of Aviation N. F. Naumenko
      216th, 217th, and 265th Fighter Aviation Divisions (plus 229th forming)
      218th Fighter-Bomber, 219th Bomber, and 230th Assault Aviation Divisions
      Reconnaissance aviation squadron
   8th Sapper Army—Colonel I. E. Salashchenko (eight sapper brigades)
   10th Guards Rifle Corps—Colonel I. A. Sevast'ianov (four brigades)
   4th Guards Cavalry Corps—Major General N. Ia. Kirichenko
      9th and 10th Guards, 30th and 110th Cavalry Divisions
   414th Rifle, 19th NKVD Rifle Divisions
   10th Rifle Brigade, three separate tank battalions
Black Sea Group of Forces—Colonel General Ia. T. Cherevichenko
   (Major General I. E. Petrov, 11 October)
   18th Army—Major General F. V. Kamkov (A. A. Grechko, 18 October)
      32nd Guards, 31st, 236th, 328th, 383rd, and 395th Rifle Divisions
      40th Motorized Rifle, 68th Naval Rifle Brigades
      12th Guards Cavalry Division, separate cavalry regiment
   46th Army—Major General K. N. Leselidze
      3rd Mountain Rifle Corps—Colonel G. N. Perekrestov
      9th, 20th, and 242nd Mountain Rifle Divisions
      61st, 351st, 394th, and 406th Rifle Divisions
      51st, 107th, 119th, and 155th Rifle Brigades
      63rd Cavalry Division
      51st Fortified Region
      One tank battalion, one naval infantry battalion, two armored train battalions,
        and ten mountain rifle detachments
   47th Army—Major General A. A. Grechko (F. V. Kamkov, 18 October)
      216th and 318th Rifle Divisions
      163rd Rifle, 81st and 83rd Naval Rifle, 255th Naval Infantry Brigades
      672nd Rifle and 137th Naval Rifle Regiments
      One separate tank battalion, one separate motorized rifle battalion
   56th Army—Major General A. I. Ryzhov
      30th, 339th, and 353rd Rifle Divisions
      76th Naval Rifle Brigade
      Rostov People's Militia Rifle Regiment

69th Fortified Region
5th Air Army—Lieutenant General of Aviation S. K. Goriunov
    236th, 237th, and 295th Fighter Aviation Divisions
    132nd Bomber, 214th Assault Aviation Divisions
    One bomber, three mixed, one reconnaissance aviation regiments
Group of Forces Control
    77th Rifle Division, 16th and 103rd Rifle Brigades
    11th Guards Cavalry Division
    151st Fortified Region
    Separate battalions of parachutists, tanks, armored trains
Tuapse Defensive Region
    408th Rifle Division (less one regiment)
    145th Naval Infantry Regiment
    Two naval infantry battalions and one special designation (SPETSNAZ)
        detachment
Front subordinate
    261st, 276th, 347th, and 349th Rifle Divisions
    34th, 164th, and 165th Rifle, 84th Naval Rifle Brigades
    2nd, 15th, 63rd, 140th, and 191st Tank Brigades
    Three separate tank battalions, one mountain ski battalion
Nonoperating forces
45th Army—Lieutenant General F. N. Remezov
    228th, 320th, 402nd, and 409th Rifle Divisions
    55th Fortified Region; 151st Tank Brigade
Forces in Iran
    75th Rifle Division
    15th Cavalry Corps (two divisions)
    207th Tank Brigade

Source: Boevoi sostav Sovetskoi armii, Chast 2 (Ianvar'-dekabr' 1942 goda) [Combat composition of the Soviet Army, part 2 (January–December 1942)] (Moscow: Voenizdat, 1966), 195–197, 204.

panzer-grenadier battalions and one tank battalion from 13th Panzer, reinforced by another tank battalion from 23rd Panzer, in an attempt to exploit southward. However, as this force approached the northern foothills of the Terek Mountains, it encountered 62nd Naval Rifle Brigade and 42nd Rifle Division, supported by 57 British Valentine and American M-3 light tanks. Simultaneously, farther to the east 10th Guards Rifle Brigade and 167th Rifle Division struck 111th Infantry Division's defenses at Terskaia. Although the Germans knocked out most of the Lend-Lease tanks, the combination of ground defenses and 500 sorties by 4th Air Army forced Herfurth to withdraw.[7] On 7–8 September 9th Army's commander, Koroteev, pressed his advantage with an attack by the reinforced 52nd Tank Brigade and, later, by 275th Rifle Division; although German assault guns broke up this assault, destroying 14 T-34s and 2 KVs, Kleist had no choice but to withdraw to the original bridgeheads at Mozdok.[8]

Urged on by Hitler, Kleist tried again. On 8–9 September he shifted Breith's 3rd Panzer Division from its bridgehead at Ishcherskaia westward to

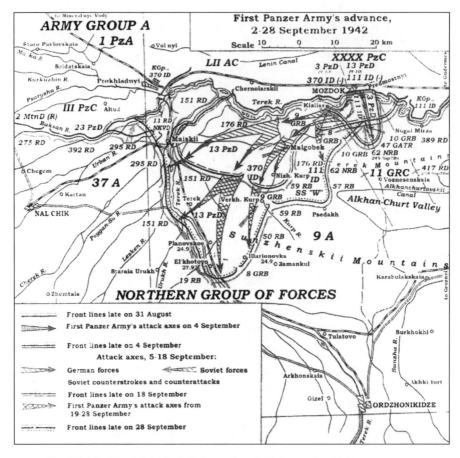

Map 56. The Mozdok-Malgobek Operation, 2–28 September 1942

the Mozdok area. Given the weakness of German units, Kleist once again had to form a *kampfgruppe* from elements of two different divisions—in this instance, one tank and one panzer-grenadier regiment from 3rd Panzer Division, reinforced by a tank battalion of 23rd Panzer, for a total of roughly 70 tanks. This task force, commanded by 3rd Panzer's acting commander, Colonel Kurt *Freiherr* von Liebenstein, was supposed to attack westward out of 370th Division's bridgehead at Kizliar. However, the Northern Group commander, Maslennikov, preempted this plan with a counterattack by 10th Guards Rifle Corps on 10 September. Forced on the defensive, most of Liebenstein's units were then transferred to *Kampfgruppe* Crisolli of 13th Panzer Division. Attacking southwestward in rainy weather, this force of some 100 tanks reached the Alkhan-Churt River, 30 kilometers from Mozdok, on 14 September; 37th Army's 151st Rifle Division finally blocked the German advance there.[9]

Once again, Maslennikov reacted forcefully to a German advance. Between 14 and 17 September three different shock groups, each supported by additional artillery, struck the corridor of Crisolli's advance. The 10th Guards Rifle Corps and 417th Rifle Division attacked near the Mozdok bridgehead, while 275th Rifle Division attacked from the west and a reinforced 52nd Tank Brigade tried to block Crisolli at the Alkhan-Churt River. By the time these attacks had exhausted themselves, 13th Panzer and 370th Infantry Divisions found themselves half encircled. After a pause to reorganize, 13th Panzer Division burst out of its confinement on 18 September, racing west toward the Terek River. There, a Brandenburger special operations detachment seized the 1,200 meter railroad bridge at Arik in the early-morning hours of 20 September. Herr's panzers captured the town of Terek, 10 kilometers south of Arik, the next day, while the weak III Panzer Corps secured the Baksan Valley, west of the Terek, on the twentieth. To the east, LII Corps' 111th Infantry Division, supported by a *kampfgruppe* of 3rd Panzer Division, also advanced out of the Mozdok bridgehead late on 18 September.[10]

The defenders continued to press First Panzer Army relentlessly, forcing the Germans to reorganize again. Hitler directed the SS *Wiking* Division to reinforce Kleist, who in turn assigned it to LII Army Corps. On 23 September 23rd Panzer Division, with approximately 80 tanks, attacked southward again, smashing 295th Rifle and 11th NKVD Divisions on 37th Army's right wing. This attack reached the town of Maiskoe the next day, where it was halted temporarily by the defenders, which included four armored trains.[11] Meanwhile, a herculean maintenance effort increased 13th Panzer Division's strength from 79 to 110 operational tanks by 24 September. The next day this division renewed the attack, with the objective of reaching the El'khotovo Pass, although the initial advance was slowed by the need to clear Soviet bunkers. In the ensuing days, General Herr succeeded in forcing 37th Army's right wing and 9th Army's left wing back, reaching the town of El'khotovo on 26 September. An epic eight-day struggle ensued before the Germans occupied most of the town on the morning of 3 October. By this time, however, 13th Panzer Division was once again exhausted.[12]

An equally bitter struggle occurred, almost simultaneously, near Verkhnyi Kurp and Nizhnyi on the Alkhan-Churt River. LII Corps' 5th SS *Wiking* and 111th Infantry Divisions attacked to capture Malgobek, the next step on the way to Ordzhonikidze and eventually Groznyi, the refinery center of the Caucasus. Unfortunately for the Germans, Koroteev had scheduled a simultaneous counterattack in the same area, using his 52nd Tank and 59th Rifle Brigades, as well as other elements. The 40 tanks of the multinational SS division encountered some 60 Soviet tanks plus elaborate antitank defenses, resulting in vicious fighting. Both German divisions suffered heavily in the process and were unable to continue the advance beyond Malgobek. Kleist, unaware of the Soviet effort, criticized a supposed lack of internal cohesion in the *Wiking* Division. The general eventually asked for additional mobile units, which Hitler vaguely promised to supply after the fall of Stalingrad. On 14 October a Führer Order officially announced the end of the summer offensive.[13]

If the German commanders all recognized that they had insufficient combat power to continue, the same could be said of their opponents. The Northern Group commander, Maslennikov, reported this through channels to the *Stavka*, and Vasilevsky, the chief of staff, responded with a long directive on 29 September. Tiulenev was authorized to disband military schools and reduce rear services units in order to bring the guards rifle brigades up to strength and create additional antitank forces. This message also specified in great detail the series of defenses to be erected to protect Groznyi, extending as far south as Ordzhonikidze.[14]

TUAPSE AGAIN

Given the shortage of German forces in the Caucasus, Hitler reluctantly decided to conduct successive rather than simultaneous offensives to continue the advance, beginning with Ruoff's Seventeenth Army attempting to take the Black Sea coast at Tuapse between 23 September and 31 October.

Deprived of the SS *Wiking* Division, Ruoff's plan for Operation Attika had to depend on his infantry divisions. General Kirchner's LVII Panzer Corps, consisting of 125th and 198th Infantry Divisions plus the Slovak Mobile Division, would begin on the western flank on 23 September, followed two days later by concentric attacks, from west to east, by XXXXIV Corps (General de Angelis, with one infantry and two *Jäger* divisions) and XXXXIX Mountain Corps (General Konrad, with two mountain divisions). Ruoff's intent was to encircle the Soviet 18th Army around Tuapse. However, this attack involved uphill advances along mountain ravines and gorges in steadily worsening weather. The Soviet defenders, the Black Sea Group of Forces under Ia. T. Cherevichenko, consisted of four armies, but the attack fell primarily against Ryzhov's 56th Army (four divisions), located west of LVII Panzer Corps, and Kamkov's 18th Army (one cavalry and five rifle divisions, plus two naval rifle brigades), opposite XXXXIV Army and part of XXXXIX Mountain Corps (see map 57).

The initial advances quickly bogged down in the face of determined Soviet resistance. On 27 September, therefore, General Ruoff sent a reinforced 1st Mountain Division (Group Lanz, named for its commander) over the

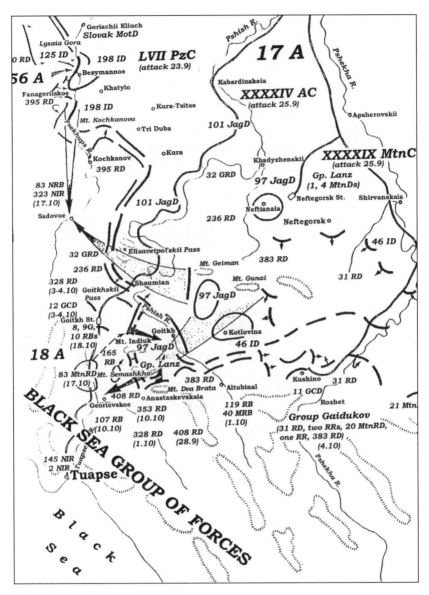

Map 57. The Tuapse Operation, 23 September–31 October 1942

forested mountains of Gunai and Geiman, defended by the overstretched 383rd and 236th Rifle Divisions. In a remarkable feat of mountain warfare, Lanz was able to force the defenders back and reach the Gunaika River Valley, near the village of Kotlovina, up to 20 kilometers deep into 18th Army's defenses. The weakened 46th Infantry Division kept pace with this advance on its eastern flank, threatening the entire Soviet defense.[15] Lanz preempted Cherevichenko's attempt at a counterattack, seizing Kotlovina on 2 October. The 18th Army commander, Kamkov, failed in his own hasty counterattack on 7 October, but on the ninth, under intense pressure from higher headquarters, he achieved a more coordinated defense that halted Group Lanz just short of the Khadyshenskii-Tuapse road.[16]

Between 10 and 13 October Seventeenth Army paused to rest and reorganize. Meanwhile, 83rd Naval Rifle Brigade and 137th Naval Infantry Regiment arrived to reinforce Kamkov's defense of Tuapse, and Moscow relieved the Black Sea Group commander, Cherevichenko, on 11 October. Major General I. E. Petrov, commander of 44th Army, replaced him. Seventeenth Army resumed its offensive on 14 October before Kamkov was able to mount a new counterattack. LVII Panzer Corps' 125th Infantry Division struck south toward Sadovoe, almost linking up with a simultaneous westward thrust by XXXXII Corps' two *Jäger* divisions, and in the process it destroyed two regiments of 395th Rifle Division. Meanwhile, Group Lanz resumed its advance despite heavy fighting, seizing the road and railroad junction 2 kilometers west of Shaumian. In 19 days of battle, Lanz's force had advanced up to 40 kilometers, but at a heavy price, losing 389 scarce mountain troops killed and 1,470 wounded.[17] This success earned Lanz the oak leaves to his Knight's Cross and later a promotion to general of mountain troops.

The defenders again acted to mass forces against the new threat. Accusing Tiulenev of favoring the Northern Group of Forces over the Black Sea Group, on 15 October the *Stavka* instructed him to transfer three rifle brigades from the former to the latter, as well as shifting 63rd Cavalry and 83rd Mountain Rifle Divisions, newly arrived from central Asia, to the Tuapse axis. Two days later, when the new commander of the Black Sea Group, Petrov, visited 18th Army, he replaced Kamkov. The latter general had lost communications with his left wing and was unaware that XXXXIV Corps had seized Shaumian and approached the Elizavetpol'skii Pass the previous day. Kamkov swapped positions with A. A. Grechko, the commander of 47th Army.[18]

Grechko promptly moved the three guards rifle brigades, just released from the Northern Group of Forces, to protect the Goitkhskii Pass area, while the fresh 83rd Mountain Rifle Division concentrated in a reserve position just north of that pass. Before Grechko could counterattack in that area, however, Ruoff preempted him with a new advance at dawn on 19

October. By nightfall, the German 198th Infantry Division had shoved 395th Rifle Division off Mount Kochkanova, 97th *Jäger* Division had completed the seizure of Elizavetpol'skii Pass, and Group Lanz had pushed 383rd Rifle Division southward from Kotlovina. The next day a German artillery barrage destroyed the headquarters of the inexperienced 408th Rifle Division, after which 97th *Jäger* Division and Group Lanz dismembered this division and captured Goitkh. Again aided by 46th Infantry Division, on 23 October Lanz cut Grechko's lateral communications by entering the Tuapsinka River Valley, only 30 kilometers from the port.[19]

Grechko was finally able to organize two shock groups, supported by 5th Air Army, to mount a series of converging counterstrokes against the flanks of the German penetration. Beginning on 23 October 353rd Rifle Division attacked the southern flank of Group Lanz, capturing Mount Semashkho. The next day the Slovak Mobile Division captured Mount Sarai, 5 kilometers northwest of Elizavetpol'skii Pass, but a counterattack by 32nd Guards and 328th Rifle Divisions forced it back. The 10th Rifle and 9th Guards Rifle Brigades joined the fray on 28 October, advancing on Pereval'nyi and Goitkh, respectively. Exhaustion and winter weather brought operations to a standstill by early November.[20]

STOPPED AT ORDZHONIKIDZE

In mid-October General Kleist had Mackensen's III Panzer Corps prepare for a renewed offensive through Nal'chik toward the Ossetian city of Ordzhonikidze (Russian name, Vladikavkaz), once again seeking to advance on Groznyi. To accomplish this, Kleist transferred 23rd Panzer Division from XXXX Panzer to III Panzer Corps, where it joined 13th Panzer in a concerted maintenance effort that brought their combined strength to some 200 tanks. The two panzer divisions would attack southwestward from the Prishibskaia-Maiskii area to the road south of Nal'chik. Mackensen also directed the Romanian 2nd Mountain Division, located some 20 kilometers west of the two panzer divisions, to attack due south toward Nal'chik itself.[21]

During this lull, General Tiulenev, the *front* commander, attempted to exploit the open German flank north and east of First Panzer Army. In late September he had transferred the four divisions of N. Ia. Kirichenko's 4th Cavalry Corps to the extreme eastern flank of the front, north of the Terek River. Moving at night across the waterless steppe between 2 and 14 October, Kirichenko finally reached his objective, the tiny town of Achikulak, some 470 kilometers south of Stalingrad. There he attacked Special Corps Fermy, an aggregation of 6,000 Muslim soldiers recruited from German POW camps and commanded by *Luftwaffe* General Helmut Fermy. Having underesti-

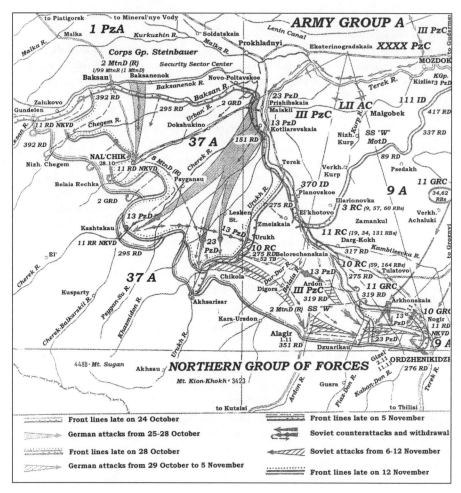

Map 58. The Nal'chik-Ordzhonikidze Operation, 25 October–12 November 1942

mated Fermy's strength, however, Kirichenko's attack failed, as did a second attempt, with an additional cavalry division, at the end of October.[22]

Always optimistic, on 23 October Tiulenev had proposed an offensive against First Panzer Army. By the time the *Stavka* approved this plan, however, Kleist had renewed his own attack on the twenty-fifth.

Recognizing that the Northern Group of Forces outnumbered him in many respects, Kleist chose to focus on a narrow sector of Kozlov's 37th Army, whose six rifle divisions were strung out along the Baksan and Terek Rivers with no armored support. When Mackensen's III Panzer Corps began its artillery preparation at dawn on 25 October, an estimated 70 German aircraft struck 37th Army's headquarters south of Nal'chik, destroying its communications and killing many staff officers. Thus, when Romanian 2nd Mountain Division attacked along the Baksan River at 1000 hours, Kozlov had neither communications nor reserves and quickly lost control of the battle. The next day Kozlov attempted to counterattack using a regiment from 295th Rifle Division, but the Romanian-German attackers swept aside this slender force. At the same time, 13th and 23rd Panzer Divisions broke out of their bridgehead and advanced some 20 kilometers in one day, reaching the Cherek River Valley east of Nal'chik.[23]

Tiulenev, who at the time was personally directing the defense of Tuapse, flew back to Northern Group headquarters. He deployed Major General P. E. Loviagin's newly formed 10th Rifle Corps into the teeth of the Axis penetration. Loviagin's corps consisted of 59th and 164th Rifle Brigades, 275th Rifle Division, two antitank artillery regiments, and three artillery battalions. Tiulenev also moved 11th Guards Rifle Corps, consisting of three brigades, to defend Ordzhonikidze itself, while 3rd Rifle Corps, also controlling three brigades, would concentrate around Zamankul, on the flank of the Axis advance.[24]

Before these defenses could gel, however, Mackensen's panzer corps completed the rout of 37th Army on 27–28 October, clearing Nal'chik and capturing the village of Kashtakau on the Cherek River. Over the next two days, Mackensen realigned the two panzer divisions to conduct a deliberate attack eastward across the Urukh River toward Ordzhonikidze. On 31 October 23rd Panzer Division broke through the left wing of 10th Rifle Corps near Chikola and overran the corps headquarters, only to be halted 10 kilometers east of the Urukh by a counterattack by 52nd Tank Brigade. That afternoon, the 60 remaining tanks of Herr's 13th Panzer Division penetrated the right wing of Loviagin's 10th Rifle Corps and, preceded by Brandenburger special operations teams, reached the town of Ardon, 20 kilometers to the southeast. III Panzer Corps' advance made excellent use of reconnaissance and air support to locate or create Soviet weak points.[25]

The two German panzer divisions attempted to encircle and destroy 10th Rifle Corps and 52nd Tank Brigade in the Ardon area. In the intense battle that ensued, the Soviets reportedly destroyed 32 German tanks. General Herr was wounded and was succeeded as commander of 13th Panzer by Major General Helmut von der Chevallerie, a veteran infantryman transferred from command of 22nd Panzer. On 1 November Loviagin withdrew his battered 10th Rifle Corps eastward to the next defensive line near the Ardon River at a point 30 kilometers northeast of Ordzhonikidze. That same day the *Luftwaffe* began to bomb Ordzhonikidze, severely damaging the forward command post of the Trans-Caucasus Front and killing both the *front* chief of staff and its commissar; both sides reported heavy aircraft losses in the skies over the city. Tiulenev redeployed 10th Guards and 11th Guards Rifle Corps, 2nd Tank and 5th Guards Tank Brigades, and numerous antitank and artillery units to defend Ordzhonikidze, but by 4 November, the two panzer divisions, now reduced to a total of perhaps 100 tanks, had captured a suburb within 9 kilometers of the town.[26]

Both sides recognized that this bold advance had left III Panzer Corps overextended, with numerous large Soviet units along the eastern flank of its thrust. Tiulenev described this opportunity in a 3 November message to the *Stavka*, which authorized a two-pronged counterattack beginning three days later. Both 10th Guards and 11th Guards Rifle Corps would attack from the area north of Ordzhonikidze to pierce the Germans' eastern wing, while 276th and 351st Rifle Divisions and 155th Rifle Brigade, located south and southwest of the city, would penetrate the Germans' right and advance northward to link up with the other thrust.[27] German intelligence apparently failed to detect these counterattack forces.

In the event, the difficult terrain and logistical situation meant that the Soviet attack was not synchronized. Major General Roslyi's 11th Guards Rifle Corps, with two rifle and two tank brigades, attacked at dawn on 6 November, forcing 23rd Panzer Division to withdraw toward Dzuarikau and encircling most of 13th Panzer Division hear Gizel', northwest of Ordzhonikidze. When 10th Guards Rifle Corps belatedly joined the assault at midday, the Germans quickly halted it. Still, Chevallerie's division was almost surrounded, and Maslennikov, the Northern Group commander, promptly committed the experienced 34th Separate Rifle Brigade in an attempt to block the road through the Suarskoe ravine, the only possible German escape route. The 34th, reinforced by 10th Guards Rifle Brigade on 10 November, halted the Romanian 2nd Mountain Division, reinforced by Brandenburgers and armor of 23rd Panzer, when that force attempted to relieve 13th Panzer Division.[28]

Kleist then redeployed 5th SS Division, one *kampfgruppe* at a time, from Malgobek to the area north of Dzuarikau. The first element to arrive, 11th SS *Nordland* Regiment, broke though the Suarskoe gorge late on 11 November, allowing most of 23th Panzer Division to escape through a gauntlet of Soviet artillery fire but leaving its heavy equipment behind. The next day forces on the left wing of Koroteev's 9th Army smashed 13th Panzer's rear guard and pushed west toward the Mairamadag River. The Soviets later reported that, during this encirclement operation, they destroyed or captured 40 tanks, 7 armored personnel carriers, and 2,533 other vehicles belonging to III Panzer Corps. German accounts acknowledge equally significant losses, with 13th Panzer Division's operational tank count dropping from 119 on 1 November to 32 on 17 November. Kleist's panzers were within 115 kilometers of Groznyi, but Maslennikov's troops had finally, if belatedly, blocked the German advance.[29]

Urged on by the *Stavka*, *front* commander Tiulenev and Northern Group commander Maslennikov prepared to mount a full counteroffensive against Kleist's troops, both to weaken them and to prevent German redeployments to reinforce Stalingrad, where the general Soviet offensive began on 19 November (see chapters 12 and 13). Koroteev's 9th Army prepared to advance in stages, with the ultimate goal of restoring defenses along the Urukh River. By this time, both sides were so worn down that Mackensen, III Panzer Corps' commander, quickly discovered that he had to recommit the shaken 13th Panzer Division in an effort to contain the Soviet advance. The 5th SS, 13th, and 23rd Panzer Divisions had a total of fewer than 140 operational tanks among them. On the Soviet side, after the counterattack towards Gizel', 275th and 319th Rifle Divisions on 9th Army's right wing had a total of only 8,000 troops, while 10th and 11th Guards Rifle Corps totaled only 13,000. Maslennikov's five tank brigades had a total of only 8 T-34s and 72 other, generally lighter, tanks.[30]

This mutual weakness made the ensuing maneuvers largely indecisive. The 10th Guards, 11th Guards, and 2nd Rifle Corps dutifully attacked northwest of Ordzhonikidze but made little progress. The 10th Guards Rifle Corps finally achieved a penetration on 17 November, only to be contained by the tanks of SS *Wiking* Division. When the Soviets encircled Stalingrad later that week, the OKH withdrew 23rd Panzer Division for an attempt to relieve Sixth Army. Deprived of its most potent remaining mechanized force, First Panzer Army was never able to resume its advance.[31]

Dissatisfied with the performance of the Trans-Caucasus Front, on 15 November Stalin summoned both Tiulenev and Maslennikov to Moscow. In addition to directing a further counteroffensive, the dictator tried again to exploit the open eastern flank of First Panzer Army. Harking back to his own experience during the Russian Civil War, he ordered the creation of a Don Guards Cavalry Corps under Major General A. G. Selivanov that would cooperate with Kirichenko's Kuban' Guards Cavalry Corps.[32] The *Stavka* also reshuffled personnel in the region, promoting Lieutenant General Aleksei Innokent'evich Antonov from chief of staff of the Black Sea Group of Forces to the same position in the Trans-Caucasus Front. Antonov eventually succeeded Vasilevsky as head of the Red Army General Staff.[33]

Given the challenges of terrain, weather, and logistics, these organizational changes had little effect on the ground. Koroteev's 9th Army again attacked III Panzer Corps on four converging axes beginning on 27 November but failed to make progress. Only the German encirclement at Stalingrad forced the eventual withdrawal of First Panzer Army.

In several respects, Operation *Blau* replicated the German problems of Operation Barbarossa the previous year. Strategically, the *Wehrmacht* of 1941 had already suffered major defeats at Leningrad and Rostov before it fell short at Moscow. Thus, in 1941 Army Groups North and South had already gone onto the defensive before Army Group Center collapsed on the approaches to the Soviet capital. Likewise, in the fall of 1942 Army Group A had already assumed the defensive in the Caucasus before Army Group B met catastrophe at Stalingrad. The same was true at the operational level. In 1941 the *Wehrmacht* had lost the battles of Tikhvin and Rostov in November 1941 before the Soviet counteroffensive at Moscow. A year later the encirclement of 13th Panzer Division north of Ordzhonikidze was a dress rehearsal, at a lower level, for the much greater defeat of German Sixth Army.

PLANNING FOR THE FINAL ACT IN STALINGRAD, 1–8 NOVEMBER

By 1 November 1942, the *Wehrmacht* controlled more than 90 percent of Stalingrad, but Sixth Army's 12 infantry divisions were short 73,996 soldiers, primarily infantrymen and combat engineers. Casualties in October alone had totaled 12,297, of which 75 percent were in the five divisions of Seydlitz's LI Corps.[34]

Despite the German attacks, the undermanned and poorly supplied 62nd Army stubbornly refused to yield its final bridgeheads along the western bank of the Volga. Chuikov's troops were in seven different groups (see map 59):

- Group Gorokhov (124th and 149th Rifle Brigades) between Rynok and Spartanovka, north of the Mokraia Mechetka River.
- 138th Rifle Division (Liudnikov) and 118th Regiment of 37th Guards Rifle Division north and northeast of the Barrikady Factory, an area less than 400 meters deep known as Liudnikov's Island.
- 339th and 344th Regiments of 308th Rifle Division (Gurt'ev) in the narrow strip east and southeast of the Barrikady Factory.
- 193rd Rifle Division (Smekhotvorov), 120th Regiment (–) of 39th Guards Rifle Division, and 61st and 253rd Regiments of 45th Rifle Division (Sokolov) holding the land between Hall 4 of the Krasnyi Oktiabr' Factory and the ravine south of the Barrikady Factory; two regiments of 95th Rifle Division joined that group on the night of 1–2 November.
- 112th Regiment and part of 120th Regiment, 39th Guards Rifle Division (Gur'ev), with 10th Regiment, 45th Rifle Division, defending from the Bannyi ravine to Halls 8a and 10 of the Krasnyi Oktiabr' Factory.
- 284th Rifle Division (Batiuk) stretching from the lower Krutoi ravine past the Dolgii ravine and the "Tennis Racket" (where Chuikov's command post was located) to the Bannyi ravine.

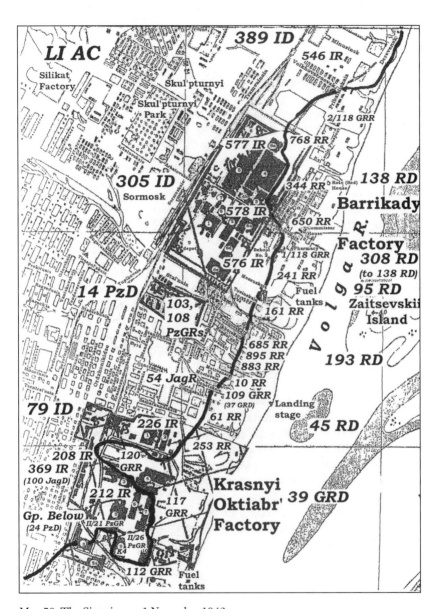

Map 59. The Situation on 1 November 1942

- 13th Guards Rifle Division (Rodimtsev), still defending strongpoints in the central city.[35]

Contemplating this enemy array, General Paulus determined to focus on the Lazur chemical factory, situated in the Tennis Racket between the Krasnyi Oktiabr' Factory and the Bannyi ravine. Capturing this headquarters would split Chuikov's defenses in half, rendering the defenses of the other factories almost irrelevant. To generate sufficient combat power from his weakened divisions, Paulus initially proposed swapping 305th Infantry Division in the factory district for 60th Motorized Division in XIV Panzer Corps' defenses northwest of the city. After extensive discussions between Sixth Army and Army Group B, however, Generals Weichs and Paulus concluded that the understrength 60th had to remain in its current location. Instead, building on a suggestion from Hitler, the commanders eventually decided to detach the four divisional pioneer (combat engineer) battalions from 22nd Panzer Division and three German infantry divisions supporting Italian Eighth Army. These four battalions, together with 45th Engineer Battalion, which was directly subordinate to Sixth Army, had a total strength of 2,171 men. Added to this was a company from 44th Infantry Division and a tank squadron from 24th Panzer, representing the last increment of trained combat troops that Paulus could eke out to tip the balance in the city fighting.[36]

Meanwhile, 389th Infantry Division, now commanded by Major General Erich Magnus, had relieved most of 24th Panzer Division on the night of 30–31 October. Rather than recuperating, however, on the following night the depleted panzer division replaced 212th Regiment of 79th Infantry Division southwest of the Krasnyi Oktiabr' Factory, opposite 39th Guards Rifle Division's 112th Regiment. To increase its effectiveness, 24th Panzer transferred approximately 700 support troops to combat roles, filling the vacancies with *Hiwi* Russian laborers.[37]

Over the next week, the Germans made a series of planning changes. No sooner had Seydlitz issued a corps order for the attack on the Lazur Factory than Hitler, hearing of the plan, inquired why Sixth Army did not clear Krasnyi Oktiabr' first. Paulus found himself responding to the dictator, through channels, with his reasons. In truth, the Germans had focused so much military and media attention on the northern factories that only people on the scene could understand the apparent shift in objective. On 6 November Hitler directed that the two large factories be captured prior to an attack on the chemical works, forcing a restructuring of the attack plans. As finally amended on 8 November, LI Corps' order directed 305th Infantry Division, with 50th, 294th, and 336th Engineer Battalions attached, to make the primary assault through the Barrikady to the riverfront. The southern wing of 389th Infantry Division, with 45th and 162nd Engineer Battalions, would support this attack on the 305th's left. The other divisions of LI Corps would conduct their own limited attacks to deceive the defenders, but the Germans' intention was to begin with the Barrikady Factory and then reduce the other strongholds in progression.[38] Still, the numerous changes and hesitations created an air of uncertainty among the German commanders.

FIGHTING DURING THE "LULL," 1–10 NOVEMBER

While senior leaders debated the next step, the fighting continued, sometimes flaring into fierce and desperate struggles. The constant pressure made it impossible for Chuikov to use the far bank of the Volga to rest his troops. Thus, on 1 November he directed that two regiments of Gorishnyi's 95th Rifle Division, resting on the eastern bank, return to the fight; although the division headquarters and staff of the 109th Regiment of Zholudev's 37th Guards Rifle Division, temporarily withdrawn from the Barrikady area, moved eastward across the river, all their combat personnel remained under Liudnikov's command.[39] Meanwhile, on 1–2 November 300th Rifle Division's amphibious battalion again landed north of Rynok, but the OKW claimed the landing was unsuccessful.[40]

With both sides preparing for another climactic struggle, combat action dropped sharply and almost ceased on 4 November. Both sides were extremely weak, holding on in some cases by their fingertips. By consolidating the number of infantry battalions from 69 to 62, German Sixth Army achieved some marginal efficiencies (see table 10.1). Still, three of LI Corps' seven divisions (94th, 295th, and 79th Infantry) were rated between "weak" and "exhausted," and the other four were only marginally better. The corps had only 21 tanks and 28 assault guns available to support the renewed effort; to its north, XIV Panzer Corps had no more than 106 functional tanks.[41]

Except in its count of German tanks, which was consistently too high, 62nd Army had a very accurate picture of its opponents' strengths and deployments.[42] With the approach of winter and dropping temperatures, Chuikov began to fear that floating ice would interrupt his communications across the Volga just as Paulus renewed the attack.[43] Intermittent German ground and air attacks continued, convincing the 62nd Army commander that a new offensive was imminent. On 8 and 10 November, therefore, he ordered renewed reconnaissance and local attacks, seeking to broaden his defensive bridgehead and disrupt Paulus's preparations.[44] In particular, a determined 10 November attack by the 112th Regiment of Gur'ev's 39th Guards Rifle Division in Hall 10 led to prolonged and indecisive struggles with elements of 24th Panzer Division. The resulting intermingling of German and Soviet units complicated preparations for LI Corps' new attack. The 24th Panzer was too hard-pressed to redeploy its *Kampfgruppe* Schelle northward to support 305th Infantry Division in the Barrikady, and both that *kampfgruppe* and 79th Infantry Division had to retake Hall 10 prior to the main offensive.[45]

Nonetheless, by late on 10 November, the Germans had completed their preparations (see map 60). On the northern (left) wing of Seydlitz's corps, 389th Infantry Division had combined three weak infantry battalions and 389th and 162nd Engineer Battalions, with the resulting *kampfgruppen* deployed from the brick factory to the northeastern edge of the Barrikady Factory. Their mission was to support Steinmetz's 305th Infantry Division, located along the eastern edge of the Barrikady to a ravine south of that factory. The 305th Division's 577th, 578th, and 576th Regiments, supported by 336th, 50th Motorized, and 294th Engineer Battalions, respectively, would make the main effort. In this sector the Volga was only 100 to 400 meters from the German forward positions, but the two infantry divisions had no more than 3,000 and 4,000 effectives, respectively.[46]

Seydlitz's main shock group was composed of 305th Division, as described above, and Group Schwerin, consisting of 79th Infantry Division with large portions of 24th Panzer subordinated to it. Schwerin's 208th Regiment and *Kampfgruppe* Schelle of 24th Panzer were opposite Hall 10. The 226th Regiment protected the left flank of this spearhead east of Halls 1 and 2, while 21st Panzer-Grenadier Regiment and 4th Motorcycle Battalion, both borrowed from the panzer division, covered the right flank north of Hall 8a. General Schwerin planned to use an assault group, consisting of 120 men from his divisional 179th Engineer Battalion plus a company of 40th Panzer Pioneer Battalion, to begin the attack on Hall 4. These pioneers, arrayed in four combat wedges, would get some support from 208th Regiment and the remnants of Croat 369th. The Germans believed their opponents were some 400 survivors of 39th Guards Rifle Division and 45th Rifle Division, but in fact, hundreds of additional Soviet troops manned various positions in the eastern part of the factory.[47] Finally, the remaining elements of 14th Panzer Division, organized as *Kampfgruppe* Seydel, were responsible for protecting Seydlitz's flank and containing Soviet forces between the Barrikady and Krasnyi Oktiabr' Factories.

THE FINAL ACT: ASSAULT ON THE BARRIKADY FACTORY SECTOR, 11–15 NOVEMBER

Paulus and Seydlitz began the long-awaited final offensive at dawn on 11 November (see map 60). To mislead the defenders concerning the true *Schwerpunkt* of this attack, neighboring German units made a number of probes and raids in the predawn hours.

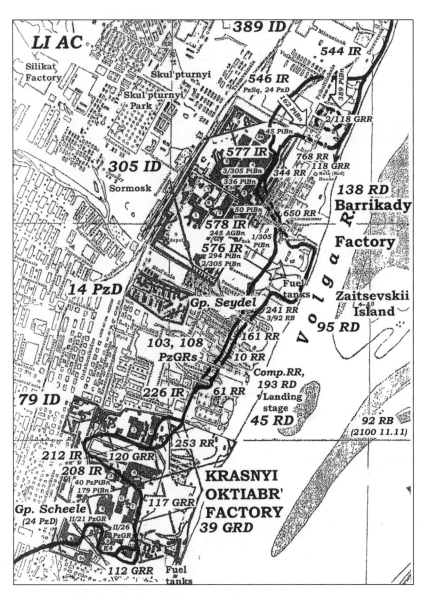

Map 60. LI Army Corps' Assault, 11–12 November 1942

After a 15-minute bombardment beginning at 0340, the assault groups of 305th and 389th Infantry Divisions began their advance, spearheaded by their attached engineers and by 244th and 245th Assault Gun Battalions. Aided by fighter-bombers, 305th Division quickly reached the Volga River along a 200 meter sector defended by 95th Rifle Division's 241st Regiment. Immediately north of this penetration and east of the center of the Barrikady Factory, German engineers caught the defenders by surprise, penetrating the boundary between 95th and 138th Rifle Divisions to reach what the Germans called the "Commissar's House." However, piles of rubble protected the nearby "Pharmacy" strongpoint from pioneer satchel charges. Because these buildings provided fields of fire in a relatively open area, the struggle continued for most of the day, preventing a further German advance there. Farther south, some elements of 39th Guards Rifle Division also had to abandon their positions inside the Krasnyi Oktiabr' Factory. However, the reinforced 179th Engineers failed to capture Hall 4, falling back after 54 of its 120 men were killed, wounded, or missing.[48] On the northern flank, 389th Division's 546th Regiment, spearheaded by 45th and 162nd Engineers and supported by 24th Panzer's squadron and 244th Assault Gun Battalion, captured several blocks from 138th Rifle Division's 768th Regiment and advanced within 200 meters of the Volga. The 389th Division's engineer battalion had similar success, splitting 118th Rifle Regiment and forcing its survivors to fight their way back to the main bridgehead of Liudnikov's main defensive position. The cost of even this limited advance was high: 305th Division reported 13 men killed and 119 wounded on 11 November, while 24th Panzer had 48 killed, 152 wounded, and 180 missing. The two assault gun battalions saw 10 of their 28 guns put out of action, at least temporarily, owing to mechanical or battle damage.[49] Paulus had to report that he had achieved only partial success, telling the OKH that he intended to regroup on 12 November and resume the attack the following day.[50]

The 138th Rifle Division's daily report provided graphic descriptions of the confused and costly fighting on the eleventh:

> Although half encircled, 118th G[uar]ds R[ifle] R[egiment] continued to repel the enemy attacks. Only at day's end, when all of its men had been put out of action, the enemy completely captured 118th Gds RR's positions since the regiment had been fully destroyed. A total of 7 men, together with the wounded commander of the regiment, Lieutenant Kolobavnikov, escaped from the fighting. . . . The advance by the enemy was halted by forces from the [768th Regiment] headquarters and a company from the division, and the penetrating group was completely destroyed by 1500 hours. . . .
>
> At 1130 hours [a] small group of enemy submachine gunners [336th Engineer Battalion] succeeded in seeping through the forward edge of

the [344th] regiment's left wing. The fighting with penetrating groups of enemy submachine gunners in the depths of the defense and constant attacks from the flanks continued until 1600 hours. . . .

Beginning at 1520 hours, having lost its personnel, 241st RR abandoned the position it occupied [to German 576th Infantry Regiment] and without advance warning, withdrew toward the south, entirely exposing the division's left flank. There is no elbow-to-elbow communication with the neighbor [95th Rifle Division].[51]

In his situation report at the end of 11 November, General Chuikov requested that Eremenko concentrate all available fire support, with additional artillery ammunition supplies, in support of 62nd Army. He also asked that the *front* send 90th Rifle Regiment across the river to reinforce its parent 95th Division. The next day, after scattered fighting and frequent German air and artillery strikes, Chuikov asked for 10,000 replacements as well as increased supplies of ammunition and river-crossing boats.[52]

Because his forces in the Krasnyi Oktiabr' Factory were too weak to conduct significant attacks on 13 November, Seydlitz decided to focus on the region east of the Barrikady Factory (see map 61). He detached 162nd Engineer Battalion from 389th Infantry Division to give Steinmetz's 305th Division a third such battalion, plus eight operational tanks from 14th Panzer Division and four vehicles from 245th Assault Gun Battalion. The plan was simple: while Steinmetz's 576th Regiment and 294th Engineer Battalion protected the southern flank near the fuel tanks, the remaining 578th and 577th Regiments (with their attachments) would seek to liquidate the encircled 138th Rifle Division. The attack would focus on the Commissar's House and the deadly open ground between that building and the fuel tanks to the south and House No. 78 to the north. The defenders had constructed dugouts both on the edge of the cliff and halfway down and received accurate fire support from the far bank of the Volga.[53]

The 13 November attack began several hours before sunrise, catching the defenders off guard. Major Eberhard Rettenmaier, a battalion commander in the 305th Infantry's 578th Regiment, described the struggle for the Commissar's House:

This time the engineers of the 50th [Battalion] had success. With the aid of ladders, they managed to penetrate into the house through the windows. The Russians fled into the cellars and fortified themselves there. The engineers tore up the floor and closed with the enemy with smoke rounds, explosive ammunition [satchel charges], and petrol. The house was smoking from all apertures, and throughout the day explosions could be heard. Only by evening the Russians disappeared from the cellars and escaped.[54]

Map 61. LI Army Corps' Assault, 13–15 November 1942

While Liudnikov and his staff officers helped defend this structure, known to the Soviets as the P-shaped building, the attacks by 576th (to the north) and 578th (to the south) Infantry Regiments were much less successful, and persistent Soviet counterattacks actually retook a few buildings. A composite regiment of 193rd Rifle Division also tried repeatedly to recapture the fuel tanks; these attacks failed but placed continuing pressure on the Germans.[55]

Still, Liudnikov acknowledged that ammunition and food were running out, while continuous German mortar fire interdicted efforts to resupply him. Despite later Soviet claims that 62nd Army had 47,000 men, the forces still defending the west bank on the evening of 13 November likely numbered no more than 8,000 effectives, the equivalent of one rifle division.[56]

By this time, all the German headquarters involved were aware of Soviet troop concentrations opposite Romanian Third Army (see chapters 12 and 13). Yet, even on 14 November the OKH's Foreign Armies East intelligence section was still downplaying the possibility of major enemy action.[57] Meanwhile, the exhausted German troops attempted to continue the offensive by local actions on the fourteenth. Using the Commissar's House as a base, 50th and 162nd Engineers moved northward and eastward. A trench leading down to the Volga enabled some of the engineers to reach the banks, but they had great difficulty consolidating this bridgehead against desperate counterattacks by the defenders. By evening, 138th Rifle Division had no more than 500 survivors clinging to their positions; they were out of ammunition and food, despite attempted airdrops by PO-2 biplanes.[58]

For 15 November, Seydlitz focused his reduced assets against specific buildings, launching two limited attacks to further compress Liudnikov's perimeter. The 305th Infantry Division's 578th Regiment, with the decimated 50th Engineers and a handful of assault guns, struck due north of the Commissar's House. The 389th Division's 546th Regiment, supported by 45th Engineer Battalion, 44th Assault Company, and perhaps ten assault guns, attacked southward toward the Rote House, defended by 138th Rifle Division's 768th Regiment. By the end of the day, Liudnikov's division acknowledged that this latter unit was destroyed; it had no supplies, and it had 250 wounded who required evacuation. Still, a resolute defense had contained the German advance to less than three blocks, and the remnants of 138th Rifle Division remained in place.[59]

Paulus and Seydlitz agreed to rest and reorganize their weakened assault forces during the period 16–18 November, but local fighting continued. After the fact, Chuikov claimed he knew the Germans were finished and that 62nd Army mounted significant attacks to relieve the encircled 138th Division. However, both German and Soviet accounts at the time indicate relatively limited fighting. At best, eight vessels of the Volga Flotilla managed to deliver some food, ammunition, and replacements on the night of 15–16 November.[60] At 1130 on 18 November the severely weakened 95th Rifle Division succeeded in retaking the oil tanks but could not break through to the encircled defenders. Liudnikov's division was reduced to an area measuring 400 by 300 meters and defended itself primarily with captured weapons, having expending all its Soviet ammunition.[61]

Seydlitz, whose combat strength had fallen to 3,530 men (only 1,600 of them infantry), husbanded his remaining force in preparation for a renewed attack on 20 November.[62] Meanwhile, at 0400 on the seventeenth 16th Panzer's Division's motorcycle battalion and 2nd Battalion, 79th Panzer-Grenadier Regiment, tried again to overrun Group Gorokhov's 124th

Rifle Brigade. In a blinding snowstorm the Germans failed to take Rynok, but they renewed their efforts the next day. Only on 19 November did XIV Panzer Corps authorize a withdrawal.[63] Also on 18 November, 305th Infantry Division's 578th Regiment, spearheaded by two engineer battalions and a squadron of tanks from 24th Panzer Division, conducted a carefully planned dawn attack against 138th Rifle Division. The first lunge captured House No. 77, 100 meters north of the Commissar's House. Later in the day, the same *kampfgruppe* pushed another 100 meters along the Volga's bank before being halted at nightfall. The defenders could not even summon artillery fires because their radios no longer functioned.[64]

Desperation motivated these final German attacks, as well as plans for a renewed assault on 20 November. Even Hitler realized that the troops could go no farther, but the sense that he was losing his last opportunity prompted him to cable a new order to Paulus on 17 November. The dictator required that this order be read to the troops:

> I am aware of the difficulties of the fighting in Stalingrad and of the decline in combat strengths. But the drift ice on the Volga poses even greater difficulties for the Russians. If we exploit this time span, we will save ourselves much blood later.
>
> I therefore expect that the leadership and the troops will once more, as they often have in the past, devote their energy and spirit to at least getting through to the Volga at the gun factory and the metallurgical plant and taking these sections of the city.[65]

In anticipation of such an effort, Chuikov yet again ordered Liudnikov and his other subordinates to stand firm, despite their extreme weakness. In reality, both sides realized that 62nd Army, for all its weaknesses, had accomplished its sacrificial mission, bleeding Sixth Army until the Germans were reduced to minuscule attacks. It was also clear to Weichs, Paulus, and their commanders that their opponents were about to mount yet another major assault on Army Group B's long flank north of Stalingrad (see chapters 12 and 13). All the Germans could do was hope their defenses would thwart the attackers yet again. Unfortunately for the Axis, however, Soviet commanders were preparing a far broader envelopment to destroy German forces by penetrating the armies of their satellite allies.

ASSESSMENT

In early November 1942 German Army Group A ground to a halt some 70 kilometers short of the refineries of Groznyi and even farther away from the main oil fields of the Caucasus. Persistent if clumsy Soviet counterattacks, in conjunction with challenging terrain and weather, had finally stopped the invaders and had come within a hair's breadth of destroying Mackensen's III Panzer Corps. At the same time, Paulus's Sixth Army came up short, only a few hundred meters from the ice-strewn Volga River. Considering the enormous challenges of logistical shortages, Red Army defenses, and hostile terrain, the *Wehrmacht* had turned in an astonishing performance by coming so close to its absurdly ambitious objectives.

In mid-September Hitler had decided to take Stalingrad by storm, a set-piece battle that deprived Sixth Army of most of its momentum and, eventually, its strength. Between 14 September and 16 November, Paulus's forces fighting in the city received 23 infantry battalions (100th *Jäger* and 305th and 79th Infantry Divisions) and at least 8 engineer battalions. This should have increased the German forces available for street fighting from 59 to 82 battalions, not counting the engineers. However, constant attrition prompted the consolidation of battalions, so the actual total stood at only 64 battalions, of which 37 were rated "weak" or "exhausted" (see tables 9.1 and 10.1).[66] The final struggles in the factory district from late October to mid-November were particularly desperate, degenerating into savage fights between platoon-sized groups struggling for control of individual bunkers, buildings, and even rooms.

The successful Soviet defense here relied on more than just the legendary courage and endurance of its soldiers. General Chuikov and his subordinate commanders used small reconnaissance patrols to assemble a clear picture of their opponents. Each German advance encountered snipers, booby traps, and ambushes. Strongpoints were organized for all-round defense with anti-tank obstacles and cleared fields of fire. Soviet assault groups of 20 to 50 soldiers, equipped with machine guns, grenades, and satchel charges, operated in between these fixed positions, crawling down sewers and breaking through walls to avoid exposing themselves in the streets. This combination of intelligence, discipline, and determination enabled 62nd Army to continue fighting when, by all conventional measures, the Germans had won.

The fighting in Stalingrad was only one element in the strategy pursued by Stalin and his *Stavka* since late July 1942. Since 23 August, Soviet forces had launched no fewer than six offensives, beginning in the Kotluban' region north of the city and eventually including Beketovka to the south. The Germans had repelled all six, although collectively, these efforts had contributed to the defense of Stalingrad by pinning down and attriting German forces that might otherwise have overwhelmed 62nd Army. Overall, Soviet efforts inside and out the city had deprived Paulus of his planned northern pincer—XIV Panzer Corps. These efforts had also forced Hitler and his Army Group B commander, Weichs, to accept increasing risks by replacing veteran German troops with inexperienced and poorly equipped Italians and Romanians.

Soviet actions far distant from Stalingrad and the Kotluban' also contributed to the final stalemate. The repeated counterattacks at Voronezh and Demiansk had little or no impact on wider events. However, the German attempt to seize both Stalingrad and the Caucasus oil fields at the same time almost guaranteed that they would come up short in both efforts. The failure of Army Group A in the Caucasus rendered the final bloody struggle in the Stalingrad factories virtually irrelevant. Zhukov's Rzhev-Sychevska offensive (30 July–23 August) not only contributed to German overextension but also established a pattern for future Soviet offensive operations, becoming a dress rehearsal for even grander efforts in November.

The defeat of Operation *Blau* came at a terrible cost. Leaving aside the battles in the Caucasus, the Soviets suffered some 1.2 million casualties on the Voronezh and Stalingrad axis from 28 June through 17 November 1942, compared with roughly 200,000 Axis casualties.[67] During the same time and in the same areas, the Soviets lost in excess of 4,862 tanks, as opposed to German losses of fewer than 700. Although accurate figures for the Caucasus fighting are unavailable, the same loss ratios (5:1 in the Germans' favor for both personnel and tanks) probably obtained. Unfortunately for the invaders, Soviet mass production and reserves of trained personnel made the Red Army far better able to replace such losses than were their opponents.

Might-have-beens are always dangerous in history. Had Germany concentrated all its forces and resources against *either* Stalingrad *or* the oil fields, it is at least conceivable that the Axis would have achieved one of these objectives in 1942. Hitler must bear a large measure of responsibility for this dispersal of effort; he gambled on achieving both goals because of his well-justified sense that he was running out of time to achieve strategic victory. On 19 November 1942 that window of opportunity closed irrevocably when the Red Army finally mounted a well-coordinated offensive.

PART THREE

The Encirclement of Sixth Army

CHAPTER TWELVE

_____ The Genesis of Operation Uranus

While Friedrich Paulus and Vasilii Chuikov sacrificed their two field armies to take and hold individual buildings in the ruined city of Stalingrad, the larger war went on around them. Adolf Hitler, as noted earlier, had to contend not only with stalemate in the Caucasus but also with defeat in North Africa. His adversary Joseph Stalin was almost equally frustrated, particularly by what he regarded as insufficient support from Britain and the United States. Although Lend-Lease weapons began to reach the Soviets in quantity during late 1941, Stalin consistently demanded a true "second front," by which he meant a major British-American invasion of northwest Europe.[1]

At the same time, the *Stavka* was planning its own major offensive, designed to regain the initiative by encircling Sixth Army and ultimately destroying Army Groups A and B. Stalin believed that he could replicate the successful counteroffensive executed outside of Moscow in December 1941.

The true story of how this plan evolved into the Soviet victory at Stalingrad is obscured by vanity on both sides. German participants, seeking to avoid responsibility for the disaster, ascribe the entire failure to Hitler. Accounts by Soviet commanders and staff officers, by contrast, have been warped by political shifts within the USSR, beginning with Nikita Khrushchev's de-Stalinization and continuing even in the present-day Russian Federation. At various times, memoirs and accounts have either exaggerated or belittled the roles of Stalin, Zhukov, Vasilevsky, Eremenko, and the other major players. What follows is an attempt to reconstruct the strategic planning for the November offensive and then to explain how and why the Germans failed to parry that offensive.

WHO FORMULATED PLAN URANUS?

The predominant interpretation of this process follows the assertions of Georgii Zhukov. Zhukov's memoirs claim that, following his strategic guidance, the *Stavka* began planning the Stalingrad counteroffensive in a series of meetings on 12–13 September 1942.[2] According to this account, the counteroffensive was to be unique, in that it would attempt a much broader or wider envelopment of Axis forces around Stalingrad than any previous Soviet attempt. Having repeatedly failed to penetrate the German flanks immediately outside the city, they would now target the weaker satellite troops farther to the northwest and south of German Sixth Army.

Vasilevsky's memoirs tell a similar story, but this account sharply contradicts the description of planning provided by General Eremenko, commander of the Stalingrad Front. Published in 1961 during Khrushchev's de-Stalinization program, Eremenko's memoirs claim that his headquarters (where Khrushchev served as commissar) gradually developed the concept of a broad encirclement of Sixth Army during August and September, a concept that he formalized in proposals to the *Stavka* on 6 and 9 October 1942.[3]

Newly released Soviet archival materials confirm Eremenko's claim to authorship, although there were significant differences between his initial proposal and the final plan for Operation Uranus. Stalin's official appointments diary reflects no meetings with Zhukov between 31 August and 26 September, nor with Vasilevsky between 9 and 21 September.[4] This does not exclude the possibility that Stalin's two trusted subordinates provided advice by telephone or teletype, but it does suggest that the true authorship of the plan lies elsewhere. The meetings to which Zhukov refers apparently occurred between 27 September and early October, when the *Stavka* formulated its concept for multiple strategic counteroffensives to take place that fall. Furthermore, the September counteroffensives launched by the Soviets on both of the near flanks of Stalingrad suggest that Soviet leaders had not yet abandoned their previous tactics or developed the concept of a wider encirclement.

Also arguing against Zhukov's claim of authorship is the fact that the *Stavka* had, in fact, planned a crude form of a general offensive in late July. Vasilevsky had become chief of the General Staff the previous month and had established a small cell of staff officers to develop alternative solutions for conducting a strategic counteroffensive. Under the leadership of Major General Fedor Efimovich Bokov, a commissar turned General Staff officer, this group drafted a number of concepts. Again, the crisis atmosphere created by the German advances in *Blau* I and II meant that, in practice, this offensive shrank into two poorly coordinated counterstrokes launched by the Stalingrad Front in the Great Bend of the Don and by the Briansk Front near Voronezh (see chapter 5). The effort enjoyed only brief success, but it did demonstrate the feasibility of what was later known as the "different solution," a broad-front counteroffensive.[5]

What follows is a description of the planning for the November counteroffensive, based on Stalin's personal calendar and on key *Stavka* and *front* planning directives.[6]

COMPETING OFFENSIVE CONCEPTS

From the first days of the German invasion in 1941, Soviet leaders consistently followed their doctrinal preference for offensive action, even when operating on the strategic defensive. During the summer and fall of 1942, Stalin and the *Stavka* launched at least eight counterstrokes against the lengthening left flank of Army Group B. Most of these operations were so hasty that the attackers achieved nothing but additional heavy losses at the hands of the Germans. These disastrous efforts have figured prominently in this narrative, especially in chapters 4, 5, and 6.

The very failure of these counterstrokes only reinforced the Germans' innate belief in their own superiority. Having held off the Soviet counterattacks, often with relative ease, the invaders had every confidence that they could repel similar efforts in the future. Some German commanders did, however, recognize the risk of a Soviet penetration through their Axis allies, as discussed below.

By late September, it was clear to many *Stavka* officers and to many field commanders that continued attacks on the immediate flanks of Sixth Army were futile. Eremenko was only the first to articulate this realization and to abandon the old solution in favor of a broader envelopment aimed at destroying all Axis forces in the Stalingrad region—a counteroffensive code-named Uranus.

In addition to changing the scope of the offensive, two factors contributed to the ultimate success of this plan. First, the attritional battle at Stalingrad led to a steady decline in the combat power of Army Group B in general and Sixth Army in particular. Weichs's forces became woefully overextended, his troops were bled white, and his flanks were increasingly entrusted to poorly equipped satellite forces. Second, Uranus involved a much longer planning time than any previous Soviet operation of the war, taking weeks and months rather than hours and days. On the one hand, this allowed staffs and logisticians to make effective preparations for an attack. There were still problems involving preparation and logistics, but by comparison to previous attempts, Operation Uranus was the first deliberate Soviet offensive of the entire war. On the other hand, the ebb and flow of battle that fall meant that the planning for Uranus occurred in fits and starts, and there was often uncertainty as to the actual terrain and situation where the offensive would begin. Despite the dire straits in which 62nd Army found itself, Stalin and his generals had to maintain an iron nerve, waiting until the Germans were completely exhausted and the Soviets were entirely ready for the counteroffensive.

Between 3 and 12 September, and again between 18 September and 2 October, Zhukov worked personally with the Stalingrad Front in planning

various counterattacks, especially around Kotluban'. These were all in the
mold of the old solution for a shallow envelopment. Even after he returned
to Moscow, Zhukov continued to demonstrate his commitment to this idea.
Thus, in late September he prompted the *Stavka* to reorganize command and
control into smaller, more manageable Stalingrad and Don Fronts, placing
his protégé Rokossovsky in command of the latter.[7] He also relieved various
commanders while insisting that the two *fronts* maintain constant offensive
pressure against Army Group B.

Between 27 and 29 September Stalin met with Zhukov, Vasilevsky, Bokov,
and other key planners, issuing a series of *Stavka* directives for major counteroffensives extending from the Western and Kalinin Fronts down to the
Trans-Caucasus Front. These meetings resembled those that Zhukov recalled as occurring two weeks earlier. On 29 September the deputy supreme
commander returned to Stalingrad, where he apparently discussed this strategic conception with field commanders.

On 5 October Eremenko and Khrushchev, commander and commissar
of the Stalingrad Front, sent a new proposal to Moscow without first coordinating it with the *Stavka* representative on the spot, Vasilevsky. Their lengthy
report questioned the wisdom of yet another shallow attack, advocating a
much wider encirclement and emphasizing the weakness of satellite forces
and German reserves in the proposed breakthrough sectors.[8]

Apparently unaware of this proposal, on the evening of 7 October Vasilevsky sent nearly identical orders to the Don and Stalingrad Fronts, directing
that they plan for a counteroffensive on the immediate flanks of Stalingrad.[9]
Both *fronts* submitted draft plans in accordance with this concept, but both
expressed reservations about the futility of such attacks. Dated 1117 hours
on 9 October, the Stalingrad Front's response read in part:

> I have thought this question over for a month and consider that the most
> favorable axis of attack from the Don Front is the axis from the Klets-
> kaia-Sirotinskaia front toward Kalach. . . .With the arrival in this region,
> we will deprive the enemy most importantly of maneuvering his mobile
> tank and mechanized forces which are operating in the Stalingrad region
> and will isolate them from the main attack. . . . The delivery of the attack
> from the Kotluban' region east of the Don River will not lead to any suc-
> cess since the enemy has the capability here of throwing in forces from
> the Stalingrad region.[10]

Eremenko cast his idea in the form of a massive raid, foreseeing large actions by cavalry and sappers to capture the Don River line from Vertiachii to
Kalach, destroy German bases and airfields at Tatsinskaia and Morozovskaia,
and demolish installations at Kotel'nikovo Station. This choice of objectives

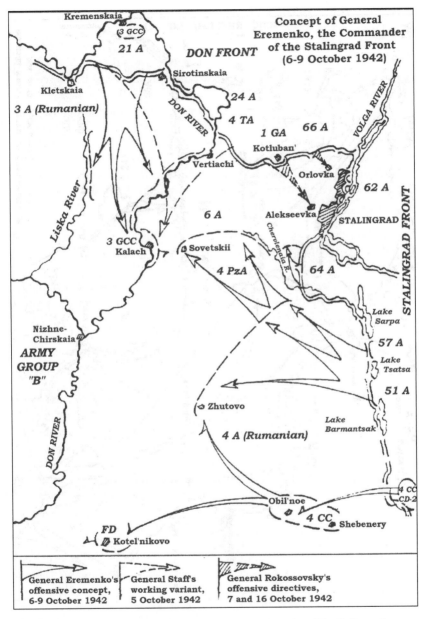

Map 62. Offensive Concept of General Eremenko, Commander of the Stalingrad Front, 6–9 October 1942

demonstrates how closely Eremenko's proposal predicted the actual Operation Uranus.

Rokossovsky's report, dated 2240 hours on 9 October, reinforced Eremenko's arguments. While dutifully producing the required plan, Rokossovsky emphasized the strong German defenses in the area chosen by Moscow, as well as the dilapidated state of his own infantry forces.[11]

In the wake of these proposals, Zhukov, Vasilevsky, and the General Staff began formulating a plan for a vastly expanded counteroffensive, which Stalin approved in concept on 13 October. Parallel to the Uranus plan for the Stalingrad region, the same group developed the so-called Mars plan for the Kalinin and Western Fronts, which called for them to attack again in the Rzhev-Sychevka area, where they had achieved only limited success in late August and September.

URANUS TAKES SHAPE, 14 OCTOBER–18 NOVEMBER

A series of *Stavka* directives elaborated upon these two plans, assembling various forces and creating new headquarters. At the same time, to protect Chuikov's hard-pressed 62nd Army and to deceive the Germans about Uranus, other orders issued on 15–16 October required the Don and Stalingrad Fronts to continue their offensive pressure on the German positions from Kotluban' and Erzovka north of Stalingrad to the lake region south of the city.

The most significant organizational development was the creation of a new Southwestern Front, located between the Voronezh and Don Fronts, to provide the wide northern pincer of the projected offensive. The *Stavka* ordered the formation of this front on 22 October but, to preserve secrecy, deferred its activation until the end of the month. The former 1st Guards Army headquarters provided the nucleus of a *front* staff, headquartered in Novo-Annenskaia, 120 kilometers north of Serafimovich. The precocious Lieutenant General N. F. Vatutin became *front* commander, with Major General G. D. Stel'makh, previously assigned to the Volkhov Front, as his chief of staff.[12] The next day the *Stavka* transferred control of 21st and 63rd Armies, as well as the battle-hardened 8th Cavalry Corps and various supporting units, to the new *front*. These transfers included elaborate secrecy measures, such as moving under cover of darkness and leaving the cavalry corps' radio transmitters in their previous locations as a deception.[13]

In a series of orders on 22–23 October, the *Stavka* also directed the NKO to form two new armies, each consisting of multiple corps based on the prewar model. Using 4th Reserve Army as its base, a new 1st Guards Army at Rtischchevo would include 4th and 6th Guards Rifle Corps, each with one rifle and two guards rifle divisions, plus the newly activated 1st Guards Mechanized Corps. Similarly, the former 1st Reserve Army at Tambov morphed into 2nd Guards Army, controlling 1st and 13th Guards Rifle Corps, each with one rifle and two guards rifle divisions, plus 2nd Guards Mechanized Corps.[14] Also on 23 October, the Red Army General Staff ordered a reorganization of logistical support for the Southwestern, Don, and Stalingrad Fronts. This involved the number of trains per day and the amounts of ammunition, fuel, and foodstuffs the GKO would provide to support the three *fronts*.[15]

After Stalin met with Bokov and Shtemenko in the early-morning hours of 25 October, a new directive authorized the transfer of various elements from Rokossovsky's Don Front to Vatutin's Southwestern Front. This included 3rd Guards Cavalry and 4th Tank Corps, four rifle divisions, eleven artillery or tank destroyer regiments, five antiaircraft regiments, and two separate antiaircraft battalions, all with ammunition supplies and transportation. In addition to the usual deception and camouflage measures, this order instructed the NKVD to "cleanse" the relevant areas and routes of "all suspicious persons."[16] In the ensuing days, Stalin personally directed not only additional rigid security measures but also the dispatch of three guards tank penetration regiments, equipped with KV heavy tanks, and two battalions of flamethrower tanks to Vatutin's 21st Army.[17]

Between 1 and 18 November field commanders and staffs made numerous adjustments and refinements to the Uranus plan under the supervision of Zhukov and Vasilevsky. An imposing entourage of experts accompanied them, including Colonel Generals N. N. Voronov and N. D. Iakovlev for artillery, A. A. Novikov and A. E. Golovanov for the air forces and long-range aviation, and Ia. N. Fedorenko for armor and mechanized forces. The two representatives of the *Stavka* also called on Major General P. P. Vechnyi, chief of the General Staff's Department for the Exploitation of War Experiences, to employ previous wartime experiences as the basis for improving Red Army performance.

Zhukov and Vasilevsky consulted extensively with *front*, field army, and mechanized corps headquarters; any issues they could not resolve went to the *Stavka*, which generated a series of directives on command, control, and coordination of operations, as well as reinforcements for the mobile forces. On 1 November, for example, a directive added three more rifle divisions to 1st Guards Army and named Lieutenant General D. D. Leliushenko as its commander, while Lieutenant General V. I. Kuznetsov became deputy commander of the Southwestern Front.[18] A second directive that same day assigned three mechanized brigades and their accompanying tank regiments to provide the nucleus for 13th Tank Corps within the Stalingrad Front, while a third order appointed a chief of staff and a deputy commander for Romanenko's 5th Tank Army.[19] During the period leading up to the actual offensive, both the *Stavka* representatives and the *Stavka* itself sharply criticized individual units that made errors in operational security, intelligence gathering, or tactics. For example, on 13 November the deputy chief of the General Staff, Major General V. D. Ivanov, singled out the Stalingrad Front for criticism, demanding corrective training after three different brigades subordinate to that *front*'s 28th Army had been defeated while functioning as forward detachments.[20]

Zhukov's work with the Southwestern Front culminated late on 4 November, when the *front*'s command and staff worked out a graphical plan for Uranus. On the sixth Zhukov returned to Moscow briefly for a coordination meeting with various commanders that apparently put the finishing touches on the overall concepts for both Uranus and Mars.[21]

With Stalin's approval, on 8 November Zhukov telegraphed Eremenko and Rokossovsky and instructed them to postpone the "resettlement" (*pereselenie*), the code word for Operation Uranus, until 13 November. Other delays followed driven by various problems, including belated troop movements, inadequate ammunition, and insufficient ground-attack aircraft.[22] It is an indication of Stalin's trust in his subordinates that on 15 November he cabled Zhukov and authorized his deputy to set the exact date for the "resettlement" at his own discretion.[23] At least temporarily, the Soviet dictator had learned that patience was required to ensure that the great offensive would be well prepared.

Ultimately, Zhukov and Vasilevsky decided that the Southwestern Front and 65th Army of the Don Front would begin their assaults on 19 November 1942, with the Stalingrad Front joining in the next day.[24] During the final three days prior to the offensive, the *Stavka* issued another series of orders, directing the forward movement of tank and rifle units to act as ready replacements for similar formations damaged in the assault.[25] On the afternoon of 18 November Vasilevsky applied the final touch, shifting the boundary between the Southwestern and Don Fronts to leave the railheads at Atkarsk, Krasnyi Iar, and Kamyshin in the latter's rear area. This mundane change rationalized the supply lines to support the Don Front's thrust.[26]

In typical Soviet fashion, army and *front* commanders did most of their own planning personally, with subordinates learning the actual date and plan for the attack only days or hours beforehand.[27] The dense cloak of secrecy and deception helps explain why German intelligence analysts were reluctant to predict when and where the counteroffensives might occur. The same secrecy, however, prompted some midlevel Red Army commanders, ignorant of the overall plan, to question the feasibility of their part in the coming offensive. One mechanized corps commander reportedly bypassed his chain of command and wrote directly to Stalin, predicting a catastrophic defeat. After showing the letter to Vasilevsky, the dictator telephoned the corps commander to reassure rather than chastise him.[28] This incident again reflects Stalin's confidence in his subordinates, but it also suggests that Soviet leaders were by no means certain of victory in Uranus.

The three *fronts* involved were to conduct the counteroffensive across a front that was 400 kilometers wide. After classic penetrations of Axis satellite defenses on both sides of Stalingrad, the exploitation would employ two major pincers. The Southwestern Front's northern pincer was to advance southward to depths of 120 to 140 kilometers, where it would meet the Stalingrad Front's northeastward thrust. The mechanized and cavalry forces of these two *fronts* would take three days to achieve this encirclement. After that, tank, mechanized, and eventually infantry forces would form the inner encirclement around the Germans, while cavalry and other rifle forces would both form the outer encirclement and expand the offensive to the west and southwest, driving the remnants of Romanian and German forces away from Stalingrad to prevent any relief effort.

SOVIET ORDER OF BATTLE

Southwestern Front

The strongest of the three attacking organizations was the Southwestern Front. In addition to the commander, Vatutin, and the chief of staff, Stel'makh, its Military Council included Corps Commissar A. S. Zheltov. Vatutin's 5th Tank and 21st Armies would make the main attack, with 1st Guards Army protecting their right (western) flank while preparing to exploit the offensive southwestward toward Rostov. This force was initially supported by 17th Air Army; later in the offensive, 2nd Air Army of the Voronezh Front also joined Vatutin's attack. The initial attacks would come out of the existing Serafimovich and Kletskaia bridgeheads on the southern bank of the Don River, 110 to 180 kilometers northwest of Stalingrad. Once these assaults had ruptured the defenses of Romanian Third Army, their component tank and cavalry corps would exploit to the southeast, aiming to link up with their Stalingrad Front counterparts along the Don River, just north of its junction with the Chir River (see map 63).

Roughly half of Vatutin's men, mostly veterans of previous battles, came from the *Stavka* Reserve. As a result, the average strength of a division in this *front* was a robust 8,800 men.

Pride of place went to the refurbished 5th Tank Army under Lieutenant General Prokofii Logvinovich Romanenko, who had already learned hard lessons of mechanized warfare as commander of 3rd Tank Army during the Western Front's Kozel'sk operation in August. The headquarters staff of 5th Tank Army had turned over considerably since its failure in the futile

Map 63. Operation Uranus: The Southwestern Front's Offensive Plan

Voronezh counteroffensives of July, but Romanenko had the veterans A. I. Danilov and L. G. Tumanian as his chief of staff and Military Council member (commissar). After refitting in the rear of the Briansk Front, this army secretly displaced southward to the area just north of Serafimovich. In the process, 5th Tank Army grew to include 6 rifle divisions; 1st and 26th Tank Corps; 8th Cavalry Corps; a separate tank brigade; 2 separate tank battalions;

27 artillery, mortar, or *katiusha* (rocket) regiments; and a host of supporting units.[29]

General Katukov, one of the rising stars among tank commanders, had led 1st Tank Corps during the July–August fighting at Voronezh, where the corps had performed better than most of its counterparts. Since September 1942 its commander had been Major General V. V. Butkov, a veteran of the 1941 Smolensk battle; he had subsequently served on the Main Armored Directorate of the General Staff. By comparison, Major General A. G. Rodin's 26th Tank Corps had missed most of the fighting since its formation in late July. These two tank corps had their full complement of 171 tanks each in mid-November, although a German air strike on 18 November weakened 1st Tank Corps.

Immediately east of 5th Tank Army, on the left flank of Vatutin's *front*, stood Lieutenant General Ivan Mikhailovich Chistiakov's 21st Army. Chistiakov's Military Council included Brigade Commissar P. I. Krainov and chief of staff Major General V. A. Pen'kovsky. This army controlled six rifle divisions, one tank corps, a guards cavalry corps, a tank destroyer brigade, three separate tank regiments, four antitank rifle battalions, six tank destroyer regiments, and a full artillery division. In addition to this last division, which included eight regiments, there were nine fire support regiments, an antiaircraft division of four regiments, and various other elements.[30]

The mobile group of this *front* included Major General A. G. Kravchenko's 4th Tank Corps and Major General I. A. Pliev's 3rd Guards Cavalry Corps. Kravchenko and Pliev were two of the most distinguished mobile commanders in the Red Army; Kravchenko, for example, had led 2nd Tank Corps well in the battles outside of Stalingrad in September. His new command, 4th Tank Corps, had suffered grievously in the futile Kotluban' attacks of late August, but it had been restored to almost full strength (143 operable tanks) by mid-November. The 3rd Guards Cavalry Corps had fought throughout the German war and consisted of 22,000 troopers in November 1942.

The final maneuver element of the Southwestern Front was Leliushenko's 1st Guards Army. The *Stavka* had changed directions several times concerning the subordinate corps of this powerful force, so some of these subordinates had not yet arrived when the offensive began. Ultimately, however, Stalin earmarked 4th Guards, 6th Guards, 14th Rifle, and 1st Guards Mechanized Corps for Leliushenko's army.

Vatutin's Southwestern Front began the offensive with no combat formations in reserve. It initially included 18 rifle divisions, 3 tank corps, 1 mechanized corps, 2 cavalry corps (each of 3 divisions), a separate tank brigade, 3 separate tank regiments and 2 separate tank battalions, a separate motorized rifle brigade, a tank destroyer brigade, a motorcycle regiment, and 4 antitank rifle battalions. This force was supported by an artillery division, 47 artillery

Table 12.1. Organization of the Southwestern, Don, and Stalingrad Fronts, 19 November 1942

Southwestern Front—Lieutenant General N. F. Vatutin
  1st Guards Army—Lieutenant General D. D. Leliushenko
    Six rifle divisions (4th Guards, 6th Guards, and 14th Rifle Corps headquarters and four guards rifle divisions en route)
    1st Guards Mechanized Corps—Major General I. N. Russianov
    22nd Separate Motorized Brigade
  5th Tank Army—Lieutenant General P. A. Romanenko
    Three guards rifle and three rifle divisions
    1st Tank Corps—Major General of Tank Forces V. V. Butkov
    26th Tank Corps—Major General of Tank Forces A. G. Rodin
    8th Cavalry Corps—Major General M. D. Borisov (three divisions)
    8th Guards Tank Brigade, 8th Motorcycle Regiment, two separate tank battalions
  21st Army—Lieutenant General I. M. Chistiakov
    Six rifle divisions
    4th Tank Corps—Major General of Tank Forces A. G. Kravchenko
    3rd Guards Cavalry Corps—Major General I. A. Pliev
    5th [Tank] Destroyer Brigade
    Three guards tank regiments, four antitank rifle battalions
  17th Air Army—Lieutenant General of Aviation S. A. Krasovsky
    1st Mixed Aviation Corps (one assault, one fighter aviation division)
    One bomber, one night bomber, one fighter, two assault aviation divisions
    One long-range reconnaissance squadron, one separate bomber squadron
  2nd Air Army (from Voronezh Front)—Major General of Aviation K. N. Smirnov
    Two fighter, one night bomber, one assault aviation divisions
    One reconnaissance regiment, one long-range reconnaissance squadron
Don Front—Colonel General K. K. Rokossovsky
  24th Army—Lieutenant General I. V. Galanin
    Nine rifle divisions, one fortified region
    16th Tank Corps—Major General of Tank Forces A. G. Maslov (assigned to the *front* after 19 November)
    10th Tank Brigade
    Three armored car battalions, two antitank rifle battalions
  65th Army—Lieutenant General P. I. Batov
    Three guards rifle and six rifle divisions
    91st and 121st Tank Brigades
    One armored train battalion, two antitank rifle battalions
  66th Army—Lieutenant General A. S. Zhadov
    Six rifle divisions
    58th Tank Brigade
    One antitank rifle battalion
  16th Air Army—Major General of Aviation S. I. Rudenko
    Two fighter, two assault, and one night bomber aviation divisions
    One guards bomber regiment, one reconnaissance squadron
  Front forces
    One fortified region
    64th and 148th Tank Brigades
    Eight antitank rifle battalions
    Three armored train battalions
Stalingrad Front—Colonel General A. I. Eremenko
  62nd Army—Lieutenant General V. I. Chuikov (all units severely understrength)
    Three guards rifle and seven rifle divisions
    Six rifle brigades

84th Tank Brigade, one separate tank battalion
64th Army—Lieutenant General M. S. Shumilov
    7th Rifle Corps—Major General S. G. Goriachev (three rifle brigades)
    One guards rifle and four rifle divisions, one fortified region
    Two naval rifle brigades
    20th [Tank] Destroyer Brigade
    Composite student regiment from Vinnitsa Infantry School
    13th and 56th Tank Brigades
    One armored train battalion
51st Army—Major General N. I. Trufanov
    One guards rifle and three rifle divisions, one fortified region
    4th Mechanized Corps—Major General of Tank Forces V. T. Vol'sky
    4th Cavalry Corps—Lieutenant General T. T. Shapkin (two divisions)
    38th Separate Motorized Infantry Brigade, 254th Tank Brigade
57th Army—Lieutenant General F. I. Tolbukhin
    Two rifle divisions, one rifle brigade
    13th Tank Corps—Major General of Tank Forces T. I. Tanaschishin
    90th and 235th Tank Brigades
    Three machine gun–artillery battalions
    One motorcycle battalion
28th Army—Lieutenant General V. F. Gerasimenko
    One guards rifle and one rifle divisions, three rifle brigades, two fortified
       regions
    6th Guards Tank Brigade
    One tank, one armored car, three armored train battalions
8th Air Army—Major General of Aviation T. T. Khriukin
    2nd Mixed Aviation Corps (one assault, two fighter aviation divisions)
    One assault, two mixed, one bomber, one night bomber, two fighter aviation
       divisions
    One reconnaissance, five mixed, one transport regiments
    Two aviation squadrons (for adjusting artillery fire), one antiaircraft artillery
       regiment
Stalingrad PVO (antiaircraft defense) Corps Region—Colonel E. A. Rainin
    One guards antiaircraft and six antiaircraft regiments
    Four separate antiaircraft battalions
    Eight armored train (antiaircraft) battalions
    One PVO fighter aviation division
Volga Military Flotilla—Vice Admiral D. D. Rogachev
    1st and 2nd Brigades of River Ships, separate armored trawlers
Front forces
    One rifle division, three fortified regions
    85th Tank Brigade, two separate tank regiments

Sources: A. M. Samsonov, *Stalingradskaia bitva* [The Battle of Stalingrad] (Moscow: Nauka, 1983), 569; V. A. Zolotarev, ed., *Velikaia Otechestvennaia: Deistvuiushchaia armiia 1941–1945gg* [The Great Patriotic (War): The operating army, 1941–1945] (Moscow: Animi Fortitudo Kuchkovo pole, 2005); M. G. Vozhakin, ed., *Velikaia Otechestvennaia Komandarmy: Voennyi biograficheskii slovar'* [The Great Patriotic (War) army commanders: A military-biographical dictionary] (Moscow-Zhukovskii: Kuchkovo pole, 2005); M. G. Vozhakin, ed., *Velikaia Otechestvennaia Komkory: Voennyi biograficheskii slovar' v. 2-h tomakh* [The Great Patriotic (War) corps commanders: A military-biographical dictionary, vol. 2] (Moscow-Zhukovskii: Kuchkovo pole, 2006); *Komandovanie korpusnogo i divizionnogo zvena Sovetskikh vooruzhennykh sil perioda Velikoi Otechestvennoi voiny 1941–1945 gg.* [The command cadre at the corps and division level of the Soviet armed forces during the Great Patriotic War, 1941–1945] (Moscow: Frunze Academy, 1964).

Table 12.2. Red Army Strengths at the Start of Uranus, 19–20 November 1942

Organization	Ration Strength (Number in Combat Units)	Guns and Mortars	Tanks (Heavy/ Medium/ Light/Other)	Aircraft (Operational)
Southwestern Front	389,902 men (331,984)	8,655	721 (145/314/262/0)	359 (311)
1st Guards Army	155,096 (142,869)	3,308	163 (0/113/50/0)	
5th Tank Army	104,196 (90,600)	2,538	359 (60/144/155/0)	
21st Army	103,270 (92,056)	2,520	199 (85/57/57/0)	
Don Front	284,373 men (192,193)	6,625	254 (72/90/88/4)	388 (329)
24th Army	68,489 (56,409)	1,899	48 (21/14/9/4)	
65th Army	74,709 (63,187)	1,922	49 (10/22/17/0)	
66th Army	51,738 (39,457)	1,568	5 (0/2/3/0)	
Stalingrad Front	367,943 men (258,317)	6,739	575 (22/308/245)	782 (637)
62nd Army	54,199 (41,667)	1,237	23 (7/15/1/0)	
64th Army	53,742 (40,490)	1,093	40 (1/27/12/0)	
51st Army	55,184 (44,720)	1,077	207 (0/118/89/0)	
57th Army	66,778 (56,026)	1,604	225 (4/122/99/0)	
28th Army	64,265 (47,891)	1,196	80 (10/26/44/0)	

Source: V. A. Zolotarev, ed., Velikaia Otechestvennaia: Deistvuiushchaia armiia 1941–1945gg [The Great Patriotic (War): The operating army, 1941–1945] (Moscow: Animi Fortitudo Kuchkovo pole, 2005).

or mortar regiments, 2 antiaircraft divisions, 12 separate antiaircraft regiments, 2 engineer brigades, and 12 engineer or bridging battalions.

Don and Stalingrad Fronts

Having battered its head repeatedly against the German defenses northwest of Stalingrad, the Don Front was by far the weakest of the three *fronts* involved in Uranus. Moreover, it had a low priority for reinforcements and a purely secondary role in the offensive plan—tying down the left wing of Sixth Army while the other two *fronts* encircled the Germans. The Don Front's Military Council consisted of Rokossovsky as commander,

Brigade Commissar A. I. Kirichenko, and chief of staff Major General M. S. Malinin.

In preparation for this secondary mission, Rokossovsky disbanded 7 of his 31 decimated divisions at the end of October, distributing the soldiers and weapons among the remaining 24 divisions.

Only the *front*'s right wing, Lieutenant General P. I. Batov's 65th Army, had an offensive mission—supporting the neighboring 21st Army of the Southwestern Front in its breakout from the Kletskaia bridgehead.[31] Batov's army had been created on 22 October from the remnants of 4th Tank Army. By the time Uranus began, this army had expanded to nine rifle divisions (three of them guards units), two tank brigades, and seven artillery, mortar, or antiaircraft regiments. Of the other two armies in the Don Front, Major General I. I. Galinin's 24th Army was significantly stronger than Major General A. S. Zhadov's 66th Army. The fourth incarnation of a "24th Army" since the war began, Galinin's force included the veteran 16th Tank Corps; if the overall offensive proved successful, this tank corps would launch a secondary attack out of the Kotluban' area to encircle the German forces defending the Don River. The 16th Tank Corps had suffered heavily in previous fighting on this front, but by mid-November, it controlled 140 tanks. Overall, Galinin commanded 9 rifle divisions, 1 fortified region, 1 tank brigade, 12 artillery and rocket regiments, 2 antiaircraft regiments, and 5 engineer battalions.

Including the weak 66th Army, the Don Front therefore totaled 24 rifle divisions, 2 fortified regions, 1 tank corps, 6 separate tank brigades, 31 artillery or rocket regiments, 9 antiaircraft regiments, and a host of supporting units, including 2 engineer brigades and 17 engineer, sapper, or bridging battalions.

In the upcoming Uranus offensive, the Stalingrad Front's mission was just as important as that of the Southwestern Front because each formed one of the pincers of the planned broad envelopment. In addition to *front* commander Eremenko, the Military Council included Brigade Commissar N. S. Khrushchev and chief of staff Major General I. S. Varennikov. Although this organization was responsible for 450 kilometers of front stretching from Rynok north of Stalingrad to the Caspian Sea, the focus of its operation would be attacks from the Beketovka bridgehead and the lakes region, 5 to 70 kilometers south of Stalingrad.

The 64th, 57th, and 51st Armies formed the shock group that would conduct the penetration in these areas, after which 13th Tank and 4th Mechanized Corps would thrust first south and then west to form the southern pincer. The 4th Cavalry Corps would advance southward, screening the left or outer flank of this thrust. Chuikov's 62nd Army inside Stalingrad and the small 28th Army on the approaches of Astrakhan' also received attack orders, but pride of place went to the shock group described above. In addition to the stalwart Volga Military Flotilla, 8th Air Army and the Stalingrad PVO (Anti-Air Defense) Corps supported these efforts.

All five of Eremenko's field armies were relatively small, ranging from 54,000 to 67,000 men in ration strength and with just over a thousand guns and mortars each.[32] Yet their opponents were equally weak—nine emaciated German divisions inside the city of Stalingrad; two German and one Romanian divisions in the southern suburbs; and four Romanian divisions, part of a cavalry division, and a motorized detachment stretching out across the vulnerable southern flank.

Unlike the Southwestern Front, which received much of its combat power from the *Stavka* Reserve, the Stalingrad Front's forces had been worn down by more than two months of combat. Including the decimated formations in 62nd Army, the average divisional strength was 4,000 to 5,000 soldiers. To achieve the breakthrough and exploitation, the *Stavka* had provided three mobile corps (13th Tank, 4th Mechanized, and 4th Cavalry), as well as two additional rifle divisions; six rifle, one motorized rifle, and three tank brigades; plus two tank destroyer and six antiaircraft artillery regiments. Even the tank corps and infantry divisions had suffered in previous fighting.

The strongest field armies in Eremenko's motley collection were Lieutenant General F. I. Tolbukhin's 57th and Major General N. I. Trufanov's 51st, which together formed the main shock group. Each of these armies had more than 200 tanks. The 57th Army's Military Council included Tolbukhin as well as Brigade Commissar N. E. Subbotin and chief of staff Colonel N. Ia. Prikhid'ko. The 57th, which had fought in the lakes region since early August, included two rifle divisions, one rifle brigade, two tank brigades, and 13th Tank Corps. Despite its designation, Colonel T. I. Tanaschishin's tank corps actually resembled a large mechanized corps, consisting of three mechanized brigades, each with a separate tank regiment, for a total of 205 medium and light tanks.[33]

The 51st Army had fought a series of bitter defensive actions going back to the defense of the Crimea in October 1941. Trufanov, an experienced officer at corps and army level, took command of this hard-luck unit on 2 October 1942. His Military Council included Brigade Commissar A. E. Khalezov and chief of staff Colonel A. I. Kuznetsov. By 20 November, the *Stavka* had reinforced the 51st to a total of four rifle divisions; one fortified region; one mechanized corps; one cavalry corps; one tank brigade; one motorized rifle brigade; nine artillery, mortar, or rocket regiments; and four engineer or bridging battalions. Major General V. T. Vol'sky commanded 4th Mechanized Corps, formed in September from the remnants of 28th Tank Corps, which the Germans had largely destroyed in the fighting in the Don River bend and on the approaches to Stalingrad. By November, Vol'sky controlled 20,000 men, mostly green replacements, with a nominal strength of 220 tanks.[34]

The other mobile formation of 51st Army, 4th Cavalry Corps, had been in existence since 17 December 1941 but had never seen combat. Lieutenant General T. T. Shapkin, one of the few surviving veterans of the Tsar's army and the anti-Bolshevik White forces during the Civil War, commanded this group of Kazakhs, Uzbeks, and other central Asian soldiers.

The third strongest army in the Stalingrad Front was Lieutenant General V. F. Gerasimenko's 28th. Gerasimenko had commanded two field armies during the disasters of 1941, followed by various staff positions before taking command of 28th Army in September. His Military Council included Corps Commissar A. N. Mel'nikov and chief of staff Major General S. M. Rogachevsky. Originally under the direct control of the *Stavka* to defend the approaches to Astrakhan', 28th Army became part of the Stalingrad Front after the reorganization on 30 September. By 20 November, it included two rifle divisions, three rifle brigades, two fortified regions, one tank brigade, and relatively weak supporting units.

Chuikov's 62nd Army and Shumilov's 64th Army have already appeared frequently in this narrative and need no introduction here.[35] Including these two weakened formations, in November Eremenko's Stalingrad Front consisted of 1 rifle corps, 24 rifle divisions, 15 rifle brigades, 7 fortified regions, 1 tank corps, 1 mechanized corps, 1 cavalry corps, 1 separate tank brigade, 1 separate motorized infantry brigade, and 1 separate tank battalion. The *front*'s fire support included 49 artillery, mortar, or rocket regiments; 1 antiaircraft division; 14 antiaircraft regiments; 3 engineer or sapper brigades; and 22 engineer, sapper, or bridging battalions.

THE BROADER STRATEGIC PLAN

Although not understood until decades after the war, Operation Uranus was part of a larger complex—a whole planetary system of plans that together constituted a Soviet offensive at least as vast as that of December 1941. In both cases, the *Stavka* planners recognized that no single operation, however successful, would defeat the *Wehrmacht*; as we have seen, this concept had been fundamental to the Red Army for decades. Instead, they planned to use forces from their strategic reserve for attacks all along the front, creating so many ruptures that the Germans would be unable to restore the situation. Just as in the previous winter, however, this strategic concept showed that the Soviet command was not only thinking big; it was also biting off more than it could chew.

If the Uranus encirclement proved successful, it would destroy the spearhead of German Army Group B. Building on this, the *Stavka* hoped to conduct Operation Saturn, launching a thrust southwestward to Rostov. The 2nd

Guards Army, a massive force held in the *Stavka* Reserve, would seize this key transportation junction, cutting off all supplies to German forces south of the Don and Volga and strangling Army Group A in the Caucasus.

Next would come Operation Mars against the Rzhev salient of Army Group Center. Here, the German line bulged northward, surrounded on three sides by the Kalinin and Western Fronts. In August 1942 Zhukov had failed to pinch off this salient, which contained portions of Ninth and Third Panzer Armies (see chapter 6). Undeterred, Zhukov proposed to attack again. At a late-September meeting with Stalin and Vasilevsky, the stubborn commander convinced the Soviet dictator that there were sufficient reserves to conduct two major offensives in the fall of 1942—one at Stalingrad, and the second at Rzhev.[36]

Originally, the Rzhev offensive, code-named Mars, was scheduled for 12 October, probably in tandem with the Don and Stalingrad Fronts' offensive in the Stalingrad region. By the time Operation Mars finally began in November, planners had greatly broadened its scope to include attacks against German forces as far distant as Velikie Luki and Demiansk, the latter 200 kilometers northwest of Rzhev.[37] If successful, Operation Mars would create an encirclement almost as large as that at Stalingrad, tearing a great hole in Army Group Center just as Army Groups A and B disintegrated.[38]

Although not yet confirmed by Soviet or Russian accounts, the final planet in the constellation of Soviet offensives was likely code-named either Jupiter or Neptune. Just as Saturn depended on the success of Uranus, so Jupiter or Neptune was designed to build on Mars. The Western Front would thrust westward through Viaz'ma, while the Kalinin Front attacked southward to link up with the victorious forces in the Rzhev salient and take Smolensk. Thus, the Uranus plan makes sense only when viewed in the context of these other plans.

CONCENTRATION OF FORCES

The initial preparations for Operation Uranus took place between 27 September, when the decision to conduct the counteroffensive was made, and 12 October, the day before Zhukov and Vasilevsky submitted their revised plan to Stalin for approval. The *Stavka* had previously withdrawn 3rd and 5th Tank Armies into its strategic reserve, where it also formed five new reserve armies and a large number of tank, mechanized, and cavalry corps, as well as artillery penetration divisions and separate tank brigades, regiments, and battalions. On 22–23 September Moscow assigned 5th Tank Army to the Briansk Front and 3rd Tank Army to the Western Front for further training and possible employment in the Uranus and Mars operations.[39] A string of similar orders followed, including one instructing the Voronezh Front to assume the defensive and transfer 17th and 24th Tank Corps to the strategic reserve for rest and refitting.[40]

The *Stavka* issued another sheaf of detailed orders shortly before Stalin approved the draft plan on 13 October. The most significant of these directed 4th Cavalry Corps to relocate "immediately" from the Central Asia Military District to the Stalingrad region (10 October) and ordered the Don Front to send its 1st Guards Army and two guards rifle divisions to the *Stavka* Reserve for refitting (11 October).[41]

After Stalin approved the Uranus plan on 13 October, a whole series of actions occurred in the Northwestern, Kalinin, and Western Fronts to prepare for Mars. The most significant developments of the period, however, were the formation of the Southwestern Front on 22 October and the allocation of its subordinate forces, including 5th Tank, 17th Air, and 63rd and 21st (Combined Arms) Armies, along with various mobile corps and brigades.[42]

The final stage of preparations, extending from 1 through 18 November, involved meticulous inspections and adjustments by the two *Stavka* representatives and the *front* and subordinate commanders. Zhukov, for example, visited the Southwestern Front and its subordinate armies on 1–5 November, the Don Front on 7–9 November, and the Stalingrad Front on 9–15 November. He returned to Moscow briefly on 6 and 16 November and then sped off to the Kalinin and Western Fronts to supervise preparations for Operation Mars.[43] Overall, between 1 October and 20 November, *Stavka* directives moved 34 divisions, 6 mobile corps, 3,391 guns and mortars (in some 20 artillery regiments), 376 tanks, and 105,211 individual replacements to the 3 *fronts*.[44]

LOGISTICAL PREPARATIONS

All these plans depended upon the success of the first one: Operation Uranus. Although the time allowed to prepare for Uranus was greater than that for any previous Soviet offensive, this preparation also involved unprecedented logistical efforts.

The same rail and road network that hampered German logistics also restricted Soviet operations. The Southwestern and Don Fronts shared a single main railway line running from Povorino to Stalingrad, while the Stalingrad Front had only one additional rail line. During late October and early November, 117,000 men labored to build six branch lines totaling 1,160 kilometers of new rail lines, while refurbishing 1,958 kilometers of existing rails and building 293 bridges. Major General P. A. Kabanov's railway troops had to move 1,300 freight cars each day over this restricted network. Although the *Luftwaffe* tended to concentrate on battlefield support, it also interdicted Soviet trains on a regular basis. Moreover, because the Soviet commanders wished to conceal the extent of their preparations from German aerial observation, most trains moved only at night.[45]

Rail movement was only the first step in distributing troops and materiel to the front. Once the trains were unloaded at railheads, Red Army trucks transported men and supplies, usually driving at night without headlights. The Stalingrad Front alone used 27,000 motor vehicles to supply Chuikov while preparing for the coming offensive. Despite this huge motor fleet, which for the first time included significant numbers of Lend-Lease vehicles, there was never sufficient transportation. This shortage had a dual effect on Uranus. First, not all the designated troops and supplies had assembled at the line of departure prior to the offensive. Second, once the offensive began, the mechanized units conducting deep penetrations often ran short of supplies, especially fuel and ammunition.[46]

In addition to rail and motor transport, most of the troops and supplies had to cross the Don or Volga River to reach their starting positions for the offensive. The problem was particularly acute south of Stalingrad, where the river level was 2 meters higher than normal, and tanks and other heavy equipment could not cross on the available floating bridges. Instead, with winter ice beginning to accumulate, Rear Admiral Dmitri Dmitrievich Rogachev's Volga River Flotilla had to ferry the heaviest loads across. Prior to 15 November, Rogachev conducted all water crossings at night to conceal the troop buildup from the Germans. Crossings that had previously required 50 minutes now took as long as 5 hours because of drifting ice. Despite these difficulties, during the first 20 days of November, 111,000 soldiers, 427 tanks, 556 guns, 14,000 trucks, and 7,000 tons of ammunition crossed the freezing Volga.[47]

Given these logistical challenges, shortfalls were inevitable. Rokossovsky's Don Front received only three of the seven rifle divisions earmarked from the *Stavka* Reserve before the offensive began; his other divisions were well below strength, despite major efforts to identify replacements from hospitals and other rear echelons.[48] The other two *fronts* had a higher priority for transportation and supply and therefore fared better than Don Front. Nevertheless, the problem of assembling enough troops and supplies was the major reason why the offensive was eventually delayed from 9 to 19 November.

This huge reinforcement of materiel was possible only because of the continued expansion of Soviet production and distribution systems. Stalin recognized how important this effort was to the success of Uranus and established a formidable hierarchy of logistical chiefs at all levels of command. The key figure in this hierarchy was Lieutenant General of the Quartermaster Service Andrei Vasil'evich Khrulev, deputy commissar for defense and chief of the Main Directorate for Rear Services. Khrulev was also responsible for railroad services, and by November, his organization had eased the severe transportation problems of earlier operations, skillfully managing the rails and roads to provide the right amount of supplies in the right places at the right times.

Even more fundamentally, the combination of ever-expanding weapons production and Lend-Lease aid provided an avalanche of new equipment. In some cases, such as T-34 tanks, production in the second half of 1942 almost doubled that in the first half. Tables 12.3 and 12.4 permit a rough comparison of Soviet and German production.

Supplementing Soviet war production, Stalin's allies (the United States, Britain, and Canada) provided critical raw materials and finished weapons to the Red Army through Lend-Lease. These materials entered the Soviet Union via convoys to Murmansk and Arkhangel'sk, on railroads through Persia, and via an air route from Alaska to Siberia.[49] Although Lend-Lease accounted for 70 percent of Red Army trucks and wheeled vehicles, the proportion was much lower in other areas. Lend-Lease tanks equaled 12 percent of Soviet tank production during the war, and in the fall of 1942 they may have accounted for 15 percent or more of Soviet tank forces fighting in the Caucasus.[50]

FRONT AND ARMY PLANS

After obtaining approval from Zhukov and Vasilevsky, the three *front* commanders issued instructions to their subordinate armies on 8 November. In turn, most of the subordinate armies, corps, and divisions developed their own orders between 9 and 11 November. In a few instances, one organization's plan could not be finalized until another had issued its instructions. For example, the Southwestern Front's 1st Mixed Aviation Corps, in support of the breakthrough attack on the ground, issued its combat order on 17 November.[51] Thus, the commanders involved had ten days to ensure that their plans meshed correctly and conformed to the overall concept of the operation. This included coordinating not only infantry, artillery, armor, and logistical support but also engineer support to clear obstacles and bridge rivers at numerous points. Artillery preparations, centrally planned at the *front* level, ranged from 40 to 80 minutes, depending on the availability of gun tubes and ammunition. Most of these preparations involved alternating periods of massive fire raids and false cessations of firing, hoping to lure the defenders out of their shelters prematurely.[52]

As previously described, Vatutin's Southwestern Front provided the northern pincer of the double envelopment (see map 63). In turn, Vatutin

Table 12.3. Growth of Soviet Production of Equipment, Weapons, and Ammunition, 1942

Type of Equipment	Number of Items Produced		Rate of Growth
	1st Half 1942	2nd Half 1942	
Combat aircraft			
Total fighters	3,871	5,973	1.54-fold
Assault (Il-2 *Shturmovik*)	2,629	5,596	2.13-fold
Bombers	1,641	1,867	1.1-fold
Total aircraft	8,141	13,436	1.65-fold
Tanks			
Heavy (KV)	1,663	890	Production stopped
Medium (T-34)	4,414	8,106	1.8-fold
Light (T-60)	5,100	4,272	Production shifting to T-70s
Total tanks	11,177	13,268	1.19-fold
Artillery			
Antitank guns (47 and 57mm)	8,957	11,142	1.24-fold
Antiaircraft guns	2,368	4,120	1.7-fold
76.2mm field guns	11,052	12,257	1.1-fold
122 and 152mm guns	3,248	3,363	—
Total guns	25,625	30,882	1.2-fold
Mortars	122,470	107,053	Production of 50mm mortars stopped
Multiple-rocket launchers	1,546	1,691	1.1-fold
Small arms			
Rifles and carbines	1,943,400	2,100,509	1.08-fold
Automatic weapons and machine guns	614,271	1,098,537	1.8-fold
Antitank rifles	114,400	134,400	1.18-fold
Total small arms	2,672,071	3,333,446	1.25-fold
Ammunition (in thousands of rounds)			
Small-arms ammunition	1,508,736	2,236,477	1.48-fold
Mortar shells (all calibers)	17,799	35,959	2-fold
Artillery shells (all calibers)	31,827	44,678	1.4-fold
MRL rockets	1,300	2,600	2-fold

Sources: K. K. Rokossovsky, ed., *Velikaia pobeda na Volge* [Great victory on the Volga] (Moscow: Voenizdat, 1965), 210–211; M. E. Morozov, ed., *Velikaia Otechestvennaia voina 1941–1945 gg. Kampanii i strategicheskie operatsii v tsifrakh v 2 tomakh. Tom 1* [The Great Patriotic War, 1941–1945. Campaigns and strategic operations in two volumes. Vol. 1] (Moscow: Ob'edinnaia redaktsiia MVD Rossii, 2010), 373, 478.

Table 12.4. German Weapons Production, 1942

Type of Weapon	Estimated Army Stocks in 1942	Number Produced in January 1942
Combat aircraft	—	15,109
Armored fighting vehicles (AFVs)		
Tanks (Pz II, III, IV, 38t)	3,365	4,759
Assault guns	625	—
Armored troop carriers	1,888	2,527
Total AFVs	5,878	9,278
Artillery		
Antitank guns	13,607	9,142
Antiaircraft guns	2,915	11,396
Infantry guns	4,684	1,687
Rocket launchers (*Werfer*)	12,615	3,864
Light guns	6,701	1,476
Heavy & extra-heavy guns	3,888	968
Total artillery	44,410	28,533
Mortars	26,494	18,199
Small arms		
Rifles & carbines	4,748,260	1,149,593
Automatic weapons and machine guns	420,070	233,882
Artillery shells (75mm or larger)	—	58,070,000

Sources: Horst Boog, Jurgen Forster, Joachim Hoffmann, Ernst Klink, Rolf-Dieter Muller, and Gerd R. Ueberschar, *Germany and the Second World War*, vol. IV, *The Attack on the Soviet Union*, trans. Dean S. McMurry, Ewald Osers, and Louise Willmot (Oxford: Clarendon Press, 1999), 1122; Horst Boog, Werner Rahm, Reinhard Stumpf, and Bernd Wegner, *Germany and the Second World War*, vol. vi, *The Global War: Widening of the Conflict into a World War and the Shift of the Initiative, 1941–1943*, trans. Ewald Osers et al. (Oxford: Clarendon Press, 2001), 613, 637–638, 668, 670–671, 678–679, 684, 687–688, 691, 700, 805.

had two different thrusts to penetrate Romanian Third Army. Attacking from the bridgehead over the Don River south of Serafimovich, Romanenko's 5th Tank Army would use 4 rifle divisions, a tank brigade, a tank battalion, 16 artillery regiments, and 1st Mixed Aviation Corps to create a 10 kilometer gap on the first day. Romanenko would then pass three mobile corps—1st Tank, 26th Tank, and 8th Cavalry—through the Romanians to exploit to the south and southeast. Simultaneously, Chistiakov's 21st Army would attack out of the Kletskaia bridgehead using a shock group of 5 rifle divisions, 3 tank regiments, and 17 artillery regiments to rip a 12 kilometer wide gap on the army's left flank. Chistiakov would then pass 4th Tank and 3rd Guards Cavalry Corps forward for a parallel exploitation. By the third day of the attack, these mobile corps were supposed to meet their counterparts from the Stalingrad Front in the Kalach and Sovetskii region and begin to destroy Axis forces in the resulting encirclement.[53]

The Stalingrad Front faced equally complex tasks. While 62nd Army attempted to tie down German forces inside Stalingrad with local attacks,

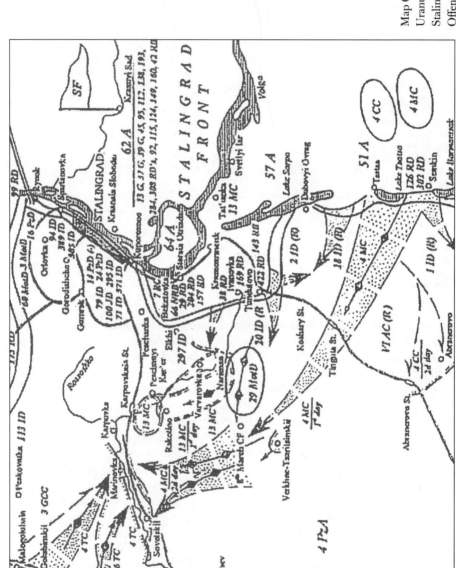

Map 64. Operation Uranus: The Stalingrad Front's Offensive Plan

three other armies—64th, 57th, and 51st—were to advance south of the city on a broad frontage (see map 64). Among them, these three headquarters involved 8 of the *front*'s 12 rifle divisions, 1 rifle brigade, all 5 of its tank brigades, and support from half of the available artillery and all of the combat power of 8th Air Army.[54] Like Vatutin, Eremenko planned two penetrations of the mostly Romanian defenders of German IV and Romanian VI Corps. General Shumilov's 64th Army would advance from the Beketovka bridgehead with Tolbukhin's 57th Army on its southern flank. Once the initial penetration occurred, Tolbukhin would commit the overstrength 13th Tank Corps into an exploitation to help form the inner edge of the future encirclement. The main attack, however, would come from General Trufanov's 51st Army between Lakes Tsata and Barmantsak, seeking to penetrate at the junction between Romanian 18th and 1st Infantry Divisions of VI Corps. Once Trufanov's rifle formations and supporting tank brigades achieved their initial lodgment, 51st Army would pass 4th Mechanized and 4th Cavalry Corps through the front lines quickly to exploit northwestward and link up with their counterparts from the Southwestern Front. Because of the shorter distances these three mobile formations had to travel, as well as continuing logistical issues, the date for the Stalingrad Front's operation was 20 November, one day later than the Southwestern Front's. In addition, a shortage of artillery meant that Eremenko's nondivisional guns would fire an initial preparation for 64th Army and then shift their fires southward to support 57th Army.

The Don Front faced two daunting problems: the weakness of its forces after months of continuous combat, and the prepared defenses of its German opponents. Nonetheless, it had two significant missions. Offensively, Rokossovsky conducted two secondary attacks—one just east of the Kletskaia bridgehead against German XI Army Corps, and the second south of Kachalinskaia to penetrate German VII Corps. The 65th Army launched the first attack with four rifle divisions and two tank brigades, while 24th Army used six rifle divisions, 16th Tank Corps, and one tank brigade. The goal was for the two attacks to defeat XI Corps and destroy its remnants before they could withdraw into the land bridge between the Don and Volga Rivers. Defensively, the remainder of 24th Army and all of 66th Army had to conduct local actions to pin down the German forces opposite them.[55]

Tactically, all three *fronts* had a shortage of forces compared with the relatively broad width of their fronts. As a result, these *fronts* attacked in a single echelon of armies; in turn, the armies generally had only a single echelon of rifle divisions, most of which were on line for the initial attack, while the mechanized and cavalry corps were retained as a separate echelon for exploitation.

A number of measurements are available to quantify the scale, scope,

Table 12.5. Operational Indices of the Stalingrad Counteroffensive

Formation	Sector Width (km)	Overall Penetration (km)	Depth (km)	Duration (days)	Movement Tempo (km/day) Rifle Units	Mobile Units
Southwestern Front	85	32	140	3	20–25	40–45
5th Tank Army	35	10	140	3	20–25	40–45
21st Army	40	12	100–110	3	20–25	30–35
1st Guards Army	10	10	30–35	3	15–17	—
Front total	—	64	30–140	3	—	—
Don Front	150	10.5	60	3	15–20	20
65th Army	80	6	60	3	15–20	20
24th Army	40	4.5	20	2	8–10	10
Front total	—	—	20–60	2	—	—
Stalingrad Front	180	40	90	2	10–15	45
64th Army	36	12	10–15	2	5–8	—
57th Army	35	16	45–50	2	8–12	20–25
51st Army	110	12	90	2	10–15	45
Front total	—	80	10–90	2	—	—

Source: K. K. Rokossovsky, ed., *Velikaia pobeda na Volge* [Great victory on the Volga] (Moscow: Voenizdat, 1965), 233, 240, 245.

form, and duration of operations. In the case of the Stalingrad counteroffensive, these so-called operational indices provide a useful picture of the complexity of the operation, as reflected in table 12.5. All of them displayed a marked increase in complexity compared with earlier Soviet offensive operations.

CHAPTER THIRTEEN

The Advent of Uranus

In mid-October 1942 the new chief of the German General Staff, Colonel General Kurt Zeitzler, made an appointment with Adolf Hitler for a private briefing on Zeitzler's estimate of the strategic situation. Because there were no witnesses to this meeting, we have only Zeitzler's account of what transpired. Still, given his known actions during the following month, it seems probable that the general did, in fact, provide Hitler with an unvarnished appraisal. If so, then two of Zeitzler's main points proved especially prescient:

> 2. The most perilous sector of the Eastern Front was undoubtedly the long, thinly-held flank stretching from Stalingrad [northwestward] to the right boundary of Army Group Center. Furthermore, this sector was held by the weakest and least reliable of our troops, Romanians, Italians, and Hungarians. . . .
> 4. The Russians [sic] were both better trained and better led than they had been in 1941.[1]

According to Zeitzler, Hitler listened without interruption but then politely dismissed the general's entire argument, assuring Zeitzler that he was too pessimistic in his appraisal.[2] The dictator was equally optimistic when he spoke with Generals Weichs and Paulus, apparently believing that even the subordinates he still trusted had become so downcast that they needed encouragement.

It would be unfair, however, to depict Hitler as a blundering amateur who ignored the threat to his flanks. During September he made repeated efforts to bolster the defenses there. Based on Weichs's recommendations, on 13 September a Führer order directed preparations for limited advances to clear and secure the flanks, eliminating Soviet bridgeheads over the Don, once Stalingrad was secured. The plan even allocated scarce reserve divisions to make such advances possible. Unfortunately for Hitler and for the future of German Sixth Army, the tenacious defense of that city continued for another two months, making the 13 September order virtually moot.[3] From the German viewpoint, Stalingrad appeared to be the last operation of 1942. To some extent, in fact, the fight for Stalingrad became a struggle by Sixth Army to acquire shelter from the impending winter.

From September onward, the dictator frequently expressed concern about the Don River flank. He often reminded his staff of Stalin's experience during the Russian Civil War, when Semen Mikhailovich Budenny's 1st Cavalry Army had conducted a rapid thrust from Stalingrad to Rostov. Hitler ordered the *Luftwaffe* to increase interdiction attacks on bridging sites and suspected assembly areas along the northern bank of the Don. Further expressing his disquiet, he issued Operational Order No. 1 on 14 October and a supplemental order on the twenty-third. These directed the implementation of a number of defensive precautions, including construction of fallback positions south of the Don. Yet Hitler was intensely human, and he resented having his subordinates remind him of risks he could do little to avert. On 27 October, for example, Zeitzler reported that the Soviet government was generating a massive propaganda campaign about a forthcoming offensive. Hitler dismissed this report and instead worried about reinforcing Army Group Center, the German force opposite Moscow that was, in fact, targeted by Operation Mars.[4]

Nor was the Eastern Front Hitler's only problem. As the tide turned against him in western Europe and the Mediterranean, he tried to shore up his defenses. This resulted in various efforts to defend Crete, the British Channel Islands, and North Africa, diverting scarce resources from the East. On 3 November one of his favorite generals, Erwin Rommel, openly disobeyed the Führer by retreating from Alamein in Egypt. This betrayal only fueled Hitler's anger at the professionals, which he vented by firing several additional staff officers. Six days later, in response to the Anglo-American invasion of northwestern Africa, Germany invaded the previously unoccupied portions of southern France.

Complicating matters further, Hitler was physically absent from his eastern headquarters, code-named *Wehrwolf*, in Vinnitsa, Ukraine, during the crucial two weeks of mid-November. On 7 November the dictator left Vinnitsa to make his annual speech at Munich, commemorating the 1923 Beer Hall Putsch. While in Germany he publicly claimed that the army had already secured Stalingrad, in the mistaken belief that this announcement would strengthen the resolve of the troops. His subordinates dutifully reported that this speech had reenergized the exhausted assault forces of Sixth Army. Thereafter, Hitler remained in Germany, traveling or vacationing at Berchtesgaden, until 23 November. Although he received constant reports, this trip isolated him from daily contact with Zeitzler and the OKH staff. It is tempting to attribute this absence to a subconscious desire to avoid an intractable situation, but the dictator certainly had other problems besides Stalingrad.

THE AXIS SATELLITES

As Army Group B prepared to face another winter in the East, it looked more like a patchwork international force than a powerful German field command. Second German Army still anchored the northwestern flank, covering the railheads at Kursk and Khar'kov, while barely retaining the disputed river bend at Voronezh. However, from a point just south of Voronezh to Kletskaia, on the left flank of Sixth German Army, more than 360 kilometers of the Don River line were protected by the forces of Germany's allies—Hungarian Second Army, Italian Eighth Army, and Romanian Third Army. South of Stalingrad, where Sixth Army and the shrunken Fourth Panzer Army were fighting, forces that would soon be designated Romanian Fourth Army extended this brittle cordon. Beyond the Romanians, the Axis line faded out into the barren steppes, except for a few patrols put out by German 16th Motorized Division.[5] The Axis soldiers of these four field armies were neither incompetent nor cowardly, but their units were understrength, lightly equipped infantry or horse cavalry formations that could do little to defend against a modern, mechanized force. They had few effective antitank weapons or materials to construct defenses. If Germany had experienced difficulties in reequipping for the 1942 campaign, its allies lacked the industrial capacity to even begin to arm their troops for modern combat.

Moreover, the various Axis armies had ongoing animosities with one another and with the sometimes overbearing Germans, all of which complicated their efforts to coordinate. The Hungarians and Romanians would have preferred to fight each other than the Soviets, which was a major reason for inserting Italian Eighth Army between them. The German soldiers themselves had such contempt for their allies that their ethnically Russian opponents in Stalingrad reported taunts shouted at them across no-man's-land: "Do you wanna swap an Uzbek for a Romanian?"[6]

A few German divisions were scattered at wide intervals along the front. Such reinforcement was limited not only by the overall scarcity of German troops but also by the mutual jealousies that meant no nationality wished to be commanded by another. Indeed, the national field armies were intended more to minimize political friction than to provide coherent tactical defenses. To mend political fences, in August 1942 Hitler had even proposed grouping the two Romanian field armies with Paulus's Sixth Army as an army group under the Romanian dictator Ion Antonescu, for whom he had considerable respect. Fortunately for the troops in the field, the deal did not reach fruition.[7] The Germans assigned small, radio-equipped liaison teams to the major headquarters of their allies; these liaison officers performed minor miracles of diplomacy to hold the front together.

Italian Eighth Army had German 294th Infantry Division anchoring its left, then Italian II Corps covering most of the front, and finally Italian XXXV Corps, in which German 62nd Infantry Division was bracketed by Italian units, on the right. The reserve for this army was Italian 3rd Mobile (*Celere*) Division, located more than 80 kilometers behind the front at the road junction and supply depot of Millerovo. This division was not a fully motorized formation but rather an odd combination of fast-marching Bersaglieri infantry with a few light tanks and self-propelled guns.[8] The Germans rated only four of the Italian infantry divisions as capable of independent missions.

Romanian Third Army was in an even more difficult tactical position. Four Romanian army corps—I, II, V, and IV—were spread out from northwest to southeast on a line of approximately 160 kilometers. Each corps headquarters controlled only two divisions, each of which, in turn, had only seven battalions. Thus, a typical Romanian division was stretched across a frontage of 20 kilometers. One-half of Third Army's reserve, Romanian 15th Infantry Division, was located at Gromki, almost on the front line between the two right-hand corps, while Romanian 7th Cavalry Division, largely without horses, was behind the western end of the line at Seniutkin, near Pronin. The total strength of these ten divisions and supporting staffs was approximately 130,000, or slightly more than one-third the size of the Southwestern Front alone.[9]

German forces available to reinforce the Romanians were laughably weak because Army Groups B and A were already stretched taut by the vast distances and attrition of the campaign. On 9 November, the originally scheduled start date for Operation Uranus, a German close support element (Group Simon) consisting of one motorized infantry battalion, one antitank company, and one section of self-propelled guns, received orders to move into position behind Romanian Third Army. A day later the Germans began to create a larger mobile reserve in this sector. XXXXVIII Panzer Corps' headquarters, commanded by Lieutenant General Ferdinand Heim, transferred from Fourth Panzer Army to Army Group Reserve behind the Romanian sector. Unfortunately, this "corps" was as flimsy as the units it was supposed to support. The 22nd Panzer Division, the victor of the Kerch' Peninsula, had sent its panzer engineer battalion to fight in Stalingrad, while its 140th Panzer-Grenadier Regiment was detached to Second German Army at Voronezh. For months, the remaining elements of 22nd Panzer Division sat behind the Italian sector, immobilized by fuel shortages and camouflaged in straw. When the division's 204th Panzer Regiment finally attempted to start its engines in November, it found that field mice had chewed the insulation off much of its wiring! This, plus the long period of inactivity and temperatures of –20 degrees Celsius (–4 degrees Fahrenheit), produced numerous short-circuits and other malfunctions when the regiment finally moved into the Romanian sector. Only 42 tanks reached the assembly area, and on 19

November only 24 were actually functional in the division. At the critical moment, the acting division commander, Colonel Eberhard Rodt, could field only a reinforced battalion task force. The 14th Panzer Division, again minus its infantry units, also moved into the region once the battle began, but it could muster only 51 tanks.[10] The Romanian 1st Armored Division had 12,196 men and 105 operable tanks on 18 November, but 84 of these were R-2 Romanian-produced light tanks, based on the Czech 38(t); 19 were German-made Panzer IIIs or IVs; and 2 were captured Soviet tanks.[11]

STRENGTH AND ORDER OF BATTLE

In mid-November Army Group B included six field armies, an air fleet, and a small operational reserve. Neither German Second Army (1 panzer and 13 infantry divisions) nor Hungarian Second Army (2 German infantry and 10 weak Hungarian divisions) were immediately involved with Uranus and are thus omitted from subsequent discussions. Those two armies apart, Army Group B included 36 infantry or mountain divisions (16 German, 7 Italian, and 13 Romanian), 5 armored divisions (4 German and 1 Romanian), 4 German motorized divisions, 3 Italian mobile divisions, 4 Romanian cavalry divisions, 2 rear-area security divisions, and 2 Italian separate brigades.[12] All the field armies deployed in a single echelon of divisions with only small reserves.

As described in previous chapters, German Sixth Army was only slightly stronger than its allied counterparts. The army headquarters' own daily assessment for 16 November indicated that the 17 divisions, which should have totaled 139 infantry or panzer-grenadier battalions, had only 96. Of this number, the headquarters assessed 4 battalions to be strong, 16 medium strong, 39 average, 26 weak, and 11 exhausted. Similarly, the 17 engineer or pioneer battalions of Sixth Army included 1 medium strong, 9 average, 5 weak, and 2 exhausted. The army's 3 panzer and 2 motorized divisions fielded a total of 218 tanks, of which 180 were operable; the 3 nondivisional assault gun battalions had 68 guns, of which 43 were operable. Not counting the 21 lightly armed Panzer II command tanks, the army had only 144 Panzer IIIs and 53 Panzer IVs, or slightly more than one full panzer division.[13] Continued restrictions on resupply limited Sixth Army's fuel and ammunition even before the Soviet counteroffensive. Sixth Army was thus incapable of mounting a major attack, and it was doubtful whether it could withstand a significant enemy offensive.

Compounding this numerical weakness, the tenuous German logistical system was unable to meet requirements for ammunition and petroleum products, nor was the army able to build up winter stocks of food. On average, Sixth Army received only about half the required daily trainloads of

Table 13.1. Organization of Army Group B, 18 November 1942

Army Group B—Colonel General Maximilian, *Freiherr* von Weichs
German Second Army—Colonel General Hans von Salmuth
  LV Army Corps (G)
    299th, 45th, 383rd, and 88th Infantry Divisions
  XIII Army Corps (G)
    82nd, 68th, 340th, 385th, and 377th Infantry Divisions
  VI Army Corps (G)
    387th, 57th, 75th, and 323rd Infantry Divisions
  27th Panzer Division
Hungarian Second Army—Colonel General Gusztáv Jány
  III Army Corps (H)
    9th and 6th Light (Infantry) Divisions (H)
  XXIV Panzer Corps (G)
    168th and 336th Infantry Divisions (G)
    7th, 13th, and 30th Light Divisions (H)
  IV Army Corps (H)
    10th and 12th Light Divisions (H)
  VII Army Corps (H)
    19th and 23rd Light Divisions (H)
  1st Armored Division (H)
Italian Eighth Army—Army General Italo Garibaldi
  Alpine Corps (I)
    2nd *Tridentina*, 3rd Julia, and 4th *Cuneense* Alpine Divisions
  II Army Corps (I)
    5th *Cosseria* and 3rd *Ravenna* Infantry Divisions (I)
    318th Infantry Regiment (of 213th Security Division) (G)
    "23 March" Blackshirt Brigade (I)
  XXXV Army Corps (I)
    9th *Pasubio* Motorized Division (I)
    298th Infantry Division (G)
    "3 January" Blackshirt Brigade (I)
  XXIX Army Corps (activated after 19 November)
    52nd *Torino* Motorized Division (I)
    3rd *Celere* Mobile Division (I)
    2nd *Sforzesca* Infantry Division (I)
    62nd Infantry Division (G)
  71st Reconnaissance Air Group (I): 32 aircraft
  22nd Fighter Air Group (I): 43 aircraft
Romanian Third Army—Army General Petre Dumitrescu
  I Army Corps (R)
    7th and 11th Infantry Divisions (R)
  II Army Corps (R)
    9th and 14th Infantry Divisions (R)
  IV Army Corps (R)
    13th Infantry and 1st Cavalry Divisions (R)
  Colonel Voicu Detachment (R), with two infantry regiments, one panzer-*Jäger*
    battalion, and one pioneer battalion
  V Army Corps (R)
    5th, 6th, and 15th Infantry Divisions (R), 7th Cavalry Division (R)
  XXXXVIII Panzer Corps
    22nd Panzer Division (–) (G)
    1st Armored Division (R)
    14th Panzer Division (–) (G) (attached after 19 November)
  1st Air Corps (I)

Two fighter groups (72 aircraft), one fighter-bomber group (22 aircraft), three
    bomber groups (54 aircraft) (I)
German Sixth Army—General of Panzer Troops Friedrich Paulus
  XI Army Corps (G)
    376th, 44th, and 384th Infantry Divisions (G)
  VIII Army Corps (G)
    76th and 113th Infantry Divisions, 177th Assault Gun Battalion (G)
  XIV Panzer Corps (G)
    60th and 3rd Motorized, 16th Panzer, and 94th Infantry Divisions (G)
  LI Army Corps (G)
    389th, 305th, 79th, 295th, 71st Infantry, and 100th *Jäger* Divisions (G)
    14th and 24th Panzer Divisions, 244th and 245th Assault Gun Battalions (G)
German Fourth Panzer Army—Colonel General Hermann Hoth
  IV Army Corps (G)
    371st and 297th Infantry Divisions (G), 20th Infantry Division (R)
  VI Army Corps (R)
    2nd, 18th, 1st, and 4th Infantry Divisions (R)
    6th *Rosiori* Motorized Regiment (of 5th Cavalry Division) (R)
  VII Army Corps (R)
    5th (–) and 8th Cavalry Divisions (R)
    16th and 29th Motorized Divisions (G)
Army Group B Reserve
  Headquarters, Romanian Fourth Army
  Headquarters, XVII Army Corps (G)
  294th Infantry Division (G)
Army Group B Rear-Area Command
  105th Light Division (H), with 46th Infantry Regiment (H)
  213th (–) and 403rd Security Divisions (G)
  156th *Vizenza* Infantry Division (I)
Fourth Air Fleet—Field Marshal Wolfram, Freiherr von Richthofen
  VIII Air Corps
    27th Bomber, 2nd Dive-Bomber, 1st Assault, 3rd Fighter, and 1st Heavy
        Fighter Wings
  9th *Flak* Division
  91st *Flak* Regiment
  172nd Transport Wing
  900th Special-Purpose Bomber Wing

Sources: Horst Boog, Werner Rahm, Reinhard Stumpf, and Bernd Wegner, *Germany and the Second World War*, vol. VI, *The Global War: Widening of the Conflict into a World War and the Shift of the Initiative, 1941–1943*, trans. Ewald Osers et al. (Oxford: Clarendon Press, 2001); Manfred Kehrig, *Stalingrad: Analyse und Dokumentation einer Schlacht* (Stuttgart, Germany: Deutsche Verlags-Anstalt, 1974), charts and map entitled "Die Lage am 19. November 1942"; *L'8 Armata Italiana nella Seconde Battaglia Digensiva Del Don (11 Decembre 1942–31 January 1943)* (Rome: Ministero della Guerra, Stato Maggiore Esercito-Ufficio Storico, 1946); *Le Operationi della Unita Italiane Al Fronte Russo (1943–1944)* (Rome: Ministero della Guerra, Stato Maggiore Esercito-Ufficio Storico, 1977); Mark Axworthy, Cornel Scafeş, and Cristian Craciunoiu, *Third Axis, Fourth Ally: The Romanian Armed Forces in the European War, 1941–1945* (London: Arms & Armour Press, 1995), 83–89.
Note: G = German, H = Hungarian, I = Italian, R = Romanian.

supplies. With winter approaching on the barren steppes around Stalingrad, German horses were so malnourished that many did not survive the trip to winter recovery centers.[14] Given these shortages and the withdrawal of most draft animals for the winter, Sixth Army was undersupplied and almost immobile even before Operation Uranus began.

Hermann Hoth's Fourth Panzer Army was equally fragile, consisting of three army corps—German IV and Romanian VI and VII—plus 16th and 29th Motorized Divisions. The 16th Motorized, reinforced by several battalions of volunteer auxiliaries from the Turkestan Autonomous Region, numbered 14,000 to 15,000 men and had 43 tanks, but it was screening the vast open southern flank around Elista. Meanwhile, since the beginning of October, 29th Motorized had rested south of Stalingrad as Hoth's reserve force. By mid-November, it was relatively strong, with roughly 12,000 men and 59 tanks.[15] As previously noted, the nonmechanized units of Hoth's army had very broad fronts to defend with only 34 75mm antitank guns, or one every 7.3 kilometers.

Beyond these overall figures, many questions linger concerning the actual strength of Axis forces at the time of the counteroffensive. Most intelligence analysts habitually assume that their opponents are at or close to full authorized strength in order to avoid underestimating the threat. Moreover, despite the Soviet emphasis on scientific accuracy, a natural pride in the achievements of Uranus probably influenced the Soviets' analysis of these correlations, exaggerating the invaders' strength to minimize the attackers' numerical advantage on the ground. What follows, therefore, is subject to considerable caveats and qualifiers concerning the accuracy of figures.

Recently discovered records for German Sixth Army have overcome some earlier problems, such as whether and how to count *Luftwaffe* elements, German service support units, and the Russian *Hiwis*, who performed valuable services for the German divisions but had limited, if any, ground combat capability. It is equally if not more difficult to determine the exact strength of the Italian, Romanian, and other Axis satellite forces that bore the brunt of initial Soviet attacks.

A comparison of Sixth Army records and a 2 November intelligence estimate of the Stalingrad Front enables us to draw general conclusions about the strength of the defenders.[16] Thus, for example, Sixth Army's ration strength (including nondivisional units) on 17 November was 175,776 soldiers, or 59 percent of its authorized strength of 297,676. In turn, the overall combat or fighting strength of that army's 17 divisions was only 64,401 soldiers, or less than half the total divisional ration strength of 149,832. Individual German combat strengths ranged from 6,748 men (64 percent) in 44th Infantry Division to only 2,924 men (29 percent) in the long-suffering 94th Infantry Division.[17]

The actual strength of the Axis satellite armies is more difficult to ascertain. Still, the standard English-language source on the Romanians estimates that, in terms of combat strength, six of the eight infantry divisions in Third Army averaged 68 percent of their authorized strength of 16,097 soldiers, while 13th and 14th Infantry Divisions, having suffered heavy casualties in October, were between 50 and 60 percent strength. A formerly classified study of 5th Tank Army's participation in Uranus estimates the average Romanian strength at 70 percent. This would place the Romanian "bayonet" strength at some 5,500 to 7,000 per division.[18] The same sources agree that the two Romanian corps subordinate to Fourth Panzer Army were substantially weaker, having suffered heavily while halting previous Soviet attacks in the lakes area. Romanian 1st, 2nd, and 4th Infantry Divisions, for example, were reportedly at 25, 30, and 34 percent, respectively, when the Stalingrad Front attacked on 20 November.[19]

Italian forces played virtually no part in the Uranus counteroffensive, so their strength is less significant to the outcome of that attack. Overall, Eighth Army fielded roughly 130,000 men, with divisional ration strengths of 9,000 to 10,000 and combat strengths of 5,000 to 7,000.

FORCE RATIOS

Taking all these factors and estimates into consideration, one can arrive at a fairly clear statement of the "correlation of forces," to use the Soviet military term, at the start of Uranus. Table 13.2 presents the overall figures, followed by breakdowns for the two attacking *fronts.*

Regardless of any flaws in these calculations, the Soviet forces in Operation Uranus clearly outnumbered their foes to a greater degree than historians have traditionally thought. Given the Soviet Union's consistent ability to outnumber and outproduce the Third Reich, this is not surprising. For the Axis, the problem was that in November 1942 the Soviet commanders and troops proved far more capable than their predecessors earlier in the war, while the Romanian defenders were much weaker than their German neighbors.

INDICATIONS AND WARNINGS

After any great military surprise, soldiers and historians naturally question how the defender could have misread the situation so badly. In 1942, as so often before and since, the answer lies in a combination of the limits of intelligence collection capabilities and the preconceived notions of the defending leaders and intelligence analysts.

Table 13.2. Correlation of Opposing Soviet and Axis Forces in Operation Uranus, 19–20 November 1942

Forces and Weapons	Soviet	Axis	Ratio
Overall			
Personnel	1,042,218 men (782,548 combat)	521,703 men (234,252 combat)	2:1 (3.3:1)
Tanks and assault guns	1,550	508	3:1
Guns and mortars	22,019	7,000 estimated	3:1
Combat aircraft	1,529 total (1,277 operable)	732 total (402 operable)	2.1:1 (3.2:1)
Southwestern Front (5th Tank and 21st Armies, 22 km breakthrough front)			
Personnel	207,466 total (182,656 combat)	166,703 total (90,000 combat)	1.24:1 (2:1)
Tanks and assault guns	558	145	3.8:1
Guns and mortars	5,058	2,000 estimated	2.5:1
Stalingrad Front (57th and 51st Armies, 28 km breakthrough front)			
Personnel	121,962 total (80,000 combat)	94,315 total (44,788 combat)	1.3:1 (1.8:1)
Tanks and assault guns	432	59	7.3:1
Guns and mortars	2,104	400 estimated	5.3:1

Sources: V. A. Zolotarev, ed., *Velikaia Otechestvennaia: Deistvuiushchaia armiia 1941–1945 gg.* [The Great Patriotic (War): The operating army, 1941–1945] (Moscow: Animi Fortitudo Kuchkovo pole, 2005), 587; Manfred Kehrig, *Stalingrad: Analyse und Dokumentation einer Schlacht* (Stuttgart, Germany: Deutsche Verlag-Anstalt, 1974), 662–663, citing reports dated 11 and 19 November; Mark Axworthy, Cornel Scafeş, and Cristian Craciunoiu, *Third Axis, Fourth Ally: The Romanian Armed Forces in the European War, 1941–1945* (London: Arms & Armour Press, 1995), 89–91, 109; Joel S. A. Hayward, *Stopped at Stalingrad: The Luftwaffe and Hitler's Defeat in the East, 1942–1943* (Lawrence: University Press of Kansas, 1998), 225, citing USAFHRA K113.106-153: *Zusammenstelling der Ist-Starken und der einstazbereiten Flugzeuge an der Ostfront 1942.*

Hitler had an instinctive concern for the security of his long left flank but was poorly served by many of his professional subordinates.[20] Colonel Reinhard Gehlen, head of the *Fremde Heere Ost* (Foreign Armies East, or FHO) branch of military intelligence, consistently misunderstood the capabilities and intentions of his opponent. Like Hitler, Gehlen believed the Red Army had exhausted its reserves in the summer battles and was capable of only limited attacks in November. The series of limited counteroffensives in August–September, together with the genuine preparations for Operation Mars, fueled Soviet deception plans and convinced Gehlen that Army Group Center was the most likely sector for any Soviet attack.[21]

Despite extreme efforts at secrecy and operational security, Soviet preparations for the coming offensive inevitably gave some clues to the Germans. In mid-October front-line units of Army Group B, as well as aerial reconnaissance flights, indicated considerable Soviet troop movements all along the Don flank. Romanian Third Army reported a steady increase in night traffic in the Serafimovich bridgehead, where 5th Tank Army was massing. Initially, the staff of Army Group B attributed this traffic to the simple replenishment of supplies. By 3 November, however, the army group headquarters became aware that some form of attack was likely in this region; the creation of the Southwestern Front headquarters reinforced this perception. Soviet prisoners indicated an offensive beginning as early as 7 November. Such reports prompted the movement of limited German reserves to the area and led the German liaison officers to urge the Romanians to move their reserves closer to the front line.[22]

Long after the battle, Gehlen claimed that Hitler and his generals had ignored the FHO's clear warnings of an impending assault. In fact, however, such warnings were often diminished by various caveats, as well as by Gehlen's continuing belief in an offensive elsewhere. On 6 November, for example, the FHO issued another assessment:

1. The point of main effort of the future Russian [*sic*] operations against the German Eastern Front looms with increasing distinctness in the sector of Army Group Center. However, it is still not clear whether, along with this, the Russians intend to conduct a major operation along the Don or they will limit their aims in the south due to the considerations that they cannot achieve success simultaneously along two axes because of insufficient forces. In any event, we can conclude that the offensive they are preparing in the south is not so far advanced that one must reckon with a major operation here in the near future simultaneously with the expected offensive against Army Group Center. Presently there is no information indicating that the Russians have given up the attack across the Don entirely, an idea which undoubtedly affected their previous intentions. The

likely demarcation of this operation . . . [is] holding the forces designated for this attack back as a reserve to throw in against Army Group Center if the situation developing there warrants their use. . . .

   b) The configuration of Army Group Center's front, with the presence of concentration areas suitable from the point of view of transport and advantageous jumping-off regions (the Sukhinichi-Toropets salient) for an operation against Smolensk, is very favorable for the development of a major operation. The Smolensk region ought to be viewed as the first objective of a decisive operation against Army Group Center. In distance, this objective fully corresponds to the resources and capabilities of the Russian command.

   c) In the event of success, after destroying the forces in the center of the German front, the possibility will exist to exploit the success by continuing the operation to the west, into the Baltic countries, to cut off German forces on the northern wing.

   d) In contradistinction with this are the greater difficulties in controlling the forces and supplying them in an operation against Rostov.[23]

Despite such ambivalent guidance, General Paulus became increasingly concerned about his flank and made various representations to the army group commander, Weichs, about the weakness of Axis units in that sector. Still, the scope and goal of the coming offensive were not apparent to the Germans until the last minute, if at all.[24] Even on 18 November, the eve of the Uranus counteroffensive, the daily FHO intelligence estimate was distinctly optimistic: "In the region of the city of Stalingrad and to the north, the enemy has not succeeded in hindering our units' forward progress. In the Romanian Third Army's sector, the enemy unsuccessfully attacked many points in the bridgehead southwest of Serafimovich." The report went on to assert that Red Army units might actually be moving *away* from the region, possibly for an offensive west of Moscow.[25]

   As so often in this war, the Germans had a fairly accurate picture of the Red Army's front-line dispositions but little knowledge of troop concentrations or logistical movements behind enemy lines. As General Hoth ruefully remarked when Uranus began, "We have overestimated the Russians at the front, but completely underestimated their reserves."[26] The 5th Tank Army went undetected, and many of the bridges attacked by German air strikes were dummies intended to distract attention from the real crossing sites. In addition, the Soviets put out false radio signals and other indications intended to convince their opponents that they planned to defend along the Don River while attacking Army Group Center. Such deception measures misled Hitler and Gehlen, even if lower-level Axis commanders became increasingly concerned by a vaguely perceived threat.[27]

Within the limitations of their resources, the Germans tried to take reasonable precautions. On 8 October 1942 the OKH had directed that all headquarters above division level release 10 percent of their personnel as replacements, while all support units not engaged in combat were to form standby *alarm abteilungen* (alert or alarm detachments) to respond to sudden emergencies. Six weeks later, these alarm detachments proved to be critical in restoring a tenuous front line after the Soviet offensive.[28] On 12 November, concerned by growing reports of Soviet preparations, Weichs ordered Paulus to "squeeze 10,000 men out of his engineer and artillery units to man a support line behind the Rumanians."[29] In reality, of course, Sixth Army was so understrength as a result of the prolonged struggle for Stalingrad that there were few if any troops available to fulfill this requirement.

More fundamentally, however, the Germans had beaten off so many previous Soviet counterattacks that they were pardonably convinced that they could handle any future threat. Unlike all the frantic, premature attacks of summer and fall, however, the coming blow was finally launched with sufficient time and resources to be decisive. Moreover, the new offensive was focused not against the veteran German units of Fourth Panzer and Sixth Armies but against the poorly equipped and badly positioned Romanians.

CHAPTER FOURTEEN

Penetration and Encirclement, November 1942

Winter came to southern Russia. It snowed on the night of 18–19 November 1942, and the temperature fell to –18 degrees Celsius (0 degrees Fahrenheit). The snow, combined with early-morning fog, muffled sounds and concealed Red Army sappers clearing lanes through the minefields along the Don front. The same weather grounded German aircraft, depriving the defenders of their most effective weapon.[1]

RECONNAISSANCE PHASE

Contrary to most accounts, the Soviet attack did not come out of the blue on the morning of 19 November. Axis commanders had come to expect that, on the evening prior to a major Soviet offensive, the first echelon of Red rifle divisions would send out reinforced companies and battalions to locate the forward edge of the Axis defenses, as well as the enemy's main firing points. To confuse the defenders as to the timing and exact focus of the attack, this time the Red Army conducted frequent patrols as early as 10 November. The main probes began on the night of 14 November, six days prior to the offensive, and reconnoitered the entire front rather than simply the intended breakthrough zones.[2]

In the Serafimovich bridgehead, all four of 5th Tank Army's first-echelon rifle divisions launched reinforced battalions on the night of 17–18 November. Supported by dedicated artillery groups, these battalion task forces overcame the forward outposts of Romanian Third Army's 5th, 14th, and 9th Infantry Divisions. By the time the actual offensive began on 19 November, the Soviet rifle divisions had advanced up to 2 kilometers and were in contact with the main line of Romanian fortifications.[3]

This staggered reconnaissance phase had its drawbacks, of course. Soviet after-action critiques noted that the early probes permitted the Romanians to adjust their minefields and obstacles and to bring reinforcements forward in key sectors. The same actions prompted Army Group B headquarters to reposition XXXXVIII Panzer Corps for counterattack; 22nd Panzer and 1st Romanian Armored Divisions seriously impeded 5th Tank Army's offensive timetable, as we shall see. Moreover, the casualties suffered by the battalion

Table 14.1. Estimated Tactical Correlation of Infantry, Sappers, and
Armor in the Main Attack Sectors of Operation Uranus

Front/Army	Soviet	Romanian/German	Ratio
Southwestern Front			
5th Tank Army			
Personnel	80,000	40,000	2:1
Tanks	359	146	2.5:1
21st Army			
Personnel	70,000	22,800	3.1:1
Tanks	199	27°	7.4:1
Don Front			
65th Army			
Personnel	28,000	13,300	2.1:1
Tanks	49	28°	1.8:1
Stalingrad Front			
64th Army			
Personnel	20,000	7,700	2.6:1
Tanks	40	—	Absolute
57th Army			
Personnel	35,000	16,800	2.1:1
Tanks	225	59	3.8:1
51st Army			
Personnel	45,000	17,500	2.6:1
Tanks	207	—	Absolute

Source: For detailed calculations of these ratios, see David M. Glantz and Jonathan M. House, *Endgame at Stalingrad*, vol. 3 of *The Stalingrad Trilogy* (Lawrence: University Press of Kansas, 2014), book 1, 190–192.
Note: Personnel includes infantry and sappers.
°Half of 14th Panzer Division's strength of 55 operating tanks against each Soviet army.

task forces effectively weakened the combat power of their parent divisions during the actual assault. After the battle, therefore, the Red Army General Staff decided that, in the future, it would be preferable to begin the reconnaissance immediately prior to the offensive and to use companies rather than battalions for most such probes.[4]

SOUTHWESTERN AND DON FRONTS' OFFENSIVE, 19–20 NOVEMBER

Just before midnight on 18–19 November, Vatutin's Southwestern Front occupied its assault positions for the offensive in the Serafimovich bridgehead. The 47th Guards and 119th Rifle Divisions moved forward behind a security screen of 14th Guards Rifle Division, which had previously held this stretch of front. In total blackout conditions, both divisional and supporting RVGK (Reserve of the High Command) artillery occupied forward positions so that

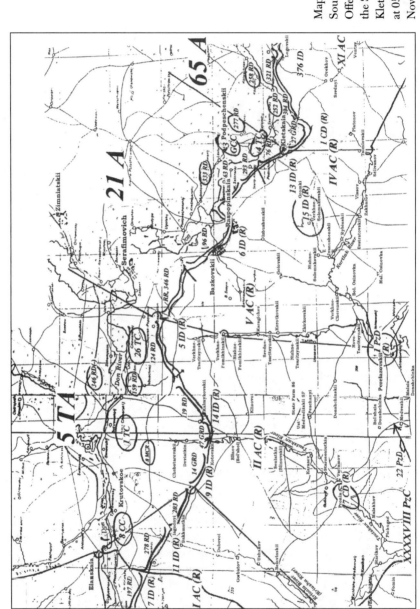

Map 65.
Southwestern Front's
Offensive Situation in
the Serafimovich and
Kletskaia Bridgeheads
at 0500 Hours, 19
November 1942

they could maximize their range in support of the coming attack. Protected by submachine gunners, sappers began to clear the remaining mines and obstacles to their front, while infantry support tanks (behind 47th Guards) and elements of 26th Tank Corps (behind 124th Rifle Division) edged into position. Echeloned behind these forces were the remainders of 1st and 26th Tank Corps, 8th Guards Motorcycle Regiment, and 8th Cavalry Corps. Crucially, however, 14th Guards and 119th Rifle Divisions had only tank destroyers, not tanks, supporting their attacks.

Fifty kilometers to the east, General Chistiakov's 21st Army made similar preparations in the Kletskaia Bridgehead. The 76th, 293rd, and 63rd Rifle Divisions, each supported by a separate tank regiment, occupied jump-off positions on a 12 kilometer stretch of front. Behind them, 4th Tank Corps arrayed its brigades in two columns, with the three divisions of 3rd Guards Cavalry Corps even farther to the rear. On Chistiakov's left flank, 304th Rifle and 27th Guards Rifle Divisions of Batov's 65th Army also moved forward; each division had a tank brigade in support, although Batov had no separate mobile exploitation force.

Not only had Romanian Third Army inherited these dangerous bridgeheads, but the terrain further hampered the defense. Beyond both bridgeheads, a series of parallel ridges and rivers running north-south, at a distance of 3 to 20 kilometers south of the Don River, provided the attackers with excellent avenues of approach while denying the Romanians observation over their entire front. The open, virtually treeless ground offered few defensible terrain features.

At 0730 hours (0530 hours Berlin time) on 19 November an impressive crash of *katiusha* rockets began an 80-minute artillery preparation along the entire 28 kilometers of penetration sector. Using the results of previous reconnaissance efforts, more than 3,500 guns, mortars, and rocket launchers fired at specific targets. After an hour of destructive fires aimed at key command, communication, and troop sites, the final 20 minutes were devoted to silencing any targets not yet identified. Although most of this artillery preparation fell on the main Romanian defensive belt, long-range artillery groups reached deeper into the rear. Fortunately for the defenders, the fog and low ceiling hampered artillery observation and prevented the scheduled attacks by 17th and 2nd Air Armies.

General Weichs at Army Group B promptly informed Zeitzler at OKH, asking permission to cease attacks inside Stalingrad and instead commit Heim's XXXXVIII Panzer Corps, then under Hitler's personal control, northeast toward Kletskaia against the developing attack.[5] As described in the previous chapter, however, Heim's force was far weaker than its name implied.

While the fire preparation was still under way, forward rifle battalions, accompanied by sappers and infantry support tanks, pushed to within 200 to

300 meters of the defenders' positions and began clearing passages through minefields and wire obstacles. Between 0848 and 0850 hours Moscow time, white-clad riflemen of the three Soviet attacking armies collided with the German and Romanian defenders. Lacking tanks and with few effective antitank weapons, the latter could offer little effective resistance. On the left wing of 5th Tank Army, Colonel A. I. Belov's 50th Guards Rifle Division and accompanying tanks tore a gaping hole in Romanian 5th Infantry Division's left wing by 1100 hours.[6] To Belov's right, Colonel I. Ia. Kulagin's 119th Rifle Division exploited its neighbor's success by thrusting due south, smashing the first defenses of Romanian 14th Infantry Division, even though Kulagin had no armor support.

To the west, however, Major General A. S. Griaznov's 14th Guards Rifle Division, attacking on a 4 kilometer wide sector just south of Kotovskii, barely dented the defending Romanian 9th Infantry Division. Without supporting tanks, Griaznov could make little headway. Across the front, Romanian resistance stiffened, indicating that the massive Red artillery preparation had been far less effective than planned. Fog and poor visibility prevented effective close air support, while slightly warmer temperatures meant that the attackers were churning up the unfrozen ground and thereby complicating movement. Overall, that morning the attacking rifle divisions of 5th Tank Army advanced only 2 to 3 kilometers, rather than the planned 15 to 18 kilometers.

Anxious to regain momentum before a German counterattack could materialize, Romanenko decided to unleash his two tank corps, even though the rifle divisions had yet to achieve a breakthrough. Throughout the war, this was often the most crucial decision for an attacking Soviet commander: committing his mobile forces early (as he did here) might well get them bogged down in the penetration battle rather than exploiting into the Axis rear. Yet, if Romanenko waited too long to release his mechanized forces, the defenders might repair their gaps and halt the entire attack.

In this instance, Romanenko judged the situation correctly, acting to thwart a muddled German counterattack. Unbeknownst to the Soviets, at 1150 General Heim received another order, originating with Hitler, directing him to wheel 22nd Panzer and Romanian 1st Armored Divisions 90 degrees to the left, heading for Blinovskii and Zhirkovskii, respectively—both of which were already well behind the Soviet front lines. Moreover, Heim had lost communications with the Romanian armored force, which continued on its northeastward march. The order also subordinated Romanian II Corps and its three infantry divisions to Heim's command, so that the German corps headquarters would control the entire penetration frontage.[7]

Acting on orders from Romanenko, at 1400 hours 1st and 26th Tank Corps entered the battle, passing through the rifle divisions of 5th Tank Army. East

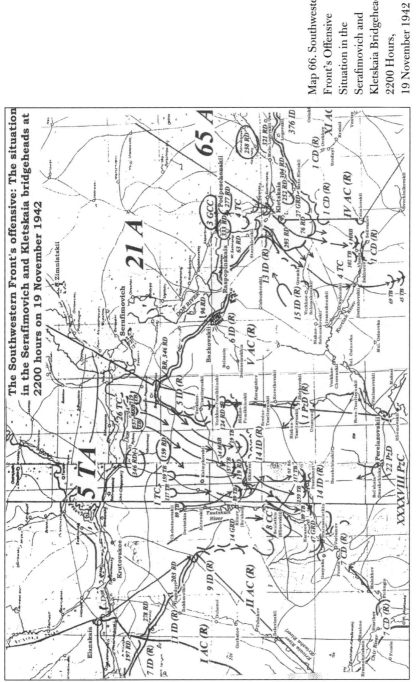

Map 66. Southwestern Front's Offensive Situation in the Serafimovich and Kletskaia Bridgeheads at 2200 Hours, 19 November 1942

of Bol'shoi, four tank brigades led this advance on a frontage of 20 kilometers, inspiring a "tank fright" that caused some Romanians to surrender and others to flee southward. Butkov's 1st Tank Corps rolled over much of Romanian 14th Infantry Division, and the neighboring 5th Infantry Division fared little better (see map 66). By nightfall, Butkov was 18 kilometers into the Romanian rear. A late-afternoon counterattack by Romanian 7th Cavalry Division and a portion of 22nd Panzer Division destroyed 17 tanks, temporarily halting 47th Guards Rifle Division and 5th Tank Army's separate 8th Motorcycle Regiment, but it could not fill the gap. Following closely behind 1st Tank Corps, Borisov's 8th Cavalry Corps helped eliminate Romanian strongpoints in a confused battle that night.[8]

To the east, the left wing of Romanian 5th Infantry Division and the right wing of 14th Infantry Division temporarily balked 26th Tank Corps, but Rodin sent his 157th Tank Brigade on an envelopment to the west that advanced 22 kilometers into the rear. Other brigades of 26th Tank Corps helped the assaulting rifle divisions reduce remaining strongpoints. Just before dark, a surprise raid by forward elements of this tank corps struck the headquarters of Romanian 1st Armored Division near Zhirkovskii, destroying the German liaison officer's radio and further disrupting any Axis counteraction.[9]

Simultaneously, General Chistiakov faced the same kind of decision as Romanenko. Attacking 35 to 50 kilometers northeast of 5th Tank Army, 21st Army achieved mixed results against the Romanians and the neighboring German XI Corps. Colonel N. T. Tavartkiladze's 76th Rifle Division penetrated 3 kilometers at the boundary between Romanian IV Corps' 13th Infantry and 1st Cavalry Divisions, while to Tavartkiladze's right, the experienced Colonel P. F. Lagutin's 293rd Rifle Division had even greater success. On the right wing of 21st Army, however, the other two assault divisions made little progress, prompting Chistiakov to commit the powerful 4th Tank Corps to finish the penetration.[10]

The Don Front commander, Rokossovsky, had gone to the forward observation post of the other attacking army, Batov's 65th, to observe the initial assault:

> Air Force General S. I. Rudenko was extremely put out. The massive air strikes provided for by the plan were ruled out by the bad weather. . . . The battlefield was obscured in dense mist, and optical instruments were of no avail. All we could see were the flashes of explosions lighting up the milky shroud. The guns rumbled ceaselessly. . . . A mighty "Hurrah" mingled with the grinding roar of the tanks. The assault had begun. We exchanged glances. Would we succeed in penetrating the enemy's fortifications? . . .
>
> Gradually the mist cleared and the battlefield came into sight. Through

field glasses I watched our troops storm the precipitous chalk hills in the Kletskaya area. I could see men clinging to ledges and climbing stubbornly. Many lost their hold and slid down, only to get up and start climbing again, helping each other up the steep slopes and rushing the enemy positions. The Nazis resisted desperately, but our infantry overcame them and drove them off the heights. The enemy's main line of defense began to show signs of cracking. The 65th Army kept pounding it steadily and pushing forward—with difficulty on the left flank, more successfully at the boundary with the 21st Army, on the right.[11]

This difference in success was not surprising, considering that 65th Army attacked at the boundary between Romanian IV Corps, on Rokossovsky's right, and German XI Corps, on his left. Batov's 304th and 321st Rifle Divisions encountered skillfully fortified German strongpoints to their front; on their left they faced counterattacks from 376th Infantry Division, supported later in the day by arriving elements of 14th Panzer Division. The same held true on the Don Front's left wing and center, where supporting attacks by Rokossovsky's 66th and 24th Armies met strong resistance from Sixth Army's XIV Panzer and VIII Army Corps.

Still, Chistiakov's commitment of 4th Tank and 3rd Guards Cavalry Corps achieved spectacular success on 19 November, threatening to split Romanian Third Army from German Sixth Army and drawing reserves away from the main attack sector of the Southwestern Front. The western column of Kravchenko's 4th Tank Corps, led by Colonel V. S. Agafonov's 69th Tank Brigade, cut rapidly through both the defenses of Romanian 13th Infantry Division and the redeploying Romanian 15th Division, which was the local reserve force. By 0100 on 20 November, Agafonov's column had advanced 35 kilometers, 20 kilometers ahead of the neighboring 102nd Tank Brigade. In the first day, Kravchenko had almost broken through the Axis defenses at a cost of 27 tanks.[12]

Moving behind Kravchenko's corps, General Pliev's 3rd Guards Cavalry Corps encountered numerous difficulties. Incessant German bombing raids destroyed 11 of the 12 pontoon bridges over the Don River in this sector, splitting his corps in half, with only 5th and 6th Guards Cavalry Divisions south of the river. The tank regiment and tank destroyer brigade that were supposed to join Pliev in the exploitation remained locked in battle supporting 76th and 293rd Rifle Divisions against remnants of Romanian 13th Infantry Division. Despite these problems and several Romanian minefields, by 1700, Pliev had all three of his divisions moving forward into the Kurtlak River Valley. After Pliev replaced the hesitant commander of 6th Guards Cavalry Division, that division reached Platonov by 2300 hours. There, in conjunction with a flank attack by 32nd Cavalry Division, 6th Guards eliminated two Romanian strongpoints in a fierce night fight; a few kilometers to the west, 5th Guards Cavalry Division was equally successful by 0700 on 20 November.[13]

The spectacular advance of Kravchenko's western column only confirmed the initial, erroneous German impression that the Kletskaia sector was the focal point of the offensive's main effort.[14] The unfortunate XXXXVIII Panzer Corps unintentionally contributed to this impression; although Hitler bitterly criticized General Heim, the corps commander, for his weak counterattacks, they had thrown 5th Tank Army off schedule and thereby obscured the threat to Sixth Army in Stalingrad. Not until 2130 that night did Army Group B express its alarm to Sixth Army headquarters, suggesting that Paulus erect a screening force to protect his supply routes.[15]

All day, Paulus and his staff had been troubled by the threat to their west. Disengaging 16th and 24th Panzer Divisions and other units from the city battle would take time. In the interim, the staff alerted *Kampfgruppe* Selle (91st *Flak* Regiment), Artillery Command (ARKO) 129, 403rd Security Division, and various alarm units to secure the main supply route.[16] Colonel Wilhelm Adam, Paulus's adjutant, asserts that he advocated an immediate withdrawal of the army to the southwest, but the general refused to violate his orders.[17] Late on the evening of 19–20 November, in response to instructions from Army Group B, Sixth Army ordered a series of troop movements on 20–21 November to deal with the undefined but growing threat. While 177th Assault Gun Battalion moved to support VIII Army Corps, 14th Panzer Division would concentrate on the western flank of XI Corps' 376th Infantry Division, around Verkhne-Buzinovka. XIV Panzer Corps, with 16th and 24th Panzer Divisions, would deploy westward into the Great Bend of the Don, on the southern flank of 14th Panzer. LI Army Corps' order implementing these redeployments recognized the obvious consequences, officially ending its assault on the Krasnyi Oktiabr' Factory.[18]

The first day of Operation Uranus was by no means a complete Soviet victory, however. Timely commitment of the weak XXXXVIII Panzer Corps and of Romanian 15th Infantry Division, together with stout resistance by other Romanian infantry units, had contained most of the attackers, especially the rifle forces of 21st and 65th Armies. The true Axis problem was a lack of operational reserves, giving the attackers time to exploit the situation before Paulus could redeploy his troops to the west. Overnight on 19–20 November, Vatutin and Rokossovsky formulated new missions for the next day. The rifle divisions of 5th Tank and 21st Armies would encircle the remainder of Romanian Third Army west of Perelazovskii, while the mobile forces of the two armies exploited southward. The 1st Tank and 8th Cavalry Corps would assist other rifle units in pushing XXXXVIII Panzer Corps southward. Meanwhile, 26th Tank and 4th Tank Corps, with 3rd Guards Cavalry Corps protecting the lengthening left flank of the advance, pushed southward to the Don at and north of Kalach.[19]

While Sixth Army began to redeploy its troops, Army Group B attempted to hold the front together with a patchwork of Axis units. General of Infantry Karl Hollidt, commander of German XVII Army Corps, moved his troops eastward from Italian Eighth Army's rear to join the battle; en route, he assumed operational control of Romanian I and II Corps.

Gradually, during the morning of 20 November, German Sixth Army headquarters pieced together an impression of the situation, but it took hours before the full magnitude of the threat was evident. For most of the day, 1st Tank Corps, 8th Motorcycle Regiment, and two divisions of 8th Cavalry Corps fought a bitter meeting engagement near the Ust'-Medveditskii State Farm, 18 to 22 kilometers northwest of Perelazovskii. The main opposition came from a *kampfgruppe* of 22nd Panzer Division, commanded by Colonel Hermann von Oppeln-Bronowski. With 30 tanks, one battalion of 129th Panzer-Grenadier Regiment, and some antitank and field artillery, this *kampfgruppe* fought so well that Butkov eventually turned this battle over to the two divisions of 8th Cavalry Corps, bypassing these defenders to refuel 1st Tank Corps and continue the advance.[20] At Romanenko's behest, Butkov also dispatched the motorcycle regiment eastward to prevent a Romanian breakout.

To the east, 26th Tank Corps had much better success on 20 November. At Perelazovskii, Major P. K. Makhur's 157th Tank Brigade captured the headquarters of Romanian V Corps so quickly that a German liaison officer who was looking for that headquarters reported to the staff of 26th Tank Corps by mistake.[21] These Soviet advances also ravaged the rear services of Romanian 1st Armored Division, leaving the combat echelons isolated northwest of Zhirkovskii. On instructions from XXXXVIII Panzer Corps, the Romanian tankers attempted to link up with 22nd Panzer Division. This effort cost 25 tanks to reach the Tsaritsa River at Sredne-Tsaritsynskii, but elements of 5th Guards Tank Army, including two rifle divisions and two brigades of 26th Tank Corps, halted the Romanians there.

Only one of Romanian Third Army's major headquarters—that of I Corps—remained intact by the second day of the offensive. Here, General Mihail Lascar, the able commander of 6th Infantry Division, assumed control of the Romanian 5th, 6th, and 15th Infantry Divisions, together with remnants of 13th and 14th Infantry. Hitler forbade any attempt by Lascar to break out, sacrificing the Romanians to delay the Soviets. Over the next two days, Lascar conducted an epic defense that thwarted Soviet efforts to create a complete breakthrough.[22] The combination of the Lascar Group and the disjoined elements of XXXXVIII Panzer Corps also stymied Butkov's 1st Tank Corps for several days; only 157th Tank and 14th Motorized Brigades of

Rodin's 26th Tank Corps were actually free to exploit south of Perelazovskii, while much of Rodin's command was still involved in clearing the area and dealing with Romanian 1st Armored.[23]

On the western flank of 5th Tank Army, General Leliushenko's newly formed 1st Guards Army had failed so completely in its initial attacks on 19 November that it was unable to resume the assault the next day. Pursuant to Vatutin's instructions, however, Leliushenko did not commit his 1st Guards Mechanized Corps, holding it in reserve until Operation Uranus could be expanded into Operation Saturn. This offensive sword remained in its sheath for the next several days.

Desperate counterattacks by Romanian I Corps' 9th and 11th Infantry Divisions, defending against the western wing of 5th Tank Army, forced Romanenko to commit his reserve 159th Rifle Division to this fight on 20 November. Aided by 8th Cavalry Corps' 21st Cavalry Division and a handful of tanks from 1st Tank Corps, the attackers west of Pronin finally pushed Romanian 7th Cavalry Division southward, which in turn prompted Romanian I Corps to withdraw as its right flank became exposed.

On the other flank of 5th Tank Army, General Chistiakov goaded his 21st Army forward on 20 November, seeking to break free of the defenders and reach the Don River before Sixth Army could redeploy westward. The seasoned General Kravchenko tried to consolidate the brigades of 4th Tank Corps, which on 20 November remained split, with one half 35 kilometers south of Kletskaia and the other half lagging behind around Evstratovskii and Platonov on the Kurtlak River. During the day, 76th Rifle Division, supported by 4th Motorized Rifle Brigade of Kravchenko's corps, finally dislodged Romanian 1st Cavalry Division and a *kampfgruppe* of 14th Panzer Division from their positions south of Platonov. By evening, all four of Kravchenko's brigades had reassembled near Mairovskii.[24] Thirty kilometers to the rear, 5th Guards Cavalry Division repelled an attempted breakout by Romanian 1st Cavalry Division, which retired to the east. The Romanian Voicu Detachment, composed of remnants of various divisions, also withdrew eastward to positions on the left flank of German XI Corps' 376th Infantry Division. Pliev's cavalry corps was thus free to move southward, protecting Kravchenko's lengthening left flank; en route, 5th Guards Cavalry Division repelled several battalion-sized Romanian and German attacks.[25] During the night of 20–21 November, Pliev's three cavalry divisions reunited and prepared to seize a German strongpoint at Verkhne-Buzinovka, hoping thereby to turn the left flank of German XI Army Corps.

Batov's 65th Army had barely dented the defenses of Sixth Army's XI Corps on 19 November, but the general spent that night preparing to exploit a minor penetration on the high ground west of Orekhovskii. He improvised a mobile group under Colonel G. I. Anisimov consisting of 45 tanks from 91st

Tank Brigade, four rifle battalions loaded in trucks, and some towed artillery. At dawn, a diversionary attack by two rifle divisions on Batov's west wing and center attempted to distract Axis reserves; following this, Colonel Z. S. Shekhtman's fresh 252nd Rifle Division advanced at the boundary between Romanian 1st Cavalry and German 376th Infantry Divisions, penetrating two lines of Romanian defenses near Orekhovskii. Shortly after noon on 20 November, Anisimov's mobile group passed through Shekhtman's riflemen and by nightfall was 23 kilometers into the Axis rear, spreading confusion and panic among support units there.[26]

In response to the growing threat, at 1445 hours on 20 November Paulus sent a message confirming his previous decision to move General Hube's XIV Panzer Corps westward. Seydlitz's LI Corps now had to assume control of the entire northern portion of Stalingrad while Hube organized a defense of Sixth Army's western flank, including the railroad line on which the entire army depended. To accomplish this, Hube received control of 16th and 24th Panzer Divisions, 295th and 389th Antitank Battalions, 244th Assault Gun Battalion, and 129th HARKO.[27] He already controlled 14th Panzer Division (reinforced by one regiment each from 44th and 384th Infantry Divisions) and 3rd Motorized Division. In reality, these divisions were mere shadows of their authorized strength, each often consisting of *kampfgruppen* built around 30 to 35 tanks. North of Hube's corps, XI Army Corps struggled to both defend its sector and send reinforcements to the hard-pressed Romanian 1st Cavalry Division.

Thus, contrary to most accounts, the combined efforts of XXXXVIII Panzer Corps and Romanian Third Army generally limited the success of the Soviet offensive during its first two days. Moreover, 17th and 16th Air Armies failed to provide effective air support to the advancing forces, while the *Luftwaffe* seemed to operate with impunity against the mobile groups of 5th Tank and 21st Armies.

STALINGRAD FRONT'S OFFENSIVE, 20 NOVEMBER

The attack by Eremenko's Stalingrad Front on 20 November made the Axis situation, already threatened by the Southwestern and Don Fronts, catastrophic. General Hoth's Fourth Panzer Army totaled approximately 110,000 men, primarily in three weak formations: German IV Army Corps (German 371st and 297th Infantry and Romanian 20th Infantry Divisions), Romanian VI Corps (Romanian 2nd, 18th, 1st, and 4th Infantry Divisions), and Romanian VII Corps (Romanian 5th and 8th Cavalry Divisions). Only the German corps had frontages sufficiently narrow for a continuous defense opposite the Soviet Beketovka bridgehead, whereas the Romanians were spread so thinly that they had to leave sizable gaps between strongpoints. German 16th Motorized Division screened the long southern flank of this force, with 29th Motorized Division as the sole army-level reserve.

Eremenko's 64th, 57th, and 51st Armies would attack on a frontage of 65 kilometers, outnumbering the defenders two to one in infantry and eight to one in armor. For the Axis, the only saving grace was that the Soviets had great difficulty moving their additional troops across the ice-choked Volga prior to their scheduled offensive. Roughly one-third of 13th Tank Corps, including many of its trucks, had not crossed the river in time, hindering the corps' operations when it encountered 29th Motorized Division on the afternoon of 20 November.

Shortly before dawn that morning, a cold front brought showers, snow, and dense ground fog to the Stalingrad Front, hampering both air operations and artillery adjustment. As a result, only General Trufanov's 51st Army was able to begin its attack on schedule at 0730. Eremenko twice delayed the attack of 57th Army, which did not commence its artillery preparation until 1000 hours. General Shumilov's 64th Army was even more tardy, beginning its bombardment at 1420 hours.[28] The resulting artillery preparations, ranging from 40 to 75 minutes, were aimed only against preplanned targets, limiting their effectiveness. Similarly, 8th Air Army was unable to support the attack, an absence that was sorely felt by 13th Tank Corps later in the day. Still, the initial infantry attacks succeeded in most areas, permitting 51st and 57th Armies to commit their mobile groups as planned at about midday.

The one failure was in 64th Army's sector, where 157th, 38th, and 204th Rifle Divisions, supported by 40 tanks from two brigades, struck German IV Corps at and south of the town of Elkhi. The attackers penetrated the positions of Romanian 20th Infantry Division with relative ease, but the German 297th Infantry Division's 523rd Regiment permitted only a minimal advance by 204th Rifle Division.[29]

In 57th Army's sector, 422nd and 169th Rifle Divisions, together with 143rd Rifle Brigade, attacked on a frontage only 8 kilometers wide on the southern bank of the Chervlenaia River. In addition to two supporting tank brigades, 176th Separate Tank Regiment of 13th Tank Corps aided the assault, in violation of doctrine.[30] The understrength Romanian 2nd Infantry Division succumbed to tank fright, allowing the two rifle divisions to advance up to 8 kilometers by midafternoon. On 57th Army's left wing, 143rd Rifle Brigade penetrated on the boundary of Romanian 2nd and 18th Infantry Divisions. It then wheeled southward to meet a matching pincer conducted by 51st Army's 15th Guards Rifle Division. These pincers linked up 12 kilometers west of Lake Sarpa, trapping much of Romanian 2nd Infantry Division as well as one regiment of 18th Infantry.

Despite this initial success, the delays in movement of 13th Tank Corps,

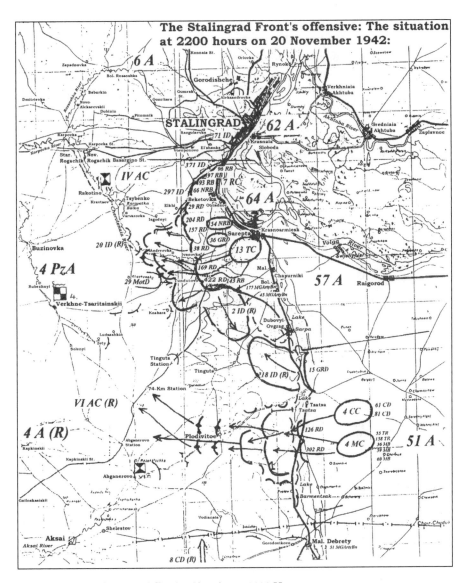

Map 67. Stalingrad Front's Offensive Situation at 2200 Hours,
20 November 1942

together with the diversion of one of its tank regiments, meant that Tanaschishin's powerful mobile force actually deployed only 78 tanks, with six to ten riflemen riding on each vehicle. Deprived of their trucks, the rest of the corps' infantrymen had to advance on foot, lagging far behind the armored spearhead. The corps became overextended, with poor radio communications between brigades. One rifle battalion of 62nd Mechanized Brigade lost its bearings during the night of 20–21 November and wandered south into the sector of 4th Mechanized Corps, rather than following 163rd Tank Regiment westward.

This dispersed deployment of 13th Tank Corps offered a rare opportunity for Lieutenant General Hans-Georg Leyser's 29th Motorized Division, which had been in an assembly area south of Karpovka, preparing to conduct a field exercise, when the offensive began. The 29th was at almost full strength, including 59 tanks (7 Panzer IIs, 32 Panzer IIIs, 18 Panzer IVs, and 2 command tanks). At 1030 on 20 November Hoth instructed Leyser to strike the advancing Soviet mobile forces on their left flank as they approached Nariman. The 29th Motorized engaged, in succession, the lead elements of 57th Army's 169th Rifle Division and 90th Tank Brigade, then 13th Tank Corps' 62nd Motorized Brigade and accompanying 163rd Tank Regiment. Unfortunately for the Soviets, most of their tank companies were still in march column rather than on line when they encountered the Germans. Leyser's division defeated the first element and decimated the second. In a separate incident, 176th Tank Regiment, supporting 422nd Rifle Division, stumbled into a Romanian minefield and lost 22 of its 28 tanks. During the night of 20–21 November the German motorized division caused further damage; when it was recalled northward early on 21 November, it launched a final counterattack en route, stabilizing the position of the beleaguered Romanian 20th Infantry Division. Soviet accounts tend to minimize the effect of Leyser's division, whose remarkable success was in fact short-lived. These sharp encounters certainly weakened and slowed 13th Tank Corps but did not change the operational outcome.[31]

In the lakes region assigned to 51st Army, General Trufanov had staggered his attacks to conceal his main effort. On his right, between Lakes Sarpa and Tsatsa, 15th Guards Rifle Division with a supporting tank battalion attacked on schedule at 0830, easily penetrating two battalions of Romanian 18th Infantry Division. Following this, as already recounted, the attack swung northward and linked up with 143rd Rifle Brigade of the neighboring 57th Army. At 0845 the left wing of 51st Army, consisting of 302nd and 126th Rifle Divisions, attacked several strongpoints of Romanian 1st Infantry Division. In yet another violation of doctrine, Trufanov ordered General Vol'sky's 4th Mechanized Corps to commit 55th and 158th Tank Regiments to support the two assault divisions. Given the thinly dispersed Axis defenses, this early commitment proved successful in helping to overcome the only substantial resistance—a strongpoint held by a reserve Romanian battalion and two batteries of 88mm German guns—by 1120. At the same time, Trufanov ordered Vol'sky's corps to assume the main effort, but an inexperienced staff, insufficient road network, and Romanian mines delayed the actual attack until 1300. Moreover, 4th Mechanized Corps had transferred 150 trucks to hasten the rifle divisions' advance, forcing many of the "motorized" rifle units to advance on foot or on tank decks. Khrushchev, the *front* commissar, was observing 57th Army's attack and personally castigated one hapless brigade commander for this delay.[32]

The mechanized corps therefore began its attack late and then had to deal with multiple Romanian minefields as well as *balkas* that obstructed its advance. Late that evening, the corps' 36th Mechanized Brigade and 26th Tank Regiment overcame intense resistance at Plodovitoe, finally capturing the town from the reconnaissance and engineer battalions of Romanian 18th Division, again supported by German 88mm guns. These accumulated mishaps meant that Vol'sky was well short of his assigned objective for the first day, Verkhne-Tsaritsynskii, which lay another 48 kilometers to the northwest. Trufanov did, however, prod Vol'sky into sending 59th and 60th Mechanized Brigades, with their supporting tank regiments, to bypass Plodovitoe. Moving all night, these brigades overcame scattered Romanian elements and captured two railroad stations, cutting the only rail line north to Stalingrad.[33] By 21 November, Romanian VI Army Corps had ceased to exist, and Vol'sky was free to exploit into the enemy rear.

Far to the south, General Gerasimenko's small 28th Army was having troubles in the region west of Astrakhan'. On 18 November a *kampfgruppe* of German 16th Motorized Division destroyed a battalion-sized forward detachment of 152nd Separate Rifle Brigade that was trying to seize a German airfield at Utta; only four Red soldiers survived. When the main advance began on 20 November, the German 60th Motorized Regiment delayed 34th Guards Rifle Division for 24 hours at Khulkhuta. The defenders then withdrew in good order, having inflicted 1,480 killed and wounded on 34th Guards. Only then could the attackers advance on Elista.[34] By 21 November, after an inauspicious start, the Stalingrad Front was moving to complete the encirclement of Sixth Army.

GERMAN DILEMMAS, 21–22 NOVEMBER

That same morning, Paulus recognized that 21st Army's advance threatened his own headquarters and directed Sixth Army's staff to relocate from Golubinskii, 20 kilometers north of Kalach, to Nizhne-Chirskaia, just south of the confluence of the Don and Chir Rivers. He had already selected Nizhne-Chirskaia as a winter headquarters because of its excellent communications facilities. The withdrawal from Golubinskii had the appearance of a rout, with the hasty burning of classified documents and Paulus and his chief of staff departing by *Storch* liaison aircraft.[35] To avoid the advance of 51st Army, Hoth also moved Fourth Panzer Army headquarters first to Buzinovka and then to Nizhne-Chirskaia. Thus, during the critical period of 21–22 November, the senior German headquarters were in transit by road, out of operation, and dodging rumored Soviet spearheads en route.

Having centralized authority in himself, Hitler had to make critical decisions at a time when he was traveling by train, away from both his east Prussian and Ukrainian headquarters. Indeed, critics have argued that his previous micromanagement had encouraged a sense of passivity among field commanders. This meant that Generals Jodl and Keitel, the senior officers of the OKW, now had to advise the dictator on matters normally handled by the OKH staff. These two men had no sense of the fragility of Army Group B, and their first solutions were totally inadequate to the scale of the threat. Moreover, in mid-November the Germans were in the process of shipping their available strategic reserves to northwestern Africa, responding to the American-British landings there. This not only distracted the OKW staff but also tied up scarce airlift assets that the Germans would need in the East.

On 20 November Hitler reacted intelligently to the crisis, placing Field Marshal von Manstein, the victor of the Crimea, in charge of a new Army Group Don to control the entire threatened sector, including Sixth, Fourth Panzer, and Romanian Third Armies. Initially, however, Manstein had no maneuver units, and only his Eleventh Army staff was available to form a new headquarters; Weichs therefore remained in charge for several more days.[36]

North of the threatened area, General Weichs and Army Group B retained control of German Second, Hungarian Second, and Italian Eighth Armies. Before Manstein assumed control, Weichs directed German IV Army Corps and 29th Motorized Division to withdraw northward and protect the southern flank of the emerging pocket. Also on the twentieth, Hitler inquired as to the possibility of the *Luftwaffe* resupplying the encircled Sixth Army for a (supposedly brief) time until Manstein could relieve the siege. Hermann Göring, titular head of the *Luftwaffe*, was in Germany chairing a petroleum conference. Thus, contrary to legend, it was not Göring but Colonel General Hans Jeshonnek, Göring's chief of staff and a trained General Staff officer, who answered the question in the affirmative. As a precedent, Jeshonnek cited the aerial resupply of the encircled II Army Corps at Demiansk during the previous winter, even though the *Luftwaffe* had barely succeeded in supplying the 100,000 men at Demiansk, which was only one-third the size of the emerging Stalingrad pocket. After offering this rash promise, Jeshonnek did a rough calculation of the supplies required and consulted the commander of Fourth Air Fleet, General von Richthofen. Richthofen convinced Jeshonnek that the task was impossible, but Hitler would not listen to second guesses. When Göring met Hitler on 22 November, he felt compelled to promise that the *Luftwaffe*, often portrayed as a more "National Socialist" force than the army, would fulfill the manifestly impossible task of aerial resupply.[37]

On 21 November Paulus and Weichs requested permission to withdraw from the Volga River to avoid encirclement. Based on Jeshonnek's response, however, Hitler flatly refused. Bypassing Army Groups B and Don, Hitler had the OKH radio the following message to Paulus: "Führer Decision: Sixth Army will hold rail line open as long as possible in spite of danger of temporary encirclement. Orders for supply by air will follow."[38] As army chief of staff, Zeitzler tried in vain to dissuade the dictator; both Zeitzler and Manstein believed that only an immediate breakout would save Sixth Army. Meanwhile, Paulus, a loyal and successful officer of the Third Reich, hesitated to disagree. He had been under enormous nervous strain since May. Now, faced with encirclement, he apparently concluded that if he withdrew without permission, Hitler would relieve him and countermand the order.[39]

The Lascar Group was equally imperiled. Lieutenant General Ilie Steflea, chief of the Royal Romanian Army General Staff, joined with General Dumitrescu, commander of Third Army, in asking that Lascar be permitted to break out. General Weichs could only repeat Hitler's stand-fast order, sacrificing the Romanians for the survival of other Axis forces. When, late on 22 November, the Romanians secretly instructed Lascar to prepare for a breakout to the southwest, Weichs partially relented, giving XXXXVIII Panzer Corps an unrealistic order to fight its way toward Chernyshevskaia to assist in the escape.[40]

EXPLOITATION BY SOUTHWESTERN AND DON FRONTS

The resistance offered by XXXXVIII Panzer Corps and Romanian Third Army had put the western pincer of Uranus 36 hours behind schedule. Until 22 November, the rifle divisions of 5th Tank and 21st Armies struggled to reduce the Lascar Group in the area southwest of Raspopinskaia. Stalin and the *Stavka* pressed the *fronts* involved to accelerate the advance of their mobile corps before Sixth Army could reorient its forces westward.[41] Butkov's 1st Tank Corps finally disengaged from Oppeln-Bronowski's *kampfgruppe* of 22nd Panzer Division on 21 November and sped to the southeast. By the end of the day, however, Butkov had advanced only 66 kilometers since the offensive began and was still at least 70 kilometers short of Kalach-on-the-Don. Behind him, 8th Cavalry Corps' 55th and 112th Cavalry Divisions, reinforced by a separate tank

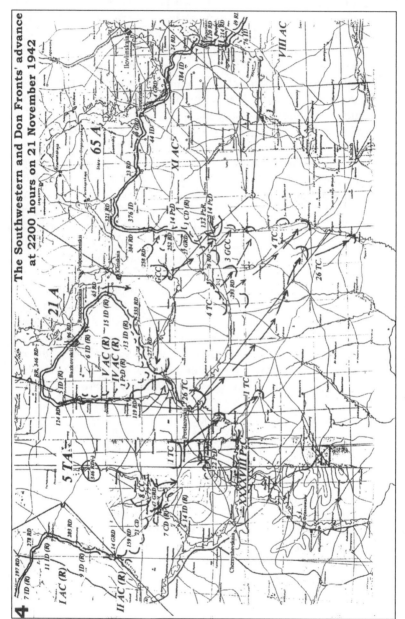

Map 68. Southwestern and Don Fronts' Advance at 2200 Hours, 21 November 1942

battalion, became entangled with the almost tankless remnants of 22nd Panzer Division northwest of Bol'shaia Donshchinka. This struggle dragged on well into the evening of 21 November, preventing both Germans and Soviets from moving eastward.[42]

In the meantime, Rodin's 26th Tank Corps had made good progress, scattering various Romanian elements en route to the town of Ostrov, just 25 kilometers west-northwest of Kalach.[43] Unbeknownst to Rodin, however, his spearheads were about to encounter the leading *kampfgruppen* of XIV Panzer Corps' 14th and 24th Panzer Divisions as the latter moved to establish a defensive line west of Stalingrad.

In 21st Army's sector, four rifle divisions helped form the eastern portion of the pocket around the Lascar Group, while Chistiakov, like Romanenko, urged his mobile corps onward to the southeast. Because it was traveling a shorter distance and had achieved greater success during the initial assault, Kravchenko's 4th Tank Corps encountered elements of XIV Panzer Corps earlier than did the mobile forces of 5th Tank Army. Lacking time to establish a coherent defense, however, the leading elements of 24th Panzer Division had to give way to Kravchenko's four brigades, which were 20 kilometers north-northwest of Kalach by the late afternoon of 21 November. Encountering almost no resistance, Kravchenko's troops passed within 15 kilometers of German Sixth Army's headquarters at Golobinskii. In the process, the Soviet tankers lost only 16 tanks (3 KV, 3 T-34, and 10 T-70) and captured an airfield and various warehouses.[44]

To Kravchenko's right rear, Pliev's 3rd Guards Cavalry Corps initially made equal progress, despite casualties inflicted by German air strikes. At 1130 elements of 24th Panzer Division counterattacked 5th Guards Cavalry Division, but that division seized and held Sukhanov overnight. The corps' other two divisions, 6th Guards and 32nd Cavalry, had less success against 14th Panzer Division at Verkhne-Buzinovka. Pliev therefore left a weak screen in front of the Germans, sidestepped to the east, and advanced another 10 kilometers closer to the Don.[45]

Between their two corps, Kravchenko and Pliev had preempted Paulus's plan for XIV Panzer Corps to launch a concerted attack to foil the developing Soviet penetration. Moreover, once Group Lascar was encircled, Chistiakov felt free to send three of his rifle divisions—76th, 293rd, and 277th—south to reinforce the mobile forces' advance and help seal the developing pocket. Chistiakov also found trucks to mount about one-quarter of this force.

To the east, Batov's 65th Army continued its costly role of keeping Sixth Army's LI Corps tied down by frontal assaults. Although reinforced by 177th Assault Gun Battalion, a regiment of 44th Infantry Division, and most of Romanian 1st Cavalry Division, the German 376th Infantry Division gradually gave ground on its left, where Colonel Anisimov's improvised mobile group

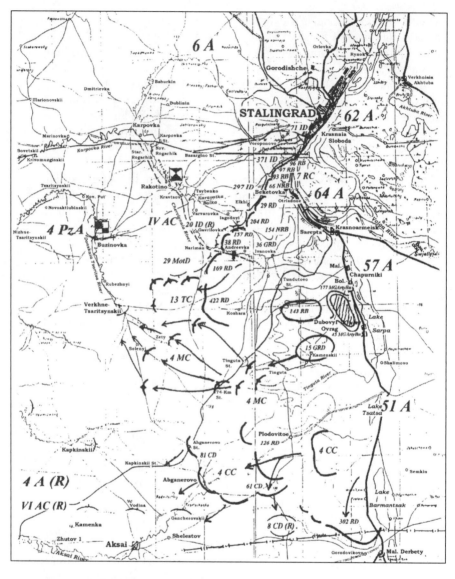

Map 69. Stalingrad Front's Offensive Situation at 2200 Hours, 21 November 1942

had pushed through the previous day. By the next morning, the Romanian cavalry was pushed off the high ground east of Orekhovskii.[46]

STALINGRAD FRONT'S OFFENSIVE, 21 NOVEMBER

Although the German 29th Motorized Division withdrew northwestward to join Paulus, its rearguard elements, as well as the damage it had previously inflicted on 13th Tank Corps, slowed the latter's movements on the twenty-first.[47] Still, by the end of the day, 57th Army had advanced sufficiently so that it threatened to outflank 29th Motorized, prompting German IV Corps to order General Leyser to accelerate his movement northwestward. Farther south, General Vol'sky's 4th Mechanized Corps traveled a greater distance on 21 November, once again forcing Fourth Panzer Army headquarters to displace northward, this time to Paulus's preferred location at Nizhne-Chirskaia. Vol'sky encountered little organized resistance, although 4th Cavalry Corps, assigned to protect his flank and eventually help form the outer front of the growing encirclement, had more difficulty. Closely supervised by General M. M. Popov, deputy commander of 51st Army, this corps seized Abganerovo with one division while attempting to outflank Romanian 4th Infantry Division with another. The lightly equipped cavalrymen awaited the arrival of 126th Rifle Division, assigned to reinforce them on the outer encirclement. The rapid advance by 57th and 51st Armies on 21 November surrounded the remnants of Romanian 2nd and 18th Infantry Divisions and overran Romanian logistical elements, leaving the remaining Axis units short of fuel and ammunition.

On the second day of the offensive for the southern pincer, 64th Army made almost no progress against the well-prepared infantry of German IV Corps. On the afternoon of 21 November General Chuikov attempted to fulfill the offensive mission of 62nd Army by having 284th Rifle Division and part of 92nd Rifle Brigade assault the positions of 100th *Jäger* Division on Mamaev Kurgan. The threadbare Soviet forces made only minor gains, prompting Chuikov to direct his units to resort to local attacks in an effort to tie down their opponents.[48] Despite the redeployment of the mobile units of Sixth Army away from the city, 62nd Army had little success even in that limited goal. After barely outlasting the prolonged German assault, the defenders of Stalingrad could do no more for the immediate future; renewed local attacks on the twenty-second, especially around Rynok and Mamaev Kurgan, made no progress.

Far to the south, in 28th Army's sector, 16th Motorized Division's 60th Panzer-Grenadier Regiment successfully broke contact and withdrew from Khulkhuta in the early hours of 21 November. Diversionary counterattacks concealed this withdrawal from 34th Guards Rifle Division, which did not occupy the town until 1000 hours. Once the Soviets realized the situation, 152nd Rifle Brigade began the pursuit, advancing westward on Utta.[49] Late that afternoon, 16th Motorized Division received a message subordinating it directly to Hoth's Fourth Panzer Army.[50] Although its screening mission did not change, the 16th was henceforth closely tied to Hoth's efforts to create a coherent front southwest of Stalingrad in preparation to relieve Sixth Army.

Hoth also received control of surviving Romanian units in the south, although only 4th Infantry, 5th Cavalry, and 8th Cavalry Divisions, together with one regiment of the Romanian 1st Infantry Division, remained relatively intact. The cavalry was deployed in screening positions from south of Abganerovo leading northward, but it could do little to stem the Soviet exploitation.

Thus, by the end of 21 November, the two Soviet pincers were within 80 kilometers of each other and closing fast. Preventing their linkup depended on XIV Panzer Corps' ability to deploy sufficient forces into this gap and halt the advance.

SOUTHWESTERN AND DON FRONTS' OFFENSIVE, 22 NOVEMBER

Overnight on 21–22 November, General Vatutin and his subordinate field army commanders assigned new missions to complete the primary goal of Operation Uranus: the encirclement of German Sixth Army. The mobile corps of 5th Tank and 21st Armies were to reach and cross the Don River, seizing Kalach and advancing across the Chir River to capture Bokovskaia, Chernyshevskaia, Oblivskaia, and Surovikino. At the same time, Rokossovsky's Don Front would expand the offensive to the southeast, sending 65th Army toward Vertiachii, while 24th Army destroyed Sixth Army's XI Army Corps at the northern edge of the Don River's Great Bend.[51]

Having left 216th Tank Brigade far in the rear to help defeat the Romanians, General Rodin now believed that the remaining three brigades of 26th Tank Corps were on the verge of victory. He therefore ordered Lieutenant Colonel G. N. Filippov, commander of 14th Rifle Brigade, to form a forward detachment that would seize the Kalach River crossings to preempt any German efforts at an organized defense. With two motorized rifle companies of his brigade, plus armored cars from a separate reconnaissance battalion, Filippov left the town of Ostrov, 23 kilometers northwest of Kalach, at 0300 on 22 November. Once he reached Kalach, a T-34 company from 157th Tank Brigade joined him, having also bypassed German resistance.[52]

At Kalach, the German area commander, Colonel Hans Mikosch, had

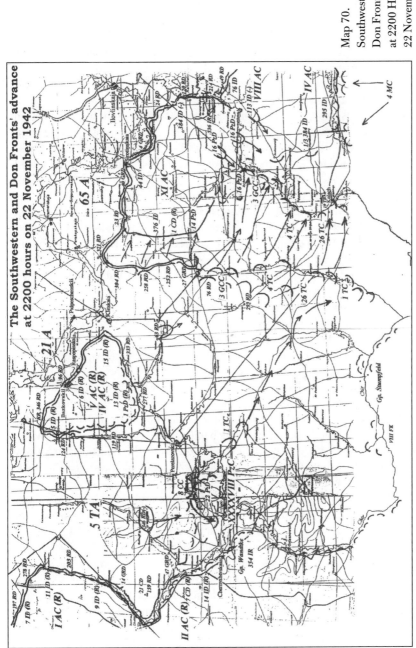

Map 70.
Southwestern and
Don Fronts' Advance
at 2200 Hours,
22 November 1942

organized the personnel of various military schools and logistical elements to defend the high ground on the eastern bank of the Don River, opposite Kalach itself, and the bridge had been prepared for demolition. Aided by information from local inhabitants, however, Filippov seized newly erected German bridges that connected the near shore to an island in the ice-choked Don River at Berezovskii, 4 kilometers north of Kalach. While one tank crossed the ice to the island, Filippov sent the remainder of his detachment in a tight column across the bridges. The German sentries, who apparently believed that the T-34s were captured vehicles, allowed this column to get too close; the Soviet soldiers overran the island and disarmed the explosive charges and nearby mines.[53] Lacking radio contact with higher headquarters, the Soviet detachment had to defend its prize for 11 hours before other troops arrived. This single stroke deprived the Germans of the obstacle value of the Don River, which might have delayed the encirclement for several days.

The remainder of 26th Tank Corps closed up along the Don River by the end of 22 November, having encountered growing resistance from Romanian troops and lead elements of 16th Panzer Division. Rodin arrived at the captured bridge late in the day and ordered Filippov, in overall command of 19th Tank and 24th Motorized Rifle Brigades, to seize Kalach itself the next morning.

Butkov's 1st Tank Corps, far to the west, moved southwestward into the Kurtlak River Valley, where it scattered the remaining rear-service elements of Romanian 1st Armored and German 22nd Panzer Divisions. Then it did an abrupt about-face, speeding up to 80 kilometers southeastward to seize bridges on the lower Liska River. Thus, at the end of the fourth day of the offensive, Butkov finally reached his objectives for the second day.[54] The cost of this belated success was significant: by nightfall on 22 November, only 24 of Butkov's original 136 tanks were still running. German air strikes, the fight with 22nd Panzer Division, and mechanical failures accounted for roughly equal numbers of the 112 missing vehicles. Until the Southwestern Front reequipped 1st Tank Corps in early December, it would have little ability to continue its mission across the Chir River.

Finally, Romanenko dispatched 5th Tank Army's 8th Motorcycle Regiment early on 22 November with orders to seize the town of Oblivskaia on the Chir River. The motorcycles infiltrated into the Axis rear, divided into five detachments, and created confusion and panic in Romanian Third Army's rear area. However, they failed in their basic mission of taking Oblivskaia.[55]

Far to the rear of the tank corps, the remaining elements of XXXXVIII Panzer Corps also continued to inflict losses on the Soviets. On 22 November Major General Radu Gheorghe's Romanian 1st Armored Division attempted to break out to the southwest. With a force of roughly 20 R-2 light tanks (the Romanian version of the Czech 35[t]) and 220 trucks, Gheorghe achieved initial surprise and thrust into the rear areas of 8th Cavalry Corps, about 8 kilometers east of Peschanyi. The two sides differ as to ensuing events. Soviet accounts assert that 55th Cavalry Division blocked the Romanian armor while inflicting heavy casualties, yet the bulk of Gheorghe's troops apparently escaped southward into the Kurtlak River Valley and seized the town of Petrovka.[56] In any event, the Romanians failed to link up with 22nd Panzer Division, which remained almost tankless and loosely encircled northeast of Medvezhyi.[57]

That day proved decisive for the Lascar Group, however. The Romanians had rejected several Soviet demands for surrender, but they lacked effective antitank weapons and were running low on food and ammunition. Lascar planned to attempt a breakout on the night of 22 November, but persistent attacks by 5th Tank Army's 50th Guards and 119th Rifle Divisions, aided by 63rd Rifle Division of 21st Army, collapsed the defense and split it in two. The Soviet seizure of Golovskii at about 2100 hours destroyed Romanian communications and, with it, all hope of an organized defense.[58] General Lascar, captured while trying to escape, survived captivity to serve as defense minister in the postwar pro-Communist government. Germany recognized Lascar's gallantry by making him the first foreign recipient of the Knight's Cross of the Iron Cross with oak leaves.[59] Despite this, the Romanians were bitter about the sacrifice Germany had demanded of them.

In 21st Army's sector, Kravchenko's 4th Tank Corps bloodied the leading *kampfgruppen* of 24th and 16th Panzer Divisions near the Krasnyi Skotovod (Red cattle breeder) State Farm and Lipo-Logovskii, respectively. Although 24th Panzer put up a stiff fight, both German elements found themselves forced backward to the east, having lost a number of tanks.[60] In the same manner as Rodin in 26th Tank Corps, Kravchenko dispatched Lieutenant Colonel P. K. Zhidkov's 45th Tank Brigade as a forward detachment to secure a bridgehead over the Don. Zhidkov crossed the river at an intact bridge near Rubezhnyi, 8 kilometers north of Kalach, and established contact with 26th Tank Corps' 157th Tank Brigade before laagering for the night.[61] To Kravchenko's east, Pliev's 3rd Guards Cavalry Corps also reached the right bank of the Don on a front some 22 to 28 kilometers north of Kalach. En route, however, the lightly equipped 6th Guards and 32nd Cavalry Divisions had more difficulty than the neighboring tankers in dealing with 16th Panzer Division's developing defenses at Evlampievskii.[62]

Behind Kravchenko and Pliev's mobile forces, some rifle divisions of 21st Army helped reduce the Lascar encirclement, while other rifle units marched southward, eliminating bypassed Romanian units as they went.

On the left wing of Leliushenko's 1st Guards Army, 203rd and 278th Rifle Divisions finally made progress westward. Cooperating with the neighboring 14th Guards Division of 5th Tank Army, these two divisions penetrated Romanian 9th and 11th Infantry Divisions. By the end of the day, they had occupied several towns on the Krivaia River, 25 to 45 kilometers north-northeast of Bokovskaia. Quite apart from their tactical progress, this advance threatened to preempt the efforts of General Hollidt's XVII Army Corps, which was supposed to organize a Romanian-German defense in the Bokovskaia area.[63]

By the end of 22 November, the decimated Romanian Third Army was trying to reconstruct a coherent defense. Its I Corps, with the relatively intact 11th and 9th Infantry Divisions, anchored the army's left wing along the Krivaia River, while the remnants of II Corps' 14th Infantry and 7th Cavalry Divisions were trying to defend the Chir River line from Bokovskaia south to Chernyshevskaia. South of the latter town, the only remaining forces available to help Romanian V Corps hold the western bank of the Chir were some rear-service units, reinforced by German rear-area security troops and hastily assembled alarm units. Group Hollidt, built around XVII Army Corps and its German 62nd and 294th Infantry Divisions, was about to assume control of Romanian I and II Corps in their current positions. General Weichs also directed Romanian Third Army to use the remnants of IV and V Corps, reinforced by German security and alarm units, as well as *Luftwaffe* antiaircraft elements, to hold the Chir River from Oblivskaia eastward to the junction with the Don. In particular, the Axis needed to defend a bridgehead over the Don at Rychkovskii, which was the best base of operations to reinforce Sixth Army from the west. Weichs also passed on Hitler's instructions that Sixth Army must hold its positions west of Kalach as long as possible, even though three Red tank corps were already east of that point.[64]

On the morning of 22 November a second army subordinate to the Don Front—Galinin's 24th—joined the Uranus offensive. With the experienced but bloodied 16th Tank Corps as its mobile group, 24th Army was supposed to attack southward from the Panshino region to link up with 21st Army's mobile corps, thereby encircling General Strecker's XI Army Corps. Galinin's initial attack lacked the combat power to dent the defenders, but it did attract German reserves needed elsewhere.[65]

The 65th Army was already making progress as the western pincer of this projected encirclement. In the course of the day, the rifle units of Batov's army forced Strecker's reinforced 376th Infantry Division to abandon Logovskii, while 14th Panzer Division found itself pushed out of Verkhne-Buzinovka and Os'kinskii. These withdrawals, in conjunction with XIV Panzer Corps' more serious setbacks, prompted General Paulus to pull both corps backward toward Stalingrad. Reporting to Army Group B, Sixth Army headquarters expressed doubt that it could stabilize even this new line, since the Don River was frozen sufficiently for foot crossing.[66] Further penetrations by 26th and 4th Tank Corps the next day also forced the Germans to pull XI Army Corps back.

STALINGRAD FRONT'S OFFENSIVE, 22 NOVEMBER

By this point, Eremenko's Stalingrad Front was in full pursuit mode. After consulting with his subordinate commanders, Eremenko directed that 64th and 57th Armies, together with 4th Mechanized Corps from 51st Army, link up with the western pincer to form the inner encirclement, while the remainder of 51st Army advanced southwestward to form an outer encirclement along the Aksai River.[67]

After an all-day struggle on 22 November, Shumilov's troops forced German IV Corps to abandon Varvarovka on the eastern bank of the Chervlenaia River and withdraw north to defend the Karavatka *balka*, closely tied to the strongpoint at Elkhi.[68] This strong defensive terrain enabled IV Corps to defend for many weeks to come, forcing the Soviet southern pincer to seek a solution west of the Chervlenaia.

This task fell to General Tolbukhin's 57th Army and General Trufanov's 51st Army. With the German 29th Motorized Division finally withdrawn from his sector, Tolbukhin's 13th Tank Corps was able to advance up to 15 kilometers on 22 November, contributing to the pressure on German IV Corps. More spectacularly, Trufanov's subordinate 4th Mechanized Corps, commanded by Vol'sky, managed to resupply his forward elements and then lunged forward to within 20 kilometers of Kalach and the spearheads of the Southwestern Front. Given conflicting orders from *front* and field army headquarters as to whether he should advance west or northeast, Vol'sky sent his 36th Mechanized Brigade westward to Sovetskii and his 59th and 60th Brigades northeastward toward Karpovka. Leading 36th Brigade, 26th Tank Regiment seized the German logistical hub at Sovetskii and severed all of German Sixth Army's communications to the west. Meanwhile, 59th Brigade's subordinate battalions fought bitter night actions with the ad hoc German defenders at the Voroshilov Camp and Karpovka Station. At the latter location, 29th Motorized Division expelled the attackers early on 23 November. Still, Vol'sky corps claimed it had killed more than 14,000 Axis troops and captured another 13,000 in three days of fighting.[69]

On 22 November General Shapkin's 4th Cavalry Corps veered sharply to the south, away from Vol'sky's advance, and drove Romanian 8th Cavalry Division back 4 kilometers, further disrupting the remnants of Romanian VI Corps on the outskirts of Aksai. The left-wing divisions of 51st Army also cleared the western shore of Lake Barmantsak and prepared to attack Romanian 4th Infantry Division defenses at Sadovoe.

In the far south, Gerasimenko mounted his 103rd Rifle Regiment on trucks, trying to bring enough forces westward to capture Iashkul'. The opposing 16th Motorized Division, using three battalions of volunteers from Turkestan, organized the defense of that town and thereby denied Elista to the Soviets.[70]

A significant portion of Fourth Panzer Army was already falling into the encirclement at Stalingrad. Clearly, Hoth required reinforcements south of the city—reinforcements that could come only from Army Group A. Until such help arrived, Eremenko's Stalingrad Front was free to focus on completing the encirclement of Sixth Army. Foreseeing this possibility, at 1900 hours on 23 November General Paulus made the first of numerous requests for "freedom of action" to escape westward if necessary.[71] As he had with the Lascar Group, however, Hitler insisted that Sixth Army stand fast to impede the Soviet offensive.

CLOSING THE RING: THE SOVIET OFFENSIVE, 23 NOVEMBER

Although his tank corps were days behind schedule, Vatutin was elated by the progress of the Southwestern Front. XIV Panzer Corps had been too slow to erect a solid defense against the western pincer of the Soviet advance. In addition to being forced eastward, German XI Corps had been required to detach various regimental and battalion groups to shore up Sixth Army's sketchy defenses, especially at Kalach and the main railroad line to Karpovka. Overnight on 22–23 November Vatutin and Rokossovsky formulated new directives to complete the initial objective of Uranus—the complete encirclement of Stalingrad and the formation of an outer encirclement along the Krivaia and Chir Rivers.

Southwestern Front, 23 November

By the end of 23 November, one of 5th Tank Army's two tank corps, plus 21st Army's 4th Tank Corps, had linked up with the Stalingrad Front's 4th Mechanized Corps at the village of Sovetskii, 15 kilometers southeast of Kalach (see map 71). Farther to the west, having been reduced to only 24 operational tanks, most of Butkov's 1st Tank Corps spent the day refitting. Despite this, small detachments of this corps' 44th Motorized Rifle Brigade captured Chir Station from various German rear-service elements. Butkov's troops also seized the village of Blizhne-Osinovskii on the Chir's northern bank, 13 kilometers west of Chir Station. These two modest gains severed the Morozovsk-Stalingrad railroad line on which Sixth Army's logistics depended. However, Group Tzchöckel, an ad hoc organization commanded by Romanian Third Army, still held a bridgehead over the Don River just south of Rychkovskii and 7 kilometers east of Chir Station. The Germans desperately defended this point because it was the best place from which they could launch a relief operation from the west toward Stalingrad.

General Rodin's 26th Tank Corps retained some 30 operational tanks on

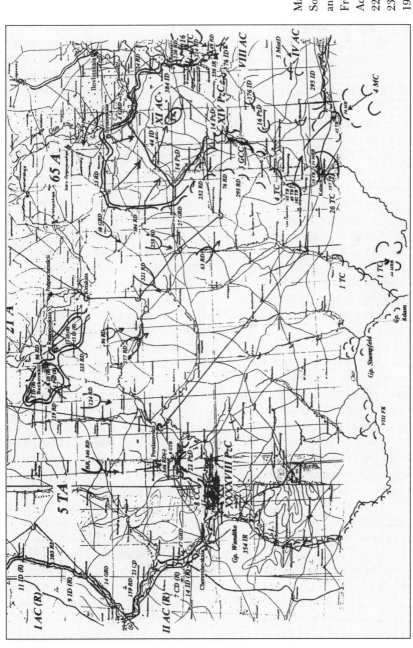

Map 71. Southwestern and Don Fronts' Advance at 2200 Hours, 23 November 1942

23 November, although its 216th Tank Brigade was still far to the north, supporting 50th Guards Rifle Division. Rodin sent his three other brigades to consolidate control of Kalach and advance southward to link up with the eastern pincer at Sovetskii.

Opposite them was a hodgepodge of German units, including 295th and 389th Panzer Antitank Battalions, 244th Assault Gun Battalion, the leading elements of 16th Panzer Division, and a variety of rear-service units controlled primarily by 3rd Motorized Division. Despite their disparate composition, these German units resisted stoutly inside Kalach, and at one point they almost broke through to the Don River. Colonel Filippenko's 19th Tank Brigade stalled in the attack, so at about 1300 hours the motorized rifle battalion of Major V. Ia. Kudriashev's 157th Tank Brigade assaulted across the frozen river to seize part of southwestern Kalach; this threat prompted the defenders to withdraw to the east.

The remainder of 5th Tank Army was still reducing the remnants of Romanian divisions, as well as 22nd Panzer Division, well to the north of Kalach. Late that evening the last organized groups of Romanian infantry surrendered to 63rd Rifle Division. Only one element of General Sion's Romanian 15th Infantry Division, numbering perhaps 3,000 men, escaped across the Tsaritsa River.[72] Meanwhile, Borisov's 8th Cavalry Corps became intermingled with elements of 22nd Panzer and Romanian 1st Armored Divisions. After destroying 28 of its own R-2 tanks that were inoperable or out of fuel, the latter division withdrew south across the Kurtlak River, where it reassembled 11 remaining Panzer III and IVs and 19 R-2s, the latter mostly towed by German vehicles. Gheorghe's bloodied division had to wait another day before making good its escape. Once 22nd Panzer crossed the river, it found itself between 112th and 55th Cavalry Divisions; fortunately for the Germans, 5th Tank Army ordered the latter division to break contact and move southward, allowing what remained of 22nd Panzer Division to survive.[73]

The 21st Army was even more successful than 5th Tank Army on 23 November. While the struggle for Kalach was still in doubt, several brigades from Kravchenko's 4th Tank Corps bypassed the town from the east and linked up with the Stalingrad Front's 4th Mechanized Corps at Sovetskii.[74]

The three divisions of Pliev's 3rd Guards Cavalry Corps advanced north of and parallel to 4th Tank Corps, seeking to separate XIV Panzer and XI Army Corps from each other, in preparation for the destruction of both. The cavalrymen seized crossings over the Don River at Golubinskii, Malo-Golubinskii, and Bol'shenabatovskii. At the latter point, 32nd Cavalry Division fought all night against a *kampfgruppe* of 16th Panzer Division. General Hube concentrated most of the remaining forces of 24th and 16th Panzer Divisions in preparation for a 24 November counterattack against 6th Guards Cavalry Division north of Bol'shenabatovskii. Pliev's men also claimed a haul (likely exaggerated) of Axis aircraft, tanks, and other vehicles that had been abandoned while inoperable. Meanwhile, the rifle elements of 21st Army, except for those still involved in liquidating bypassed Romanians, advanced behind and to the left wing of Pliev's corps. On that wing, Colonel Tavartkiladze's 76th Rifle Division succeeded in forcing a *kampfgruppe* of 14th Panzer Division, together with two supporting infantry regiments, to withdraw eastward from their defensive positions near Os'kinskii.

On 23 November 1st Guards Army limited its operations to probes across the Krivaia River from Verkhne-Krivskaia south to Gorbatovskii. Kuznetsov sought to determine the new positions of Romanian I Corps and German XVII Corps, waiting for the completion of the Uranus encirclement so that he could launch the grander Saturn offensive. As *front* commander, Vatutin was equally anxious to begin Saturn, but first he had to focus on the persistent German bridgehead at Rychkovskii.

Don Front, 23 November

Rokossovsky's relatively weak *front* continued the unglamorous but necessary work of pushing back the German defenders on the eastern shoulder of the penetration. The right (western) wing of Batov's 65th Army advanced up to 10 kilometers that day, forcing General Strecker's XI Corps to withdraw its flank to a line from Khmelevskii southwestward to Os'kinskii. Farther east, Batov's troops continued to inflict casualties but made smaller advances against the well-prepared defenses of 44th Infantry Division. Strecker managed to maintain a coherent defensive front but was weakened by the requirement to send 384th Division's 536th Regiment southward across the Don to shore up the defenses east of Kalach, where it joined a regiment of 44th Division that had moved there several days earlier. Increasingly, Paulus's need to reinforce his western front at the expense of his northern front reflected the growing Soviet success in achieving encirclement.

The Soviet 24th Army, commanded by I. V. Galanin, had even less success on the 23 November. In a vain effort to crack the German 76th Infantry Division, Galinin ordered two brigades of 16th Tank Corps to support the assaulting 120th, 214th, 49th, and 233rd Rifle Divisions as they launched southward attacks converging on Vertiachii. This plan not only abandoned the doctrinal exploitation role assigned to the 16th but also caused the armor to stumble into two uncleared minefields, losing a total of 55 tanks to mines and German antitank defenses. Batov, commander of the neighboring 65th Army, bitterly criticized Galinin for this failure, although Rokossovsky later absolved Galinin of blame.[75]

Stalingrad Front, 23 November

In the two days of fighting on 22–23 November, Eremenko's *front* not only linked up with the northern pincer to complete the encirclement but also destroyed the equivalent of a full Romanian army south of Stalingrad. While broadening his grip on the Morozovsk-Stalingrad railroad line east and west of Sovetskii, Eremenko began the task of digesting the encircled Axis forces in that area and erecting an outer encirclement front along and south of the Aksai River. A double perimeter, defending both inward and outward, was essential to hold and ultimately reduce the Axis encirclement. To accomplish this, 62nd and 64th Armies used local attacks to tie down as many German forces as possible, while the distant 28th Army continued its advance toward Elista to fix 16th Motorized Division.

This left the Stalingrad Front's main effort, as on the previous day, to Tolbukhin's 57th Army and Trufanov's 51st Army. In the former area, Tanaschishin's 13th Tank Corps, already damaged by German 29th Motorized Division's counterattacks on the first day of the offensive, again attempted to attack the 29th's defenses, primarily in the 8 kilometer wide sector from Kravtsov south to Varvarovka. This attack failed at a heavy cost, as did a supporting attack by 36th Guards Rifle Division. Thereafter, Tolbukhin's army was reduced to siege operations against the southern front of Sixth Army's encirclement.

For most of 23 November, individual battalions of 59th Mechanized Brigade, 4th Mechanized Corps, continued their losing battle with German defenders along the railroad line from Voroshilov Camp to Karpovka. *Kampfgruppen* from 3rd and 29th Motorized Divisions, respectively, defended these two points. That evening, however, 51st Army's 15th Guards Rifle Division arrived on the scene to stabilize this flank of the encirclement.

About 1600 that afternoon, 4th Mechanized Corps' 36th Brigade finally met with a forward detachment of 4th Tank Corps' 45th Tank Brigade on the northern outskirts of Sovetskii. The encounter was not without incident, however, as each side fired on the other before establishing their identities.[76]

Farther south, 61st Cavalry Division, 302nd Rifle Division, 76th Fortified Region, and 91st Rifle Division all advanced concentrically on Sadovoe. These actions forced Romanian 4th Infantry and 5th Cavalry Divisions to abandon Sadovoe early on the twenty-fourth. Rounding out 51st Army's actions on 23 November, 126th Rifle Division hurried through Aksai to shore up the outer encirclement, which was still tenuously outlined by 4th Cavalry Corps.

Late that evening, German 371st and 297th Infantry and 29th Motorized Divisions, together with the survivors of Romanian 20th Infantry Division, formed a coherent defensive front along the Karavatka *balka* and the Cherv-

Ienaia River. These former subordinates of Fourth Panzer Army now fell under General Erwin Jänecke's IV Army Corps on the southern boundary of Sixth Army's developing encirclement.

THE STALINGRAD POCKET

The Soviet execution of Uranus included numerous errors, and the Romanian and German defenders were far more determined and effective than most accounts admit. As a result, the operation took five days rather than the planned three, and it cost the Soviet mobile units up to 80 percent of their tanks. Against a stronger foe, the attackers might have failed. Nonetheless, the Red Army had achieved a strategic-level victory by destroying two Romanian armies and, for the first time in the war, encircling an entire German field army. Yet the victory would be complete only if the attackers could contain and destroy what they had encircled. This would require not only a complete penetration of Axis tactical defenses but also the first instance of Soviet mobile forces defeating the (admittedly weak) Axis operational reserves and conducting mechanized maneuver more quickly and effectively than their opponents.

Trapped within the resulting pocket were the headquarters of 2 armies—Fourth Panzer and Sixth—as well as 5 corps headquarters and 20 German Army divisions, 1 *Luftwaffe Flak* division, and 2 Romanian divisions. German accounts also identified 149 separate regiments and battalions, although Soviet accounts reckoned this figure at 160. Such nondivisional units were by no means unimportant; they included 4 assault gun battalions, 17 artillery and rocket units, 3 antitank battalions, and 23 pioneer or engineer battalions of various types. The total number of soldiers encircled is difficult to determine precisely, with the best estimate being 264,000 Germans, 20,000 Romanians, and 60,000 Russian *Hiwi* volunteers, for a total of 344,000; this compares closely with the postwar Soviet estimate of 330,000.[77]

Axis casualties during Uranus also remain a source of considerable controversy. At its basis, however, Romanian forces on both flanks of Stalingrad totaled some 230,000 soldiers prior to the Soviet offensive, but by 8 December, their combined strength was 122,000 men. Allowing for approximately 20,000 Romanians caught within the Stalingrad pocket, this suggests that Romanian losses from 19 to 23 November amounted to 88,000 men, of which the Soviets claim to have captured 37,000.[78] During the same time period, recent Russian assessments conclude that the Germans lost 24,000 killed or captured, while another 39,000 escaped encirclement. Soviet claims for tank trophies are more problematic, including a total Axis loss of 457 tanks. Given that the Germans possessed about 340 tanks and 44 self-propelled guns, plus an additional 140 Romanian tanks (both functional and not), the actual Axis armored loss was more likely 350 vehicles.[79]

Hitler had already overruled Paulus's 22 November request for freedom of action. The next evening, both Weichs at Army Group B and Paulus within the encirclement again argued that withdrawal was the only hope of saving the bulk of Sixth Army.[80] General Zeitzler made every effort to persuade Hitler on the evening of 23 November but failed.

That day, General Seydlitz, commander of LI Army Corps, issued Order No. 118, directing 3rd Motorized and 94th Infantry Divisions to withdraw from the northeastern corner of the pocket, south of Erzovka, on the night of 23–24 November. General Zhadov's 66th Army detected the withdrawal and promptly launched an attack that inflicted serious losses on the Germans. Seydlitz had apparently intended this action to force the issue of withdrawal, but instead it only irritated Hitler, who wrongly suspected Paulus of violating orders. Hitler therefore forbade any further discussion of withdrawal, eliminating any chance for XI Army and XIV Panzer Corps to break out. The Sixth Army commander concluded that even if he disobeyed orders, Hitler would only appoint Seydlitz to replace him.[81]

CHAPTER FIFTEEN

Tightening the Noose, November 1942

With the encirclement completed at Kalach and Sovetskii, the *Stavka* had to coordinate three related operations. First, between 24 and 27 November the Don Front's 65th Army and the Southwestern Front's 21st Army forced German XI Army and XIV Panzer Corps back into the Stalingrad encirclement. Simultaneously, the Southwestern Front (less 21st Army) and the Stalingrad Front launched twin efforts to push other German units southward and westward to prevent a relief effort. Vatutin aimed to seize the towns of Oblivskaia and Surovikino on the Chir's northern bank, as well as the Rychkovskii bridgehead. Meanwhile, Trufanov's 51st Army sought to seize the Don's eastern bank opposite Nizhne-Chirskaia and Kotel'nikovo, the road and rail center from which the Germans would try to relieve Stalingrad from the southwest. Contrary to the *Stavka's* expectations, Trufanov's army was too weak to contend with such relief efforts, especially after Vol'sky's 4th Mechanized Corps was reassigned from 51st to 57th Army. Indeed, throughout this period, the encircled Axis force proved both stronger and more resistant than the Soviets had anticipated, eventually forcing the *Stavka* to modify its plans to exploit Uranus.

THE BATTLE IN THE SKIES, 19–30 NOVEMBER

During the first five days of the Stalingrad offensive, a cold front curtailed most of the air activity on both sides. General Martin Fiebig's VIII *Fliegerkorps* had managed to send up some 120 sorties, primarily Ju-87 Stuka dive-bombers, on 19 November, but this was insufficient to impede the Southwestern Front's penetration and exploitation of Romanian Third Army.[1]

Between 19 and 23 November the Southwestern Front's 17th Air Army flew 546 sorties, primarily against the Romanian ground troops and redeploying mobile elements of XIV Corps. The Don Front's 16th Air Army reported 238 sorties during the same time period, while 8th Air Army supported the Stalingrad Front with 438 sorties, of which 170 were bombing and ground attacks, from 20 to 23 November.[2]

Weather conditions began to improve on 24 November, resulting in a marked increase in air activity on both sides. On 25 November, for example,

German airpower killed or wounded 4 regimental commanders, 12 squadron commanders, 500 troopers, and up to 1,500 horses of 8th Cavalry Corps.[3] However, the *Luftwaffe* was hampered by the need to transfer aircraft to new airfields as their former bases were overrun. The three Soviet air armies recorded 5,760 combat sorties between 24 and 30 November, or five times the sortie rate of German and Romanian air units.[4]

CONTINUING THE OFFENSIVE, 24 NOVEMBER

As chief of staff and representative of the *Stavka*, General Vasilevsky drew up the initial plans to reduce the Stalingrad pocket, which the Soviets initially estimated at 80,000 to 90,000 men. This false estimate made the attackers overly optimistic about the resulting plans. The Southwestern Front's 21st Army, reinforced by 26th and 4th Tank Corps, would attack from the west to push the defenders back from the Don to the Volga River and into the encirclement. The Don Front's 65th, 24th, and 66th Armies would attack from the north to isolate German forces west of the Don, then turn eastward to link up with the Stalingrad Front's 62nd Army near Rynok. That *front's* 57th Army would clear the enemy from the Chervlenaia River by 24 November, after which it, along with 51st and 64th Armies, would attack northward. All three *fronts* would be aiming for the area of Gumrak on the high ground northwest of the city.

In trying to secure the Chir River on 24 November, Vatutin's Southwestern Front continued to face the stubborn defenses of XXXXVIII Panzer Corps' 22nd Panzer and Romanian 1st Armored Divisions. In preparation for subsequent operations, Vatutin ordered Romanenko's 5th Tank Army to rest 26th Tank Corps and then transfer it to Chistiakov's 21st Army on 25 November. This meant that Romanenko had to accomplish his immediate objectives with only rifle units plus Butkov's 1st Tank Corps, which had been reduced to some 20 operational tanks. This weakness, in combination with repeated German ground attacks and air strikes of 20 to 30 aircraft, meant that Butkov made almost no progress in achieving his objectives on 24 November.[5] This left Romanenko with 346th, 50th Guards, and 119th Rifle Divisions; 8th Guards and 216th Tank Brigades; and 8th Motorcycle Regiment to contend with various dispersed *kampfgruppen* of 22nd Panzer Division north of the Kurtlak River. As the panzer division moved south and then west toward the Chir, 8th Cavalry Corps' 21st and 55th Cavalry Divisions attacked eastward along and south of the Kurtlak River to block the German withdrawal. Despite this effort, XXXXVIII Panzer Corps' surviving elements reached the relative safety of the western bank of the Chir during the night of 24–25 November. In turn, this allowed General Borisov to send his cavalrymen south-

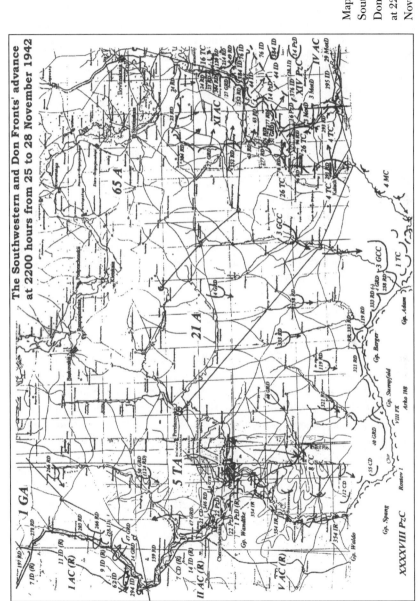

Map 72.
Southwestern and
Don Fronts' Advance
at 2200 Hours, 25–28
November 1942

ward, with 55th Cavalry Division seeking to capture Oblivskaia and cut the rails and roads north of the Chir River, while 112th Cavalry joined 21st Cavalry Division in seeking bridgeheads over the Chir both north and south of Chernyshevskaia. The rifle elements on Romanenko's right wing also closed up along the Chir, with 159th Rifle Division probing toward Bokovskaia.

North of Romanenko, Leliushenko's 1st Guards Army attempted to crush Romanian I Corps (7th and 11th Infantry Divisions) between the Don and Krivaia Rivers. Instead, the attackers encountered well-coordinated Romanian defensive fires, with only 14th Guards Rifle Division making any progress. General Hollidt, commander of the army detachment named for him, dispatched the German 62nd and 294th Infantry Divisions to support the Romanians in a counterattack, seeking to drive the Soviets back across the Krivaia.[6]

Meanwhile, in 21st Army's sector, General Chistiakov planned to push Sixth Army eastward in the area northeast of Kalach, while the Stalingrad Front's 4th Mechanized Corps thrust northward into the German flank. Until 26th Tank Corps could arrive, however, this left Kravchenko's 4th Tank Corps dispersed across a 15 kilometer front against 3rd Motorized Division, while Pliev's 3rd Guards Cavalry Corps, with at least one rifle division attached, tried to defeat 16th Panzer Division east of the Golubaia River. Kravchenko and Pliev made little progress against these skeletonized German units.[7] Fortunately for the attackers, General Hube was in the process of reorganizing XIV Panzer Corps into a defensive line east of the Don; he hoped to redeploy 3rd Motorized, 24th, and 16th Panzer Divisions on this line by the end of 26 November, with 14th Panzer eventually becoming his reserve.[8]

In the Don Front, Batov's 65th Army continued to press XI Army Corps' shrinking perimeter west of the Don River, advancing 7 to 15 kilometers on 24 November as Strecker's corps made a fighting withdrawal to new defensive positions. For the third straight day, however, General Galinin kept the armor of Maslov's 16th Tank Corps dispersed in a vain effort to support the rifle divisions attacking toward Vertiachii. With poor infantry-armor cooperation, Maslov lost another 33 tanks, while the rifle units advanced no more than 4 kilometers.[9] As noted in chapter 14, 66th Army made some progress against LI Army Corps, but only because it disrupted Seydlitz's risky withdrawal during the night.

Overall, none of the three Soviet *fronts* achieved significant advances on 24 November. Eremenko's Stalingrad Front experienced much the same problems as its counterparts, making little progress against Sixth Army's defenses along the railroad line from Marinovka to Karpovka, thence along the Karpovka and Chervlenaia Rivers to the Karavatka *balka* and then the southern suburb of Kuporosnoe. In particular, *Kampfgruppe* Willig of 3rd Motorized Division thwarted efforts by 4th Mechanized Corps and 15th Guards

Rifle Division to capture the strongpoint at Marinovka.[10] Only Shapkin's 4th Cavalry Corps and the rifle divisions of 51st Army had any success, pushing the outer encirclement farther away from the inner one (see map 73). The 81st Cavalry Division of Shapkin's corps seized the town of Aksai on the river of the same name and continued pressing westward. This, in turn, cut communications lines of Romanian 4th Infantry Division, which withdrew southwestward from Sadovoe; other elements of Romanian VI Corps, including 8th Cavalry Division, also retreated from the encirclement, much to the frustration of Fourth Panzer Army headquarters.

Even this Soviet success was short-lived, for the next day Colonel Helmuth von Pannwitz occupied Kotel'nikovo. This charismatic cavalryman had recruited a brigade of Cossack volunteers, to which he added a motorized Romanian artillery battalion and 18 tanks liberated from a repair facility.[11] Two days later this *kampfgruppe*, along with Romanian 8th Cavalry, inflicted a series of defeats on Shapkin's cavalry. Far to the south, General Schwerin's 16th Motorized Division received orders to defend Iashkul'.[12] It would take 28th Army more than a month to reduce this Stalingrad in miniature.

Inside the encircled city, Paulus attempted to implement Hitler's declaration of Stalingrad as a fortress. Having dispatched his mobile divisions westward, however, Paulus had no capacity to retake the positions that Seydlitz had so rashly abandoned the previous night. Similarly, Chuikov's troops were too weak to retake any significant territory.

TIGHTENING THE RING, 25–27 NOVEMBER

Despite the meager results achieved on 24 November, Vasilevsky insisted on continuing the offensive, seeking to prevent any German reinforcement or relief of Sixth Army. The only significant change he made to his orders that night was to transfer 4th Mechanized Corps from 51st to 57th Army in order to seize the eastern bank of the Don south of Rychkovskii, thereby eliminating the German bridgehead there. Otherwise, the costly struggles for the city itself, as well as for the Chir and Aksai River areas, continued unabated.

Southwestern Front, 25–27 November

Vatutin's Southwestern Front continued to operate in two directions simultaneously, with Romanenko's 5th Tank Army focused south toward the Chir River, and Chistiakov's 21st Army fighting along the western face of Sixth Army's pocket. For Soviet commanders accustomed to directing the fighting from forward observation posts, this bifurcated arrangement was awkward at best.

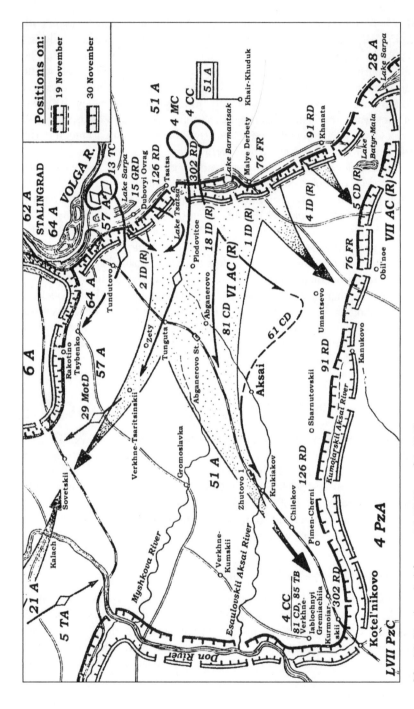

Map 73. 51st Army's Advance, 19–30 November 1942

Positions on:
19 November
30 November

Chistiakov ordered the newly transferred 26th Tank Corps to capture the towns of Sokarevka and Peskovatka from XIV Panzer Corps on 25 November, but this corps was far too weak—numbering only 40 tanks—for such a major assignment. The 26th and 4th Tank Corps came to an abrupt halt, facing a well-organized defense erected by 3rd Motorized Division—later reinforced by 14th Panzer Division—along the deep Vaniukova *balka*. To their north, 3rd Guards Cavalry Corps (less 6th Cavalry Division, detached to the outer wing) had forced the Don River at Luchenskii and Peskovatka, but even this success was due mainly to the temporary redeployments of the defending German XI Corps; at the end of the day, 16th Panzer Division helped stabilize the front again.[13]

On 26 November Chistiakov resumed his attacks north of the Don. In a confused situation, Colonel A. F. Chudesov's 32nd Cavalry Division infiltrated a regiment into the town of Peskovatka, filled with numerous German units moving east or west to new defensive positions. Most of this regiment was lost in the ensuing struggle, but 32nd Cavalry and 277th Rifle Divisions rendered Peskovatka untenable to the defenders.[14]

To the south, Rodin's 26th Tank Corps continued to attack eastward, despite having fewer than 25 tanks; these were now formed into two groups and supported by 293rd Rifle Division. Rodin made almost no progress along the Vaniukova *balka*.

By 27 November, 21st Army was almost entirely on the eastern bank of the Don, although Vatutin now ordered Pliev's cavalry corps, together with 66th Army's 40th Guards, 321st, and 285th Rifle Divisions, to reinforce 5th Tank Army's forces struggling to seize the German strongpoints of Oblivskaia, Surovikino, and (on the Don) Rychkovskii. Chistiakov's forces were virtually exhausted and made little further progress. His two tank corps had no more than 60 tanks, consolidated into a single brigade for each corps. Opposite them, 16th and 14th Panzer Divisions were also reduced, with perhaps 35 to 40 tanks between them. That night, Vasilevsky transferred control of 21st Army from the Southwestern to the Don Front, ending the awkward command situation and marking the end of this phase of combat.

To the south, 5th Tank Army also lunged forward on 25–26 November, seeking to take Rychkovskii on the Don and the upper Chir River before the Axis could reinforce its weak and fragmented defenders. Butkov's 1st Tank Corps, supported by the main body of Borisov's 8th Cavalry Corps, aimed at Rychkovskii, while 21st Cavalry Division and most of the tank army's rifle divisions aimed to clear the Chir River.

Opposite this advance in late November were two ad hoc Axis formations. Army Group (literally Attack Group, or *Angriffsgruppe*) Hollidt had four clusters to defend outside the western face of the outer Soviet encirclement:

- German XVII Corps (62nd and 294th Infantry Divisions) and Romanian I Corps (7th and 11th Infantry Divisions), defending along the Krivaia River north of Bokovskaia.
- Romanian II Corps (9th Infantry and 7th Cavalry Divisions), defending the Chir River front from Bokovskaia south to Chernyshevskaia.
- XXXXVIII Panzer Corps (22nd Panzer and Romanian 1st Armored Divisions), not yet ready to defend the Chir from Chernyshevskaia south.
- Remnants of Romanian V and IV Corps west of the Chir.

To the south, Romanian Third Army headquarters was responsible for defending the Chir River from roughly 10 kilometers south of Chernyshevskaia and then east to Rychkovskii on the Don. This included a variety of ad hoc combat groups formed from alarm and rear-area forces, including the following:

- Group Wandtke: 610th Regiment of 403rd Security Division from Chernyshevskaia south to Ust'-Griaznovskii.
- Group Waldow (merged with Wandtke into Group Spang on 24 November): 354th Regiment of 403rd Division from Ust'-Griaznovskii south to Lagutin.
- Group Fiebig (renamed Group Stahel) of VIII *Flieger* Corps: the Oblivskaia sector.
- Group von Stumpfeld (108th Artillery Command): the Surovikino sector.
- Group Adam: the Chirskii Station sector, headed by Paulus's adjutant.
- Group Tzschöckel (former Kalach garrison): the Rychkovskii sector.
- Group Schmidt (14th Panzer Division rear): east of Rychkovskii initially, but then to the Surovikino sector.
- Group Korntner (to Group Selle on 28 November): the Ostrovskii sector.
- Group Selle (14th Panzer Division rear support elements): the Nizhne-Chirskaia sector, but to the Ostrovskii sector by 30 November.[15]

Butkov's 1st Tank Corps attacked south of Kalach toward Rychkovskii and Surovikino on 25 November. It pushed in some German security outposts but encountered stubborn resistance from Group von Stumpfeld at Surovikino. With only 20 operable tanks, the corps halted at the end of the day to await rifle forces. Thirty kilometers to the west, 8th Motorcycle Regiment similarly halted at the outskirts of Oblivskaia, awaiting reinforcement from Borisov's cavalry corps. The 112th Division of that corps captured a small bridgehead over the Chir at Osinovskii, beginning a prolonged sequence of moves and countermoves between the Soviet cavalry and Group Waldow's security troops.[16]

Far behind the main body of this cavalry corps, General N. P. Iakunin's 21st Cavalry Division, then operating independently north of Chernyshevskaia, received orders late on 24 November to seize a bridgehead across the Chir the next day. Iakunin crossed the Chir 6 kilometers northwest of Chernyshevskaia, encircling one regiment of Romanian 7th Cavalry Division.[17] Emulating Iakunin's boldness, General Ia S. Fokanov's 47th Guards Division divided into three sectors, with one regiment taking up a position on 21st Cavalry's left, another regiment supporting 112th Cavalry Division's crossing at Osinovskii, and the third regiment trying to screen the Chernyshevskaia area.

Iakunin's surprise crossing prompted Hollidt to order Group Wandtke, together with surviving elements of 22nd Panzer and Romanian 1st Armored Divisions, to attempt a rescue. On the morning of 26 November the two worn-out armored units surprised 47th Guards' overextended 437th Regiment and retook Chernyshevskaia and the bridge over the Chir.

Romanenko in turn sent Colonel A. I. Belov's 50th Guards Division and 8th Guards Tank Brigade to relieve the 47th. When Belov's regiments reached the upper Chir River about midday on 26 November, they captured Chernyshevskaia and again threatened Romanian 14th Infantry Division. Over the next several days, XXXXVIII Panzer Corps and Romanian II Corps struggled for and ultimately regained Chernyshevskaia from Belov, but north and south of that point, 5th Tank Army held the river.[18]

If Romanenko's command achieved only partial success on the Chir, on 24–26 November it also fell short of its assigned missions on the Don. Reduced to fewer than 20 tanks, Butkov's 1st Tank Corps reported on the twenty-sixth that its forces "occupied the Bol'shaia Osinovka, Novomaksimovskii, and Rychkovskii line, 15–35 kilometers southeast of Surovikino."[19] As they became available, Romanenko dispatched 119th Rifle Division on 25 November and four more divisions the next day to consolidate the Chir-Don River line from Oblivskaia to Rychkovskii. Until these divisions arrived, the weak German defenders had time to consolidate their positions, and higher headquarters accepted Romanenko's excuses for the lack of progress. On the twenty-seventh Group Selle repelled a battalion of Soviet infantry with three T-34 tanks in the Nizhne-Chirskaia area; this proved to be the advance guard of Vol'sky's 4th Mechanized Corps, which posed a new threat from the east.[20]

That same day, 8th Cavalry Corps' 55th and 112th Cavalry Divisions, having turned their Chir River bridgeheads over to 346th Rifle Division, engaged Group Stahel north of Oblivskaia but failed to capture the strongpoint.[21]

Nor were the Germans completely passive. At dawn on 25 November the two divisions of XVII Army Corps launched a double envelopment against part of Leliushenko's 1st Guards Army along and west of the Krivaia River on the western edge of the Southwestern Front. The 62nd Infantry Division advanced eastward from Kruzhilin, while 294th Infantry Division thrust northeastward from Bokovskaia. This attack caught 14th Guards and 203rd Rifle Divisions just as they had been transferred to the control of 14th Rifle Corps. The Red troops retreated in considerable disorder, with their pursuers even crossing the river and driving into Leliushenko's rear area. An attempted counterattack early on 27 November failed, costing an entire regiment of 266th Rifle Division and leaving a threat to the Southwestern Front's flank.[22]

Don Front, 25–27 November

Unlike the Southwestern Front, all three armies of Rokossovsky's Don Front shared a common mission: to smash and begin liquidating the northern part of German Sixth Army. Yet all three armies were relatively weak, and with the exception of Batov's 65th Army, they were still facing well-prepared German defenses.

On the morning of 25 November Batov's 24th, 304th, and 252nd Rifle Divisions pressed southward along a 14 kilometer arc defended by a *kampfgruppe* of 16th Panzer Division and five regiments of XI Army Corps' 44th and 384th Infantry Divisions. The 91st Tank Brigade supported 304th Division, and 121st Tank Brigade supported 24th Division. These troops advanced 8 kilometers that day against the truck-mounted rear guards left by the Germans. That evening, therefore, Rokossovsky reassigned four rifle divisions from Batov to Romanenko's overstretched tank army. This left Batov with only 27th Guards Rifle Division in reserve, a force he committed at about noon on 26 November when the pursuit stalled short of the river. However, the defenders conducted a methodical withdrawal that afternoon and evening, exploding the remaining bridge at about 0340 hours on the twenty-seventh. Batov had failed to destroy the German defenders but had inflicted significant materiel damage.[23]

Later that same morning, General Strecker's XI Corps informed Sixth Army that because its new positions were untenable, it would continue a withdrawal southward. Paulus identified the crest of the ridgeline dividing the Rossoshka River from the Don River to the west as the natural line for his northern defensive front. German VIII Army Corps, commanded by General Walter Heitz, assumed control of this sector, which consisted of 376th Infantry Division, portions of 384th Infantry Division, a task force from Sikenius's regiment of 16th Panzer Division, and 522nd Construction Battalion. Paulus's defensive plan called for 24th Panzer Division and much of 384th Infantry Division to go into army reserve.

On Batov's eastern flank, Galinin's 24th Army made little progress during

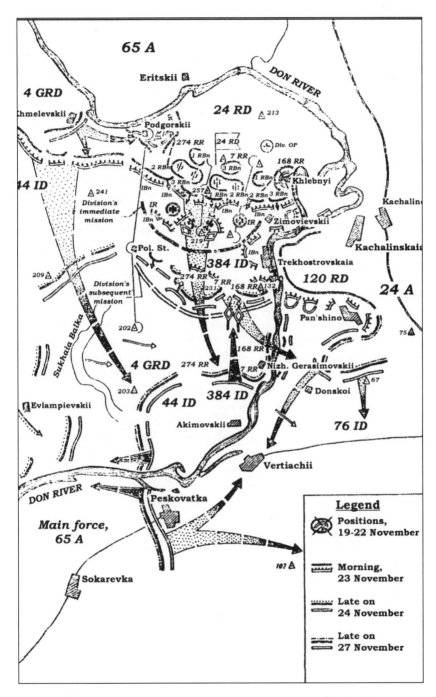

Map 74. Advance by the Don Front's 65th and 24th Armies toward Vertiachii,
19–27 November 1942

five costly days of attacks (22–26 November) against VIII Army Corps' 76th Infantry Division. The resulting heavy losses reduced 16th Tank Corps to a single group of fewer than 20 tanks.[24] Batov's advances on the west threatened 76th Division's left flank at about midday on the twenty-seventh, finally forcing it to begin withdrawing that evening. By failing to capture Vertiachii, Galinin's army permitted XI Corps to withdraw south across the Don while still relatively intact.

After mauling the German 94th Division during Seydlitz's ill-timed withdrawal on 24–25 November, 66th Army likewise failed to make significant progress against LI Corps in the Spartakovka-Orlovka sector. During this period, Zhadov's troops did inflict some 350 casualties on the 94th, a division that had numbered only 5,025 combat soldiers on 15 November.[25] Reduced to 18 tanks, 24th Panzer Division counterattacked on Hill 135.4 on 26–27 November, regaining much of the ground lost to 66th Army's 64th Rifle Division in previous days.[26] Zhadov, Rokossovsky, and Vasilevsky all agreed that further attacks would accomplish nothing, and 66th Army attempted little more than local raids until late December.

To simplify the tasks of his subordinate *fronts*, on 26 November Vasilevsky proposed a restructuring so that the Don Front would control all forces along the northern and western sides of the developing pocket. Approved by Stalin the next day, this change gave 21st Army to the Don Front, while Vatutin's Southwestern Front gained four additional rifle divisions (three of them from 65th Army), plus the three divisions of 3rd Guards Cavalry Corps and the new 5th Mechanized Corps for 5th Tank Army.[27] The senior Soviet leadership had recognized that much greater efforts would be required to reduce the stubborn Axis pocket.

Nonetheless, the reality of being encircled rapidly struck home for the German defenders. On 25 November General Seydlitz's LI Corps directed that the survivors of the pioneer troops that had been brought into the city at the start of the month be incorporated into existing divisional engineer battalions. Later that same day, Sixth Army reduced daily bread rations from 750 to 400 grams per soldier, meat from 250 to 120 grams, and so on.[28]

Stalingrad Front, 25–27 November

Mirroring the Southwestern Front, the Stalingrad Front initially devoted most of its troops to collapsing the Sixth Army pocket on its eastern and southern faces, while assigning only part of 51st Army to expand the outer encirclement. Events soon forced Eremenko to commit all of 51st Army to the struggle around Kotel'nikovo, however.

Most of the besiegers lacked the combat power to make significant progress against the strong German defensive positions, although they dutifully

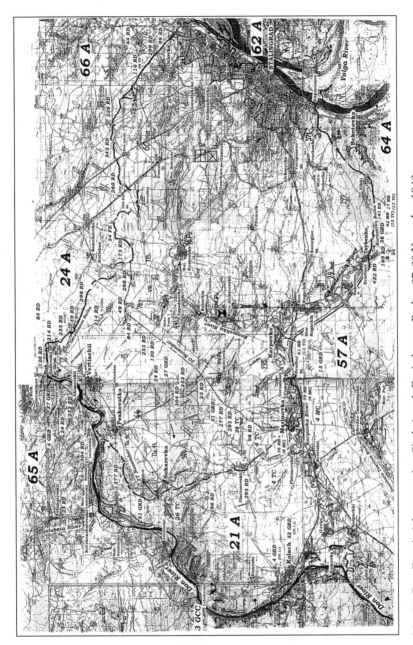

Map 75. Don Front's Advance against Sixth Army's Encirclement Pocket, 27–30 November 1942

tried to do so. Late on 24 November Vasilevsky transferred 36th Guards Rifle Division—the only portion of 64th Army that had made any progress against German IV Corps defending the Karavatka *balka*—to 51st Army, with both armies directed to renew the attack the next day. In fact, Shumilov paid only lip service to this directive, sending two battalions of 97th Rifle Brigade, 7th Rifle Corps, to attack at the junction of 371st and 297th Infantry Divisions southeast of Tsybenko. In 57th Army, Tolbukhin sent 169th Rifle Division to relieve the successful 36th Guards in place, but this new division, supported by the neighboring 422nd Division, made little further progress against Tsybenko. There, 670th Regiment, resubordinated from 371st to 297th Infantry Division, as well as the reinforced 74th Panzer-Grenadier Regiment of 29th Motorized Division, held on stubbornly for the rest of the month.[29]

On 25 November Vasilevsky also gave 4th Mechanized Corps a new, divided mission. In the sector from Marinovka eastward to Karpovka, one portion of Vol'sky's corps, supported by 15th Guards Rifle Division, made repeated, unsuccessful probing attacks against the various German defenders along the vital railroad line. More significantly, a reinforced 158th Separate Tank Regiment was dispatched to the Liapichev and Logovskii regions, 30 to 40 kilometers southwest of Sovetskii, to assist 1st Tank Corps in its efforts against the vital Rychkovskii bridgehead. The 158th promptly blundered into a minefield that wounded its commander. His successor, political officer P. D. Sinkevich, seized Liapichev at dusk on 25 November but wrongly concluded that Logovskii, defended by the small Group Tzschöckel of 53rd Heavy Mortar Regiment, was too strong to attack without reinforcements.[30] When 60th Mechanized Brigade arrived two days later, the combined force captured Logovskii, although Sinkevich died in the attack. However, Group Tzschöckel retained a marshy bridgehead on the east bank of the Don; two weeks later, sufficient Soviet infantry finally arrived to eliminate this threat. Thus 57th Army, like its neighbor 64th Army, failed to take its objectives and instead lapsed into siege operations.

On the night of 24–25 November Eremenko ordered Shapkin's 4th Cavalry Corps, in tandem with 126th Rifle Division, to traverse some 90 kilometers and capture Kotel'nikovo.[31] Shapkin began the advance the next day, with the two cavalry divisions soon ranging ahead of the riflemen. At the village of Sharnutovskii, 45 kilometers east of Kotel'nikovo, Colonel Pannwitz's ad hoc group of Cossacks, infantry, and tanks, together with another group led by Colonel Radu Korne, commander of Romanian 8th Cavalry Division, ambushed Colonel A. V. Stavenko's 61st Cavalry Division. After an all-night fight, the Red cavalrymen withdrew in some disorder, and Korne attacked north toward Aksai.[32] Ignoring this setback, 4th Cavalry Corps' 81st Cavalry Division bypassed Sharnutovskii to the southeast and reached the lower portion of the Aksai River, 40 kilometers north of Kotel'nikovo. The 126th and

302nd Rifle Divisions followed close behind, pushing Romanian VI Corps' 1st and 18th Infantry Divisions west of the Aksai River. The next morning, 27 November, leading elements of 81st Cavalry Division, together with about 35 tanks of 85th Tank Brigade, attacked into the heart of Kotel'nikovo.

Yet the Soviets were a few hours too late. Romanian support troops in the town briefly panicked, but Pannwitz's Cossacks arrived almost simultaneously with the lead trains carrying the full-strength 6th Panzer Division, redeployed from France in preparation for a relief attempt toward Stalingrad.[33] The Soviet cavalry escaped the trap and withdrew northward 20 kilometers to set up new defenses along a *balka* around Verkhne-Iablochnyi. Having pushed the remnants of five Romanian divisions westward with relative ease, 51st Army fell short in the face of the arriving German reinforcements.

ORGANIZING OPERATION SATURN

After coordinating by telephone with the three *front* commanders, on 24 November General Vasilevsky set out to visit the neighboring headquarters of General Golikov's Voronezh Front at Verkhne Mamon. Ice and fog forced the general's AN-2 biplane, as well as five other AN-2s carrying his immediate staff, to make an emergency landing, so he did not reach Verkhne Mamon (by car) until the twenty-sixth. There he adjusted the plan for Operation Saturn and gained Stalin's approval on the twenty-seventh (see map 76).[34]

Vasilevsky proposed to divide 1st Guards Army into a smaller headquarters of the same name, commanded by V. I. Kuznetsov, and a new 3rd Guards Army, led by Leliushenko. Advancing to converge on Millerovo, these two forces would encircle Italian Eighth Army and destroy the patchwork Army Detachment Hollidt. Once there, the reserve 2nd Guards Army would continue the advance to Rostov-on-the-Don, cutting off the retreat of Army Group A from the Caucasus. Fifth Tank Army would meanwhile continue efforts to isolate Stalingrad, advancing southwestward to capture the German transport airfield at Tatsinskaia and reach the Northern Donets River on Leliushenko's west.

Kuznetsov's operational group, which became the new 1st Guards Army in early December, consisted of six rifle divisions under 4th and 6th Guards Rifle Corps headquarters, plus 18th Tank Corps, 22nd Motorized Rifle Brigade, and supporting artillery.

By husbanding these and other forces in preparation for Saturn, the *Stavka* and General Vasilevsky deprived their *fronts* of sufficient forces to block relief efforts and complete the destruction of Sixth Army. Once they realized that the encirclement actually contained three times the number of

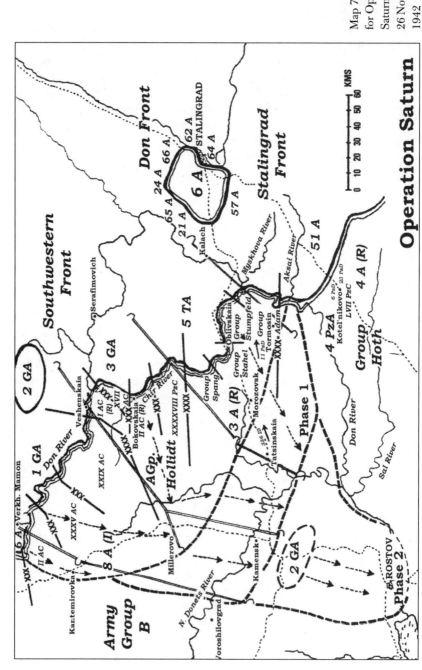

Map 76. Plan for Operation Saturn, 26 November 1942

Axis troops they had originally estimated, the Soviet leaders would have to make major changes in their plans.

CONTINUING THE URANUS OFFENSIVE

Southwestern Front, 28 November–1 December

While this planning continued, the three *fronts* attempted to solidify the inner and outer encirclements of Stalingrad. On 28 November Leliushenko's 278th and 266th Rifle Divisions counterattacked and contained the two German infantry divisions that had attacked along the Krivaia River, but Group Hollidt as a whole continued to defend the Krivaia and Chir Rivers energetically with multiple local attacks.[35] In 5th Tank Army's area, 3rd Guards Cavalry Corps briefly relieved 1st Tank Corps along the lower Chir River on 27–28 November so that Butkov's men could incorporate new tanks. On the army's right wing, 346th Rifle Division likewise relieved 112th Cavalry Division of its bridgeheads over the Chir at Varlamovskii and Klinovoi. Borisov was therefore able to concentrate his entire 8th Cavalry Corps for an attack on Oblivskaia. However, fighting along the tank army's front remained inconclusive on 28–30 November. German air raids and the limited combat power of dismounted cavalry meant that Borisov failed to take Oblivskaia, forcing him to wait for the arrival of 321st Rifle and 40th Guards Rifle Divisions. At and west of Chernyshevskaia, 22nd Panzer Division continued to block efforts by 21st Cavalry and 50th Guards Rifle Divisions to take the town. Meanwhile, though reduced to 28 tanks and 30 percent overall strength, Romanian 1st Armored Division was still able to parry encircling rifle forces south of the town, resulting in a stalemate.[36]

To the southeast, on 28 and 29 November threadbare Red Army forces made additional attempts to take Nizhne-Chirskaia and isolated Rychkovskii. Leaving 32nd Cavalry Division in reserve, Pliev ordered 5th and 6th Guards Cavalry Divisions, with the few surviving tanks of 1st Tank Corps, to attack south toward Nizhne-Chirskaia.

Both attacks failed, just as the German defenders received encouragement in the form of reinforcements. Late on 28 November the leading three battalions of General of Artillery Walter Lucht's 336th Infantry Division began arriving on the lower Chir, filling in the gap between Group Adam at Nizhne-Chirskaia and Group Schmidt at Surovikino. The 11th Panzer and 7th *Luftwaffe* Field Divisions followed 336th Infantry over the next several days, as a reorganized XXXXVIII Panzer Corps gathered to launch a relief attack on Stalingrad eastward from Nizhne-Chirskaia and Rychkovskii.

Farther to the west, however, 119th Rifle Division broke into Group

Schmidt's defenses at Surovikino on 29 November. The next day, 333rd Rifle Division advanced farther, seizing a 3 by 6 kilometer bridgehead over the Chir River at the village of Ostrovskii. Group Selle quickly stabilized the situation, but this bridgehead threatened any German attempts to relieve Stalingrad from the west. At Oblivskaia, the largest northern-bank town on the Chir that was still in German hands, two fresh Soviet divisions also entered the fray on the twenty-ninth. The 321st Rifle and 40th Guards Rifle Divisions attacked the town concentrically, joining 8th Cavalry Corps' assault on Group Stahel. The next day Borisov made a renewed assault on Oblivskaia, while his cavalrymen seized several small bridgeheads west of the town, but the scattered line of German strongpoints held on.[37] Frustrated, Romanenko ordered 21st Cavalry Division to break contact with 22nd Panzer and Romanian 14th Infantry Divisions north of Chernyshevskaia, turn over its sector to 50th Guards Division, and rejoin the rest of its corps, but this process took almost three days. On 30 November 346th Rifle, 47th Guards Rifle, and two tank brigades combined their bridgeheads over the Chir into a large one around Chernyshevskaia. Romanian 1st Armored Division once again fought these troops to a standstill on 1 December, but that encounter, in conjunction with frostbite, reduced the Romanian division to 944 combat troops and three tanks.[38] In fact, this fighting reduced divisions on both sides to regimental strength.

The Romanian and German defenses along the Chir River had proved far more effective than their chaotic organization suggested. XXXXVIII Panzer Corps had not only delayed 5th Tank Army's advance but also survived in sufficient strength to defend key locations along the Chir. The much-maligned 22nd Panzer Division actually proved to be the most effective impediment to the Southwestern Front during the first two weeks of Operation Uranus. Until 1st Tank Corps could absorb its replacement tanks, Romanenko was effectively stalled.

Don Front, 28 November–1 December

At the end of November the Don Front's 21st, 65th, and 24th Armies all pushed eastward from Kalach toward the Don River, capturing Peskovatka and Vertiachii. Rokossovsky suggested to Stalin that reduction of the Sixth Army pocket would require a deliberate attack coordinated by a single *front* headquarters, but the *Stavka*, preoccupied with the outer encirclement, did not reply immediately; instead, it transferred additional units from the Don and Stalingrad Fronts.[39]

Now under the Don Front, Chistiakov's 21st Army armored force had been reduced to a single brigade from the remnants of 4th and 26th Tank Corps. Opposite it, 3rd Motorized, 376th Infantry, and 44th Infantry Divi-

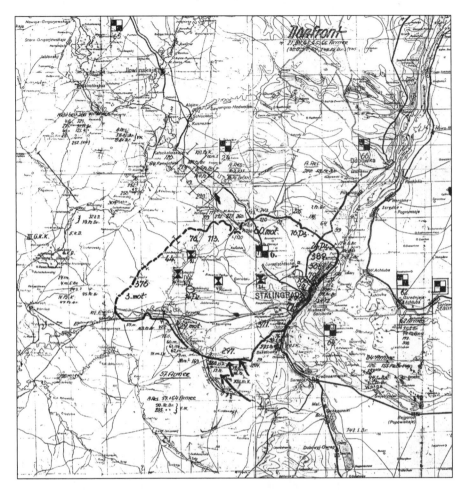

Map 77. Sixth Army's Stalingrad Pocket (*Kessel*), 29–30 November 1942

sions defended from south to north. The two infantry divisions were reinforced by *kampfgruppen* from 14th and 16th Panzer Divisions, respectively.
These German forces provided their usual stubborn resistance as 21st Army
advanced eastward at an agonizingly slow pace.

Reduced to only five rifle divisions, Batov's 65th Army crossed the ice of
the Don River on the night of 27–28 November, converging on and capturing
Vertiachii by midnight.[40] The pursuing rifle divisions ground to a halt when
they approached Paulus's new defensive line, which XI Army Corps occupied with the usual German skill, despite its pursuers. The 24th Army, as

previously described, was even less effective, simply following 76th Infantry Division as it methodically withdrew to the new defensive line.

The 66th Army launched a series of strong attacks on 28 and 29 November, despite sharp counterattacks by elements of 16th Panzer and 60th Motorized Divisions at Spartakovka and Hill 135.4 on the twenty-eighth. On 30 November Zhadov committed his second-echelon 299th Rifle Division to join 166th and 99th Rifle Divisions in assaulting the same hill, but the regrouping effort was so clumsy that the German defenders, especially 24th Panzer Division, anticipated and thwarted the renewed attack. Paulus's northern defensive line had indeed become the "fortress" that Hitler had demanded.[41]

Stalingrad Front, 28 November–1 December

Although Vasilevsky had simplified the command and control problem on the northern faces of Stalingrad, the Stalingrad Front was still trying to besiege the southern and eastern fronts of the pocket, while its 51st Army tried in vain to advance south toward Kotel'nikovo.

Within the city, 62nd Army dutifully attempted to attack on 28 and 29 November but was hampered by ice that prevented resupply and evacuation of the wounded until late on the twenty-ninth. Light transport aircraft dropped a few dozen boxes of ammunition and sacks of food to sustain the skeletal defenders of Stalingrad.[42]

Early on 28 November 57th and 64th Armies launched a coordinated attack against German IV Army Corps' defenses along the Karavatka *balka*, northwest of Iagodnyi. In ferocious fighting over the next two days, 64th Army's 38th and 157th Rifle Divisions, supported by up to 60 tanks of 56th and 235th Tank Brigades as well as Soviet fighter-bombers, penetrated 2 kilometers into the sector of Romanian 82nd Infantry Regiment, but they were ejected by a counterattack that included a handful of tanks from 14th Panzer Division. The 57th Army was equally ineffective, attacking 29th Motorized and 197th Infantry Divisions with 36th Guards and 169th Rifle Divisions, as well as tanks from 13th Tank Corps. Both attacking armies paid a high price in human and tank casualties for virtually no progress.[43] Some 45 kilometers to the west, 60th Mechanized Brigade and 158th Tank Regiment of 4th Mechanized Corps seized the villages on the eastern bank of the Don opposite Rychkovskii and Nizhne-Chirskaia, but they lacked sufficient infantry to clear the marshlands of German defenders.

Farther south, faced with the full strength 6th Panzer Division, General Trufanov recognized that his 51st Army had insufficient force even to contain a German counterstroke from Kotel'nikovo, let alone secure the railhead there. Shapkin's 4th Cavalry Corps headquarters, along with 81st Cavalry Division and 85th Tank Brigade, had fled some 20 kilometers north of the town after losing their initial struggle with 6th Panzer. From there, Shapkin began to reassemble his forces for a renewed advance. Egged on by Eremenko, the remainder of Trufanov's 51st Army moved very cautiously on 28–30 November, setting up a defensive perimeter halfway between the Aksai Rover and Kotel'nikovo.

THE STALINGRAD POCKET ON 1 DECEMBER

During the last 12 days of November 1942, the attacking Southwestern and Stalingrad Fronts had torn a 250 kilometer hole in the Axis front. By the end of the month, better-organized and better-equipped German units had begun to arrive to supplement the string of security and rear-area units along the Krivaia, Chir, Don, and Aksai Rivers.

At that point, Sixth Army and other associated units had completed most of their withdrawal into the resulting pocket, seeking to create a strong, relatively short front that would free up troops to act as local reserves (see map 77). Headquartered at Gumrak airfield, 15 kilometers west of the city, Paulus initially organized the pocket into five sectors, subordinate to XI, VIII, IV, and LI Army Corps, plus XIV Panzer Corps (see table 15.1). Each of these five corps faced one or two Soviet field armies, with each German division or special group opposing three to six Soviet rifle divisions or separate brigades (see table 15.2). One should recall, however, that most of the German organizations, as well as the formations within 62nd and 64th Armies, had already been extremely weakened by city fighting, making a direct comparison of forces highly subjective.

THE OUTER ENCIRCLEMENT ON 1 DECEMBER

The correlation of forces along the outer encirclement is difficult to determine, as it shifted on a daily basis. Romanian Third Army had prevented 5th Tank Army from capturing Oblivskaia, Surovikino, and Rychkovskii before Axis reinforcements reached the region at the end of November; thereafter, each side built up its forces rapidly.

Most significantly, Field Marshal Manstein's Army Group Don, placed in charge of the entire threatened area around Stalingrad, began planning an eventual relief effort toward the city. Initially, both the OKW and Manstein had contemplated launching such an effort from the upper Chir River, north of Chernyshevskaia, using Hollidt's XVII Corps and the survivors of XXXXVIII Panzer Corps. But strong Soviet action in that area soon showed

Table 15.1. Sixth Army Order of Battle, 1 December 1942

Sixth Army—General of Panzer Troops Friedrich Paulus
IV Army Corps—General of Engineers Erwin Jänecke
    371st Infantry Division (two regiments)—Lieutenant General Richard Stempel
    297th Infantry Division (three regiments, plus 82nd Regiment from Romanian
        20th Division and 670th Regiment from 371st Division)—General of Artillery
        Max Pfeffer
    29th Motorized Division (two regiments, plus 1st Battalion of 191st Regiment)—
        Major General Hans-George Leyser
XIV Panzer Corps—General of Panzer Troops Hans-Valentin Hube
    295th Infantry Division (Group Korfes)—Major General Dr. Otto Korfes
        Groups Domaschk, Grahms, von Hanstein (two *Luftwaffe* battalions), Willig
        (two companies [+] of 60th Motorized Division)
    3rd Motorized Division (two regiments)—Lieutenant General Helmuth
        Schlömer
    376th Infantry Division (three regiments, plus 2nd Battalion of 536th
        Regiment)—Lieutenant General Alexander Edler von Daniels
VIII Army Corps—Colonel General Walter Heitz
    44th Infantry Division (three regiments, plus 177th Assault Gun Battalion)—
        Lieutenant General Heinrich Deboi
    76th Infantry Division (three regiments, plus 2nd Panzer Regiment of 16th
        Panzer Division and 244th Assault Gun Battalion)—General of Artillery
        Maximilian de Angelis
    113th Infantry Division (three infantry battalions, plus 754th Pioneer
        Battalion)—Lieutenant General Hans-Heinrich Sixt von Arnim
XI Army Corps—Colonel General Karl Strecker
    60th Motorized Division (five motorized and one machine gun battalions, 16th
        Pioneer Battalion)—Major General Hans-Adolf Arenstorff
    16th Panzer Division (two motorized and one pioneer battalions, plus 2nd
        Battalion, 276th Infantry Regiment)—Major General Günther Angern
    24th Panzer Division (Group Lenski) (two motorized regiments, one motorcycle
        battalion, four infantry battalions, one *Luftwaffe* battalion)—Lieutenant
        General Arno von Lenski
LI Army Corps—General of Artillery Walter von Seydlitz-Kurzbach
    389th Infantry Division (three regiments)—Major General Erich Magnus
    305th Infantry Division (three regiments)—Lieutenant General Bernhard
        Steinmetz
    79th Infantry Division (three regiments)—Lieutenant General Richard Schwerin
    100th *Jäger* Division (two *Jäger* regiments, plus Croat 369th Infantry
        Regiment)—Lieutenant General Werner Sanne
    295th Infantry Division (three regiments [–])—Major General Dr. Otto Korfes
        (part-time with Group Korfes in XIV Panzer Corps)
    71st Infantry Division (three regiments)—Lieutenant General Alexander von
        Hartmann
    245th Assault Gun Battalion
Reserve
    14th Panzer Division (one panzer, two panzer-grenadier regiments)—Colonel
        Martin Lattmann
    384th Infantry Division (three regiments [–])—Lieutenant General Eccard
        Freiherr von Gablenz (to XIV Panzer Corps in mid-December)

Table 15.2. Opposing Forces around the Stalingrad Pocket, 1 December 1942

Stalingrad Front	Sixth Army
64th Army	IV Army Corps
7th Rifle Corps (three brigades)	371st Infantry Division
29th Rifle Division	
204th, 157th, 38th Rifle Divisions	297th Infantry Division
66th, 154th Naval Rifle Brigades	
56th, 235th Tank Brigades	
57th Army	
169th Rifle, 36th Guards Rifle	
Divisions	
17th Mechanized Brigade (13th	
Tank Corps)	
422nd Rifle Division	29th Motorized Division
90th Tank, 62nd, 61st Mechanized	
Brigades (13th Tank Corps)	
15th Guards Rifle Division	XIV Panzer Corps
59th, 36th Mechanized Brigades	Group Korfes
(4th Mechanized Corps)	
Don Front	
21st Army	
52nd Guards Rifle Division	
96th Rifle Division (with 4th Tank	3rd Motorized Division
Corps)	
293rd Rifle Division (with 26th Tank	
Corps)	
51st Guards Rifle Division	376th Infantry Division
277th Rifle Division	
65th Army	
23rd Rifle Division	VIII Army Corps
252nd, 27th Guards Rifle Divisions	44th Infantry Division
91st, 121st Tank Brigades	
304th, 24th Rifle Divisions (second	
echelon)	
24th Army	
120th, 233rd, 84th, 49th Rifle	76th Infantry Division
Divisions	
214th Rifle Division (second	
echelon)	
298th, 273rd, 173rd Rifle Divisions	113th Infantry Division
173rd Fortified Region	
	XI Army Corps
260th Rifle Division	60th Motorized Division
66th Army	
343rd Rifle Division	
226th, 64th, 116th Rifle Divisions	16th Panzer Division
299th, 99th Rifle Divisions	24th Panzer Division
Stalingrad Front	
62nd Army	LI Army Corps
Group Gorokhov	389th Infantry Division
138th, 95th Rifle Divisions	305th Infantry Division
45th, 39th Guards Rifle Divisions	79th Infantry Division
92nd Rifle Brigade	Group Sanne
284th Rifle Division	100th *Jäger*, 295th Infantry
	Divisions
13th Guards Rifle Division	71st Infantry Division

Map 78. Army Group Don's Plan *Wintergewitter* (Winter Tempest),
1 December 1942

the fallacy of such a plan.[44] At the same time, Manstein learned that the *Luft-waffe* would be unable to resupply Paulus by air, making a relief effort more urgent. He therefore shifted his focus southward and eventually proposed two different axes of advance.

General of Panzer Troops Friedrich Kirchner's LVII Panzer Corps, transferred from Army Group A, began to assemble at Kotel'nikovo under the command of General Hoth's ad hoc army group (see table 15.4). Manstein originally planned to have Kirchner attack as early as 3 December, recognizing that the other force, a reborn XXXXVIII Panzer Corps now commanded

Table 15.3. Opposing Forces along the Don, Krivaia, and Chir Rivers,
1 December 1942

Southwestern Front	Army Detachment Hollidt
1st Guards Army	Romanian I and German XVII Army Corps
197th, 278th Rifle Divisions	7th Infantry Division (R)
14th Rifle Corps	11th Infantry Division (R) + 2 regiments, 62nd Infantry Division
203rd Rifle Division	
266th Rifle Division (to 6th Guards Rifle Corps)	
4th Guards Rifle Corps (reserve)	Remnants, 9th Infantry Division (R)
35th Guards, 41st Guards, 195th Rifle Divisions	
22nd Motorized Rifle Brigade (reserve)	
14th Guards Rifle Division	294th Infantry Division
6th Guards Rifle Corps (reserve)	
38th Guards, 44th Guards, 266th Rifle Divisions	
1st Guards Mechanized Corps (reserve)	
5th Tank Army	Romanian II Army Corps
159th Rifle Division	14th Infantry Division (R)
216th Tank Brigade (second echelon)	
50th Guards Rifle Division	7th Cavalry Division (R)
	XXXXVIII Panzer Corps
1 regiment, 47th Guards Rifle Division	22nd Panzer Division
1 regiment, 21st Cavalry Division	1st Armored Division (R)
	336th Infantry Division (en route)
	11th Panzer Division (en route)
	7th Luftwaffe Field Division (en route)
346th Rifle Division	**Romanian Third Army**
	Group Spang
2 regiments, 47th Guards Rifle Division	Group Wandtke (610th Security Regiment +)
21st Cavalry Division (en route)	
8th Cavalry Corps (en route)	Group Waldow (354th Grenadier Regiment +)
112th, 55th Cavalry Divisions	Group Stahel (VIII Air Corps)
40th Guards Rifle Division (en route)	3rd Battalion, 177th Security Regiment
	63rd Construction Battalion
	1st Battalion, 8th *Luftwaffe* Field Division
321st Rifle Division (en route)	
8th Guards Tank Brigade	Group Obergehtmann (99th *Flak* Battalion)
119th Rifle Division	Group Stumpfeld (108th ARKO)
	Group Schmidt (520th Pioneer Battalion): 301st Tank Detachment, 36th Front Battalion

(continued on next page)

Table 15.3. (*continued*)

333rd Rifle Division	Group Selle (alarm battalions)
258th Rifle Division	Group Adam (to XXXXVIII Panzer Corps)

1st Tank Corps
  89th, 117th, 159th Tank Brigades
  44th Motorized Rifle Brigade
3rd Guards Cavalry Corps
  5th Guards, 6th Guards, 32nd
    Cavalry Divisions
60th Mechanized Brigade (4th
  Mechanized Corps)
	Group Heilmann (*kampfgruppen*
	  from 14th Panzer, 29th
	  Motorized)
	306th, 304th Infantry Divisions (en
	  route)

Front Reserves	**Army Group Hoth** (see table 15.4)
5th Mechanized Corps 18th Tank Corps 57th Army 4th Mechanized Corps	

by General of Panzer Troops Otto von Knobelsdorff, would take an additional six days to advance eastward from the Rychkovskii bridgehead. To accomplish this task, XXXXVIII Panzer Corps gained control of 11th Panzer Division and 336th Infantry Division and was originally slated to receive Lieutenant General Fridolin von Senger und Etterlin's 17th Panzer Division, dispatched southward from Orel.[45] Hitler eventually decided not to release the latter division in time for the attack. All told, some 240 tanks and assault guns prepared for a relief operation code-named *Wintergewitter* (Winter Tempest). This attack ultimately kicked off on 12 December. Yet even Manstein assumed that when the relief effort approached Sixth Army's perimeter, Hitler would relent and permit Paulus to abandon some of his gains in order to break out and link up. This assumption, like the rest of Manstein's concept, proved to be overly optimistic.

Based on his experience during the previous winter's Soviet offensive, Hitler insisted that Sixth Army stand fast in Stalingrad, relying on the *Luftwaffe* to resupply the pocket while the German panzer forces broke in and relieved it. The ill-considered promises made by General Jeschonnek and Marshal Göring had encouraged him in this belief. Of equal significance, however, were Manstein's assurances that relief was possible. From the moment he arrived on the scene to command Army Group Don, Manstein broke up the nearly unanimous assessment by Weichs, Paulus, and other German generals that an immediate breakout was the best if not the only solution to the threat posed by the Uranus encirclement. Manstein's self-confidence helped eliminate this option, committing Sixth Army to wait for external re-

Table 15.4. Composition of Army Group Hoth, 3 December 1942

Army Group Hoth (former Fourth Panzer Army)—Colonel General Hermann
    Hoth
Group von Pannwitz—Colonel Helmuth von Pannwitz
VI Army Corps (R)—Lieutenant General Corneliu Dragalina
    2nd, 18th, 1st Infantry Divisions (R)
VII Army Corps (R)—Lieutenant General Florea Mitrănescu
    4th Infantry Division (R)
    5th and 8th Cavalry Divisions (R)
16th Panzer-Grenadier Division—General of Panzer Troops Gerhard Graf von
    Schwerin
Subordinate to Army Group Don, en route to Army Group Hoth
LVII Panzer Corps—General of Panzer Troops Friedrich Kirchner
    6th Panzer Division
    23rd Panzer Division
    15th Luftwaffe Field Division

Note: R = Romanian.

lief. Manstein's arguments confirmed Hitler's natural tendencies, encouraging the dictator to believe that even if the *Luftwaffe* were unable to resupply the pocket completely, it could provide sufficient help to allow Sixth Army to hold on long enough.

PART FOUR

The Death of Sixth Army

CHAPTER SIXTEEN

Relief Attempts and Pressuring the Pocket, 1–15 December 1942

AERIAL RESUPPLY

After the fact, participants and historians calculated the true requirements for a successful airlift. General Jeschonnek concluded that to supply Sixth Army fully, Göring's pilots had to bring in 750 tons of supplies per day. Zeitzler had suggested a figure of 300 tons per day to Hitler, but this was an absolute minimum for subsistence and did not include the materials necessary to maintain a fighting force. The 750 tons represented at least 375 Ju-52s, each with a 2-ton payload, landing inside the encirclement every 24 hours. In fact, considering the distances to be flown, the practical load limit was probably closer to 1.5 tons per Ju-52. Given an operational readiness rate of 35 percent for the overworked transports, this meant that the *Luftwaffe* needed at least 1,050 Ju-52s. Yet the entire *Luftwaffe* had only about 750 of these aircraft in November 1942, and only 47 of them were immediately available for Stalingrad. Furthermore, during the time Stalingrad was encircled, Hitler ordered the commitment of at least one-third of the German transport fleet to airlift German troops into Tunisia in response to the Allied landings in northwestern Africa.[1]

Moreover, the *Luftwaffe* itself, like Army Group B, was operating at the end of a long supply line because of the poor Soviet road network and the difference in railroad gauges between Germany and the Soviet Union. Consequently, not all Ju-52s could be dedicated to the actual airlift; some would be needed to bring critical parts and time-sensitive supplies to the departure airfields of the lower Don. Thus, even before factoring in the weather and the Red Air Force, a sustained airlift was a logical and logistical impossibility.

Still, Jeschonnek and Göring had promised Hitler, and no one in the *Luftwaffe* wanted to abandon the soldiers of Sixth Army. On 23 November the *Luftwaffe* staff began shifting transports eastward. The training command surrendered aircraft and skilled instructor pilots; these diversions, in combination with combat losses in the airlifts to Tunisia and Stalingrad, meant that the German air transport fleet never recovered from the crisis of late 1942. Even *Lufthansa* civil aircraft found themselves pressed into service in the crisis. Yet moving these aircraft, many of them already worn and in need of repair, a distance of more than 2,000 kilometers from Germany to southeastern Russia took time. Bomber aircraft, including the Ju-86 bombing trainer, the He-111, and the newly fielded He-177, required additional time to convert to a transport role. On 2 December, when the siege was already a week old, Fourth Air Fleet could muster a total of only 200 transports, a figure that rose to 300 by 8 December. By that time, Richthofen controlled nine wings of Ju-52s, four wings plus two additional groups of He-111s, two wings of Ju-86s, a wing of He-177s, and even some FW-200 Condors and other long-range aircraft. Subsequent arrivals barely kept pace with losses in the airlift.[2]

While the aircraft gathered, Lieutenant General *der Flieger* Martin Fiebig, commander of VIII Air Corps under Richthofen's Fourth Air Fleet, began to organize the airlift effort. On 26 November, however, Richthofen conducted a radical reorganization to maximize that effort. Under Fiebig's supervision, Major General Victor Carganico became responsible for the overall airlift. Richthofen and Carganico segregated the aircraft, concentrating all transports of a single type at a single airfield to simplify maintenance and loading. Tatsinskaia, 211 kilometers from Pitomnik, was the base for all Ju-52s, as well as for 14 Me-109 fighters that patrolled the air corridor. He-111 units operated out of Morozovskaia, the most advanced base, located 168 kilometers from Pitomnik, while the long-range bombers and reconnaissance aircraft were based at Stalino, a full 440 kilometers away from the pocket. The airfields, especially the arrival field at Pitomnik and four smaller airstrips within the pocket, soon became congested. In addition to Pitomnik, there was an airstrip at Gumrak, 15 kilometers west of the city, but it was not fully developed because it was too close to Sixth Army's headquarters, and any activity there might attract Soviet strikes.[3]

This German organizational effort had to deal with severe problems of maintenance, adverse weather, and Soviet opposition. The Red Air Force had been outclassed in the summer and fall, but by the time of the airlift, it was able to mount a major effort to thwart Richthofen's pilots. The air armies in the Stalingrad region totaled more than 1,350 aircraft by mid-November, compared with 732 German aircraft (not including the influx of air transports) in Fourth Air Fleet. Moreover, most of these Red aircraft were newer, more capable types than those used during the summer months. La-5 and Iak-7 fighters had replaced virtually all the obsolete LaGG-3s, while Pe-2 twin-engine bombers and Il-2 *Shturmovik* assault aircraft gave the Soviets a much greater ground-attack capability. Particularly at lower altitudes, where most German transports flew, such aircraft could compete effectively against their German counterparts. Newer aircraft also tended to have higher maintenance readiness than the worn-out planes of Fourth Air Fleet. For the first time in the war, virtually all Soviet aircraft were radio-equipped, which facilitated the task of ground-controlled intercept.[4]

By early December, Red air commanders had organized an effective air defense system. Over the German airfields, 17th and 8th Air Armies bombed transports on the ground at night and interdicted them on takeoff in the daytime. Around Stalingrad, the Red Air Force's commander, General Aleksandr Alexandrovich Novikov, organized three concentric zones. The outer zone, corresponding roughly to the area between the inner and outer fronts of the ground encirclement, was subdivided into five sectors. Here, 16th and 8th Air Armies, reinforced with a division of national air defense fighters, assigned specific fighter units to particular sectors so they would be familiar with their operational areas. Kotluban' airfield served as the headquarters for a ground intercept control network, vectoring fighters toward any transports it detected. The middle zone was a band of approximately 30 kilometers, where Soviet antiaircraft batteries put up barrages along the most likely axes of German flight. Finally, over the German pocket itself, Soviet fighters tried to intercept the transports while Red bombers attacked the arrival airfields.[5]

By one German account, Fourth Air Fleet lost 488 transports and bombers converted to the transport role; this figure included 266 Ju-52s, more than one-third of Germany's entire inventory. It also lost more than 1,000 airmen. By contrast, according to a Soviet estimate, 903 transports and bombers, including 676 Ju-52s, had been destroyed, together with another 162 fighter aircraft. Discrepancies of this type are common when computing aerial combat losses and do not necessarily represent intentional deception by either side. For example, the German figure may not include 47 transports destroyed on the ground when 24th Tank Corps overran Tatsinskaia field in late December (see chapter 17).[6]

What did the *Luftwaffe* accomplish for this terrible price? By any measure—the ideal of 750 tons per day, the minimum of 300 tons, or whatever intermediate figure one might suggest—the airlift failed. During the first five days (25–29 November), an average of 53.8 tons arrived each day in Stalingrad. This average rose in early December, when the influx of transports brought the airlift to its height. Nevertheless, on only two days did the airlift even approach the 300 ton mark. Fourth Air Fleet reached its high-water mark on 19 December, when 154 aircraft moved a total of 289 tons into Pitomnik and evacuated 1,000 wounded from the pocket. Overall, during the 71 days of the airlift, the *Luftwaffe* transported 8,350.7 tons of food and supplies, or an average of 117.6 tons per day. Although the airlift failed to supply Sixth Army, it did rescue at least 24,900 wounded soldiers who otherwise would have died or become prisoners.[7] During the final days, the airlift evacuated a number of key German commanders and staff officers, including Generals Hube and Jänecke.

As a result of the aerial resupply failure, Sixth Army reduced each soldier's intake from 2,500 calories to 1,500 calories on 26 November and to 1,000 calories on 8 December.[8] By mid-December, it was clear to Paulus that, unless something was done to relieve or resupply the army, it would perish by starvation if not enemy action.

PLANNING: THE *STAVKA*, VASILEVSKY, AND VATUTIN

The *Stavka*'s original plan (see chapter 12) had been to follow a successful Operation Uranus with an even more ambitious Operation Saturn, designed to push Axis forces out of the eastern Donbas region and trap Army Group A in the Caucasus. Vatutin's Southwestern Front, aided by 6th Army from Golikov's Voronezh Front, was to advance southwestward to capture Rostov-on-the-Don, thereby cutting the German logistics south of that key node.

However, the unexpectedly large size of the force trapped at Stalingrad, together with German preparations to relieve that encirclement, meant that the *Stavka* now faced two other tasks—reducing the encircled Sixth Army and defeating German rescue attempts—in addition to launching Saturn. Like Hitler four months earlier, the Soviet leaders had inadequate forces to achieve simultaneous but geographically separate goals. Ultimately, these other missions compelled the Soviets to truncate Operation Saturn into the more modest Little Saturn.

The immediate issue was Malinovsky's 2nd Guards Army. Originally constructed around 1st and 13th Guards Rifle Corps with 2nd Guards Mechanized Corps, it eventually gained control of 7th Tank and 6th Mechanized Corps, for a total of more than 450 tanks.[9] Malinovsky's army was originally assigned as the exploitation instrument for Operation Saturn. On 9 December the *Stavka* reluctantly diverted Malinovsky to help reduce the Stalingrad pocket, only to decide a few days later that 2nd Guards Army would have to block the German relief effort at Kotel'nikovo.

In the interim, on 2 December Vatutin had issued the attack order for Operation Saturn, with Leliushenko's 1st Guards Army, supported by 5th Tank Army, directed to encircle Italian Eighth Army and Group Hollidt by concentric thrusts. On 5 December, after considerable internal debate, the Soviet leadership subdivided 1st Guards Army, placing Leliushenko in command of the newly created 3rd Guards Army to manage the thrust from the Chir westward, and leaving Kuznetsov to command a shrunken 1st Guards Army from Verkhne Mamon southward.[10] Similarly, after 5th Tank Army continued to falter against the Germans on the Chir River, Stalin again intervened to subdivide command and control. On 8 December, at Vasilevsky's request, the Soviet dictator ordered the vigorous Lieutenant General Markian Mikhailovich Popov to activate a new 5th Shock Army (using the staff of a reserve army) subordinate to the Stalingrad Front. This new army was to assume control of 5th Tank Army's 4th Guards and 25th Rifle Divisions, as well as 3rd Guards Cavalry Corps. The same order gave Popov command of P. A. Rotmistrov's 7th Tank Corps, coming from the *Stavka* Reserve, and Vol'sky's 4th Mechanized Corps, previously assigned to 57th Army. Thus, Popov ended up with three mobile corps plus two rifle divisions to attack the German bridgehead at Rychkovskii.[11] To replace the units transferred to Popov's new command, on 9 December Vatutin gave Romanenko's 5th Tank Army control of 5th Mechanized Corps and returned 47th Guards Rifle Division, allowing Leliushenko to focus on Saturn.

Late on 9 December Vasilevsky reluctantly concluded that Saturn could not be executed as originally planned. He offered Stalin a detailed concept of how 2nd Guards Army could reduce the Stalingrad encirclement, while indicating that Saturn's replacement would have to be sufficient to smash Eighth Army and block German relief attempts toward the encirclement.[12] After consulting with Zhukov, who was directing the unsuccessful Operation Mars, early on the morning of 11 December Stalin ordered the initiation of Operation Ring (*Kol'tso*). Given the difficulties involved in transferring and supporting Malinovsky's army, Vasilevsky had to request a delay of this operation until 15 December.

On 12 December, however, Vasilevsky was dismayed to learn that Kirchner's LVII Panzer Corps had launched its drive from Kotel'nikovo northeastward to relieve Paulus. By 13 December, 6th Panzer Division had pushed north of the Aksai River. Vasilevsky met with Rokossovsky at the headquarters of the Don Front, where Malinovsky happened to be visiting. The *Stavka* representative felt compelled to divert 2nd Guards Army to block the relief effort; after a considerable delay, Stalin approved his decision on the morning of 13 December.[13]

Starting from Rychkovskii, XXXXVIII Panzer Corps had a much shorter distance (52 kilometers) to cover in relieving Stalingrad than did LVII Panzer Corps (140 kilometers). For this reason, both the *Stavka* and the Southwestern Front commander, Vatutin, considered Rychkovskii the more threatening location, so they reinforced Romanenko's 5th Tank Army with 5th Mechanized Corps, as well as adding 216th Tank Brigade to Butkov's 1st Tank Corps (which had been reequipped with 5 KVs, 75 T-34s, and 66 T-70s). The new 5th Mechanized Corps was equipped with 213 British Lend-Lease vehicles, including 114 Valentine III cruiser tanks and 99 Matilda II infantry support tanks.[14] In turn, Romanenko also diverted a few tanks and an M-13 multiple-rocket launcher battalion to support Pliev's 3rd Cavalry Corps. This helped Pliev reach the banks of the town east and west of Rychkovskii, placing heavy pressure on subordinate units of Group Adam.[15] Although the Soviets were overly optimistic about Romanenko's ability to eliminate the threat from Rychkovskii, his operations along the lower Chir River were sufficient to disrupt XXXXVIII Panzer Corps' initial relief preparations.

THE CHIR (TORMOSIN) OFFENSIVE, 7–15 DECEMBER

Pursuant to a *Stavka* directive, Romanenko prepared his principal attack against Rychkovskii to begin on 7 December. Romanenko's main shock group consisted of Butkov's reinforced 1st Tank Corps and Colonel M. I. Matveev's 33rd Rifle Division, with 8th Guards Heavy Tank Brigade (38 KV-1s) and 8th Motorcycle Regiment in reserve. While Butkov penetrated the German defenses west of Rychkovskii and then wheeled southeast toward Nizhne-Chirskaia, Pliev's 5th Guards and 32nd Cavalry Divisions, together with 258th Rifle Division, would make a supporting attack east of Rychkovskii (see map 79). Following these attacks on 7–8 December, Romanenko envisioned 5th Mechanized Corps exploiting southwest, toward Tormosin, on the ninth.

Romanenko's intelligence staff had correctly noted the arrival of the German 336th Infantry Division beginning on 5 December, but they did not identify 11th Panzer Division until the day of the attack. Moreover, the Soviets were unaware that on 3 December Manstein had transferred the panzer corps, together with Group Adam, which was defending the Rychkovskii area, to Fourth Panzer Army. This meant that the new right wing of Romanian Third Army was the now divided Group Stumpfeld (108th Artillery Command) and, specifically, Group Schmidt (the understrength 672nd Sapper Battalion), Group Weicke (301st Panzer Detachment), and various other small formations. These elements defended the Chir River from Ostrovskii through Rychkovskii to Nizhne-Chirskaia on the Don. General Knobelsdorff, commander of XXXXVIII Panzer Corps, had assigned 7th *Luftwaffe* Field Division to protect his left flank in the area of Romanenko's main effort, while his other divisions were in assembly areas to the southeast.

On 7 December, therefore, 1st Tank Corps easily overran the army and *Luftwaffe* units west of Rychkovskii, advancing to State Farm No. 79. Simultaneously, 8th Motorcycle Regiment raced southeastward, halting about 10 kilometers west of Verkhne-Solonovskii when it encountered an unidentified element of 336th Infantry or 11th Panzer Division. Although the latter division was still detraining at Tormosin, its commander, Major General Hermann Balck, sent a detachment from his 15th Panzer Regiment northward to contain the penetration. Meanwhile, 336th Infantry Division launched its own counterattack farther east, inflicting a sharp defeat that kept Pliev's cavalry and some of Butkov's mounted infantry from supporting the main effort.[16]

Undeterred by this resistance, Romanenko reiterated his order to Butkov to seize Nizhne-Chirskaia.[17] In response, during the night of 7–8 December, Butkov redeployed 89th Tank Brigade and one battalion of 44th Motorized Rifle Brigade from his right wing and reserve, sending them to reinforce 258th Rifle Division attacking Group Adam east of Lisinskii.

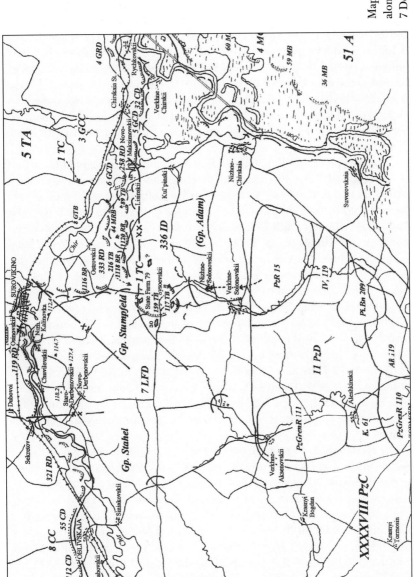

Map 79. Situation
along the Chir River,
7 December 1942

The Germans were planning their own attacks for 8 December. Balck concentrated some 70 tanks of his 15th Panzer Regiment, supported by 111th Panzer-Grenadier Regiment, to attack north to the vicinity of State Farm No. 79. This attack would then turn eastward, forcing the enemy into a horseshoe set of defenses formed by 336th Infantry Division, one regiment of 7th *Luftwaffe* Field Division, and (on the southern side) Balck's third regiment, 110th Panzer-Grenadiers.[18] The German advance surprised and severely damaged 44th Motorized Rifle Brigade and briefly encircled three of Butkov's tank brigades at State Farm No. 79, destroying some 60 Soviet tanks at a cost of 10 German vehicles. The survivors of these three brigades exfiltrated the encirclement to the north.[19] The *Stavka* still hoped to destroy or weaken the German group, issuing orders for 1st Tank Corps to renew its advance on 9 December while Major General M. V. Volkov's 5th Mechanized Corps made its own attack across the frozen Chir River, west of 1st Tank Corps, as planned.

This two-pronged effort failed. On 9 December two regiments each of 119th and 321st Rifle Divisions, with two brigades of 5th Mechanized Corps behind them, attempted to cross the river west of Surovikino, but they were stopped cold by the defensive fire of *Kampfgruppe* Weicke, including 301st Panzer Detachment, 36th Estonian Police Battalion, and other scratch elements. A surprise night crossing by dismounted infantry of 5th Mechanized Corps did achieve a small bridgehead by 10 December, but it failed to dislodge the main German defenses at Surovikino.[20] Also on the tenth, 11th Panzer Division counterattacked an attempted advance by 47th Guards Rifle Division and 1st Tank Corps' 159th Tank Brigade; by the end of the day, Romanenko's bridgehead was significantly reduced in size.[21] The next day, 3rd Guards Cavalry Corps achieved a similar minor success at Lisinksii, east of Surovikino, further distracting and dividing the attention of the German defenders. On 12 December, therefore, 11th Panzer Division dispatched half its panzer regiment, together with its pioneer battalion, northeastward to push back 1st Tank Corps' bridgehead at Ostrovskii; it then used almost the entire division to compress 5th Mechanized Corps' bridgehead at Nizhniaia Kalinovka.[22]

As recounted by Friedrich von Mellenthin in his famous book *Panzer Battles*, these German tactical successes overlook the broader threat posed by the Red Army. The appearance of 11th Panzer Division on 8 December had convinced the General Staff that the Germans did, indeed, intend to conduct a major relief effort from the Tormosin region. Recognizing that 5th Tank Army by itself might be insufficient to halt this effort, the *Stavka* ordered Eremenko's Stalingrad Front to activate the new 5th Shock Army. Commanded by General Popov, this force included the experienced 7th and 23rd Tank Corps. Major General P. A. Rotmistrov, who later commanded the famous 5th Guards Tank Army during 1943–1944, headed 7th Tank Corps throughout 1942. Refurbished after heavy losses in the Kotluban' region during August and September, Rotmistrov's corps had moved into assembly areas southwest of Stalingrad in early December.[23] Repeatedly decimated in the summer 1942 fighting, 23rd Tank Corps, once again commanded by Major General E. G. Pushkin, had rebuilt itself on the eastern bank of the Volga.

While 5th Tank Army continued largely ineffective attacks to keep XXXXVIII Panzer Corps fully occupied on 10–12 December, Popov's new army moved in on both sides of the Chir-Don River junction, assuming control of 4th Mechanized Corps in the process. The intelligence staff of Romanian Third Army had noted the advent of two new (but misidentified) tank corps in the area as early as 10 December, but they did not identify a new army headquarters until after 17 December. By contrast, the staffs of the Southwestern Front, 5th Tank Army, and 5th Shock Army had an accurate picture of the German forces facing them.[24] Meanwhile, 11th Panzer Division declined from 70 operational tanks on 7 December to 58 four days later, and 336th Infantry Division's combat effectiveness also declined.[25]

Popov's army attacked at dawn on 13 December, striking the various German *kampfgruppen* now subordinate to the newly formed 384th Infantry Division. In a full day of fighting, Rotmistrov's 7th Tank Corps captured Rychkovskii, while 315th Rifle Division cleared the enemy from the woods east of Verkhne-Chirskii and 4th Guards Rifle Division captured the Rychkovskii railway station and cut off the German retreat. This sudden attack broke through at the boundary between 110th Panzer-Grenadier Regiment and 336th Infantry Division southwest of Ostrovskii, encircling one battalion of the panzer-grenadiers.[26] Balck rescued this battalion by committing most of his division at Ostrovskii the next day, leaving his 61st Motorcycle Battalion and an artillery battalion to contain 5th Mechanized Corps at Nizhniaia Kalinovka. More importantly, Knobelsdorff's panzer corps expended its energy countering the Soviet attacks from the Kalinovka and Ostrovskii bridgeheads, leaving 5th Shock Army to seize the more important objectives of Rychkovskii and Verkhne-Chirskii. After extensive discussions between Popov and Rotmistrov, a deeply echeloned attack, supported by artillery from 5th Tank Army, unrolled smoothly on 13 December. The 3rd Guards Heavy Tank and 62nd Tank Brigades, the latter carrying motorized riflemen on the decks of its tanks, bypassed the German strongpoint at Hill 110.7 and thundered into Rychkovskii. By 0900, all German forces were cleared from the town, withdrawing southwestward 2 kilometers to Verkhne-Chirskii.[27]

By nightfall on 13 December, the Soviet Ostrovskii bridgehead was 19 kilometers wide and up to 8 kilometers deep. Knobelsdorff authorized the abandonment of Surovikino to free forces for defense elsewhere,[28] but for the moment, the Soviet attackers concentrated on eliminating any possible

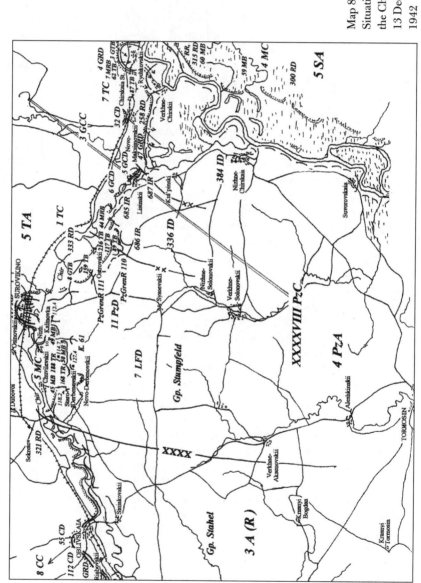

Map 80.
Situation along
the Chir River,
13 December
1942

German relief attempt launched from Verkhne-Chirskii. This was especially critical because that same day, LVII Panzer Corps launched its rescue attempt from Kotel'nikovo.

On 14 December, therefore, 5th Mechanized and 1st Tank Corps withdrew into 5th Tank Army's reserve, while 4th Guards Rifle Division and 7th Tank Corps fought their way into the heavily fortified strongpoint at Verkhne-Chirskii. This was defended by Group Göbel and the remnants of Group Mikosch, a total of perhaps 3,500 troops. Rotmistrov attempted to achieve surprise by launching his attack at 0200, but the German and Romanian defenders resisted bitterly.[29] Meanwhile, 5th Tank Army conducted local attacks from the Ostrovskii bridgehead in an effort to pin down 11th Panzer Division's armor. Contrary to General von Mellenthin's recollections, 11th Panzer Division was unable to break through to Nizhne-Chirskaia on 15 December; instead, it was tied up in a series of operations to limit Soviet attacks at Ostrovskii on the seventeenth.[30]

Thus, by 15 December, 5th Tank and 5th Shock Armies had ended any German hope of a relief effort from the west. Indeed, their success was so complete that two of the mobile corps involved along the Don—Rotmistrov's 7th Tank and Pliev's 3rd Guards Cavalry Corps—were available to help stop the other relief effort by LVII Panzer Corps. Both the ad hoc German defense groups and Knobelsdorff's XXXXVIII Panzer Corps achieved notable tactical victories in this struggle, but at the operational level, the Soviets were victorious. Clearly, Soviet mechanized formations were far more effective against the Germans than either the summer campaigns or Mellenthin's memoirs suggest. In turn, this often overlooked Chir-Tormosin offensive helped secure the eastern flank of the developing Operation Little Saturn.

FIGHTING FOR POKHLEBIN, 3–4 DECEMBER

While the Southwestern Front fought, with ultimate success, to contain XXXXVIII Panzer Corps around Rychkovskii, the Stalingrad Front remained shorthanded to deal with the parallel threat of LVI Panzer Corps at Kotel'nikovo. In early December General Trufanov's 51st Army had only a single echelon of overstretched divisions to cover the southeastern portion of the outer encirclement from the lake district, southeast of Sadovoe, westward past Kotel'nikovo to the Don River at Verkhne-Kurmoiarskaia. Across this 140 kilometer front, Trufanov had one fortified region, three rifle divisions, two cavalry divisions, and a separate tank brigade. Having been repulsed by 6th Panzer Division on 27–28 November, Lieutenant General T. T. Shapkin's 4th Cavalry Corps headquarters, controlling 81st Cavalry Division and 85th Tank Brigade, was concentrated some 20 kilometers north of Kotel'nikovo.

Shapkin had perhaps 5,500 horsemen, 60 tanks, and a battalion of *katiusha* multiple-rocket launchers. During the first two days of December, these relatively light forces reconnoitered the rapidly developing German defenses in front of them. Early on 2 December Trufanov directed Shapkin to conduct a double envelopment of Kotel'nikovo, but lack of fuel for the tank brigade delayed this attack until the following day.[31]

That day, Shapkin achieved some initial success, capturing the village of Pokhlebin, situated on a low ridge some 12 kilometers northwest of Kotel'nikovo. An initial counterattack by two companies of German 11th Panzer Regiment, which had just detrained at the railhead, failed to dislodge the Soviets.[32] The 6th Panzer's commander, General Raus, therefore accelerated the arrival of the rest of his division. On 4 December the entire 11th Panzer Regiment, numbering up to 150 tanks and supported by at least 2nd Battalion, 114th Panzer-Grenadier Regiment, surrounded the reinforced 81st Cavalry Division south of Pokhlebin by 1400 hours. After fighting all day, the surviving Soviet soldiers broke out of the encirclement that night. The Soviet force lost at least 10 tanks and 26 guns, while 81st Cavalry lost 1,897 men and almost as many horses.[33] Among the dead were the cavalry division's acting commander, chief of staff, and chief of the political section. In total, 4th Cavalry Corps lost as many as 3,500 men and likely half a tank brigade on 4 December. The defeat at Pokhlebin prompted the dispatch of 13th Tank Corps and four tank and artillery regiments to reinforce 51st Army; it also contributed to the decision to form the new 5th Shock Army.

Although 6th Panzer Division pursued the remnants of this force northward after the battle, Trufanov ordered them to establish an antitank defensive system north of the Iablochnaia River. He also directed Colonel A. V. Stavenkov's 61st Cavalry Division to continue its advance on Kotel'nikovo from the east, apparently seeking to distract the defenders. This division was reinforced by at least part of 254th Tank Brigade. On 5 December General Raus positioned his panzer regiment and his reconnaissance battalion to encircle this force, as he had done with the previous Soviet advance, but Stavenkov wisely retreated before the Germans could strike.[34]

LAUNCHING *WINTERGEWITTER*

While Eremenko moved 13th Tank Corps and other reinforcements to support Trufanov, combat operations near Kotel'nikovo were relatively light from 6 through 11 December. During this time, Field Marshal von Manstein argued for additional combat power to reinforce Kirchner's LVII Panzer Corps for Operation *Wintergewitter*.[35] Manstein became increasingly frustrated by Hitler's reluctance to withdraw more forces from Army Group A, apparently ignoring the fact that the Caucasus oil fields were the true goals of the campaign. Ultimately, the only units available were 6th and 23rd Panzer Divisions, together with two relatively weak Romanian army corps: VI Corps controlled 1st, 2nd, and 18th Infantry Divisions, while VII Corps had 4th Infantry and 5th and 8th Cavalry Divisions. In a lengthy report to the OKH on 9 December, Manstein dismissed these divisions as consisting of one or two battalions each and lacking both antitank defenses and "necessary energy."[36]

Manstein's report also failed to identify the presence of 5th Shock and 2nd Guards Armies in his area, two large organizations that significantly reduced German chances of success. Moreover, Army Group Don's planning was already complicated by the successful Soviet Chir-Tormosin offensive, which effectively removed XXXXVIII Panzer Corps from the relief plan. A paucity of air support also complicated Kirchner's task: originally, Fourth Air Fleet had allocated 179 combat aircraft to support LVII Panzer Corps, but for the period 11–13 December, two air groups were temporarily reassigned to support the threatened Italian Eighth Army.[37] In short, the relief attempt was a shoestring operation at best.

At midnight on 5–6 December LVII Panzer Corps issued Directive No. 1 (*Korpsbefehl Nr. 1*) for the relief of Stalingrad. Attacking north-northeastward out of Kotel'nikovo, Raus's 6th Panzer Division would make the main effort, with General Boineburg-Lengfeld's 23rd Panzer Division to its right and the three divisions of Romanian VI Corps screening its western (left) flank. Although the corps believed it had destroyed most of 51st Army's armor at Pokhlebin, it acknowledged that the Stalingrad Front could commit roughly 300 tanks from 4th and 13th Mechanized Corps.[38] Protecting the right flanks of 23rd Panzer Division and the corps fell to Cavalry Group Popescu, an ad hoc combination of General Korne's Romanian 8th Cavalry Division reinforced by two regiments of 5th Cavalry Division and Pannwitz's volunteers. In his own planning, General Raus envisioned a two-stage attack before exploiting to the Aksai River. Rather than detach forces he would need later in the penetration, he intended to break through the Soviet rifle divisions to his front and then lunge sideways with 11th Panzer and 4th Panzer-Grenadier Regiments to crush the remnants of 4th Cavalry Corps on his left.[39] To accomplish all this, Raus had 141 functioning tanks and 40 self-propelled guns, while Boineburg-Lengfeld's 23rd Panzer had only 30 operable tanks.[40] Trufanov's 51st Army had 34,000 men and 116 tanks initially, but it gained 107 tanks when 4th Mechanized Corps entered battle on 14 December, followed by a growing stream of vehicles from 13th Mechanized, 7th Tank, and other mobile corps.[41] Kirchner had to win quickly or not at all.

The attack began auspiciously at 0430 on 12 December (see map 81). The two panzer divisions, supported by Romanian 18th Infantry Division on their left, shattered the center and right wing of 51st Army's defenses in a matter of hours. Raus's 6th Panzer Division surprised and routed 81st Cavalry Division and 85th Tank Brigade, while 23rd Panzer overran the headquarters of 302nd Rifle Division, driving it backward in disorder. To the east, one *kampfgruppe* of 23rd Panzer Division plus Group Popescu also forced 126th Rifle Division back, while to the west, the remainder of 4th Cavalry Corps, including remnants of 81st Cavalry Division, withdrew toward Verkhne-Kurmoiarskaia.[42] After several hours of rest in the early evening, Kirchner's divisions resumed their advance shortly after midnight on 12–13 December, seeking to catch the defenders off guard. The 6th Panzer Division seized crossings over the Aksai River by 0800 and reached the village of Verkhne-Kumskii, 13 kilometers farther north, at noon.[43]

On the evening of 13 December Stalin placed Vasilevsky in charge of the defense in that area and approved the chief of staff's recommendation to divert 2nd Guards Army yet again, this time to stop LVII Panzer Corps. Operation Saturn would have to be reduced in scale. The next evening the dictator reluctantly sanctioned the temporary abandonment of Operation Ring to defeat Manstein's relief efforts.[44]

For five days, 14–18 December, LVII Panzer Corps and its Soviet opponents fought a brutal struggle on both sides of the Aksai River. Upon Vasilevsky's request, Eremenko dispatched numerous forces from the Stalingrad Front's reserve. At 1100 on 12 December Eremenko ordered Major General Tanaschishin to move his 13th Mechanized Corps immediately to halt 23rd Panzer Division. Not only did this daylight advance expose the corps to German aerial attack, but the formation was also short of troops, tanks, and trucks, so Tanaschishin was unable to attack until the next morning.[45]

More significantly, Eremenko had already dispatched Vol'sky's 4th Mechanized Corps, with 107 tanks and 105 guns, southward into an assembly area with orders to block 6th Panzer Division at the Aksai River. Eremenko also sent his deputy *front* commander, Lieutenant General G. F. Zakharov, and a staff to coordinate the actions of all three mobile corps—13th Mechanized, 4th Mechanized, and 4th Cavalry—as well as 234th Separate Tank Regiment (39 tanks), 20th Tank Destroyer Brigade, and two rifle divisions in the defense of the Aksai.

The first lunge of 6th Panzer Division placed it well north of 23rd Panzer, and General Hoth subsequently delayed the latter division's northward movement because of the reported approach of Soviet armor. To screen the gap between the two units, General Raus detailed 6th Panzer Reconnaissance Battalion, later joined by 2nd Battalion, 114th Panzer-Grenadier Regiment. That decision brought these two battalions into contact with the western flank of 13th Mechanized Corps when Tanaschishin engaged 23rd Panzer Division.[46]

Writing from memory, General Raus later described a series of tank

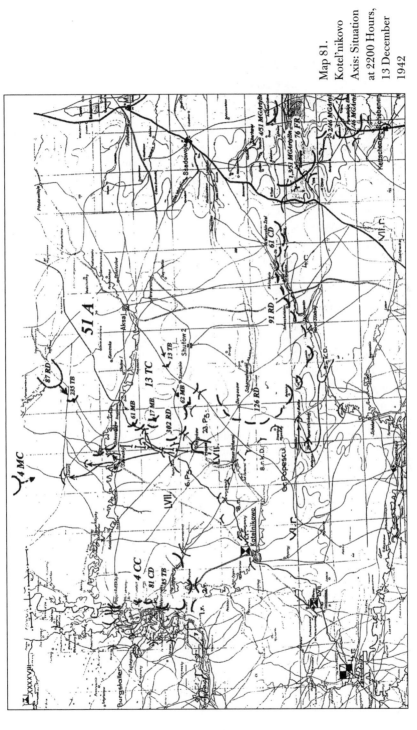

Map 81.
Kotel'nikovo
Axis: Situation
at 2200 Hours,
13 December
1942

clashes to his front, presumably with 4th Mechanized Corps, on 13 December.[47] In fact, Vol'sky's brigades did not reach Verkhne-Kumskii until late on 14 December and entered battle the following day. Instead, on the thirteenth the mauled elements of 4th Cavalry Corps tried in vain to impede the Romanian-German elements on Raus's left flank, while 13th Mechanized Corps had more success blocking 23rd Panzer Division and the two battalions Raus had put out on his right flank.[48]

On 14 December 4th Mechanized Corps fought a swirling battle with various elements, especially *Kampfgruppe* Hünersdorff (named for the commander of Raus's 15th Panzer Regiment). Hünersdorff rebuffed Vol'sky's advance guards, although 235th Tank Brigade and 234th Tank Regiment briefly encircled two panzer-grenadier battalions.[49] That same day, 23rd Panzer Division had more success against 13th Mechanized Corps, with *Kampfgruppe* Heydebreck, consisting of 201st Panzer Regiment and 1st Battalion, 125th Panzer-Grenadier Regiment, capturing a small bridgehead over the Aksai.

Based on reconnaissance of the German positions, General Zakharov approved Vol'sky's plan for a 15 December concentric attack aimed at Verkhne-Kumskii using his 59th and 60th Mechanized Brigades, each led by its tank regiment, with 55th Separate Tank Regiment behind 59th Brigade's western flank (see map 82). Zakharov also ordered one regiment of the newly arrived 87th Rifle Division to join the remnants of 235th Tank Brigade east of the village.

It is difficult to reconcile the German and Soviet accounts of the climactic battle at Verkhne-Kumskii on 15 December. The Soviet version neglects the role of 60th Brigade, suggesting that Raus's panzers did, in fact, thwart its advance. However, 59th Brigade began its attack at 0900, just as the fog blew away and the skies cleared. With motorized riflemen riding on tank decks, this brigade quickly rode into the village. In a series of attacks and counterattacks, the two sides struggled all day, but ultimately, *Kampfgruppe* Hünersdorff had to withdraw south to the Zalivskii bridgehead over the Aksai River, having lost at least 19 tanks.[50] By contrast, on 15 December 23rd Panzer Division pursued withdrawing forces of 13th Mechanized Corps and 126th Rifle Division, seizing yet another bridgehead over the Aksai.[51] This finally brought the two panzer divisions on line with each other, but by this time, 4th Mechanized Corps and its reinforcing units were digging in south of Verkhne-Kumskii, posing a much stronger obstacle to further German advances.

Throughout 16 and 17 December 60th Mechanized Brigade conducted a fighting withdrawal, protecting the damaged 36th Mechanized Brigade and preventing a breakthrough by 6th Panzer Division. Although reinforced by some self-propelled guns, General Raus later blamed General Hoth for a plan that dispersed his limited armor over a broad frontage, but he ac-

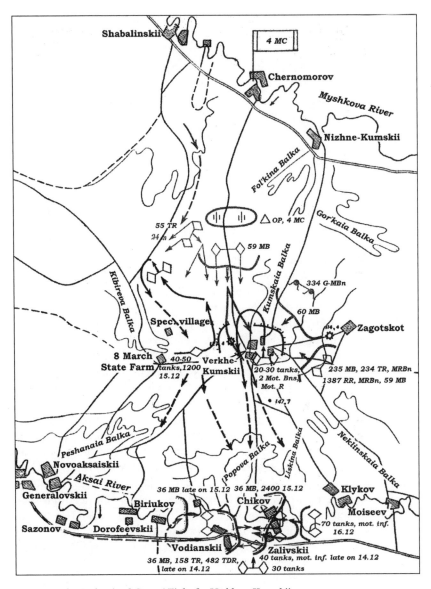

Map 82. 4th Mechanized Corps' Fight for Verkhne-Kumskii,
14–15 December 1942

knowledged his division's inability to get beyond Verkhne-Kumskii. To the west, Vol'sky used armored patrols to secure his flank, especially because 4th Cavalry Corps had so little combat power.[52] To the east, 13th Mechanized Corps' 17th and 62nd Brigades held firm to their defenses at Krugliakov and Kovalevka, respectively, denying 23rd Panzer Division much progress on 16 December. The next day a counterattack by 13th Mechanized Corps against 23rd Panzer forced General Raus to divert some of his armor eastward, again stalemating the advance.[53]

ADVANCE TO THE MYSHKOVA RIVER

At the end of 17 December frustrated Generals Hoth and Kirchner decided to resolve the Aksai River battles by a coordinated attack of three panzer divisions. Hitler had released 17th Panzer Division to Hoth's control on the thirteenth, but the veteran division did not reach the battlefield until the seventeenth. Lieutenant General Fridolin von Senger und Etterlin's division had only 30 tanks, no armored cars, and less than two-thirds of its authorized trucks; this last shortage meant that one company of each of the division's panzer-grenadier battalions was dismounted and would be left behind as their comrades advanced. When the division assembled northeast of Kotel'nikovo on 15 December, its commander reminded Hoth of these facts, but Fourth Panzer Army's commander replied, "At the front some divisions are in [an] even worse state. Yours has an excellent reputation. I rely on you."[54]

A hard freeze on the night of 16–17 December allowed the new division to begin refueling and rearming after its rail movement; a *kampfgruppe* from the division's 63rd Panzer-Grenadier Regiment moved north on 6th Panzer's western flank, pushing 81st Cavalry Division back and seizing its own bridgehead over the Aksai near Generalovskii, 20 kilometers west-southwest of 4th Mechanized Corps' western flank.[55] Thus, Kirchner had all three of his divisions on line along the river, waiting to attack on 18 December. By this time, those three divisions fielded about 125 functional tanks, while German intelligence estimated that the two opposing mechanized corps had perhaps 60 combat vehicles between them.[56]

On 18 December Vol'sky's 4th Mechanized, which had just been awarded the honorific 3rd Guards Mechanized Corps, again defended Verkhne-Kumskii from 6th Panzer Division. This tactical success became irrelevant, however, when 17th Panzer Division outflanked Vol'sky to the west and defeated many of the available Soviet tanks at 8 March Collective Farm, 7 kilometers west of the village.[57] This allowed 6th Panzer Division to overrun 87th Rifle Division's 1378th Regiment and envelop the rear of 59th Mecha-

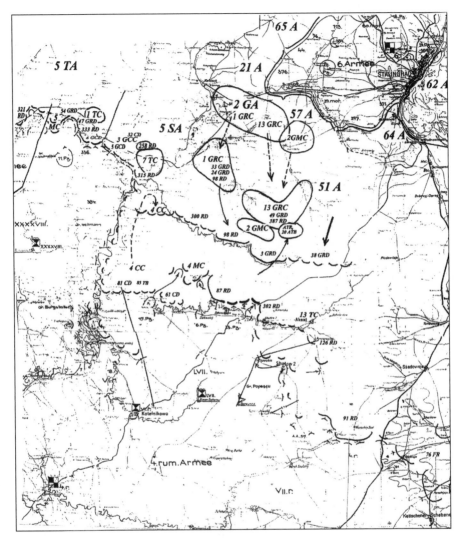

Map 83. Kotel'nikovo Axis: Situation at 2200 Hours, 18 December 1942

nized Brigade, severely mauling both units. The newest guards mechanized corps barely retained control of the village. To the east, 23rd Panzer Division, Cavalry Group Popescu, and Romanian 4th Infantry Division also captured several positions from 91st Rifle Division.[58]

While the battle still raged on 18 December, Vasilevsky sent a detailed report to Stalin.[59] By this time, 2nd Guards Army, which was moving south toward the Aksai battlefield, had assumed command of the area, while Rot-mistrov's 7th Tank Corps was en route to reinforce it. Vasilevsky asked Stalin to approve a plan for a general assault across the Myshkova River on the morning of 22 December, with 51st Army supporting 2nd Guards' eastern flank while Popov's 5th Shock Army completed its drive on Tormosin. With 5th Shock Army supported by 5th Tank Army and Operation Little Saturn encircling Italian Eighth Army, the Kotel'nikovo and Tormosin attacks were part of a major offensive effort. If successful, this effort would not only seal the fate of Sixth Army but also threaten to destroy Army Group A. Stalin approved the plan soon after midnight on 19 December. At best, LVII Panzer Corps now had only three days to drive to the Myshkova River before Mali-novsky's 2nd Guards Army intercepted it.

Kirchner's corps redoubled its efforts on 19 December, finally reaching the Myshkova. Preceded by groups of 20 to 30 *Luftwaffe* ground-attack air-craft, 17th Panzer Division closed up on the river by dark that same day, fol-lowed by 6th Panzer shortly before midnight. Crushed at Verkhne-Kumskii, the survivors of 3rd Guards Mechanized Corps withdrew to establish a new defensive position along the river. Having lost most of his tanks, artillery, and radios, Vol'sky had difficulty coordinating his units. By 20 December, he had only 6,333 men with 50 tanks (31 T-34s and 19 T-70s).[60] Still, the Germans did not achieve this advance without effort. Northeast of Krugliakov, 13th Mechanized Corps again halted 23rd Panzer's attacks on 19 December. That day, LVII Panzer Corps reported that it had lost 1,613 officers and men, about 10 percent of its strength, since 12 December. Fourth Panzer Army calculated that by the morning of 21 December, the three panzer divisions had lost 33 tanks destroyed and 83 others in need of repair, leaving no more than 92 operational tanks on hand.[61]

Thus, the Soviet defenders had completely absorbed the combat power of XXXXVIII Panzer Corps at Rychkovskii, while significantly delaying and degrading LVII Panzer Corps' advance from Kotel'nikovo. Recognizing this, Manstein sent a report to the OKH at 1435 hours on 19 December, virtually demanding that Sixth Army do its part to break out of its pocket; LVII Panzer Corps could not achieve victory on its own.[62] Later that evening, Manstein transmitted a message to General Paulus, pleading with him to initiate a breakout that would reach the Donskaia Tsaritsa River, some 20 to 25 kilome-ters south of the Stalingrad pocket's perimeter. The army group commander had previously sent his intelligence officer, Major Eismann, into the pocket to coordinate such a linkup. Yet neither Paulus nor his chief of staff, Major General Arthur Schmidt, believed that Sixth Army was sufficiently mobile or robust to assist in a linkup.[63]

The traditional explanation depicts Paulus as a defeatist, but even if this were so, Manstein should have already visited the city, assessed the situation, and replaced the Sixth Army commander. Given Hitler's suspicions about LI Corps' unauthorized withdrawal on 23 November, the dictator almost certainly would have agreed.

Quite apart from Hitler's refusal to consider a withdrawal from the city, Paulus and Schmidt were undoubtedly correct about their ability to conduct a breakout. Their subordinates had been expending ammunition at twice the rate it was being replaced by air. Even before the Red Army launched Operation Uranus, Sixth Army had ordered all but 25,000 of its 90,000 horses evacuated to a warmer clime for the winter. Those horses that remained in the city required fodder in vast quantities, complicating logistical planning for both the airlift and the subsequent ground relief convoys.[64] Without adequate ammunition, fuel, and horses, any breakout would have to be accomplished on foot, abandoning Sixth Army's heavy weapons and many of its wounded. In any event, LVII Panzer Corps was about to meet a Soviet force that would prevent it from reaching the pocket.

SIXTH ARMY HEMMED IN, 1–6 DECEMBER

While the outer encirclement prepared to fight the German relief columns, the Don and Stalingrad Fronts had to deal with the unexpectedly strong forces they had encircled. Despite frequent changes in *Stavka* plans, especially the diversion of 2nd Guards Army, these two *fronts* tried to reconnoiter, contain, and weaken the encircled Sixth Army. During 1–9 December 1942 a slugging match ensued, with little progress by either side. Within the Don Front, 21st and 65th Armies, as well as part of 24th Army, conducted limited attacks against German strongpoints along the pocket's western face, while the remainder of 24th Army, along with 66th Army, fought to tie down the German reserves. Similarly, the Stalingrad Front's 64th and 57th Armies launched supporting attacks on 2 December, while the threadbare 62nd and 64th Armies attempted the same on 3 December. None of these forces had sufficient combat power to make any real progress, especially as most of the available mechanized forces had to focus on the two relieving panzer corps. Thus, *front* commanders Rokossovsky and Eremenko had to wait for the defeat of the German relief efforts. In the meantime, however, Sixth Army's resources and energy continued to dwindle.

A few of the many minor actions had some effect on the ground. On 1 December, for example, 65th Army's 27th Guards Rifle Division sent a reconnaissance detachment against VIII Army Corps' 44th Infantry Division on the northwestern face of the German pocket (see map 84). This attack cost the Germans 11 dead, 42 wounded, and 1 missing, in return for an estimated 70 Red casualties. Although ultimately repulsed, this advance left the

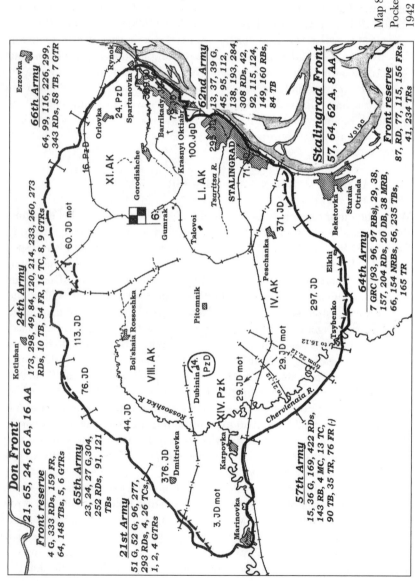

Map 84. Stalingrad Pocket, 1 December 1942

Soviets with a foothold in the German defenses north and northeast of Hill 124.5 (Chernyi Kurgan), offering a chance for later exploitation.[65]

On 2–4 December the Don Front's 21st and 65th Armies, together with two divisions on the right wing of 24th Army, renewed attacks all along the defensive lines of XIV Panzer and VIII Army Corps. Despite a few local successes, Rokossovsky's offensive action failed. Still, the panzer corps was so hard-pressed that it committed its last tactical reserves; this, in turn, forced General Hube to move one battalion each from three other infantry regiments, plus a *Luftwaffe* battalion from Sixth Army's slender reserves.[66] Late on 5 December Hube also sent the 11 tanks of 3rd Motorized Division's Panzer Detachment Warmbold to halt an attack on 384th Division; the detachment reported destroying seven Soviet tanks but lost the same number damaged. Moreover, this division suffered total casualties of 1,585 men between 21 November and 5 December.[67]

A history of 24th Rifle Division, which reinforced the right wing of 65th Army during this period, reflects the miserable conditions under which both sides fought:

> The steppe in this region constituted broken terrain subdivided by a series of heights. The Chernyi Kurgan rose 15–17 meters above the surrounding terrain. There was no vegetation, water, or lodgings in the region but, on the other hand, it abounded in dry gullies and ravines. Supplying water and heat to the subunits and especially the medical [aid] points represented a particularly difficult problem. The temperatures approached up to –42 degrees Centigrade [–44 degrees Fahrenheit]. The soldiers were in sheepskin coats, felt boots, quilted trousers and jackets, and caps with ear flaps; but the cold gripped the men.
>
> Movement was possible only by crawling on all fours.[68]

Supported by a tank brigade, this rifle division plus 304th Rifle Division achieved the greatest, if short-lived, success of Rokossovsky's attack when it seized Hill 124.5 on 4 December, prompting Sixth Army to direct a counterattack by VIII Corps to restore the main defensive line using *kampfgruppen* from 14th Panzer and 3rd Motorized Divisions. Again, the defenders succeeded on 5 December, but only after a significant effort.[69]

By 6 December, Sixth Army had dismembered its reserve 384th Infantry Division and assigned virtually all its component parts to reinforce VIII Corps' 44th Infantry Division and XIV Panzer Corps' 376th Infantry Division.[70] Sixth Army's personnel and tank strengths continued to dwindle, while Rokossovsky's tank regiments continued to get replacements. Unlike the mobile corps, however, most of these separate tank regiments were broken up into handfuls of tanks to support rifle units. This made them relatively vulnerable to German antitank guns as well as the famous 88mm *Flak* guns, thereby enabling the Germans to defend their positions against numerically superior Red tank forces.

Within the city, bitter small-unit struggles erupted periodically in the ruins. Both sides were reduced to skeleton formations. On 3 December, for example, the two brigades of Group Gorokhov achieved nothing when they attacked LI Army Corps' 389th Infantry Division in the western portion of Spartakovka village. At the start of the attack, Gorokhov had only 1,936 effectives, 13 heavy machine guns, and 22 guns ranging from 45mm to 122mm. The opposing German division, which had 4,021 combat effectives on 15 November, reported losing 152 of them between 21 November and 6 December, largely during the early December fighting.[71]

PREPARING FOR 2ND GUARDS ARMY, 6–15 DECEMBER

Rokossovsky continued to mount limited offensive operations against Sixth Army throughout the middle of December, preparing the way for the anticipated commitment of 2nd Guards Army to complete the task. Because that army was diverted to the Kotel'nikovo axis, Soviet memoirs and historical accounts tend to gloss over these frustrating and ultimately vain efforts, but in fact, they came close to unhinging XIV Panzer Corps' defenses at the Marinovka salient, the westernmost protrusion of the Stalingrad pocket.

While the Don Front's soldiers licked their wounds after the fighting of 2–5 December, the Germans shored up their defenses and conducted local counterattacks of their own. In particular, they focused on recapturing Hill 124.5 from 24th Rifle Division. On 6 December VIII Army Corps used *kampfgruppen* from 14th Panzer and 3rd Motorized Divisions, as well as 534th Infantry Regiment, 177th Assault Gun Battalion, and various antitank units, all supported by two division's worth of artillery and *Werfer* (rocket launcher) units. In response, 65th Army shifted its 252nd Rifle Division to reinforce the 24th. These German attacks retook a number of nearby heights, but the 24th clung to its dominant positions on Hill 124.5 itself.[72]

With the exception of 57th Army, which was preoccupied with German relief efforts, all the other Don and Stalingrad Front armies around the Stalingrad pocket attempted to resume offensive operations shortly after dawn on the brief winter day of 8 December. However, most of these armies remained so weak that they faltered almost immediately. The exception was along Sixth Army's western front and, in particular, Chistiakov's 21st Army when it attempted to collapse the German Marinovka salient (see map 85).

All five of Chistiakov's rifle divisions took part. With some armored support from 4th Tank and 1st Guards Tank Corps, 293rd Rifle and 51st Guards

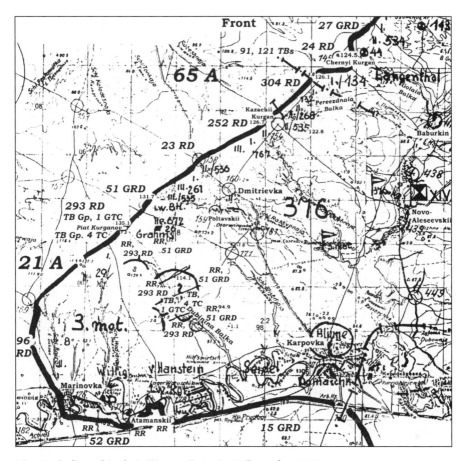

Map 85. Stalingrad Pocket's Western Front, 7–10 December 1942

Rifle Divisions had the most success, attacking southeastward in the center of their army and advancing 6 kilometers at the junction between XIV Panzer Corps' 3rd Motorized and 376th Infantry Divisions.[73] This advance gave the attackers control of the entire Dubinina *balka*, bringing them within 8 kilometers of Marinovka. Sixth Army reports confirm the sparse record in Soviet General Staff summaries, showing that, with considerable difficulty, the defenders contained and expelled this penetration by the evening of 11 December. The Germans had to defend Marinovka while continuing to counterattack just north of 376th's sector to restore 44th Infantry Division's front. On 8 December alone, 376th Infantry Division suffered 337 casualties, while 3rd Motorized and 44th Infantry Divisions reported casualties of 140 and 241, respectively.[74] Sixth Army continued to bleed at a lesser but still significant rate through 11 December, while the defeat of Rokossovsky's offensive depleted German stocks of fuel and ammunition.

With the start of LVII Panzer Corps' attack on 12 December, followed quickly by the diversion of 2nd Guards Army to halt it, Vasilevsky obtained Stalin's permission to postpone the start of Operation Ring until 15 December. The pace of fighting around the pocket slackened, but Sixth Army continued to suffer casualties, including 723 on 11 December, 705 on the twelfth, 723 on the thirteenth, 666 on the fourteenth, and 653 on the fifteenth. Most German combat battalions dwindled to 150 to 250 effectives, with some as low as 70.[75] Faced with such casualties, Army Group Don repeatedly urged Paulus to convert support troops into infantrymen or panzer-grenadiers, a task that was far easier said than done in an army that had been doing so for several months.

Despite repeated tactical failures under horrendous weather conditions, the course of events in the Stalingrad region tilted decisively in favor of the Red Army during the first half of December 1942. The Red Army not only foiled relief attempts but also forced Sixth Army to continue its losing battle of attrition, exacerbated by inadequate replacements and supplies. With the clear failure of aerial resupply, only rescue by an outside force could save Sixth Army, and that hope died during the third week of December.

CHAPTER SEVENTEEN

Little Saturn and the Failure
of Relief Efforts

LVII Panzer Corps' controversial effort to relieve Stalingrad, and the Stalingrad Front's efforts to block that relief, did not occur in a vacuum. Just as Kirchner's panzer corps belatedly advanced to the Myshkova River, the *Stavka* launched Operation Little Saturn, an effort to encircle the bulk of Italian Eighth Army and force Army Detachment Hollidt to retreat toward the main railroad line in the Morozovsk region. Then, while Army Group B struggled to plug the resulting gap by piecing together Army Detachment Fretter-Pico, the Southwestern Front unleashed 24th and 25th Tank Corps in an extended raid into the rear of Army Group Don. By attacking the airfields and supply bases at Tatsinskaia and Morozovsk, this raid seriously disrupted the airlift sustaining Sixth Army, as well as German efforts to defend along the lower Chir River.

OPERATION LITTLE SATURN, 16–31 DECEMBER

On 13 December Stalin approved Vasilevsky's plan for Operation Little Saturn. As described earlier, 1st Guards and 3rd Guards Armies, commanded by Generals Kuznetsov and Leliushenko, respectively, were to destroy Italian Eighth Army, while the Southwestern Front's 5th Tank Army protected the offensive's left (eastern) flank by continuing its own advance to Tormosin (see map 86).[1] To achieve the encirclement, four tank corps with a total of 700 tanks had concentrated behind the extreme northern (right) flank of Kuznetsov's army. Once the initial penetration was achieved, 17th Tank Corps would provide a flank guard moving west and then south of Strel'tsovka. At the same time, 24th, 25th, and 18th Tank Corps, operating parallel to one another from west to east, would continuously envelop the Axis rear by moving south-southeast. The first two corps would head for Tatsinskaia and Morozovsk, respectively, on the Northern Donets River. If the situation permitted, 5th Tank Army would join the southeastern movement by advancing to capture Tormosin and then wheeling westward to link up with 3rd Guards Army at Morozovsk.

In addition to the four tank corps, 1st Guards Army controlled 4th and 6th Guards Rifle Corps and was supported by the neighboring 6th Army of

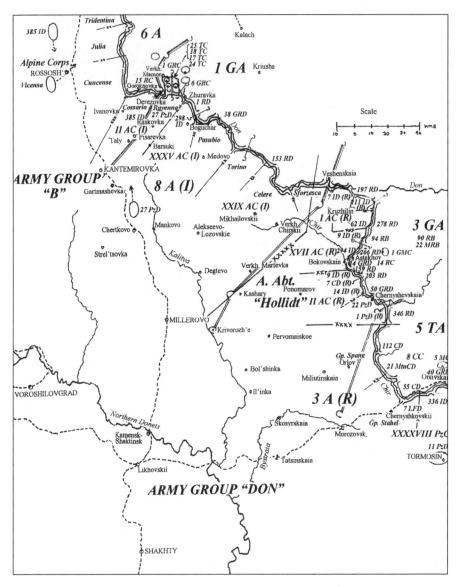

Map 86. Operation Little Saturn: Opposing Force, 16 December 1942

the Voronezh Front, for a total of nine rifle divisions attacking on a front of only 27 kilometers.

Opposite this assembly of Soviet offensive power, Army General Italo Garibaldi's Eighth Army controlled one German and ten Italian infantry or mobile divisions subordinate to four corps headquarters along a 125 kilometer wide sector. Only two of these divisions—5th *Cosseria* and 3rd *Ravenna* from II Army Corps, reinforced by German 318th Security Regiment—were deployed opposite the main attack area of 1st Guards Army. At that point, the attackers had a four-to-one advantage in battalions and even greater superiorities in field guns and tanks.[2] Like the Romanians in November, the Italian defenders were short of effective antitank weapons and local counterattack forces. Finally, Army Group B kept the weak 27th Panzer Division in reserve behind Eighth Army, with 38th and 387th Infantry Divisions behind Hungarian Second Army but in position to support the Italians if necessary.[3]

In turn, 3rd Guards Army controlled seven rifle divisions, two separate rifle brigades, 1st Guards Mechanized Corps, and 22nd Separate Motorized Rifle Brigade. Four of Leliushenko's rifle divisions would attack on a frontage of only 9 kilometers. His exploitation force consisted of the mechanized corps, one rifle brigade, and the motorized rifle brigade, totaling 234 tanks.

Leliushenko was facing Army Group Hollidt, controlled by General of Infantry Karl Hollidt's XVII Army Corps, plus Romanian I and II Corps. Unlike the Italians, who were subordinate to Army Group B, Hollidt belonged to the newly formed Army Group Don. In total, Hollidt's force consisted of the remnants of six Romanian divisions (7th, 9th, 11th, and 14th Infantry; 7th Cavalry; and 1st Armored), as well as German 62nd and 294th Infantry and 22nd Panzer Divisions.[4] Two other units—306th Infantry and 8th *Luftwaffe* Field Divisions—were in the area, and Hollidt received control of them after Little Saturn began. Until then, however, Hollidt had only part of 294th Infantry Division as a reserve.

Finally, Romanenko's 5th Tank Army, in cooperation with 5th Shock Army, was to demolish the defenses of Fourth Panzer Army's XXXXVIII Panzer Corps along the lower Chir River. By 12 December, Romanenko controlled six rifle divisions, three mobile corps (1st Tank, 5th Mechanized, and 8th Cavalry), 8th and 15th Guards Tank Brigades, and a number of smaller units.

Despite an enormous superiority in combat power, Operation Little Saturn did not begin smoothly. Leliushenko's main fire-support element, 9th Artillery Division, was late in arriving, and heavy fog covered the battlefield. Italian II Corps therefore contained the first attack on the morning of 16 December, and when the tank corps began to pass through the assault infantry, they became disorganized by uncleared minefields. Perhaps because of these initial Soviet setbacks, German headquarters did not realize the significance of the offensive until later in the day.

Frustrated, 1st Guards and 6th Armies reorganized to integrate armor more closely with infantry and rapidly routed the Italians on the second day, 17 December. Late that afternoon, 17th Tank Corps was committed to battle and exploited about 20 kilometers into the Italian rear. The Axis commanders moved to hold the shoulders of the penetration, so that by 18 December, German 385th and 298th Infantry Divisions were on the western and eastern flanks, each supported by a *kampfgruppe* of 27th Panzer, which had moved forward from Army Group B's reserve. Still, the Italian center continued to hemorrhage; by the end of the third day, 24th and 25th Tank Corps had also entered the exploitation, the latter capturing the town of Alekseevo-Lozovskie, 70 kilometers south of its original position. The poorly armed Italian infantry collapsed.[5]

Group Hollidt also had some success in containing 3rd Guards Army on 16 December. This may have been due to a change in Soviet tactics, with the attackers seeking to infiltrate enemy defenses rather than systematically clearing them. By the evening of 19 December, 1st Guards Mechanized Corps had begun its exploitation, meaning that all five of the Southwestern Front's mobile corps were loose in the Axis rear areas. Sizable Italian and German forces were either already encircled or about to fall prey to envelopments.

Shortly after midnight on 22 December, Hitler issued an order to establish a new defensive line extending from the Chir River northwestward to Degtevo to protect Millerovo, Morozovskaia, and the rail lines in the area.[6] By that time, however, both 24th and 25th Tank Corps were already well south of his proposed line.

More constructively, the OKH borrowed XXX Corps headquarters, commanded by General Maximilian von Fretter-Pico, from Army Group North. On 23 December Fretter-Pico received command of 304th Infantry Division, just assembling around Kamensk on the Northern Donets River; the remnants of 27th Panzer and 298th Infantry Divisions, which had been reinforcing the Italians; Group Kreysing (built around 3rd Mountain Division's 144th Mountain *Jäger* Regiment); and surviving elements of two German security divisions and of XXIX Army Corps.[7] Army Detachment Fretter-Pico attempted to screen the Northern Donets River crossings and cover the gap between the Italians and Hollidt. Hitler's concern was evident in his odd decision to ship the first experimental battalion of Panzer VI Tiger tanks to the region.

Such patchwork solutions were clearly inadequate; by the evening of 22 December, Manstein had concluded that stopping Little Saturn must take precedence over relieving Sixth Army. He convinced Hitler that this was necessary to protect the crucial airfields south of the Donets. With the dictator's reluctant approval, the next day Manstein removed XXXXVIII Panzer Corps headquarters and 11th Panzer Division from the defense of the lower Chir, leaving that task to an ad hoc corps command headed by General of Infantry Friedrich Mieth, previously chief of Army Group Don's security forces. More significantly, Manstein also diverted 6th Panzer Division, leaving LVII Panzer Corps along the Myshkova River with only 19 functional tanks in its other two panzer divisions.[8]

By Christmas Eve, the Soviet mobile corps were 200 kilometers into Army Group B's rear area. Major General P. P. Pavlov's 25th Tank Corps was within artillery range of the German airfield at Morozovsk, while Major General V. M. Badanov's 24th Tank Corps had actually overrun the principal Ju-52 airlift base at Tatsinskaia. As a result, there was no airlift into Stalingrad that day, and the next day, nine He-111s delivered only seven tons of cargo.[9]

Badanov, whose corps had already been reduced to 58 tanks, paid a high price for his audacity. On Christmas Day the weather cleared, and German bombers savaged the invaders. Having assembled southwest of Morozovsk, 11th Panzer Division drove southwest toward 24th Tank Corps. A *kampfgruppe* from 6th Panzer Division split the two tank corps and engaged Badanov from the northwest, while 306th Infantry Division's 579th Regiment attempted to complete the encirclement on the southern side of Tatsinskaia. Stalin and Zhukov urged Vatutin to rescue the talented tank commander, and Badanov did escape the encirclement; he then assumed command of the 40 tanks that remained of the two tank corps. Still, the multicorps attack became the model for the creation in 1943 of the first five (of six) new tank armies that led Soviet offensive operations for the remainder of the war.[10]

Although XXXXVIII Panzer Corps had recaptured Tatsinskaia, Army Detachment Fretter-Pico faced the unenviable task of containing 1st Guards Army's southwestward push using scattered units that had been rushed into the area. Much of this effort fell on the understrength Group Kreysing, fighting an epic battle of encirclement to defend Millerovo.

The 3rd Mountain Division had been split into three different elements to hold these locations, with Millerovo falling to the group headed by and named for the division commander, Lieutenant General Hans Kreysing. With him, Kreysing had brought his 144th Mountain *Jäger* Regiment plus two artillery battalions and elements of his reconnaissance, engineer, and support units. At Millerovo, he found ample ammunition supplies, two panzer-*Jäger* (antitank) companies, three engineer battalions, and five *Luftwaffe* antiaircraft batteries, two of which were equipped with 88mm guns. Between 24 December and 15 January this composite force was besieged, repulsing 38 different attacks, most of them conducted by 6th Guards Rifle Corps' 38th Guards Rifle Division and a few tanks from 18th Tank Corps. Kreysing finally broke out to the southwest and, after a running three-day fight with two other divisions of 6th Corps, rejoined German lines 48 kilometers to the southwest.[11]

Other isolated detachments had similar experiences. A *kampfgruppe* based on 19th Panzer Division's 73rd Panzer-Grenadier Regiment defended the communications center of Chertkovo, 80 kilometers south of the original breakthrough by 1st Guards Army. For ten days beginning on 28 December, this *kampfgruppe* fended off frequent attacks from three different divisions of 4th Guards Rifle Corps. The 73rd Regiment rejoined its parent division on 16 January, but together with the threadbare 27th Panzer, now under the control of XXIV Panzer Corps, they could only slow the advance of 1st Guards Army.[12]

By New Years' Eve, XXIV Panzer Corps (with a mixture of infantry, armored, and ad hoc units) and the Italian Alpine Corps had temporarily stabilized a 60 kilometer front from Novaia Kalitva southwest to the Kantermirovka area. Farther south, Army Detachment Fretter-Pico's 19th Panzer and 304th Infantry Divisions held a discontinuous string of outposts about 170 kilometers down to the area of Kamensk-Shakhtinsk, while the besieged forces at Chertkovo and Millerovo tied down large portions of 1st Guards Army. The southern boundary of this flimsy perimeter belonged to Army Detachment Hollidt, controlling XXXXVIII Panzer Corps and the remnants of XVII and XXIX Army Corps. Meanwhile, the withdrawal of 11th Panzer Division from the lower Chir River had inevitably led to a collapse in that area as well.

THE TORMOSIN OFFENSIVE CONTINUED, 16–31 DECEMBER

After the fighting on the lower Chir and Don Rivers during the first half of December, a brief respite began on the evening of 15 December. The 11th Panzer Division turned over its defensive front to 7th *Luftwaffe* Field Division and moved south into assembly areas, preparing for another attempt to capture a bridgehead over the Don near Nizhne-Chirskaia and thereby support the relief of Sixth Army.[13] At the same time, Southwestern Front commander Vatutin, realizing that 5th Tank Army had transferred much of its combat power to 5th Shock Army, assigned Romanenko a supporting role for Operation Little Saturn: 48 hours after the main attack by 1st and 3rd Guards Army, 5th Tank Army would resume the attack in its own area, seeking to at least tie up 11th Panzer Division and other German forces on the lower Chir.

To accomplish this mission, shortly after dawn on 18 December the inexperienced 5th Mechanized Corps attacked southward from its shallow bridgehead over the Chir near Chuvilevskii. Supported by 321st Rifle Division on its right, General Volkov's corps first captured the village of Dal'ne-Podgorskii, one of the few remaining German bridgeheads over the Chir River. By the

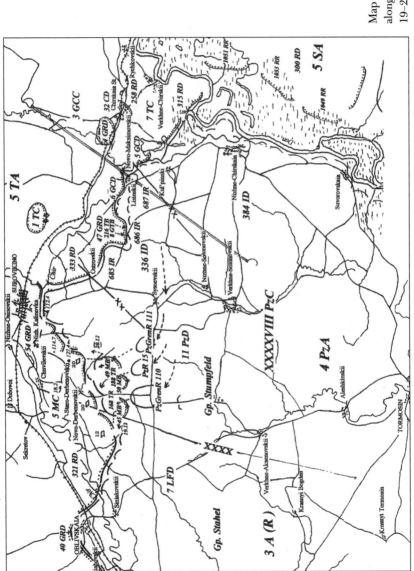

Map 87. Situation
along the Chir River,
19–20 December 1942

end of the day, Volkov had also advanced up to 12 kilometers south of the river, threatening to envelop both 7th *Luftwaffe* Field Division and the western flank of 336th Infantry Division.

In response, XXXXVIII Panzer Corps sent 11th Panzer Division back to the same area. In a classic meeting engagement on 19 December south of State Farm No. 79, 15th Panzer Regiment's 25 functional tanks engaged the largely British-made armor of 5th Mechanized Corps (see map 87). Although General von Mellenthin claimed the Germans had destroyed 65 Red tanks without losses, the chief of staff of the Soviet corps later insisted that, at shorter ranges, the British 40mm guns had some effect on the Germans' Panzer II and III vehicles.[14] Heavy fighting continued throughout 19–22 December, with Volkov attempting a night advance on the twentieth, even though 11th Panzer had gone on the defensive. On the twenty-third XXXXVIII Panzer Corps had to abandon its salient toward Surovikino as Red pressure made its grip on the lower Chir increasingly tenuous. Both 5th Mechanized and 11th Panzer withdrew from the area on the twenty-second—the one to refit, and the other to help plug the gaps created by Operation Little Saturn. Despite repeated tactical successes, as recorded by Mellenthin in *Panzer Battles*,[15] 11th Panzer Division had been neutralized at the operational level. Butkov's tank corps and Volkov's mechanized corps demonstrated an increasing and (for the Germans) disconcerting ability to attack, absorb defeat, and attack again as Soviet commanders and staffs became almost as experienced and effective as their German counterparts.

The withdrawal of 5th Mechanized Corps and 11th Panzer Division was only the curtain-raiser for a much more significant change in the same area. This occurred when, in conjunction with 2nd Guards Army's counterattacks on the Kotel'nikovo axis, 5th Tank and 5th Shock Armies burst from their confines and cleared Axis forces from the entire lower Chir area.

The *Stavka* planned for 5th Tank Army, using 8th Cavalry Corps and a refurbished 5th Mechanized Corps, to penetrate Army Group Hollidt's Group Spang northwest of Oblivskaia. Launched on 27 December, this penetration would form the right or northern arm of a pincer movement to cut the main railroad line running through the Chir valley to Stalingrad. Two days later, the southern or left pincer of this Tormosin offensive, composed of two groups from 5th Shock Army plus a portion of 2nd Guards Army, would begin. In this phase, Pliev's 3rd Guards Cavalry Corps would overrun the weak Corps Group Mieth, advance west to capture Tormosin, and then meet up with 5th Tank Army south of Morozovsk. The second shock group would consist of the rifle divisions of 5th Shock, possibly joined by 23rd Tank Corps, attacking westward from the lower Chir River and advancing in tandem with Pliev's cavalrymen.

Finally, if 2nd Shock Army succeeded in its 24 December counterattack

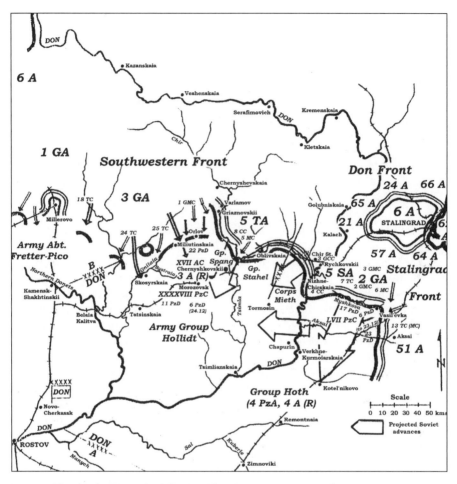

Map 88. Plan for the Tormosin Offensive: Situation on 23–24 December 1942

along the Myshkova, 2nd Guards Mechanized Corps and up to a full rifle corps would pivot westward, force the Don River in the Potemkinskaia region, and then advance parallel with 5th Shock Army but south of Tormosin. The *Stavka* was so confident that Malinovsky's guards army would be able to deal with LVII Panzer Corps that on 25 December Stalin directed the transfer of 23rd Tank Corps, just assigned to Malinovsky, to 5th Shock Army. At the same time, the *Stavka* reassigned 1st Guards (formerly 26th) Tank Corps from the Don Front to the Southwestern Front's 5th Tank Army, thereby giving 5th Tank and 5th Shock Armies the offensive capability they needed for the Tormosin offensive. Early on 26 December the *Stavka* restored unity of command in the area, transferring 5th Shock Army from the Stalingrad to the Southwestern Front. At the same time, 5th Shock Army's successful commander Popov became Vatutin's deputy at Southwestern Front head-quarters, succeeded by Lieutenant General V. D. Tsvetaev in command of 5th Shock.[16]

Army Group Don also had to reorganize after the transfer of XXXXVIII Panzer Corps from the lower Chir to Morozovsk on 22 December. On the twenty-seventh Manstein assigned the remnants of Romanian Third Army to Army Group Hollidt. This moved the boundary between Hollidt and Fourth Panzer Army westward to Chernyshkovskii. In addition to 336th and 384th Infantry Divisions in the Chir-Don area, Group Mieth assumed command of Group Stahel and 7th *Luftwaffe* Field Division.[17]

As temperatures dropped just below freezing, Romanenko's 5th Tank Army began its attack at dawn on 27 December. Whereas his previous efforts had been conducted on the eastern wing of his army, closer to the junction of the Chir and Don Rivers, this time Romanenko's main effort was in the west, between Popov and Karachev, 12 and 22 kilometers, respectively, northwest of Oblivskaia. General Volkov's 5th Mechanized Corps, General Borisov's 8th Cavalry Corps, and 8th Guards Tank Brigade attacked, their first objective being Chernyshkovskii, on the main railroad line some 25 kilometers southwest of Oblivskaia. This attack brought them into contact with Army Detachment Hollidt's Group Spang, a mixture of two battalions of 354th Infantry Regiment, 63rd Construction Battalion, and three alarm battalions. General Hollidt ordered Group Spang to fall back to a preplanned defensive *Stellung* (stronghold position) on a line about 15 kilometers north of the key centers of Morozovsk and Chernyshkovskii (see dashed line on map 89). This defensive line was tied in with Knobelsdorff's XXXXVIII Panzer Corps to the west; Hollidt's own XVII Army Corps, protecting the two cities; and Group Stahel, the left wing of Corps Group Mieth, to the east.[18]

This defensive line brought Romanenko's rapid advance to a halt. He reached the Tsimla River line in the Sivolobov area on 28 December, where he encountered the decimated 22nd Panzer Division. At Hollidt's direction, XXXXVIII Panzer Corps sent *Kampfgruppe* Hünersdorff, part of 6th Panzer Division, to reinforce the defense of the area. With 20 tanks, a battalion of panzer-grenadiers, an artillery battalion, and two panzer-*Jäger* companies, Hünersdorff launched two counterattacks between Chernyshkovskii and Sivolobov on 28–29 December. These actions administered a sharp rebuff to 8th Cavalry Corps and 8th Guards Tank Brigade, but then the *kampfgruppe* had to race to another threatened spot west of Morozovsk.[19] This departure made it impossible for Group Spang to expel a portion of 5th Mechanized Corps that controlled the railroad at Parshin Station, 14 kilometers east of Chernyshkovskii. The result was a stalemate, as Soviet tank strength plum-

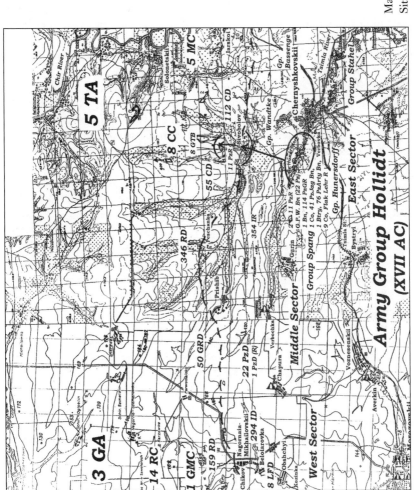

Map 89. 5th Tank Army's Advance: Situation on 28 December 1942

meted and Axis intelligence estimated that 5th Mechanized and 8th Cavalry Corps were at about one-third their authorized strength.[20]

This stalemate was the final straw for Romanenko, whose inability to control the tank army had repeatedly disappointed both Vatutin and the *Stavka* since the beginning of the Uranus offensive in November. After an extended discussion by teletype between Vatutin and Moscow on 28 December, Stalin ordered that General Popov would replace Romanenko as commander of 5th Tank Army, while retaining his new post as deputy commander of the Southwestern Front.[21]

The next day, 29 December, 5th Shock Army attacked across the Don River south of Nizhne-Chirskaia. Despite making no major progress, the combined pressure of 5th Tank and 5th Shock Armies kept Corps Group Mieth fully occupied along the lower Chir River.[22] Thus, the defenders were ill prepared to deal with 2nd Guards Army's crossings farther south, where General A. I. Utvenko's 33rd Guards Division, with light tanks from General K. V. Sviridov's 2nd Guards Mechanized Corps, crossed successfully near Krasnoiarskii and Verkhne-Kurmoiarskii. These were part of an operations group that General Malinovsky had created under his deputy, General Ia. G. Kreizer, because the *Stavka* wanted to liquidate the German wedge between the twin large-scale offensives conducted by the Southwestern and Stalingrad Fronts.[23] During the night of 29–30 December the remainder of 2nd Guards Mechanized Corps crossed the river in this area, while 3rd Guards Cavalry Corps crossed farther north, in 5th Shock Army's area (see map 90).

That same night, the *Stavka* again acted to bring its command structure in line with the developing situation. Eremenko's Stalingrad Front became the new Southern Front, transferring its 57th, 62nd, and 64th Armies to Rokossovsky's Don Front, which now commanded all the forces involved in the liquidation of Sixth Army. Eremenko retained control of 2nd Guards, 51st, and 28th Armies, while Rokossovsky continued to coordinate the offensives of that *front* and the Southwestern Front in the lower Chir–Tormosin–Kotel'nikovo area.[24]

On 30 December 3rd Guards Cavalry and 2nd Guards Mechanized Corps moved so quickly that they preempted some of General Mieth's intended defensive positions, so instead he tried to fortify the Tsimla River to protect his southern flank. The 384th Infantry Division and the right wing of the 336th withdrew westward through the Tormosin area, while Army Group Don directed 11th Panzer Division to backstop the new Tsimla position. Corps Group Mieth had hastily dispatched a small intervention group, *Eingreifgruppe* Bassenge, in an attempt to slow Sviridov's 2nd Guards Mechanized Corps, but Bassenge quickly withdrew toward the Tsimla as well.[25]

On 30 December Sviridov reported taking Balabanovskii, 18 kilometers south-southeast of Tormosin, almost without loss, in part because the situ-

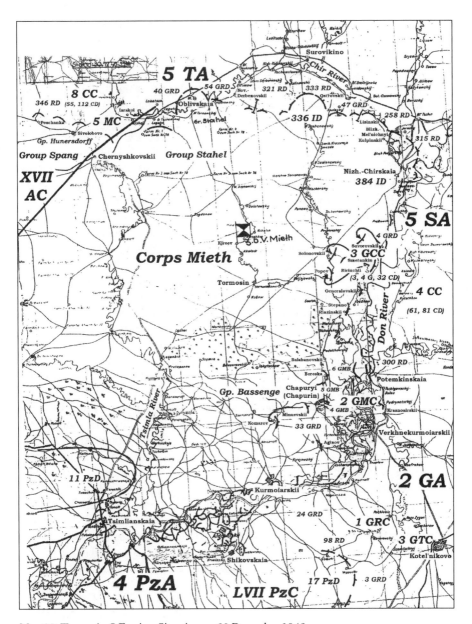

Map 90. Tormosin Offensive: Situation on 30 December 1942

ation had changed so quickly that the *Luftwaffe* bombed friendly troops by mistake.[26] The corps reached Tormosin itself late on New Year's Eve.

Thus, both 5th Shock and 2nd Guards Armies accomplished their missions in the often forgotten Tormosin offensive. The *Stavka* won the chess game played along the Don, Chir, and Aksai Rivers in the final three weeks of 1942 and, in the process, seriously depleted German forces in the area.

PLANNING *DONNERSCHLAG*

As the difficulties of relieving Stalingrad from the outside, either by air or on the ground (Operation *Wintergewitter*), increased, Field Marshal von Manstein increasingly insisted that Paulus mount some effort to assist General Kirchner's advance. Once LVII Panzer Corps became enmeshed in heavy fighting around Verkhne-Kumskii and Krugliakov on 16 December, Paulus initiated detailed planning for such a breakout operation, known as *Donnerschlag* (Thunderclap). General Hube's XIV Panzer Corps would conduct the breakout to link up with relief forces in the hills west of Buzinovka, 20 to 25 kilometers south of Marinovka.[27] In turn, Hube planned for Colonel Lattmann's 14th Panzer Division, with 29th Motorized and 3rd Motorized Divisions on his flanks, to make the main attack. Although there are no documents showing that Paulus approved Hube's plan, subsequent German troop movements indicate that he did. On 26 December Paulus expanded *Donnerschlag* to include Jänecke's IV Corps, operating on Hube's southern (left) flank (see map 91). In addition to its own 297th Infantry Division, IV Corps received 60th Motorized and 79th Infantry Divisions, which were withdrawn from other portions of the pocket.[28] However, Paulus operated under the restriction, imposed by Hitler, that if a breakout occurred, Sixth Army would retain its position inside the pocket; both Sixth Army and Army Group Don realized that this requirement was impossible.

This was the background for the ongoing discussions among Hitler, Manstein, and Paulus concerning the fate of Sixth Army. The concerned parties fenced over the matter from 19 through 23 December, after which Operation *Wintergewitter* no longer seemed to have any chance of success. Various teletype conversations involving Paulus, Manstein, and the army group chief of staff, Lieutenant General Friedrich Schulz, on 18–19 December indicate that LVII Panzer Corps still faced strong opposition on the Myshkova River, a situation that reinforced Paulus's doubts.[29] The Sixth Army chief of staff, General Schmidt, also exchanged views with Schulz on 20 and 22 December, emphasizing the logistical constraints of a breakout and the necessity of Kirchner reaching Buzinovka on the first day of the projected breakout.[30] Schulz, like Manstein, was optimistic that Sixth Army had the

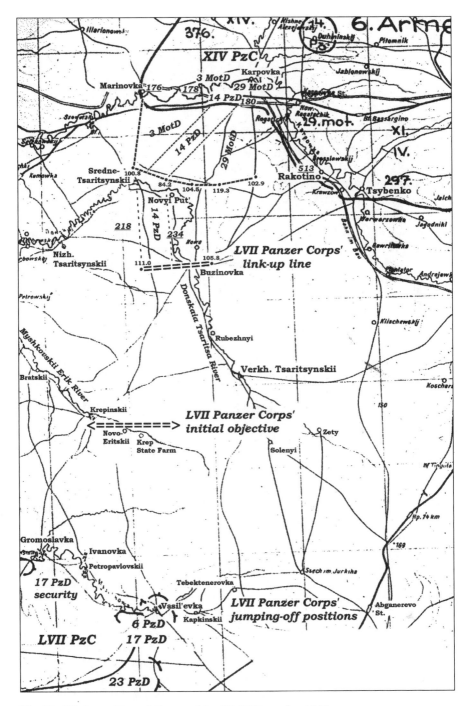

Map 91. *Wintergewitter* and *Donnerschlag*, 19–23 December 1942

power to break out, but Paulus and his staff provided details of their logistical constraints. As late as 1740 hours on 23 December, the field marshal urged Paulus to prepare for the breakout, even though Hitler had not yet authorized it, and by that time, Manstein had been forced to divert 6th Panzer Division elsewhere.[31]

Three facts decided the fate of Sixth Army. First, Paulus never initiated a breakout, either because Hitler had forbidden it or because the Soviets had blocked any escape routes, or perhaps a combination of the two. Second, Manstein never *ordered* Paulus to break out; he may have hoped Sixth Army would take action on its own, but he never openly violated Hitler's wishes. In fact, the field marshal had, in effect, sided with Hitler in rejecting any withdrawal by Sixth Army. Finally, even if Sixth Army had initiated *Donnerschlag*, it appears highly unlikely that Paulus and Kirchner could have linked up in the face of the powerful forces of 2nd Guards Army; any attempted breakout would have been a disaster.

CLIMAX OF *WINTERGEWITTER*, 19–24 DECEMBER

On 19 December the spearhead of LVII Panzer Corps reached the Myshkova River, but its forces had been sadly depleted by the fighting with Vol'sky's mechanized corps. As of the twentieth, Kirchner had 15,666 officers and men, having lost 10 percent of his combat strength since 12 December.[32] According to reports issued the following day, the German tank strength had shrunk to 92 vehicles, with another 83 supposedly repairable. Kirchner was hardly in a position to engage a guards army with three times the tanks and well over 100,000 men.

It would take three additional days, 20–22 December, for the opposing sides to bring their forces fully on line with each other. This period involved intense fighting between the armored elements of 6th and 17th Panzer Divisions on one side and at least two divisions of Malinovsky's guards army. On 20 December *Kampfgruppe* Hünersdorff from 6th Panzer Division (which one week later would be struggling along the Tsimla River) was trying to defend its new bridgehead at Vasil'evka on the north bank of the Myshkova. Hünersdorff reported that Soviet resistance was constantly increasing, while "our own forces were weak, and 21 tanks without fuel and two weak companies of motorized infantry on armored transporters were not sufficient to widen the bridgehead and advance further."[33] Similar struggles were occurring in the other panzer divisions, which had to fight simultaneously to take bridgeheads north of the river and reduce Soviet forces south of it. Despite signals and imagery intelligence of Malinovsky's forward movement, on 20 December Army Group Don did not realize that 2nd Guards Army was already op-

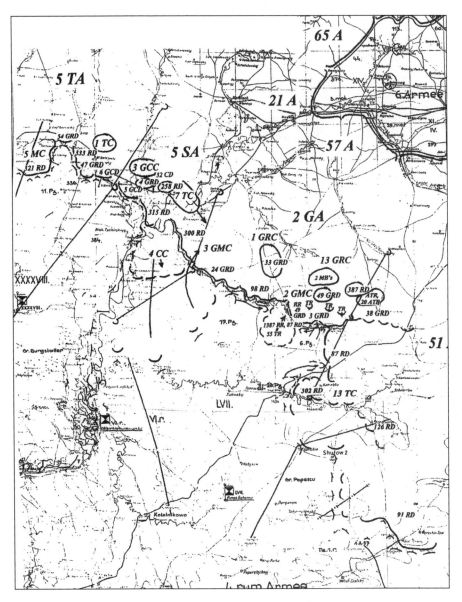

Map 92. Kotel'nikovo Axis: Situation at 2200 Hours, 21 December 1942

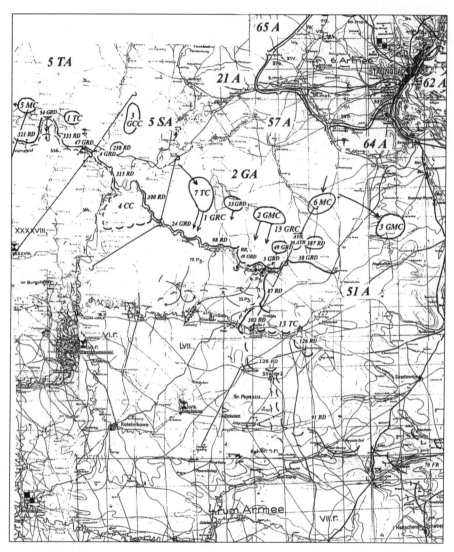

Map 93. Kotel'nikovo Axis: Situation at 2200 Hours, 23 December 1942

posite Fourth Panzer Army. The army group headquarters was clearly distracted by the alarming developments in the sectors of Italian Eighth Army, Army Group Hollidt, and Corps Group Mieth, developments that took up 80 percent of the headquarters' daily records on 20–21 December.[34] On the twenty-second the tank elements of 17th Panzer Division belatedly shifted eastward to the Vasil'evka sector, where they formed a second attack wave behind 6th Panzer Division, which was facing several divisions of 13th Guards Rifle Corps.[35] However, this shift in tanks meant that 17th Panzer had to abandon its own bridgehead at Nizhne-Kumskii, which was also under heavy pressure from 1st Guards Rifle Corps. In fact, by the night of 22 December, LVII Panzer Corps was essentially involved in a defensive struggle.

The continued fighting along the Myshkova River on 23 December is the subject of considerable controversy. General Raus clearly argues that, had it been allowed to continue, LVII Panzer Corps would have broken through 13th Guards Rifle Corps and advanced to relieve Stalingrad. However, Raus recalls having had 120 tanks, 40 StuG assault guns, and 24 Sd Kfz 233 reconnaissance cars on that day, whereas 6th Panzer Division's *Kriegstagebuch* recorded only 41 Panzer III and IV tanks operational in that division, with an additional 36 available in the other two panzer divisions combined.[36] Thus, even before Raus's division was redeployed elsewhere, Kirchner's corps had, at most, some 80 to 100 tanks and assault guns available to continue the advance, with 7th Tank Corps on its western flank and 13th Tank Corps threatening its right rear (see map 93). German operational summaries do confirm Raus's recollection that the Soviets—primarily 49th Guards Rifle Division—suffered hundreds of infantry casualties fighting against 6th Panzer Division on 23 December. The same documents also correctly record Soviet attacks across the Myshkova River from Nizhne-Kumskii east to Ivanovka.[37] These attacks forced 17th Panzer Division to withdraw its left and center southward, and they caused 23rd Panzer to dispatch an element to fill the gap between 17th Panzer's right wing and 6th Panzer's left wing to the west of Vasil'evka.

It was during this crisis that, as described earlier, the Soviet tank raid toward the German airfields prompted the diversion of 6th Panzer Division to Morozovsk. Numerous German military leaders have blamed Hitler, Manstein, or both for this diversion, but given subsequent events, it seems unlikely that the presence of one additional division with fewer than 50 tanks would have changed the outcome of *Wintergewitter*.

On the afternoon of 24 December, however, Army Group Don's headquarters continued to pretend that Sixth Army could be saved. Despite the threat to the airfields and the stalemate on the Myshkova, Manstein's chief of staff, Schulz, misled Schmidt at Sixth Army headquarters about the prospects for a relief effort.[38] At 1730 the same day, Manstein sent a more realistic assessment to OKH headquarters. In it, he proposed reinforcing Kirchner's corps with Army Group A's III Panzer Corps by the end of the month, an unlikely schedule at best.[39] Thinking strategically, the field marshal still sought some drastic solution, even if it meant withdrawing three army groups to shorten the front. Hitler, however, was still thinking politically, hoping to both retain the Caucasus oil and avoid the humiliation of abandoning Stalingrad.

THE STALINGRAD FRONT'S KOTEL'NIKOVO OFFENSIVE, 24–27 DECEMBER

By 23 December, Eremenko's Stalingrad Front had accomplished its initial mission of halting LVII Panzer Corps at the Myshkova River. However, its larger mission was to destroy the elements of Fourth Panzer Army and Romanian Fourth Army in the Kotel'nikovo area, eliminating any possibility of relieving Sixth Army. The 2nd Guards Army would make the main attack, with a supporting effort by 51st Army to the east. After Stalin approved the concept on 19 December, Eremenko and his two army commanders, Malinovsky and Trufanov, prepared their detailed plans over the next four days, plans that Vasilevsky and Stalin approved (see map 94). This left only 18 hours to disseminate the plan and prepare for the attack. After enveloping LVII Panzer Corps and forcing it back to the Aksai River, the two armies would seize crossings over that river to permit exploitation. In this final phase, the most important effort was the advance of 13th Mechanized (formerly Tank) and 3rd Guards (formerly 4th) Mechanized Corps to Dubovskoe, 35 kilometers south of Kotel'nikovo, with the aim of cutting off all Axis forces in the area. Support from 8th Air Army went by priority to these mechanized corps.

Eremenko's attacking force consisted of 149,000 men, 635 tanks, 1,728 guns and mortars, and 294 combat aircraft. Opposite them, Kirchner's corps had a combat strength of perhaps 15,500 men with only 36 operational tanks. The results were predictable.

After a brief artillery preparation, Malinovsky's 1st Guards and 13th Guards Rifle Corps attacked southward across the Myshkova River beginning at 0800 on Christmas Eve. At noon Rotmistrov's 7th Tank and Sviridov's 2nd Guards Mechanized Corps passed through the assaulting infantry.[40]

By the end of the first day, 17th and 23rd Panzer Divisions had withdrawn southward to defensive positions more than halfway between the Myskhova and Aksai Rivers. By Christmas afternoon, these two divisions had only 19 operable tanks between them, and LVII Panzer Corps continued to retreat under immense pressure.[41] Instead of holding on to a bridgehead to relieve Stalingrad, Kirchner's corps was fighting for survival.

On 26 December the two attacking armies crushed German defenses along the Aksai River with relative ease and advanced halfway from there to Kotel'nikovo. General Bogdanov, having assumed command of 6th Mechanized Corps, struck the seam between the right wing of LVII Panzer Corps and the supporting Romanian Group Popescu. The next day two more mobile corps—Tanaschishin's 13th Mechanized and Vol'sky's 3rd Guards Mechanized—each with about 100 tanks, attacked from the east.[42] They brushed aside a thin screen made up of remnants of Romanian 1st and 4th Infantry

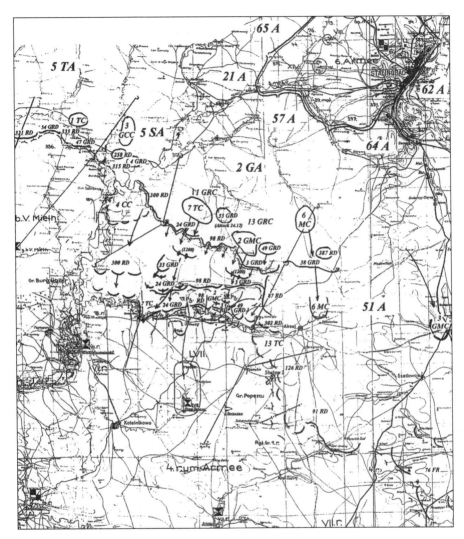

Map 94. Kotel'nikovo Axis: Situation on 24 and 25 December 1942

Divisions, backed by 16th Motorized Division's 156th Regiment, which had been rushed north to protect the communications around Dubovskoe. In a desperate attempt to contain the Soviet advance, Manstein had also ordered 5th SS *Wiking* Division to the same area.

After two more days of confused fighting, 2nd Guards Army secured Kotel'nikovo on the evening of 29 December; the next day the two mechanized corps of 51st Army seized the Dubovskoe area. After spending nine days

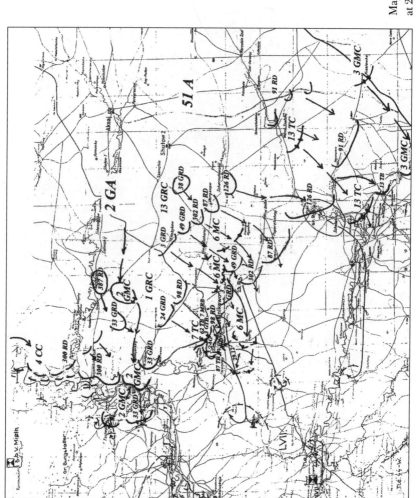

Map 95. Kotel'nikovo Axis: Situation at 2200 Hours, 29 December 1942

(12–20 December) advancing from Kotel'nikovo to the Myshkova River, LVII Panzer Corps found itself driven back through Kotel'nikovo in only six days. Between 12 and 31 December Kirchner's command suffered some 16,000 casualties and lost more than 160 tanks and assault guns, plus 177 guns and mortars. Moreover, in retreat, the Germans had fewer opportunities to evacuate and repair their damaged weapons, making temporary damage permanent. The lightly equipped Romanians were equally affected.[43]

CONSEQUENCES

By defeating LVII Panzer Corps, the Stalingrad Front not only kept Sixth Army isolated but also, in conjunction with Operation Little Saturn, threatened to reach Rostov and thereby cut off German withdrawal routes out of the Caucasus.

Under respectful but persistent pressure from Zeitzler, Hitler issued a new Führer directive on 27 December. He insisted that "the liberation of Sixth Army" remained the primary goal, with Army Group Don assigned to hold the Kotel'nikovo region while Army Group B regained the railroad line from Millerovo eastward. He also promised a handful of reinforcements, such as SS *Wiking* and 7th Panzer Divisions.[44] The next day the OKH published Operations Order No. 2 implementing this directive, which included resubordinating Army Group B to Army Group Don as soon as Manstein was prepared to assume command.[45]

By contrast, Soviet staff actions at the end of December were relatively minor. In addition to redesignating the Stalingrad Front as the Southern Front, the *Stavka* addressed the issues that arose because 2nd Guards Army was simultaneously engaged in two offensives, against Tormosin and Kotel'nikovo. General Antonov, the new chief of the Red Army General Staff, insisted that the People's Commissariat for Defense provide Malinovsky with additional communications equipment to facilitate command and control, a problem that became more serious in the new year.[46] The *Stavka* also issued orders for continued offensives toward Kamensk-Shakhtinskii and Rostov. After its victories in Little Saturn and at Tormosin and Kotel'nikovo, the Red Army planned to continue its exploitation while liquidating the Stalingrad pocket.

CHAPTER EIGHTEEN

_____ The Condemned Army

As noted in the previous chapter, on 15 December General Paulus issued an order for General Hube's XIV Panzer Corps to prepare for the implementation of *Donnerschlag* (Thunderclap). As a result of this order, Hube transferred 376th Infantry Division, together with its defensive sector on the corps' right wing, to General Heitz's VIII Army Corps. In return, the panzer corps gained control of 29th Motorized Division, together with half its former sector on the right wing of Jänecke's IV Army Corps, as well as 14th Panzer Division from the army reserve. Hube had to transfer the ten-tank Panzer Detachment Langenthal to support the 376th, but after these changes, the panzer corps mustered about 50 tanks—the minimum number Paulus had estimated would be required for the breakout.[1] IV Army Corps also shifted its boundary to give Hube a slightly narrower sector.

SIXTH ARMY'S STRENGTH AND CAPABILITIES, DECEMBER 1942

As of 18 December, Sixth Army had a ration strength of 249,000 men, including 13,000 Romanians, 19,300 *Hiwis* and attached troops, and 6,000 wounded. The actual bayonet strength, however, was only 25,000 infantry and 3,200 pioneers, compared with a total of some 40,000 combatants on 21 November.[2] The prolonged struggle for control of Stalingrad had left Paulus's army weak even before Operation Uranus began, but now its combat power and maneuverability had decreased significantly. Moreover, in the absence of most of their draft animals, many units (including 389th Infantry Division) were virtually immobile; this problem grew as the remaining draft animals died and were eaten during the siege. Even on 15 December, staff officers rated only 29th Motorized Division qualified to perform offensive tasks, and only 60th Motorized and 371st Infantry Divisions were rated fully qualified for defensive tasks (see table 18.1). Of course, the opposing Soviet units, especially in 62nd Army, were equally depleted.

In terms of armored strength, as of 15–17 December, Sixth Army had a total of 103 functioning tanks and 35 assault guns. Rather than being concentrated in one command, however, these vehicles were divided into numerous

Table 18.1. Combat Ratings of German Infantry and Pioneer Battalions
Fighting in Stalingrad, 16 November–28 December 1942

16 November	15 December	28 December
96 infantry battalions	115 infantry battalions	113 infantry battalions
4 strong	5 strong	4 strong
16 medium strong	15 medium strong	11 medium strong
39 average	36 average	31 average
26 weak	53 weak	53 weak
11 exhausted	6 exhausted	14 exhausted
17 pioneer battalions	19 pioneer battalions	19 pioneer battalions
1 medium strong	1 medium strong	1 medium strong
9 average	6 average	2 average
5 weak	7 weak	12 weak
2 exhausted	5 exhausted	4 exhausted

Source: "Betr.: Zustand der Divisionen, Armee-Oberkommando 6. Abt. 1a, A.H.Qu., 16 November 1942, 12:00 Uhr," "Fernschreiben am Heeresgruppe Don, Armee-Oberkommando 6. 1a Bt. Nr. 4745/42 g., A.H.Qu., 14 Dezember 1942, 10.15 Uhr," and "Betr.: Zustand der Divisionen, Armee-Oberkommando 6. Abt. 1a, A.H.Qu., 09 November 1942, 16.20 Uhr," in Florian *Freiherr* von und zu Aufsess, *Die Anlagenbänder zu den Kriegstagebüchern der 6. Armee vom 14.09.42 bis 24.11.42*, book 1 (Schwabach, Germany: self-published, 2006), 284–290; ibid., *24.11.1942 bis 24.12.1942*, book 2, 228–323; ibid., *24.12.1942 bis 02.02.1943*, book 3, 44–49.
Note: The total number of battalions increased between 16 November and 15 December because additional divisions, trapped in the pocket, fell under Sixth Army control.

small groups, primarily to support the infantry and pioneers against enemy mechanized attacks.[3]

On 16 December Sixth Army faced seven Soviet armies—the Don Front's 21st, 65th, 24th, and 66th, and the Stalingrad Front's 62nd, 64th, and 57th (see map 95). Except for the northeast, opposite Chuikov's emaciated 62nd Army, each German division faced at least two and as many as five Soviet division equivalents.[4] However, the *Stavka* and Vasilevsky postponed Operation Ring, the actual offensive against the pocket, until 10 January in order to build up the besieging forces to a ratio of at least three to one. In the meantime, starvation would further weaken the defenders.

COMBAT OPERATIONS, 16–31 DECEMBER

In the interim, Rokossovsky and Eremenko maintained their pressure on the pocket, occasionally provoking local engagements with the defenders. On 17 December 24th Army used 49th Rifle Division and a battalion from 16th Tank Corps to achieve a local penetration of VIII Army Corps' 76th Infantry Division on the pocket's northwestern face. That afternoon, a local counterattack force, supported by a battery of assault guns, retook most of the lost ground. The Germans claimed to have killed or damaged 8 of the 19 Soviet tanks involved but acknowledged that 76th Division suffered 151 casualties on 17–18 December.[5] On the eighteenth Chuikov's 138th and 95th Rifle Divisions launched heavy local attacks to consolidate their defensive front in the Barrikady Factory; this action cost 305th Infantry Division another 127 casualties.[6]

On 19–20 December, as LVII Panzer Corps advanced from Verkhne-Kumskii to the Myshkova River, fighting broke out along the western and southwestern faces of Sixth Army's pocket, the obvious goal of the relief effort. In particular, 21st Army launched two local attacks, each supported by tanks, artillery, and air, against defending battalions of 3rd Motorized Division. These assaults failed, but they inflicted significant casualties on the defenders. Sixth Army lost 1,141 men on 19 December and another 800 on the twentieth, significantly higher than the loss rates for previous days.[7]

Such fighting not only contributed to the steady decline of combat power in Sixth Army but also emphasized that the besiegers were fully prepared to contest any possible breakout from Stalingrad. Indeed, strong evidence exists that Vasilevsky, Rokossovsky, and Eremenko either anticipated an attempted breakout or had direct intelligence of the *Donnerschlag* plan. On 19–20 December Eremenko transferred 422nd Rifle Division, 235th Separate Tank Brigade, and 234th Separate Tank Regiment to reinforce 21st and 57th Armies on the southern face of the pocket, opposite XIV Panzer Corps. The Don and Stalingrad Fronts also intensified air strikes against German positions between Marinovka and Karpovka. Such actions undoubtedly contributed to Paulus's decision not to attempt a breakout.

Meanwhile, the bitter fighting dragged on inside the ruined city. At 0500 on 21 December Colonel Liudnikov's 138th Rifle Division again attacked southwestward, capturing four houses and then repelling three German counterattacks. At the same time, Colonel Gorishnyi's 95th Rifle Division pushed northwestward, encircling several German strongpoints and capturing a fortified building in house-to-house fighting.[8] This struggle continued for a week, with local German counterattacks against the modest gains achieved by these two rifle divisions.

In preparation for the eventual assault on the pocket, on 19 December the *Stavka* reassigned General N. N. Voronov from coordinating the *fronts* involved in Little Saturn to serving as Vasilevsky's deputy representative, tasked specifically with planning Operation Ring. Three days later Moscow also directed the withdrawal of three rifle divisions (37th Guards, 112th, and 193rd) and three rifle brigades (42nd, 115th, and 160th) from 62nd Army into the Reserve of the High Command (RVGK). All six had been bled white in the city fighting under Chuikov and needed to rebuild for future attacks.[9]

Meanwhile, the cold and dark contributed to the psychological isolation of Sixth Army. This mood influenced even Paulus's headquarters, which was installed in 12 earth bunkers located 6 kilometers west of the city center, close to the Gumrak rail station.[10]

Once LVII Panzer Corps retreated from the Myshkova River on and after 24 December, there was no realistic chance of a breakout. The *Stavka* therefore directed that, except for the 62nd, all the Don and Stalingrad Front armies should go over to the defensive and improve their positions from 24 through 31 December. Even the resulting low levels of Soviet activity continued to inflict casualties, however. Local fighting between 66th Army's rifle divisions and XI Corps' 16th and 24th Panzer Divisions north of Orlovka cost the Germans 221 casualties on 26 December, 112 on the twenty-eighth, 203 the next day, and 176 on 31 December.[11] Moreover, the rate of casualties caused a bottleneck in evacuating the wounded by air; not until 1–3 January was the *Luftwaffe* able to evacuate the more than 1,200 seriously wounded who had accumulated inside the pocket.[12]

Vasilevsky wanted 62nd Army to expand its bridgehead so that it could accommodate more troops for the coming offensive. As a result, Chuikov ordered the two brigades of Group Gorokhov to attack the German positions in the western portion of Spartakovka village on 26 December. Two days later he directed 39th Guards, 45th, and 284th Rifle Divisions, reinforced by 92nd Rifle Brigade, to attack westward from the Krasnyi Oktiabr' Factory and Mamaev Kurgan, seeking to gain the dominant Hill 107.5 between the upper and lower halves of Krasnyi Oktiabr' village. The struggle for the ruins of Stalingrad dragged on, with neither side achieving any significant advantage.[13]

DONNERSCHLAG AND *WINTERGEWITTER* REVISITED

Given the declining situation, Sixth Army continued to hope and plan for a breakout as late as 28 December. Paulus and his staff bombarded Army Group Don with requests for both a renewed relief attempt and authorization to break out. On 26 December a frustrated Paulus radioed a bleak assessment to Manstein:

> Bloody losses, the cold, and inadequate supplies have recently made serious inroads on the combat strength of the divisions. For that reason, I must report:
>
> 1. The army is weaker than in the past to repulse enemy attacks and clean up local crises. The prerequisite remains better supply and speedier influx of replacements.
>
> 2. If the Russians withdraw stronger forces from Hoth and employ

these or other troops to launch mass assault on the fortress, we cannot resist this for long.

3. *Donnerschlag* will no longer be feasible if a corridor is not punched through beforehand and if the army is not replenished with men and supplies.

I therefore ask you to make representations to the highest level to ensure energetic measures be taken for the rapid link up with the army. If not you will force the sacrifice of the entire force.

The army will do everything possible to hold out to the last.[14]

In teletype conversations that evening, General Schulz at Army Group Don continued to assure General Schmidt, Paulus's chief of staff, that Manstein was working to get more mobile divisions assigned, while Richthofen was obtaining another 270 transport aircraft.[15] Two days later Schulz blamed the Romanians for the Axis's failure to hold Kotel'nikovo but reported that the Germans had recaptured Tatsinskaia and that Army Group A would now provide additional forces for the relief effort.[16]

By this time, Manstein had recognized that neither 7th Panzer nor 5th SS *Wiking* Division would be of much help to Hoth, so he pinned his hopes on First Panzer Army's III Panzer Corps to relieve Stalingrad. As noted in the previous chapter, Manstein's version of events, written from memory, dated the Soviet offensive against LVII Panzer Corps as 27 rather than 24 December.[17] This discrepancy implied that Paulus was at fault for not launching *Donnerschlag* earlier, but in fact, rescue was already impossible by Christmas Eve.

Hitler was also grasping at straws. On 31 December he issued a supplement to his 27 December directive concerning the relief of Sixth Army. This supplement called for his best units—SS Divisions *Leibstandarte Adolf Hitler*, *Das Reich*, and *Totenkopf*; *Grossdeutschland* Motorized Division; and three infantry divisions from the West—to concentrate southeast of Khar'kov and advance on Stalingrad.[18] However, the date specified for this concentration—mid-February—was obviously too late to save Paulus's men from starvation or destruction. In a New Year's message to Paulus, the dictator wrote, "Every man of the Sixth Army can start the New Year with the absolute conviction that the Führer will not leave his heroic soldiers on the Volga in the lurch and that Germany can and will find a means to relieve them."[19] Quite apart from the disingenuous tone of this message, it is clear that Hitler still wanted Sixth Army to hold its position on the Volga, not break out to save itself.

Paulus's biographer, Walter Goerlitz, claims that the general had become passive and fatalistic, but in fact, his response to this message was to order his corps commanders to prepare for the breakout. These plans, especially for an attack by IV Army Corps to support XIV Panzer Corps' main attack, became quite detailed.[20] To launch this attack, Sixth Army still had 127 tanks, 37 assault guns, and 42 88mm guns, but as Paulus quite accurately insisted, he needed the *Luftwaffe* to provide fuel for such an attack.[21] Even though the *Luftwaffe*'s daily deliveries increased during late December, these shipments, averaging 118 tons daily, were barely enough to keep Paulus's army alive.

Thus, both Hitler and Manstein continued to offer Paulus false hope, either pledging or (in the field marshal's case) implying relief long after it had become impossible. Nor did Manstein ever order or authorize Sixth Army to launch *Donnerschlag*. Instead, he kept Paulus hanging in limbo, leaving the decision to disobey the Führer firmly on the army commander's shoulders.

On 24 December Paulus separated General Strecker's XI Army Corps from Seydlitz's LI Corps, leaving the former controlling 16th and 24th Panzer, 60th Motorized, and elements of 389th Infantry Division in the northeastern corner of the pocket. On 27 and 30 December, respectively, the army headquarters subordinated 14th Panzer and 376th Infantry Divisions to XIV Panzer Corps, providing Hube with greater capabilities if *Donnerschlag* were implemented.[22]

Between 16 and 31 December the army suffered 11,066 casualties, compared with roughly 15,000 losses from 21 November through 5 December and 7,032 casualties from 6 through 15 December.[23] Combat strength fell from about 40,000 on 21 November to 34,000 on 6 December and to 28,200 on 18 December. Although the army systematically reassigned noncombat soldiers to fill resulting vacancies, many of these replacements were less well trained than their predecessors, resulting in reduced effectiveness and increased future casualties. Paulus repeatedly requested combat replacements, but every such replacement constituted an additional drain on food, ammunition, and fuel.

Beginning on 19 December Sixth Army added three new categories to the daily casualty reports from the corps: soldiers frostbitten, soldiers dead from starvation or exhaustion, and those who died from disease in hospitals. These losses rose quickly, with 127 frostbite cases reported on 28 December alone.

OVERALL PLANNING FOR OPERATION RING

N. N. Voronov, Vasilevsky's deputy, began revising the plan for Operation Ring on 19 December. It was no coincidence that Voronov was the Red Army's senior artilleryman. Given previous failures to reduce the pocket with tanks and infantry, the *Stavka* planned to use a crushing fire preparation before launching mechanized forces into the shattered Germans.

Basing his plan on Rokossovsky's initial estimate that the German force

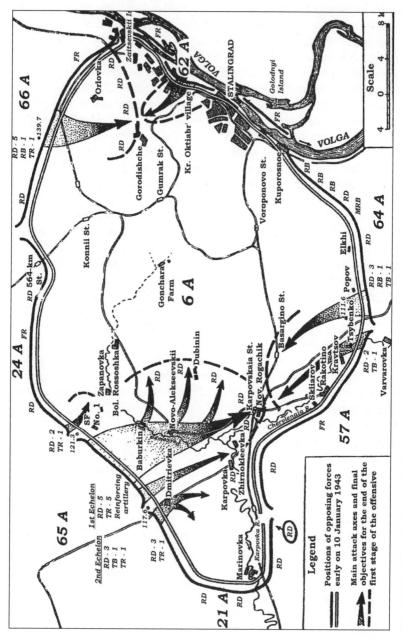

Map 96. Final Plan for the First Stage of Operation *Kol'tso* (Ring), with *Slavka* Corrections

numbered 86,000, Voronov grossly underestimated the size of Sixth Army.[24] As finally presented to Moscow on 27 December, Voronov's plan involved a three-stage offensive to destroy Sixth Army in seven days. Rokossovsky's 24th, 65th, and 21st Armies would make the main attack from the northwest face of the pocket eastward. This main attack would employ 14 rifle divisions supported by 8 tank and 41 artillery and guards-mortar (multiple-rocket) regiments. Their initial target was VIII Army Corps, consisting of 376th, 384th, 44th, and 76th Infantry Divisions, with remnants of 14th Panzer in reserve. Voronov also envisioned two supporting attacks. Five rifle divisions of 66th Army would strike 60th Motorized and 16th Panzer Divisions northwest of Orlovka, while 57th and 64th Armies attacked at the extreme southern point of the pocket between Rakotino and Popov, an area defended by Romanian 20th and German 297th Infantry Divisions. Between them, these two Soviet armies would use 4 rifle divisions plus 3 motorized and 2 mechanized brigades, supported by 16 artillery and rocket regiments. After two days of penetration attacks, the main German resistance in Stalingrad, Gumrak, and Peschanka would require two more days to defeat, followed by three days of mopping up. Voronov estimated that logistical preparations would require nine days, permitting the attack to begin on 6 January 1943.[25]

In 24 hours the *Stavka* reviewed Voronov's plan and mandated several changes (see map 96). In essence, Moscow changed the direction of the initial thrusts so that those attacks would divide the pocket into easily digestible parts, beginning by lopping off the extreme eastern and western lobes of the encirclement. On the twenty-ninth the *Stavka* endorsed General Eremenko's suggestion to narrow the assigned attack frontages for his 57th and 64th Armies.[26] Finally, effective 1 January 1943, the *Stavka*, probably at Rokossovsky's suggestion, placed all seven armies of Operation Ring under one headquarters, the Don Front.

By the end of December, therefore, the Red Army had decisively defeated German relief efforts and planned to eliminate the Stalingrad pocket. Both chief of staff Zeitzler and Sixth Army commander Paulus had prodded their superiors to recognize the reality of the situation and radically reallocate combat power to save the encircled force. However, Hitler and his senior commanders had fallen into the habit of expecting too much from their troops, and Manstein, as the responsible operational commander, would not join Zeitzler and Paulus in forcing a reassessment.

THE EXPANDING SOVIET OFFENSIVES

In fairness to the German commanders, the Soviet offensive machine continued to function at the same disorienting speed that had characterized the

German blitzkrieg for the past four years. On 29 December Zhukov persuaded Stalin to broaden Operation Little Saturn to include the original goal of seizing Rostov and thereby cutting off Army Group A. Malinovsky's pursuit southwestward from Kotel'nikovo already threatened to do just that. On 30 December the OKH directed 7th Panzer Division, which was redeploying from Army Group A to the relief forces of Army Group Don, to halt at Rostov and defend the city.

The other offensives in the *Stavka's* planetary system of plans—especially Mars, with its possible follow-ons Jupiter and Neptune—had achieved only minor success. They had, however, absorbed Axis operational reserves and thereby complicated German efforts to relieve Stalingrad.

In a series of directives issued between 1 and 4 January, the *Stavka* expanded Operation Little Saturn into Operation Don, directing the Southwestern, Southern, and Trans-Caucasus Fronts to advance westward on several cities, including Kamensk, Voroshilovgrad, Rostov, and Bataisk (see map 97). The goal was to defeat Army Detachment Hollidt north of the Don River and Fourth Panzer Army to the south, in preparation for capturing Rostov and Bataisk and thereby trapping Army Group A before it could escape from the Caucasus.

Soon thereafter, Moscow attempted to exploit its previous victories along the middle reaches of the Don River. On 13 January the Voronezh and Southwestern Fronts began the Ostrogozhsk-Rossosh' offensive, which decimated Hungarian Second Army and its cooperating Italian Alpine Corps in just ten days. Then, on 24 January, the Briansk and Voronezh Fronts commenced the Voronezh-Kastornoe offensive against German Second Army, forcing it to retreat in disarray toward Belgorod and Kursk.

Throughout January the Southwestern Front conducted a painfully slow offensive toward Kamensk and Voroshilovgrad while the Southern Front, with its 2nd Guards Army still straddling the Don River, advanced on Shakhty and Rostov. Although the *Stavka* committed ten tank, six mechanized, and three cavalry corps to these offensives, they ultimately failed to achieve their objectives. Fretter-Pico and Hollidt, ably supported by four dwindling panzer divisions (19th, 6th, 7th, and 11th), slowed the advance on Voroshilovgrad to a crawl, while seriously weakening the Soviet mobile corps involved. Similarly, by early February, an artful defense by Fourth and First Panzer Armies, supported by five additional mobile divisions (3rd, 17th, 23rd, 5th SS *Wiking* Panzer, and 16th Motorized) and (for part of this period) by 11th Panzer, had enabled most of both armies to escape from the Caucasus region via Rostov. Thus, by 13 February, Manstein commanded a combined Army Group South, using First and Fourth Panzer Armies as well as Army Detachment Hollidt to defend the Donbas industrial region. These massive struggles provide the context for the destruction of Paulus's Sixth Army.

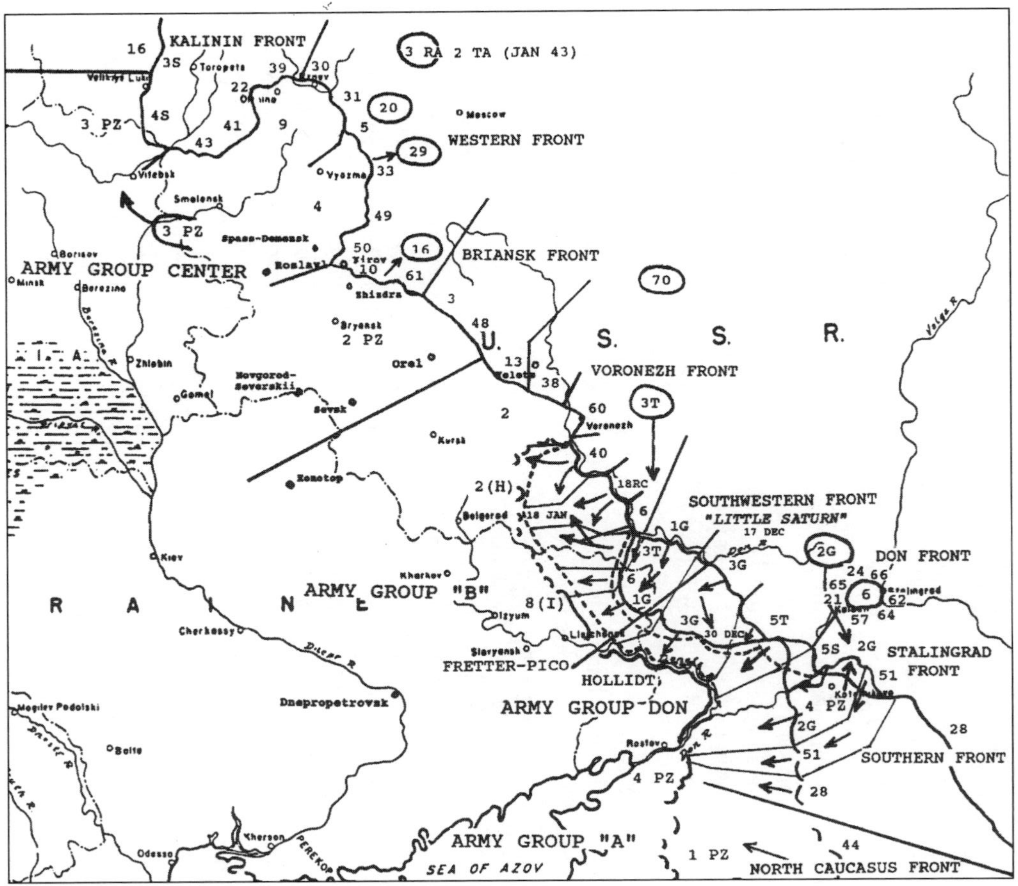

Map 97. *Stavka*'s Offensive Plans, 13 December 1942–20 January 1943

LULL BEFORE THE STORM

On 30 December General Paulus sent a candid order (No. 6015) to all his subordinates.[27] While assuring them that supplies and reinforcements would arrive eventually, he directed a number of practical actions to improve the defenses of the pocket. These actions included an expanded program to retrain support personnel to fight as infantrymen and infantrymen to fight as panzer-grenadiers, as well as the construction of multiple alternate (secondary) and fallback defensive positions. The general assigned Colonel Martin Lattmann, commander of the weak 14th Panzer Division (with 23 tanks) in army reserve, to coordinate these measures. Paulus concluded with a frank statement: "This is about the life of the army. The slightest fault anywhere can mean the loss of the entire fortress."[28]

After suffering 9,991 combat casualties between 18 and 31 December, the army's ration strength, which had been 211,300 unwounded German soldiers on 18 December, fell to 201,309 unwounded and 7,818 wounded by the end of the month. The only solution, as Paulus had noted, was to convert support personnel into line soldiers. On 6 January General Seydlitz indicated that he had converted 4,088 support troops in this manner within LI Corps.[29] Assuming the other corps took similar drastic measures, Sixth Army's combat strength of 25,000 was probably maintained or exceeded.

Moreover, Paulus's reassignment of units also contributed to the pocket's security.[30] By 5 January, for example, 376th Infantry Division, with five exhausted battalions, had moved into strong defensive positions along the Chervlenaia River southeast of Karpovka, while the much stronger 29th Motorized was alongside 44th Infantry Division in the more open and vulnerable western front of the pocket. Such measures increased the armored strength of the western sector, which was the intended site of Voronov's attack, from 42 tanks and 19 assault guns on 30 January to 60 tanks and 16 assault guns on 9 January. However, since shuffling units in this manner was a zero-sum game, the pocket's southern front became weaker. Despite dedicated maintenance efforts, the number of functioning armored vehicles in the pocket declined from 159 (122 tanks and 37 assault guns) on 24 December to 124 (102 and 22) on 9 January; even these vehicles were severely limited by shortages of fuel and spare parts, leaving commanders no choice but to dig in their tanks as virtual pillboxes.[31]

Once the Don Front began its offensive on 10 January, attrition sharply reduced the quantity of tanks and assault guns. On 13 January, for example, XI Army Corps reported that the combined armor strength of 16th and 24th Panzer Divisions had fallen from 32 to 9 tanks, with only a single Panzer IV remaining.[32]

Aside from armored vehicles, the most important weapons in the German inventory were the ubiquitous *Pak* (*Panzerabwerekanone*) antitank guns, supplemented by the 88mm dual-purpose *Flak* antiaircraft guns. The total number of *Paks* and infantry support guns declined only slightly from 317 on 17 December to 309 on 9 January. Once the Soviet offensive began, this number fell to only 102 by 12–13 January, with heaviest losses in VIII Army and XIV Panzer Corps, which bore the brunt of the attack.[33]

Despite the *Luftwaffe's* best efforts, aerial resupply remained grossly inadequate in early January. No aircraft at all arrived on 2 January, and the daily average from 1 to 9 January was only 69 sorties and 158 tons.[34] Instead of the 2,500 calories per day needed for soldiers fighting in winter, the official ration had been only 1,500 calories since mid-November. In reality, continued shortfalls meant that the actual ration included only 80 grams of bread and well under 1,000 calories by 31 December. Paulus ordered a new ration, with 75 grams of bread but increased horse meat, to begin on 9 January, but this still amounted to less than 1,000 calories.[35] A mid-December anecdote illustrates this desperate situation: A battalion commander in 44th Infantry Division received the Knight's Cross, and along with the decoration, General Paulus sent him something more valuable—a package containing a loaf of bread and a tin of herring.[36]

Chuikov's soldiers were scarcely better off, receiving 100 grams per day as of 31 December. Iosif Solomonovich "Vasily" Grossman, a novelist and Red Army newspaper correspondent, described Stalingrad:

> The Volga froze on December 16, and the smashed barges are lying there, frozen in the ice . . . the battle now is one of long lulls and sharp clashes . . . the Germans have crawled into deep holes and stone cellars. . . . Only a well-aimed explosive or thermite shell can get at them there.
>
> It is morning. The sun is shining on the stone ruins of the factories, on those factory yards that became battlefields for whole regiments and divisions. It is lighting up the edges of those enormous craters made by one-ton bombs . . . it shines through the holes of the factory chimneys and into the marshalling yards, where cisterns lie like dead horses with their bellies ripped open, and hundreds of [trucks] are piled one on top of another. . . . It shines on the twisted metal girders of the factories red with rust, and on the common graves of our soldiers who fell in the area of the main German drive.[37]

PRELIMINARY OPERATIONS

During the first six days of 1943 the Don Front conducted a number of preliminary operations to both weaken the defenders and obtain further intelligence about German dispositions. Even such minor actions inflicted up to 560 German casualties daily, especially in 44th Infantry Division on the western face of the pocket and in 79th and 305th Divisions, which were still locked in a struggle in the factory district.

On 6 January these reconnaissances-in-force gave way to heavier attacks by 65th and 66th Armies, yet the Red Army General Staff made no mention of this increased fighting. By contrast, the OKH noted on 7 January: "Sixth Army halted enemy units that penetrated in 16th Pz and 29th MotDs' sectors but was unable to drive them back. Repeated enemy attacks have been repulsed."[38] In the northeast, 116th Rifle Division had carved a breach at least 300 meters wide in 16th Panzer Division's defenses and inflicted some 50 casualties.[39] Simultaneously, in the western sector, 65th Army's 214th Rifle Division had a similar effect on 44th Infantry Division, which lost a 1.5 kilometer stretch of its main defensive line (see upper right-hand corner of map 98). This threat was so significant that VIII Army Corps committed virtually its entire reserves, including two infantry battalions and various armored detachments totaling 23 assault and infantry guns, 24 tanks, and 7 *Paks*.[40] In three days of fighting (6–8 January), 44th Infantry Division lost 480 casualties, the equivalent of almost two reduced-strength battalions.

As the attackers intended, this fighting absorbed most of the reserves of VIII and XI Army Corps before the main offensive began. It also contributed to the rapid deterioration in ammunition reserves within the pocket. Having built up German expectations of an imminent general assault, on 9 January the besiegers virtually stopped their attacks, leaving the front in an eerie calm.

That evening at 2300, General Chuikov issued his attack order, timed for 0900 the next day. The 95th, 45th, 39th Guards, and 184th Rifle Divisions, together with 92nd Separate Rifle Brigade, were given specific objectives that generally envisioned advancing to the outskirts of Krasnyi Oktiabr' village and completely clearing Hill 102.0 and Mamaev Kurgan.[41] However, his maneuver units remained incredibly emaciated. Just as during the bitter fall fighting, Chuikov had received only a trickle of reinforcements to continue the fight. Given the withdrawal of some units and continued attrition among others, his ration strength declined from 41,199 on 20 November to 26,480 men on 9 January, with a total bayonet strength of only 5,850 to 7,700 men.

By comparison, German units had suffered so heavily from cold, starvation, and casualties that 79th Infantry Division, which faced the Krasnyi Oktiabr' and bread factories, was folded into 305th Infantry Division on 8 January.[42] Even allowing for the reprogrammed support troops thrust into the line, the five remaining divisions of LI Corps had perhaps 7,500 bayonets by 9 January. Regardless of what happened on the open steppes west of the

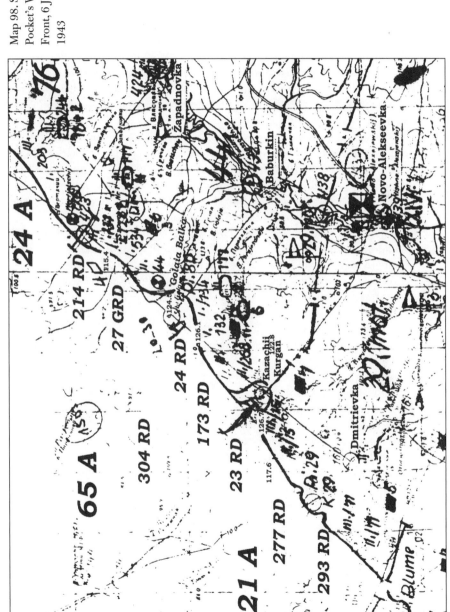

Map 98. Stalingrad Pocket's Western Front, 6 January 1943

city, the urban fighting remained as vicious and balanced as it had been for the past three months. Neither side would request or receive quarter.

FINAL PLANNING FOR OPERATION RING

In preparation for the final offensive, the *Stavka* ensured that Rokossovsky's Don Front received massive quantities of artillery and 20,000 personnel replacements. This increased the average strength of its rifle divisions from 4,900 to 5,900 men, with most of 65th Army's units growing to about 7,000 soldiers.[43]

Based on prisoner interrogations, the intelligence directorates of the *Stavka* and the Don Front estimated Sixth Army's combat strength at 75,550 combat soldiers, with 1,997 guns of various calibers, 366 mortars, 6,881 machine guns, and 245 tanks and assault guns.[44] These figures continued the Soviet tendency to overestimate the true combat power of the defenders while underestimating the total number of Axis soldiers.

Using this estimate and working with Rokossovsky and his army commanders, General Voronov refined his assault plan to allow for enemy strength, weather, and the flat, treeless terrain (see map 99).[45] The plan called for the Don Front's main attack, conducted by Batov's 65th Army, to penetrate the defensive sector of 44th Infantry Division and lop off the western lobe of the pocket by the third day of operations. Galanin's 24th Army protected Batov's left flank, while Chistiakov's 21st Army operated on the extreme western end of the bulge, opposite XIV Panzer Corps' 29th Motorized Division. These attacks would clear the way for an advance east toward the Barrikady and Krasnyi Oktiabr' villages to eliminate all resistance. The other armies of the Don Front—Zhadov's 66th in the north, Chuikov's 62nd inside the city, and Shumilov's 64th and Tolbukhin's 57th in the south—would conduct supporting attacks to prevent the Germans from withdrawing forces from any part of their perimeter.

Overall, the three main assault armies had ten rifle divisions in first echelon and four in second, supported by eight guards heavy tank regiments, against 44th Infantry and 29th Motorized Divisions, which had 32 tanks and 16 assault guns between them. Assuming an average of 3,500 infantrymen and sappers per Soviet rifle division, this represented 50,000 combat troops against about 10,000 infantry, panzer-grenadiers, and sappers. The direct infantry-support tanks numbered 264, including 110 heavy KVs (in the guards units), 72 medium T-34s, 60 light T-60 or T-70 tanks, plus 1 British-supplied Valentine Mark III and 21 Churchill Mark IVs.[46] Except in 65th and 57th Armies, which held tank brigades in reserve for German counterattacks, the remaining armies used all their tanks in an infantry-support role, including

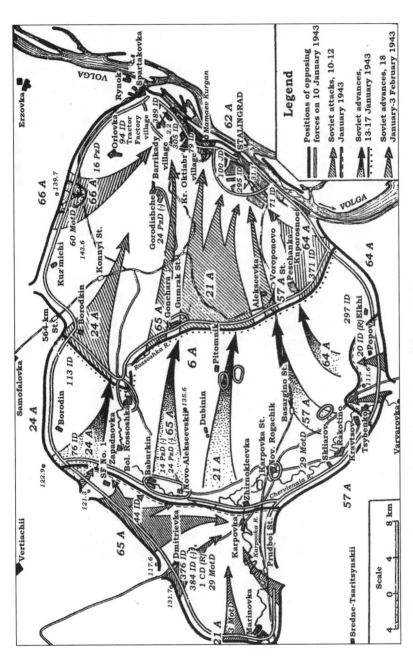

Map 99. Don Front's Operation *Kol'tso* (Ring), 10 January–2 February 1943

authorization for the tanks to dig in if necessary to help the infantry hold terrain.

If the infantry and armor were not sufficient, Voronov organized an overwhelming artillery preparation that, by 9 January, included 50 RVGK artillery regiments, 2 guards-mortar divisions (with 5 brigades), 9 mortar regiments, and 17 tank destroyer artillery regiments. This meant a total of 6,860 guns and mortars of 76mm or greater, plus 1,323 antitank and 222 antiaircraft guns.[47] This artillery was grouped into special mission groups at every level. Divisions organized infantry-support groups (*podderzhka pekhoty*) as well as general-support groups at division level. Armies formed long-range artillery groups (*dal'nye deistviia*); 65th Army, for example, had nine artillery regiments in three groups to support its assaulting infantry, as well as an artillery destruction group (*razrusheniia*) composed of two high-power artillery regiments and four heavy guards-mortar brigades. As the principal assault force, only 65th Army had sufficient artillery to form an artillery destruction group. In addition, the same army had a tank destroyer and a guards-mortar regiment in reserve. Other armies had less fire support, although Chuikov received limited help from the guns of 19 vessels of the Volga River Flotilla.[48]

Nor were these units simply firing at will. On the contrary, Voronov planned a 55-minute preparation in the main attack sector, consisting of three fire raids of 5 minutes each against the forward edge of the enemy's defenses, interspersed with longer periods of fires into the depths of the German positions. This pattern was intended to lure the Germans out of their bunkers in anticipation of an imminent assault, only to be struck by renewed fires. Once the ground assault began, a creeping barrage up to a depth of 2 kilometers would precede the infantry and armor.

On the eve of the offensive, 16th Air Army had approximately 400 combat aircraft, 150 of which were fighters.[49] These aircraft were divided among two bomber, two fighter, one assault, and one night bomber divisions, plus a reconnaissance regiment. Principal targets included German command posts and reserves. In addition, each day, long-range aviation regiments under *Stavka* control bombed German airfields, headquarters, communications centers, and troop concentrations in the eastern half of Sixth Army's pocket, especially in the area of Gumrak, Gorodishche, and Kamennyi Buerak.

The attack involved multiple engineer tasks, including reconnaissance, road and position construction, camouflage, deception, obstacle clearing, and direct support to the advance, all of which were complicated by bitter cold and heavy snow. The *Stavka* therefore reinforced Rokossovsky's *front* with numerous engineer units. By 9 January, the Don Front controlled the following (asterisks indicate reinforcements arriving after 1 December):

- 5th and 8th° Engineer-Miner Brigades
- 16th Special Designation (*Spetznaz*) Engineer Brigade
- 57th° and 61st° Sapper Brigades
- 14th Guards Miner Battalion
- 4 pontoon bridge battalions (1°)
- 2 separate engineer battalions
- 2 separate sapper battalions (1°)[50]

The guards miner battalion conducted engineer reconnaissance and diversionary operations inside Sixth Army's rear area, while the *Spetznaz* brigade created a false or notional tank corps concentration, including dummy equipment, positions, and communications, on 24th Army's left wing, seeking to deceive the Germans as to the main attack.[51]

FORCE RATIOS

The traditional accounts of Operation Ring indicate that Rokossovsky had a combat strength of 212,000 men, supported by 6,860 guns and mortars and 257 tanks. This force supposedly faced 250,000 Axis troops supported by 4,130 artillery tubes and 300 tanks. However, such a comparison uses Sixth Army's strength as of 18 December and assumes that all the Axis troops, *Hiwis*, and wounded in the pocket were skilled combat soldiers.[52] Table 18.2 reflects more realistic figures, but even those numbers exaggerate Sixth Army's combat power. By concentrating most of its forces in the main attack sectors, the Don Front increased its tactical superiority in those sectors to as much as 8 to 1 in manpower, 5 to 1 in armor, and 20 to 1 in artillery.

Table 18.2. Correlation of Don Front and Sixth Army Forces, 10 January 1943

Forces and Weapons	Don Front	Sixth Army	Ratio
Overall personnel	281,158	197,034 German (212,000 Axis)	1.4:1
Total tanks and assault guns	264	102 (plus 23 without fuel)	2.6:1
Total guns and mortars	7,949	1,222° (162 Paks, 29 88mm)	6.5:1
Total combat aircraft	400	100 (estimated)	4.5:1

Sources: Aleksei Isaev, Stalingrad: *Za Volgoi dlia nas zemli net* [Stalingrad: There is no land for us beyond the Volga] (Moscow: Iauza, Eksmo, 2008), 398–399, 401–402; Sixth Army's daily reports for 8–10 January 1943, in Florian *Freiherr* von und zu Aufsess, *Die Anlagenbänder zu den Kriegstagebüchern der 6. Armee vom 24.12.1942 bis 02.02.1943*, book 3 (Schwabach, Germany: self-published, 2006), 189–209.
°Sixth Army's gun and mortar strength is from the formerly classified Red Army General Staff work *Sbornik materialov po izucheniiu opyta voiny, No.7* [Collection of materials for the study of war experiences, no. 7] (Moscow: Voenizdat, 1943), 20.

One reason for this overwhelming tactical superiority was that Rokoss-ovsky employed six field fortified regions—54th, 115th, 156th, 77th, 118th, and 159th—in their doctrinal role, covering wide portions of each army's sector to permit the concentration of other units at breakthrough points. In 24th Army, for example, 54th Fortified Region, reinforced with one conventional rifle regiment, protected almost 80 percent of the army's frontage, while four rifle divisions focused on the remaining 20 percent.[53]

This Soviet advantage, on top of the half-starved condition of the German troops and Voronov's careful planning, made the destruction of Sixth Army inevitable.

CHAPTER NINETEEN

The Destruction

On 8 January 1943, having previously established radio contact with Sixth Army, General Rokossovsky sent his personal representative along with a translator to deliver an ultimatum to the beleaguered force. This message promised honorable terms of surrender, with all soldiers retaining their badges and senior officers keeping their sidearms; at the end of the conflict, the Soviet Union would return the prisoners to Germany or to any other country of their choosing.[1] Paulus again requested freedom of action to break out, which Hitler refused. The next day the Soviets used loudspeakers and leaflets to communicate the surrender terms directly to the troops, who feared for their lives if captured. At this stage, the German commanders believed that their continued resistance would tie up Soviet forces and thereby prevent a much larger catastrophe.

ADVANCE TO THE ROSSOSHKA RIVER, 10–14 JANUARY

Throughout the day and overnight on 9–10 January, the Soviets tried to replicate normal, low levels of activity to disguise the exact timing and location of the main attack. The one exception was heightened activity in the north, opposite 60th Motorized Division, which was part of the deception effort to conceal the main point of attack.

Once the offensive began on 10 January, German corps headquarters again shuffled their slender reserves to limit Soviet inroads. These corps submitted their daily reports to Paulus's headquarters between 1557 and 1730 hours, after which Sixth Army's operations officer sent a grim summary to Army Group Don:

> On 10 January, after several hours of a fierce barrage by all calibers, including 100 Stalin organs [*katiushas*], the Russians attacked against the West Front with 9–10 divisions and 90–100 tanks, the South Front with 3–4 divisions and 40 tanks, and the Northeast Front with 2–3 divisions and 20 tanks. We could not respond to the attack with our own artillery because of ammunition shortages. It was not possible to move our tanks and assault guns behind the threatened fronts because of material (repair

parts) shortages. The Russians succeeded in breaking through 44th ID's front, and local reserves are being assembled in a position west of the Rossoschka [River].[2]

The report then detailed specific actions, noted that enemy air attacks were heavy, and acknowledged receiving 180 tons of supplies. At 2100 that evening Paulus sent his own characteristically blunt message to Manstein. Observing that another strong attack would exhaust the defenders, the army commander declared that a breakout attempt was "no longer possible" and urged that "multiple unified battalions with weapons must be flown in immediately if the Fortress is not to be overwhelmed in the future."[3]

After the artillery preparation, the Don Front's armies began their attacks at 0900 hours Moscow time. The five-division shock group of General Batov's 65th Army, supported on each flank by three divisions of Galinin's 24th Army and Chistiakov's 21st Army, savaged VIII Army Corps' 44th Infantry Division and the right wing of XIV Panzer Corps' 29th Motorized Division. Few of the defending German battalions fielded more than 300 men each, making it a very uneven contest. The deepest penetration, some 7 kilometers at the east end of the Golaia *balka*, was achieved by 27th Guards Rifle Division of 65th Army. To the right of this division, 24th and 304th Rifle Divisions, supported by about 40 tanks, overran three weak battalions of 44th Division plus a battalion-sized *kampfgruppe* of 29th Motorized. Paulus acknowledged a 2 kilometer wide breach in this area; the devastation was so great that a battalion commander of 132nd Infantry Regiment reportedly committed suicide the next day.[4] Nonetheless, the desperate defense by 44th Division prevented Batov's shock group from penetrating into the Rossoshka River Valley on the first day of the offensive. Hube's XIV Panzer Corps also contained the attack by 21st Army, but only by shifting all available reserves to reinforce 29th Motorized Division. On 65th Army's left, 24th Army penetrated up to 2 kilometers to seize positions along the Zapadnovka *balka* against the defenses of 76th Infantry Division, reinforced by ten vehicles of 244th Assault Gun Battalion. Together, the coordinated assault by 65th, 21st, and 24th Armies crumbled the western defenses of Sixth Army. The extent of this damage is suggested by an overnight report from XIV Panzer Corps, indicating that 29th Motorized Division had only 19 operable tanks and had lost 11 of its 18 *Paks*.[5] Paulus had to begin withdrawing behind the Rossoshka River far earlier than he had hoped.

Soviet advances on the southern face of the pocket were less dramatic but still boded ill for the integrity of the German defense. General Shumilov's 64th Army deepened its existing bridgehead on the northern bank of the Karavatka *balka* by 1 to 2 kilometers. To the west, the right wing of Tolbukhin's 57th Army tore large gaps and advanced up to 3 kilometers into the defenses

Map 100. Operation Ring, 10–13 January 1943

of IV Army Corps' 297th Infantry Division around Tsybenko, on both sides
of the frozen Chervlenaia River.

Within the city itself, General Chuikov used 156th Fortified Region in
its economy-of-force role, occupying strongpoints to free up rifle units for
attacks elsewhere. On the morning of 10 January, 45th Rifle Division retook
the last German-held building in the Krasnyi Oktiabr' Factory, while Bati-

uk's 284th Division seized the summit of Mamaev Kurgan and a cistern 75 meters southeast of that crest. Elsewhere, however, the defenders contained Soviet probes.[6]

Amidst this carnage, General Hartmann, commander of LI Corps' 71st Infantry Division, tried to maintain civility by holding an evening musical recital in his headquarters, the icy basement of a half-ruined building in southern Stalingrad. In addition to various classical piano pieces, he read inspirational selections from Goethe, Frederick the Great, and Hitler.[7]

Overnight on 10–11 January Generals Rokossovsky and Voronov adjusted the tactical objectives of units in 65th and 24th Armies to eliminate the remaining resistance of 76th Infantry, 44th Infantry, and 29th Motorized Divisions, thereby clearing the way for a further advance to the Rossoshka River at and south of Baburkin. In the process, they urged subordinates to focus on improving tank-infantry cooperation in response to the loss of one-third of the 100 infantry-support tanks on the first day. Division commanders also formed special assault groups to take specific German strongpoints.

The commanders on both sides focused on the Marinovka salient, the angle at the extreme western tip of the pocket. There, Paulus ordered Hube's XIV Panzer Corps to make a risky withdrawal, moving five battalions of 3rd Motorized Division a total of 9 to 10 kilometers eastward and northward to shore up 29th Motorized Division's defenses opposite 21st Army. Similarly, *Kampfgruppen* Willig, von Hanstein, and Seidel, composed of the remnants of 14th Panzer Division's panzer-grenadiers and reinforced by ad hoc battalions of service troops and *Luftwaffe* personnel, also planned to conduct a staged withdrawal from Marinovka east to Karpovka. In both cases these movements were undertaken hastily and under conditions of bitter cold, deep snow, and frequent Soviet artillery fire. The Germans attempted to leave sufficient troops behind to hold their previous defensive lines, but this was an almost impossible task.

For his part, Rokossovsky planned to roll up XIV Panzer Corps from north to south. The main effort fell to 21st Army's leftmost unit, Major General N. T. Tavartkiladze's 51st Guards Rifle Division, and its neighbor on the right wing of 65th Army, Colonel V. S. Askalenov's 173rd Rifle Division. They were to advance on both sides of the Dmitievka-Karpovka road and capture the latter town, while 120th Rifle Division attacked northward from a position in second echelon and then wheeled around to meet Tavartkiladze at Karpovka. The remaining divisions of 21st Army would attempt to pin down 3rd Motorized Division to prevent precisely the kind of withdrawal the Germans were planning.

By 0820 on 11 January, Hube's corps was already under heavy pressure,[8] while to the north, 44th Infantry Division was in dire circumstances. On the southern face of the pocket, the methodical German reporting system broke down, and Sixth Army received no situation reports from IV Army Corps as it tried in vain to contain 57th and 64th Armies. Communicating to Army Group Don, one report from Paulus's headquarters early on the eleventh poignantly declared, "the army has no more reserves," with the comment underlined for emphasis.[9] The supply situation was equally bleak.

The 65th and 21st Armies, which outnumbered the defenders by as much as four to one, pressed hard on Heitz's VIII Army Corps along the pocket's northwestern face. These attacks again failed to break through, although 27th Guards and 304th Rifle Divisions, part of Batov's original shock group, advanced 3 kilometers southeastward on either side of Hill 103.1. The 76th Infantry Division reported 12 separate attacks of company or battalion strength on 11 January. Six vehicles of 177th Assault Gun Battalion broke up the strongest of these attacks in the late morning, but later the division had to fall back to new positions along the Zapadnovka *balka* and burial mound. Still, the Germans restored the connection between the left flank of 76th Infantry and the right flank of 44th Infantry. The latter division, however, barely repulsed Soviet attacks resulting in heavy losses on both sides, and it lost contact with 29th Motorized Division on its left.[10] Batov exploited this gap, committing his second-echelon 23rd Rifle Division into it. This brought 65th Army's shock group to within a kilometer of the Rossoshka valley around Baburkin by day's end, thereby rendering VIII Corps' defense of that river completely untenable.

Against the Marinovka salient at the western tip of the pocket, the Don Front's designated main effort—65th Army's 173rd Rifle Division and 21st Army's 51st Guards Rifle Division, supported by two other divisions of 21st Army—pushed back 29th Motorized Division's 15th Panzer-Grenadiers. Reaching Otorvanovka and the Rassypnaia *balka* by nightfall on 11 January, the two rifle divisions pressed forward overnight, leaving only a narrow corridor at the southern base of the salient through which the survivors of 29th and 3rd Motorized Divisions could withdraw. XIV Panzer Corps reported that it had completed its withdrawal here as intended, but it clearly lost significant assets in the process. The stay-behind units of 3rd Motorized Division suffered heavily. The division was reduced to 11 operable tanks and had 4 fewer *Paks* than the day before; however, it claimed it had destroyed 20 Soviet tanks, most of them British models.[11]

Along the southern face of the pocket, Jänecke's IV Army Corps reported halting the attacks of 57th and 64th Armies, but it could not restore its previous defensive positions. In reality, General Shumilov had paused to move second-echelon units, including 29th Rifle Division and 154th Naval Rifle Brigade, forward for his next assault. Elements of 297th Infantry Division still clung to a strongpoint in Tsybenko, but they were surrounded, and no rescue attempt was possible.[12] Worse still for IV Corps, there was no defensible terrain to its rear; once 297th and 376th Infantry Divisions lost their current positions, the "fortress defense" would be completely untenable on the open steppe west of Stalingrad.

North of the city, additional Soviet tank-infantry attacks that afternoon carved multiple breaches in the defenses of 16th Panzer Division. Fortunately for the Germans, the hilly terrain they occupied here was much more defensible than that at the western end of the pocket, and 66th Army was one of the weakest formations in the Don Front. While 16th Panzer claimed it killed 800 to 900 Red soldiers on 11 January, it also lost 29 killed, 87 wounded, and 20 missing itself.[13] Like its counterparts in the west, 16th Panzer would soon have to pull back, in this instance to positions northwest of Orlovka.

Within the city itself, Chuikov continued to substitute machine gun–artillery battalions of 156th Fortified Region to free up more capable units; on 11 January this involved the relief of 138th Rifle Division. LI Corps lost several houses and other strongpoints between the Krasnyi Oktiabr', bread, and Barrikady factories. The corps also suffered a rising toll of casualties; 100th *Jäger* and 305th Infantry Divisions lost a total of 42 killed, 202 wounded, and 12 missing on 11 January.[14] As Seydlitz's units ran low on riflemen, 62nd Army's advance gradually accelerated.

In addition to dour reports from his staff, Paulus sent a personal message to Manstein at 2135 hours, describing his army's plight:

> Despite heroic resistance in recent days, the heavy fighting has led to repeated deep enemy penetrations that cannot be halted. Reserves are no longer available, without which we can do no more. Ammunition is sufficient for only 3 days. Supplies are at an end. Heavy weapons can no longer be moved.
>
> The high losses and poor supply situation associated with the cold have caused the resistance of the troops to fall significantly. It is to be expected that the enemy's attacks on the fortress will continue to be as strong as previously, and we can hold out for only a few days. Resistance will then dissolve into separate fights.[15]

Higher German headquarters, reflecting Hitler's will, remained disconnected from reality. Later that evening the OKH radioed Sixth Army: "The line Zybenko-Karpowka-Rossoschka will be held at all costs . . . Zybenko will in all circumstances be recaptured."[16]

Overnight on 11–12 January Rokossovsky urged all his subordinates in the west, but particularly 24th, 65th, and 21st Armies, to liquidate the Marinovka salient and breach the Rossoshka River line if possible.

This time, the center of combat shifted slightly northward, to State Farm No. 1 and the hills north of it, defended by 44th Infantry Division's reinforced 131st Regiment. Around noon on 12 January, 24th Army's right-wing 84th Rifle Division and 65th Army's left-wing 214th Rifle Division, aided by 10 tanks each, finally broke the back of German resistance at the State Farm. To the south, four rifle divisions plus about 40 tanks of 65th Army continued to make the main assault, breaking through the other two regiments of 44th Infantry Division. By nightfall, 304th Rifle Division had seized a narrow bridgehead on the east bank of the Rossoshka River, northeast of the village of Karpovka. Just south of this penetration, Batov committed his army's second-echelon 252nd Rifle Division through the widening gap between VIII Army Corps and XIV Panzer Corps. This fresh unit pivoted southward across the lower part of the Rassypnaia *balka*, reaching the river midway between Novo-Alekseevskii and Karpovka. This maneuver further narrowed 29th Motorized Division's route of withdrawal. Meanwhile, concentric attacks by Chistiakov's 21st Army crushed 29th Motorized's defenses at Poltavskii and along the Rassypnaia *balka*. The same army's 52nd Guards Division cleared German stay-behind forces from strongpoints at Marinovka eastward, while other divisions loosely encircled about half of 3rd Motorized Division. The two motorized divisions lost approximately one-half to two-thirds of their original strength in this fighting. At day's end, a corridor less than 2 kilometers wide still existed at and north of Karpovka, through which the surviving elements of XIV Panzer Corps withdrew eastward. It was apparent to Paulus that the Rossoshka River line could not be held when so many elements had been destroyed or were trapped west of that line. By the end of 12 January, Paulus's troops had no choice but to fight to the end without hope of rescue.

The chaotic situation that day produced a number of rumors in the German rear area. The most famous one involved a small group of Soviet tanks headed for the main airfield at Pitomnik. If these tanks existed at all, they were likely a reconnaissance party. However, the rumor produced disorderly crowds of soldiers seeking places on *Luftwaffe* evacuation flights; supply troops and some of the wounded were hastily evacuated based on what turned out to be a false alarm.[17]

On the southern face of the pocket, Shumilov's 64th Army continued to eliminate German defenses methodically, expanding its bridgehead north of the Karavatka *balka*. To Shumilov's right, 57th Army's 422nd Rifle Division captured Tsybenko, while 38th Rifle Division exploited to within 2 kilometers of Rakotino, beginning the attrition of the already weak left wing of 376th Infantry Division in that area. All IV Corps could do was create a cordon of artillery strongpoints around the penetration.[18]

On the northeast face of the pocket, 16th Panzer Division, reinforced with virtually all of XI Army Corps' available armor, held out stubbornly against Zhadov's 66th Army, which had focused two rifle divisions and a separate rifle brigade against it. Sheer attrition would force the panzer unit to withdraw to more coherent defenses on 13 January. Within the city, Chuikov's troops continued to inch forward without achieving decisive results. In the last casualty report it submitted, LI Army Corps reported losing 23 dead and 85 wounded on 12 January, figures that did not include losses for 305th Infantry Division.[19]

In preparation for the third day of the offensive, Rokossovsky transferred 65th Army's 173rd and 252nd Rifle Divisions, together with additional multiple-rocket launchers and two heavy mortar brigades, to 21st Army. This placed Chistiakov in sole command of the effort to capture Karpovka and advance to the Rossoshka River. The *front* commander expected 21st Army, now reinforced to 23 artillery and 7 tank regiments, to finish this task by 14 January, after which it would lead the advance eastward to seize the Pitomnik airfield and link up with 57th Army.[20] Batov's 65th Army, protected on its left flank by 24th Army, would then advance in parallel, striking through Novo-Alekseevskii to attack Baburkin.[21]

The attackers achieved most of this plan as scheduled on 13–14 January. The 120th and 96th Rifle Divisions of 21st Army helped capture Karpovka from 3rd Motorized Division and then moved east about a kilometer, into jumping-off positions along the Rossoshka River. Meanwhile, 293rd, 277th, and 289th Rifle Divisions, cooperating with 52nd Guards Division, destroyed or captured large portions of 29th and 3rd Motorized Divisions encircled west of Karpovka; with the exception of 289th Rifle Division, which moved into army reserve, the other divisions then advanced eastward to the Rossoshka on 14 January to join those preparing to advance eastward.

Shumilov's 64th and Tolbukhin's 57th Armies pushed the defenses of IV Army Corps and the neighboring 376th Infantry Division of XIV Panzer Corps to the breaking point on the thirteenth. On Tolbukhin's left wing, 15th Guards Rifle Division rolled up the defenses of 376th Infantry from west to east. By the end of the day, this stricken German division was caught in a pincer between 15th Guards moving east across the Chervlenaia River, as 422nd Rifle Division advanced northwestward, and 21st Army's 120th Rifle Division moving southeast along the northern bank of the Chervlenaia. On the same day, 38th Rifle Division, supported by 254th Tank Brigade, advanced north several kilometers from the Tsybenko area into Gornaia Poliana State Farm, brushing off 297th Infantry Division's efforts to retard its progress. The right wing of this German division was overrun, while 7th Rifle Corps' 97th Rifle Brigade split 297th from 371st Infantry Division, its neighbor to the east. In its final recorded reports, IV Army Corps continued to plan in vain for weak counterattacks using a bicycle-mounted battalion borrowed from LI Corps.[22] In fact, however, by 14 January, IV Corps had been penetrated on its right wing and center and could no longer keep up any pretense of containing the

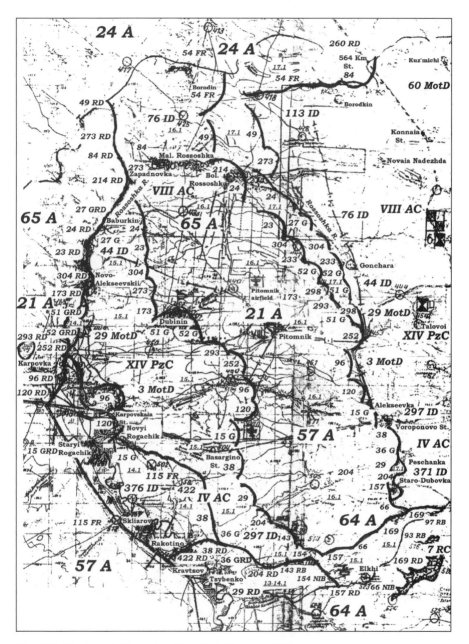

Map 101. Don Front's Operation Ring, 13–17 January 1943

Soviet attacks. Like the western salient, the southern face of the German pocket was ripe for total collapse.

Within the city, 62nd Army completed the first stage of its offensive on 13 January. It had pushed 100th *Jäger* and 305th Infantry Divisions westward from most of the factory district, leaving the bread factory as its next major target. Symptomatic of the progressive German breakdown throughout the pocket, after that date, Sixth Army's records contain no further corps reports, only intermittent communications with higher headquarters.

On the morning of 14 January, 65th Army's 24th Rifle and 27th Guards Divisions entered the outskirts of Baburkin, but the remnants of 44th Infantry Division held on to the town; late in the day, 27th Guards reverted to army reserve to rest for future attacks. To the south, Batov's right-wing divisions, 23rd and 304th Rifle, enveloped other elements of 44th Infantry Division defending Novo-Alekseevskii but again failed to clear the town.[23]

Distracted by 65th Army's attacks, VIII Corps was unable to prevent Chistiakov's 21st Army from concentrating its 173rd, 51st and 52nd Guards, and 298th Rifle Divisions on a 6 kilometer wide sector of the Rossoshka River south of Novo-Alekseevskii. The first three of these divisions forced the river and pushed the weak, dismounted elements of the two German motorized divisions east up to 2 kilometers. While Chistiakov's left wing pressed eastward in this manner, his right-wing 252nd, 96th, and 120th Rifle Divisions had even greater success, lunging forward to reach the Karpovka River and beyond, seizing Karpovka Station and shattering the remnants of 3rd and 29th Motorized Divisions in the process.[24]

The advance by Chistiakov's 120th Rifle Division contributed to 57th Army's encirclement of the remnants of 376th Infantry Division on the collapsing southern face of the pocket. On 14 January Tolbukhin sent two pincers—one composed of 38th Rifle Division and 254th Tank Brigade, the other consisting of 15th Guards Rifle Division—deep into IV Army Corps' rear. They linked up on the railway line near Barsargino Station and trapped 376th Infantry between them. Lacking artillery support, the surviving German infantrymen died in place, surrendered, or disappeared into the cold winter night. Moreover, the Germans lost an auxiliary airstrip near Barsargino, and there was little left of XIV Panzer or IV Army Corps to prevent a Soviet advance eastward to Pitomnik.[25]

Inside Stalingrad proper, LI Army Corps' 305th Infantry Division clung to positions in the Barrikady and bread factories, while 100th *Jäger* Division retained a line on the western slope of Mamaev Kurgan. Between them, however, the combined forces of 45th Rifle, 138th Rifle, and 39th Guards Rifle Divisions advanced up to ten blocks into the lower Krasnyi Oktiabr' village on 14 January. Just before midnight that evening, Army Group Don reported the dire situation to the OKH, adding that "the army group no longer expects that the situation of the [Sixth] Army can be restored because of inadequate remaining supplies."[26]

FROM THE ROSSOSHKA RIVER TO PITOMNIK, 15–17 JANUARY

On 15 January, as the Don Front resumed its offensive soon after dawn, Rokossovsky received a promotion to colonel general.

Snowdrifts, severe cold, and Soviet air and ground attacks hampered the efforts of VIII Army Corps and XIV Panzer Corps to withdraw toward the Bol'shaia Rossoshka–Dubininskii–Peschanyi line. This bleak position was only a way station to defensive positions extending south from the village of Borodkin through Gonchara to Alekseevka. By 1700, the OKH liaison officer at Sixth Army reported that he doubted whether even those "end positions" could be held for a significant period of time.[27]

That day, the shock groups of 65th, 21st, and 24th Armies, attacking on a 25 kilometer front, advanced eastward 6 to 10 kilometers. Chistiakov's 21st Army lunged within 3 kilometers of Pitomnik. In the process, the three Red armies took Baburkin and Novo-Alekseevskii on the Rossoshka, as well as Dubininskii and Iablonovskii to the east, savaging the remnants of 44th and 297th Infantry Divisions as well as 29th and 3rd Motorized Divisions. As a result, Paulus had no choice but to evacuate the Pitomnik airfield that evening. He also had to instruct the commanders of VIII and IV Army Corps to use their shattered units, along with two other weakened infantry divisions (76th and 371st), to assemble a new defensive front. The line selected ran from the Korennaia *balka* south to a point some 4 kilometers northeast of Dubinin and then southward again to Staro-Dubovka. However, establishing a serious defense in one frozen night (15–16 January) with such exhausted troops was a virtually impossible task. Within the city, the remnants of two regiments of 79th Infantry Division faced the equally challenging task of containing 138th Rifle Division, which was pushing into the lower Krasnyi Oktiabr' village from the factory of the same name.

By 15 January, Sixth Army had suffered more than 60,000 troops killed, frozen, or captured, roughly one-third of the force it had fielded six days before. Although the desperate Germans were short of food, ammunition, and fuel, they were still far more numerous than the planners of Operation Ring had anticipated. Moreover, as they retreated eastward, Paulus's troops were now occupying some of the same positions 62nd Army had tried to defend in August and September 1942. On the Soviet side, the first six days had reportedly cost 24,000 soldiers killed, wounded, missing in action, or otherwise injured, as well as at least 143 of the original 264

tanks. The weakened Don Front would have to wage a protracted struggle
for each separate German defensive position.[28] A letter written by one German noncommissioned officer reflected his dedication under these extreme
circumstances:

> On Tuesday, I knocked out two T-34s with my mobile anti-tank gun. . . .
> Afterwards I drove past the smoking remains. From the hatch there hung
> a body, head down, his feet caught, and his legs burning up to this knees.
> . . . And there was no possibility of freeing him. Even if there had been,
> he would have died after a few hours of torture. I shot him and, as I did
> it, the tears ran down my cheeks. . . .
>   I have now taken over a heavy anti-tank gun and organized eight men,
> four Russians [*Hiwis*] among them. The nine of us drag the cannon from
> one place to another. Every time we change position, a burning tank re-
> mains on the field. The number has grown to eight already, and we intend
> to make it a dozen. However, I have only three rounds left . . . during the
> night I cry without control, like a child.[29]

By the end of 16 January, 65th, 21st, and 57th Armies had penetrated
Sixth Army's designated intermediate defensive line before it had even been
formed. In the process, 21st Army's 51st Guards and 252nd Rifle Divisions
occupied the Pitomnik airfield, while the same army's 298th and 293rd Rifle
Divisions captured Pitomnik village, some 3 kilometers to the south. There,
the Soviets encountered an 88mm battery that fought to the last round
against advancing T-34s.[30]

That afternoon, Paulus launched a counterattack east of Pitomnik using
most of 14th Panzer Division's surviving tanks.[31] At a cost of four tanks, this
weak effort slowed the advance of 65th and 21st Armies and inflicted some
damage on 252nd Rifle Division. By this stage, however, each Soviet field
army commander was rotating one division back from the front line each day
to rest and recuperate. With the Germans now anchored in the western suburbs of the city, the Red forces would have to take a longer pause to prepare
for the final push.

With Pitomnik lost, the last German defensive fighter aircraft flew out,
and the already difficult German supply situation became impossible. Paulus
moved his own staff back into the city, occupying the former headquarters of
General Alexander von Hartmann's decimated 71st Infantry Division. It soon
earned the nickname "Hartmannstadt."[32]

On 17 January the German defenses generally held firm except in VIII
Army Corps' sector east of Pitomnik, where the attackers penetrated from 1
to 4 kilometers. The 65th Army's 27th Guards Division pushed its lead elements eastward across the Rossoshka and paused only because Rokossovsky

wanted to rest and replenish his divisions. For the Germans, loss of the main airfield meant that Sixth Army received less than ten tons of air-dropped supplies, and it demanded that the *Luftwaffe* resume landings at the auxiliary strip. That evening Paulus appealed through Army Group Don to the OKH, lamenting, "My Führer, your orders regarding the delivery of supplies to Sixth Army are not being carried out. . . . Request quickest possible intervention."[33]

In other sectors, the Soviet advance was slow and bloody. The 66th Army concentrated its attacks against the hapless 16th Panzer Division at the northeast corner of the pocket but advanced only 2.5 kilometers over five days. Inside the city, Chuikov ordered yet another attack by his skeletal forces, committing Rodimtsev's 13th Guards Rifle Division against the southern half of Krasnyi Oktiabr' village after the guardsmen had redeployed from the city center.[34] By the end of 17 January, Chuikov had expanded his "bridgehead" by more than 50 percent since the crisis of November.

By nightfall that day, six days into the battle, the pocket's dimensions had decreased sharply: its perimeter shrank from 170 to 110 kilometers, its depth from 53 to 20 kilometers west to east, and its width from 35 to 30 kilometers north to south.[35] Five German divisions—3rd and 29th Motorized, 44th, 297th, and 376th Infantry Divisions—were severely depleted if not destroyed. The Red Air Force had achieved daylight air superiority, pounding German defensive positions and airstrips. The *Luftwaffe* was forced to conduct its aerial resupply at night.[36] At this point, the besieging forces paused to rest and refit for four days while Rokossovsky and Voronov worked out a new plan to complete the destruction of Sixth Army.

THE LULL, 18–21 JANUARY

On the morning of 18 January General Voronov proposed his plan for the next stage of the offensive, a plan that Stalin approved without change that same afternoon.[37] Voronov's concept was to continue the successful advance from west to east. Beginning on 20 January—later delayed by two days—24th, 65th, and 21st Armies would renew their attack along a 22 kilometer sector of the Rossoshka River, stretching from 2 kilometers north of Borodkin to 2.5 kilometers north of Alekseevka (see map 102). In the center of this sector, Chistiakov's 21st Army would launch the main effort against the already shattered forces of VIII Army and XIV Panzer Corps. For this attack, Chistiakov had 9 rifle divisions (from north to south, 173rd, 51st and 52nd Guards, 293rd, 298th, 252nd, 277th, 96th, and 120th) supported by 1st and 4th Artillery Divisions and 12 separate artillery and rocket regiments or brigades. He also had 7 heavy tank regiments, 5 antiaircraft regiments, and a host of

Map 102. Don Front's Operation Ring, 17–25 January 1943

other supporting units. While 65th Army pushed east to seize Aleksandrovka and the outskirts of Krasnyi Oktiabr' village, 21st Army aimed to split the Germans in two and ultimately link up with Chuikov's 62nd and Zhadov's 66th Armies somewhere near Gorodishche. Meanwhile, Tolbukhin's 57th and Shumilov's 64th Armies would conduct concentric attacks against the southern part of the German pocket and enter the southern half of the city.

This was the plan, at least, even though Zhadov, Chuikov, Tolbukhin, and Shumilov had only limited combat power to achieve such ambitious goals.

Even during the intended lull, fighting went on. On 18 January 65th Army's 27th Guards Rifle Division, supported by 91st Tank Brigade, broke through the defenses of VIII Corps' 44th Infantry Division, leaving part of that division isolated south of Bol'shala Rossoshka. Late in the day, 44th and 76th Infantry Divisions, aided by the remnants of 14th Panzer, managed to contain 65th Army along the high ground north of Gonchara.

With the loss of Pitomnik, German casualties accumulated, with little means of providing medical treatment or chance of evacuation. Front-line troops received virtually no food, and casualty clearing stations became charnel houses. On 17 January Hitler belatedly put General Milch in direct command of the airlift, with unlimited authority to requisition assets. However, Milch learned that Paulus's staff had resisted developing the remaining airstrip at Gumrak for fear that flights landing there would attract Soviet bombing raids on Sixth Army's nearby headquarters.[38] Now there was no choice, and Gumrak did indeed come under intermittent air attack. On the night of 18 January Milch managed to have seven aircraft deliver supplies to Gumrak. At Hitler's request, one of these aircraft brought out Lieutenant General Hans Hube, the wounded commander of XIV Panzer Corps. Hube described the declining fortunes of Sixth Army and bluntly told Hitler that the airlift had failed. Given the great favoritism shown toward the supposedly modern, pro-Nazi *Luftwaffe*, Hube was understandably bitter. "Why don't you kill off some of your *Luftwaffe* generals?" he reportedly asked Hitler. "It's always the army generals who go to the wall."[39] Hube provided additional graphic details of the situation to General Zeitzler, but with little apparent effect.

In truth, however, the airlift had been impossible from the start. Despite Milch's herculean efforts to reorganize the transports, the stream of supplies dwindled and was reduced to parachute drops after Gumrak fell on 23 January.

Early on 19 January Paulus sent another somber message through the OKW liaison officer:

The fortress can be held for only a few days longer. The failure of supplies has exhausted the men and rendered vehicles immobile. The last airfield will be lost shortly, so that supplies will sink to a minimum. The basis for continuing the struggle for Stalingrad no longer exists. From now on the Russians can pierce every front. The heroism of the soldiers is still unbroken. In order to exploit this to the last measure, on the verge of collapse I intend to command all the units to make an organized breakthrough to the south. Individual groups will get through and at least create confusion in the Russian front. . . . Suggest a few men, officers and crews, that is, specialists, still fly out in order for you to make them available for further warfare. This order must be given soon. There is expected to be only a short period for possible flights. Request you determine these officers by name. I, myself, as a matter of course, will separate myself from them.[40]

Even at this stage, however, Hitler would not authorize a breakout. By this point, both the dictator and his operational commander, Manstein, had, in effect, written Sixth Army off, sacrificing it to absorb the enemy's combat power.

In any event, the developing series of Soviet offensives gave the Germans other urgent problems. On 13 January the Voronezh and Southwestern Fronts opened their offensive against Hungarian Second Army. By the sixteenth, the same day the Germans lost the Pitomnik airfield, these two *fronts*, led by 3rd Tank Army, had encircled almost the entire Hungarian army and its supporting Italian Alpine Corps. This offensive carved a 160 kilometer gap in the Axis front south of Voronezh; the continued resistance of Sixth Army was essential to prevent six additional Soviet armies from exploiting the Axis disarray.

By 20 January, fuel shortages inside the pocket forced the Germans to abandon their heavy weapons when they withdrew. That day, the defenders noted a number of strong reconnaissance efforts, both along the western face and in the northeast, where 60th Motorized and 16th Panzer Divisions were withdrawing to more favorable defensive terrain. The defenders fought, starved, and died in an indescribable frozen hell.[41]

Although the final stage of Operation Ring officially began on 22 January, in reality, it started on the previous day. The three principal attacking forces —24th, 65th, and 21st Armies—began their now customary reconnaissances-in-force against the entire northwestern corner of Sixth Army's defenses. At the same time, 66th Army pursued XI Army Corps' 60th Motorized and 16th Panzer Divisions as they withdrew to new positions. Both these operations forced the weakened defenders to withdraw farther than they had planned, and 44th Infantry Division ceased to exist in all but name. Deep snow and lack of fuel hampered Paulus's efforts to fill the resulting 6 kilometer gap north of Gonchara, leaving 76th and 113th Infantry Divisions to erect new defenses as best they could from Novaia Nadezhda State Farm southward to the rail line. Sixth Army's intelligence also identified significant Soviet troop concentrations west of XIV Panzer Corps, foretelling an even greater push the next day.

Sixth Army was clearly dying. While some German units withdrew in good order into the city, in other instances, individual German soldiers sought shelter in the ruins. The rapid dissolution was illustrated by a message to Army Group Don, sent shortly after noon on 21 January: "No longer intend a breakthrough toward the west since it is impossible to announce it to all the commanders."[42] Manstein's headquarters nonetheless emphasized the importance of the continued airdrops of supplies to permit some units to escape the encirclement. That night, Sixth Army tersely radioed that no more flights should be sent to Gumrak airstrip after 0400 on the twenty-second, although Paulus's headquarters optimistically promised to open a new airstrip west of Hill 102.0.[43]

The 21 January reconnaissances conducted by Galinin's 24th and Batov's 65th Armies were so successful that Rokossovsky simply ordered them to continue the advance, thus denying any opportunity for XI and VIII Army Corps to reestablish a defensive front. To the south, however, 21st, 57th, and 64th Armies had completed their preparations for a final deliberate offensive. These three armies had a total of 4,100 guns and mortars (76.2mm or higher) and 75 tanks. Overall, the Don Front still numbered perhaps 245,000 soldiers; the Axis defenders had roughly 110,000 men, but only 20,000 of them were considered combat troops. At this stage, every soldier was a potential combatant, but the Germans had so little fuel and ammunition that they often could not defend themselves effectively. Nonetheless, Sixth Army did not die easily or quickly.

THE SOVIET ADVANCE, 22–25 JANUARY

After a 70-minute artillery preparation, 21st, 57th, 64th, and 62nd Armies resumed their offensive at 1000 hours on 22 January. Despite dense clouds and light snow, hand-picked crews of 16th Air Army struck German troop concentrations, firing positions, and other key objectives while fighter pilots blocked the last German airstrips. By midmorning, Batov's 65th and Galinin's 24th Armies drew even with Chistiakov's 21st Army, although all units reported "stubborn enemy resistance." Indeed, Rokossovsky was disappointed with the limited progress made on 22 January, especially against 371st Infantry Division's strong positions south of Kuporosnoe and El'shanka. Chistiakov overcame his enemy's defenses but advanced only 3 to 4 kilometers, bringing his troops within 2 kilometers of Gumrak, well within artillery range. Only in the evening did 36th Guards and 29th Rifle Divisions, deployed on 64th Army's right wing, exploit a breakthrough by 57th Army along the railroad line; by the next day, these divisions had captured Peschanka.

Both sides were worn down by prolonged fighting and hampered by the cold and snow. The Germans, however, had the additional handicap of starvation. In one instance, Chistiakov claimed he had witnessed a field kitchen deliberately advancing in front of the riflemen of his 293rd Division; the German defenders reportedly surrendered to the field kitchen and were promptly fed.[44]

That evening, Hitler responded to Paulus's hints of a possible surrender, effectively directing the beleaguered command to commit suicide:

> Capitulation is out of the question.
>
> The troops will defend themselves to the last. If possible, the size of the fortress is to be reduced so that it can be held by the troops still capable of fighting.
>
> The courage and endurance of the fortress have made it possible to establish a new front and begin preparing a counter-operation.
>
> Thereby, Sixth Army has made an historic contribution to Germany's greatest struggle.[45]

Despite the limited Soviet advance on 22 January, Rokossovsky decided to press forward, reasoning that the Germans on the western face of the pocket had lost their last prepared defensive line. He also decided to confuse the defenders by changing the time of his attacks, attacking earlier (0900) on 23 January and later (1030) on the next day. This denied the Germans the effective use of their remaining shelters.

On 23 January 66th Army was still consolidating its recent capture of Kuz'michi. The other six armies resumed (or continued) their attacks. In the west, 65th, 21st, and 57th Armies advanced as much as 8 kilometers, prompting Paulus to relocate his headquarters to the vicinity of Station No. 1 in central Stalingrad.[46] Equally ominous for the defenders was 64th Army's systematic destruction of 297th Infantry Division's positions near Peschanka. Exploiting this success, 157th and 169th Rifle Divisions in 64th Army's center wheeled northeastward to seize Zelenaia Poliana, 4 kilometers from the southern suburbs of the city. Within Stalingrad, Chuikov's forces continued their bitter house-to-house struggle against LI Army Corps.

That night, Paulus shifted elements of 24th Panzer, 60th Motorized, and Romanian 1st Cavalry and 20th Infantry Divisions southward from the factory district in a final effort to bolster defenses near Gumrak Station, opposite 21st Army's left wing. However, German and Soviet accounts differ sharply with regard to the intensity of the ensuing fight.

Rokossovsky later recalled that fighting reached a crescendo on 24–25 January as the defenders fought to protect the approaches to Gumrak and cover the withdrawal of other German units into the city. He even committed a *front* reserve unit, 121st Tank Brigade with 41 tanks, to reinforce 21st Army's left wing.[47] German resistance was so effective that the *Stavka* was unable to withdraw any significant numbers of troops from the Stalingrad region until 27 January, when it ordered Galinin's 24th Army into strategic reserve in the Voronezh region. Tolbukhin's 57th Army, together with two *front*-level artillery divisions, followed Galinin's headquarters into reserve, although the combat forces of these two armies were transferred to 64th, 65th, and 66th Armies on 1 February. Eventually, the *Stavka* dispatched 65th and 21st Armies northward to the Livny area, east of Kursk. There, they joined the new Central Front, formed from the Don Front headquarters with Rokossovsky still in command, on 15 February. Not until 25 February did this new *front* launch its next offensive, which came close to succeeding.[48] In this respect, therefore, Sixth Army performed its designated purpose of tying down Soviet combat power as long as possible. This outcome must be recognized when pondering the hypothetical effects of a formal surrender by Paulus in late January.

The fighting on 24 January reduced the size of Sixth Army's pocket by almost one-third. The 21st Army captured Gumrak and Opytnaia Station, while on its left, 24th and 65th Armies advanced to the outskirts of Gorodishche and Aleksandrovka. In the south, 57th and 64th Armies reached the western outskirts of El'shanka and the center of Kuporosnoe.[49]

The inexorable but costly advance of the Red Army continued on 25 January. Spearheaded by 121st Tank Brigade, 51st, 52nd, and 66th Guards Rifle Divisions on 21st Army's left pushed east up to 3 kilometers, coming within 3.5 kilometers of 62nd Army's farthest advances in the Krasnyi Oktiabr' village and Mamaev Kurgan. Farther south, the other six divisions of Chistakov's army advanced north of the Tsaritsa River toward the western edge of Stalingrad's center city. The divisions of Batov's 65th Army converged on and captured Aleksandrovka and Gorodishche, while Tolbukhin's 57th Army lunged eastward along the railroad line into the southern part of the city. In the process, Tolbukhin's men cut off most of 297th Infantry Division; the division's commander, Major General Moritz von Drebber, surrendered his headquarters to 57th Army's 38th Rifle Division.[50] In the extreme southern part of the city, Shumilov's 64th Army also pushed forward, with 157th Rifle Division recapturing the infamous grain elevator and pushing north toward the Tsaritsa River. The remnants of IV Army Corps' 371st Infantry Division withdrew north across the El'shanka River and railroad line, although they still held some buildings near Railroad Station No. 2.

At the northern end of the city, Galinin's 24th and Zhadov's 66th Armies converged on XI Army Corps' defenses, forcing that corps to abandon its strongpoints around Orlovka and begin a slow withdrawal to the tractor factory and its associated village. The 24th and 16th Panzer and 60th Motorized Divisions, having lost or abandoned their heavy weapons, were about halfway back to these new positions at day's end.

The Soviet advances on 24–25 January were so effective that Chuikov ordered his men to rest, consolidate, and conduct reconnaissance on the twenty-fifth. Late that evening, Rokossovsky assigned 62nd Army a key role in the final destruction of Sixth Army.

By now, the overstretched divisions of Army Groups B and Don were between 270 and 400 kilometers distant from the shrunken Stalingrad pocket, and airdrops had become inaccurate and rare. On 25 January Field Marshal von Manstein issued a circular order to all commanders, staff officers, and other officials within his army group. Ostensibly to maintain morale, he ordered all officers to discontinue any discussions concerning the "responsibility" for what had happened to the Stalingrad pocket.[51] This gag order also prevented any discussion of the role of the army group and its commander in the demise of Paulus's army. By contrast, Stalin issued an order to the entire Red Army congratulating his soldiers on their achievements over the previous two months. The Soviet dictator intended nothing less than the collapse of all Axis forces in the East.

THE LIQUIDATION OF SIXTH ARMY'S SOUTHERN POCKET, 26–30 JANUARY

On the evening of 25 January General Rokossovsky found himself in much the same position General Paulus had confronted all fall: having to attack from west to east and clear the difficult terrain of a half-destroyed city against a determined foe. This time, however, the defenders were cut off, without food or ammunition, having been abandoned by their higher headquarters.

The obvious next step was to chop Sixth Army into two pieces, north and south, and then destroy those elements piecemeal. As before, 21st and 65th Armies would perform the major effort, met by a matching assault from 62nd Army in the east. To achieve surprise, Rokossovsky decided to forgo a preliminary artillery preparation on the twenty-sixth.[52]

In turn, General Chistiakov assigned the task of achieving the linkup to Major General N. T. Tavartkiladze's 51st and Major General N. D. Kozin's 52nd Guards Rifle Divisions, supported by 121st Tank Brigade and 9th and 48th Guards Heavy Tank Regiments. These formations would attack due east at first light, link up with 62nd Army's troops somewhere near the western end of Krasnyi Oktiabr' village, and then wheel south to begin destroying the southern grouping of German divisions.[53]

Rokossovsky's effort to divide Sixth Army in half began shortly after dawn on 26 January. The disorganized and exhausted Germans, short of all types of ammunition, had little chance of thwarting the Soviet commander. Piercing the weak defenses of VIII Army Corps' 44th and 76th Infantry Divisions, Chistiakov's two guards divisions with supporting tanks linked up with

62nd Army's 13th Guards Rifle Division near the western edge of the upper Krasnyi Oktiabr' village and the Bannyi ravine. Cautiously identifying each other, the leading troops of these two armies were soon hugging, with characteristic shouts of "Urrah!" ringing in the frozen air.[54] Kozin's 52nd Guards Division, led by 121st Tank Brigade, then turned southeast through the woods toward the western slope of Mamaev Kurgan, where they encountered Batiuk's 284th Rifle Division. Anticipating such a development, Batiuk had posted an operations officer, Captain G. M. Malitsky, at an observation post. When he saw approaching armor at about 1120 hours, Malitsky promptly fired off red signal rockets and received an answering signal from the leading tank platoon. After a brief celebration, 52nd Guards turned back northward to clear 100th *Jäger* Division from Krasnyi Oktiabr' village, while 284th Rifle Division turned southward to engage the newly created southern pocket of Sixth Army.

North of this linkup, 65th Army had considerable difficulty against the remainder of 76th Infantry Division, penetrating 3 to 5 kilometers eastward but still not reaching the factory villages.[55] On Chistiakov's right, the other rifle divisions of 21st Army advanced just south of the Tsaritsa River, despite surprisingly strong resistance from XIV Panzer Corps' shattered divisions. In part, the slow pace of this advance was due to the previous casualties in the Don Front's rifle units, which left some divisions at regimental strength. German reports described the advancing Red infantry as moving "timidly" and "hesitantly," but they were still better organized and better equipped than the defenders. Although some extraordinary German commanders held their troops together, other units degenerated into leaderless groups seeking shelter from incessant air and artillery strikes.

In the northeastern corner of the city, 66th Army pursued XI Army Corps' withdrawing 60th Motorized, 24th, and 16th Panzer Divisions, capturing Orlovka from the north and west and reaching the western bank of the Mechetka River west of the tractor factory village. This advance isolated elements of 24th Panzer, along with attached troops from 94th Infantry Division, in a narrow pocket between Orlovka and Spartanovka.

In the southern part of the city, IV Army Corps prepared to make a final stand along the Tsaritsa River. Sixth Army headquarters was in the basement of the State Department Store (*Univermag*), adjacent to the Square of the Fallen Fighters in the center of the city. Around this headquarters stood the remains of XIV Panzer Corps, VIII Army Corps, and the southern third of LI Army Corps. Paulus himself traveled under fire to a number of locations, encouraging his subordinates to continue resistance and avoid a formal surrender. Individual units surrendered when their ammunition and food were exhausted, but Rokossovsky freely acknowledged the incredible bravery and sustained resistance of his opponents.[56]

This resistance was fully apparent on 27 January. While General Strecker controlled the defense of the northern German pocket, Paulus himself commanded in the southern half. There, elements of Shumilov's 64th Army crossed the Tsaritsa River and advanced to within four blocks of Sixth Army headquarters, but 71st Infantry Division, now commanded by newly promoted Major General Fritz Roske, hemmed them in and halted the attack. To the west, Tolbukhin's 57th Army was unable to force a crossing of the Tsaritsa against the survivors of 371st Infantry Division. West of Stalingrad's center city, the first-line divisions of 21st Army labored slowly through the hills separating them from the urban areas on low ground. On Chistiakov's left, 51st and 52nd Guards Divisions spent the day preparing to attack south from positions west of Mamaev Kurgan. Still farther north, the combined forces of 233rd Rifle Division from 65th Army and 13th and 39th Guards Divisions from 62nd Army made equally slow progress, pushing northward into the Barrikady village. Over the next several days, the dug-in LI Army Corps, with the remains of VIII Corps covering its northern flank, continued to slow these two armies to a crawl.

As noted earlier, 27 January marked the first significant Soviet troop withdrawals from the ongoing battle. Galinin's 24th Army transferred most of its subordinate units to the control of 65th and 66th Armies, after which the army headquarters and 49th Rifle Division withdrew into an assembly area to rest and refit for future operations elsewhere. Overall, the *Stavka* detached five rifle divisions and three brigades from the various armies in Operation Ring, a clear indication that Moscow was anxious to generate additional forces for other operational and strategic tasks. Indeed, throughout the destruction of Sixth Army, *Stavka* guidance stressed the need to conserve infantry manpower by relying on artillery and tanks. This guidance explains the very deliberate pace at which Rokossovsky reduced the German defenses. This approach, in concert with his previous command tours, gave Rokossovsky a reputation among Red Army veterans as an "unbloody" general who took pains to preserve the lives of his subordinates. By this stage, German soldiers began to surrender in larger groups, and 64th Army alone captured 15,000 prisoners between 27 and 29 January.[57]

On 28 January Sixth Army reported that XI Army Corps had established a hedgehog at the tractor and Barrikady factories, but the continued failure to locate and recover parachuted supplies meant that the wounded and sick were no longer receiving any rations.[58] In the northern sector, 66th Army performed the bulk of the fighting that day. Three of its divisions, led by 226th Rifle Division, crossed the Mokraia Mechetka River and gained lodgments in the northern edge of the tractor factory village. To the west, 65th Army advanced eastward, south of the Mechetka River, but again, German resistance limited their gains to no more than 200 meters inside the Barrikady village.

Map 103.
Destruction of
Sixth Army's
Southern Pocket,
28–31 January
1943

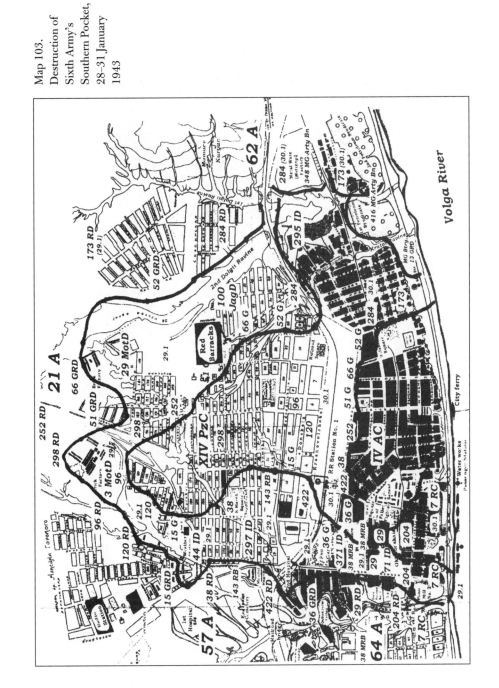

Map 104. Destruction of Sixth Army's Northern Pocket,
28 January–2 February 1943

While the defenders kept 64th Army's rifle units pinned down, to the west, Tolbukhin's 57th and Chistiakov's 21st Armies made the most significant progress on 28 January. Attacking north across the Tsaritsa River west of the railroad bridge, 57th Army's 15th Guards and 38th Rifle Divisions, along with 143rd Rifle Brigade, seized the ruins of two hospitals, captured the headquarters of 44th Infantry Division, and forced the remaining elements of 44th and 371st Infantry Divisions to withdraw northward.[59] On 57th Army's left, five divisions of 21st Army forced their way down the bluff into the western outskirts of the city center that afternoon. Advancing up to 600 meters, these divisions pushed back the remnants of XIV Panzer Corps. On 21st Army's left (northern) wing, two other rifle divisions advanced southward from the Mamaev Kurgan area, forcing the survivors of 100th *Jäger* and 295th Rifle Divisions to fall back to the southern bank of the Dolgii ravine.

By evening on 28 January, the northern pocket measured about 3.5 kilometers from east to west and 4 kilometers from north to south; the southern pocket was slightly more than 3 kilometers in each dimension. The 90,000 remaining men of Sixth Army, many of them wounded or sick, were crowded into an area measuring about 25 square kilometers. With such a small area under German control, the proportion of parachuted supplies going astray increased. German resistance in the southern pocket weakened significantly from this date forward, with soldiers of XIV Panzer and VIII Army Corps surrendering in large groups.

The 64th, 57th, and 21st Armies conducted the strongest attacks on 29 January, with 36th Guards and 29th Rifle Divisions of Shumilov's army making the greatest advance, nearing the main railroad station and Gogolia Street by late afternoon. During the previous night, a surprise thrust had captured XIV Panzer Corps' headquarters and wounded its commander.[60] Shortly after dawn on the twenty-ninth, Lieutenant General Alexander von Daniels surrendered the 3,000 survivors of 376th Infantry Division to the commander of 422nd Rifle Division, part of 57th Army, near Railroad Station No. 1. After reconnaissance probing in the morning, the three Red armies resumed large-scale attacks on the afternoon of 29 January, further compressing the southern pocket. That evening a captured Romanian staff officer led the Germans to the grain elevator in Flour Milling Factory No. 2, where Brigadier General Romulus Dumitriu commanded the remnants of Romanian 20th Division, now formed into the composite 82nd Regiment. Under threat of *katiusha* bombardment, Dumitriu surrendered his command.[61] Both Dumitriu and captured German staff officers independently informed the Soviets of the location of Sixth Army headquarters, and General Shumilov ordered Colonel I. D. Burmakov's 38th Separate Motorized Rifle Brigade, in 64th Army's reserve, to launch an attack toward the Square of the Fallen Fighters to seize that headquarters.[62]

In the northern pocket, three divisions of Zhadov's 66th Army advanced across the Mechetka and Mokraia Mechetka Rivers, gaining small footholds in the tractor factory village in the face of increasingly desperate resistance by 24th Panzer and 389th Infantry Divisions. While 65th and 66th Armies gnawed their way into the northern and western portions of XI Army Corps' hedgehog, LI Corps' 305th Infantry Division, along with portions of other divisions, stubbornly blocked 62nd Army's progress in the factory district. Batov's and Chuikov's men struggled to clear the upper and lower Barrikady village, respectively. Once again, Chuikov failed to eject Seydlitz's forces from the Barrikady and bread factories.[63]

By the evening of 29 January, the success against the southern pocket enabled the *Stavka* to withdraw two artillery divisions as well as the headquarters of Tolbukhin's 57th Army from the fight effective 31 January; three divisions and a brigade under Tolbukhin's control would then revert to Shumilov's 64th Army to continue the battle. Rokossovsky prepared to deliver the final blow against the southern pocket on the thirtieth; the swastika would cease flying there within 48 hours.

Once again, Shumilov's army made the greatest advances on 30 January. As planned, 36th Guards and 29th Rifle Divisions, spearheaded by 38th Motorized Rifle Brigade, attacked northward into the center city from positions near Railway Station No. 1 and southward along Gogolia Street. By the end of the day, these three units had encircled the *Univermag* building on the western and northern sides. To the east, the right wing of 64th Army, consisting of 204th Rifle Division and three brigades of 7th Rifle Corps, advanced due north to within a few hundred meters of the main Stalingrad landing stage; there, they formed the eastern side of the encirclement. To assist in clearing buildings, Shumilov assigned one sapper company to this eastern group, while the balance of 329th Engineer-Sapper Battalion reinforced 38th Motorized Brigade.[64]

In its last days of operation at Stalingrad, Tolbukhin's 57th Army as well as Chistiakov's 21st Army swept into the heart of the center city from the west and northwest, snuffing out any remaining resistance from the demolished XIV Panzer and VIII Army Corps. By the end of the day, they held positions along the railroad both north and south of Station No. 1 and had freed 300 Soviet prisoners at Hospital No. 2 (see map 103). On 21st Army's left (northern) wing, its 173rd Rifle Division, cooperating with 62nd Army's 284th, advanced a kilometer southward from the Krutoi ravine, breaking the back of 295th Infantry Division's defenses on the northern face of the southern pocket.

By contrast, LI Corps continued to defend its northern pocket stoutly, although it was running short of ammunition. This situation confirmed Rokossovsky's decision to liquidate the southern grouping first.

PAULUS'S SURRENDER AND THE LIQUIDATION OF THE
NORTHERN POCKET, 31 JANUARY–2 FEBRUARY

Overnight on 30–31 January Colonel Burmakov's 38th Motorized Brigade with its attached sapper companies cordoned off the area around the Square of the Fallen Fighters and the *Univermag*, cutting off telephone connections between Paulus and his subordinate units. Upon hearing that the headquarters was about to fall, Adolf Hitler announced 117 promotions for officers inside Stalingrad, including Paulus's elevation to field marshal. The clear intent of this announcement was to pressure Paulus to commit suicide, since no field marshal had ever surrendered. Possibly influenced by his Roman Catholicism, Paulus was about to break the precedent, although he hoped to avoid signing any surrender document.[65]

The final radio messages were sent by the OKH liaison officer. At 0615 on 31 January he reported, "The Russians are at the door. We are preparing to destroy [papers and equipment]." Fifty-nine minutes later the same radio confirmed that the headquarters was engaged in this destruction.[66] At 0700 Paulus's adjutant, Colonel Adam, had emerged from the basement under a white flag and announced to the nearest Soviet officer that he wished to arrange a surrender. After two hours of negotiation, at about 1000 hours, the army headquarters surrendered unconditionally to Major General I. A. Laskin, chief of staff of 64th Army. Paulus refused to instruct the northern group to surrender, on the grounds that he had neither communications with nor authority over it once he was captured.

As the day progressed, other German generals surrendered to their immediate opponents. Fittingly, Chuikov's subordinates accepted the surrenders of Lieutenant General von Seydlitz (LI Corps), Lieutenant General Pfeffer (IV Corps), Lieutenant General Schlömer (XIV Panzer Corps), Lieutenant General Deboi (44th Infantry Division), and Major General Korfes (295th Infantry Division). With them, at least 50,000 Axis survivors went into captivity.

The Soviet leaders naturally wished to save lives by persuading the Sixth Army commander to surrender the northern pocket, but Paulus clearly believed in the value of prolonging resistance, which had been his mission for the past five weeks. Still, Rokossovsky directed the commanders of 65th and 66th Armies to limit their actions on 31 January to reconnaissance, hoping that defeat and insufficient supplies would prompt more surrenders. Only Chuikov's 62nd Army continued the house-to-house fighting that had consumed it for the preceding five months. In the process, 284th Rifle Division pushed south to 9 January Square, where it linked up with troops of 64th Army.

Meanwhile, Rokossovsky began to shuffle forces northward after the col-

lapse of the southern pocket. By nightfall on 31 January, the first such reinforcement, 66th Guards Rifle Division, had arrived to join Zhadov's army of
the same number.

At 0830 on 1 February 62nd, 65th, and 66th Armies fired a massive artillery preparation against the defenders of the northern pocket, under the
control of General Strecker's XI Army Corps. Tactical air strikes added to the
rain of fire, which prompted some German units to raise white flags.[67] Attacking at 1000 hours, 66th Army broke through Strecker's defenses and entered
the tractor factory village, enveloping much of 16th Panzer Division and forcing other elements of that division and of 60th Motorized to withdraw in
disorder into the village and the nearby tractor factory. At 1100 hours Batov's
65th Army punched more gaping holes into the industrial district, taking
the northwestern part of the upper Barrikady village and surrounding the
strongpoint on Hill 107.5. Despite Hitler's demand that the defenders hold
out to the last gasp, that evening XI Corps radioed a warning: "Resistance is
expected to come to an end on 2 February as a result of overwhelming superiority and the expenditure of all of the ammunition."[68]

Meanwhile, Chuikov transferred Batiuk's 284th Rifle Division north to
reinforce 45th Rifle Division, in preparation for a 2 February attack on the
eastern part of the Barrikady village and the rear of the bread factory. In addition to returning recovered wounded soldiers to the 45th, Chuikov added
newly arrived engineer tanks and antitank guns to this last effort. All this
time, the struggle between 62nd Army and its German opponents continued
with unabated ferocity, although both sides were so skeletal that the scale of
the fighting was much smaller than in other areas of the city. Chuikov's chief
of staff, Krylov, later recorded only 116 Germans surrendering on 1 February, while his army lost another 42 killed and 105 wounded.[69]

While the struggle continued to reduce the northern pocket, islands of
resistance remained in the center of the city. During the first several days
of February, 64th Army directed the liquidation of many of these recalci-
trant forces, which Soviet sources often incorrectly identified as fanatical SS
troops.

Overnight on 1–2 February General Strecker reportedly rejected several
requests by his subordinates to surrender. General von Lenski, commander
of 24th Panzer Division, supposedly told Strecker that he had already sent
an emissary to the Russians. Strecker then gave in. At 0700 on 2 February he transmitted a message to his subordinates directing that they cease
fighting and destroy their weapons.[70] At 0800 hours the corps sent its formal
announcement to Army Group Don: "The XI Army Corps, consisting of 6
divisions, has fulfilled its duty by the heaviest fighting to the very last. Hail to
the Führer! Hail to Germany!"[71] XI Army Corps sent its last radio message

at 0920 hours, stating, "The Russians are penetrating . . . fighting . . . Tractor Works . . ." and then the radio fell silent.[72]

Soviet unit histories speak of a massive but bloodless assault on the morning of 2 February, with perhaps 40,000 Germans laying down their arms, while a few went to ground or headed off into the frozen and desolate steppes. Strecker surrendered to 66th Army, and four division commanders surrendered to the nearest Red units. Lieutenant General Günther von Angern, commander of 16th Panzer Division, committed suicide. Shortly after noon, 62nd Army sent Combat Report No. 32 to the Don Front: "The troops of 62nd Army have completely fulfilled the combat mission at 1200 hours on 2 February 1943."[73] At 1600 hours Voronov and Rokossovsky reported the complete liquidation of the encircled forces to Moscow.[74] Preoccupied with developments elsewhere, the *Stavka* had not even waited for this formal announcement. At 1420 hours Moscow had ordered that the headquarters, support, and logistical elements of 21st and 64th Armies be withdrawn into reserve for reassignment.[75] The very next day, these units began entraining for assembly areas in the Briansk Front's rear areas.

AFTERMATH

For several days after XI Corps surrendered, German aerial surveillance continued, primarily to locate and drop supplies to any escaping German troops. On 3 February, for example, one last He-111 flew over the city but could find no indication of continued resistance. The pilot dropped his load of food over what he thought was a small group of Germans and flew home. Perhaps hundreds of soldiers made a vain effort to reach friendly lines. Only one sergeant from a *Flak* battery allegedly escaped, and 48 hours after reaching 11th Panzer Division lines, he was killed by a mortar round. Regardless of the veracity of such tales, Sixth Army had ceased to exist.[76]

After 2 February Batov assigned two divisions of his 65th Army, 67th Guards and 214th Rifle, to comb the factory district and clear the remaining German forces.[77] They were accompanied by elements of 62nd Army as well as the ubiquitous NKVD forces, the latter resuming their responsibility for rear-area security and order. The 21st NKVD Separate Rifle Brigade recorded that most of the Germans were captured within a few days, although armed groups persisted into March. During this two-month period, the brigade reported killing 2,418 officers and soldiers and capturing 8,646, the latter being handed over to POW camps.[78]

Although focused on generating forces for other operations, the *Stavka* left an operational group behind to deal with any remaining resistance in Stalingrad. On 5 February Moscow appointed Rokossovsky's deputy *front* commander, Lieutenant General K. P. Trufanov, to head this group. Trufanov took control of divisions conducting security operations as well as other units, especially the understrength divisions of 62nd Army, that were resting and refitting in place.

After the experienced army headquarters were moved out of the city, Moscow recognized their contributions to victory. In April Galinin's 24th, Chistiakov's 21st, and Shumilov's 64th Armies became 4th, 6th, and 7th Guards Armies, respectively. Tolbukhin's 57th Army, redesignated the 68th, was earmarked for Marshal Zhukov's Operation Polar Star in late February. Zhadov's 66th and Chuikov's 62nd Armies initially controlled the security divisions remaining in Stalingrad. At the end of February 62nd Army was transferred to the Southwestern Front, where it used its experience erecting defenses along the eastern bank of the Oskol River. The 62nd Army became 8th Guards Army on 16 April. Overall, 5 armies; 1 rifle, 1 cavalry, and 1 tank corps; 19 rifle divisions; and 3 tank brigades that had fought during Operation Ring received the guards designation by 16 April 1943.[79]

Acting on instructions from Hitler, on 31 January Field Marshal von Manstein issued an order to re-create the German units destroyed at Stalingrad using any elements outside the encirclement.[80] In some instances, only support units such as bakery companies had survived. General Hube, former commander of XIV Panzer Corps, supervised this process. Eventually, Germany replaced the headquarters of Sixth Army and all five corps, while re-forming the 20 divisions lost at Stalingrad. Replacing the experienced manpower and scarce equipment of the lost units was far more difficult.

By moving cautiously and using firepower to replace manpower, General Rokossovsky had managed to conduct Operation Ring for the relatively modest cost of 48,000 casualties, or 17 percent of the 280,000 Soviet soldiers involved. Admittedly, both Hitler and his senior commanders made significant blunders that facilitated Rokossovsky's task. Whether through timidity or misplaced loyalty, Manstein failed to confront Hitler about such errors in a timely manner. After the fact, the field marshal manipulated dates, implying that he had acted sooner and Paulus had acted later than the actual sequence of events, hoping to pass the blame for this failure onto the Sixth Army commander.

Controversy still surrounds estimates of German losses in Operation Ring. In his victory report to the *Stavka*, Rokossovsky placed German losses at 91,000 prisoners plus 42,000 evacuated, the majority of the latter being wounded.[81] Yet on 9 January, prior to the final offensive, Sixth Army records indicated a strength of 197,000 German officers and soldiers, including some 5,100 wounded or sick. By adding perhaps 10,000 Romanian, 5,000 Croatian, and miscellaneous other Axis troops, the army's total ration strength was roughly 212,000 to 217,000 on that date. Moreover, a recent study based largely on *Luftwaffe* records suggests that, throughout the siege, the number of evacuees was about 30,000, not the 42,000 figure used by many Russian historians.[82] Regardless of the actual figures, the Axis lost an entire army either killed or captured, with the exception of the evacuees and a handful of soldiers who went to ground or escaped. It was the German *landser* and their Axis comrades in arms who paid for the incompetence and hubris of their leaders. All but 5,000 perished either during the battle or in captivity that extended for years after the end of the war.

Civilian casualties are equally difficult to establish. The city of Stalingrad had a population of roughly 400,000 in August 1942. Official Soviet histories claim that the state had evacuated 125,000 civilians by early October, but this figure is optimistic at best. An NKVD report after the fact stated that more than 200,000 civilians fell into German hands that fall,[83] suggesting that at least 75,000 civilians perished in the German bombing before occupation. Between 185,000 and 187,000 civilians were shipped to German factories and slave labor camps, and perhaps 5,000 of the remaining civilians died during Operation Ring. The NKVD found 7,655 surviving civilian occupants, and it arrested 502 of them as enemy agents, traitors, or criminals. Among the Axis prisoners of war were 91 "official employees or collaborators of German and Romanian intelligence, counterintelligence, police and other administrative organs," all of whom presumably perished.[84]

Finally, one must consider the fate of the two protagonists in the struggle for Stalin's namesake city. Vasilii Ivanovich Chuikov led the redesigned 8th Guards Army throughout the war, culminating in the conquest of Berlin in 1945. After the war he commanded first the Group of Soviet Forces in Germany and then the Kiev Military District; in 1955, while serving in the latter post, he received a belated promotion to marshal of the Soviet Union. Friedrich Paulus eventually joined the Soviet-sponsored National Committee for a Free Germany and testified at the Nuremberg trials. He died in East Germany in 1957.

CHAPTER TWENTY

Conclusions

The original objective of Operation *Blau*, the Germans' second major offensive in the conflict with the Soviet Union, was to seize the Caucasus oil fields, thereby obtaining essential fuel for themselves while denying that fuel to the Soviets. This objective required the invaders to project combat power over vast and inhospitable terrain while protecting their ever-lengthening left flank against Soviet counterattacks. Given the *Wehrmacht*'s experienced commanders and the repeated blunders of their Red counterparts, it is at least conceivable that Germany might have achieved this goal. However, once the Germans became involved in the additional mission of seizing Stalingrad—a diversion of resources that had not been included in the original plan—their chances of success became virtually nil. Faced with determined resistance and growing competence on the part of the Red Army, General Paulus had neither the combat power nor the logistical support to take the city in a single lunge, before his opponents could prepare its defense. This forced Paulus to conduct four successive, deliberate attacks simply to reach the city. Once there, Chuikov's 62nd Army tied the invaders down and bled them white for months. The combination of densely urbanized terrain and an opponent that "hugged" German front-line units negated the *Wehrmacht*'s previous advantages of rapid maneuver and close air support. Recognizing this, Chuikov's superiors provided him with a thin but steady flow of reinforcements and supplies, enabling him to hang on, if just barely, while severely attriting his foes.

Throughout the late summer and fall of 1942, Stalin took every opportunity to organize counteroffensives against the advancing German forces. In addition to numerous attacks on the immediate flanks of Stalingrad, the Soviets launched repeated efforts at Voronezh and as far north as Demiansk. However, all these counterattacks were so hastily planned and rushed in execution that they failed, resulting in bloody losses. In most instances, these operations did not even divert German units away from Stalingrad and the Caucasus, although they may have prevented redeployments to help those operations. Only the Rzhev-Sychevka offensive against Army Group Center succeeded in further extending the invaders, drawing in two panzer divisions from the Voronezh area that otherwise might have reinforced Sixth Army at Stalingrad or Army Group A in the Caucasus. As for local attacks outside of

Stalingrad, these actions diverted most of XIV Panzer Corps from partici-
pating in the struggle for the city while denying German units any rest when
they rotated away from the urban struggle.

These Soviet defeats also helped convince senior German leaders of
their own invincibility, even though tactical commanders were well aware of
the growing competence of their opponents. Meanwhile, the manpower demands of the three missions—seizing the Caucasus, protecting the left flank
along the Don, and reducing Stalingrad—forced the Germans to rely increasingly on their poorly equipped allies to perform the second mission of flank
guard. Over time, the OKH entrusted virtually the entire Don River front
to Hungarian Second, Italian Eighth, and Romanian Third Armies, none of
which had sufficient troops, antitank weapons, or construction materials to
build an effective defense against the increasingly lethal Soviet mechanized
formations. By November, the Axis was on the verge of turning over the flank
south of Stalingrad to yet another weak satellite formation: Romanian Fourth
Army. Adolf Hitler and his generals were clearly aware of the risks involved,
but they had become hyperfocused on the streets of Stalingrad and deferred
the question of flank security until that battle had been won.

In November 1942 the luck of the Axis ran out just as the drained Sixth
Army came within 100 meters of the Volga River. The Red Army finally
focused its resources and coordinated its troops for an effective counteroffensive and bold encirclement. Worse still from the Axis viewpoint, this
counteroffensive was deliberately aimed at the weak satellite troops rather
than the veteran German infantry that had thwarted previous attacks closer
to Stalingrad.

PLANNING OPERATION URANUS

On 6 October 1942 General Eremenko, commander of the Stalingrad Front,
proposed an alternative to yet another vain attack against the German infantry defending just outside the city. Eremenko's "different solution" involved
a broader, deeper envelopment of all Axis forces in the Stalingrad region.
Moreover, he suggested that the breakthrough efforts should focus against
Romanian rather than German forces.[1] Thus it was Eremenko, not Zhukov,
who conceived of the plan that became Operation Uranus, although Zhukov
had the discernment to endorse the idea strongly.[2] Moreover, whereas Eremenko had conceived of the operation as a giant raid, Zhukov helped convert
it into a full-scale counteroffensive.

Prior to November 1942 the Red Army had rarely penetrated well-
prepared German defenses. Moreover, the plan to attack Romanian Third
Army at Serafimovich offered an opportunity for exploitation by the newly

developed tank, mechanized, and guards cavalry corps. By this stage in the war, the commanders and staffs of these mobile corps were becoming more proficient at deep maneuvers in enemy rear areas, allowing the Soviet attackers to achieve the desired encirclement before the enemy could react.

Of equal importance, for the first time in the war, the *Stavka* and *front* commanders took sufficient time to both plan the attack and concentrate the necessary forces and supplies for the operation. This was in marked contrast to the hurried, ill-prepared attacks that had produced so many disasters in the preceding 17 months of the war. Thanks to the continued sacrifices of 62nd Army in the industrial district of Stalingrad, the newly formed Southwestern Front, the Don Front, and the remainder of the Stalingrad Front could prepare their attack without any German interference. Indeed, the absence of such careful preparation in subsequent Soviet operations that winter goes far to explain Manstein's "miraculous" success in restoring the front during February and March 1943.

The *Stavka*, the People's Commissariat of Defense, and the Red Army General Staff did everything in their power to provide the resources and guidance necessary for success. In addition to forming and deploying a kaleidoscope of units to support the Southwestern Front, these three staffs had to replace the 1.2 million casualties, including nearly 700,000 killed or captured, lost along the Voronezh and Stalingrad axes between 28 June and 18 November, as well as another 3 million casualties along the rest of the Soviet-German front.

What Moscow and the three *front* headquarters could not control were the underdeveloped Soviet rail network, the general lack of trucks, and the challenging weather conditions. As a result, some of the forces, weapons, and supplies needed for the new offensive arrived late or in insufficient quantities, contributing to the delay in the counteroffensive's start. Moreover, these conditions combined with months of fighting meant that the attacking units, especially the rifle divisions, sometimes lacked manpower and training. Nonetheless, the *Stavka* finally assembled more than 1 million men and 1,550 tanks to conduct Uranus, and Soviet preparations were sufficiently concealed to confuse a complacent German intelligence with regard to when, where, and in what strength the Red Army would strike.

The German commanders made this looming threat worse by accepting enormous risks and committing ever-increasing proportions of their strength to the urban struggle. Unlike his predecessor, Bock, General Weichs at Army Group B did little to slow this commitment or to apprise Hitler and the OKH of the danger. Determined to fulfill his orders, General Paulus permitted the bulk of his army to be drawn into the meat grinder. In particular, all three of his panzer divisions (14th, 16th, and 24th) and two of his three motorized divisions (3rd and 60th) were worn down to the nub by the time the Soviets struck back. Pressed to win quickly, Paulus never resolved the logistical and personnel shortfalls that hampered his attack, so his army was already drained by the time of the Soviet counterattack. Although authorized a force of almost 300,000 men, by mid-November, Sixth Army was short 121,900 soldiers, or 41 percent; the weakness in actual combat forces was even more pronounced. When Operation Uranus began, Sixth Army numbered less than 200,000 men, while Fourth Panzer Army had roughly 120,000, Romanian Third Army had some 155,000, and Army Group B had another 45,000 troops in the area. Thus, Axis forces fielded perhaps 520,000 men to oppose the 1 million Red soldiers assembled for Operation Uranus. Worse still for Paulus's men, Sixth Army had only 218 operational tanks. In addition to these vehicles, there were 59 tanks in 29th Motorized Division (Fourth Panzer Army), 40 tanks in 22nd Panzer Division (Army Group B reserve), 105 indifferent tanks in Romanian 1st Armored Division, and 43 assault guns, giving the defenders a total of 465 tanks and assault guns, or less than one-third of their opponents' force. Even these Axis mobile divisions were dispersed to perform various roles, making them slow to respond to the massed assaults by multiple Soviet tank and mechanized corps.

BATTLES OUTSIDE STALINGRAD, NOVEMBER–DECEMBER 1942

The Uranus counteroffensive was an unprecedented success, completely surrounding Sixth Army and the bulk of Fourth Panzer Army in five days. The Soviet performance was by no means flawless, however. Initial attacks against German divisions barely dented the defenders, while the Romanians put up a surprisingly stiff fight. General Lascar's group of Romanian infantry offered gallant resistance that slowed the initial attack, while the much-maligned XXXXVIII Panzer Corps, consisting of 22nd Panzer and Romanian 1st Armored Divisions, was a persistent thorn to the Soviets. Between them, these unexpected centers of resistance delayed the planned Soviet encirclement by two days and inflicted far higher rates of attrition in armor than the Red commanders had anticipated. Moreover, the Southwestern and Stalingrad Fronts failed to push the outer encirclement far enough away from Stalingrad, offering the Germans a chance to relieve Sixth Army. This threat later prompted the Soviets to divert major formations away from the reduction of Stalingrad and the planned subsequent operation toward Rostov. Furthermore, once the Stalingrad pocket took shape, the Soviets proved unable to liquidate it with the forces originally allocated to this task, primarily because the besieged Axis force was almost three times the Soviet estimate of 90,000.

Nonetheless, the understrength and poorly supplied German forces in

Stalingrad were in peril within a week of the start of Operation Uranus. Given the shortages of armor, fuel, draft animals, and other transport, Paulus would have been hard-pressed to extract his entire force, along with its equipment, even if he had been free to break out. One might argue that, although an immediate flight to the west could have saved the core of experienced troops in Sixth Army, such a decision required too great a change in perspective for senior German commanders to contemplate. Paulus and his corps commanders understood the need for radical action, but Hitler and his entourage categorically rejected the thought, and Manstein failed to force the issue.

Had Paulus's army attempted (in late November or early December) to break out west toward the Don River or south toward Kotel'nikovo, at least half of its personnel might have escaped, albeit without most of their heavy equipment and weapons. This did not occur for several reasons. First, Hitler stubbornly refused to abandon Sixth Army's gains and believed General Jeschonnek's optimistic promise (reinforced by Göring) to resupply the pocket by air. This apparently allowed the dictator to persuade himself that Paulus could survive well into February, when a full relief expedition could be mounted. Second, Manstein broke the consensus among field commanders that an immediate breakout was necessary; Manstein was both overly confident of German abilities and insufficiently bold in the face of Hitler's will. Manstein repeatedly urged Paulus to break out, but he never made a serious attempt to obtain permission from Hitler. Third, Paulus needed time to organize a breakout. Moreover, he would not order a breakout without both permission from Hitler and assurances from Manstein that a strong relief force would meet him halfway. Although sometimes depicted as too timid, Paulus was simply being realistic; he believed Hitler would relieve him of command if he ordered the breakout on his own, and he thought Sixth Army had little chance of breaking through the growing Soviet forces to his south and west. Thus, although he made meticulous plans for Operation *Donnerschlag*, Paulus never attempted to carry it out.

With Sixth Army pinned to the ruins of Stalingrad, Manstein's Army Group Don had to contend with the three Soviet *fronts* in a deadly series of attacks and counterattacks during the first three weeks of December. The field marshal's initial plan was to form a two-pronged relief expedition, with XXXXVIII Panzer Corps attacking eastward across the Don River near Verkhne-Chirskii and Rychkovskii while LVII Panzer Corps advanced northeastward from Kotel'nikovo across the Aksai and Myshkova Rivers. However, each of these corps had only two German divisions and a miscellaneous collection of lightly armed Romanian and improvised security units, far below the combat power needed for a major counteroffensive.

Anticipating the German effort to relieve Sixth Army, the *Stavka* continued with a truncated Operation Saturn aimed at destroying Italian Eighth

Army and exploiting south toward Rostov. This renewed offensive not only destroyed a second satellite army but also unleashed three tank corps that disrupted and panicked the German rear areas, including the vital resupply airfields. Meanwhile, during early to mid-December, the Southwestern Front committed first the poorly handled 5th Tank Army and later the newly formed 5th Shock Army around Verkhne-Chirskii and Rychkovskii. Despite some errors by the attackers, this determined effort prevented XXXXVIII Panzer Corps from ever launching a relief attempt toward Stalingrad, contrary to the faulty memories of the German commanders involved.

The pivotal formation for the Soviets was Malinovsky's 2nd Guards Army, originally assigned to Operation Saturn. The unexpected resistance offered by the Stalingrad pocket prompted the *Stavka* to divert this army first (on 10 December) to spearhead Operation Ring and then (two days later) to block LVII Panzer Corps' strong attack northward from Kotel'nikovo. These diversions meant that the Soviets had to truncate Operation Saturn into Little Saturn and delay the reduction of Stalingrad by four weeks. However, these twin decisions determined the ultimate fate of Paulus's army. After a decisive four-day battle (20–23 December) along the Aksai River near the village of Verkhne-Kumskii, Malinovsky's guardsmen first halted and then threw back LVII Panzer Corps, ending any chance of relief for Paulus's troops in Stalingrad. A day later, on Christmas Eve, the Stalingrad Front's 2nd Guards and 51st Armies crushed LVII Panzer Corps' defenses and thrust the Germans back, south of their start point at Kotel'nikovo. To the west of this Kotel'nikovo operation, 5th Shock and 5th Tank Armies, aided by the right wing of 2nd Guards Army, attacked toward Tormosin, pushing the would-be relievers even farther away from the stricken city named for the Soviet dictator.

OPERATION RING

From this point onward (if not several weeks earlier), Paulus's army was doomed. German commanders from Hitler to Manstein to Paulus worked to prolong the agony of Sixth Army for as long as possible, preventing the seven Red armies around Stalingrad from exploiting the widespread havoc along the Axis's main front. At enormous human cost, Sixth Army kept those seven armies tied down for a month, ultimately giving Manstein the opportunity to assemble a major counterattack force, but this assembly was far too late to save the Germans at Stalingrad.

While the Germans sought to prolong the resistance of Sixth Army, the *Stavka*'s main priority was to reduce the pocket as quickly and cheaply as possible, minimizing casualties while freeing up combat power for other operations in its planetary system of plans. In Operation Ring, Generals Voronov and Rokossovsky set the standard for subsequent deliberate offensives, using reconnaissance-in-force followed by massed artillery fire and heavy tanks to overwhelm the defenders while minimizing their own infantry losses.

On 20 January General Paulus again requested freedom of action to authorize an attempted breakout to the south. The next day Hitler categorically refused, demanding that the army fight to the end. The day after that, 22 January, Paulus described the deteriorating situation and asked, "What order should I give the troops?"[3] Hitler again forbade capitulation, although a few days later it became apparent that some commanders had authorized their subordinates to break out. By that time, however, it was too late to save any significant portion of Sixth Army.

THE CONTEXT OF OPERATION RING

Following the Little Saturn and Kotel'nikovo offensives in late 1942, the Red Army's *fronts* in the southern USSR capitalized on German misfortune by launching seven offensive operations during January 1943.[4] These offensives sought to drive German forces away from the Voronezh, Donbas, and Rostov regions, destroying major portions of Army Groups A, B, and Don in the process and projecting the Red Army as far west as the Dnepr River by the time of the spring thaw.

Spearheaded by 3rd Tank Army and two independent mobile corps, the Briansk and Voronezh Fronts, assisted by the right wing of the Southwestern Front, decimated Hungarian Second Army and the Italian Alpine Corps, while defeating German Second Army and reaching the approaches to Kursk, Belgorod, and Khar'kov. During the same period, the Southwestern Front made a much slower and more costly advance to capture Millerovo, Kamensk, and the Northern Donets River east of Voroshilovgrad. The 11 tank and mechanized corps committed to this Donbas operation suffered heavy losses in armor, making them vulnerable to the counteroffensive mounted by Manstein's redesignated Army Group South when the latter counterattacked in mid-February. Farther south, the Southern (formerly Stalingrad) Front's 3rd Guards Tank Corps advanced some 150 kilometers during the first week of January, seizing a bridgehead over the Don about 80 kilometers northeast of Rostov. However, the remaining four mechanized corps of the Southern Front lagged well behind, covering the same distance only by the end of the month. In the process of making this advance, they lost much of their combat power. This delay allowed First Panzer Army to escape through Rostov, while the remainder of Army Group A formed a bridgehead in the Kuban'. The additional divisions of First Panzer Army, in conjunction with the SS panzer corps that arrived from the west in mid-February, gave

Manstein the mobile forces he had lacked two months earlier. Beginning on 20 February Manstein launched a brilliant series of counterstrokes, known to the Germans as the Donetz campaign and to the Russians as the Donbas and Khar'kov operations, which were classics of mobile warfare. In a vain attempt to halt Manstein's attacks, the *Stavka* had to divert major forces, including the refurbished 62nd and 64th Armies, which otherwise might have aided Rokossovsky's redesignated Central Front in its new offensives farther north. By the time the spring thaw returned in mid-March, the Germans had recaptured Khar'kov and thwarted the remaining portions of the Soviets' series of planetary offensive plans. Stalingrad was a distant memory, as both sides began to rebuild for what became the Kursk campaign in July.[5]

THE COST OF BATTLE

By official Soviet count, during Operation *Blau* the Red Army's *fronts* suffered a total of 1,212,189 casualties, of which 694,108 were irrevocable losses and 517,811 were wounded or ill. Including the fighting from Rostov down into the Caucasus, this toll rose to the almost inconceivable figure of 1,586,100 casualties, including 886,899 irrevocable losses and 698,931 wounded or sick.[6] Although difficult to calculate precisely, Fourth Panzer and Sixth Armies probably lost about 130,000 men during Operation *Blau*. The additional losses of 40,000 Romanians and 30,000 Hungarians, plus the casualties of German Second and Italian Eighth Armies, increased the Axis casualty count to as many as 250,000 by early November.

Soviet offensive operations between 19 November 1942 and 2 February 1943 resulted in another 485,777 Red casualties, including 154,885 irrevocable and 330,892 wounded or sick.[7] Soviet sources estimate Axis losses at 800,000 troops, including roughly 580,000 killed, wounded, missing, or evacuated from the combat zone, plus about 220,000 prisoners of war, of whom 91,000 were captured at Stalingrad.[8] Although Soviet estimates of Axis losses are often inflated, these figures seem roughly correct. Perhaps 300,000 Axis troops were inside the Stalingrad pocket, while the Romanian and Italian losses, together with other German elements of Army Groups B and Don, probably approached 200,000 between November and February.

Equipment losses are even more difficult to assess. The Soviets admitted to losing approximately 3,000 tanks, 3,500 guns, and more than 200 combat aircraft during their Stalingrad strategic offensive. The Soviet claims for Axis losses—1,666 tanks and assault guns, 7,074 guns and mortars, and 805 aircraft—are clearly inflated, probably because the Soviets originally credited their opponents with more weapons than they possessed. The total number of German tanks operating along the Voronezh and Stalingrad axes, including reinforcements brought in after Operation Uranus, was 1,168, plus roughly 50 assault guns. Of these, the Germans probably lost somewhere between 700 and 800, including the 218 tanks inside the Stalingrad pocket.[9] Virtually all the Romanian tanks (115) and Italian light tanks (55) were lost in battle, together with 70 to 90 percent of the heavy weapons for the satellite armies.

German accounts acknowledge that the *Luftwaffe* lost some 488 transport aircraft during the aerial resupply effort from 24 November through 2 February.[10] Adding perhaps 100 German, Romanian, and Italian fighters and bombers lost during this same time period gives an estimated total of 588 Axis aircraft lost, or 73 percent of the Soviet estimates.

Although German Fourth Panzer and Romanian Fourth Armies were being reconstituted, by 2 February 1943, the better part of five armies had disappeared from the Axis order of battle in ten weeks. These included 300,000 soldiers from German Sixth and Fourth Panzer Armies, 230,000 from Romanian Third and Fourth Armies, 221,875 troops from Italian Eighth Army, and 204,334 from Hungarian Second Army. After Stalingrad, Hitler's allies withdrew virtually all their remaining forces from the theater, except for a few lightly equipped rear-area security divisions. Germany was unable to replace the nearly 1 million soldiers in these formations. Only Romania fielded a significant force in the East for the rest of the war, and the Germans had to provide large amounts of heavy weapons to equip the rebuilt Romanian army.[11]

There remains the question of Stalingrad's place in the Soviet-German conflict, of the extent to which it was, in fact, a "turning point" in the war. The failure of Operation Barbarossa at the end of 1941 had already demonstrated that Germany could not win a short war based on blitzkrieg. The failure of Operation *Blau* a year later, including the grievous loss of Sixth Army, established that Germany could not win on any terms. Six months after that, the Battle of Kursk dictated that Germany's ultimate defeat would be total.

Notes

Abbreviations

BA-MA   *Bundesarchiv-Militärarchiv*, Freiburg, Germany
JSMS   *Journal of Slavic Military Studies*
KTB   *Kriegstagebuch* (combat jurnal)
NAM   National Archives Microfilm
SVIMVOV   *Sbornik voenno-istoricheskikh materialov Velikoi Otechestvennoi voiny*
            [Collection of military-historical materials of the Great Patriotic War]
            (Moscow: Voenizdat, various dates)
TsAMO   *Tsentral'nyi arkhiv Ministerstva Oborony* (Central Archives of the
            Ministry of Defense)
VE   *Voennaia Entsiklopediia v vos'mi tomakh* [Military encyclopedia in
            eight volumes] (Moscow: Voenizdat, 1994–2004)
VIZh   *Voenno-istoricheskii zhurnal* (Military-historical journal)

Prologue

1. On the Mechelen incident, see Karl-Heinz Frieser, *The Blitzkrieg Legend: The 1940 Campaign in the West* (Annapolis, MD: Naval Institute Press, 2005), 62–63.

2. At the time, the official designation of German mobile corps was still "motorized," although during July 1942 the Germans began to refer to them as panzer corps, a term that became official at the end of the year. The most complete account of the Reichel incident is in Paul Carell [pseud. of Paul Karl Schmidt], *Stalingrad: The Defeat of the German 6th Army*, trans. David Johnston (Atglen, PA: Schiffer Military/Aviation History, 1993), 50–58. Unlike his earlier works, which were often based on hearsay evidence, this study is well researched, albeit biased toward the German viewpoint.

3. *Stavka* Directive Nos. 994076 (26 June 1942), 170466 (28 June), and 170465 (28 June), in V. A. Zolotarev, ed., "Stavka VGK: Dokumenty i materialy 1942" [The *Stavka* Supreme High Command: Documents and materials 1942], in *Russkii arkhiv: Velikaia Otechestvennaia*, 16 (5-2) [The Russian archives: The Great Patriotic (War), 16 (5-2)] (Moscow: Terra, 1996), 264–266; hereafter cited as Zolotarev, "*Stavka* 1942."

Chapter 1. Opposing Forces

1. G. F. Krivosheev, ed., *Soviet Casualties and Combat Losses in the Twentieth Century*, trans. Christine Barnard (London: Greenhill Books; Mechanicsburg, PA: Stackpole Books, 1997), 94.

2. Horst Boog, Jurgen Forster, Joachim Hoffmann, et al., *Germany and the Second World War*, vol. IV, *The Attack on the Soviet Union*, trans. Dean S. McMurry, Ewald Osers, and Louise Willmot (Oxford: Clarendon Press, 1999), 140, 293–297.

3. David M. Glantz, *The Military Strategy of the Soviet Union: A History* (London: Frank Cass, 1992), 91–95.

4. See especially Adam Tooze, *The Wages of Destruction: The Making and Breaking of the Nazi Economy* (New York: Viking, 2006), 358–361. Germany had 3 million foreign forced laborers even before invading the USSR.

5. Bernard R. Kroener, Rolf-Dieter Muller, and Hans Umbreit, *Germany and the Second World War*, vol. V, pt. I, *Wartime Administration, Economy, and Manpower Resources, 1939–1941*, trans. Ewald Osers et al. (Oxford: Clarendon Press, 2000), 983, 839.

6. Ibid., 939, 984, lists the replacement forces in June 1941.

7. Klaus Reinhardt, *Moscow—The Turning Point: The Failure of Hitler's Strategy in the Winter of 1941–1942*, trans. Karl Keenan (Oxford: Oxford University Press, 1992), 367–368.

8. Ibid., 369–370. Artillery losses included 4,262 antitank guns, 5,990 mortars, 1,942 howitzers, and 1,411 infantry support guns.

9. George E. Blau, *The German Campaign in Russia: Planning and Operations, 1940–1942*, Department of the Army Pamphlet No. 20-261a (Washington, DC: Department of the Army, 1955), 120.

10. See Reinhardt, *Moscow*, 381–387; Tooze, *Wages of Destruction*, 509–545.

11. Reinhardt, *Moscow*, 381.

12. Tooze, *Wages of Destruction*, 509.

13. Earl F. Ziemke and Magna Bauer, *Moscow to Stalingrad: Decision in the East* (Washington, DC: US Army Center of Military History, 1987), 177, 293–295; Franz Halder, *The Halder War Diaries, 1939–1942*, ed. Charles Burdick and Hans-Adolf Jacobsen (Novato, CA: Presidio Press, 1988), 613–615.

14. Horst Boog, Werner Rahm, Reinhard Stumpf, and Bernd Wegner, *Germany and the Second World War*, vol. VI, *The Global War: Widening of the Conflict into a World War and the Shift of the Initiative, 1941–1943*, trans. Ewald Osers et al. (Oxford: Clarendon Press, 2001), 965, shows slightly more aircraft in June 1942; older studies, such as Williamson Murray's *Luftwaffe* (Baltimore: Nautical & Aviation Publishing Co. of America, 1985), 112–119, assert that the *Luftwaffe* began the 1942 campaign with 2,750 aircraft.

15. Blau, *German Campaign in Russia*, 131. On Mussolini, see Hope Hamilton, *Sacrifice on the Steppe: The Italian Alpine Corps in the Stalingrad Campaign, 1942–1943* (Philadelphia: Casemate, 2011), 7–17.

16. J. Lee Ready, *The Forgotten Axis: Germany's Partners and Foreign Volunteers in World War II* (Jefferson, NC: McFarland, 1987), 205–206. See also Mark Axworthy, Cornel Scafeş, and Cristian Craciunoiu, *Third Axis, Fourth Ally: The Ro-*

manian Armed Forces in the European War, 1941–1945 (London: Arms & Armour Press, 1995); Boog et al., *Germany and the Second World War*, VI:904–923.

17. For a detailed description of Soviet force regeneration in 1942, see David M. Glantz, *Colossus Reborn: The Red Army at War, 1941–1943* (Lawrence: University Press of Kansas, 2005), 135–369.

18. Ibid., 180–184, 201–206. The basic reorganization document was *Stavka* Circular 01, dated 15 July 1941; this circular and its changes are discussed in Iu P. Babich and A. G. Baier, *Razvitie vooruzheniia i organizatsii sovetskikh sukhoputnykh voisk v gody Velikoi Otechestvennoi voiny* [Development of the armament and organization of the Soviet ground forces in the Great Patriotic War] (Moscow: Izdanie Akademii, 1990).

19. Babich and Baier, *Razvitie vooruzheniia i organizatsii*, 42–43.

20. On the actual effects of Lend-Lease, which Soviet accounts always downplayed, see the works of Alexander Hill, especially *The Great Patriotic War of the Soviet Union, 1941–45: A Documentary Reader* (London: Routledge, 2009), 163–191.

21. Babich and Baier, *Razvitie vooruzheniia i organizatsii*, 42–43. See also O. A. Losik, ed., *Stroitel'stvo i boevoe primenenie sovetskikh tankovykh voisk v gody Velikoi Otechestvennoi voiny* [The formation and combat use of Soviet tank forces in the years of the Great Patriotic War] (Moscow: Voenizdat, 1979).

22. Babich and Baier, *Razvitie vooruzheniia i organizatsii*, 44–45; Glantz, *Colossus Reborn*, 228.

23. Babich and Baier, *Razvitie vooruzheniia i organizatsii*, 46. In theory, the rifle units created the penetration through which the tank corps exploited while the cavalry corps screened the flanks.

24. Steve Zaloga and Peter Sarson, *T-34/76 Medium Tank, 1941–1945* (London: Osprey, 1994), esp. 17–23.

25. On Soviet armaments production, see Walter S. Dunn Jr., *Stalin's Keys to Victory: The Rebirth of the Red Army* (Westport, CT: Praeger Security International, 2006), 28–41.

26. Van Hardesty and Ilya Grinberg, *Red Phoenix Rising: The Soviet Air Force in World War II* (Lawrence: University Press of Kansas, 2012), 105–108.

27. N. I. Nikoforov et al., *Velikaia Otechestvennaia voina 1941–1945 gg.: Deistvuiushchaia armiia* [The Great Patriotic War, 1941–1945: The operating army] (Moscow: Animi Fortitudo, Kuchkovo pole, 2005), 541–542.

28. Boog et al., *Germany and the Second World War*, VI:962.

29. Ibid., 965.

30. *Boevoi sostav Sovetskoi armii, Chast' 2 (ianvar'–dekabr' 1942 goda)* [Combat composition of the Soviet Army, part 2 (January–December 1942)] (Moscow: Voenizdat, 1966), 103–107, 113 (prepared by the Military-Scientific Directorate of the General Staff).

31. Nikoforov et al., *Velikaia Otechestvennaia voina 1941–1945*, 541–542.

32. Joel S. A. Hayward, *Stopped at Stalingrad: The Luftwaffe and Hitler's Defeat in the East, 1942–1943* (Lawrence: University Press of Kansas, 1998), esp. 70–73. See also James S. Corum, *Wolfram von Richthofen: Master of the German Air War* (Lawrence: University Press of Kansas, 2008), 286–294. Promoted to field marshal in February 1943, Richthofen died of complications from surgery in 1945.

33. Helmut Heiber and David Glantz, *Hitler and His Generals: The Military Conferences, 1943–1945* (New York: Enigma Books, 2002), 829. Hitler relieved Hoth of command in December 1943, after which he spent most of the war without an assignment.

34. See Richard Carver, "Manstein," in *Hitler's Generals*, ed. Correlli Barnett (New York: Grove Weidenfeld, 1989), 221–246; Marcel Stein, *Field Marshal von Manstein: The Janus Head/A Portrait* (Solihull, UK: Helion, 2007). Stein documents Manstein's active involvement in genocide during the Russian war, which led to his imprisonment by a British court after the war.

35. Samuel W. Mitcham Jr., "Kleist," in Barnett, *Hitler's Generals*, 249–263; Heiber and Glantz, *Hitler and His Generals*, 896–897. Kleist survived relief from command and suspicion of involvement in the 20 July 1944 plot, only to die in a Soviet prison camp after the war.

36. This account is based largely on the sympathetic biography by Walter Goerlitz, *Paulus and Stalingrad: A Life of Field-Marshal Friedrich Paulus with Notes, Correspondence, and Documents from His Papers*, trans. B. H. Stevens (New York: Citadel Press, 1963). See also Martin Middlebrook, "Paulus," in Barnett, *Hitler's Generals*, 361–373.

37. Goerlitz, *Paulus and Stalingrad*, 21–28, 35. On the Barbarossa war game and Paulus's resulting concerns, see David Stahel, *Operation Barbarossa and Germany's Defeat in the East* (Cambridge: Cambridge University Press, 2009), 54–60.

38. On Weichs, see Konstantin Zalessky, *Vermacht: Sukhoputnye voiska i Verkhovnoe komandovanie* [The *Wehrmacht*: Ground forces and high command] (Moscow: Iauza, 1942), 81–83. Weichs commanded a series of army groups for most of the war until he was retired by Hitler in March 1945. Imprisoned by a war crimes tribunal in 1945, he was released for ill health two years later.

39. *Komandarmy. Voennyi biograficheskii slovar'* (Velikaia Otechestvennaia) [Army commanders. Military-bibliographic dictionary (Great Patriotic War)] (Moscow: Institute of Military History, Russian Federation Ministry of Defense, OOO Kuchkovo pole, 2005), 48–50. After a variety of commands during 1942, Golikov suffered defeat as head of the Voronezh Front in March 1943. Stalin still valued him politically, however, retaining him as a staff officer for the rest of the war and allowing him various commands after 1945.

40. Ibid., 139–141. Despite his embarrassing defeat in the Crimea (see chapter 3), Malinovsky commanded the powerful 2nd Guards Army in blocking German efforts to relieve Stalingrad and then served as a *front* commander for the remainder of the war. He became minister of defense in 1957, a position he held until his death ten years later.

41. Ibid., 95–96.

42. See Richard Woff's biography of Rokossovsky in Harold Shukman, ed., *Stalin's Generals* (New York: Weidenfeld & Nicholson, 1993), esp. 177–185.

43. *Komandarmy. Voennyi biograficheskii slovar'*, 153–155. Moskalenko commanded, in succession, four other armies during the 1942 campaign before returning to lead 38th Army for the remainder of the war. After helping to thwart an attempted coup by Lavrenti Beriia in 1953, Moskalenko finished his career as deputy minister of defense from 1955 to 1962.

44. Peter Antill, "Andrei Ivanovich Yeremenko," 2006, http://www.historyofwar
.org/articles/people_yeremenko.html (accessed 19 February 2016).

45. See Woff's biography of Chuikov in Shukman, *Stalin's Generals*, 67–76.

46. Timothy A. Wray, *Standing Fast: German Defensive Doctrine on the Russian Front during World War II, Prewar to 1943*, Research Survey No. 5 (Ft. Leavenworth, KS: Combat Studies Institute, 1986), 113.

47. Omer Bartov, *The Eastern Front, 1941–45: German Troops and the Barbarization of Warfare* (New York: St. Martin's Press, 1986), 51, 66.

48. Roger Reese, *Why Stalin's Soldiers Fought: The Red Army's Military Effectiveness in World War II* (Lawrence: University Press of Kansas, 2011), 163–165, 241–242. See also Glantz, *Colossus Reborn*, 536–608.

49. On ethnic friction, see Waling T. Gorter-Gronvik and Mikhail N. Suprun, "Ethnic Minorities and Warfare in the Arctic Front, 1939–1945," *JSMS* 13, 1 (March 2000): 127–142. See also Reese, *Why Stalin's Soldiers Fought*, 198–199.

50. Ready, *Forgotten Axis*, 255–384.

51. Reina Pennington, "Women," in *The Soviet Union at War, 1941–1945*, ed. David R. Stone (Barnsley, UK: Pen & Sword Books, 2010), 93–115. See also Reina Pennington, "Offensive Women: Women in Combat in the Red Army in the Second World War," *JSMS* 74, 3 (July 2010): 775–820.

Chapter 2. Plans and Preparations

1. Halder, *War Diaries*, 611–612; Ziemke and Bauer, *Moscow to Stalingrad*, 291–292.

2. Hayward, *Stopped at Stalingrad*, 4, 9.

3. Ibid., 2–11, 19–20, provides an excellent discussion of Germany's petroleum problem.

4. Blau, *German Campaign in Russia*, 109–118.

5. On Case Blue, see ibid., 121–124; Carell, *Stalingrad*, 14–23.

6. Quoted in Hugh R. Trevor-Roper, ed., *Blitzkrieg to Defeat: Hitler's War Directives 1939–1945* (New York: Holt, Rinehart & Winston, 1964), 117; this volume provides the entire order in translation. The full text is also included, in Russian, in *SVIMVOV*, issue 18 (Moscow: Voenizdat, 1960), 257–262 (originally classified secret).

7. This analysis is based on Trevor-Roper, *Blitzkrieg to Defeat*, 119; Blau, *German Campaign in Russia*, 122–123; and Ziemke and Bauer, *Moscow to Stalingrad*, 289–290. See also Robert M. Citino, *Death of the Wehrmacht: The German Campaigns of 1942* (Lawrence: University Press of Kansas, 2007), 160–162.

8. Quoted in Trevor-Roper, *Blitzkrieg to Defeat*, 119.

9. For a description of and documents concerning this deception, see "Operatsiia 'Kreml'" [Operation Kremlin], *VIZh* 8 (August 1961): 9–90.

10. Ziemke and Bauer, *Moscow to Stalingrad*, 322.

11. For a discussion of this dilemma, see David M. Glantz, *The Strategic and Operational Impact of Terrain on Military Operations in Central and Eastern Europe* (Carlisle, PA: self-published, 1998).

12. David M. Glantz, *The Role of Intelligence in Soviet Military Strategy in World War II* (Novato, CA: Presidio Press, 1990), 42–48.

13. See Vasilevsky's memoir *Delo vsei zhizni* [Life's work] (Moscow: Izdatel'stvo politicheskoi literatury, 1983); Geoffrey Jukes, "Alexander Mikhailovich Vasilevsky," in Shukman, *Stalin's Generals*, 275–285; Nikoforov et al., *Velikaia Otechestvennaia voina 1941–1945*, 288–291. Vasilevsky finished the war as theater commander for the invasion of Manchuria in 1945 and went on to become first deputy defense minister in 1953; he retired in 1956 for health reasons.

14. G. K. Zhukov, *Reminiscences and Reflections*, vol. 2 (Moscow: Progress Publishers, 1985), 72–73.

15. Vasilevsky, *Delo vsei zhizni*, 183–185. These offensives included the Crimea, the Khar'kov region, the L'vov-Kursk and Smolensk axes, and Demiansk and Leningrad.

16. See Viktor Anfilov, "Semen Konstantinovich Timoshenko," in Shukman, *Stalin's Generals*, 239–253; "Timoshenko, Semen Konstantinovich," in *Sovetskaia Voennaia Enksiklopediia v vos'mikh tomakh, 8* [Soviet military encyclopedia in eight volumes, vol. 8] (Moscow: Voenizdat, 1980), 43–44.

17. David M. Glantz, *Kharkov 1942: Anatomy of a Military Disaster* (Rockville Centre, NY: Sarpedon, 1998), 24–26.

18. K. S. Moskalenko, *Na iugo-zapadnom napravlentii* [On the southwestern axis], vol. 1 (Moscow: Nauka, 1969), 176–177.

19. The 22 March estimate of the Southwestern Direction is reprinted as an appendix to Glantz, *Kharkov 1942*, 252–255.

20. I. Kh. Bagramian, *Tak shli my k pobeda* [As we went on to victory] (Moscow: Voenizdat, 1977), 54–67.

21. Zolotarev, "*Stavka 1942*," 152.

22. Ibid., 171–174.

23. On Soviet planning for the 1942 offensives, see also A. N. Grilov, "Nekotorye osobennosti planirovaniia letne-osennei kampanii 1942 goda" [Some features of planning for the 1942 summer-autumn campaign], *VIZh* 9 (September 1991): 4–11.

24. The 10 April plan of the Southwestern Direction is reproduced in translation as an appendix to Glantz, *Kharkov 1942*, 256–258.

25. Ibid., 42–43.

26. V. V. Beshanov, *God 1942—"Uchebnyi"* [The year 1942—educational] (Minsk: Harvest, 2002), 212–214.

Chapter 3. Preliminary Battles, April–June 1942

1. V. A. Zolotarev, ed., *Velikaia Otechestvennaia voina 1941–1945: Voenno-istoricheskie ocherki v chetyrekh knigagh, kniga 1: Surovye ispytaniia* [The Great Patriotic War, 1941–1945: A military-historical survey in four books, book 1: A harsh education] (Moscow: Nauka, 1998), 332; hereafter cited as *VOV*.

2. *Boevoi sostav Sovetskoi armii* [Combat composition of the Soviet army], 3 parts (Moscow: Voenizdat, 1966), pt. 2, 67.

3. Sergei M. Shtemenko, *The Soviet General Staff at War, 1941–1945*, vol. 1 (Moscow: Progress Publishers, 1985), 69.

4. See David M. Glantz, *Forgotten Battles of the Soviet-German War (1941–1945)*, vol. 2, *The Winter Campaign (5 December 1941–April 1942)* (Carlisle, PA:

self-published, 1999), 118–154; A. A. Volkhov, *Kriticheskii prolog: Nezavershennye frontovye nastupatel'nye operatsii pervykh kampanii Velikoi Otechestvennoi voiny* [Critical prologue: Incomplete *front* offensive operations of the initial campaign of the Great Patriotic War] (Moscow: AVIAR, 1992), 128–143; *Soviet Documents on the Use of War Experience*, vol. 3, *Military Operations, 1941–1942*, trans. Harold S. Orenstein (London: Frank Cass, 1993), 122–161; Beshanov, *God 1942*, 130–191. See also Shtemenko, *Soviet General Staff at War*, 1:68–70; Erich von Manstein, *Lost Victories*, trans. Anthony G. Powell (Chicago: Henry Regnery, 1958), 233–235; and Hayward, *Stopped at Stalingrad*, 68–85.

    5. Volkhov, *Kriticheskii prolog*, 131.

    6. Ziemke and Bauer, *Moscow to Stalingrad*, 262–263.

    7. Hayward, *Stopped at Stalingrad*, 68–70, 85.

    8. This account of the German assault on Kerch' is based primarily on Carell, *Stalingrad*, 25–29. See also Boog et al., *Germany and the Second World War*, VI:930–933.

    9. Quoted in Shtemenko, *Soviet General Staff at War*, 1:69–70. See Zolotarov, "*Stavka* 1942," 196, 198–199, for other caustic exchanges between the two.

    10. See Zolotarev, *VOV*, book 1, 332; Hayward, *Stopped at Stalingrad*, 84–85; Werner Haupt, *Army Group South: The Wehrmacht in Russia, 1941–1945*, trans. Joseph P. Welsh (Atglen, PA: Schiffer Press, 1998), 112–114. Official Soviet records indicate 176,566 casualties at Kerch', including 162,282 killed or captured. Kozlov also lost 347 tanks, 3,476 guns and mortars, and 400 aircraft. See Krivosheev, *Soviet Casualties and Combat Losses*, 108.

    11. Beshanov, *God 1942*, 51–56.

    12. Ibid., 51, 54.

    13. For a complete description of the battle, see Glantz, *Kharkov 1942*; Andrei Galushko and Maksim Kolomiets, "Boi za Khar'kov v mae 1942 god" [The battle for Khar'kov in May 1942], in *Frontovaia illustratsiia, 6-2000* [Front illustrated, June 2000] (Moscow: Strategiia KM, 1999); Beshanov, *God 1942*, 220–238.

    14. Zhukov, *Reminiscences and Reflections*, 1:75.

    15. Anthony Beevor, *Stalingrad: The Fateful Siege, 1942–1943* (New York: Viking, 1998), 65; Glantz, *Kharkov 1942*, 126–128; Hayward, *Stopped at Stalingrad*, 275–278.

    16. Halder, *War Diaries*, 616–617; Ziemke and Bauer, *Moscow to Stalingrad*, 275–278.

    17. III Corps' counterattack is summarized in Eberhard von Mackensen, *Vom Bug zum Caucasus: Das III. Panzerkorps im Feldzug gegen Sowjetrussland 1941/42* (Neckargemund, Germany: Kurt Vowinkel Verlag, 1967), 68–75.

    18. Galushko and Kolomiets, "Boi za Khar'kov," 73; Aleksei Isaev, *Kratkii kurs Istorii Velikoi Otechestvennoi voyny: Nastuplenie Marshala Shaposhnikova* [A short course in the history of the Great Patriotic War: The offensives of Marshal Shaposhnikov] (Moscow: Iauza Eksmo, 2005), 352–353.

    19. Beshanov, *God 1942*, 240.

    20. Blau, *German Campaign in Russia*, 140.

    21. Ibid., 140–141; Beevor, *Stalingrad*, 69–70.

    22. *Boevoi sostav Sovetskoi armii*, pt. 3, 106; Isaev, *Kratkii kurs*, 288–289.

23. Alex Buchner, *Sewastopol: Der Angriff auf die Stärkste Festung der Welt 1942* (Friedberg, Germany: Podzun-Pallas-Verlag, 1978), 1098–110; Isaev, *Kratkii kurs*, 289–290.

24. On the siege artillery, see Buchner, *Sewastopol*, 110–113; Ziemke and Bauer, *Moscow to Stalingrad*, 309; Hayward, *Stopped at Stalingrad*, 91–92; Carell, *Stalingrad*, 43.

25. For details on the final defense of Sevastopol', see G. I. Vaneev, S. L. Ermash, I. D. Malakhovsky, S. T. Sakhno, and A. F. Khrenov, *Geroicheskaia oborona Sevastopolia 1941–1942* [The heroic defense of Sevastopol', 1941–1942] (Moscow: Voenizdat, 1969); A. Dukachev, *Kurs na Sevastopol'* [The path to Sevastopol'] (Kiev: Politicheskoi literatury Ukrainy, 1986); S. G. Gorshkov, *Na Iuzhnom flange, osen' 1941 g.–vesna 1944 g.*[On the southern flank, fall 1941–spring 1944] (Moscow: Voenizdat, 1989); *SVIMVOV*, issue 14 (Moscow: Voenizdat, 1954), 88–114; F. D. Vorov'ev, *Oborona Sevastopolia* [The defense of Sevastopol'] (Moscow: Voenizdat, 1943); Buchner, *Sewastopol*.

26. This description of LIV Corps' attack is quoted in Haupt, *Army Group South*, 121.

27. Ziemke and Bauer, *Moscow to Stalingrad*, 316–318.

28. See the evocative account in Carell, *Stalingrad*, 44–49.

29. Ziemke and Bauer, *Moscow to Stalingrad*, 316–318.

30. Haupt, *Army Group South*, 123–124.

31. Ziemke and Bauer, *Moscow to Stalingrad*, 319–321; Manstein, *Lost Victories*, 248–258.

32. Beshanov, *God 1942*, 210.

33. The German advance in Operation Wilhelm is reflected in the daily situation maps in "Ia Lagenkarten zum KTB 12, May–Jul 1942," AOK 6 [Sixth Army command], 22855/Ia, NAM T-312, roll 1448. The Soviet side is best described by Moskalenko (commander of 38th Army) in *Na iugo-zapadnom napravlenii*, 224–227.

34. See "Notes of Conversations by Direct Line of the Supreme High Commander and the Deputy Chief of the General Staff with the High Command of the Southwestern Direction," in Zolotarev, *"Stavka 1942,"* 247–249. The directives transferring additional tank units are in the same volume, pp. 251, 255–256.

35. *Stavka* Directive No. 270458, 0235 hours, 21 June 1942, ibid., 258.

36. See the daily situation maps in "Ia, Lagenkarten zum KTB 12, May–Jul 1942," AOK 6, 22855/Ia, NAM T-312, roll 1446; and "Lagenkarten Pz. AOK 1, Ia (Armee-Gruppe v. Kleist), 1–29 Jun 1942," PzAOK 1, 24906/12, NAM T-313, roll 35. See also Ziemke and Bauer, *Moscow to Stalingrad*, 318–319; Wolfgang Werthen, *Geschichte der 16. Panzer-Division 1939–1945* (Friedberg, Germany: Podzum-Pallas Verlag, 1958), 96. On Beloborodov, see *Komandarmy. Voennyi biograficheskii slovar'*, 22–25.

Chapter 4. Punch and Counterpunch

1. *SVIMVOV*, issue 15, 128.

2. Carell, *Stalingrad*, 58–59; Ziemke and Bauer, *Moscow to Stalingrad*, 333; Ferdinand von Senger und Etterlin, *Die 24. Panzer-Division vormals 1. Kavallerie-Division 1939–1945.* (Neckargemünd, Germany: Kurt Vowinkel Verlag, 1962), 71–74.

3. *SVIMVOV*, issue 15, 128.

4. This fratricidal air attack is described in Helmuth Spaeter, *The History of the Panzerkorps Grossdeutschland*, vol. 1, trans. David Johnston (Winnipeg, MB: J. J. Fedorowicz, 1992), 323–324.

5. Zolotarev, "*Stavka* 1942," 262–276.

6. Maksim Kolomiets and Aleksandr Smolinov, "Boi v izluchine Dona, 28 ii-unia–23 iiulia 1942 goda" [The battle in the bend of the Don, 28 June–23 July 1942], in *Frontovaia illiustratsiia, 6-2002* [Front illustrated, June 2002] (Moscow: Strategiia KM, 2002), 26–28, 71–73.

7. David M. Glantz, *Forgotten Battles of the German-Soviet War, 1941–1945*, vol. 3, *The Summer Campaign (12 May–18 November 1942)* (Carlisle, PA: self-published, 1999), 36–37.

8. "Boevye rasporiazhenie i boevye doneseniia shtaba 28 Armii (12.5–12.7.1942)" [Combat orders and combat reports of the headquarters of 28th Army (12-5–12-7-1942)], TsAMO, f. 382, op. 8452, ed. khr. 37, 55–56; for discussions between the *Stavka* and Golikov, see Zolotarev, "*Stavka* 1942," 272–279; *SVIMVOV*, issue 15, 131–132.

9. Kolomiets and Smolinov, "Boi v izluchine Dona," 33.

10. See *Stavka* Directive Nos. 170471–170474 and 994089, 2 July 1942, in Zolotarev, "*Stavka* 1942," 280–282.

11. *SVIMVOV*, issue 15, 134.

12. Spaeter, *History of Panzerkorps Grossdeutschland*, 1:351.

13. Glantz, *Forgotten Battles*, 3:11–13, 21; Ziemke and Bauer, *Moscow to Stalingrad*, 336–337.

14. See *Stavka* Directive No. 170475, 0030 hours, 3 July 1942, in Zolotarev, "*Stavka* 1942," 284. For a complete description of 5th Tank Army's organization, see Kolomiets and Smolinov, "Boi v izluchine Dona," 41.

15. For the mission of 5th Tank Army, see M. E. Katukov, *Na ostrie glavnogo udara* [At the point of the main attack] (Moscow: Voenizdat, 1976), 133. For the overall history of this counterstroke, see David M. Glantz, "Forgotten Battles of the Soviet-German War, Part 7: The Summer Campaign, 12 May–18 November 1942: Voronezh, July 1942," *JSMS* 14, 3 (2001): 150–220.

16. A. I. Golobordov, "Kontrudar 5-i tankovoi armii pod Voronezhem" [The 5th Tank Army's counterstroke at Voronezh], *Voennaia mysl'* [Military thought] 4 (April 1993): 42–48. The armor of 2nd Tank Corps became mired in mud.

17. See *Stavka* Directive No. 170483, 2100 hours, 7 July 1942, in Zolotarev, "*Stavka* 1942," 291–292.

18. Kolomiets and Smolinov, "Boi v izluchine Dona," 46.

19. Katukov, *Na ostrie glavnogo udara*, 160–162.

20. Glantz, *Forgotten Battles*, 3:48–52.

21. I. I. Iushchik, *Odinnadtsatyi tankovyi korpusa v boiakh za Rodinu* [The 11th Tank Corps in combat for the Motherland] (Moscow: Voenizdat, 1962), 6–13; Zolotarev, "*Stavka* 1942," 295, 309–310; Glantz, *Forgotten Battles*, 3:40–46. Vatutin was known as the "boy wonder of the *Stavka*," rising rapidly to command the Southwestern Front at Stalingrad at age 42.

22. Klaus Gerbet, ed., *Generalfeldmarschall Fedor von Bock: The War Diary*,

1939–1945, trans. David Johnson (Atglen, PA: Schiffer Military History, 1996), 512; hereafter cited as *Bock Diary*.

23. Ibid.

24. On the Poltava conference, see ibid., 512–514; Geoffrey Jukes, *Hitler's Stalingrad Decisions* (Berkeley: University of California Press, 1985), 35–38; Ziemke and Bauer, *Moscow to Stalingrad*, 337–339.

25. Halder, *War Diaries*, 633–634; *Bock Diary*, 514–517.

26. *Bock Diary*, 520.

27. Carell, *Stalingrad*, 65–68. On the fuel shortage, see Friedrich W. von Mellenthin, *German Generals of World War II as I Saw Them* (Norman: University of Oklahoma Press, 1977), 108–109.

28. See, for example, Moskalenko, *Na iugo-zapadnom napravlenii*, 252–253; Kolomiets and Smolinov, "Boi v izluchine Dona," 58.

29. Moskalenko, *Na iugo-zapadnom napravlenii*, 253–255.

30. See TsAMO, f. 382, op. 8452, ed. khr 37, II. 432, for 28th Army's report on the situation.

31. See *Stavka* Directive No. 17040, 0115 hours, 10 July 1942; No. 735/up, 1245 hours, 10 July 1942; No. 170491, 1910 hours, 10 July 1942, in Zolotarev, "*Stavka* 1942," 298–299.

32. Citino, *Death of the Wehrmacht*, 174–175, 180–182.

33. Shtemenko, *Soviet General Staff at War*, 1:84–87.

34. The order deploying 62nd Army forward was No. 170435, 0215 hours, 11 July 1942, in Zolotarev, "*Stavka* 1942," 300. See also Aleksei Isaev, *Stalingrad: Za Volgoi dlia nas zemli net* [Stalingrad: There is no land for us beyond the Volga] (Moscow: Iauza, Eksmo, 2008), 12.

35. See *Stavka* Directive No. 170495, 0215 hours, 12 July 1942, in Zolotarev, "*Stavka* 1942," 302.

36. *Komandarmy. Voennyi biograficheskii slovar'*, 99–100.

37. Ibid., 116–118.

38. See *Stavka* Directive Nos. 1035055, 170501, and 170502, 12 July 1942, in Zolotarev, "*Stavka* 1942," 306–307.

39. *Stavka* Directive No. 170508, 0240 hours, 14 July 1942; No. 170513, 17 July 1942; No. 170512, 1525 hours, 15 July 1942; No. 170515, 0015 hours, 17 July 1942, ibid., 306–312.

40. Halder, *War Diaries*, 639.

41. Ibid., 639–640; *Bock Diary*, 526. On Bock's relief, see also Jukes, *Hitler's Stalingrad Decisions*, 43; Ziemke and Bauer, *Moscow to Stalingrad*, 347–348; Boog et al., *Germany and the Second World War*, VI:971–973, 977.

42. See Blau, *German Campaign in Russia*, 148; Ziemke and Bauer, *Moscow to Stalingrad*, 351.

43. Halder, *War Diaries*, 635; Jukes, *Hitler's Stalingrad Decisions*, 39.

44. Führer Directive No. 43 is reproduced in Trevor-Roper, *Blitzkrieg to Defeat*, 124–127.

45. Ziemke and Bauer, *Moscow to Stalingrad*, 349–351; Moskalenko, *Na iugo-zapadnom napravlenii*, 259–262.

46. Blau, *German Campaign in Russia*, 149–150.

47. Boog et al., *Germany and the Second World War*, VI:983–984.

48. Ibid., 150.

49. M. M. Povalyi, *Vosemnadtsataia v srazheniia za Rodiny* [The 18th (Army) in the defense of the Motherland] (Moscow: Voenizdat, 1962), 106–109.

50. Beevor, *Stalingrad*, 79; Haupt, *Army Group South*, 180–181; Carell, *Stalingrad*, 71–76.

51. Official figures in Krivosheev, *Soviet Casualties and Combat Losses*, 123–125. On routine underestimation, see S. A. I'lenkov, "Concerning the Registration of Soviet Armed Forces Wartime Irrevocable Losses, 1941–1945," *JSMS* 9, 2 (June 1996): 440–442.

52. Il'ia Moshchansky and Sergei Smolinov, "Oborona Stalingrada: Stalingradskaia strategicheskaia obornitel'naia operatsiia, 17 iiulia–18 noiabria 1942 goda" [The defense of Stalingrad: The Stalingrad strategic defensive operation, 17 July–18 November 1942], in *Voennaia letopis'*, 6-2002 [Military chronicle, June 2002] (Moscow: BTV, 2002), 12.

53. Führer Directive No. 45 is reproduced in English in Trevor-Roper, *Blitzkrieg to Defeat*, 129–131, and in Russian in *SVIMVOV*, issue 18, 265–267. See also Blau, *German Campaign in Russia*, 152–155, for analysis.

54. Trevor-Roper, *Blitzkrieg to Defeat*, 130; *SVIMVOV*, issue 18, 265.

55. *SVIMVOV*, issue 18, 266.

56. Ibid.

57. These force ratios are calculated from a number of different sources, including *Boevoi sostav Sovetskoi armii*, pt. 2, 146–150; Maksim Kolomiets and Il'ia Moshchansky, "Oborona Kavkaz (iiuli'–dekabr' 1942 goda)" [Defense of the Caucasus (July–December 1942)], in *Frontovaia illiustratsiia, 2-2002* [Front illustrated, February 2002] (Moscow: Strategiia KM, 2002), 5; "Lagenkarten, 8 July–5 October 1942," AOK II, Ia, 2595/207a, NAM T-312, roll 1207; "Ia, Lagenkarten Nr. 1 zum KTB Nr. 13, Jul–Oct 1942," AOK 6, 23948/1a, NAM T-312, roll 1446; "Feindlagekarten, PzAOK 1, 1c, 29 Jun–31 Jul 1942," PzAOK 1, 24906/24, NAM T-313, roll 38; "Anlage 3 zum Tatigkeisbericht, OAK 17, Ic, 20 Jul–25 Jul 1942," AOK 17, 24411/33, NAM T-312, roll 679.

58. See Blau, *German Campaign in Russia*, 149–150, 155. Kolomiets and Moshchansky, "Oborona Kavkaz," 5, which does not include 16th Panzer, 22nd Panzer, and *Grossdeutschland* Divisions, calculated First Panzer Army's strength at 29 tanks.

59. See *Stavka* Directive Nos. 170516 (1610 hours) and 170519 (1800 hours), 17 July 1942; No. 994121, 18 July 1942, in Zolotorev, "*Stavka* 1942," 313–315.

60. *Stavka* Directive Nos. 994124 and 9904125, 2030 hours, 22 July 1942, ibid., 320–321.

61. Boog et al., *Germany and the Second World War*, VI:980–989.

Chapter 5. The German Advance to the Don and the Volga

1. For strength figures, see "Ia, Lagenkarten Nr. 1 zum KTB Nr. 13, Jul–Oct 1942," AOK 6, 23948/Ia, NAM T-312, roll 1446. On Paulus's plan, see Ziemke and Bauer, *Moscow to Stalingrad*, 357.

2. *Boevoi sostav Sovetskoi armii*, pt. 2, 148–149; Moshchansky and Smolinov, "Oborona Stalingrada," 12. See also Isaev, *Stalingrad*, 26.

3. Vasili I. Chuikov, *The Battle for Stalingrad*, trans. Harold Silver (New York: Holt, Rinehart & Winston, 1964), 19–20 (Chuikov's divisions began to occupy their forward positions only on 22–24 July); V. A. Zhilin, ed., *Stalingradskaia bitva: Khronika, fakty, liudi v. 2 kn.* [The Battle of Stalingrad: Chronicles, facts, people in two books] (Moscow: OLMA, 2002), 232.

4. Chuikov, *Battle for Stalingrad*, 17–20.

5. V. E. Tarrant, *Stalingrad: Anatomy of an Agony* (London: Leo Cooper, 1992), 39. On aerial resupply, see Hayward, *Stopped at Stalingrad*, 183.

6. For the question of Chuikov's command status, compare his *Battle for Stalingrad*, 17–19, with Moshchansky and Smolinov, "Oborona Stalingrada," 9. On the *front* change of command, see *Boevoi sostav Sovetskoi armii*, pt. 2, 148–149; Shtemenko, *Soviet General Staff at War*, 1:89–90.

7. For details on this encirclement battle, see Halder, *War Diaries*, 646–647; Moshchansky and Smolinov, "Oborona Stalingrada," 15; K. K. Rokossovsky, ed., *Velikaia pobeda na Volge* [Great victory on the Volga] (Moscow: Voenizdat, 1965), 64–65; Zhilin, *Stalingradskaia bitva*, 1:252.

8. "Ia Lagenkarten Nr. 1 zum KTB Nr. 13, Jul–Oct 1942," AOK 6, 23948/1a, NAM T-312, roll 1446.

9. Rokossovsky, *Velikaia pobeda na Volge*, 66–67.

10. Zhilin, *Stalingradskaia bitva*, 256. On Soviet tank losses, see Isaev, *Stalingrad*, 48–49.

11. Werthen, *Geschichte der 16. Panzer-Division*, 100. See also Halder, *War Diaries*, 648.

12. Zhilin, *Stalingradskaia bitva*, 265–274; Werthen, *Geschichte der 16. Panzer-Division*, 102; Rokossovsky, *Velikaia pobeda na Volge*, 69–70; Isaev, *Stalingrad*, 53; Halder, *War Diaries*, 649; Moshchansky and Smolinov, "Oborona Stalingrada," 15.

13. Moskalenko's 1st Tank Army reported destroying or capturing 116 tanks between 23 and 30 July; if this figure is interpreted to include disabled tanks that were later repaired, it appears accurate. Moshchansky and Smolinov, "Oborona Stalingrada," 20.

14. "Nekotorie vyvody po operatsiiam levogo kryla Zapodnogo fronta" [Some conclusions concerning the operations of the Western Front's left wing], in *Sbornik materialov po izucheniiu opyta voiny* [Collection of materials for the study of war experience], no. 5 (Moscow: Voenizdat, 1943), 60–75. See K. K. Rokossovsky, "Soldatskii dolg" [A soldier's duty], *VIZh* 2 (February 1990): 52, for his critique of the operation.

15. *Stavka* Directive No. 170516, 1630 hours, 17 July 1942, in Zolotarev, "*Stavka* 1942," 313–314.

16. Glantz, *Forgotten Battles*, 3:55.

17. I. Iu Sdvizhkov, "Kak pogib i gde pokhoronen general Liziukov?" [How did General Liziukov perish and where was he buried?], *Voenno-istoricheskii arkhiv* [Military-historical archives] 9, 81 (2006): 149–165, and 10, 82 (2006): 39–56.

18. Katukov, *Na ostrie glavnogo udara*, 163–164, provides the conventional account, complete with an inaccurate date, of Liziukov's death. This account was

apparently intended to assuage Stalin's fears that Liziukov was a traitor. Sdvizhkov reconstructed the actual circumstances in "Kak pogib i gde pokhoronen general Liziukov?"

19. For details of the German counterattack, see Carl Hans Hermann, *Die 9. Panzerdivision, 1939–1945* (Friedberg, Germany: Podzun-Pallas-Verlag, 2004).

20. Order No. 227, signed by Stalin, is reproduced in V. A. Zolotarev, ed., "Prikazy narodnogo komissara oborony SSSR, 22 iiunia 1941 g.–1942" [Orders of the People's Commissariat of Defense of the USSR, 22 June 1941–1942], in *Russkii arkhiv: Velikaia Otechestvennaia [voina]*, 13 (2-2) [The Russian archives: The Great Patriotic (War), vol. 13 (2-2)] (Moscow: Terra, 1997), 276–279.

21. Ibid., 278–279.

22. For additional orders related to No. 227, see P. N. Lashchenko, "Prodiktovan surovoi neobkhodimost'iu" [Severe measures are dictated], *VIZh* 8 (August 1989): 76–80; Alexander Statiev, "Blocking Units in the Red Army," *Journal of Military History* 76, 2 (April 2012): 475–495.

23. See Zhilin, *Stalingradskaia bitva*, 248, 252, 254.

24. Chuikov, *Battle for Stalingrad*, 30–38. The quotation is from Senger und Etterlin, *Die 24. Panzer-Division*, 96. The blocking detachments were included in *Stavka* Directive No. 170524, 1940 hours, 31 July 1942, in Zolotarev, "*Stavka* 1942," 337.

25. Halder, *War Diaries*, 646.

26. Ibid. For the organization of Fourth Panzer Army in August, see Boog et al., *Germany and the Second World War*, VI:964.

27. For the gradual shifts in Army Group B's order of battle, see "Ia Lagenkarten Nr. 1 zum KTB Nr. 13, Jul–Oct 1942," AOK 6, 23948/1a, NAM T-312, roll 1446.

28. See *Stavka* Directive No. 994129, 1920 hours, 29 July 1942, and unnumbered directive, 2 August 1942, in Zolotarev, "*Stavka* 1942," 333, 338–339.

29. Joachim Lemelsen, Walter Fries, and Wilhelm Schaeffer, *29. Division: 29. Infanteriedivision, 29. Infanteriedivision (mot.), 29. Panzergrenadier-Division* (Bad Nauheim, Germany: Podzun-Verlag, 1960), 194; Rolf Grams, *Die 14. Panzer-Division 1940–1945* (Bad Nauheim, Germany: Verlag Haus-Henning Podzun, 1957), 50; Zhilin, *Stalingradskaia bitva*, 277, 282; S. M. Sarkis'ian, *51-ia Armiia* [The 51st Army] (Moscow: Voenizdat, 1963), 81.

30. Rokossovsky, *Velikaia pobeda na Volge*, 76.

31. Chuikov, *Battle for Stalingrad*, 44–54.

32. The exact timing of this split into two *fronts* is debated. See A. I. Eremenko, *Stalingrad: Zapiski komanduiushchevo frontom* [Stalingrad: The notes of a *front* commander] (Moscow: Voenizdat, 1961), 38–39; Vasilevsky, *Delo vsei zhizni*, 210; Rokossovsky, *Velikaia pobeda na Volge*, 78. For the order creating the two *fronts*, see *Stavka* Directive No. 994140, 0530 hours, 4 August 1942, and No. 170554, 0415 hours, 5 August 1942, in Zolotarev, "*Stavka* 1942," 342–343.

33. *Stavka* Directive No. 170562, 2300 hours, 9 August 1942, ibid., 354.

34. Moshchansky and Smolinov, "Oborona Stalingrada," 28–30; Zhilin, *Stalingradskaia bitva*, 325, 328, 336–337, 342–344; "Ia Lagenkarten Nr. 1 zum KTB Nr. 13, Jul–Oct 1942," AOK 6, 23948/1a, NAM T-312, roll 1446. The two German mobile divisions suffered a total of 3,464 casualties on top of previous losses in July. See

George W. S. Kuhn, *Ground Force Casualty Rate Patterns: The Empirical Evidence*, Report FP301TR1 (Bethesda, MD: Logistics Management Agency, 1989), for tables based on German records.

35. See daily situation maps in "Ia Lagenkarten Nr. 1 zum KTB Nr. 13, Jul–Oct 1942," AOK 6, 23948/1a, NAM T-312, roll 1446. On German air superiority, see Hayward, *Stopped at Stalingrad*, 183–185.

36. Rokossovsky, *Velikaia pobeda na Volge*, 86.

37. For details, see Werthen, *Geschichte der 16. Panzer-Division*, 103–107; Zhilin, *Stalingradskaia bitva*, 316–322. On prisoners versus escapees, see Ziemke and Bauer, *Moscow to Stalingrad*, 384; Isaev, *Stalingrad*, 67–68, 74–75, citing TsAMO RF, f. 220, op. 230, d. 71, ll. 141, 171.

38. The 24th Panzer Division, for example, began the operation with 116 tanks and ended it with only 82. Thomas L. Jentz, *Panzertruppen* (Atglen, PA: Schiffer Publishing, 1996), 248.

39. Rokossovsky, *Velikaia pobeda na Volge*, 96.

40. Ibid., 97–100.

41. On 1st Guards Army, see Moskalenko, *Na iugo-zapadnom napravlenii*, 294–298.

42. Rokossovsky, *Velikaia pobeda na Volge*, 103–105.

43. Werthen, *Geschichte der 16. Panzer-Division*, 105.

44. Moskalenko, *Na iugo-zapadnom napravlenii*, 298–303; Rokossovsky, *Velikaia pobeda na Volge*, 114–115. I. M. Chistiakov, ed., *Po prikazu Rodiny: boevoi put' 6-i gvardeiskoi armii v. Velikoi Otechestvennoi voine, 1941–1945 gg* [By order of the Motherland: The combat path of 6th Guards Army in the Great Patriotic War, 1941–1945] (Moscow: Voenizdat, 1971), 18–20, describes the role of 21st Army in this defense. See also Gerhard Dieckhoff, *3. Infanterie-Division, 3. Infanterie-Division (Mot.), 3. Panzer-Grenadier-Division* (Cuxhaven, Germany: Oberstudienrat Gerhard Dieckhoff, 1960), 192–193.

45. Werthen, *Geschichte der 16. Panzer-Division*, 115–117. On the remnants of 4th Tank Army, see Isaev, *Stalingrad*, 80. German troop movements are reflected in daily situation maps in "Ia Lagenkarten Nr. 1 zum KTB Nr. 13, Jul–Oct 1942," AOK 6, 23948/1a, NAM T-312, roll 1446.

46. Grams, *Die 14. Panzer-Division*, 51. See also Jentz, *Panzertruppen*, 248.

47. The Sixth Army order is quoted in full in Heinz Schröter, *Stalingrad* (New York: Ballantine, 1958), 24. See also Haupt, *Army Group South*, 161; Zhilin, *Stalingradskaia bitva*, 386–387.

48. Werthen, *Geschichte der 16. Panzer-Division*, 106.

49. Rokossovsky, *Velikaia pobeda na Volge*, 119–122; Glantz, *Forgotten Battles* 3:66–74.

50. Schröter, *Stalingrad*, 28.

51. The casualty figures are from Tarrant, *Stalingrad*, 51.

52. Werthen, *Geschichte der 16. Panzer-Division*, 106–107; Carell, *Stalingrad*, 124–125; Rokossovsky, *Velikaia pobeda na Volge*, 127.

53. Rokossovsky, *Velikaia pobeda na Volge*, 124–133.

54. Ibid., 133.

55. *Stavka* Directive No. 994170, 2015 hours, 24 August 1942, in Zolotarev, "*Stavka* 1942," 372–373.

56. Ibid.; Ziemke and Bauer, *Moscow to Stalingrad*, 87; Werthen, *Geschichte der 16. Panzer-Division*, 110–111.

57. Hayward, *Stopped at Stalingrad*, 187–189; Beevor, *Stalingrad*, 104–106.

58. Hardesty and Grinberg, *Red Phoenix Rising*, 125–134.

59. Rokossovsky, *Velikaia pobeda na Volge*, 142–144, See also *Stavka* Instruction No. 170585, 0515 hours, 25 August 1942, in Zolotarev, "*Stavka* 1942," 373; and daily situation maps in "Ia Lagenkarten Nr. 1 zum KTB Nr. 13, Jul–Oct 1942," AOK 6, 23948/1a, NAM T-312, roll 1446.

60. Jentz, *Panzertruppen*, 248, provides the tank strength of 24th Panzer. For the campaign operations of this division, see Jason D. Mark, *Death of the Leaping Horseman: 24. Panzer-Division in Stalingrad, 12th August–20th November 1942* (Sydney, Australia: Leaping Horseman Books, 2003), 14–44.

61. Rokossovsky, *Velikaia pobeda na Volge*, 99–100.

62. *Boevoi sostav Sovetskoi armii*, pt. 2, 172.

63. Zhilin, *Stalingradskaia bitva*, 401, 407; Mark, *Death of the Leaping Horseman*, 30–31.

64. Zhilin, *Stalingradskaia bitva*, 407.

65. Mark, *Death of the Leaping Horseman*, 49–64; Rokossovsky, *Velikaia pobeda na Volge*, 147.

66. Zhilin, *Stalingradskaia bitva*, 458; Rokossovsky, *Velikaia pobeda na Volge*, 151; Zolotarev, "*Stavka* 1942," 381; Mark, *Death of the Leaping Horseman*, 94, 107–108.

67. Rokossovsky, *Velikaia pobeda na Volge*, 152; "Ia Lagenkarten Nr. 1 zum KTB Nr. 13, Jul–Oct 1942," AOK 6, 23948/1a, NAM T-312, roll 1446.

68. For the advance of 24th Panzer, see Mark, *Death of the Leaping Horseman*, 108–109. The tank strength of the Southeastern Front is described in Moshchansky and Smolinov, "Oborona Stalingrada," 36.

69. Pliev had a distinguished wartime record for cavalry-mechanized operations in the enemy rear. In 1962 Khrushchev chose the aging cavalryman to command the Soviet forces in Cuba during the missile crisis.

70. Zhilin, *Stalingradskaia bitva*, 400, 422–433; Rokossovsky, *Velikaia pobeda na Volge*, 129.

71. Zhilin, *Stalingradskaia bitva*, 411, 417, 427, 433, 438; Moskalenko, *Na iugo-zapadnom napravlenii*, 303–307; "Ia Lagenkarten Nr. 1 zum KTB Nr. 13, Jul–Oct 1942," AOK 6, 23948/1a, NAM T-312, roll 1446. See also Rolf Stoves, *Die 22. Panzer-Division, Die 25. Panzer-Division, Die 27. Panzer-Division, und die 233. Reserve-Panzer-Division* (Friedberg, Germany: Podzun-Pallas-Verlag, 1985), 34–35.

72. Schröter, *Stalingrad*, 33.

Chapter 6. Struggles on the Flanks, 25 July–11 September 1942

1. *SVIMVOV*, issue 18, 265; Trevor-Roper, *Blitzkrieg to Defeat*, 130.

2. For German plans, see Ziemke and Bauer, *Moscow to Stalingrad*, 397; Wilhelm Tieke, *The Caucasus and the Oil: The German-Soviet War in the Caucasus 1942/43*, trans. Joseph G. Welsh (Winnipeg, MB: J. J. Fedorowicz, 1995), 4–16. The order of battle is found in "Lagenkarten. Anlage 9 zum Kriegstagebuch Nr. 3, AOK

17, Ia., 31 Jul–13 Aug 1942," AOK 17. 24411/19, NAM T-312, roll 696; and "Ia. La-genkarten Pz AOK 1, 1–31 Aug 1942," Pz AOK 1, 24906/14, NAM T-313, roll 36.

3. Zolotarev, *Velikaia Otechestvennaia voina*, book 1, 370; A. A. Grechko, *Bitva za Kavkaz* [The battle for the Caucasus] (Moscow: Voenizdat, 1973), 53–54. Kri-vosheev, *Soviet Casualties and Combat Losses*, 125–126, gives somewhat larger fig-ures.

4. Haupt, *Army Group South*, 187; Sarkis'ian, *51-ia Armiia*, 77–78. Carell, *Stal-ingrad*, 85–86, claims that a "Russian tank corps" ambushed 23rd Panzer, but the opponents were actually 135th and 155th Tank Brigades of 51st Army.

5. Tieke, *Caucasus and the Oil*, 29–33; Grechko, *Bitva za Kavkaz*, 60, 76–77.

6. North Caucasus Front Report No. 4198, 0751 hours, 27 July 1942, and *Stavka* Directive Nos. 170534 (0245 hours, 28 July 1942) and 156400 (1730 hours, 29 July 1942), in Zolotarev, "*Stavka* 1942," 530–532, 330, 332.

7. Grechko, *Bitva za Kavkaz*, 61.

8. See *Stavka* Directive No. 994139, 0305 hours, 31 July 1942, in Zolotarev, "*Stavka* 1942," 336.

9. *Geschichte der 3. Panzer-Division, Berlin-Brandenburg 1935–1945* (Berlin: Verlag der Buchhandlung Gunter Richter, 1947), 308.

10. Tieke, *Caucasus and the Oil*, 34–36.

11. For the defense by 17th Cavalry Corps and 18th Army, see Grechko, *Bitva za Kavkaz*, 78.

12. For tank strengths, see Kolomiets and Moshchansky, "Oborona Kavkaz," 8. According to Jentz, *Panzertruppen*, 251, 13th Panzer Division declined from 129 tanks (29 July) to 80 (26 September).

13. Shukman, *Stalin's Generals*, 64–65, 119–120; John Erickson, *The Road to Stalingrad: Stalin's War with Germany* (New York: Harper & Row, 1975), 378–379.

14. This advance is reflected in the daily situation maps of "Lagenkarten. Anlage 9 zum Kriegstagebuch nr. 3, AOK 17, Ia, 31 Jul–13 Aug 1942," AOK 17. 24411/19, NAM T-312, roll 696; and "Ia. Lagenkarten Pz AOK 1, 1–31 Aug 1942," Pz AOK 1, 24906/14, NAM T-313, roll 36.

15. Tieke, *Caucasus and the Oil*, 27–28, 63.

16. See *Stavka* Directive Nos. 170553 (0445 hours, 5 August 1942), 170555 (same date and time), 170551 (0600 hours, 5 August 1942), and 170552 (0615 hours, 5 August 1942), in Zolotarev, "*Stavka* 1942," 344, 346–347; Grechko, *Bitva za Kavkaz*, 80.

17. Zolotarev, "*Stavka* 1942," 350–352.

18. Tieke, *Caucasus and the Oil*, 52–53.

19. Mackensen, *Vom Bug zum Kaukasus*, 91–93; Carell, *Stalingrad*, 83–95; Hay-ward, *Stopped at Stalingrad*, 157–159; Ziemke and Bauer, *Moscow to Stalingrad*, 370. On the deliberate Soviet destruction, see Grechko, *Bitva za Kavkaz*, 85.

20. Grechko, *Bitva za Kavkaz*, 85; *Stavka* Directive No. 170565, 11 August 1942, in Zolotarev, "*Stavka* 1942," 358.

21. Haupt, *Army Group South*, 185–187; Carell, *Stalingrad*, 91–93.

22. Tieke, *Caucasus and the Oil*, 68–82; Grechko, *Bitva za Kavkaz*, 86–88.

23. Budenny's complete 13 August report is included in V. A. Shapovalov, ed.,

Bitva za Kavkaz v dokumentakh i materialov [The battle for the Caucasus in documents and materials] (Stavropol': Stavropol' State University, 2003), 142–144.

24. Ziemke and Bauer, *Moscow to Stalingrad*, 372–373; Tieke, *Caucasus and the Oil*, 94–101.

25. "Ia. Lagenkarten Pz AOK 1, 1–31 Aug 1942," Pz AOK 1, 24906/14, NAM T-313, roll 36; Grechko, *Bitva za Kavkaz*, 112; Tieke, *Caucasus and the Oil*, 139–142, 149–162. For details of the Soviet defensive plans, see Shapovalov, *Bitva za Kavkaz v dokumentakh*, 163–169.

26. Tieke, *Caucasus and the Oil*, 138–142.

27. Grechko, *Bitva za Kavkaz*,109–110, 114; Shtemenko, *Soviet General Staff at War*, 1:123–127; Kolomiets and Moshchansky, "Oborona Kavkaz," 19.

28. *Stavka* Directive Nos. 170596 (1440 hours, 1 September 1942) and 170598 (0250 hours, 3 September 1942), in Zolotarev, "*Stavka* 1942," 386–287. For Beria's recommendations and report, see Shapovalov, *Bitva za Kavkaz v dokumentakh*, 185–186, 189–192.

29. Grechko, *Bitva za Kavkaz*, 115; V. F. Mozolev, "Mozdok-Malgrobekskaia operatsiia 1942" [The Mozdok-Malgrobek operation, 1942], in *VE*, 5:196.

30. Tieke, *Caucasus and the Oil*, 87.

31. Grechko, *Bitva za Kavkaz*, 128–134; I. S. Shiian, *Ratnyi podvig Novorossiiska* [Feat of arms at Novorossiisk] (Moscow: Voenizdat, 1977), 35–52. The Novorossiisk Defensive Region was formed in accordance with Directive No. 170575, 1945 hours, 18 August 1942, in Zolotarev, "*Stavka* 1942," 367.

32. Grechko, *Bitva za Kavkaz*, 133–134; Axworthy et al., *Third Axis, Fourth Ally*, 82.

33. Shiian, *Ratnyi podvig*, 41–43; Tieke, *Caucasus and the Oil*, 88–89.

34. Shiian, *Ratnyi podvig*, 46–54; Grechko, *Bitva za Kavkaz*, 142–154; Shapovalov, *Bitva za Kavkaz v dokumentakh*, 204–209; Tieke, *Caucasus and the Oil*, 85.

35. "Novorossiiska operatsiia 1942" [The Novorossiisk operation, 1942], in *VE*, 5:501.

36. Tieke, *Caucasus and the Oil*, 101.

37. Grechko, *Bitva za Kavkaz*, 154–156.

38. Ibid., 164–169, especially the insightful discussion of tactics on 167–169; Shapovalov, *Bitva za Kavkaz v dokumentakh*, 175–182, 187–189, 219–222, 227–229; Tieke, *Caucasus and the Oil*, 110–117.

39. See Glantz, *Forgotten Battles*, 3:67–68.

40. For details, see Katukov, *Na ostrie glavnogo udara*, 166–168; *Stavka* Directive Nos. 156675 (1850 hours, 15 August 1942) and 994176 (0300 hours, 30 August 1942), in Zolotarev, "*Stavka* 1942," 363, 376–377.

41. See *Stavka* Directive Nos. 270593 (30 August 1942), 170593 (1610 hours, 30 August 1942), 170601 (1810 hours, 7 September 1942), and 170627 (28 September 1942), in Zolotarev, "*Stavka* 1942," 378, 388, 403. For further operational details, see Glantz, *Forgotten Battles*, 3:76–86.

42. A. M. Sandalov, *Pogoreloe-Gorodishchenskaia operatsiia: Nastupatel'naia operatsiia 20-i armii Zapadnogo fronta v avguste 1942 goda* [The Pogoreloe-Gorodishche operation: The offensive operation of the Western Front's 20th Army in August 1942]

(Moscow: Voenizdat, 1960), 74; N. M. Ramanichev and V. V. Gurkhin, "Rzhevsko-Sy-chevskie operatsii 1942" [The Rzhev-Sychevka operation, 1942], in *VE*, 7:233. See also "Freindlage, AOK 9, IC/A, 1–31 Aug 1942," AOK 9, 27970/5, pt. II, NAM T-312, roll 304. On the German defense, see Anton Detlev von Plato, *Die Geschichte der 5. Panzerdivision 1938 bis 1945* (Regensberg, Germany: Walhalla u. Praetoria Verlag, 1978), 230–240.

43. Halder, *War Diaries*, 653–654; Ziemke and Bauer, *Moscow to Stalingrad*, 402–403.

44. Glantz, *Forgotten Battles*, 3:156–167; Ziemke and Bauer, *Moscow to Stalingrad*, 406–407; Halder, *War Diaries*, 657.

45. A. M. Zvartsev, ed., *3-ia gvardeiskaia tankovaia armiia* [The 3rd Guards Tank Army] (Moscow: Voenizdat, 1982), 19–20.

46. Ibid., 19–24; Glantz, *Forgotten Battles*, 3:122–129.

47. G. I. Berdnikov, *Pervaia udarnaia: Boevoia pyt' 1-i udarnoi armii v Velikoi Otechestvennoi voine* [First Shock: The combat path of 1st Shock Army in the Great Patriotic War] (Moscow: Voenizdat, 1985), 106; Glantz, *Forgotten Battles*, 3:178.

48. Glantz, *Forgotten Battles*, 3:180–188; Berdnikov, *Pervaia udarnaia*, 109.

49. Glantz, *Forgotten Battles*, 3:190–193; Ziemke and Bauer, *Moscow to Stalingrad*, 421–422; Berdnikov, *Pervaia udarnaia*, 111–116.

50. Halder, *War Diaries*, 649.

51. Zhukov, *Reminiscences and Reflections*, 2:86.

Chapter 7. The Initial Battles for Stalingrad, September 1942

1. Rokossovsky, *Velikaia pobeda na Volge*, 133, 153.

2. As is typical in wartime, the Soviets credited the Germans with more armored vehicles than they actually had available. Rokossovsky, ibid., claimed that 62nd Army alone faced 390 tanks. According to Moshchansky and Smolinov, "Oborona Stalingrada," 38, the Germans fielded 500 tanks.

3. See Beshanov, *God 1942*, 527–529; Rokossovsky, *Velikaia pobeda na Volge*, 154. Estimates of ground force weaponry vary widely.

4. Hayward, *Stopped at Stalingrad*, 195. Rokossovsky, *Velikaia pobeda na Volge*, 155, placed Soviet aircraft strength at 137 operable aircraft in 8th Air Army and 89 in 16th Air Army.

5. Moskalenko, *Na iugo-zapadnom napravlenii*, 315.

6. On the composition and strength of 1st Guards Army, see Isaev, *Stalingrad*, 141–142.

7. Moskalenko, *Na iugo-zapadnom naprvalenii*, 318–319; Zhukov, *Reminiscences and Reflections*, 2:89.

8. For German dispositions and movements, see "Ia Lagenkarten Nr. 1 zum KTB Nr. 13, Jul–Oct 1942," AOK 6, 23948/1a, NAM T-312, roll 1446. See also Dieckhoff, *3. Infanterie-Division*, 199–202.

9. Rotmistrov's 7th Tank Corps lost 53 of its 169 tanks in this action. See Isaev, *Stalingrad*, 145.

10. See *Stavka* Order No. 170599, 2230 hours, 3 September 1942, in Zolotarev, "*Stavka* 1942," 387.

11. Quoted in Ziemke and Bauer, *Moscow to Stalingrad*, 391.

12. Rokossovsky, *Velikaia pobeda na Volge*, 157.

13. "Boevoe rasporiazhenie no. 0075/op, Shtab IuVF, 1.9.42.2215" [Combat order no. 0075/op, headquarters, Southeastern Front, 2215 hours, 1 September 1942], in *62nd Army Combat Journal*, copy of the original.

14. Zhilin, *Stalingradskaia bitva*, 485. See also "Ia Lagenkarten Nr. 1 zum KTB Nr. 13, Jul–Oct 1942," AOK 6, 23948/1a, NAM T-312, roll 1446.

15. Kravchenko's counterattack included two tank brigades and elements of 112th Rifle Division; he lost 27 of his 62 tanks in the process. Isaev, *Stalingrad*, 154.

16. See the details of this fighting in *62nd Army Combat Journal*.

17. Mark, *Death of the Leaping Horseman*, 118; Zhilin, *Stalingradskaia bitva*, 493. See also "Ia Lagenkarten Nr. 1 zum KTB Nr. 13, Jul–Oct 1942," AOK 6, 23948/1a, NAM T-312, roll 1446.

18. Mark, *Death of the Leaping Horseman*, 124–126.

19. Rokossovsky, *Velikaia pobeda na Volge*, 159; Zhilin, *Stalingradskaia bitva*, 500.

20. Zhilin, *Stalingradskaia bitva*, 511; Isaev, *Stalingrad*, 156.

21. Rokossovsky, *Velikaia pobeda na Volge*, 159.

22. Zhilin, *Stalingradskaia bitva*, 519.

23. See, for example, General von Richthofen's complaints about the slow pace and hesitation of the Sixth Army commanders, as quoted in Goerlitz, *Paulus and Stalingrad*, 191.

24. Lopatin's relief is in *Stavka* Directive No. 160603, 0440 hours, 8 September 1942, and Chuikov's appointment is in *Stavka* Directive No. 994200, 2310 hours, 9 September 1942, in Zolotarev, "*Stavka* 1942," 389, 390.

25. Chuikov, *Battle for Stalingrad*, 76.

26. Ibid., 80–81.

27. Gurov joined the Red Army in 1919 and served as a junior officer and commissar during the Civil War. From the start of the German invasion in 1941, he was commissar for a series of field armies until his death, from an unspecified illness, on 25 August 1943. See "Gurov, Kuz'ma Akimovich," in *VE*, 2:534.

28. See, for example, Chuikov, *Battle for Stalingrad*, 81–82, and NKVD reports on disciplinary matters in *Stalingradskaia epopeia* [The Stalingrad epoch] (Moscow: Evonnitsa-MG, 2000), 192–208.

29. Isaev, *Stalingrad*, 161–162 (citing TsAMO RF, f. 345, op. 5487, d. 6, l. 3) and 64 (citing TsAMO RF, f. 48, op. 468, d. 25, ll. 33, 35). The armor included 22 heavy, 51 medium, and 42 light tanks, with only 23rd Tank Corps having even a modicum of vehicles (48).

30. Lemelsen et al., *29. Division*, 198.

31. Zhilin, *Stalingradskaia bitva*, 533, quoting an OKW bulletin.

32. Ibid., 532–536.

33. Ziemke and Bauer, *Moscow to Stalingrad*, 393.

34. Mark, *Death of the Leaping Horseman*, 149–150.

35. Hayward, *Stopped at Stalingrad*, 194–195. Khriukin was far younger than most ground commanders, having taken command of 8th Air Army in June 1942 at the age of 32. However, he had already fought in Spain and in the undeclared 1939 war with Japan. See *Komandarmy. Voennyi biograficheskii slovar'*, 393–394.

36. *Stavka* Directive No. 170600, 0235 hours, 6 September 1942, in Zolotarev, "*Stavka* 1942," 388. For Rudenko's tactics, see Hardesty and Grinberg, *Red Phoenix Rising*, 122–123. For Stepanov's biography, see *Komandarmy. Voennyi biograficheskii slovar'*, 391–392.

Chapter 8. The Battle for Central and Southern Stalingrad, 13–26 September 1942

1. Senger und Etterlin, *Die 24. Panzer-Division*, 120.
2. Shtemenko, *Soviet General Staff at War*, 1:116.
3. "Lagenkarten zum KTB. Nr. 5 (Teil III), PzAOK 4, Ia, 21 Oct–24 Nov 1942," PzAOK 4, 28183/12, NAM T-313, roll 359.
4. See Paulus's account of this conference in Goerlitz, *Paulus and Stalingrad*, 159–160.
5. Zhilin, *Stalingradskaia bitva*, 2:545, quoting the order in KTB OKW, Bd. II, Hb. 2, s. 530.
6. Ziemke and Bauer, *Moscow to Stalingrad*, 395; Blau, *German Campaign in Russia*, 168.
7. A. M. Samsonov, *Stalingradskaia bitva* [The Battle of Stalingrad] (Moscow: Nauka, 1983), 176, which exaggerates the German armored total by including all of XIV Panzer Corps and other elements that were not actually engaged in the city.
8. Jentz, *Panzertruppen*, 248; Mark, *Death of the Leaping Horseman*, 157. The daily returns of the assault gun battalions are in Sixth Army's daily reports for the period 1 September–18 November, NAM T-312, roll 1453.
9. Mark, *Death of the Leaping Horseman*, 156–158.
10. Samsonov, *Stalingradskaia bitva*, 173, asserts that German firepower killed 42,754 civilians and wounded tens of thousands more during September–October, but by early November, he claims that only a few thousand inhabitants remained in the city. The Germans impressed many other civilians as forced laborers.
11. Moshchansky and Smolinov, "Oborona Stalingrada," 45.
12. For the slow pace of Kempf's advance, see Mark, *Death of the Leaping Horseman*, 157. Chuikov, *Battle for Stalingrad*, 86–87, describes the bunker change. This passage also misidentifies 76th Infantry Division as part of LI Corps, an error repeated in many other accounts of the campaign.
13. "Boevoi prikaz no. 145 Shtarm 62. 13.9.42. 22.30" [Combat order no. 145, headquarters, 62nd Army, 2230 hours, 13 September 1942], and "Opersvodka no. 150–151" [Operational summary no. 150–151], in *62nd Army Combat Journal*.
14. "Opersvodka no. 151–152" [Operational summary no. 151–152], ibid.; Rokossovsky, *Velikaia pobeda na Volge*, 172; Moshchansky and Smolinov, "Oborona Stalingrada," 46; Chuikov, *Battle for Stalingrad*, 90–91. What the Germans referred to as Red Square was actually named the Square of the Fallen Fighters.
15. Zhilin, *Stalingradskaia bitva*, 555.
16. The 13th Guards Rifle Division was a combination of green recruits and veterans who had recovered from their wounds. Its 9,603 men reportedly had 7,774 rifles, 170 submachine guns, and 46 machine guns when they arrived. See S. I. Samchuk, *Trinadtsataia gvardsaia* [The 13th Guards] (Moscow: Voenizdat, 1971), 97–99.

Chuikov's staff apparently found additional weapons for this division over the next two days; see Isaev, *Stalingrad*, 173. On the division commander, see "Rodimtsev, Aleksandr Il'ich," in *VE*, 7:251.

17. Chuikov, *Battle for Stalingrad*, 95.

18. Mark, *Death of the Leaping Horseman*, 160–170.

19. "Opersvodka no. 153 Shtarm 62" [Operational summary no. 153, headquarters, 62nd Army], in *62nd Army Combat Journal*.

20. Mark, *Death of the Leaping Horseman*, 173. Hoth's panzer army was still responsible for the logistical support of Kempf's corps.

21. Zhilin, *Stalingradskaia bitva*, 562.

22. "Donesenie OO NKVD STF v NKVD SSSP o khode boev v Stalingrad, 16 sentiabria 1942 g." [Report by the OO (Special Department) of the Stalingrad Front's NKVD to the NKVD of the USSR about the course of battles in Stalingrad, 16 September 1942], in *Stalingradskaia epopeia*, 197, 199, citing TsA FSB RF (Central Archives of the Russian Federation's FSB), f. 14, op. 4, d. 326, ll. 220–223. This report is translated in full in David M. Glantz and Jonathan M. House, *Armageddon in Stalingrad: September–November 1942*, vol. 2 of *The Stalingrad Trilogy* (Lawrence: University Press of Kansas, 2009), 131–134.

23. Florian *Freiherr* von und zu Aufsess, "Betr.: Zustand der Divisionen, Armee-Oberkommando 6. Abt. 1A, A.H. Qu., den 14 September 1942, 12:35 Uhr," in *Die Anlagenbänder zu den Kriegstagebüchern der 6. Armee vom 14.09.42 bis 24.11.42*, book 1 (Schwabach, Germany: self-published, 2006), 12.

24. Mark, *Death of the Leaping Horseman*, 181; "Opersvodka No. 154," in *62nd Army Combat Journal*.

25. Mark, *Death of the Leaping Horseman*, 184–186.

26. Chuikov, *Battle for Stalingrad*, 99.

27. Ziemke and Bauer, *Moscow to Stalingrad*, 395.

28. Chuikov, *Battle for Stalingrad*, 103.

29. Quoted in ibid., 100–102.

30. Mark, *Death of the Leaping Horseman*, 189–191.

31. Chuikov, *Battle for Stalingrad*, 84–85.

32. Rokossovsky, *Velikaia pobeda na Volge*, 173–174.

33. Moskalenko, *Na iugo-zapadnom napravlenii*, 336–337.

34. Pavel A. Rotmistrov, *Stal'naia gvardiia* [Steel guards] (Moscow: Voenizdat, 1964), 124–125.

35. Isaev, *Stalingrad*, 184, 192–193, citing TsAMO RF, f. 220, op. 220, d. 72, 1. 36.

36. For details on the defense by XIV Panzer Corps, see Dieckhoff, *3. Infanterie-Division*, 204; Werthen, *Geschichte der 16. Panzer-Division*, 118–120.

37. See the *front* daily report in Zhilin, *Stalingradskaia bitva*, 580–581, and translated in Glantz and House, *Armageddon in Stalingrad*, 175; Moskalenko, *Na iugo-zapadnom napravlenii*, 342–344.

38. Isaev, *Stalingrad*, 205–206, citing TsAMO RF, f. 220, op. 220, d. 72, 1. 85 and f. 38, op. 11360, d. 120, ll. 14, 16, 16.ob.

39. Zhilin, *Stalingradskaia bitva*, 594–595, 610–616. See also "Ia Lagenkarten Nr. 1 zum KTB Nr. 13, Jul–Oct 1942," AOK 6, 23948/1a, NAM T-312, roll 1446.

40. Isaev, *Stalingrad*, 209.

41. "Ia Lagenkarten Nr. 1 zum KTB Nr. 13, Jul–Oct 1942," AOK 6, 23948/1a, NAM T-312, roll 1446. For the declining strength of 76th Infantry Division, see Aufsess, *Die Anlagenbänder zu den Kriegstagebüchern der 6. Armee*, book 1, 12–13, 59–62, 128–130.

42. Ziemke and Bauer, *Moscow to Stalingrad*, 395.

43. "Boevoi prikaz no. 151 Shtarm IuVF 18.9.42 1800" [Combat order no. 151, headquarters, Southwestern Front, 1800 hours, 18 September 1942], in *62nd Army Combat Journal*. See also Zhilin, *Stalingradskaia bitva*, 581.

44. "Boevoe donesenie nos. 122–123, Shtarm 62, 19.9.42," in *62nd Army Combat Journal*.

45. See 24th Panzer Division's Order No. 62 in Mark, *Death of the Leaping Horseman*, 193.

46. N. I. Afanas'ev, *Ot Volgi do Shpree: Boevoi put' 35-i gvardeiskoi strelkovoi Lozovskoi Krasnoznamennoi,ordena Suvorova i Bogdan Khmel'nitskogo divizii* [From the Volga to the Spree: The combat path of 35th Guards Lozovaia, Red Banner, and Orders of Suvorov and Bogdan Khmel'nitsky Rifle Division] (Moscow: Voenizdat, 1982), 77–81.

47. Zhilin, *Stalingradskaia bitva*, 600–601; "Boevoe rasporiazhenie no. 156 Shtarm 62 21.9.42" [Combat instructions no. 156, 62nd Army, 21 September 1942], in *62nd Army Combat Journal*. On 94th Division's fight, see Adelbert Holl, *An Infantryman in Stalingrad: From 24 September 1942 to 2 February 1943*, trans. Jason D. Mark and Neil Page (Sydney, Australia: Leaping Horseman Books, 2005).

48. Because Batiuk was Ukrainian and Rodimtsev was Russian, the latter received greater praise and attention in Soviet accounts of the battle. Promoted to major general, Batiuk continued to command his division, redesignated 79th Guards Rifle, until his death from disease in July 1943.

49. Chuikov, *Battle for Stalingrad*, 140.

50. "Betr.: Zustand der Divisionen, Armee-Oberkommando 6, Abt. 1A, A.H. Qu., den 14 September 1942, 12:35 Uhr," compared to the same report for 26 September, in Aufsess, *Die Anlagenbänder zu den Kriegstagebüchern der 6. Armee*, book 1, 12–13, 59–62.

51. Chuikov, *Battle for Stalingrad*, 132–133.

52. Zhilin, *Stalingradskaia bitva*, 611, 616–617, 622, 627. See also multiple reports in *62nd Army Combat Journal*.

53. Rokossovsky, *Velikaia pobeda na Volge*, 176–177.

54. Chuikov, *Battle for Stalingrad*, 133–134.

55. Fragmentary reports in Sixth Army records indicate that 71st, 295th, and 389th Divisions alone suffered about 1,000 dead, 3,000 wounded, and 100 missing from 14 to 26 September. Soviet estimates of total German casualties were 6,000 dead plus the loss of 170 tanks or assault guns, although many of the latter were repaired. Rokossovsky, *Velikaia pobeda na Volge*, 178.

56. Mark, *Death of the Leaping Horseman*, 205, 208–209; "Betr.: Zustand der Divisionen, Armee-Oberkommando 6, Abt. 1A, A.H. Qu., den 14 September 1942, 12:35 Uhr," compared to the same report for 5 October, in Aufsess, *Die Anlagenbänder zu den Kriegstagebüchern der 6. Armee*, book 1, 12–13, 128–132. Other divisions suffered similarly.

57. Rokossovsky, *Velikaia pobeda na Volge*, 178. For unit strengths of 62nd Army on 25 September, see Isaev, *Stalingrad*, 180, citing TsAMO RF, f. 48, op. 451, d. 41, l. 129.

Chapter 9. The German Assault on the Workers' Villages

1. Mark, *Death of the Leaping Horseman*, 211. See German dispositions and troop movements in "Ia Lagenkarten Nr. 1 zum KTB Nr. 13, Jul–Oct 1942," AOK 6, 23948/1a, NAM T-312, roll 1446; Rokossovsky, *Velikaia pobeda na Volge*, 179. Jäger divisions normally had only two maneuver regiments, hence the attachment of the Croatian unit to the 100th.

2. Mark, *Death of the Leaping Horseman*, 213.

3. "Boevoi prikaz no. 164 Shtarm 62, 25.9.42" [Combat order no. 164, headquarters, 62nd Army, 25 September 1942], in *62nd Army Combat Journal*. See also Chuikov, *Battle for Stalingrad*, 137–138.

4. "Boevoi prikaz no. 166/op, Shtarm 62, 26.9.42" [Combat order no. 166/op, headquarters, 62nd Army, 26 September 1942], in *62nd Army Combat Journal*. See also Chuikov, *Battle for Stalingrad*, 149–150.

5. Quoted in Mark, *Death of the Leaping Horseman*, 218.

6. The third (685th) regiment of 193rd Rifle Division was already committed in the city center. See F. N. Smekhotvorov, "Ispytaniia na stoikost" [An ordeal in determination], in *Pomnit Dnepr-reka . . . : Vospominaniia veteranov 193-i strelkovoi Dneprovskoi ordena Lenina, Kraznoznamennoi, ordena Suvorova i Kutuzova divizii* [Remember the Dnepr River . . . : Recollections of veterans of the Dnepr, Order of Lenin, Red Banner, and Orders of Suvorov and Kutuzov 193rd Rifle Division] (Minsk: Belarus, 1986), 12. See also Chuikov, *Battle for Stalingrad*, 154–155.

7. Mark, *Death of the Leaping Horseman*, 228–234; Moshchansky and Smolinov, "Oborona Stalingrada," 56; Aufsess, "Betr.: Zustand der Divisionen, Armee-Oberkommando 6. Abt. 1A, A.H. Qu., den 14 September 1942, 12:35 Uhr," in *Die Anlagenbänder zu den Kriegstagebüchern der 6. Armee*, book 1, 76; Hans Neidhardt, *Mit Tanne und Eichenlaub: Kriegschronik der 100.Jäger-Division vormals 100.leichte Infanterie-Division.* (Graz-Stuttgart, Germany: Leopold Stocker Verlag, 1981), 212; Chuikov, *Battle for Stalingrad*, 155.

8. Chuikov, *Battle for Stalingrad*, 155–156.

9. Mark, *Death of the Leaping Horseman*, 234.

10. Neidhardt, *Mit Tanne und Eichenlaub*, 212.

11. Isaev, *Stalingrad*, 225–226.

12. Samchuk, *Trinadtsataia gvardsaia*, 125–130.

13. See the relevant directives in V. A. Zolotarev, ed., "General'nyi shtab v gody Velikoi Otechestvennoi voiny: Dokumenty i materially, 1942 god, T. 23 (12-2)" [The General Staff in the Great Patriotic War: Documents and materials, 1942, vol. 23 (12-2)], in *Russki arkhiv: Velikaia Otechestvennaia [voina]* [The Russian archives: The Great Patriotic (War)] (Moscow: Terra, 1999), 334–339; hereafater cited as "General Staff 1942."

14. The newly arrived units were reflected in the *62nd Army Combat Journal* report for 30 September; the casualties are recorded in Isaev, *Stalingrad*, 226, citing TsAMO RF, f. 220, pp. 220, d. 72, l. 85.

15. *62nd Army Combat Journal*, entry for 1800 hours, 1 October 1942.

16. Chuikov, *Battle for Stalingrad*, 160.

17. This description of the fighting in the Orlovka salient is based on Moshchansky and Smolinov, "Oborona Stalingrada," 57–60. The authors assert that the Germans lost 1,200 dead and 50 tanks destroyed or damaged during the first two days of the fighting. See also Zhilin, *Stalingradskaia bitva*, 650, 659–677.

18. Moshchansky and Smolinov, "Oborona Stalingrada," 58.

19. Ibid., 59; Chuikov, *Battle for Stalingrad*, 166.

20. Aufsess, "Betr.: Zustand der Divionen, Armee-Oberkommando 6. Abt. 1A, A.H. Qu., den 5 Oktober 1942," in *Die Anlagenbänder zu den Kriegstagebüchern der 6. Armee*, book 1, 128–132.

21. Mark, *Death of the Leaping Horseman*, 242.

22. Ibid., 246.

23. Holl, *Infantryman in Stalingrad*, 93; Zhilin, *Stalingradskaia bitva*, 659.

24. Mark, *Death of the Leaping Horseman*, 241.

25. Chuikov, *Battle for Stalingrad*, 168–169.

26. Mark, *Death of the Leaping Horseman*, 246.

27. Moshchansky and Smolinov, "Oborona Stalingrada," 55; Chuikov, *Battle for Stalingrad*, 170.

28. Mark, *Death of the Leaping Horseman*, 250.

29. Chuikov, *Battle for Stalingrad*, 171. See also daily report for 4 October in *62nd Army Combat Journal*.

30. Mark, *Death of the Leaping Horseman*, 251–258, as confirmed by the 4 October entry in the *308th Rifle Division's Daily Combat Journal.*

31. For additional details on the deployment of 37th Guards Rifle Division, see N. I. Volostnov, *Na ognennykh rubezhakh* [In firing positions] (Moscow: Voenizdat, 1983), 70–77.

32. Ziemke and Bauer, *Moscow to Stalingrad*, 396, quoting "AOK 6, Ia Kriegstagebuch Nr. 13, 4 Oct 42," in AOK 6 2394811 file.

33. Mark, *Death of the Leaping Horseman*, 258–259.

34. Rokossovsky, *Velikaia pobeda na Volge*, 186.

35. See the daily reports on this fighting in *62nd Army Combat Journal*, as well as Chuikov, *Battle for Stalingrad*, 171.

36. "Boevoe donesenie no. 295, Shtarm 62, 7.10.42" [Combat report no. 295, headquarters, 62nd Army, 7 October 1942], in *62nd Army Combat Journal.* See also the somewhat exaggerated accounts in Moshchansky and Smolinov, "Oborona Stalingrada," 64; Chuikov, *Battle for Stalingrad*, 173–174.

37. Rokossovsky, *Velikaia pobeda na Volge*, 182–183.

38. A. Vasilevsky, "Nezabyvaemye dni" [Unforgettable days], *VIZh* 10 (October 1965): 19.

39. Samsonov, *Stalingradskaia bitva*, 215; Axworthy et al., *Third Axis, Fourth Ally*, 85.

40. Grams, *Die 14. Panzer-Division*, 53. This Soviet attack reminded Eremenko of the Romanian forces' vulnerability to a concerted attack, which led him to propose an offensive that ultimately evolved into the Uranus plan.

41. I. K. Morozov, "Na iuzhnom uchaske fronta" [In the *front's* southern sector],

in *Bitva za Volge* [The battle for the Volga] (Stalingrad: Knizhnoe izdatel'stvo, 1962), 108–109; Zhilin, *Stalingradskaia bitva*, 665–666, 672, 677.

42. Tarrant, *Stalingrad*, 86–87; Jukes, *Hitler's Stalingrad Decisions*, 78.

43. *62nd Army Combat Journal* for 9–10 October 1942. This gave Batiuk's 284th responsibility for defending all of Mamaev Kurgan. For other minor Soviet attacks during the lull, see Zhilin, *Stalingradskaia bitva*, 704, 714, 722, 727, 731, 738.

44. "Ia Lagenkarten Nr. 1 zum KTB Nr. 13, Jul–Oct 1942," AOK 6, 23948/1a, NAM T-312, roll 1446.

45. By mid-October, Romanian Third Army consisted of four corps headquarters with seven infantry and one cavalry division on the front line, plus 7th Infantry and 7th Cavalry Divisions in reserve. In addition, Army Group B held Romanian 1st Armored, 18th Infantry, and 5th Cavalry Divisions in reserve behind Third Army, and OKH controlled the depleted 22nd Panzer Division for the same purpose. "Ia Lagenkarten Nr. 1 zum KTB Nr. 13, Jul–Oct 1942," AOK 6, 23948/1a, NAM T-312, roll 1446; Axworthy et al., *Third Axis, Fourth Ally*, 84–85.

46. Axworthy et al., *Third Axis, Fourth Ally*, 86–87; Goerlitz, *Paulus and Stalingrad*, 195–196.

47. Rokossovsky, *Velikaia pobeda na Volge*, 191; Moshchansky and Smolinov, "Oborona Stalingrada," 63, 65.

48. On 13 October, for example, 14th Panzer had a total of 50 tanks, including 3 Pz. II, 9 Pz. III short-barreled gun, 13 Pz. III long-barreled gun, 3 Pz. IV short, 2 Pz. IV long, and 2 command tanks; 24th Panzer had 33 tanks, including 6 Pz. II, 7 Pz. III short, 13 Pz. III long, 3 Pz. IV short, 2 Pz. IV long, and 2 command tanks; between them, the two assault gun battalions had 31 operational vehicles, including 13 short and 18 long. Aufsess, *Die Anlagenbänder zu den Kriegstagebüchern der 6. Armee*, book 1, 164, 166.

49. Hayward, *Stopped at Stalingrad*, 206, quoting H. Schröter, *Stalingrad: ". . . bis letzten Patrone"* (Lengerich, Germany: Kleins Druck- und Verlagsanstalt, n.d.), 45.

50. *Stavka* Directive No. 170634, 1430 hours, 5 October 1942, in Zolotarev, "*Stavka* 1942," 411.

51. *Stavka* Order No. 0789, 5 October 1942, ibid., 410.

52. *Stavka* Directive Nos. 170640 and 170641, 6 October 1942, and Nos. 994226, 170642, and 170643, 7 October 1942, ibid., 414–417.

53. Report of the Don Front commander no. 0028/op, 2240 hours, 9 October 1942, in Zhilin, *Stalingradskaia bitva*, 549–550.

54. These dispositions are described in Rokossovsky, *Velikaia pobeda na Volge*, 191–193. In addition, the Stalingrad Front officially included eight rifle divisions, seven tank brigades, and one motorized rifle brigade, all in reserve. Most of these units had been decimated in the battle and withdrawn for refitting.

55. Isaev, *Stalingrad*, 235.

56. Hardesty and Grinberg, *Red Phoenix Rising*, 93–104; William Craig, *Enemy at the Gates: The Battle for Stalingrad* (New York: Reader's Digest Press, 1973), 136–137.

Chapter 10. The Struggle for the Factories

1. For the Sixth Army attack order concerning this assault, see Hans J. Wijers, *The Battle for Stalingrad: The Battle for the Factories, 14 October–19 November 1942* (Heerenveen, The Netherlands: self-published, 2003), 11–12.

2. For details of 24th Panzer's plans, see Mark, *Death of the Leaping Horseman*, 269–270.

3. Entry for 14–15 October in *37th Guards Rifle Division Combat Journal*; Wijers, *Battle for Stalingrad*, 14, 32; Volostnov, *Na ognennykh rubezhakh*, 100–104.

4. Mark, *Death of the Leaping Horseman*, 273–278.

5. "Boevoe donesenie no. 198, Shtarm 62, 14.10.42" [Combat report no. 198, headquarters, 62nd Army, 14 October 1942], in *62nd Army Combat Journal*.

6. Ibid.

7. Chuikov, *Battle for Stalingrad*, 181.

8. Ibid., 182. German casualties are derived from "Morgenmeldung, A.O.K. 6, Ia, Datum 15.10.42," in Aufsess, *Die Anlagenbänder zu den Kriegstagebüchern der 6. Armee*, book 1, 172.

9. Chuikov, *Battle for Stalingrad*, 183–184. He failed to convince the *front* that most of his army headquarters should withdraw to the eastern bank to better coordinate fire support.

10. "Boevoe rasporiazhenie no. 205 Shtarm 62 15.10.42 01.00" [Combat instructions no. 205, headquarters, 62nd Army, 0100 hours on 15 October 1942], in *62nd Army Combat Journal*.

11. Werthen, *Geschichte der 16. Panzer-Division*, 114–115. See *62nd Army Combat Journal* for the Soviet perspective.

12. Werthen, *Geschichte der 16. Panzer-Division*, 115.

13. Wijers, *Battle for Stalingrad*, 34–38; Zhilin, *Stalingradskaia bitva*, 755, quoting OKW information bulletins.

14. Isaev, *Stalingrad*, 238–239. For Liudnikov's illustrious career, see I. I. Liudnikov, *Doroga dlinoiu v zhizn'* [The long road in life] (Moscow: Voenizdat, 1969), and the entry for Liudnikov in *Komandarmy. Voennyi biograficheskii slovar'*, 81–82.

15. Mark, *Death of the Leaping Horseman*, 278–281.

16. Zolotarev, "Stavka 1942," 372; Chuikov, *Battle for Stalingrad*, 187.

17. Mark, *Death of the Leaping Horseman*, 281–282; Holl, *Infantryman in Stalingrad*, 51.

18. Mark, *Death of the Leaping Horseman*, 283.

19. Ibid., 284; entry for 17–18 October 1942 in *308th Rifle Division Combat Journal*. See also *138th Rifle Division Combat Journal*; Zhilin, *Stalingradskaia bitva*, 764–766.

20. Werthen, *Geschichte der 16. Panzer-Division*, 115; Chuikov, *Battle for Stalingrad*, 187–188; "Boevoe donesenie no. 201" [Combat report no. 201], in *62nd Army Combat Journal*.

21. Chuikov, *Battle for Stalingrad*, 188; "Morgenmeldung Gen. Kdo. VIII A.K. meldit 04.08 uhr, A.O.K. 6, Ia, Datum: 18.10.42," in Aufsess, *Die Anlagenbänder zu den Kriegstagebüchern der 6. Armee*, book 1, 180.

22. Holl, *Infantryman in Stalingrad*, 57, 109–111; Mark, *Death of the Leaping Horseman*, 287–288.

23. Chuikov, *Battle for Stalingrad*, 189.

24. Quoted in Holl, *Infantryman in Stalingrad*, 116.

25. See "Boevoe donesenie no. 202, Shtarm 62 18.10.42" [Combat report no. 202, headquarters, 62nd Army, 18 October 1942], in *62nd Army Combat Journal*. This portion is quoted directly from 308th Rifle Division's daily report (pp. 328, 335).

26. Chuikov, *Battle for Stalingrad*, 190. See the full order, "Chastnyi boevoi prikaz no. 214 Shtarm 62 18.10.42 2000" [Individual combat order no. 214, headquarters, 62nd Army, 2000 hours, 18 October 1942], in *62nd Army Combat Journal*.

27. Isaev, *Stalingrad*, 241; Chuikov, *Battle for Stalingrad*, 190. See also "Boevoe donesenie no. 215, Shtarm 62 18.10.42" [Combat report no. 215, headquarters, 62nd Army, 2000 hours 18 October 1942], in *62nd Army Combat Journal*.

28. Ziemke and Bauer, *Moscow to Stalingrad*, 462, 460.

29. See the entry for 19 October 1942 in *62nd Army Combat Journal*; Mark, *Death of the Leaping Horseman*, 296–298. For a description of the Soviet counterattack, see B. S. Venkov and P. P. Dudinov, *Gvardeiskaia doblest': Boevoi put' 70-i gvardeiskoi strelkovoi glukhovskoi ordena Lenina, dvazhdy krasnoznamennoi, ordena Suvorova, Kutuzova i Bogdana Khmel'nitskogo divizii* [Guards valor: The combat path of 70th Guards Glukhov, Order of Lenin and Order of Suvorov, Kutuzov, and Bogdan Khmel'nitsky Rifle Division] (Moscow: Voenizdat, 1979), 40–42.

30. "Morgenmeldung LI. A.K. meldet 06.35 Uhr, A.O.K. 6, Ia, Datum 20.10.42," in Aufsess, *Die Anlagenbänder zu den Kriegstagebüchern der 6. Armee*, book 1, 190.

31. Mark, *Death of the Leaping Horseman*, 301–302; Holl, *Infantryman in Stalingrad*, 102.

32. Mark, *Death of the Leaping Horseman*, 301–304; "Boevoe donesenie no. 206, Shtarm 62 21.10.42" [Combat report no. 206, headquarters, 62nd Army, 2000 hours, 18 October 1942], in *62nd Army Combat Journal*.

33. "Boevoe donesenie no. 206," in *62nd Army Combat Journal*.

34. Zhilin, *Stalingradskaia bitva*, 786.

35. Rokossovsky, *Velikaia pobeda na Volge*, 197–198.

36. Moskalenko, *Na iugo-zapadnom napravlenii*, 351. The nickname of 4th Tank Army is traced in Pavel Ivanovich Batov, *V pokhodakh i boiakh* [In marches and battles] (Moscow: Golos, 2000), 153.

37. *Stavka* Directive No. 994273, 0250 hours, 22 October 1942, in Zolotarev, "*Stavka* 1942," 440–441. The order is reproduced in translation in Glantz and House, *Armageddon in Stalingrad*, 442.

38. *Stavka* Directive Nos. 170668 (0523 hours, 15 October 1942) and 170669 (0530 hours, 15 October 1942), in Zolotarev, "*Stavka* 1942," 434–435.

39. Ibid., 553; Rokossovsky, *Soldatskii dolg*, 137–138. See also A. S. Zhadov, *Chetyre goda voyny* [Four years of war] (Moscow: Voenizdat, 1978), 54–57.

40. *Stavka* Directive No. 170670, 0300 hours, 16 October 1942, in Zolotarev, "*Stavka* 1942," 436.

41. Dieckhoff, *3. Infanterie-Division*, 206.

42. Quoted in V. K. Vinogradov et al., *Stalingradskaia epopeia, Materialy NKVD*

USSR, based on working notes of the 2nd Special Section of the NKVD in the Directorate of OO's, 251–252.

43. On LI Corps' Order No. 67, see Mark, *Death of the Leaping Horseman*, 239; Holl, *Infantryman in Stalingrad*, 87.

44. "Meldung Über Verpflegungs—und Gefechtsstärken der Division, Armee-Oberkommando 6, Ia, Nr. 4150/42 geh., A. H. Qu., 24. Oktober 1942," in Aufsess, *Die Anlagenbänder zu den Kriegstagebüchern der 6. Armee*, book 1, 201–205.

45. Ibid.

46. Quoted in Wijers, *Battle for Stalingrad*, 80.

47. "Boevoe donesenie no. 208, Shtarm 62 23.10.42" [Combat report no. 208, headquarters, 62nd Army, 23 October 1942], in *62nd Army Combat Journal*.

48. A. V. Morozov, *39-ia Barvenkovskaia: Boevoi put' 39-i gvardeiskoi strelkovoi Barvenkovskoi ordena Lenina, dvazhdy Krasnoznamennoi,, ordenov Suvorov i Bogdana Khmel'nitskogo II stepeni divizii* [The 39th Barvenkovo: The combat path of 39th Guards Rifle Barvenkovo, Order of Lenin, twice Red Banner, and Orders of Suvorov and Bogdan Khmel'nitsky second degree division] (Moscow: Voenizdat, 1981), 15–17; "Boevoe donesenie no. 208," in *62nd Army Combat Journal*.

49. Wijers, *Battle for Stalingrad*, 108.

50. Ibid., 308–309; "Boevoe donesenie no. 208," in *62nd Army Combat Journal*. See also daily entries in *138th Rifle Division Combat Journal*.

51. Zhilin, *Stalingradskaia bitva*, 790–791; "Boevoe donesenie no. 208," in *62nd Army Combat Journal*.

52. "Boevoe donesenie no. 209, Shtarm 62 24.10.42" [Combat report no. 209, headquarters, 62nd Army, 24 October 1942], in *62nd Army Combat Journal*; Zhilin, *Stalingradskaia bitva*, 799, quoting OKW informational bulletin.

53. "Boevoe donesenie no. 209," in *62nd Army Combat Journal*; *138th Rifle Division Combat Journal*.

54. "Boevoe donesenie no. 209," in *62nd Army Combat Journal*.

55. "Frontfahrt des Oberbefehlshavers am 24.10.42, A.O.K. 6, Ia, Datum: 24.10.42," in Aufsess, *Die Anlagenbänder zu den Kriegstagebüchern der 6. Armee*, book 1, 200.

56. "Tagesmeldung, Armee—Oberkommando 6. Abt. Ia, A. H. Qu., 24 Oktober 1942," ibid., 210.

57. Chuikov, *Battle for Stalingrad*, 193.

58. Entry for 25 October in *62nd Army Combat Journal*.

59. Werthen, *Geschichte der 16. Panzer-Division*, 115.

60. Chuikov, *Battle for Stalingrad*, 195; "Boevoe donesenie no. 212, Shtarm 62 27.10.42" [Combat report no. 212, headquarters, 62nd Army, 27 October 1942], in *62nd Army Combat Journal*.

61. Chuikov, *Battle for Stalingrad*, 196. According to Isaev, *Stalingrad*, 244, 45th Rifle Division numbered 6,358 men on 5 November.

62. Chuikov, *Battle for Stalingrad*, 197.

63. Zhilin, *Stalingradskaia Bitva*, 819–820; "Boevoe donesenie no. 213, Shtarm 62 28.10.42" [Combat report no. 213, headquarters, 62nd Army, 28 October 1942], in *62nd Army Combat Journal*.

64. The casualty figures are from the daily morning reports of VIII and LI Army

Corps for 28–30 October, reproduced in Aufsess, *Die Anlagenbänder zu den Kriegstagebüchern der 6. Armee*, book 1, 212, 229, 232.

65. Mark, *Death of the Leaping Horseman*, 333–334.

66. Zhilin, *Stalingradskaia bitva*, 823–842; Werthen, *Geschichte der 16. Panzer-Division*, 115–117.

67. Report No. 3864 by commander, Stalingrad Front, to Deputy Supreme Commander [Zhukov], 1800 hours, 17 October 1942, and *Stavka* Directive No. 170676, 2030 hours, 19 October 1942, in Zolotarev, "*Stavka* 1942," 570–571, 438–439. See Fourth Panzer Army situation map for 24 October in "Lagenkarten zum KTB, Nr. 5 (Teil III), PzAK 4, Ia, 21 Oct–24 Nov 1942," PzAOK 4, 28/183/42, NAM T-313, roll 359.

68. Zhilin, *Stalingradskaia bitva*, 801–827.

Chapter 11. The Final German Advances

1. Jukes, *Hitler's Stalingrad Decisions*, 43–60; Halder, *War Diaries*, 664. On Maikop oil, see Hayward, *Stopped at Stalingrad*, 159–160.

2. Ziemke and Bauer, *Moscow to Stalingrad*, 375.

3. Seymour Friedin and William Richardson, eds., *The Fatal Decisions* (New York: William Sloane Associates, 1956), 135–136; Jukes, *Hitler's Stalingrad Decisions*, 63–67.

4. Halder, *War Diaries*, 668–669, 671.

5. Boog et al., *Germany and the Second World War*, VI:1035.

6. Grechko, *Bitva za Kavkaz*, 116–117; Tieke, *Caucasus and the Oil*, 153–154; "Lagenkarten PzAOK I, Ia, 1–30 Sep 1942," PzAOK I, 24906/15, NAM T-313, roll 36.

7. Grechko, *Bitva za Kavkaz*, 117; Tieke, *Caucasus and the Oil*, 155–156; Kolomiets and Moshchansky, "Oborona Kavkaz," 22–24. See also the candid report from Beria and Tiulenev to Stalin, sent at 2325 hours on 9 September, in Shapovalov, *Bitva za Kavkaz v dokumentakh*, 215–219.

8. Tieke, *Caucasus and the Oil*, 157; Kolomiets and Moshchansky, "Oborona Kavkaz," 22–23.

9. Tieke, *Caucasus and the Oil*, 157–162; Kolomiets and Moshchansky, "Oborona Kavkaz," 24–25.

10. Mackensen, *Vom Bug zum Kaukasus*, 96–100; Ziemke and Bauer, *Moscow to Stalingrad*, 379; Kolomiets and Moshchansky, "Oborona Kavkaz," 26. The Brandenburger incident is recounted in Haupt, *Army Group South*, 197–198.

11. Kolomiets and Moshchansky, "Oborona Kavkaz," 26–27.

12. Tieke, *Caucasus and the Oil*, 165; Kolomiets and Moshchansky, "Oborona Kavkaz," 26. For a description of the Soviet defenses at El'khotovo, see Grechko, *Bitva za Kavkaz*, 121.

13. Ziemke and Bauer, *Moscow to Stalingrad*, 379, 453; Tieke, *Caucasus and the Oil*, 165–185; Kolomiets and Moshchansky, "Oborona Kavkaz," 28–29.

14. *Stavka* Directive No. 170628, 0230 hours, 29 September 1942, in Zolotarev, "*Stavka* 1942," 404–405.

15. Tieke, *Caucasus and the Oil*, 200–204; Grechko, *Bitva za Kavkaz*, 180.

16. Grechko, *Bitva za Kavkaz*, 180–183.

17. Tieke, *Caucasus and the Oil*, 204–205.

18. *Stavka* Directive No. 170660, 0510 hours, 15 October 1942, in Zolotarev, "*Stavka 1942*," 434; Grechko, *Bitva za Kavkaz*, 184.

19. Grechko, *Bitva za Kavkaz*, 186–188.

20. Ibid., 190–191; Tieke, *Caucasus and the Oil*, 192, 207–208.

21. Tieke, *Caucasus and the Oil*, 221. For German dispositions prior to the offensive, see "Lagenkarten PzAOK I, Ia, 1–31 Oct 1942," PzAOK I, 24906/16, NAM T-313, roll 36. Jentz, *Panzertruppen*, 251, places 13th Panzer Division's strength at 130 tanks on 20 October.

22. Grechko, *Bitva za Kavkaz*, 196–199; Tieke, *Caucasus and the Oil*, 145–148. Kirichenko's report, dated 5 November, is included in Shapovalov, *Bitva za Kavkaz v dokumentakh*, 263–266.

23. Grechko, *Bitva za Kavkaz*, 202–203; Tieke, *Caucasus and the Oil*, 221–222.

24. Grechko, *Bitva za Kavkaz*, 204.

25. Tieke, *Caucasus and the Oil*, 222–225; Grechko, *Bitva za Kavkaz*, 205. Tiulenev's Order No. 4405, dated 30 October 1942, to Maslennikov regarding the defense of the Urukh River is in Zolotarev, "*Stavka 1942*," 558.

26. Grechko, *Bitva za Kavkaz*, 205–208; Tieke, *Caucasus and the Oil*, 224–231.

27. Tiulenev's report to the *Stavka*, 3 November 1942, in Shapovalov, *Bitva za Kavkaz v dokumentakh*, 260–263; Grechko, *Bitva za Kavkaz*, 208–209; Tieke, *Caucasus and the Oil*, 231–233.

28. Grechko, *Bitva za Kavkaz*, 209–210.

29. Ibid., 210–211; Tieke, *Caucasus and the Oil*, 235–237.

30. Tieke, *Caucasus and the Oil*, 237–239; Kolomiets and Moshchansky, "Oborona Kavkaz," 64.

31. Kolomiets and Moshchansky, "Oborona Kavkaz," 65–66; Grechko, *Bitva za Kavkaz*, 215–216; Tieke, *Caucasus and the Oil*, 239–242.

32. *Stavka* Directive No. 170692, 20 November 1942, in Zolotarev, "*Stavka 1942*," 450–451.

33. After joining the Red Army in 1919, Antonov (1896–1962) served as a brigade chief of staff during the Civil War. A product of the Frunze Academy (1931) and General Staff Academy (1937), he served as chief of staff, in succession, of the Kiev Special Military District, the Southern Front, the North Caucasus Front, and the Black Sea Group of Forces before becoming Tiulenev's chief of staff. M. M. Kozlov, ed., *Velikaia Otechestvennaia voina 1941–1945: Entsiklopediia* (The Great Patriotic War, 1941–1945: An encyclopedia] (Moscow: Sovetskaia entsiklopediia, 1985), 59.

34. "Personeller Fehlbestand der Infanterie Divisionen (Stand 01.11.42), Armee—Oberkommando 6, Ia Nr. 4534/42 geh., A.H.Qu., 12. November 1942," in Aufsess, *Die Anlagenbänder zu den Kriegstagebüchern der 6. Armee*, book 1, 271.

35. See *62nd Army Combat Journal* entries for 1–2 November 1942.

36. Ziemke and Bauer, *Moscow to Stalingrad*, 463–464, quoting "AOK 6, Ia Kriegstagebuch Nr. 14, 3 Nov 42," AOK 6 33224/2 file. For a discussion of the German planning meetings, see Jason D. Mark, *Island of Fire: The Battle for the Barrikady Gun Factory in Stalingrad, November 1942–February 1943* (Sydney, Australia: Leaping Horseman Books, 2006), 14, 25–49.

37. Mark, *Death of the Leaping Horseman*, 316–335.

38. Ibid., 342; Mark, *Island of Fire*, 56–61; Ziemke and Bauer, *Moscow to Stalingrad*, 465, quoting "AOK 6, Ia Kriegstagebuch Nr. 14, 8–10 Nov 42," AOK 6 33224/2 file.

39. "Chastnyi boevoi prikaz no. 218 KP Shtarma 62 1.11.42 13.35" [Separate combat order no. 218, CP, headquarters, 62nd Army, 1 November 1942]; "Boevoe rasporiazhenie no. 227, Shtarm 62 1.11.42" [Combat instructions no. 227, headquarters, 62nd Army, 1 November 1942], in *62nd Army Combat Journal*.

40. Zhilin, *Stalingradskaia bitva*, 832–834.

41. "Morgenmeldung LI A.K. meldet 06.00 Uhr, A.O.K. 6, Ia, Datum 11.11.42," and "Tagesmeldung XIV A.K. meldet 20.30 Uhr, A.O.K. 6, Ia, Datum 14.11.42," in Aufsess, *Die Anlagenbänder zu den Kriegstagebüchern der 6. Armee*, book 1, 257, 275.

42. "Spravka o Gruppirovke I Deistviiakh protivnika pered frontom 62 Armii k ishkody 4.11.42g" [Information about the grouping and actions of the enemy in front of 62nd Army], in *62nd Army Combat Journal*.

43. Chuikov, *Battle for Stalingrad*, 206–207.

44. "Boevoe donesenie no. 224, Shtarm 62 8.11.42" [Combat report no. 224, headquarters, 62nd Army, 8 November 1942], in *62nd Army Combat Journal*.

45. Mark, *Death of the Leaping Horseman*, 353–354. By the end of 10 November, *Kampfgruppe* Scheele had only seven functioning tanks and as many self-propelled antitank guns.

46. Wijers, *Battle for Stalingrad*, 160–162. Strength figures are based on "Meldungen uber Verpflegungs—und Gefechtsstarken der Divisionen, Armee-Oberkommando 6, Ia, Nr. 4548/42 geh, A.H. Qu., 24 Oktober 1942, 08.30, 13 November 42," in Aufsess, *Die Anlagenbänder zu den Kriegstagebüchern der 6. Armee*, book 1, 201–202, 268–269.

47. Wijers, *Battle for Stalingrad*, 139, 141, 150; Mark, *Death of the Leaping Horseman*, 356–359.

48. Mark, *Island of Fire*, 98–99, 101–148; Mark, *Death of the Leaping Horseman*, 356–362; "Boevoe donesenie no. 227, Shtarm 62 11.11.42" [Combat report no. 227, headquarters, 62nd Army, 11 November 1942], in *62nd Army Combat Journal*; entry for 11 November 1942 in *138th Rifle Division Combat Journal*; Zhilin, *Stalingradskaia bitva*, 870; Wijers, *Battle for Stalingrad*, 168–172, which discusses the struggle for the Commissar's House and Pharmacy as well as the failure of 179th Engineers.

49. "Morgenmeldung LI A.K. meldet 06.45 Uhr, A.O.K. 6, Ia, Datum 12.11.42," in Aufsess, *Die Anlagenbänder zu den Kriegstagebüchern der 6. Armee*, book 1, 266.

50. Ziemke and Bauer, *Moscow to Stalingrad*, 467.

51. Entry for 11 November 1942 in *138th Rifle Division Combat Journal*.

52. "Boevoe donesenie nos. 227 and 228," in *62nd Army Combat Journal*.

53. Mark, *Island of Fire*, 159–160.

54. Wijers, *Battle for Stalingrad*, 171.

55. Entry for 13 November 1942 in *138th Rifle Division Combat Journal*; "Boevoe donesenie no. 229, Shtarm 62 13.11.42" [Combat report no. 229, headquarters, 62nd Army, 13 November 1942], in *62nd Army Combat Journal*.

56. Entry for 13 November in *138th Rifle Division Combat Journal*. The 47,000

strength figure is from Rokossovsky, *Velikaia pobeda na Volga*, 201. However, Liud-nikov reported only 123 riflemen in 344th Regiment, 31 in 650th Regiment, and a few hundred in the other two regiments under his command. The estimate of 8,000 men fighting on the Volga's right bank is based on 62nd Army's overall strength and reports in the combat journals of most of the army's subordinate divisions and brigades fight-ing in Stalingrad.

57. Zhilin, *Stalingradskaia bitva*, 879, citing TsAMO RF, f. 500, op. 12462, d. 89, ll. 392–394.

58. Wijers, *Battle for Stalingrad*, 172; entry for 14 November 1942 in *138th Rifle Division Combat Journal*.

59. Ziemke and Bauer, *Moscow to Stalingrad*, 468; entry for 15 November 1942 in *138th Rifle Division Combat Journal*; Zhilin, *Stalingradskaia bitva*, 884, quoting the OKW informational bulletin for 15 November.

60. Chuikov, *Battle for Stalingrad*, 216–217. But see "Boevoe donesenie no. 232, Shtarm 62 16.11.42" [Combat report no. 232, headquarters, 62nd Army, 16 Novem-ber 1942], in *62nd Army Combat Journal*; Zhilin, *Stalingradskaia bitva*, 890–891.

61. Mark, *Island of Fire*, 220–222; entry for 17 November 1942 in *138th Rifle Division Combat Journal*.

62. Mark, *Island of Fire*, 216.

63. Holl, *Infantryman in Stalingrad*, 144–145; Werthen, *Geschichte der 16. Pan-zer-Division*, 119.

64. Mark, *Island of Fire*, 228–232; entry for 18 November 1942 in *138th Rifle Division Combat Journal*.

65. Zhilin, *Stalingradskaia bitva*, 892, quoting "Ia, AOK 6, No. 4640/42," in *Kriegstagebuch OKW*, Bd. 2, hb. 2.

66. "Betr.: Zustand der Divisionen, Armee-Oberkommando 6. Abt. 1a, A.H. Qu., 14 September 1942, 12.35 Uhr," and "Betr.: Zustand der Divisionen, Armee-Oberkommando 6. Abt. 1a, A.H. Qu., 16. November 1942, 12.00 Uhr," in Aufsess, *Die Anlagenbänder zu den Kriegstagebüchern der 6. Armee*, book 1, 12–14, 284–290.

67. Krivosheev, *Soviet Casualties and Combat Losses*, 122–125, 184–187. For a detailed discussion of these estimates, see Glantz and House, *Armageddon in Stalin-grad*, 714–718.

Chapter 12. The Genesis of Operation Uranus

1. On the second-front debate in 1942, see Erickson, *Road to Stalingrad*, 394–402.

2. Zhukov, *Reminiscences and Reflections*, 2:94.

3. Eremenko, *Stalingrad: Zapiski komanduuishcevo frontom*, 325–326.

4. For Stalin's complete calender, see A. A. Chernobaev, ed., *Na prieme u Stalina. Tetradi (zhurnaly) zapisei lits, priniatykh I. V. Stalinym (1924–1953gg.). Spravochnik* [Received by Stalin. The notebooks (journals) of entries of those per-sons admitted by I. V. Stalin (1924–1953)] (Moscow: Novyi khronograf, 2008), 379. A truncated version appears in Geoffrey Roberts, *Stalin's Wars: From World War to Cold War, 1939–1953* (New Haven, CT: Yale University Press, 2006), 149, citing "Posetiteli Kremlevskogo Kabineta I. V. Stalina," *Istoricheskii Archiv* 2 (1996): 35–38.

5. Shtemenko, *Soviet General Staff at War*, 121; S. Mikhalev, "O razrabotke zamysla i planirovanii kontrnastupleniia pod Stalingradom" [About the concept and planning of the counteroffensive at Stalingrad], *Voennaia mysl'* [Military thought] 8 (August 1992): 1.

6. For a more detailed discussion, see appendix 2, "Soviet Strategic Planning and the Genesis of Plan Uranus," in David M. Glantz, *Companion to Endgame at Stalingrad* (Lawrence: University Press of Kansas, 2014), 82–104.

7. Zolotarev, "*Stavka* 1942," 440–441, citing TsAMO, f. 148a, op. 3763, d. 1071, l. 240. See chapter 5 for details of the Soviet command reorganization and counterattacks.

8. Message quoted in A. I. Eremenko, *Stalingrad: Uchastnikam Velikoi bitvy pod Stalingradom posviashchaetsia* [Stalingrad: A participant in the great battle for Stalingrad explains] (Moscow: Khranitel', 2006), 352–353.

9. "Direktiva Stavki VGK No. 170644 komanduiushchemu Donskim frontom T. Rokossovskomu" [*Stavka* VGK Directive No. 170644 to the commander of the Don Front, Comrade Rokossovsky], in Zhilin, *Stalingradskaia bitva*, 1:694, archival citation TsAMO RF, f.48a, op. 1640, d. 27, ll. 246–247.

10. "Doklad komanduiushchego voiskami Stalingradskogo fronta No. 2889 Verkhovnomu Glavnokomanduiushchemu o plane operatsii po ob'edineniiu s voiskami, oboroniaiushchimisia v Stalingrada" [Report of the commander of the forces of the Stalingrad Front No. 2889 to the Supreme High Commander on a plan of operations for uniting with the forces defending in Stalingrad], in Zhilin, *Stalingradskaia bitva*, 1:707–709, archival citation TsAMO RF, f. 48a, op. 1161, d. 6, ll. 259–264; telegram, copy no. 3. The text is reproduced, in translation, in Glantz, *Companion to Endgame at Stalingrad*, 88–91.

11. Rokossovsky's report is reproduced in Zolotarev, "*Stavka* 1942," 549–550, archival citation TsAMO RF, f. 48a, op. 1159, d. 2, ll. 339–345; telegram, copy no. 2.

12. Zolotarev, "*Stavka* 1942," 440–441, archival citation TsAMO RF, f. 48a, op. 1159, d. 107, l. 240. Golikov succeeded Vatutin at deputy commander of the Voronezh Front. See also Vasilevsky, *Delo vsei zhizni*, 219.

13. Zolotarev, "General Staff 1942," 379, archival citation TsAMO RF, f. 48a, op. 3408, d. 99, ll. 280, 279.

14. Zolotarev, "*Stavka* 1942," 442, archival citation TsAMO RF, f. 148a, op. 3763, d. 111, ll. 282–283.

15. Zolotarev, "General Staff 1942," 380–381, archival citation TsAMO RF, f. 48a, op. 3408, d. 99, ll. 282–283.

16. Zolotarev, "*Stavka* 1942," 443–444, archival citation TsAMO RF, f. 148, op. 3408, d. 113, l. 297.

17. Ibid., 445–446, archival citation TsAMO RF, f. 148a, op. 3763, d. 126, ll. 289–190; Zolotarev, "General Staff 1942," 380–381, archival citation TsAMO RF, f. 48a, op. 3408, d.113, l. 297.

18. Zolotarev, "*Stavka* 1942," 446–447, archival citation TsAMO RF, f. 148a, op. 3763, d. 124, ll. 291–292.

19. Ibid., 447–448, archival citation TsAMO RF, f. 48a, op. 3408, d. 72, ll. 358–360.

20. Ibid., 393, archival citation TsAMO RF, f. 48a, op. 3408, d. 114, l. 50.

21. Mikhalev, "O razrabotke zamysla," 5, citing TsAMO, f. 232, op. 590, d. 73. Neither Zhukov's memoirs nor his published wartime calendar mention the 6 November meeting, but see the entry on Stalin's meeting with Zhukov and others that day in Chernobaev, *Na prieme u Stalina*, 389.

22. Mikhalev, "O razrabotke zamysla," 5, citing TsAMO, f. 220, op. 451, d. 3, ll. 327–331, and d. 92 (map); Zhukov, *Reminiscences and Reflections*, 404–405; Zolotarev, "Stavka 1942," 448–449, archival citation TsAMO RF, f. 148a, op. 3763, d. 126, l. 193.

23. Zolotarev, "Stavka 1942," 449–450, archival citation TsAMO RF, f. 148a, op. 3763, d. 126, l. 195.

24. Zhukov, *Reminiscences and Reflections*, 2:427; this agrees with Stalin's daily schedule.

25. Zolotarev, "Stavka 1942," 392–394, 396.

26. Ibid., 450, archival citation TsAMÓ RF, f. 48a, op. 3408, d. 72, l. 360.

27. Louis C. Rotundo, ed., *Battle for Stalingrad: The 1943 Soviet General Staff Study* (Washington, DC: Pergamon-Brassey's International Defense Publishers, 1989), 15. Marshal Rokossovsky describes a 4 November planning conference of senior commanders in *Soldatskii dolg*, 195–196.

28. Vasilevsky, *Delo vsei zhizni*, 224–225. A more detailed account of this incident, based on a 1967 interview with Vasilevsky, appears in Isaev, *Stalingrad*, 285–296.

29. See Samsonov, *Stalingradskaia bitva*, 569, for the entire order of battle as of 19–20 November 1942.

30. Ibid.

31. Batov's memoirs, *V podkhodakh i boiakh*, serve as a history of 65th Army.

32. V. A. Zolotarev, ed., *Velikaia Otechestvennaia: Deistvuiushchaia armiia 1941–1945 gg* [The Great Patriotic (War): The operating army, 1941–1945] (Moscow: Animi Fortitudo Kuchkovo pole, 2005), 584.

33. For the history of 13th Tank Corps, see V. F. Tolubko and N. I. Baryshev, *Na iuzhnom flange: Boevoi put' 4-go gvardeiskogo mekhanizirovanogo korpusa (1942–1945 gg.)* [On the southern flank: The combat path of 4th Guards Mechanized Corps (1942–1945)] (Moscow: Nauka, 1973). The corps was redesignated 4th Guards Mechanized Corps on 9 January 1943.

34. For a history of 4th Mechanized Corps, see A. M. Samsonov, *Ot Volgi do Baltiki: Ocherk istorii 3-go Gvardeiskogo mekhanizirovannogo korpusa 1942–1945 gg* [From the Volga to the Baltic: A study of the history of 3rd Guards Mechanized Corps, 1942–1945] (Moscow: Nauka, 1963). For its brilliant defense against LVI Panzer Corps around Verkhne-Kumskii, this formation was redesigned 3rd Guards Mechanized Corps.

35. For a history of 64th Army, see D. A. Dragunsky et al., eds., *Ot Volgi do Pragi* [From the Volga to Prague] (Moscow: Voenizdat, 1966). The 64th Army was redesignated 7th Guards Army on 1 May 1943.

36. David M. Glantz, *Zhukov's Greatest Defeat: The Red Army's Epic Disaster in Operation Mars, 1942* (Lawrence: University Press of Kansas, 2005), 20–22. Additional planning documents for Operation Mars are included in the Russian-

language edition, *Krupneishee porazhenie Zhukova. Katastrofa Krasnoi Armii v operatsii "Mars" 1942 g.* (Moscow: Astrel', 2006), 404–602.

37. V. A. Zolotarev, ed., *Velikaia Otechestvennaia voina 1941–1945: Voenno-istoricheskie ocherki v chetyrekh knigagh, kniga 2: Perelom* [The Great Patriotic War, 1941–1945: A military-historical survey in four books, book 2: The turning point] (Moscow: Nauka, 1998), 38. See also David M. Glantz, *Forgotten Battles of the German-Soviet War, 1941–1945*, vol. 4, *The Winter Campaign (19 November 1942–21 March 1943)* (Carlisle, PA: self-published, 1999), 67–82.

38. Glantz, *Zhukov's Greatest Defeat*, 22–30. The assault on the city of Rzhev was code-named Venus; see Zolotarev, "*Stavka 1942*," 394, 543–544.

39. The various directives issued by the *Stavka* and the People's Commissariat of Defense are found in Zolotarev, "*Stavka 1942*." The specific directives requiring *fronts* to send forces to the *Stavka* Reserve and to activate the new reserve armies were dated 0745, 31 August 1942, and are in ibid., 380–383. The directives withdrawing 3rd Tank and 5th Tank Armies, No. 994176, 30 August 1942, and No. 170606, 9 September 1942, are in ibid., 376–389.

40. *Stavka* Directive No. 170627, ibid., 403. See appendix 2A in Glantz, *Companion to Endgame at Stalingrad*, 82–83, for detailed orders issued in late September.

41. *Stavka* Directive No. 170647, in Zolotarev, "*Stavka 1942*," 423; *Stavka* Directive Nos. 990157 and 990154, in Zolotarev, "General Staff 1942," 358–360.

42. *Stavka* Directive No. 994273, in Zolotarev, "*Stavka 1942*," 440–441; *Stavka* Directive No. 990373, in Zolotarev, "General Staff 1942," 379. See appendix 2B in Glantz, *Companion to Endgame at Stalingrad*, 83–88, for directives issued during the second period of planning in October.

43. See appendix 2G in Glantz, *Companion to Endgame at Stalingrad*, 97–100, for the orders issued during the third period of planning in early November.

44. M. E. Morozov, ed., *Velikaia Otechestvennaia voina 1941–1945 gg. Kampanii i strategicheskie operatsii v tsifrakh v 2 tomakh. Tom 1* [The Great Patriotic War, 1941–1945. Campaigns and strategic operations in two volumes. Vol. 1] (Moscow: Ob'edinnaia redaktsiia MVD Rossii, 2010), 481.

45. Erickson, *Road to Stalingrad*, 448–449; Zhukov, *Reminiscences and Reflections*, 2:116; Rotundo, *Battle for Stalingrad*, 15; Tarrant, *Stalingrad*, 96; Rokossovsky, *Velikaia pobeda na Volge*, 226–227.

46. Erickson, *Road to Stalingrad*, 448–452; Zhukov, *Reminiscences and Reflections*, 2:115.

47. Erickson, *Road to Stalingrad*, 449; Zhukov, *Reminiscences and Reflections*, 2:116; Rotundo, *Battle for Stalingrad*, 15.

48. Rokossovsky, *Soldatskii dolg*, 138–140.

49. See G. A. Kumanov and L. M. Chuzavkov, "Sovetskii soinz i lend-liz 1941–1945 gg.," in M. N. Supron, ed., *Lend-liz i Russiia* [Lend-Lease and Russia] (Archangel'sk: OAO IPP Pravda Severa, 2006), 92–123. See also Hill, *Great Patriotic War of the Soviet Union*, 163–192.

50. For additional details on Lend-Lease, see V. A. Zolotarev, ed., *Velikaia Ote-chestvennaia voina 1941–1945: Voenno-istoricheskie ocherki v chetyrekh knigagh, kniga 4: Narod i voina* [The Great Patriotic War, 1941–1945: A military-

historical survey in four books, book 4: The people and the war] (Moscow: Nauka, 1999), 205–217.

51. See, for example, the complete planning documents for 5th Tank Army and its subordinate headquarters in I. M. Kravchenko, *Nastupatel'naia operatsiia 5-i Tankovoi Armii v kontrnastuplenii pod Stalingradom (19–25 noiabria 1942 g.)* [The offensive operation of 5th Tank Army in the counteroffensive at Stalingrad (19–25 November 1942)] (Moscow: Voroshilov Academy of the General Staff, 1978), classified secret.

52. Rokossovsky, *Velikaia pobeda na Volge*, 245–246.

53. Ibid., 228–232; Chistiakov, *Po prikazu Rodiny*, 32–33.

54. Rokossovsky, *Velikaia pobeda na Volge*, 237.

55. Ibid., 243–244. For 65th Army's planning, see Batov, *V pokhodakh i boiakh*, 165–176. I. A. Samchuk, P. G. Skachko, Iu. N. Babikov, and I. L. Gnedoi, *Ot Volgi do El'by i Pragi (Kratkii ocherk o boevom puti 5-i Gvardeskoi Armii)* [From the Volga to the Elbe and Prague (A short study of the combat path of 5th Guards Army)] (Moscow: Voenizdat, 1970), 32–33, describes 24th Army's limited missions.

Chapter 13. The Advent of Uranus

1. Quoted in Friedin and Richardson, *Fatal Decisions*, 139.

2. Ibid., 137–149.

3. Boog et al., *Germany and the Second World War*, VI:1084–1086.

4. Jukes, *Hitler's Stalingrad Decisions*, 83–88; Friedin and Richardson, *Fatal Decisions*, 142–143; Blau, *German Campaign in Russia*, 170–171; Boog et al., *Germany and the Second World War*, VI:1114–1118.

5. Blau, *German Campaign in Russia*, 168, map 17.

6. Quoted in Vasily S. Grossman, *A Writer at War: Vasily Grossman with the Red Army, 1941–1945*, ed. and trans. Anthony Beevor and Luba Vinogradova (New York: Pantheon Books, 2005), 162. Grossman's real name was Iosif Solomonovich Grossman, but he used the pseudonym Vasili Semenovich when writing for the army newspaper *Krasnaia Zvezda* (Red Star).

7. For a discussion of Axis relations, see Richard L. Dinardo, *Germany and the Axis Powers: From Coalition to Collapse* (Lawrence: University Press of Kansas, 2005), 136–157. See also Hamilton, *Sacrifice on the Steppe*.

8. For the Axis order of battle, see "Ia Lagenkarten Nr. 1 zum KTB Nr. 13, Jul–Oct 1942," AOK 6, 23948/1a, NAM T-312, roll 1446. For detailed Italian dispositions, see David M. Glantz, *Atlas of the Battle of Stalingrad: Red Army Operations, 19 November 1942–2 February 1943* (Carlisle, PA: self-published, 2000), map 7. See also "Gruppirovka i sostav 3 Rumynskoi i 8 Italianskoi armii na Donu" [The grouping and composition of 3rd Romanian and 8th Italian Armies on the Don], in *Sbornik materialov po izucheniiu opyta voiny, No. 8, avgust–oktiabr' 1943 g.* [Collection of materials for the study of war experience, no. 8, August–October 1943] (Moscow: Voenizdat, 1943), 24–36. On the shortage of weapons in Eighth Army, see, for example, Friedrich Schultz, *Reverses on the Eastern Wing (1942–1943)*, MS T-15 (Historical Division, Headquarters US Army Europe, ca. 1966), annex 6.

9. Tarrant, *Stalingrad*, 98. For extended discussions of Romanian efforts to deal

with this situation, see Axworthy et al., *Third Axis, Fourth Ally*, esp. 85–87; DiNardo, *Germany and the Axis Powers*, 141.

10. Stoves, *Die 22. Panzer-Division*, 45–49; Tarrant, *Stalingrad*, 92–93; Carell, *Stalingrad*, 154–155; Goerlitz, *Paulus and Stalingrad*, 218–219; Samuel W. Mitcham Jr., *The Panzer Legions: A Guide to the German Army Tank Divisions of World War II and Their Commanders* (Westport, CT: Greenwood Press, 2001), 165–166. The story of the mice immobilizing 22nd Panzer Division has become a minor legend, but the same problem affected the Soviet forces in a more insidious manner. On the eve of the Uranus offensive, 16th Air Army, assigned to support Rokossovsky attacking the Romanians, found that rodents had damaged the wiring on a number of aircraft. Worse still, the mice infected the aircrews with tularemia, a blood-borne bacterial fever. See Rokossovsky, *Soldatskii dolg*, 139.

11. Axworthy et al., *Third Axis, Fourth Ally*, 89; Goerlitz, *Paulus and Stalingrad*, 199.

12. For the German order of battle in Army Group B, see William McCrodden's five-volume unpublished manuscript "The Organization of the German Army in World War II: Army Groups, Armies, Corps, Divisions, and Combat Groups." For the Romanians, see Axworthy et al., *Third Axis, Fourth Ally*, 89–90.

13. "Betr.: Zustand der Divisionen, Armee-Oberkommando 6. Abt. 1a, A.H. Qu., 09. November 1942, 16.20 Uhr," and "Betr.: Zustand der Divisionen, Armee-Oberkommando 6. Abt. 1a, A.H. Qu., 16. November 1942, 12.00 Uhr," in Aufsess, *Die Anlagenbänder zu den Kriegstagebüchern der 6. Armee*, book 1, 285–290.

14. Boog et al., *Germany and the Second World War*, VI:1091–1095.

15. Lemelsen et al., *29. Division*, 204. For a breakdown of tanks in these two motorized divisions, see Isaev, *Stalingrad*, 295.

16. "Intelligence Summary No. 033a of the Stalingrad Front Headquarters, Dated 2 November 1942," in Isaev, *Stalingrad*, 289–290, citing TsAMO RF, f. 38, op. 11360, d. 251, ll. 135–136. See also Aufsess, *Die Anlagenbänder zu den Kriegstagebüchern der 6. Armee*, book 1; Manfred Kehrig, *Stalingrad: Analyse und Dokumentation einer Schlacht* (Stuttgart, Germany: Deutsche Verlag-Anstalt, 1974), 662–663.

17. For a full calculation of Axis strengths, see David M. Glantz and Jonathan M. House, *Endgame at Stalingrad*, vol. 3, book 1 of *The Stalingrad Trilogy* (Lawrence: University Press of Kansas, 2014), 151–165.

18. Axworthy et al., *Third Axis, Fourth Ally*, 85–86, 89; V. T. Minov, *Nastupatel'naia operatsiia 5-i Tankovoi armii v kontrnastuplenii pod Stalingradom (19–25 noiabria 1942 goda)* [The offensive operation of 5th Tank Army in the counteroffensive at Stalingrad (19–25 November 1942)] (Moscow: Voroshilov Academy of the General Staff, 1979), 5.

19. Axworthy et al., *Third Axis, Fourth Ally*, 85, 89.

20. Boog et al., *Germany and the Second World War*, VI:1118–1119.

21. David M. Glantz, *Soviet Military Deception in the Second World War* (London: Frank Cass, 1989), 109–110; Beevor, *Stalingrad*, 222.

22. Blau, *German Campaign in Russia*, 170–171; Goerlitz, *Paulus and Stalingrad*, 198–199, 227.

23. Zhilin, *Stalingradskaia bitva*, 849–850, citing KTB, OKW, Bd. II, hb. II, 1305–1306. See a condensed version of Gehlen's report in David Kahn, "An Intel-

ligence Case Study: The Defense of Osuga, 1942," *Aerospace Historian* 28, 4 (December 1981): 248. Gehlen's *The Service: The Memoirs of General Reinhard Gehlen*, trans. David Irving (New York: World Publishing, 1972), omits any mention of the 6 November report.

24. Goerlitz, *Paulus and Stalingrad*, 218.

25. Zhilin, *Stalingradskaia bitva*, 897–898, citing OKH intelligence summary no. 521 in TsAMO RF, f. 500, op. 12462, d. 89, ll. 430–432.

26. Quoted in Carell, *Stalingrad*, 158. For the state of German signals intelligence with regard to the Red buildup, see *Concentration of Russian Troops for Stalingrad—Offensive*, manuscript P-096 (Historical Division, US Army European Command, 1952).

27. Blau, *German Campaign in Russia*, 171–172; Beevor, *Stalingrad*, 227–228. On Soviet deception measures, see M. Kozlov, "Strategy and Operational Art at Stalingrad," *VIZh* 11 (November 1982): 9–16.

28. Boog et al., *Germany and the Second World War*, VI:1114–1115.

29. Quoted in Ziemke and Bauer, *Moscow to Stalingrad*, 466.

Chapter 14. Penetration and Encirclement, November 1942

1. Beevor, *Stalingrad*, 239; Ziemke and Bauer, *Moscow to Stalingrad*, 468.

2. Batov, *V pokhodakh i boiakh*, 180–181; Rokossovsky, *Velikaia pobeda na Volge*, 260–261.

3. Kravchenko, *Nastupatel'naia operatsiia 5-i Tankovoi Armii*, 26.

4. Rokossovsky, *Velikaia pobeda na Volge*, 260–262.

5. Initially, the Germans believed the Soviet main attack was from the Kletskaia bridgehead.

6. The most detailed accounts of these Soviet assaults are in Rokossovsky, *Velikaia pobeda na Volge*, 261–265; Kravchenko, *Nastupatel'naia operatsiia 5-i Tankovoi Armii*, 26–29; Chistiakov, *Po prikazu Rodiny*, 36–38; Axworthy et al., *Third Axis, Fourth Ally*, 89–92. For detailed maps of the entire operation, see Glantz, *Atlas of the Battle of Stalingrad*.

7. "HGr B/Ia an XXXXVIII Pz K vom 19.11.42, 1150 Uhr," in XXXXVIII Pz K./ Ia, 26 775/2 file.

8. Samsonov, *Stalingradskaia bitva*, 368; Kravchenko, *Nastupatel'naia operatsiia 5-i Tankovoi Armii*, 27; Goerlitz, *Paulus and Stalingrad*, 200; Axworthy et al., *Third Axis, Fourth Ally*, 91–92.

9. Carell, *Stalingrad*, 159.

10. On 21st Army's offensive, see Chistiakov, *Po prikazu Rodiny*, 36–37; Samsonov, *Stalingradskaia bitva*, 371; Axworthy et al., *Third Axis, Fourth Ally*, 91.

11. Rokossovsky, *Soldatskii dolg*, 200.

12. See General Heim's report in Goerlitz, *Paulus and Stalingrad*, 199–200; Axworthy et al., *Third Axis, Fourth Ally*, 91; Isaev, *Stalingrad*, 317.

13. I. A. Pliev, *Pod gvardeiskim znamenem* [Under the guards banner] (Ordzhonikidze: Izdatel'stvo IR, 1976), 124–125; Axworthy et al., *Third Axis, Fourth Ally*, 93.

14. Samsonov, *Stalingradskaia bitva*, 405 n107, citing a Russian translation of

Joachim Wieder, *Die Tragödie von Stalingrad. Erinnerungen eines Überlebenden* (Deggendorf: Nothhaft, 1955).

15. "KR-Fernschreien an AOK.6 Oberkommando der Heeresgruppe B, 19.11.1942 21.30 Uhr," in Aufsess, *Die Anlagenbänder zu den Kriegstagebüchern der 6. Armee*, book 1, 302.

16. Ibid., 300–301.

17. Wilhelm Adam, *Der Schwere Entschluss* (Berlin: Verlag der Nation, 1965), 155–156.

18. Untitled message in Aufsess, *Die Anlagenbänder zu den Kriegstagebüchern der 6. Armee*, book 1, 301; Mark, *Island of Fire*, 256.

19. Kravchenko, *Nastupatel'naia operatsiia 5-i Tankovoi Armii*, 266–267; Rokossovsky, *Velikaia pobeda na Volge*, 266–267. The result was summarized in Red Army General Staff, "Izvlechenie iz operativnoi svodkoi No. 325," in Zhilin, *Stalingradskaia bitva,*book 2, 36, citing TsAMO RF, f. 16, op. 1072ss, d. 11, ll. 132–136.

20. Stoves, *Die 22. Panzer-Division*, 53–66; Kravchenko, *Nastupatel'naia operatsiia 5-i Tankovoi Armii*, 31.

21. On the fight at Perelazovskii, see M. F. Panov, *Na napravlenii glavnogo udara* [On the axis of the main attack] (Moscow: Shcherbinskaia tipografiia, 1993), 22; Kravchenko, *Nastupatel'naia operatsiia 5-i Tankovoi Armii*, 31.

22. Axworthy et al., *Third Axis, Fourth Ally*, 94–95.

23. Kravchenko, *Nastupatel'naia operatsiia 5-i Tankovoi Armii*, 48, severely criticized Butkov's performance in this battle.

24. For the situation around Kletskaia on 20 November, see Samsonov, *Stalingradskaia bitva*, 374–376; Rokossovsky, *Velikaia pobeda na Volge*, 268–269; Axworthy et al., *Third Axis, Fourth Ally*, 92–93.

25. Axworthy et al., *Third Axis, Fourth Ally*, 92–93. Pliev, *Pod gvardeiskim znamenem*, 126, probably exaggerates the Romanian casualties in these actions.

26. Batov, *V pokhodakh i boiakh*, 193–202. For the German perspective, see Army Group B reports for 20 November reproduced in Aufsess, *Die Anlagenbänder zu den Kriegstagebüchern der 6. Armee*, book 1, 306–307, 314.

27. "Fernschreiben an Gen. Kdo. XIV. Pz.K, Gen Kdo. LI. A.K., Gen. Kdo. VIII A.K., Gen. Kdo. XI. A.K., nachr.: VIII. Fliegerkorps, 1445 Uhr, Armee-Oberkommando 6, Abt. Ia, A.H. Qu., 20.11.1942," in Aufsess, *Die Anlagenbänder zu den Kriegstagebüchern der 6. Armee*, book 1, 311–312.

28. On the Stalingrad Front's offensive, see Rokossovsky, *Velikaia pobeda na Volge*, 268–270; Samsonov, *Stalingradskaia bitva*, 382–385; Eremenko, *Stalingrad: Zapiski komanduiushchego frontom*, 325–351.

29. On 64th Army, see Samsonov, *Stalingradskaia bitva*, 284; Dragunsky et al., *Ot Volgi do Pragi*, 42–43; Axworthy et al., *Third Axis, Fourth Ally*, 101–102.

30. Isaev, *Stalingrad*, 525.

31. The corps' history focuses on 21 November to avoid acknowledging the German successes of the previous 24 hours. See Tolubko and Baryshev, *Na iuzhnom flange*, 56–57; Rokossovsky, *Velikaia pobeda na Volge*, 270. For a flamboyant account of the German side, see Carell, *Stalingrad*, 161–162.

32. On 57th Army operations, see Sarkis'ian, *51-ia Armii*, 101–102; Samsonov, *Ot Volgi do Baltiki*, 40–45.

33. Samsonov, *Ot Volgi do Baltiki*, 43, 46.

34. Oleg Shein, *Neizvestnyi front Velikoi Otechestvennoi* [The unknown front of the Great Patriotic War] (Moscow: Eksmo Iauza, 2009), 162–188.

35. Adam, *Der Schwere Entschluss*, 165–168.

36. Jukes, *Hitler's Stalingrad Decisions*, 104–105; John Erickson, *The Road to Berlin: Continuing Stalin's War with Germany* (Boulder, CO: Westview Press, 1983), 7.

37. See the excellent discussion of the airlift decision in Hayward, *Stopped at Stalingrad*, 234–239.

38. "H. Gr. B/Ia, Funkspruch Nr. 1352 an AOK 6 vom 21.11.1942," BA-MA, RH 20-6/241.

39. Tarrant, *Stalingrad*, 112–113; Beevor, *Stalingrad*, 245.

40. Axworthy et al., *Third Axis, Fourth Ally*, 96; Goerlitz, *Paulus and Stalingrad*, 201–203; Kehrig, *Stalingrad*, 158–159.

41. Kravchenko, *Nastupatel'naia operatsiia 5-i Tankovoi Armii*, 32–33. For a list of the missions of specific Soviet units, see appendix 5N in Glantz, *Companion to Endgame at Stalingrad*, 157–159.

42. For the struggles of 22nd Panzer Division on 21 November, see Stoves, *Die 22. Panzer-Division*, 57–59.

43. Samsonov, *Stalingradskaia bitva*, 386, quoting TsAMO SSSR. f. 1st Guards Tank Corps, op. 33764, d. 2, l. 3; Panov, *Na napravlenii glavnogo udara*, 23.

44. Isaev, *Stalingrad*, 317. Senger und Etterlin, *Die 24. Panzer-Division*, 126–131, provides a full account of *Kampfgruppe* Don, the leading element of 24th Panzer, on 21 November.

45. Pliev, *Pod gvardeiskim znamenem*, 126–129.

46. Batov, *V pokhodakh i boiakh*, 202; Rokossovsky, *Soldatskii dolg*, 200–201; "Morgenmeldung XI A.K., 0540 Uhr, A.O.K. 6 Ia, a. 22.11.42," in Aufsess, *Die Anlagenbänder zu den Kriegstagebüchern der 6. Armee*, book 1, 318.

47. For Stalingrad Front operations generally, see Rokossovsky, *Velikaia pobeda na Volge*, 270–271. On 51st Army, see Sarkis'ian, *51-ia Armii*, 101–102. Samsonov, *Ot Volgi do Baltiki*, 48–49, addresses 4th Mechanized Corps' operations.

48. See *62nd Army Combat Journal* reports for 21 November 1942.

49. Shein, *Neizvestnyi front*, 187–193; Tieke, *Caucasus and the Oil*, 135.

50. Tieke, *Caucasus and the Oil*, 135.

51. Kravchenko, *Nastupatel'naia operatsiia 5-i Tankovoi Armii*, 35. For the missions of specific Soviet units, see appendix 5R in Glantz, *Companion to Endgame at Stalingrad*, 164–166.

52. Panov, *Na napravlenii glavnogo udara*, 25–26.

53. Gans Dërr, *Pokhod na Stalingrad* [The approach to Stalingrad] (Moscow: Voenizdat, 1957), 70–71; a translation of Hans von Dörr, *Der Feldzug nach Stalingrad: Versuch eines operative Überblickes* (Darmstadt: E. S. Mittler und Sohn, 1955). Filippov was later named a Hero of the Soviet Union for his exploits.

54. Kravchenko, *Nastupatel'naia operatsiia 5-i Tankovoi Armii*, 35–37.

55. Ibid.

56. *Sbornik materialov po izucheniiu opyta voiny, No. 6, aprel'–mai 1943 g.*

[Collection of materials for the study of war experiences, no. 6, April–May 1943] (Moscow: Voenizdat, 1943), 91; Axworthy et al., *Third Axis, Fourth Ally*, 96.

57. Stoves, *Die 22. Panzer-Division*, 61–62.

58. Axworthy et al., *Third Axis, Fourth Ally*, 96–97. See Chistiakov, *Po prikazu Rodiny*, 42–44, on the final reduction of the Romanian pocket.

59. Ithiel de Sola Pool, *Satellite Generals: A Study of Military Elites in the Soviet Sphere*, Hoover Institute Studies Series B: Elites. No. 5 (Stanford, CA: Stanford University Press, 1955), 86–87.

60. Senger und Etterlin, *Die 24. Panzer-Division*, 129–130. The 16th Panzer Division apparently declined from 34 tanks on 20 November to 15 on 26 November; see "Zwischenmeldung XIV Pz. K., 1810 Uhr, A.O.K. 6, Ia, 26.11.42," in Aufsess, *Die Anlagenbänder zu den Kriegstagebüchern der 6. Armee*, book 2, 24.

61. Anna Stroeva, *Komandarm Kravchenko* [Army commander Kravchenko] (Kiev: Politicheskoi literatury Ukrainy, 1984), 38.

62. Pliev, *Pod gvardeiskim znamenem*, 129–130.

63. "Izvlechenie iz operativnoi svodki No. 327 General'nogo shtaba Krasnoi Armii na 8:00 23.11.42 g." [Excerpt from operational summary no. 327 of the General Staff of the Red Army at 0800 hours on 23 November 1942], in Zhilin, *Stalingradskaia bitva*, book 2, 48–49; reproduced in translation as appendix 5 in Glantz, *Companion to Endgame at Stalingrad*, 166–168.

64. Axworthy et al., *Third Axis, Fourth Ally*, 98; Army Group B message, "Ia Nr. 4018/42.g. Kdos, Chefsache, Heeresgruppe B, O. Qu., 22.11.1942," in Aufsess, *Die Anlagenbänder zu den Kriegstagebüchern der 6. Armee*, book 1, 326–327.

65. Rokossovsky, *Soldatskii dolg*, 201.

66. "Funkspruch an Heeresgruppe B, 1900 Uhr, Armee-Oberkommando 6 Abt.-Ia, A.H. Qu., 22.11.1942," in Aufsess, *Die Anlagenbänder zu den Kriegstagebüchern der 6. Armee*, book 1, 327.

67. Rokossovsky, *Velikaia pobeda na Volge*, 274–276.

68. K. V. Amirov, *Ot Volgi do Al'p: Boevoi put' 36-t Gvardeiskoi strelkovoi verkhnedneprovskoi Krasnoznamennoi ordenov Suvorova i Kutuzova II stepeni divizii* [From the Volga to the Alps: The combat path of 36th Guards Verkhne-Dnepr, Red Banner, and Orders of Suvorov and Kutuzov Rifle Division] (Moscow: Voenizdat, 1987), 47. See also German IV Army Corps' daily operational map for 22 November 1942 and "Izvlechenie iz operativnoi svodki No. 327," in Zhilin, *Stalingradskaia bitva*, book 2, 50–51, translated as appendix 5Y in Glantz, *Companion to Endgame at Stalingrad*, 172–173.

69. Isaev, *Stalingrad*, 329–330; Samsonov, *Ot Volgi do Baltiki*, 55.

70. These volunteers have often been misidentified because of the annotation "Turk" on German operational maps.

71. "Funkspruch an Heeresgruppe B, 1900 Uhr, Armee-Oberkommando 6 Abt.-Ia, A.H. Qu 22.11.42," in Aufsess, *Die Anlagenbänder zu den Kriegstagebüchern der 6. Armee*, book 1, 327.

72. Samsonov, *Stalingradskaia bitva*, 392–393.

73. Axworthy et al., *Third Axis, Fourth Ally*, 99. For 22nd Panzer's fight on 23 November, see Stoves, *Die 22. Panzer-Division*, 62–63.

74. Stroeva, *Komandarm Kravchenko*, 39–40.

75. Red Army General Staff summary, "Izvlechenie iz operativnoi svodkoi No. 328," in Zhilin, *Stalingradskaia bitva*, book 2, 59; Batov, *V pokhodakh i boiakh*, 207.

76. Samsonov, *Ot Volgi do Baltiki*, 58–60; this account is translated in Glantz, *Companion to Endgame at Stalingrad*, 184–185.

77. Sources for these estimates include Aufsess, *Die Anlagenbänder zu den Kriegstagebüchern der 6. Armee*, book 1, 330–336, and book 2, 4–25; Hans Dörr, *Pokhod na Stalingrad* [March to Stalingrad] (Moscow: Voenizdat, 1957), 79–80; *Stalingrad: Tsena Pobedy* [Stalingrad: The cost of victory] (Moscow: AST, 2005), 66–67; Tarrant, *Stalingrad*, 123; and Red Army General Staff daily operational summaries for 19–25 November 1942.

78. Axworthy et al., *Third Axis, Fourth Ally*, 101, 109.

79. Zolotarev, *Velikaia Otechestvennaia voina 1941–1945*, book 2, 66. Tarrant, *Stalingrad*, 123, suggests similar numbers without citing a specific source.

80. Weichs's radio message to OKH/GenstdH/OpAbt fur Chef GenStdH, 1845 hours, 23 November 1942, in Kehrig, *Stalingrad*, 561; "Funkspruch geh. Kds., Chefsache! An OKH 2345 Uhr, 23.11.42," in Aufsess, *Die Anlagenbänder zu den Kriegstagebüchern der 6. Armee*, book 1, 333.

81. Mark, *Island of Fire*, 282–283; Carell, *Stalingrad*, 174–177.

Chapter 15. Tightening the Noose, November 1942

1. Hayward, *Stopped at Stalingrad*, 229.

2. S. I. Rudenko et al., eds., *Sovetskie voenno-vozdushnye sily v Velikoi Otechestvennoi voine, 1941–1945 gg.* [The Soviet air force in the Great Patriotic War, 1941–1945] (Moscow: Voenizdat, 1968), 139, 99.

3. M. S. Dokuchaev, *V boi shli eskadrony: Boevoi put' 7-go gvardeiskogo ordena Lenina, Krasnoznamennogo, ordena Suvorova korpusa v Velikoi Otechestvennoi voine* [The squadrons went into battle: The combat path of 7th Guards Order of Lenin, Red Banner, and Order of Suvorov (Cavalry) Corps in the Great Patriotic War] (Moscow: Voenizdat, 1987), 28.

4. M. N. Kozhevnikov, *Komandovanie i shtab VVS Sovetskoi Armii v Velikoi Otechestvennoi 1941–1945 gg.* [Command and staff of the air force of the Soviet army in the Great Patriotic War, 1941–1945] (Moscow: Nauka, 1977), 110. For a detailed comparison of Soviet and German sorties, see Glantz, *Companion to Endgame at Stalingrad*, appendix 7L, 244.

5. "Izvlechenie iz operativnoi svodkoi No. 329," 24 November 1942, in Zhilin, *Stalingradskaia bitva*, book 2, 67–69, archival citation TsAMO RF, f. 167, op. 1072ss, d. 11, ll. 159–168; Kravchenko, *Nastupatel'naia operatsiia 5-i Tankovoi Armii*, 42.

6. Rokossovsky, *Velikaia pobeda na Volge*, 290; "Izvlechenie iz operativnoi svodkoi No. 329," 67.

7. "Izvlechenie iz operativnoi svodkoi No. 329," 68; Pliev, *Pod gvardeiskim znamenem*, 133.

8. See Paulus's order, "Armeebefehl für die Weiterführung des Kampfes, Armee-Oberkommando 6, Abt.-Ia, A.H.Qu., 24.11.1942," in Aufsess, *Die Anla-*

genbänder zu den Kriegstagebüchern der 6. Armee, book 2, 4; Grams, *Die 14. Panzer-Division*, 57–58; Senger und Etterlin, *Die 24. Panzer-Division*, 130–132.

9. "Izvlechenie iz operativnoi svodkoi No. 329," 68.

10. "Morgenmeldung IV A.K., A.O.K. 6, I.a, 25.11.42," in Aufsess, *Die Anlagenbänder zu den Kriegstagebüchern der 6. Armee*, book 2, 6.

11. Samuel J. Newland, *Cossacks in the German Army, 1941–1945* (London: Frank Cass, 1991), 105–107.

12. See "Lagenkarte 16. I.D. (Mot), Stand: 25.11.2200 [Uhr]," in *Fourth Panzer Army's Combat Journal.*

13. Panov, *Na napravlenii glavnogo udara*, 31; Pliev, *Pod gvardeiskim znamenem*, 133; Sixth Army situation reports for morning, midday, and evening on 25 November 1942, in Aufsess, *Die Anlagenbänder zu den Kriegstagebüchern der 6. Armee*, book 2, 10–11, 18.

14. "Izvlechenie iz operativnoi svodkoi No. 331," 26 November 1942, in Zhilin, *Stalingradskaia bitva*, book 2, 88; Pliev, *Pod gvardeiskim znamenem*, 134. This fighting is confirmed by various Sixth Army reports in Aufsess, *Die Anlagenbänder zu den Kriegstagebüchern der 6. Armee*, book 2, 23–24, 27.

15. These groups, whose designations and compositions changed frequently, are reflected on the daily intelligence maps of Romanian Third Army in War Journal—Maps (KTB-Karten), November 1942–January 1943, AOK 6, 30155/37, NAM T-312, roll 1459.

16. Dokuchaev, *V boi shli eskadrony*, 27.

17. Ibid., 26.

18. A. V. Tuzov, *V ogne voiny: Boevoi put' 50-i Gvardeiskoi dvazhdy Krasnoznammennoi ordena Suvorova i Kutuzova strelkovoi divizii* [In the flames of battle: The combat path of 50th twice Red Banner and Orders of Suvorov and Kutuzov Rifle Division] (Moscow: Voenizdat, 1970), 65–67.

19. "Izvlechenie iz operativnoi svodkoi No. 331," 88.

20. See annotations on "Lage, 27.11.42," AOK 6, 30155/37, NAM T-312, roll 1459, for German and Romanian positions on that day.

21. "Izvlechenie iz operativnoi svodkoi No. 332," 27 November 1942, in Zhilin, *Stalingradskaia bitva*, book 2, 99; "Lage, 27.11.42," AOK 6, 30155/37, NAM T-312, roll 1459.

22. Morozov, *Velikaia Otechestvennaia voina*, 495–496; K. E. Naumenko, *266-ia Artemovsko-Berlinskaia: Voenno-istoricheskii ocherk boevogo puti 266-i strelkovoi Artemovsko-Berlinskoi Krasnoznammenoi, Ordena Suvorova II stepeni divizii* [The 266th Artemovsk-Berlin: A military-historical study of the combat path of 266th Red Banner and Order of Suvorov II Degree Rifle Division] (Moscow: Voenizdat, 1987), 7.

23. Beevor, *Stalingrad*, 261–262. Batov, *V pokhodakh i boiakh*, 210, in effect confirms the methodical withdrawal by making no mention of 24th or 23rd Rifle Divisions' advance that day. For a calculation of German losses during the bridgehead, see Glantz and House, *Endgame at Stalingrad*, book 1, 444–445.

24. "Izvlechenie iz operativnoi svodkoi Nos. 330, 331, 332," 80, 89, 99; Isaev, *Stalingrad*, 321.

25. Holl, *Infantryman in Stalingrad*, 151. See the original German reports in Aufsess, *Die Anlagenbänder zu den Kriegstagebüchern der 6. Armee*, book 2, 9–10, 19.

26. Senger und Etterlin, *Die 24. Panzer-Division*, 137.

27. "Direktiva Stavki VGK No. 170694 komanduiushchim voiskami Iugo-zapadnogo i Donskogo frontovo perepodchinenii 21-i Armii" [*Stavka* VGK Directive No. 170694 to the commanders of the forces of the Southwestern and Don Fronts about the resubordination of 21st Army], in Zolotarev, "*Stavka* 1942," 453, archival citation TsAMO MD RF, f. 148a, op. 3763, d. 124, l. 299.

28. Mark, *Island of Fire*, 126, 297–298.

29. "Izvlechenie iz operativnoi svodkoi Nos. 330, 331, 332," 81, 89, 101; "Morgenmeldung IV A.K. meldet 28.11.05.00 Uhr an A.O.K. 6/Ia.," in Aufsess, *Die Anlagenbänder zu den Kriegstagebüchern der 6. Armee*, book 2, 41. The 29th Motorized Division had 15 tanks in this sector.

30. Samsonov, *Ot Volgi do Baltiki*, 65–67.

31. Sarkis'ian, *51-ia Armii*, 105.

32. "Izvlechenie iz operativnoi svodkoi No. 330," 81. According to Axworthy et al., *Third Axis, Fourth Ally*, 104, Pannwitz captured 500 prisoners, ten antitank guns, and a complete artillery battery.

33. Sarkis'ian, *51-ia Armii*, 105; Wolfgang Paul, *Brennpunkte: Die Geschichte der 6. Panzerdivision (1. Leichte) 1937–1945* (Osnabrück, Germany: Biblio Verlag, 1984), 232–233.

34. Vasilevsky, *Delo vsei zhizni*, 230–231; this passage is translated in Glantz, *Companion to Endgame at Stalingrad*, 218–219.

35. Naumenko, *266-ia Artemovsko-Berlinskaia*, 8–9; Axworthy et al., *Third Axis, Fourth Ally*, 100.

36. Stoves, *Die 22. Panzer-Division*, 72; Axworthy et al., *Third Axis, Fourth Ally*, 100.

37. "Stand v, 30.11.42, Lagenkarten Anlagen zu K.T.B. 1, Armee Abt. Hollidt," 26624/6 file, NAM T-312, roll 1452.

38. Army Group Hollidt's daily maps for 30 November and 1 December show the fighting north of Chernyshevskaia; see also Axworthy et al., *Third Axis, Fourth Ally*, 100.

39. Rokossovsky, *Soldatskii dolg*, 204.

40. Batov, *V pokhodakh i boiakh*, 212–214; this passage is translated in Glantz, *Companion to Endgame at Stalingrad*, 235.

41. "Izvlechenie iz operativnoi svodkoi No. 335, 0800 hours, 1 December 1942," in Zhilin, *Stalingradskaia bitva*, book 2, 122; "Morganmeldung, LI A.K., 0600 Uhr, A.O.K. 6, I.a, Datum 30.11.42," in Aufsess, *Die Anlagenbänder zu den Kriegstagebüchern der 6. Armee*, book 2, 64; Holl, *Infantryman in Stalingrad*, 157. LI Corps' hourly account of the 30 November attacks is translated in Glantz, *Companion to Endgame at Stalingrad*, 237–238.

42. "Mogenmeldung LI. SW.K., 0600 Uhr, A.O.K. 6, I.a, Datum 30.11.42," 65; "Boevoe donesenie 246" [Combat report no. 246], 30 November 1942, in *62nd Army's Combat Journal*.

43. Dragunsky et al., *Ot Volgi do Pragi*, 45–46. See various reports for 28–29

November by IV Corps and Sixth Army in Aufsess, *Die Anlagenbänder zu den Krieg-stagebüchern der 6. Armee*, book 2, 43–62.

44. Manstein, *Lost Victories*, 301.

45. Ibid., 318–319, quoting from the OKH directive of 26 November. See also Friedrich W. von Mellenthin, *Panzer Battles*, trans. H. Betzler (Norman: University of Oklahoma Press, 1956), 175. Mellenthin was chief of staff of XXXXVIII Panzer Corps.

Chapter 16. Relief Attempts and Pressuring the Pocket, 1–15 December 1942

1. Hardesty and Grinberg, *Red Phoenix Rising*, 107; Tarrant, *Stalingrad*, 145; Hayward, *Stopped at Stalingrad*, 245.

2. Murray, *Luftwaffe*, 147; Hayward, *Stopped at Stalingrad*, 246.

3. Hayward, *Stopped at Stalingrad*, 249; Tarrant, *Stalingrad*, 149.

4. Hardesty and Grinberg, *Red Phoenix Rising*, 106–107; Hayward, *Stopped at Stalingrad*, 225.

5. Hardesty and Grinberg, *Red Phoenix Rising*, 112–114.

6. Ibid., 110; Hayward, *Stopped at Stalingrad*, 272, 310, 322.

7. Carell, *Stalingrad*, 310, claims that 30,000 were evacuated. For a table of daily airlift operations, see Boog et al., *Germany and the Second World War*, VI:1150.

8. Tarrant, *Stalingrad*, 151.

9. Zolotarev, *Velikaia Otechestvennaia voina*, book 2, 82.

10. "Prikaz Stavki VGK o formirovanii 3-i Gvareiskoi Armii" [*Stavka* VGK order about the formation of 3rd Guards Army] and "Prikaz Stavki VGK o formirovanii 1-i Gvareiskoi Armii" [*Stavka* VGK order about the formation of 1st Guards Army], in Zolotarev, "*Stavka* 1942," 460–461; translated in Glantz, *Companion to Endgame at Stalingrad*, 273.

11. "Prikaz Stavki VGK No. 170699 o formirovanii 5-i Udarnoi Armii" [*Stavka* VGK order no. 170699 about the formation of 5th Shock Army], in Zolotarev, "*Stavka* 1942," 461–462, archival citation TsAMO, f. 148a, op. 3763, d. 124, ll. 302–304; translated in Glantz, *Companion to Endgame at Stalingrad*, 272. The 5th Shock Army was originally slated to receive 23rd Tank Corps, but that unit eventually went to the Southwestern Front's reserve later in December.

12. "Doklad predstavitelia Stavki No. 15 Verkhovnomu Glavnokomanduiush-chemu plana ispol'zovaniia 2-i Gvardeiskoi Armii dlia likvidatsii okruzhennoi v Stalingrade gruppirovki protivnika" [Report of the representative of the *Stavka* no. 15 to the supreme high commander on a plan for the employment of 2nd Guards Army for the liquidation of the enemy grouping encircled in Stalingrad], in Zolotarev, "*Stavka* 1942," 565–566, archival citation TsAMO, f. 48a, op. 3408, d. 139, ll. 674–678.

13. Vasilevsky, *Delo vsei zhizni*, 243–244.

14. Vitalii Belokon' and Il'ia Moshchansky, *Na flangakh Stalingrada: Operatsii na Srednom i Verkhnem Donu 17 iiulia 1942–2 fevralia 1943 goda* [On the flanks of Stalingrad: The operations on the middle and upper Don, 17 July 1942–2 February 1943] (Moscow: PKV, 2002), 52, 54.

15. Pliev's near success prompted the Red Army General Staff to report, falsely, that he had captured Rychkovskii on 4 December. See "Izvlechenie iz operativnoi

svodki No. 339," in Zhilin, *Stalingradskaia bitva*, book 2, 144–148; translated in Glantz, *Companion to Endgame at Stalingrad*, 282.

16. *Kriegstagebuch*, Gen. Kdo. XXXXVIII Panzer Corps, entry for 7 December 1942, 16–18, photocopy of the original (hereafter cited as KTB, XXXXVIII Panzer Corps); Mellenthin, *Panzer Battles*, 175–177; David M. Glantz, ed., *1984 Art of War Symposium: From the Don to the Dnepr: Soviet Offensive Operations—December 1942–August 1943* (Carlisle, PA: Center for Land Warfare, US Army War College, 1984; reprint, Foreign Military Studies Office, 1992), 99–113. On 336th Infantry's counterattack, see the intelligence report for 11 December in Documents from 5th Tank Army, archival citation TsAMO RF, f. 331, op. 5041, d. 130, l. 55.

17. Combat Orders of 1st Tank Corps, archival citation TsAMO RF, f. 3398, op. 1, d. 3, l. 47.

18. See 11th Panzer's attack plan in KTB, XXXXVIII Panzer Corps, 23.

19. For slightly different estimates of tank losses, see Mellenthin, *Panzer Battles*, 178; KTB, XXXXVIII Panzer Corps, entry for 8 December 1942; and the Romanian report, "Ic Tagesmeldung v. 9.12.42," in *Tatigkeitsbericht*, 5–31. Dez. 1942, AOK 6, Ic, Rom. AOK 3, Chef des Deutschen Gen. Stabes dann Armeegruppe Hollidt, 2. 1. Text (copy of the original). For his part, Romanenko downplayed the incident in his daily report to higher headquarters. See "Izvlechenie iz operativnoi svodkoi No. 343," 8 December 1942, in Zhilin, *Stalingradskaia bitva*, book 2, 166–169, archival citation TsAMO RF, f. 16, op. 1072ss, d. 12, ll. 66–73.

20. M. Shaposhnikov, "Boevye deistviia 5-go mekhanizirovannogo korpusa zapadnee Surovikino v dekabre 1942 goda" [Combat operations of 5th Mechanized Corps west of Surovikino in December 1942], *VIZh* 10 (October 1982): 33–36.

21. See XXXXVIII Panzer Corps' daily situation map. The corps KTB confirmed the timing and general strength of the Soviet attacks.

22. Mellenthin, *Panzer Battles*, 178. See XXXXVIII Panzer Corps' daily situation maps for 11 and 12 December.

23. Rotmistrov, *Stal'naia gvardiia*, 130–146.

24. See, for example, "Operativnye svodki, boevye doneseniia, razvedsvodki 5 TA (1942 g.)" [Operational summaries, combat reports, and intelligence summaries of 5th Tank Army (1942)], archival citation TsAMO RF, f. 331, op. 5041, d. 130, ll. 50–56; translated in Glantz, *Companion to Endgame at Stalingrad*, 287–290.

25. Jentz, *Panzertruppen*, 2:31.

26. "Izvlechenie iz operativnoi svodki No. 348," 14 December 1942, in Zhilin, *Stalingradskaia bitva*, book 2, 209–210, archival citation TsAMO RF, f. 16, op. 1072ss, d. 12, ll. 105–111; N. Z. Kadyrov, *Ot Minska do Veny: Boevoi put' 4-i gvardeiskoi strelkovoi Apostolovsko-Venskoi Krasnoznamennoi divizii* [From Minsk to Vienna: The combat path of 4th Guards Apostolovo-Vienna Red Banner Rifle Division] (Moscow: Voenizdat, 1985), 65–66. For the German side, compare Mellenthin's lecture in Glantz, *1984 Art of War Symposium*, 108, with his *Panzer Battles*, 178–179; see also KTB, XXXXVIII Panzer Corps, entries for 13–14 December 1942, 45–55.

27. Rotmistrov, *Stal'naia gvardiia*, 139–144; "Operativnye svodki 5 Ud.A. 15 dekabria 1942–31 marta 1943" [Operational summaries of 5th Shock Army, 15 December 1942–31 March 1943], archival citation TsAMO RF, f. 333, op. 4885, d. 25,

l. 1; translated in Glantz, *Companion to Endgame at Stalingrad*, 293–298. See also KTB, XXXXVIII Panzer Corps, entry for 13 December 1942, 49–50.

28. KTB, XXXXVIII Panzer Corps, entry for 13 December 1942, 48.

29. Rotmistrov, *Stal'naia gvardiia*, 143–144.

30. KTB, XXXXVIII Panzer Corps, entries for 14 and 15 December 1942, 53–60.

31. Isaev, *Stalingrad*, 349–350.

32. Paul, *Brennpunkte*, 238–239. The division's KTB records the initial stages of the engagement. Writing from memory, the division commander, General Raus, apparently telescoped a number of engagements into an inaccurate summary in *Panzer Operations: The Eastern Front Memoir of General Raus, 1941–1945*, comp. and trans. Steven H. Newton (n.p.: Da Capo Press, 2003), 146–147.

33. Isaev, *Stalingrad*, 351–352; Paul, *Brennpunkte*, 239. Jentz, *Panzertruppen*, 2:26–29, contains extracts from 11th Panzer Regiment's war diary of the incident.

34. Raus, *Panzer Operations*, 154–156. Raus apparently believed that he faced an entire tank corps.

35. The debates about reinforcing Manstein are included in his memoirs, *Lost Victories*, as well as in Earl F. Ziemke, *Stalingrad to Berlin: The German Defeat in the East* (Washington, DC: US Army Office of the Chief of Military History, 1968), 61–62.

36. Manstein, *Lost Victories*, 557–558.

37. Boog et al., *Germany and the Second World War*, VI:1145.

38. Paul, *Brennpunkte*, 239–240.

39. Raus, *Panzer Operations*, 156–157.

40. Paul, *Brennpunkte*, 242–243. These figures are as of 11 December; other reports that 23rd Panzer Division had received new tanks en route to its location are likely incorrect.

41. Rokossovsky, *Velikaia pobeda na Volge*, 370, 375; Samsonov, *Ot Volgi do Baltiki*, 71, 74.

42. Paul, *Brennpunkte*, 245–246; Ernst Rebentisch, *The Combat History of the 23rd Panzer Division in World War II* (Mechanicsburg, PA: Stackpole Books, 2012), 207; Sarkis'ian, *51-ia Armiia*, 108.

43. Paul, *Brennpunkte*, 246–247.

44. "Direktiva Stavki VGK komanduiushchim voiskani Iugo-Zapadnogo i Voruneghskogo frontov, predstaviteliu Stavki ob izmenii plana operatsii 'Saturn'" [*Stavka VGK directive to the commanders of the forces of the Southwestern and Voronezh Fronts and the representative of the Stavka about changes in operational plan* "Saturn"], in Zolotarev, "*Stavka 1942*," 466–467, archival citation TsAMO RF, f. 148a, op. 3763, d. 126, ll. 211–214. This and Stalin's subsequent directive suspending Operation Ring are translated in Glantz, *Companion to Endgame at Stalingrad*, 277–278.

45. Tolubko and Baryshev, *Na iuzhnom flange*, 62–63; Sarkis'ian, *51-ia Armiia*, 109.

46. Although termed a tank corps at its creation, Tanaschishin's 13th was in reality a mechanized corps, a term routinely used to describe the formation by early December.

47. Raus, *Panzer Operations*, 164. See also Dërr, *Pokhod na Stalingrad*, 92–93.

48. Tolubko and Baryshev, *Na iuzhnom flange*, 63–64.

49. Dërr, *Pokhod na Stalingrad*, 93; Raus, *Panzer Operations*, 168; Samsonov, *Ot Volgi do Baltiki,* 75. For a detailed comparison of these various accounts, see Glantz and House, *Endgame at Stalingrad*, book 2, 121–123.

50. Samsonov, *Ot Volgi do Baltiki*, 76–80; Sarkis'ian, *51-ia Armiia*, 110; Dërr, *Pokhod na Stalingrad*, 93; The German tank loss figure is from Paul, *Brennpunkte*, 255.

51. Rebentisch, *Combat History of 23rd Panzer Division*, 207–208.

52. Raus, *Panzer Operations*, 176; Dërr, *Pokhod na Stalingrad*, 94; Samsonov, *Ot Volgi do Baltiki*, 81; "Izvlechenie iz operativnoisvodkoi No. 351," 16 December 1942, in Zhilin, *Stalingradskaia bitva*, book 2, 225, archival citation TsAMO RF, f. 16, op. 1072ss, d. 12, ll. 131–132.

53. Dërr, *Pokhod na Stalingrad*, 94; Paul, *Brennpunkte*, 257–258; entry for 1630 hours, 17 December 1942, in Headquarters, Army Group Don, Kriegstagebuch, 16.12.42–31.12.42, 215 (copy of original). All these accounts contradict Raus's more optimistic recollections in *Panzer Operations*, 176, 180.

54. Fridolin von Senger und Etterlin, *Neither Fear nor Hope: The Wartime Career of General Frido von Senger und Etterlin, Defender of Casino* (New York: E. P. Dutton, 1964), 63–64.

55. Ibid., 64–66.

56. Samsonov, *Ot Volgi do Baltiki*, 85; archival citation TsAMO SSSR, f. 605, op. 420575, d. 1, l. 6 ob.

57. Dërr, *Pokhod na Stalingrad*, 94; "Izvlechenie iz operativnoisvodkoi No. 353," 18 December 1942, in Zhilin, *Stalingradskaia bitva*, book 2, 238, archival citation TsAMO RF, f. 16, op. 1072ss, d. 12, l. 155.

58. Horst Scheibert, *Nach Stalingrad—48 Kilometers! Der Einsatzvorstoss der 6. Panzerdivision. Dezember 1942* (Neckargemünd, Germany: Kurt Vowinckel Verlag, 1956), 101; Paul, *Brennpunkte*, 261; Samsonov, *Ot Volgi do Baltiki*, 90–91.

59. "Doklad predstavitelia Stavki No. 42 Verkhovnomu glavnokomaduiush-chemu ob obstanovke i plane dal'neishego ispol'zovaniia 2-i Gvardeiskoi Armii" [Report of the representative of the *Stavka* no. 42 to the supreme high commander about the situation and plan for the further employment of 2nd Guards Army], in Zolotarev, "*Stavka 1942*," 567–568, archival citation TsAMO, f. 48a, op. 2294, d.1, ll. 47–51; translated in Glantz, *Companion to Endgame at Stalingrad*, 338–340.

60. Dërr, *Pokhod na Stalingrad*, 94–95; "Izvlechenie iz operativnoisvodkoi No. 354," 19 December 1942, in Zhilin, *Stalingradskaia bitva*, book 2, 243–246, archival citation TsAMO RF, f. 16, op. 1072ss, d. 12, ll. 146–153; Samsonov, *Ot Volgi do Baltiki*, 92–95. The 3rd Guards Mechanized Corps strength is from Isaev, *Stalingrad*, 374, citing TsAMO RF, f. 48, op. 468, d. 24, l. 221.

61. Paul, *Brennpunkte*, 262. The tank strength report is in "Pz. AOK.4/Ia, Meldung über Ausfälle an personal und Material seit Beginn Operation 'Wintergewitter' vom 21.12.1942, 0215 Uhr," in HGr Don/Ia, 39 694/5, BA-MA, EH 19 VI/30-42.

62. Kehrig, *Stalingrad*, document 35; translated in Glantz, *Companion to Endgame at Stalingrad*, 240–241.

63. Manstein, *Lost Victories*, 333–335; Boog et al., *Germany and the Second World War*, VI:1148–1149.

64. On ammunition, see Boog et al., *Germany and the Second World War*, VI:1151. On horses, see Richard L. Dinardo, *Mechanized Juggernaut or Military Anachronism? Horses and the German Army of World War II* (Westport, CT: Greenwood Press, 1991), 59–61.

65. "Zwischenmeldung, VIII. A.K. 1605 Uhr, A.O.K. 6 I.a, Datum 1.12,42," in Aufsess, *Die Anlagenbänder zu den Kriegstagebüchern der 6. Armee*, book 2, 81.

66. "Morganmeldung, XIV. Pz.K. 0605 Uhr, A.O.K. 6 I.a, Datum 04.12.42," ibid., 108. See VIII Army Corps' and Sixth Army's daily operations maps for 30 November and 1 and 4–5 December 1942, in K.T.B. AOK. 6, Ia, Karten, Nov 1942–Jan 1943, AOK 6, 30155/37 file, NAM T-312, roll 1459.

67. "Tagesmeldung, XIV. Pz.K. 2200 Uhr, A.O.K. 6 I.a, Datum 05.12.42," in Aufsess, *Die Anlagenbänder zu den Kriegstagebüchern der 6. Armee*, book 2, 126. Not counting Warmbold's 11 tanks, 3rd Motorized Division had 20 functioning tanks late on 4 December.

68. I. N. Pavlov, *Legendarnaia zheleznaia: Boevoi put' motostrelkovoi Samarov-Ul'ianovskoi, Berdicheskoi Zheleznoi ordena Oktiabr'skoi Revolutsii, trizhdy Krasnoznamennoi, ordenov Suvorova i Bogdana Khmel'nitskogo divisii* [The legendary iron: The combat path of the Samara-Ul'ianovsk and Berdichev, Order of the October Revolution, thrice Red Banner, and Orders of Suvorov and Bogdan Khmel'nitsky Motorized Rifle Division] (Moscow: Voenizdat, 1987), 108.

69. Ibid., 109–110. See various situation reports from VIII Army Corps on 4–5 December in Aufsess, *Die Anlagenbänder zu den Kriegstagebüchern der 6. Armee*, book 2, 114, 123, 126–127.

70. "KR-Fernschreiben an Gen. Kdo. VIII. A.K. Armee-Oberkommando 6, Abt.-Ia, A.H. Qu., 06.12.42," ibid., 137–138.

71. "Opersvodka, No. 309, 2.12.42," in *62nd Army's Combat Journal*; "Verluste der 6. Armee in der Zeit vom 21.11–05.12.42 nur im Kessel, Armee-Oberkommando 6, Abt-Ia, A.H. Qu., 06.12.1942," in Aufsess, *Die Anlagenbänder zu den Kriegstagebüchern der 6. Armee*, book 2, 133, and strength reports on 248–249.

72. "Tagesmeldung, VIII. A.K. 2300 Uhr, A.O.K. 6 I.a, Datum 06.12.42," and "Morganmeldung, VIII. A.K. 0530 Uhr, A.O.K. 6 I.a, Datum 07.12.42," in Aufsess, *Die Anlagenbänder zu den Kriegstagebüchern der 6. Armee*, book 2, 141–142, 144.

73. "Izvelechenie iz operativnoi svodki No. 342," 8 December 1942, in Zhilin, *Stalingradskaia bitva*, book 2, 160. Glantz, *Companion to Endgame at Stalingrad*, 359–365, provides translated summaries of Soviet General Staff reports for 6–10 December 1942.

74. "Morganmeldung, VIII. A.K. 0550 Uhr, A.O.K. 6 I.a, Datum 09.12.42," and "Morganmeldung, XIV Pz.K. 0600 Uhr, A.O.K. 6 I.a, Datum 10.12.42," in Aufsess, *Die Anlagenbänder zu den Kriegstagebüchern der 6. Armee*, book 2, 167, 176.

75. See Glantz, *Companion to Endgame at Stalingrad*, 375–378, for German strength figures, based on Aufsess, *Die Anlagenbänder zu den Kriegstagebüchern der 6. Armee*, book 2, 205–206, 216–217, 226, 239, 248–251.

Chapter 17. Little Saturn and the Failure of Relief Efforts

1. "Iz Direktivy General-polkovnika Vatutina General-leitenantu Kuznetsovu" [From a directive of Colonel General Vatutin to Lieutenant General Kuznetsov], 14 December 1942, and "Iz Direktivy General-polkovnika Vatutina General-leiten-antu Kuznetsovu" [From a directive of Colonel General Vatutin to Lieutenant General Kuznetsov], 15 December 1942, both in *Razgrom Italo-Nemetskikh voisk na Donu (Dekabr' 1942 r.): Kratkii operativno-takticheskii ocherk* [The destruction of Italian-German forces on the Don (December 1942): A brief operational-tactical summary] (Moscow: Voenizdat, 1945), 121–125; translated in Glantz, *Companion to Endgame at Stalingrad*, 380–385.

2. *Razgrom Italo-Nemetskikh voisk na Donu*, 28–30; details reproduced in Glantz, *Companion to Endgame at Stalingrad*, 386–387.

3. See Glantz, *Companion to Endgame at Stalingrad*, 1–81, for the opposing forces' complete orders of battle from 19 November 1942 through 1 February 1943.

4. For a history of Army Group Hollidt, see Horst Scheibert, *Zwischen Don und Donez: Winter 1942/43* (Neckargemünd, Germany: Kurt Vowinckel Verlag, 1961).

5. For the Italian view of this breakthrough, see Hope Hamilton, *Sacrifice on the Steppe: The Italian Alpine Corps in the Stalingrad Campaign, 1942–1943* (Philadelphia: Casemate, 2011), 72–75.

6. Hitler's order is reproduced in KTB 1, *Heeresgruppe* Don, 292.

7. "Kriegstagebuch Nr. 1, Armee-Abteilung Fretter-Pico, 18.12.1942–2.2.1943," BA-MA, XXX A.K. 31783/1 (copy of the original); hereafter cited as KTB, Fretter-Pico.

8. Boog et al., *Germany and the Second World War*, VI:1157–1158; Ziemke and Bauer, *Moscow to Stalingrad*, 486–488, 491; Manstein, *Lost Victories*, 338–345. See also associated reports in KTB 1, *Heeresgruppe* Don, 338.

9. "OKL/Stab Milch, III L., 78/3," BA-MA, RH 1/41-44; Hermann Plocher and Harry R. Fletcher, eds., *The German Air Force versus Russia, 1942*, USAF Historical Studies No. 154, Aerospace Studies Institute (Maxwell Air Force Base, AL: Air University, 1966), 294. According to Plocher, German aircrews saved all but 56 aircraft from this attack, but the Soviets claimed they destroyed large logistical stocks and up to 350 aircraft, including 50 unassembled planes on railroad cars. In either case, Badanov's capture of Tatsinskaia cost two precious days of airlift operations.

10. See KTB 1, *Heeresgruppe* Don; KTB, XXXXVIII Panzer Corps, December 1942. See also Erickson, *Road to Berlin*, 19–22; Hayward, *Stopped at Stalingrad*, 278. Stalin redesignated 24th Tank Corps as 2nd Guards Tank Corps and made Badanov the first recipient of the new Order of Suvorov. The general later commanded 4th Tank Army; see Richard N. Armstrong, *Red Army Tank Commanders: The Armored Guards* (Atglen, PA: Schiffer Military/Aviation History, 1994), 268–269.

11. KTB, Fretter-Pico, 8–20; Karl Ruef, *Odysee einer Gebirgsdivision: Die 3. Geb. Div. Im Einsatz* (Graz, Austria: Leopold Stocker Verlag, 1976), 293–294, 298, 301–323. See also "Iz dnevnika boevykh deistvii Verkhovnogo Glavno-komandovaniia Vermakhta," in Zhilin, *Stalingradskaia bitva*, book 2, 457.

12. Albert Krull, *Die Hannoversche Regiment 73: Geschichte des Panzer-*

Grenadier-Regiments 73 (vorm. Inf. Regt. 73), 1939–1945 (published by the regiment's Kameradschaft, ca. 1967), 254–274.

13. KTB, XXXXVIII Panzer Corps, 53–54, 57–59; Mellenthin, *Panzer Battles*, 179.

14. Mellenthin, *Panzer Battles*, 181–182; M. Shaposhnikov, "Boevye deistviia 5-go mekhanizirovovannogo korpusa zapadnee Surovikino" [Combat operations of 5th Mechanized Corps west of Surovikino in December 1942], *VIZh* 10 (October 1982): 37.

15. Mellenthin, *Panzer Battles*, 182.

16. See the various directives reassigning tank corps in Zolotarev, "*Stavka* 1942," 468–469. The relevant portions are translated, with archival citations, in Glantz, *Companion to Endgame at Stalingrad*, 402–403.

17. For German command changes, see entries in KTB 1, *Heeresgruppe* Don; Scheibert, *Zwischen Don und Donez*, 49–55.

18. See daily report for 27 December 1942, in KTB 1, *Heeresgruppe* Don.

19. Paul, *Brennpunkte*, 278–279, 282; entries for 28 and 29 December 1942, in KTB 1, *Armee Abteilung* Hollidt.

20. Intelligence report for 29 December 1942 in "Tatigkeitsbericht, 5. 31. Dez. 1942, Ic, Rom. AOK 3., der Chef des Deutschen Gen.-Stabes, dann Armeesgruppe Hollidt," BA-MA, 26624/7 (copy of the original in David Glantz's possession).

21. "Zapis' peregovorov po priamomu provodu Verkhovnogo Glavnokomanduiushchego i ego zamestitelia s komanduiushchim Iugo-Zapadnogo fronta" [Notes of a conversation by direct line of the supreme high commander and his deputy with the commander of the forces of the Southwestern Front], in Zolotarev, "*Stavka* 1942," 470–473, archival citation TsAMO, f. 96a, op. 2011, d. 26, ll. 206–216.

22. *Operativnye svodki 5 Ud. A. 15 dekabria 1942–31 marta 1943* [Operational summaries of 5th Shock Army, 15 December 1942–31 March 1943], archival citation TsAMO MO RF, f. 333, op. 4885, d. 25, l. 39.

23. V. M. Domnikov, ed., *V nastuplenii gvardiia: Ocherk o boevom puti 2-i Gvardeiskoi Armii* [Guards on the offensive: A study of the combat path of 2nd Guards Army] (Moscow: Voenizdat, 1971), 66.

24. "Direktiva Stavka VGK No. 170720 o likvidatsii Stalingradskogo i obrazovanii Iuzhnogo fronta" [*Stavka* VGK directive no. 170720 about the abolition of the Stalingrad Front and the formation of the Southern Front], in Zolotarev, "*Stavka* 1942," 476–477, archival citation TsAMO, 48a, op. 3408, d. 71, l. 369.

25. See entries for 29–31 December 1942, in KTB 1, *Heeresgruppe* Don, 382–414.

26. Domnikov, *V nastuplenii gvardiia*, 67.

27. "KR-Fernschreiben an Gen. Kdo. XIV Pz. K., 1220 Uhr, A.H. Qu, 16.12.1942, Armee-Oberkommando 6 Ia Nr. 4738/42, g. Kdos.Chefs," in Aufsess, *Die Anlagenbänder zu den Kriegstagebüchern der 6. Armee*, book 2, 242–243.

28. Sixth Army's daily situation maps for 19–21 December reflect the regrouping of forces called for by Paulus's 16 December plan.

29. "Fernschreiben von Generaloberst Paulus an Generalfeldmarschall von Manstein, 1730–1850 Uhr, 18.12.1942," and "Fernschreiben von Generaloberst Pau-

lus an Heeresgruppe Don, 0040–0215 Uhr, 19.12.1942," in Aufsess, *Die Anlagen-bänder zu den Kriegstagebüchern der 6. Armee*, book 2, 273, 277–278.

30. "Fernschreiben von General Schulz an General Schmidt, 1800–1900 Uhr, 20.12.1942 [and] 1710–1745 Uhr, 20.22.1942," ibid., 296–298, 321–322.

31. Teleprinter conversation between Field Marshal von Manstein and General Paulus, ibid., 276–278.

32. Paul, *Brennpunkte*, 262.

33. Scheibert, *Nach Stalingrad*, 115.

34. KTB 1, *Heeresgruppe* Don, 270–272.

35. Rokossovsky, *Velikaia pobeda na Volge*, 390–391.

36. Raus, *Panzer Operations*, 183–184; Paul, *Brennpunkte*, 272, citing 6th Panzer's KTB.

37. KTB 1, *Heeresgruppe* Don, 307, 313. For the Soviet view, see "Izvlechenie iz operativnoi svodkoi No. 358," in Zhilin, *Stalingradskaia bitva*, book 2, 268–281, archival citation TsAMO RF, f. 16,op. 1072ss, d. 12, ll. 176–183.

38. Teleprinter conversation between General Schmidt, chief of staff of Sixth Army, and General Schulz, chief of staff of Army Group Don, in Goerlitz, *Paulus and Stalingrad*, 278–279.

39. Message from the General Officer Commanding in Army Group Don to Chief of the General Staff, ibid., 279–280.

40. In *Lost Victories*, Manstein erroneously notes, "On 27 December 57 Panzer Corps was attacked in the Mishkova sector, where a steady enemy build-up had been going on, and was pushed back to the Aksai River." This misdating of the Soviet offensive by three days may have been an intentional act designed to place blame on Paulus for failing to break out of Stalingrad.

41. KTB 1, *Heeresgruppe* Don, 337.

42. Tolubko and Baryshev, *Na iuzhnom flange*, 68–69.

43. Dërr, *Pokhod na Stalingrad*, 97, 108–109. See Axworthy et al., *Third Axis, Fourth Ally*, 111, for the effects on Romanian Fourth Army.

44. "Prikaz Gitlera ot 27 Dekabria 1942 g. 'O dal'neishikh boevykh deistviiakh na iuzhnom flange Vostochnogo fronta'" [Order of Hitler of 27 December 1942 "About the future combat operations on the southern wing of the Eastern Front"], in Zhilin, *Stalingradskaia bitva*, book 2, 292–294.

45. Ibid., 301–302.

46. "Direktiva General'nogo Shtaba No. 158396 nachal'niku shtaba Stalingradskogo fronta ob obespechenii 2-i Gvardeiskoi Armii sredstvami sviazi" [General Staff directive no. 158396 to the chief of staff of the Stalingrad Front about providing 2nd Guards Army with communications equipment], in Zolotarev, "General Staff 1942," 429, archival citation TsAMO, f. 48a, op. 3408, d. 115, l. 93.

Chapter 18. The Condemned Army

1. "KR-Fernschreiben an Gen. Kdo. IV. A.K., XIV Pz.K., VIII A.K., nachr.: 9. Flak Division, O. Qu.-AOK 6 (durch Melder), Nr. 4737/42 geh., Armee-Oberkommando Abt.-Ia, A.H. Qu., 15.12.1942, 2010 Uhr," in Aufsess, *Die Anlagenbänder zu den Kriegstagebüchern der 6. Armee*, book 2, 237.

2. "Funkspruch An Chef Gen. Stab Geh. Kdos, Bezug: Chef Gen. St. 4068/42 geh. Kdos, 0700 Uhr 22. Dezember 1942," ibid., 317–319.

3. See daily corps reports for 15–17 December in ibid., 222–246. Actual counts of operational vehicles changed on a daily basis, as illustrated in Kehrig, *Stalingrad*, 670.

4. Comparison of Sixth Army's situation maps for 15–18 December 1942 and Red Army General Staff daily operational summaries in Zhilin, *Stalingradskaia bitva*, book 2, 196–220. For a detailed comparative order of battle as of 16 December, see Glantz and House, *Endgame at Stalingrad*, book 2, table 6, 340–341.

5. KTB I, *Heeresgruppe* Don, 214; "Tagesmeldung, VIII A. K. meldet 1630 Uhr, 17.12.42, A.O.K. 6 I.a, Datum 17.12.42," and Sixth Army reports for 17–19 December in Aufsess, *Die Anlagenbänder zu den Kriegstagebüchern der 6. Armee*, book 2, 257–278. By way of comparison, Sixth Army as a whole suffered 590 and 626 casualties, respectively, on 17 and 18 December. See Kehrig, *Stalingrad*, 670, for slightly different casualty figures.

6. Aufsess, *Die Anlagenbänder zu den Kriegstagebüchern der 6. Armee*, book 2, 257–278. See also entries for 17 and 18 December 1942 in *62nd Army's Combat Journal*.

7. See XIV Panzer Corps' daily reports for 20–21 December in Aufsess, *Die Anlagenbänder zu den Kriegstagebüchern der 6. Armee*, book 2, 289, 308–309.

8. "Opersvodka Nos. 347–348, Boevoi donesenie No. 266, 21 December 1942," in *62nd Army's Combat Journal*. Various reports of the mid-December city fighting are translated in Glantz, *Companion to Endgame at Stalingrad*, 643–679.

9. "Direktiva General'nogo Shtaba No. 991175 komanduiushchemu voiskami Stalingradskogo fronta o vyvode soedinenii v rezerv Verkhovnogo Glavnokomandovaniia" [General Staff directive no. 991175 to the commander of forces of the Stalingrad Front about the withdrawal of formations into the reserve of the Supreme High Command], in Zolotarev, "*Stavka* 1942," 413, archival citation TsAMO, f. 48, op. 3408, d. 114, l. 400.

10. Carell, *Stalingrad*, 177.

11. See corps' daily reports for 27 December–1 January in Aufsess, *Die Anlagenbänder zu den Kriegstagebüchern der 6. Armee*, book 2, 38, 65, 77, 92, 112. For details of this fighting, see Senger und Etterlin, *Die 24. Panzer-Division*, 140–144.

12. See Sixth Army's daily log of wounded soldiers by division and rank from 22 December through 30 January in "Heeresgruppe Don Kriegstagebuch vom 22.12.42–31.1.43, Anlagen Band 6," NAM T-311, roll 270.

13. See translations of Chuikov's reports and orders in Glantz, *Companion to Endgame at Stalingrad*, 667–679.

14. "KR-Fernshreiben g. Kdos. Chefs' an Oberbefehlshaber H. Gr. Don, 1315 Uhr, 26.12.42," in Aufsess, *Die Anlagenbänder zu den Kriegstagebüchern der 6. Armee*, book 3, 20–21.

15. "Fernschreiben von General Schulz an General Schmidt, 1715 Uhr 26.12.42," and "Fernschreiben von General Schulz an General Schmidt, 1835 Uhr 26.12.42," ibid., 27–28, 30–31.

16. "Fernschreiben von General Schulz an General Schmidt, 1650 Uhr 28.12.42," ibid., 58–60.

17. Manstein, *Lost Victories*, 346.

18. OKH, GenStdH, Op. Abt. (I S/B) Nr. 421053-42, Ergaenzung zum Operationsbefehl Nr. 2, 1.1.31, H. Gr. Don, in 39694/6 file. The key passages are translated in Glantz, *Companion to Endgame at Stalingrad*, 480.

19. Quoted in Goerlitz, *Paulus and Stalingrad*, 260.

20. "Operationsabsicht IV A. K. Fall 'Donnerschlag,' Generalkommando IV A. K. Chef d. Gen. Stabes, Armee-Oberkommando 6. Abt.-Ia, A.H.Qu., 24. Dezember 1942," in Aufsess, *Die Anlagenbänder zu den Kriegstagebüchern der 6. Armee*, book 3, 22–23. For specific missions and a map of the plan, see Glantz and House, *Endgame at Stalingrad*, book 2, 361–363.

21. Ibid. Armored strength is based on Sixth Army's reports for 24–28 December, in Aufsess, *Die Anlagenbänder zu den Kriegstagebüchern der 6. Armee*, book 3, 5–63.

22. "KR-Fernshreiben an Gen. Kdos. LI A.K., Gen. Kdos. VIII A.K., Gen. Kdos. XI A.K., Armee-Oberkommando 6. Abt.-Ia, A.H.Qu., 24. Dezember 1942," "KR-Fernshreiben an Gen. Kdos. XIV Pz.K., Fernspruch 14. Pz. Div., 1740 Uhr, Armee-Oberkommando 6. Abt.-Ia, A.H.Qu., 27.12.1942," and "Fernspruch an Heeresgruppe Don, Armee-Oberkommando 6. Abt.-Ia, A.H.Qu., 30. Dezember 1942," ibid., book 2, 336, and book 3, 41, 87.

23. For daily casualty figures, see Glantz, *Companion to Endgame at Stalingrad*, 483–488.

24. N. N. Voronov, *Na sluzhbe voennoi* [In military service] (Moscow: Voenizdat, 1963), 299–300.

25. See the complete plan in "Doklad predstavitelia Stavki Verkhovnomu Glavokomanduiushchemu plana razgroma okruzhennoi v Stalingrade gruppirovki protivnika" [Report of the representative of the *Stavka* to the supreme high commander on a plan for the destruction of the enemy grouping encircled in Stalingrad], in Zolotarev, "*Stavka* 1942," 475, archival citation TsAMO, f. 16-A, op. 1002, d. 1, ll. 26–29. This report is translated in Glantz, *Companion to Endgame at Stalingrad*, 488–489.

26. "Direktiva Stavka VGK No. 170718 predstaviteliu Stavki o dorabotke plan operatsii 'Kol'tso'" [*Stavka* VGK directive no. 170718 to the representative of the *Stavka* about completing work on the plan of Operation "Ring"], and "Direktiva Stavka VGK No. 61629 predstaviteliu Stavki i komanduiuschemu voiskami Stalingradskogo fronta o perenose napravleniia udara" [*Stavka* VGK directive no. 61629 to the representative of the *Stavka* and the commander of the forces of the Stalingrad Front about shifting the axis of attack], in Zolotarev, "*Stavka* 1942," 475, archival citations TsAMO, f. 148a, op. 3763, d. 124, ll. 314–315 and f. 48a, op. 3408, d. 72, l. 367. The former directive is translated in Glantz, *Companion to Endgame at Stalingrad*, 490.

27. "Armee-Oberkommando 6, I a [Befehl] Nr. 6015/42 g. Kdos, A.H.Qu., 30.12.42," in Aufsess, *Die Anlagenbänder zu den Kriegstagebüchern der 6. Armee*, book 3, 81.

28. Ibid.

29. Mark, *Island of Fire*, 417.

30. For detailed tables of how Sixth Army reorganized its defenses and armored

vehicles in the ten days prior to the Soviet assault, see Glantz, *Companion to Endgame at Stalingrad*, 492–496.

31. See Sixth Army's daily reports from 28 December 1942 to 13 January 1943 in Aufsess, *Die Anlagenbänder zu den Kriegstagebüchern der 6. Armee*, book 3, 50–250. Once again, Kehrig, *Stalingrad*, 670, gives slightly different figures, including 128 armored vehicles (95 tanks and 33 assault guns) on 9 January.

32. "Nachtrag zur Tagesmeldung, XI. A.K. meldet 2000 Uhr, A.O.K. 6 I.A, Datum 13.01.43," in Aufsess, *Die Anlagenbänder zu den Kriegstagebüchern der 6. Armee*, book 3, 249.

33. See Sixth Army's daily reports in ibid., book 2, 262–340, and book 3, 4–250.

34. Kehrig, *Stalingrad*, 635–636.

35. "Funkspruch an OKH, 2100 Uhr, V.O. bei AOK. 6, 08.01.43," in Aufsess, *Die Anlagenbänder zu den Kriegstagebüchern der 6. Armee*, book 3, 194. See also the message from the commander of Army Group Don to chief of the OKH in Goerlitz, *Paulus and Stalingrad*, 275–276.

36. Carell, *Stalingrad,* 202.

37. Quoted in Alexander Werth, *The Year of Stalingrad: A Historical Record and a Study of Russian Mentality, Methods, and Policies* (New York: A. A. Knopf, 1947), 434.

38. "Iz dnevnika boevykh deistvii Verkhovnogo Glavnokomandovaniia Vermakhta," in Zhilin, *Stalingradskaia bitva*, book 2, 380–381, quoting OKW *Kriegstagebuch* book 2, hb.2.

39. "Nachtrag zur Tagesmeldung, XI A.K., 2000 Uhr, A.O.K. 6 I.a., Datum 06.01.43," in Aufsess, *Die Anlagenbänder zu den Kriegstagebüchern der 6. Armee*, book 3, 173.

40. "Morgenmeldung, VIII A.K. 0545 Uhr, A.O.K. 6 I.a., Datum 07.01.43," "Tagesmeldung, VIII A.K. 1630 Uhr, A.O.K. 6 I.a., Datum 06.01.43," and "Funkspruch, Tagesmeldung 1805 Uhr, Armee-Oberkommando 6, Abt.-Ia. A.H.Qu., 07.01.43," ibid., 273–279, 181.

41. See the combat journals of 62nd Army and subordinate formations.

42. See Mark, *Island of Fire*, 374, 395, 427, for the decline of 79th Infantry Division.

43. Rokossovsky, *Velikaia pobeda na Volge*, 430–431, 442. See also Isaev, *Stalingrad*, 399.

44. "Likvidatsiia okruzhennoi Stalingradskoi gruppirovki protivnika" [The liquidation of the enemy's encircled Stalingrad grouping], in *Sbornik materialov po izucheniiu opyta voiny, No. 6,* 73, copy no. 6065; hereafter cited as *SMPIOV*.

45. For details of the final plan, see Rokossovsky, *Velikaia pobeda na Volge*, 432–439.

46. Ibid., 436. Rokossovsky listed a total of 257 tanks because he erroneously counted 6th Guards Tank Regiment, which was still subordinated to the Southern Front.

47. Ibid., 433; Isaev, *Stalingrad*, 399. For a detailed report, see "Adequate Provision of Artillery Means for the Operation Directed to Destroying an Encircled Enemy in the Stalingrad Area," extracted from *SMPIOV* and translated by US Army

Assistant Chief of Staff for Intelligence, No. F-9093, declassified 1964, in Combined Arms Research Library, Ft. Leavenworth, KS.

48. Rokossovsky, *Velikaia pobeda na Volge*, 433–434.

49. *SMPIOV*, 156, and Isaev, *Stalingrad*, 401, list a total of 400 operational aircraft. The most likely mix was 150 fighters, 100 bombers, 50 assault aircraft, and 100 night bombers.

50. See the organization and functions of these engineer units in Glantz, *Colossus Reborn*, 333–343.

51. Rokossovsky, *Velikaia pobeda na Volge*, 438–439.

52. Ibid., 443.

53. See the history of 54th Fortified Region in I. N. Vinogradov, *Oborona, shturm, pobeda* [Defense, assault, victory] (Moscow: Nauka, 1968). In late 1942 a typical fortified region consisted of six machine gun–artillery battalions, each with 48 76.2mm guns, 48 50mm mortars, 48 45mm antitank guns, 168 antitank rifles, and 284 machine guns.

Chapter 19. The Destruction

1. "Ultimatum komanduiushchemu okruzhennoi pod Stalingradom 6-i Germanskoi Armiei general-polkovniki Pauliusu ili ego zamestiteliu" [Ultimatum to the commander of Sixth German Army encircled at Stalingrad Colonel-General Paulus or his deputy], in Zhilin, *Stalingradskaia bitva*, book 2, 396.

2. "Funkspruch an Heeresgruppe Don, Tagesmeldung, 1900 Uhr, Armee-Oberkommando 6, Abt.-Ia, A.H.Qu., 10.01.1943," in Aufsess, *Die Anlagenbänder zu den Kriegstagebüchern der 6. Armee*, book 3, 216.

3. Ibid., 218.

4. *Historical Study: Small Unit Actions during the German Campaign in Russia*, Department of the Army Pamphlet No. 20-269 (Washington, DC: Department of the Army, 1953), 64.

5. "Fernspruch XIV. Pz.K. an AOK 6-Ia, 0045 Uhr, 11.01.43," in Aufsess, *Die Anlagenbänder zu den Kriegstagebüchern der 6. Armee*, book 3, 219.

6. See various orders and reports from both sides, translated in Glantz, *Companion to Endgame at Stalingrad*, 703–707.

7. "Program einer Feierstunde des Stabes Der 71. Inf. Div. am 10.1.1943 in Stalingrad," with the heading, "Vertrag: General v. Hartmann, Klavier: Hauptmann Ilse," copy of the original.

8. "Morgenmeldung, XIV. Pz. K., 0820 Uhr, A.O.K. 6, I.a, Datum 11.01.43," in Aufsess, *Die Anlagenbänder zu den Kriegstagebüchern der 6. Armee*, book 3, 221.

9. "Funkspruch an Heeresgruppe Don, Morgenmeldung 0640 Uhr, Armee-Oberkommando 6, Abt.-Ia, A.H.Qu., 11.01.43," ibid.

10. "Tagesmeldung, VIII. A.K., 1930 Uhr, A.O.K. 6, I.a, Datum 11.01.43," ibid., 226.

11. "Nachtrag zur Tagesmeldung, XIV. Pz.K., 2230 Uhr, A.O.K. 6, I.a, Datum 11.01.43," ibid., 232. For additional, fragmentary information on the escape from the Marinovka pocket, see Ronald Seth, *Stalingrad: Point of No Return: The Story*

of the Battle August 1942–February 1943 (New York: Coward-McCann, 1959), 239; Lemelsen et al., 29. Division, 234–235; Dieckhoff, 3. Infanterie-Division, 224–227.

12. "Nachtrag zur Tagesmeldung, IV. A.K.,2140 Uhr, A.O.K. 6, I.a, Datum 11.01.43," in Aufsess, Die Anlagenbänder zu den Kriegstagebüchern der 6. Armee, book 3, 231.

13. "Tagesmeldung, XI. A.K. meldet 2030 Uhr, A.O.K. 6, I.a, Datum 11.01.43," and "Nachtrag zur Tagesmeldung, LI. A.K. meldet 2110 Uhr, A.O.K. 6, I.a, Datum 11.01.43," ibid., 229, 231.

14. "Morgenmeldung, LI. A.K., 0625 Uhr, A.O.K. 6, I.a, Datum 12.01.43," ibid., 235.

15. "An Heeresgruppe Don, Oberbefehlshaber, 2135 Uhr, den 11.01.43," ibid., 233.

16. Schröter, Stalingrad, 175, asserts that Army Group Don sent this message on the night of 10–11 January; even if true, it was likely received on the night of 12 January.

17. Ibid., 180. For a broader Soviet perspective, see Samsonov, Stalingradskaia bitva, 496–497.

18. For the German version of the fighting at Tsybenko, see "Morgenmeldung, IV. A.K., 0600 Uhr, A.O.K. 6, I.a, Datum 12.01.43," and "Tagesmeldung, IV. A.K., 1720 Uhr, A.O.K. 6, I.a, Datum 12.01.43," in Aufsess, Die Anlagenbänder zu den Kriegstagebüchern der 6. Armee, book 3, 234, 240, and supplement 244.

19. "Morgenmeldung, LI A.K., 0550 Uhr, A.O.K. 6 I.a, Datum 13.01.43," ibid., 247.

20. Chistiakov, Po prikazu Rodiny, 104.

21. Rokossovsky, Velikaia pobeda na Volge, 450–451; Rokossovsky, Soldatskii dolg, 223.

22. "Nachtrag zur Tagesmeldung, IV. A.K. 2150 Uhr, A.O.K. 6, I.a, Datum 13.01.43," in Aufsess, Die Anlagenbänder zu den Kriegstagebüchern der 6. Armee, book 3, 248–250.

23. "Izvlechenie iz operativnoi svodkoi No. 15 (688)" [Extract from operational summary no. 15 (688)], 14 January 1943, in Zhilin, Stalingradskaia bitva, book 2, 428–431, citing TsAMO RF, f. 16, op. 1072ss, d. 1, ll. 129–138.

24. Ibid.

25. "Fernschreiben an OKH/Op. Abt, nachr: Bef. H. Gebiet Don, Morgen-meldung, Heeresgruppe Don Abt.-Ia, A.H.Qu., 15.01.1943," in Aufsess, Die Anla-genbänder zu den Kriegstagebüchern der 6. Armee, book 3, 252–253. See also Boog et al., Germany and the Second World War, VI:1162.

26. "Fernschreiben an OKH/Op. Abt, nachr: Bef. H. Gebiet Don, 2320 Uhr, Heeresgruppe Don Abt.-Ia, A.H.Qu., 14.01.1943," in Aufsess, Die Anlagenbänder zu den Kriegstagebüchern der 6. Armee, book 3, 252–253.

27. "Funkspruch an OKH, V.O. bei AOK 6, 1700 Uhr 15.01.43," ibid., 254.

28. Rokossovsky, Soldatskii dolg, 223–226. Casualty figures are from Isaev, Stal-ingrad, 410–413.

29. Quoted in Franz Schneider and Charles Gullans, trans., Last Letters from Stalingrad (Westport, CT: Greenwood Press, 1974), 112–114.

30. I. M. Chistiakov, *Sluzhim otchizne* [In service to the Fatherland] (Moscow: Voenizdat, 1975), 118. Because the airfield and village were at different locations, Batov believed he had captured the airfield when his troops actually occupied the town; see Batov, *V pokhodakh i boiakh*, 258. For German views of the airfield's seizure, see Ziemke and Bauer, *Moscow to Stalingrad*, 497–489; Hayward, *Stopped at Stalingrad*, 284–285.

31. "Funkspruch an OKH, 1715 Uhr, V.O. bei AOK 6, 16.01.43," in Aufsess, *Die Anlagenbänder zu den Kriegstagebüchern der 6. Armee*, book 3, 257.

32. Adam, *Der Schwere Entschluss*, 292.

33. Quotation from "Funkspruch an Heeresgruppe Don. Tagesmeldung, 2051 Uhr, Armee-Oberkommando 6, Abt.-Ia., A.H. Qu., 17.01.43," and "Funkspruch an General Zeitzler zur Weitergabe, 2102 Uhr, Armee-Oberkommando 6, Abt.-Ia, A.H.Qu., 17.01.1943," in Aufsess, *Die Anlagenbänder zu den Kriegstagebüchern der 6. Armee*, book 3, 259.

34. Samchuk, *Trinadtsataia gvardeiskaia*, 161–162.

35. Samsonov, *Stalingradskaia bitva*, 499; Rokossovsky, *Velikaia pobeda na Volge*, 453.

36. On the air battle, see Hayward, *Stopped at Stalingrad*, 281–310; Hardesty and Grinberg, *Red Phoenix Rising*, 104–164; Plocher and Fletcher, *German Air Forces versus Russia,* 260–355.

37. "Doklad predstavitelia Stavki No. 1191 Verkhovnomu Glavnokomanduiushchemu plana razgrom okruzhennogo v raione Staligrada protivnika" [Report of the representative of the *Stavka* no. 1191 to the supreme high commander on a plan for the destruction of the enemy encircled in the Stalingrad region], in Zolotarev, "*Stavka* 1942," 270–271, archival citation TsAMO, f. 206, op. 268, d. 123, ll. 17–18. Key portions are translated in Glantz, *Companion to Endgame at Stalingrad*, 537–538.

38. On the airlift controversy, see Hayward, *Stopped at Stalingrad*, 286–310; Plocher and Fletcher, *German Air Forces versus Russia*, 306–330.

39. Quoted in Hayward, *Stopped at Stalingrad*, 295.

40. "Funkspruch vom 20.01.43, 1150 Uhr. Absendende Stelle: V.O. AOK 6, 19.01.43, 03.45 Uhr KR-Drigend!" in Aufsess, *Die Anlagenbänder zu den Kriegstagebüchern der 6. Armee*, book 3, 266–267. Manstein records the same message in *Lost Victories*, 358. However, as in other cases, Manstein gives an erroneous date (24 January).

41. For accounts of German combat conditions at Stalingrad, see Craig, *Enemy at the Gates*; Beevor, *Stalingrad*. For the Soviet experience, see Michael K. Jones, *Stalingrad: How the Red Army Survived the German Onslaught* (Philadelphia: Casemate, 2007); Frank Ellis, *The Damned and the Dead: The Eastern Front through the Eyes of Soviet and Russian Novelists* (Lawrence: University Press of Kansas, 2011); P. P. Popov, A. V. Kozlov, and B. G. Usik, *Turning Point: Recollections of Russian Participants and Witnesses of the Stalingrad Battle*, trans. James F. Gebhardt (Sydney, Australia: Leaping Horseman Books, 2008). NKVD reports on prisoner of war interrogations as well as censored letters of Red Army soldiers are reproduced in *Stalingradskaia epopeia.*

42. "Funkspruch an Heeresgruppe Don, 1235 Uhr, Armee Oberkommando 6,

Abt.-Ia, A.H.Qu., 21.01.1943," in Aufsess, *Die Anlagenbänder zu den Kriegstage-büchern der 6. Armee*, book 3, 268.

43. "Funkspruch an Heeresgruppe Don, 2050 Uhr, Armee-Oberkommando 6, Abt.-Ia, A.H.Qu., 21.01.1943," ibid.

44. Chistiakov, *Sluzhim otchizne*, 119–120.

45. "Abschrift von Funkspruch an 6. Armee Zur Vorlage an Herrn Generalfeld-marschall von Manstein an Herrn Generaloberst Paulus, 1900 Uhr, 22 Januar 1943," in Aufsess, *Die Anlagenbänder zu den Kriegstagebüchern der 6. Armee*, book 3, 272.

46. "Funkspruch an Heeresgruppe Don, 1115 Uhr, Armee-Oberkommando 6, Abt.-Ia, A.H.Qu., 23.01.1943," ibid., 274.

47. Rokossovsky, *Velikaia pobeda na Volge*, 459.

48. For the Central Front's planned offensive, see David M. Glantz, *After Stalingrad: The Red Army's Winter Offensive, 1942–43* (Solihull, UK: Helion, 2008), 228–389.

49. "Izvlechenie iz operativnoi svoedkoi No. 25 (698) General'nogo shtaba Krasnoi Armii na 8.00 25. 1. 43. g" [Excerpt from operational summary no. 25 (698) of the Red Army General Staff at 0800 on 25 January 1943], in Zhilin, *Stalingradskaia bitva*, book 2, 487–490, archival citation TsAMO RF, f. 16, op. 1072ss, d. 1, ll. 235–242; portions translated in Glantz, *Companion to Endgame at Stalingrad*, 560–561.

50. *73-ia Gvardeiskaia Sbornik vospominanii, dokumentov i materialov o boevom puti 73-i guardeiskoi strelkovoi Stalingradsko-Dunaiskoi Krasnoznamennoi divizii* [The 73rd Guards: A collection of recollections, documents, and materials about the combat path of 73rd Guards Stalingrad-Danube Red Banner Rifle Division] (Alma-Ata: Kazakhstan, 1986), 68–72.

51. "Der Oberbefehlshaber der Heeresgruppe Don, H.Q., den 25.01.43, FPNr. 23079," in Aufsess, *Die Anlagenbänder zu den Kriegstagebüchern der 6. Armee*, book 3, 278.

52. Rokossovsky, *Velikaia pobeda na Volge*, 460–461.

53. Chistiakov, *Po prikazu Rodiny*, 65.

54. Ibid., 66–67. Schröter, *Stalingrad*, 211–212, alleges that the Soviet break-through occurred because a Romanian regiment, located between 44th Infantry and 29th Motorized Divisions, surrendered secretly during the night. In fact, however, the Axis was too weak to halt 21st Army's two guards divisions with supporting armor. Moreover, many Germans made a habit of blaming the Romanians for failures, despite the enormous losses suffered by that satellite army.

55. Batov, *V pokhodakh i boiakh*, 261.

56. Rokossovsky, *Velikaia pobeda na Volge*, 464.

57. Ibid.; Isaev, *Stalingrad*, 416.

58. "Funkspruch an Heeresgruppe Don, 0712 Uhr, Armee-Oberkommando 6, Abt.-Ia, A.H.Qu., 28.01.1943," in Aufsess, *Die Anlagenbänder zu den Kriegstage-büchern der 6. Armee*, book 3, 283.

59. I. Vasil'ev and A. P. Likan', *Gvardeitsy piatnadtsatoi: Boevoi put' Piatnadtsatoi Gvardeiskoi strelkovoi divizii* [Guardsmen of the 15th: The combat path of 15th Guards Rifle Division] (Moscow: Voenizdat, 1960), 74–75.

60. "Funkspruch an Heeresgruppe Don, 0655 Uhr, Armee-Oberkommando 6,

Abt.-Ia, A.H.Qu., 29.01.1943," in Aufsess, *Die Anlagenbänder zu den Kriegstage-büchern der 6. Armee*, book 3, 284.

61. I. A. Laskin, *Na puti k perelomu* [On paths to the turning point] (Moscow: Voenizdat, 1977), 315–316.

62. Rokossovsky, *Velikaia pobeda na Volge*, 464.

63. For details of 62nd Army's actions in the final days, see the translated summaries in Glantz, *Companion to Endgame at Stalingrad*, 749–773.

64. Amirov, *Ot Volgi do Al'p*, 69.

65. Schröter, *Stalingrad*, 244. For the German version, see Carell, *Stalingrad*, 206–207.

66. "Funkspruch an OKH, 0615 Uhr, V.O. b. AOK 6," and "Funkspruch an OKH, 0714 Uhr, V.O. b. AOK 6," in Aufsess, *Die Anlagenbänder zu den Kriegstage-büchern der 6. Armee*, book 3, 292, 293.

67. Rokossovsky, *Velikaia pobeda na Volge*, 467; Batov, *V pokhodakh i boiakh*, 263–264.

68. "XI. A.K., 2130 Uhr, Gef. Std., den 01.02.1943," in Aufsess, *Die Anlagen-bänder zu den Kriegstagebüchern der 6. Armee*, book 3, 294.

69. N. I. Krylov, *Stalingradskii rubezh* [The Stalingrad line] (Moscow: Voenizdat, 1979), 366.

70. Mark, *Island of Fire*, 469.

71. "Funkspruch XI. A.K. an H. Gru. Don /Ia, nachr. Chef, HNW, 0800 Uhr, 2.2.43," in Aufsess, *Die Anlagenbänder zu den Kriegstagebüchern der 6. Armee*, book 3, 295.

72. "XI A.K. 0920 Uhr, Gef. Std., den 02.02.43," ibid., 296.

73. See Glantz, *Companion to Endgame at Stalingrad*, 773, quoting from Krylov, *Stalingradskii rubezh*, 369.

74. Samsonov, *Stalingradskaia bitva*, 506.

75. "Direktiva Stavki VGK No. 46038 komanduiushchemu voiskami Donskogo fronta o vyvode v reserv Verkhovnogo Glavnokomandovaniia upravlenii 21-i i 64-i armii" [*Stavka* VGK directive no. 46038 to the commander of the forces of the Don Front about the withdrawal of 21st and 64th Armies into the reserve of the Supreme High Command], in Zolotarov, "*Stavka* 1943," 58; archival citation TsAMO, f. 48a, op. 3409, d. 8, l. 30, signed by Zhukov.

76. Carell, *Stalingrad*, 209.

77. Batov, *V pokhodakh i boiakh*, 265.

78. These figures are quoted in Mark, *Island of Fire*, 479, but are consistent with other reports from 21st NKVD Brigade.

79. See Glantz, *Companion to Endgame at Stalingrad*, 604, for a table of all units receiving the guards designation. This table is based on *Boevoi sostav Sovetskoi armii*, pt. 3, and Zolotarev, *Velikaia Otechestvennaia: Deistvuiushchaia armiia*.

80. "Neuaufstellung der Divisionen 6. Armee, Oberkommando der Heerees-gruppe Don, Abt. Ia, Nr. 310/43 geh. Kdos. H.QAu., den 31 Januar 1943," in Aufsess, *Die Anlagenbänder zu den Kriegstagebüchern der 6. Armee*, book 3, 296. Manstein's order omitted 94th Infantry Division, which had been disbanded in November, but eventually that division was also reactivated.

81. Rokossovsky, *Velikaia pobeda na Volge*, 468.

82. Hayward, *Stopped at Stalingrad*, 310. Carell, *Stalingrad*, 208, accepts the

42,000 figure, but Dörr, *Pokhod na Stalingrad*, 119, follows Schröter in placing the evacuated wounded at 29,000, perhaps half of whom were flown out between 10 and 24 January.

83. "No. 93. Iz dokladnoi zapiski UNKVD CO v NKVD SSSR 'O polozhenii v g. Stalingrade v period ego chastichnoi okkupatsii i nosle izgnansiia okkupantov,' 1 aprelia 1943 g." [No. 93. From a report by the NKVD Directorate of Stalingrad *oblast'* to the NKVD of the USSR "about the situation in the city of Stalingrad in the period of its occupation and after the expulsion of the occupiers," 1 April 1943], in *Stalingradskaia epopeia*, 393–407.

84. Ibid., 406–407.

Chapter 20. Conclusions

1. Eremenko, *Stalingrad: Uchastnikam velikoi bitvy pod Stalingradom posviashchadetsia*, 352–353.

2. Stalin's appointments diary listed no meetings with Zhukov between 31 August and 26 September, suggesting that Zhukov's claim that he planned Uranus on 12–13 September was an inaccurate recollection at best. See A. A. Chernobaev, ed., *Na prieme u Stalina: Tetradi (zhurnaly) zapisei lits, priniatykh I. V. Stalinym (1924–1953 gg.)* [Received by Stalin: The notebooks (journals) of entries of those persons admitted by I. V. Stalin (1924–1953)] (Moscow: Novyi khronograf, 2008), 389.

3. "Funkspruch an Heeresgruppe Don, 0905 Uhr, Armee-Oberkommando 6, Abt.-Ia, A.H.Qu., 22.01.43," in Aufsess, *Die Anlagenbänder zu den Kriegstagebüchern der 6. Armee*, book 3, 273. See also Manstein, *Lost Victories*, 360. In this English-language version, Manstein reverses the sequence and changes the dates, stating that Paulus asked permission to surrender on 22 January and to authorize a desperate breakout on the twenty-fourth.

4. For a summary of these operations, see Glantz, *Companion to Endgame at Stalingrad*, 803.

5. On the formation of the Kursk bulge, see Dieter Ose, ed., *Manstein's Gegenangriff Fruhjahr 1943* (Bonn, Germany: Führungsakademie der Bundeswehr, 1987); Dana M. Sadarananda, *Beyond Stalingrad: Manstein and the Operations of Army Group Don* (New York: Praeger, 1990); V. A. Zolotarev et al., eds., *Russkii arkhiv: Velikaia Otechestvennaia: Preliudiia Kurskoi bitvy. Dokumenty i materialy 6 dekabria 1942 g.–25 aprelia 1943 g. T 15 (4-3)* [The Russian archives: The Great Patriotic (War): Prelude to the Battle of Kursk. Documents and materials, 6 December 1942–25 April 1943. Vol. 15 (4-3)] (Moscow: Terra, 1997).

6. Krivosheev, *Soviet Casualties and Combat Losses*, 123–128.

7. Ibid., 127.

8. See Glantz, *Companion to Endgame at Stalingrad*, 805, for a table of Soviet and Axis estimates of these casualties.

9. See ibid., 806–807, for detailed calculations.

10. Hayward, *Stopped at Stalingrad*, 310.

11. Ready, *Forgotten Axis*, 247–250; Hamilton, *Sacrifice on the Steppe*, 300–303; Axworthy et al., *Third Axis, Fourth Ally*, 114, 145–146.

Selected Bibliography

Abbreviations

BA-MA *Bundesarchiv-Militärarchiv*, Freiburg, Germany
NAM   National Archives Microfilm

Primary Sources

COMBAT JOURNALS (*KRIEGSTAGEBUCH*): GERMAN

Army Detachment Fretter-Pico. *Kriegstagebuch Nr. 1, Armee-Abteilung Fretter-Pico, 18.12.1942–2.2.1943.* BA-MA XXX A.K. 31783/1 file. Copy of the original.

Army Detachment Hollidt. *Anlagen zu K.T.B. 1, Armee Abteilung Hollidt, Lagen-karten, Dez. 1942.* AOK 6, 22624/6 file. NAM series T-312, roll 1542.

———. *Anlagen zu K.T.B. 1, Armee Abteilung Hollidt, Skizzen, Nov 1942.* AOK 6, 26624/5 file. NAM series T-312, roll 1452.

———. *Anlagen zu K.T.B. 1., Armee Abt. Hollidt, Tagl. Meldungen, Teil A: 23–27.11.42, Teil B: 28.11–31.12.42.* BA-MA RH 20-6/249. Copy of the original.

———. *Kriegstagebuch Armee Abteilung Hollidt, 23.11.42 bis 27.12.42, Deutscher Generalstab bei 3. rum. Armee, 27.12.42 bis 31.12.42 Armeegruppe Hollidt.* BA-MA RH 20-6/246. Copy of the original.

Army Group Don. *Heeresgruppe Don Kriegstagebuch vom 22.12.42–31.1.43, Anlagen Band 6.* NAM series T-311, roll 270.

———. *Kriegstagebuch Nr. 1, Oberkommando der Heeresgruppe Don/Süd, 20. November 1942–23. März 1943.* BA-MA (number illegible). Copy of the original.

11th Panzer Division. *K.T.B. 11th Panzer-Divizion* for December 1942. Copy of the original.

XXXXVIII Panzer Corps. *Generalkommando XXXXVIII. Pz. Korps., Lagenkarten, 16.11.1942–31.12.1942.* BA-MA RH 26775/6. Copy of the original.

———. *Kriegs-Tagebuch, Dezember 1942., Gen. Kdo. XXXXVIII. Panzer Korps.* BA-MA RH 26-776/3. Copy of the original.

Fourth Panzer Army. *Lagenkarten zum KTB. Nr. 5 (Teil III.), PzAOK 4, Ia, 21 Oct–24 Nov 1942.* PzAOK. 4, 28183/12 file. NAM series T-313, roll 359.

———. *Lagenkarten zum KTB. Nr. 5 (Teil IV.), PzAOK 4, Ia, 21 Nov–Dec 1942.* PzAOK. 4, 28183/13 file. NAM series T-313, roll 359.

Romanian Third Army. *Anlagen zu K.T.B 1, Armee Abt. Hollidt, Befehl und sonst. Anlagen, Teil A: 1-29 & Teil B: 30-143.* AOK 6/2624/2 file. NAM series T-312, roll 1452.

———. *Anlagen zu. K.T.B. 1, Armee Abt. Hollidt, Skizzen, Teil A: 1-5, Teil B: 6-26.* AOK 6/26624/5. NAM series T-312, roll 1452.

———. *Tatigkeitsbericht 5.–31. Dez. 1942, Ic, Rum. AOK. 3, der Chef des Deutschen Gen.-Stabes, dann Armeegruppe Hollidt, 1. Text, 2. Anlagen, 1-11 Feindlagenkarten, 3. Zwischen u. Tagesmeldungen.* AOK 6, 26624/7 and 26624/9 files. Activities Report, Romanian Third Army. NAM series T-312, roll 1452.

Sixth Army. *K.T.B. AOK. 6, Ia., Karten, Nov 1942–Jan 1943.* AOK 6, 30155/37 file. NAM series T-312, roll 1459.

———. *6. Armee.* NAM series T-312, roll 1453.

62nd Infantry Division. *62. I.D., K.T.B. Nr. 7, Buch 2 vom 1.8.42 bis 28.2.43.* BA-MA RH 26-62/70. Copy of the original.

XXX Army Corps. *K.T.B. Gen. Kdo. XXX. A.K. vom 6.11.42–13.12.42.* 31296/1-2 file, BA-MA (number missing). Copy of the original.

22nd Panzer Division. *Kriegstagebuch Nr. 3 Anlagenband I der 22 Panzer Division vom 1.12.42–5.3.43.* BA-MA RH 27-22/16. Copy of the original.

———. *Kriegstagebuch Nr. 3 Anlagenband II der 22 Panzer Division vom 1.12.42–5.3.43.* BA-MA RH 27-22/17. Copy of the original.

———. *Kriegstagebuch Nr. 3 vom 12.42–5.3.43 d. 22. Pz. Division Ia.* BA-MA RH 27-22/15. Copy of the original.

294th Infantry Division. *Anlagenband. 1, Kriegstagebuch Nr. 4, 294. I.D. vom 1.12.42–21.12.42., Nr. 1559–1683.*, BA-MA 26-294/34. Copy of the original.

———. *Anlagenband. 2, Kriegstagebuch Nr. 4, 294. I.D. vom 22.12.42–14.1.43, Nr. 1685–1819.*, BA-MA 26-294/35. Copy of the original.

COMBAT JOURNALS (*ZHURNAL BOEVYKH DEISTVII*): SOVIET

62nd Army, September–November 1942.

5th Shock Army (15 December 1942–31 March 1943). F. 333, op. 4885, d. 25 and ed. khr. 24.

5th Tank Army (1942). F. 333, op. 5041, d. 130.

7th Tank Corps (25 August 1942–20 January 1943). F. 3401, op. 1, d. 8.

2nd Guards Mechanized Corps (1942–43). F. 3426, op. 1, d. 6.

3rd Guards Mechanized Corps (December 1942). F. 3428, op. 1, ed. khr. 3.

7th Guards (8th) Cavalry Corps (1942–1943). F. 3475, op. 1, ed. khr. 12.

9th Guards (5th) Mechanized Corps (1942). F. 3443, op. 1, d. 11.

95th Rifle Division.

112th Rifle Division.

138th Rifle Division. *138-ia Krasnoznamennaia strelkovaia diviziia v boiakh za Stalingrada* [The 138th Red Banner Rifle Division in the battle for Stalingrad].

284th Rifle Division.

308th Rifle Division.

37th Guards Rifle Division.

39th Guards Rifle Division.

10th Rifle Brigade.

42nd Rifle Brigade.

GERMAN SIXTH ARMY'S REDISCOVERED DAILY RECORDS

Aufsess, Florian *Freiherr* von und zu. *Die Anlagenbänder zu den Kriegstagebüchern der 6. Armee vom 14.09.42 bis 24.11.42*, book 1. *Die Anlagenbänder zu den Kriegstagebüchern der 6. Armee vom 24.11.42 bis 24.12.42*, book 2. *Die Anlagenbänder zu den Kriegstagebüchern der 6. Armee vom 24.12.1942 bis 02.02.1943*, book 3. Schwabach, Germany: self-published, 2006.

Other Primary Sources

Operativnye svodki 5 Ud. A. 15 dekabria 1942–31 marta 1943 [Operational summaries of 5th Shock Army, 15 December 1942–31 March 1943]. Extracts from the original.

Sbornik materialov po izucheniiu opyta voiny, No. 6, aprel'–mai 1943 g. [Collection of materials for the study of war experiences, no. 6, April–May 1943]. Moscow: Voenizdat, 1943. Classified secret but now declassified.

Sbornik materialov po izucheniiu opyta voiny, No. 8, avgust–oktiabr' 1943 g. [Collection of materials for the study of war experience, no. 8, August–October 1943]. Moscow: Voenizdat, 1943. Classified secret but now declassified.

Sbornik voenno-istoricheskikh materialov Velikoi Otechestvennoi voiny [Collection of military-historical materials of the Great Patriotic War]. Moscow: Voenizdat, various dates. Classified secret but now declassified.

Stalingradskaia epopeia: Vpervye publikuemye dokumenty rassekrechennye FSB RF: Vospominaniia.feld' marshala Pauliusa; Dnevniki i pis'ma soldat RKKA i vermakhta; Agenturnye doneseniia; Protokoly doprosov, Dokladnye zapiski osobykh frontov i armii [The Stalingrad epoch: Declassified documents of the Russian Federation's FSB, published for the first time: The recollections of Field Marshal Paulus; diaries and letters of soldiers of the RKKA and *Wehrmacht*; agent reports; protocols of interrogations; and report notes of the Special Department of *Fronts* and Armies]. Moscow: Evonnitsa-MG, 2000.

Zolotarev, V. A., ed. "General'nyi shtab v gody Velikoi Otechestvennoi voiny: Dokumenty i materially, 1942 god" [The General Staff in the Great Patriotic War: Documents and materials, 1942]. In *Russki arkhiv: Velikaia Otechestvennaia [voina]*, 23 (12-2) [The Russian archives: The Great Patriotic (War), vol. 23 (12-2)]. Moscow: Terra, 1999.

———. "Prikazy narodnogo komissara oborony SSSR, 22 iiunia 1941 g.–1942" [Orders of the People's Commissariat of Defense of the USSR, 22 June 1941–1942]. In *Russkii arkhiv: Velikaia Otechestvennaia [voina]*, 13 (2-2) [The Russian archives: The Great Patriotic (War), vol. 13 (2-2)]. Moscow: Terra, 1997.

———. "Stavka VGK: Dokumenty i materialy 1942" [The *Stavka* Supreme High Command: Documents and materials, 1942]. In *Russkii arkhiv: Velikaia Otechestvennaia [voina]*, 16 (5-2) [The Russian archives: The Great Patriotic (War), vol. 16 (5-2)]. Moscow: Terra, 1996.

———. *Velikaia Otechestvennaia: Deistvuiushchaia armiia 1941–1945 gg* [The Great Patriotic (War): The operating army, 1941–1945]. Moscow: Animi Fortitudo Kuchkovo pole, 2005.

———. *Velikaia Otechestvennaia voina 1941–1945: Voenno-istoricheskie ocherki v chetyrekh knigagh, kniga 1: Surovye ispytaniia* [The Great Patriotic War, 1941–1945: A military-historical survey in four books, book 1: A harsh education]. Moscow: Nauka, 1998.

————. *Velikaia Otechestvennaia voina 1941–1945: Voenno-istoricheskie ocherki v chetyrekh knigagh, kniga 2: Perelom* [The Great Patriotic War, 1941–1945: A military-historical survey in four books, book 2: The turning point]. Moscow: Nauka, 1998.

Published Sources

Adam, Wilhelm. *Der Schwere Entschluss*. Berlin: Verlag der Nation, 1965.

Afanas'ev, N. I. *Ot Volgi do Shpree: Boevoi put' 35-i gvardeiskoi strelkovoi Lozovskoi Krasnoznamennoi,ordena Suvorova i Bogdan Khmel'nitskogo divizii* [From the Volga to the Spree: The combat path of 35th Guards Lozovaia, Red Banner, and Orders of Suvorov and Bogdan Khmel'nitsky Rifle Division]. Moscow: Voenizdat, 1982.

Amirov, K. V. *Ot Volgi do Al'p: Boevoi put' 36-i gvardeskoi strelkovoi Verkhnedneprovskoi Krasnoznamennoi, ordenov Suvorov i Kutuzova II stepeni divizii* [From the Volga to the Alps: The combat path of 36th Guards Upper Dnepr Red Banner and Orders of Suvorov and Kutuzov II Degree Rifle Division]. Moscow: Voenizdat, 1987.

Axworthy, Mark, Cornel Scafeş, and Cristian Craciunoiu. *Third Axis, Fourth Ally: The Romanian Armed Forces in the European War, 1941–1945*. London: Arms & Armour Press, 1995.

Barnett, Correlli, ed. *Hitler's Generals*. New York: Grove Weidenfeld, 1989.

Bartov, Omer. *The Eastern Front, 1941–45: German Troops and the Barbarization of Warfare*. New York: St. Martin's Press, 1986.

Batov, Pavel Ivanovich. *V pokhodakh i boiakh* [In marches and battles]. Moscow: Golos, 2000.

Beevor, Anthony. *Stalingrad: The Fateful Siege, 1942–1943*. New York: Viking, 1998.

Belokon', Vitalii, and Il'ia Moshchansky, *Na flangakh Stalingrada: Operatsii na Srednom i Verkhnem Donu 17 iiulia 1942–2 fevralia 1943 goda* [On the flanks of Stalingrad: The operations on the middle and upper Don, 17 July 1942–2 February 1943]. Moscow: PKV, 2002.

Berdnikov, G. I. *Pervaia udarnaia: Boevoia pyt' 1-i udarnoi armii v Velikoi Otechestvennoi voine* [First Shock: The combat path of 1st Shock Army in the Great Patriotic War]. Moscow: Voenizdat, 1985.

Beshanov, Vladimir Vasilevich. *God 1942—"Uchebnyi"* [The year 1942—educational]. Minsk: Harvest, 2002.

Blau, George E. *The German Campaign in Russia: Planning and Operations, 1940–1942*. Department of the Army Pamphlet No. 20-261a. Washington, DC: Department of the Army, 1955.

Boevoi sostav Sovetskoi armii [Combat composition of the Soviet army], 3 parts. Moscow: Voenizdat, 1966.

Boog, Horst, Jurgen Forster, Joachim Hoffmann, Ernst Klink, Rolf-Dieter Muller, and Gerd R. Ueberschar. *Germany and the Second World War*, vol. IV, *The At-*

tack on the Soviet Union, trans. Dean S. McMurry, Ewald Osers, and Louise Willmot. Oxford: Clarendon Press, 1999.

Boog, Horst, Werner Rahm, Reinhard Stumpf, and Bernd Wegner. *Germany and the Second World War*, vol. VI, *The Global War: Widening of the Conflict into a World War and the Shift of the Initiative, 1941–1943*, trans. Ewald Osers et al. Oxford: Clarendon Press, 2001.

Carell, Paul [pseud. of Paul Karl Schmidt]. *Stalingrad: The Defeat of the German 6th Army*, trans. David Johnston. Atglen, PA: Schiffer Military/Aviation History, 1993.

Chistiakov, I. M., ed. *Po prikazu Rodiny: Boevoi put' 6-i Gvardeiskoi armii v. Velikoi Otechestvennoi voine, 1941–1945 gg* [By order of the Motherland: The combat path of 6th Guards Army in the Great Patriotic War, 1941–1945]. Moscow: Voenizdat, 1971.

———. *Sluzhim otchizne* [In service to the Fatherland]. Moscow: Voenizdat, 1975.

Chuikov, Vasili I. *The Battle for Stalingrad*, trans. Harold Silver. New York: Holt, Rinehart & Winston, 1964.

Citino, Robert M. *Death of the Wehrmacht: The German Campaigns of 1942*. Lawrence: University Press of Kansas, 2007.

Craig, William. *Enemy at the Gates: The Battle for Stalingrad*. New York: Reader's Digest Press, 1973.

Dërr, Gans. *Pokhod na Stalingrad*. [The approach to Stalingrad]. Moscow: Voenizdat, 1957. A translation of Hans von Dörr. *Der Feldzug nach Stalingrad: Versuch eines operative Überblickes*. Darmstadt, Germany: E. S. Mittler und Sohn, 1955.

Dieckhoff, Gerhard. *3. Infanterie-Division, 3. Infanterie-Division (Mot), 3. Panzer-Grenadier-Division*. Cuxhaven, Germany: Oberstudienrat Gerhard Dieckhoff, 1960.

Dinardo, Richard L. *Germany and the Axis Powers: From Coalition to Collapse*. Lawrence: University Press of Kansas, 2005.

———. *Mechanized Juggernaut or Military Anachronism? Horses and the German Army of World War II*. Westport, CT: Greenwood Press, 1991.

Dokuchaev, M. S. *V boi shli eskadrony: Boevoi put' 7-go gvardeiskogo ordena Lenina, Krasnoznamennogo, ordena Suvorova korpusa v Velikoi Otechestvennoi voine* [The squadrons went into battle: The combat path of 7th Guards Order of Lenin, Red Banner, and Order of Suvorov (Cavalry) Corps in the Great Patriotic War]. Moscow: Voenizdat, 1987.

Domnikov, V. M., ed. *V nastuplenii gvardiia: Ocherk o boevom puti 2-i Gvardeiskoi Armii* [Guards on the offensive: A study of the combat path of 2nd Guards Army]. Moscow: Voenizdat, 1971.

Dragunsky, D. A., et al., eds. *Ot Volgi do Pragi* [From the Volga to Prague]. Moscow: Voenizdat, 1966.

Eremenko, Andrei Ivanovich. *Stalingrad: Uchastnikam Velikoi bitvy pod Stalingradom posviashchaetsia* [Stalingrad: A participant in the great battle for Stalingrad explains]. Moscow: Khranitel', 2006.

———. *Stalingrad: Zapiski komanduiushchevo frontom* [Stalingrad: The notes of a front commander]. Moscow: Voenizdat, 1961.

Erickson, John. *The Road to Berlin: Continuing Stalin's War with Germany*. Boulder, CO: Westview Press, 1983.

———. *The Road to Stalingrad: Stalin's War with Germany*. New York: Harper & Row, 1975.

Friedin, Seymour, and William Richardson, eds. *The Fatal Decisions*. New York: William Sloane Associates, 1956.

Gerbet, Klaus, ed. *Generalfeldmarschall Fedor von Bock: The War Diary, 1939–1945*, trans. David Johnson. Atglen, PA: Schiffer Military History, 1996.

Geschichte der 3. Panzer-Division, Berlin-Brandenburg 1935–1945. Berlin: Verlag der Buchhandlung Gunter Richter, 1947.

Glantz, David M. *After Stalingrad: The Red Army's Winter Offensive, 1942–43*. Solihull, UK: Helion, 2008.

———. *Atlas of the Battle of Stalingrad: Red Army Operations, 19 November 1942–2 February 1943*. Carlisle, PA: self-published, 2000.

———. *Colossus Reborn: The Red Army at War, 1941–1943*. Lawrence: University Press of Kansas, 2005.

———. *Companion to Endgame at Stalingrad*. Lawrence: University Press of Kansas, 2014.

———. *Forgotten Battles of the German-Soviet War, 1941–1945*, vol. 3, *The Summer Campaign (12 May–18 November 1942)*. Carlisle, PA: self-published, 1999.

———. *Kharkov 1942: Anatomy of a Military Disaster*. Rockville Centre, NY: Sarpedon, 1998.

———. *Soviet Military Deception in the Second World War*. London: Frank Cass, 1989.

———. *Zhukov's Greatest Defeat: The Red Army's Epic Disaster in Operation Mars, 1942*. Lawrence: University Press of Kansas, 2005.

———, ed. *1984 Art of War Symposium: From the Don to the Dnepr: Soviet Offensive Operations—December 1942–August 1943*. Carlisle, PA: Center for Land Warfare, US Army War College, 1984; reprint, Foreign Military Studies Office, 1992.

Glantz, David M., and Jonathan M. House. *Armageddon in Stalingrad: September–November 1942. The Stalingrad Trilogy*, vol. 2. Lawrence: University Press of Kansas, 2009.

———. *Endgame at Stalingrad. The Stalingrad Trilogy*, vol. 3, books 1 and 2. Lawrence: University Press of Kansas, 2014.

———. *To the Gates of Stalingrad: Soviet-German Combat Operations, April–August 1942. The Stalingrad Trilogy*, vol. 1. Lawrence: University Press of Kansas, 2009.

———. *When Titans Clashed: How the Red Army Stopped Hitler*. Rev. ed. Lawrence: University Press of Kansas, 2015.

Goerlitz, Walter. *Paulus and Stalingrad: A Life of Field-Marshal Friedrich Paulus with Notes, Correspondence, and Documents from His Papers*, trans. B. H. Stevens. New York: Citadel Press, 1963.

Grams, Rolf. *Die 14. Panzer-Division 1940–1945*. Bad Nauheim, Germany: Verlag Haus-Henning Podzun, 1957.

Grechko, A. A. *Bitva za Kavkaz* [The battle for the Caucasus]. Moscow: Voenizdat, 1973.

Grossman, Vasily S. *A Writer at War: Vasily Grossman with the Red Army, 1941–*

1945, ed. and trans. Anthony Beevor and Luba Vinogradova. New York: Pantheon Books, 2005.

Halder, Franz. *The Halder War Diaries, 1939–1942*, ed. Charles Burdick and Hans-Adolf Jacobsen. Novato, CA: Presidio Press, 1988.

Hamilton, Hope. *Sacrifice on the Steppe: The Italian Alpine Corps in the Stalingrad Campaign, 1942–1943*. Philadelphia: Casemate, 2011.

Hardesty, Van, and Ilya Grinberg. *Red Phoenix Rising: The Soviet Air Force in World War II*. Lawrence: University Press of Kansas, 2012.

Haupt, Werner. *Army Group South: The Wehrmacht in Russia, 1941–1945*, trans. Joseph P. Welsh. Atglen, PA: Schiffer Press, 1998.

Hayward, Joel S. A. *Stopped at Stalingrad: The Luftwaffe and Hitler's Defeat in the East, 1942–1943.* Lawrence: University Press of Kansas, 1998.

Hill, Alexander. *The Great Patriotic War of the Soviet Union, 1941–45: A Documentary Reader*. London: Routledge, 2009.

Historical Study: Small Unit Actions during the German Campaign in Russia. Department of the Army Pamphlet No. 20-269. Washington, DC: Department of the Army, 1953.

Holl, Adelbert. *An Infantryman in Stalingrad: From 24 September 1942 to 2 February 1943*, trans. Jason D. Mark and Neil Page. Sydney, Australia: Leaping Horseman Books, 2005.

Isaev, Aleksei V. *Stalingrad: Za Volgoi dlia nas zemli net* [Stalingrad: There is no land for us beyond the Volga]. Moscow: Iauza, Eksmo, 2008.

Jentz, Thomas L. *Panzertruppen*. Atglen, PA: Schiffer Publishing, 1996.

Jukes, Geoffrey. *Hitler's Stalingrad Decisions*. Berkeley: University of California Press, 1985.

Kadyrov, N. Z. *Ot Minska do Veny: Boevoi put' 4-i gvardeiskoi strelkovoi Apostolovsko-Venskoi Krasnoznamennoi divizii* [From Minsk to Vienna: The combat path of 4th Guards Apostolovo-Vienna Red Banner Rifle Division]. Moscow: Voenizdat, 1985.

Katukov, Mikhail Efremovich. *Na ostrie glavnogo udara* [At the point of the main attack]. Moscow: Voenizdat, 1976.

Kehrig, Manfred. *Stalingrad: Analyse und Dokumentation einer Schlacht*. Stuttgart, Germany: Deutsche Verlag-Anstalt, 1974.

Kolomiets, Maksim, and Il'ia Moshchansky. "Oborona Kavkaz (iiul'–dekabr' 1942 goda)" [Defense of the Caucasus (July–December 1942)]. In *Frontovaia illiustratsiia, 2-2000* [Front illustrated, February 2002]. Moscow: OOO Strategiia KM, 2002.

Komandarmy. Voennyi biograficheskii slovar' (Velikaia Otechestvennaia) [Army commanders. Military-bibliographic dictionary (Great Patriotic War)]. Moscow: Institute of Military History, Russian Federation Ministry of Defense, OOO Kuchkovo pole, 2005.

Kozlov, M. M., ed. *Velikaia Otechestvennaia voina 1941–1945: Entsiklopediia* [The Great Patriotic War, 1941–1945: An encyclopedia]. Moscow: Sovetskaia entsiklopediia, 1985.

Kravchenko, I. M. *Nastupatel'naia operatsiia 5-i Tankovoi Armii v kontrnastuplenii pod Stalingradom (19–25 noiabria 1942 g.)* [The offensive operation of 5th Tank

Army in the counteroffensive at Stalingrad (19–25 November 1942)]. Moscow: Voroshilov Academy of the General Staff, 1978. Classified secret but now declassified.

Krivosheev, G. F., ed. *Soviet Casualties and Combat Losses in the Twentieth Century*, trans. Christine Barnard. London: Greenhill Books; Mechanicsburg, PA: Stackpole Books, 1997.

Lemelsen, Joachim, Walter Fries, and Wilhelm Schaeffer. *29. Division: 29.Infanteriedivision, 29. Infanteriedivision (Mot.), 29. Panzergrenadier-Division.* Bad Nauheim, Germany: Podzun-Verlag, 1960.

Losik, O. A., ed. *Stroitel'stvo i boevoe primenenie sovetskikh tankovykh voisk v gody Velikoi Otechestvennoi voiny* [The formation and combat use of Soviet tank forces in the years of the Great Patriotic War]. Moscow: Voenizdat, 1979.

Mackensen, Eberhard von. *Vom Bug zum Caucasus: Das III. Panzerkorps im Feldzug gegen Sowjetrussland 1941/42.* Neckargemund, Germany: Kurt Vowinkel Verlag, 1967.

Manstein, Erich von. *Lost Victories*, trans. Anthony G. Powell. Chicago: Henry Regnery, 1958.

Mark, Jason D. *Death of the Leaping Horseman: 24. Panzer-Division in Stalingrad, 12th August–20th November 1942.* Sydney, Australia: Leaping Horseman Books, 2003.

———. *Island of Fire: The Battle for the Barrikady Gun Factory in Stalingrad, November 1942–February 1943.* Sydney, Australia: Leaping Horseman Books, 2006.

Mellenthin, Friedrich W. von. *Panzer Battles*, trans. H. Betzler. Norman: University of Oklahoma Press, 1956.

Morozov, A. V. *39-ia Barvenkovskaia: Boevoi put' 39-i gvardeiskoi strelkovoi Barvenkovskoi ordena Lenina, dvazhdy Krasnoznamennoi,, ordenov Suvorov i Bogdana Khmel'nitskogo II stepeni divizii* [The 39th Barvenkovo: The combat path of 39th Guards Rifle Barvenkovo, Order of Lenin, twice Red Banner, and Orders of Suvorov and Bogdan Khmel'nitsky second degree division]. Moscow: Voenizdat, 1981.

Morozov, M. E., ed. *Velikaia Otechestvennaia voina 1941–1945 gg. Kampanii i strategicheskie operatsii v tsifrakh v 2 tomakh. Tom 1* [The Great Patriotic War, 1941–1945. Campaigns and strategic operations in two volumes. Vol. 1]. Moscow: Ob'edinnaia redaktsiia MVD Rossii, 2010.

Moshchansky, Il'ia, and Sergei Smolinov. "Oborona Stalingrada: Stalingradskaia strategicheskaia obornitel'naia operatsiia, 17 iiulia–18 noiabria 1942 goda" [The defense of Stalingrad: The Stalingrad strategic defensive operation, 17 July–18 November 1942]. In *Voennaia letopis'*, 6-2002 [Military chronicle, June 2002]. Moscow: BTV, 2002.

Moskalenko, Kirill Semenovich. *Na iugo-zapadnom napravlenii* [On the southwestern axis]. Moscow: Nauka, 1969.

Murray, Williamson. *Luftwaffe*. Baltimore: Nautical & Aviation Publishing Co. of America, 1985.

Naumenko, K. E. *266-ia Artemovsko-Berlinskaia: Voenno-istoricheskii ocherk boevogo puti 266-i strelkovoi Artemovsko-Berlinskoi Krasnoznammenoi, Ordena Suvorova II stepeni divizii* [The 266th Artemovsk-Berlin: A military-historical study of the combat path of 266th Red Banner and Order of Suvorov II Degree Rifle Division]. Moscow: Voenizdat, 1987.

Neidhardt, Hans. *Mit Tanne und Eichenlaub: Kriegschronik der 100. Jäger-Division vormals 100. leichte Infanterie-Division.* Graz-Stuttgart, Germany: Leopold Stocker Verlag, 1981.

Newland, Samuel J. *Cossacks in the German Army, 1941–1945.* London: Frank Cass, 1991.

Nikoforov, N. I., et al. *Velikaia Otechestvennaia voina 1941–1945 gg.: Deistvuiush-chaia armiia* [The Great Patriotic War, 1941–1945: The operating army]. Moscow: Animi Fortitudo, Kuchkovo pole, 2005.

Panov, M. F. *Na napravlenii glavnogo udara* [On the axis of the main attack]. Moscow: Shcherbinskaia tipografiia, 1993.

Paul, Wolfgang. *Brennpunkte: Die Geschichte der 6. Panzerdivision (1. Leichte) 1937–1945.* Osnabrück, Germany: Biblio Verlag, 1984.

Pavlov, I. N. *Legendarnaia zheleznaia: Boevoi put' motostrelkovoi Samarov-Ul'ianovskoi, Berdicheskoi Zheleznoi ordena Oktiabr'skoi Revolutsii, trizhdy Krasnoznamennoi, ordenov Suvorova i Bogdana Khmel'nitskogo divisii.* [The legendary iron: The combat path of the Samara-Ul'ianovsk and Berdichev, Order of the October Revolution, thrice Red Banner, and Orders of Suvorov and Bogdan Khmel'nitsky Motorized Rifle Division]. Moscow: Voenizdat, 1987.

Pliev, I. A. *Pod gvardeiskim znamenem* [Under the guards banner]. Ordzhonikidze: Izdatel'stvo IR, 1976.

Plocher, Hermann, and Harry R. Fletcher, eds. *The German Air Forces versus Russia, 1942.* USAF Historical Studies No. 154, Aerospace Studies Institute. Maxwell Air Force Base, AL: Air University, 1966.

Pomnit Dnepr-reka . . .: Vospominaniia veteranov 193-i strelkovoi Dneprovskoi ordena Lenina, Krasnoznamennoi, ordena Suvorova i Kutuzova divizii [Remember the Dnepr River . . . : Recollections of veterans of the 193rd Dnepr, Order of Lenin, Red Banner, and Orders of Suvorov and Kutuzov Rifle Division]. Minsk: Belarus, 1986.

Razgrom Italo-Nemetskikh voisk na Donu (Dekabr' 1942 r.): Kratkii operativno-takticheskii ocherk [The destruction of Italian-German forces on the Don (December 1942): A brief operational-tactical summary]. Moscow: Voenizdat, 1945. Originally classified secret but now declassified.

Ready, J. Lee. *The Forgotten Axis: Germany's Partners and Foreign Volunteers in World War II.* Jefferson, NC: McFarland, 1987.

Rebentisch, Ernst. *The Combat History of the 23rd Panzer Division in World War II.* Mechanicsburg, PA: Stackpole Books, 2012.

Reinhardt, Klaus. *Moscow—The Turning Point: The Failure of Hitler's Strategy in the Winter of 1941–1942*, trans. Karl Keenan. Oxford: Oxford University Press, 1992.

Rokossovsky, Konstantin K. *Soldatskii dolg* [A soldier's duty]. Moscow: Golos, 2000.

———, ed. *Velikaia pobeda na Volge* [Great victory on Volga]. Moscow: Voenizdat, 1965.

Rotmistrov, Pavel A. *Stal'naia gvardiia* [Steel guards]. Moscow: Voenizdat, 1964.

Rotundo, Louis C., ed. *Battle for Stalingrad: The 1943 Soviet General Staff Study.* Washington, DC: Pergamon-Brassey's International Defense Publishers, 1989.

Rudenko, S. I., et al., eds. *Sovetskie voenno-vozdushnye sily v Velikoi Otechestven-noi voine, 1941–1945 gg.* [The Soviet air force in the Great Patriotic War, 1941–1945]. Moscow: Voenizdat, 1968.

Samchuk, I. A. *Trinadtsataia gvardeiskaia* [The 13th Guards]. Moscow: Voenizdat, 1971.

Samchuk, I. A., P. G. Skachko, Iu. N. Babikov, and I. L. Gnedoi. *Ot Volgi do El'by i Pragi (Kratkii ocherk o boevom puti 5-i Gvardeskoi Armii)* [From the Volga to the Elbe and Prague (A short study of the combat path of 5th Guards Army)]. Moscow: Voenizdat, 1970.

Samsonov, A. M. *Ot Volgi do Baltiki: Ocherk istorii 3-go Gvardeiskogo mekhaniziro-vannogo korpusa 1942–1945 gg* [From the Volga to the Baltic: A study of the history of 3rd Guards Mechanized Corps, 1942–1945]. Moscow: Nauka, 1963.

———. *Stalingradskaia bitva* [The Battle of Stalingrad]. Moscow: Nauka, 1983.

Sarkis'ian, S. M. *51-ia Armii* [The 51st Army]. Moscow: Voenizdat, 1983.

Scheibert, Horst. *Nach Stalingrad—48 Kilometers! Der Einsatzvorstoss der 6. Panzerdivision. Dezember 1942.* Neckargemünd, Germany: Kurt Vowinckel Verlag, 1956.

———. *Zwischen Don und Donez: Winter 1942/43.* Neckargemünd, Germany: Kurt Vowinckel Verlag, 1961.

Schröter, Heinz. *Stalingrad.* New York: Ballantine, 1958.

Senger und Etterlin, Ferdinand von. *Die 24. Panzer-Division vormals 1. Kavalerie-Division 1939–1945.* Neckargemünd, Germany: Kurt Vowinkel Verlag, 1962.

Senger und Etterlin, Fridolin von. *Neither Fear nor Hope: The Wartime Career of General Frido von Senger und Etterlin, Defender of Casino.* New York: E. P. Dutton, 1964.

Seth, Ronald. *Stalingrad: Point of No Return: The Story of the Battle August 1942–February 1943.* New York: Coward-McCann, 1959.

Shaposhnikov, M. "Boevye deistviia 5-go mekanizirovannogo korpusa zapadnee Surovikino v dekabre 1942 goda" [Combat operations of 5th Mechanized Corps west of Surovikino in December 1942]. *Voenno-istoricheskii zhurnal* [Military-historical journal] 10 (October 1982): 32–36.

Shapovalov, V. A., ed. *Bitva za Kavkaz v dokumentakh i materialov* [The battle for the Caucasus in documents and materials]. Stavropol': Stavropol' State University, 2003.

Shtemenko, Sergei M. *The Soviet General Staff at War, 1941–1945,* vol. 1. Moscow: Progress Publishers, 1985.

Shukman, Harold, ed. *Stalin's Generals.* New York: Weidenfeld & Nicholson, 1993.

Sovetskaia Voennaia Entsiklopediia v vos'mi tomakh [Soviet military encyclopedia in eight volumes]. Moscow: Voenizdat, 1980.

Stalingradskaia epopeia [Stalingrad epoch]. Moscow: Evonnitsa-MG, 2000.

Stein, Marcel. *Field Marshal von Manstein: The Janus Head/A Portrait.* Solihull, UK: Helion, 2007.

Stoves, Rolf. *Die 22. Panzer-Division, Die 25. Panzer-Division, Die 27. Panzer-Division, und die 233. Reserve-Panzer-Division.* Friedberg, Germany: Podzun-Pallas-Verlag, 1985.

Stroeva, Anna. *Komandarm Kravchenko* [Army commander Kravchenko]. Kiev: Politicheskoi literatury Ukrainy, 1984.

Tarrant, V. E. *Stalingrad: Anatomy of an Agony.* London: Leo Cooper, 1992.

Tieke, Wilhelm. *The Caucasus and the Oil: The German-Soviet War in the Caucasus 1942/43*, trans. Joseph G. Welsh. Winnipeg, MB: J. J. Fedorowicz, 1995.

Tolubko, B. F., and N. I. Baryshev. *Na iuzhnom flange: Boevoi put' 4-go gvardeiskogo mekhanizirovanogo korpusa (1942–1945 gg.)* [On the southern flank: The combat path of 4th Guards Mechanized Corps (1942–1945)]. Moscow: Nauka, 1973.

Tooze, Adam. *The Wages of Destruction: The Making and Breaking of the Nazi Economy.* New York: Viking, 2006.

Trevor-Roper, Hugh R., ed. *Blitzkrieg to Defeat: Hitler's War Directives 1939–1945.* New York: Holt, Rinehart & Winston, 1964.

Tuzov, A. V. *V ogne voiny: Boevoi put' 50-i Gvardeiskoi dvazhdy Krasnoznammennoi ordena Suvorova i Kutuzova strelkovoi divizii* [In the flames of battle: The combat path of 50th twice Red Banner and Orders of Suvorov and Kutuzov Rifle Division]. Moscow: Voenizdat, 1970.

Vasilevsky, A. M. *A Lifelong Cause.* Moscow: Progress Publishers, 1970.

———. *Delo vsei zhizni* [Life's work]. Moscow: Izdatel'stvo politicheskoi literatury, 1983.

Vinogradov, V. K., A. T. Zhalobin, V. V. Markovchin, Ia. F. Pogony, Iu. B. Sigachev, B. S. Venkov, and P. P. Dudinov. *Gvardeiskaia doblest': Boevoi put' 70-i gvardeiskoi strelkovoi glukhovskoi ordena Lenina, dvazhdy krasnoznamennoi, ordena Suvorova, Kutuvova i Bogdana Khmel'nitskogo divizii* [Guards valor: The combat path of 70th Guards Glukhov, Order of Lenin and Order of Suvorov, Kutuzov, and Bogdan Khmel'nitsky Rifle Division]. Moscow: Voenizdat, 1979.

Voennaia Entsiklopediia v vos'mi tomakh [Military encyclopedia in eight volumes]. Moscow: Voenizdat, 1994–2004.

Volostnov, N. I. *Na ognennykh rubezhakh* [In firing positions]. Moscow: Voenizdat, 1983.

Voronov, N. N. *Na sluzhbe voennoi* [In military service]. Moscow: Voenizdat, 1963.

Vozhakin, M. G., ed. *Velikaia Otechestvennaia Komandarmy: Voennyi biograficheskii slovar'* [The Great Patriotic (War) army commanders: A military-biographical dictionary]. Moscow-Zhukovskii: Kuchkovo pole, 2005.

———. *Velikaia Otechestvennaia Komkory: Voennyi biograficheskii slovar' v. 2-h tomakh* [The Great Patriotic (War) corps commanders: A military-biographical dictionary, vol. 2]. Moscow-Zhukovskii: Kuchkovo pole, 2006.

Werthen, Wolfgang. *Geschichte der 16. Panzer-Division 1939–1945.* Friedberg, Germany: Podzun-Pallas Verlag, 1958.

Wijers, Hans J. *The Battle for Stalingrad: The Battle for the Factories, 14 October–19 November 1942.* Heerenveen, The Netherlands: self-published, 2003.

Wray, Timothy A. *Standing Fast: German Defensive Doctrine on the Russian Front during World War II, Prewar to 1943.* Research Survey No. 5. Ft. Leavenworth, KS: Combat Studies Institute, 1986.

Zhadov, A. S. *Chetyre goda voiny* [Four years of war]. Moscow: Voenizdat, 1978.

Zhilin, V. A., ed. *Stalingradskaia bitva: Khronika, fakty, liudi v. 2 kn.* [The Battle of Stalingrad: Chronicles, facts, people in two books]. Moscow: OLMA, 2002.

Zhukov, G. K. *Reminiscences and Reflections*. Moscow: Progress Publishers, 1985.
Ziemke, Earl F., and Magna Bauer. *Moscow to Stalingrad: Decision in the East*. Washington, DC: US Army Center of Military History, 1987.

Index